Time's River

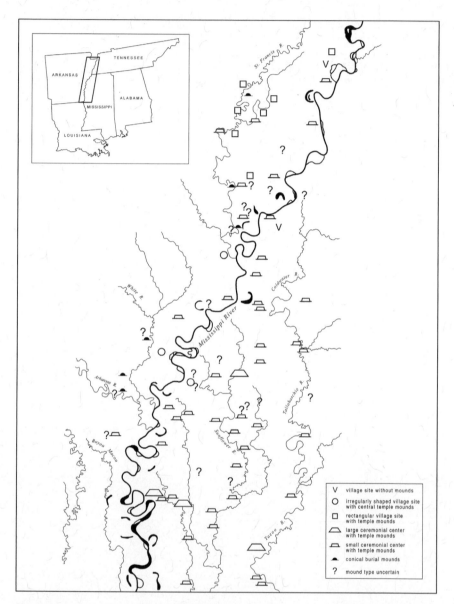

Distribution of occupation patterns in the early Mississippian Period (based on Phillips, Ford, and Griffin 2003).

Time's River

Archaeological Syntheses from the Lower Mississippi River Valley

Edited by
JANET RAFFERTY AND EVAN PEACOCK

THE UNIVERSITY OF ALABAMA PRESS
Tuscaloosa

Funding for and sponsorship of this research provided by
the Mississippi Department of Transportation.

A Dan Josselyn Memorial Publication

∞

The paper on which this book is printed meets the minimum requirements of American
National Standard for Information Science—Permanence of Paper for Printed Library
Materials, ANSI Z39.48-1984.

Library of Congress Cataloging-in-Publication Data

Time's river : archaeological syntheses from the lower Mississippi River Valley / edited by
Janet Rafferty and Evan Peacock.
p.   cm.
Includes bibliographical references and index.
ISBN 978-0-8173-1614-3 (cloth : alk. paper) — ISBN 978-0-8173-5489-3 (pbk. : alk.
paper) — ISBN 978-0-8173-8112-7 (electronic) 1. Mississippi River Valley—Antiquities.
2. Interstate 69—Antiquities. 3. Archaeology—Mississippi River Valley. 4. Excavations
(Archaeology)—Mississippi River Valley. 5. Mississippi River Valley—History.
6. Prehistoric peoples—Mississippi River Valley. 7. Indians of North America—Mississippi
River Valley—Antiquities. I. Rafferty, Janet, 1947– II. Peacock, Evan, 1961–
F350.8.T56 2008
977—dc22

2007046797

Contents

Contents

Illustrations

Figures

Tables

Time's River

1
Introduction

Reconsidering the Archaeology of the Lower Mississippi River Valley

Janet Rafferty and Evan Peacock

> I mention the incestuous nature of archaeology in the [southern Central Mississippi Valley] area because it is sometimes advantageous to introduce new blood into old debates.
>
> —Starr 2003:27

Much of the archaeology done in the world today is carried out via cultural resource management, or CRM. We believe that CRM is first and foremost a research pursuit, in the sense that documenting the archaeological record in order to learn from it is the main justification for the field. But it is a research pursuit with its own particular set of difficulties. The gray literature status of most CRM reports, and the fact that CRM archaeologists publish journal articles on their projects only infrequently (a result of job expectations, time pressures, and other influences), lessen the scholarly impact of this kind of work. It also allows agencies to tolerate workmanlike description rather than insisting on new approaches and demonstrable increments to knowledge. There are admirable exceptions, but all too often CRM work languishes in the backwaters of archaeology, not only in terms of theory but also in terms of method and contributions to substantive knowledge. One can see this in many recent synthetic volumes, where CRM reports are poorly represented in the bibliographies.

It could be argued that CRM is primarily a vocation, a set of methods for retrieving materials so that their research potential remains intact. But, because methods derive from theory, an emphasis on method alone cannot be defended. Clearly there is more than one way to do things, and clearly there should be theoretically justifiable reasons for doing things one way rather than another. CRM archaeologists—indeed, all archaeologists—also must contend with the need to accommodate future investigations using the materials they have collected. No one set of research problems should be an excuse for collecting data in such a way as to preclude addressing other problems. This is in accord with the other main concern of archaeological work, which is preservation of the record—in place, if possible, or in the form of artifacts and documentation if archaeological recovery is necessary. We believe that the choice of methods should be rationalized in terms of both concerns: in terms of theory, which leads to tackling particular scientific problems in particular ways, and in terms of using proveniencing and sampling methods that are attentive to preserving the maximum amount of information possible.

One way the tension between problem-oriented research and preservation can be lessened is to employ recovery methods designed to meet preservation requirements, assuring that the resulting data will be suitable for addressing many different kinds of research interests. If field methods are designed to be spatially extensive, to include the full range of artifact sizes, and to incorporate detailed proveniencing from all kinds of contexts, they will produce data that can be used repeatedly for many different purposes (Peacock and Rafferty 2007). The rationale for using such methods is already well-developed, as they derive from general archaeological theory, which archaeologists mostly hold in common whatever specific explanatory theory they subscribe to. Unfortunately, while both preservation and research goals ostensibly are met by the research-design approach to CRM, expedient field methods currently in use typically do not produce truly representative samples at a full range of scales. Thus, they create systematic bias in what is left for future generations of archaeologists to study (Dunnell 1984). This is evidenced by the continuing fixation on large, deep sites at the expense of smaller, less artifact-rich ones, and by the rote application of stripping and other methods that sacrifice surface or other contexts without a scientific rationale for doing so.

The analysis phase of a project is more amenable than the recovery phase to being oriented toward research goals. As properly curated artifacts can be reanalyzed numberless times in light of various research topics, and as most analytic methods are non- to minimally destructive, there is much scope for problem-oriented research to be carried out during the analysis stage. However, despite broad acknowledgment that there is no one correct way to classify artifacts, but that this should depend on the problem being investigated, general descriptive categories are routinely employed across the board, minimizing the generation of new knowledge. This is true both in prehistoric archaeology, where pottery and point types, flake stages, and other traditional categories are used as a matter of course, and historic archaeology, where folk categories are employed as though they were units created for scientific analysis.

This methodological and analytical homogenization is visible at the outset of most CRM products. Archaeologists who work in the United States and who have had any contact with CRM are familiar with the "cultural background" chapter of technical reports. All too often these chapters are rote cut-

and-paste exercises in which the culture history of the region is summarized in general terms, using periods, phases, and diagnostic artifact types. Broad generalizations about subsistence, settlement, and technology are used to characterize each period. The information in this section of a report rarely informs the remainder.

The current volume is meant to provide an alternative to such formulaic background overviews. The Mississippi Department of Transportation (MDOT) has sponsored this new kind of overview in an attempt to provide a more useful approach to compiling cultural background information (Underwood et al., this volume). It is aimed at upcoming projects in the Yazoo Basin, and especially at archaeology to be done in connection with construction of Interstate 69 through northwest Mississippi. The hope, in practical terms, is to preclude the need for each project report to contain a background section on which much time and effort has been spent to reiterate what is already known. The existing culture historical framework for the I-69 area has been ably summarized recently (Weinstein 2004a, 2004b), as has the later prehistory of the LMV in general (Kidder 2004; Rolingson 2004). To complement these overviews, the current volume is focused on compiling data, critically reviewing our current understandings, and proposing fruitful ways to tackle regional archaeological questions: to identify gaps in our knowledge, to understand why such gaps exist, and to determine how those gaps might best be filled.

These goals were reflected in the charge to authors and in the resulting chapters. Participants were asked to summarize current knowledge for the immediate study area (the Yazoo Basin, a.k.a. the Delta) and the surrounding region (broadly speaking, the Lower Mississippi Valley [LMV]), each focusing on his or her area of expertise. Counties and parishes included in the study area are shown in Figure 1.1. As used in this volume, this region subsumes the central Mississippi Valley (cf. Morse and Morse 1983:1; O'Brien and Dunnell 1998:1) from the mouth of the Ohio to the mouth of the Arkansas River. Farther south, it includes the area from the Red River to the Arkansas River's confluence with the Mississippi. In total, it includes all or parts of 17 counties in Arkansas, 19 counties in Mississippi, 2 counties in Missouri, 10 counties in Tennessee, and 11 parishes in Louisiana. This entire region, forming the northern and central lower Mississippi Alluvial Valley of Phillips et al. (2003 [1951]:11), establishes the context for the archaeology of the Yazoo Basin and the route of I-69 through Mississippi. The information provided here will necessarily be augmented as time passes and new work is done, but this compendium of the current state of knowledge from this archaeologically rich area is expected to be useful for many years to come.

Much of the information on the Delta (and more generally the LMV) that has been accumulated in the years since the major monographs of Phillips

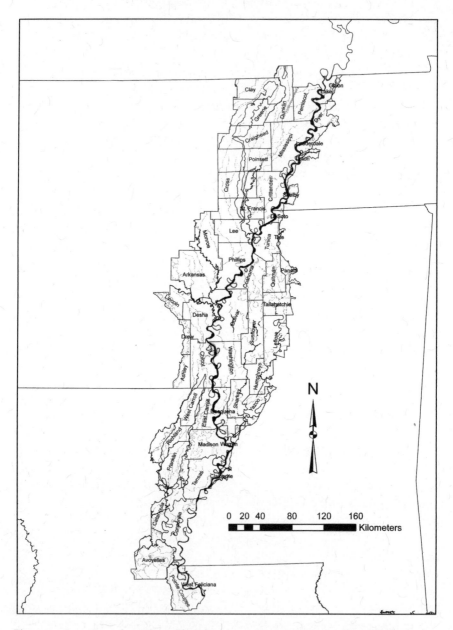

Figure 1.1. Counties and parishes included in the study area. Courtesy of Carl Lipo.

et al. (2003 [1951]) and Phillips (1970) has been provided by CRM work. We therefore made a concerted effort to identify and obtain copies of CRM reports to provide to the authors, allowing them to encompass these important but poorly circulated data in their reviews. The authors also have relied heavily on the archaeological publications of the Mississippi Department of Archives and History (MDAH) and the Arkansas Archeological Survey, the site files maintained by the states of Mississippi, Arkansas, Louisiana, and Missouri, and the state archaeology journals, especially *Mississippi Archaeology.* For the sake of future researchers who wish to obtain them and for historical clarity, unless otherwise noted, reprinted works are cited both by their reprint and original dates, the latter in brackets.

The authors have largely focused on the compilation of primary data rather than propounding on broad issues such as trade, political hierarchy, demography, cultural complexity, and the like. Many recent books in Southeastern archaeology have treated such larger issues but suffer from a lack of consideration of fundamental problems related to recovery and analytical biases, formation processes, and the articulation between theory and method. One result has been the resurgence of ethnographic analogy as an explanatory device, despite the logical flaws with such an approach. Another recurrent theme in recent literature is the invocation of human agency or intentionality, a teleological approach reliant upon ascribed motives: i.e., interpretation rather than explanation. Tackling broad issues from an explicitly scientific standpoint requires combining data from a number of different research domains. If such data are lacking or have been cast in terms that are too general, robust scientific explanations will be hard to come by. It is therefore necessary to consider how more, and more useful, data might be generated.

Although not included as an explicit instruction to the authors, another thing we hoped to accomplish was to break with the major concern that archaeologists working in the Delta often have shown with phases, pottery types and varieties, and culture historical description. Overall organization of the volume by cultural periods was rejected because we wished to discard the straitjacket too often imposed by culture historical units. Such units, and the diagnostic types on which they are based, have tended to become reified, as though they were objects of research rather than mere tools in its furtherance. This traditional approach has been roundly criticized in a host of recent publications (e.g., Claassen 1991; Dunnell 1982; Fox 1998; Mainfort 2003a; O'Brien and Lyman 2000) but continues to be the norm, even though its units may be poorly suited for addressing current archaeological problems (Brown, this volume; Dunnell, Chapter 4 this volume; Lipo and Dunnell, this volume; Starr 2003:25). Whether one chooses to adopt any particular alternative approach, the theoretical bases of the criticisms are real, and it is incumbent upon Southeastern archaeologists to rise to the challenge of addressing those criticisms rather than simply dismissing them as iconoclasm (e.g., Williams 2003).

One issue that must be taken up in this regard involves usage: i.e., "Mississippi" vs. "Mississippian." Authors often have distinguished between these, with the former said to refer to a period and the latter to a culture (Phillips et al. 2003 [1951]:239–240; Steponaitis 1983:1). We (the editors) have chosen to use the term Mississippian throughout. Our reasoning is that researchers, when using either word, overwhelmingly are referring to a cultural period—i.e., one which is defined by its cultural content (usually mussel shell-tempered pottery, but sometimes including other cultural traits) and not by time. The temporal boundaries of this cultural period vary depending on the author and by sub-region (and, of course, by the traits considered to be important). Thus, there is no meaningful difference between the Mississippi period and the Mississippian "culture." This poorly understood conflation of terms was clarified for Hopewell by Mason (1970) years ago; it continues to be an important problem in the archaeology of the LMV.

To the extent possible, the authors in this volume have incorporated raw data into their chapters; none have wed their data summaries or problem statements to specific phases or typological frameworks beyond the limits imposed by how the available data have been reported. Matters of theory, method, and technique are covered to varying degrees throughout. If needed for reference, phase-based, descriptive background accounts are available in the many CRM reports from the study area (e.g., Weinstein 2004a, 2004b) and in the Delta section of Mississippi's comprehensive state plan (Morgan 1992). The state plan also includes questions to be addressed by archaeologists, and these have informed research designs for some major projects in the Delta (e.g., Walling and Chapman 1999). But fundamental issues of theory and method, such as classification, have not received proper attention in the region in modern times, despite the extraordinary richness of the archaeological record there. We hope that this volume will make a substantial contribution in this regard.

Acknowledgments

Many people have helped as we assembled information for this book, showing a generosity of spirit typical among archaeologists and especially gracious, given our attempts to offer researchers something other than the traditional approaches. This project was the brainchild of Kevin Bruce when he worked at MDOT; we are grateful to Claiborne Barnwell, Bruce Gray, Kevin Bruce, John Underwood, Jim Turner, and Lizbeth Velasquez at MDOT for having the vision to see it through. Others who deserve special thanks include David Abbott, Jeffrey Alvey, Keith Baca, Drew Buchner, Sam Brookes, John Connaway, David

Dye, Ann Early, Pam Edwards-Lieb, Thomas Eubanks, Nick Fielder, Marisa Fontana, Thurston Hahn, Donald Hunter, Cliff Jenkins, Marvin Jeter, Rick Kanaski, Lucretia Kelly, David Kelley, T. R. Kidder, Patrick Livingood, Jim McNeil, Chip McGimsey, Charles McNutt, Sr., John Miller, Mike Moore, Mark Norton, Anthony Ortmann, Elenanora Reber, Koretta Reed, Duke Rivet, Joe Saunders, Jim Turner, Lizbeth Velasquez, Rachel Watson, Guy Weaver, and Rich Weinstein. Nicole Palmer served as a research assistant, helping to compile gray literature and other sources for all the authors. Many of the papers were presented in preliminary form at the 2004 Southeastern Archaeological Conference in St. Louis. We wish to thank John House and Richard Weinstein for serving as discussants for the symposium and for their encouragement then and since. Sam Brookes and T. R. Kidder read the book in draft and provided many useful and insightful comments. Finally, we would like to thank Joe Seger, Director of the Cobb Institute of Archaeology, for his continuing support.

2
The Interstate 69 Project in Mississippi

Generation of an Archaeological Synthesis

John R. Underwood, James H. Turner, and Kevin L. Bruce

Introduction

The Interstate 69 (I-69) proposed project corridor crosses the northwestern quarter of the state of Mississippi, a region better known to residents of the Southeast as the Mississippi Delta. The Phase I cultural resources survey of this project was conducted in 2002 and 2003 by Coastal Environments, Inc. (CEI), under contract to Neel-Schaffer, Inc., and the Mississippi Department of Transportation (MDOT). Dozens of previously recorded cultural resources were relocated, and hundreds of unrecorded cultural resources were identified, a substantial number of which were determined potentially eligible for the National Register of Historic Places (NRHP). Given the volume of significant resources that may be impacted and therefore require data recovery/mitigation, archaeologists from the Cobb Institute of Archaeology at Mississippi State University (MSU) and MDOT proposed creation of an up-to-date regional environmental and archaeological synthesis to help streamline the Phase III cultural resources management (CRM) process and direct new research. This chapter is devoted to discussing the near-completion and potential of this study.

General Corridor Background

The portion of the I-69 project corridor that crosses northwest Mississippi constitutes less than 10 percent of the project corridor's total length. This approximately 1,600-mile national highway project extends from the Canadian border and passes through 11 states (Arkansas, Indiana, Kentucky, Illinois, Louisiana, Michigan, Missouri, Ohio, Mississippi, Tennessee, and Texas) en route to its terminus at the Mexican border in the lower Rio Grande valley of southwest Texas (Federal Highway Administration [FHWA] 2001) (Figure 2.1). The

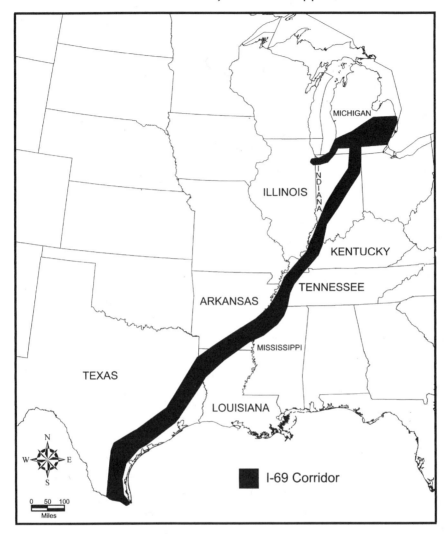

Figure 2.1. Location of the proposed Interstate 69 corridor across the United States (see http://www.nationali69.org/servlet/com).

northern 400 miles of this interstate between Port Huron, Michigan, and Indianapolis, Indiana, were built in the 1960s and 1970s to service the Great Lakes region following the 1956 passage of the Federal Aid-Highway Act, which authorized the creation of the interstate highway system (Cox and Love 1996). The remaining 1,200 miles were given preliminary definition and clear direction of purpose through a series of federal legislative acts between 1991 and 1998 (AA Roads 2004).

In 1991 Congress passed the Intermodal Surface Transportation Efficiency Act (ISTEA), which established and defined "high-priority" highway corridors of national importance. After the passage of the North American Free Trade Agreement, or NAFTA, in 1992, a steering committee composed of representatives from these eleven states began actively researching and evaluating high-priority transportation corridors from Indianapolis, Indiana, to the Texas/Mexico border to address the anticipated increase in commercial traffic among the three NAFTA partners (FHWA 2001). Two of these corridors merged in 1995 and were later subsumed under the Interstate 69 designation following the 1998 passage of the Transportation Equity Act for the 21st Century (TEA-21) (AA Roads 2004; FHWA 2001).

Once completed, I-69 will provide a more efficient means of overland shipping from border to border, significantly reducing travel times and costs while servicing regions and communities that currently do not have direct access to the U.S. Interstate Highway System (Tennessee Department of Transportation [TDOT] 2004). In particular, the Mississippi Delta and portions of Texas are notably underserved by interstate highways. Development of this interstate will provide these regions new opportunities for economic growth as well as improved access to education, health, and commercial services that accompany improved transportation networks (MDOT 2004).

To accomplish this Herculean task, the overall length of the I-69 corridor was divided into 32 Sections of Independent Utility, or SIUs, that address state and local needs, schedules, and funding constraints (FHWA 2001; TDOT 2004). Each section falls under the purview of the agencies in each state responsible for the planning, design, and construction of interstate highways; in Mississippi this is MDOT and its contracted consultants. Because specific highway locations vary greatly in terms of services required, the SIU process gives state transportation agencies the responsibility of addressing each particular location's distinctive needs and the freedom to develop innovative and creative planning strategies for the management of required work. This also means that work associated with each section will have its own intrinsic value and significance (AA Roads 2004; FHWA 2001; TDOT 2004).

I-69 Corridor: Section 11

The portion of the I-69 project corridor that most interests archaeologists crosses the "upper" or "northern" Yazoo Basin of Mississippi, encompassing large sections of Tunica, Coahoma, Bolivar, and Sunflower counties and amounting to approximately 100 linear miles of project corridor (Figure 2.2). Given the sensitivity of this project, steps were taken fairly early on in the planning process to actively involve cultural resources specialists. Prior to the selec-

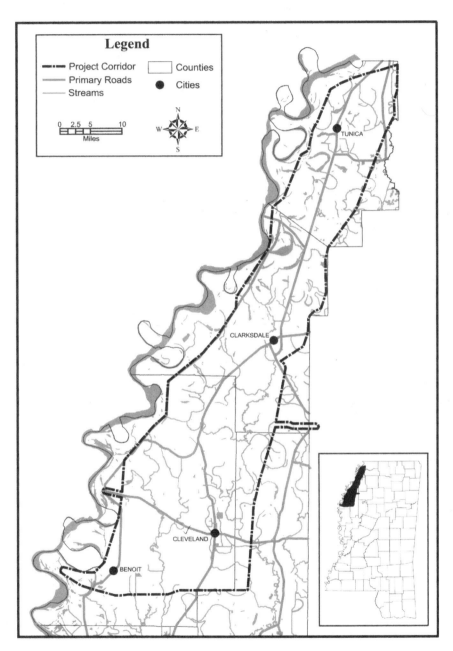

Figure 2.2 Location of Interstate 69 corridor across northwestern Mississippi (after Ryan et al. 2004:Figure 1–1).

tion of potential corridor alternatives, Coastal Environments, Inc., compiled data on all cultural resources within a 100-mile long by 10–20-mile-wide project area. These data, along with other variables, were then converted to GIS image files for use by project planners, designers, and engineers in the selection of potential corridor alternatives. These selections were then presented privately to regulatory agencies and publicly through a series of public hearings in the fall of 2001. Based upon comments and questions raised during these meetings, revised and modified versions of these alternatives were presented through a second series of public hearings in the spring of 2002. Following this second series of public hearings, a total of four final alternatives were chosen for detailed cultural resources studies.

The initial scope of work called for 100-percent coverage of each alternative to provide specific information concerning the nature and distribution of cultural resources within each alternative, including preliminary determinations of NRHP eligibility. However, due to the sheer size of the proposed alternatives, it was not feasible to survey each in its entirety. A 33-percent survey sample of each alternative, focusing on high-probability areas as defined by geomorphology and existing cultural resources data, was jointly recommended by MDOT and the Mississippi Department of Archives and History (MDAH) in lieu of 100-percent survey coverage. The resulting information would then be used by project planners to select a final alternative that would be subjected to additional cultural resources surveys to ensure 100-percent coverage and full compliance with federal guidelines.

Thirty-three percent survey samples of the combined alternatives resulted in the identification of 197 previously unrecorded archaeological sites, the relocation of an additional 20 archaeological sites, and the recording of 287 standing architectural resources. Forty-three archaeological sites and five structures were recommended as potentially eligible for the National Register (Ryan et al. 2004:7-1, 8-1).

Recognition of Existing Data Gaps

One of the benefits of this project has been a recent and comprehensive review of archaeological and related studies conducted in and immediately adjacent to the Interstate 69 project corridor. The area's archaeological richness has been well acknowledged and studied since the mid-nineteenth century through large-scale site-identification surveys, location studies, and village and prehistoric mound investigations sponsored by museum and academic institutions; small prehistoric sites and Historic-period resources in general have received a disproportionately small amount of attention (Ryan et al. 2004) (see Dunnell, Chapter Three of this volume). Furthermore, the majority of what can be considered "professional" work conducted within the project corridor has consisted of numerous, mostly small-scale, compliance-driven cultural resources surveys and only a small handful of data-recovery projects generated by transportation or United States Army Corps of Engineers projects within the past 35 years (Ryan et al. 2004). The result is a collection of data that has yet to be effectively integrated (see Dunnell, Chapter Three of this volume for further discussion on this topic).

Considering these shortcomings, MDAH has developed a number of research questions to be addressed during the investigation of prehistoric sites in the state. Of particular relevance here are those concerned with the overall pattern, expression, and development of the Middle and Late Woodland and Mississippian cultures in the Upper Yazoo Basin (Walling and Chapman 1999:3–5; Morgan 1992). These research questions specifically reference the lack of developed regional chronologies as well as the lack of well-documented settlement, subsistence, stratigraphic, and feature data, data attainable only through more intensive evaluation and data recovery/mitigation-level investigations (Morgan 1992).

In light of this, and given the spatial and temporal range of the survey results, survey data were analyzed to further assess and refine existing notions concerning prehistoric settlement in the Upper Yazoo Basin portion of the Lower Mississippi Valley (LMV) generated from existing syntheses (see Phillips 1970; Phillips et al. 2003 [1951]; Weinstein et al. 1979). Meaningful statements concerning the Historic settlement of the region were also generated through the joint analyses of archaeological and architectural data, contemporary cartographic resources and aerial photography, and local histories. While these results are highly informative in their own right, survey-level data, by design, are somewhat limited in research potential and are generally restricted to prehistoric and Historic-period settlement, culture history, and land-use reconstruction studies (Underwood et al. 2004).

As stated earlier, very few modern data-recovery excavations have taken place within the region, with fewer still finalized and readily available (see Hahn et al. 1994; Mooney et al. 2004; Walling and Chapman 1999; Weinstein et al. 1995). While few in number, these projects have begun the process of addressing prehistoric intrasite settlement patterns, subsistence and diet, and material culture chronologies through more sophisticated recovery and analytical methodologies and techniques. Modern study of these research topics is crucial to the development of a more complete understanding of the Upper Yazoo Basin's prehistory. To date, only one Historic site has been subjected to intensive archaeological investigations and has provided a new perspective on mid- to late-nineteenth through early-twentieth-century plantation life, use of space, and participation in both local and regional economic markets (Hahn et al. 1994).

Goals and Objectives of Regional Overview Volume

Perhaps the two most significant points the above discussions have raised are that: 1) the I-69 project may potentially impact a large number of prehistoric and Historic resources, and 2) no recent archaeological syntheses of the Upper Yazoo Basin exist to aid in the development of pertinent research questions and strategies for the mitigation of such resources. Due to planning constraints, MDOT currently approaches all potentially eligible archaeological sites as subject to data recovery and/or mitigation-level investigations. Given these circumstances and the state of our current archaeological knowledge of the region, MDOT and MSU began collaborating on ways to streamline and expedite the overall Phase III process without limiting the recovery of significant information.

Close collaboration between MDOT and MSU archaeologists resulted in the conceptualization of a synthesis of environmental and archaeological knowledge within the I-69 corridor and immediate surrounding areas. This overview volume was envisioned with two primary purposes in mind. First, it was to provide an up-to-date and thorough environmental and archaeological context for the I-69 project corridor as it will occur in northwest and west-central Mississippi; second, it would highlight gaps in our current archaeological and cultural understanding of the Upper Yazoo Basin in particular and the LMV in general.

The first goal will serve as a cost-saving and efficiency measure, designed to eliminate redundancy and maintain consistency in the preparation and use of environmental and archaeological contexts. To accomplish this, thorough reviews of the published and gray literature detailing work conducted within the project area, and enough of the surrounding area to provide meaningful context, were planned on a topical basis. Respected regional specialists in environmental, prehistoric, historic, biological, zoological, and geophysical archaeology were invited to contribute to the volume, charged with compiling rather than summarizing previous interpretations within their given specialties. These contributions, submitted in the form of individual chapters, were to be accompanied by suggestions for new research strategies and questions, reviews of promising methods for addressing them, defined lists of crucial terms, and complete bibliographies.

The desired result of these topical reviews will be recognition of significant gaps in the environmental and archaeological knowledge of the region and suggestions for how these informational gaps may be addressed. In this way, the volume will provide a procedural framework for the data recovery/mitigation process that can be supplemented by emerging ideas, techniques, and methodologies and a mutual point of reference between cultural resource managers and project planners. By not functioning as a restrictive step-by-step manual, this volume will hopefully encourage and facilitate innovative, problem-oriented research strategies and approaches for archaeological data recovery and/or mitigation efforts and possibly spur further specialist studies in the region as well.

The concept of creating a regional environmental and archaeological overview in association with the I-69 project was born of the need to streamline the Phase III process while simultaneously encouraging archaeological research. By concentrating on the creation of a single, thoroughly researched and indexed volume detailing the current environmental and archaeological knowledge of the Upper Yazoo Basin and the needed direction for future studies, MDOT and MSU will have eliminated needless redundancy in the compliance process while promoting and encouraging new and innovative archaeological research. In short, this overview will greatly assist both planners and consultants by providing all involved a clearly defined, concise, and easily usable point of reference throughout the archaeological data recovery/mitigation process. It has been envisioned that this volume will serve as a standard reference for all compliance projects, not only in the Mississippi Delta, but in surrounding regions for years to come.

3
Archaeology in the Lower Mississippi Valley

Robert C. Dunnell

Introduction

There is ample evidence that the way we view ourselves and our past exerts a significant, sometimes profound, influence on the practice of archaeology. History does matter; it does have lessons for the present.

After a long period of neglect, the Lower Mississippi Valley (LMV), and the Southeast generally, have been blessed with a number of excellent histories of archaeological endeavors (e.g., Hoffman 1999; Johnson, ed. 1993; Johnson 2002; Lyon 1996; Rolingson 1999, 2001; Rolingson, ed. 2001; Tushingham et al. 2002) in recent years. Further, the University of Alabama Press series of Southeastern Classics, edited by Stephen Williams, has made many of the scarce original sources available to a broad audience, promising to stimulate additional interest in historical research. O'Brien and Lyman (ed. 2001) have also reprinted key documents. The seemingly obligatory section on "history of research" or "archaeological background" seen in modern cultural resources management (CRM) reports appears to have led to a competition that ferrets out new historical details with regularity. As a result, I wondered how one might make a contribution in such a densely populated, well-researched field in a brief essay.

Most of the history of archaeology has been written within the same paradigm as current among archaeologists for constructing prehistory. Thus the dominant mode employed in structuring the history of archaeology has been culture-historical—a set of periods are devised, a characteristic approach for each period identified, and exemplars recited in support of the characterization (e.g., Daniel 1975, 1981; Willey and Sabloff 1970, 1980, 1993). Other tacks have been taken occasionally (e.g., Brown 1994; O'Brien 1996a; Trigger 1989), but none of this history was organized in a manner relevant to the conservation and management of the archaeological record, the central theme of this volume.

To realize the promise of archaeological history for present practice, one not only has to get the "facts"[1] right, but to identify relevant descriptive parameters and an appropriate theory with which to explain the facts. These are plainly choices made by writer and reader. Here, I have focused on what might be described as the growth of scientific[2] knowledge about the archaeological record, rather than what archaeologists and others believe and/or say about it. The latter tack has been the usual target of archaeological histories. This is not to say that that kind of interpretive approach is unimportant, but that our knowledge about the archaeological record is critical in a resource-management context, whereas interpretations are not (or should not be, Resource Protection Planning Process [RP3] and "state plans" notwithstanding) of the same importance.

To understand the growth of archaeological knowledge, I look at three factors: 1) motivations—i.e., why an observation/investigation was made; 2) source of funding; and 3) conceptions of the nature of the record. Motivation is tough enough to ascertain even contemporaneously—traditionally in this country we have twelve people vote on it. From a scientific perspective, motivation pertains only to reason-giving rather than explanation (Sellars 1963). Even so, the stories we tell ourselves about why we do what we do, do pass for cause in our culture and provide a link between our history and the literature we generate about it. For the purpose of assessing the impact and shifting emphases of motivation in archaeology in the LMV, I have distinguished five classes of motives: commercial, curiosity, heritage, political, and scientific. Of course, not many acts or individuals can be neatly assigned a single motive, but this complexity does not preclude linkages between archaeological knowledge and motive.

Commercial motives are those that treat the archaeological record as a commodity. For professionals this conjures up looting and other pejoratives, but anyone who makes a living from the archaeological record can have commercial motives. Commercial motives are and have been a powerful shaper of archaeological knowledge. Curiosity designates the desire to know about something that lies outside contemporary common experience. Heritage motivation is part of a larger preservationist ethic that construes surviving elements of the past as significant just because they are surviving symbols of someone's real or imagined past. This motivation underlay most of the initial CRM legislation. Political motives entail the use of the record to further contemporary political objectives. While one normally associates such motives with European archaeology in the first half of the last century, they also clearly underlie many contemporary practices and even legislation, such as the Native American Graves Protection and Repatriation Act (NAGPRA), that sadly governs archaeology and archaeological practice in this country today. Scientific motivation is taken to be the desire to develop a body of knowledge suitable for testing hypotheses about how we came to be the way we are, i.e., the unfolding of human history. Science is and has often been claimed as motivation by archaeologists, even when no science is in evidence; consequently, such claims need close scrutiny. Missing from this list is conservation. It is a secondary goal, inasmuch as conservation is always attributable to one or more of the factors outlined above.

The second parameter, source of funding, is conceived in terms of private sources, local public sources, state government, and federal government. While source of funding certainly interacts with motivation, they are not two measures of the same thing. Funding source should impact archaeology primarily in determining where and on what archaeology gets done rather than how it is done. In this manner funding links archaeology to, and thereby identifies, different constituencies. As we are all aware, however, how archaeology is done can become entangled with funding source, usually to the detriment of archaeology.

Archaeological theories, conceptions of the nature of the archaeological record, are discussed in terms of three major paradigms or approaches: historical, more or less synonymous with culture history; functional, which embraces reconstructionism (*sensu* Dunnell 1982, 1986a) and most elements of processualism; and scientific, being represented by evolutionary archaeology and integrating historical and functional approaches. The essay itself is written from the last perspective. To these archaeological paradigms must be added the pre-paradigmatic "common sense," i.e., our own cultural biases and values (*sensu* Dunnell 1982; *contra* Watson 1991). Missing are the various postprocessualisms, because they are concerned almost exclusively with the meaning of the record and have no relevance to the central task here.

Abjuring classical periods, these considerations are organized only roughly by chronology; "nineteenth-century archaeology" means the archaeology of the nineteenth century, and not a particular way of practicing archaeology. The result differs from the usual episodic accounts, periods of stasis separated by abrupt, revolutionary "transitions." A picture of continuous development emerges, driven by multiple motivations, funding sources, and conceptions of the record. This developmental continuum is punctuated by a few key events.

Knowledge of the Archaeological Record

Literate encounters are but one factor influencing the recognition of regional archaeological records. The nature of the remains and the environment(s) of the region interact with the attitudes of the reporting population. In the low-relief landscape of the Mississippi valley, the presence of large earthen architecture was easily recognized as artificial by both the indigenes and the Europeans. Not surprisingly, they are the initial focus of attention.

Early Notices: Travelers' Accounts

Archaeological remains began to come to notice as soon as literate Europeans started to traverse the Mississippi alluvial valley. The environment of the valley, however, insured that there was great variability in when particular elements were identified. The earliest discoveries followed the river itself and its major tributaries. For example, what is certainly the Troyville site, with its ca. 70-foot-tall, tiered mound is repeatedly noted from 1717 on (Jones 2005). Nothing of lasting archaeological value is contained in the eighteenth-century literature of the region. One does well even to associate these earliest reports with locations and structures known from later literature. Troyville is the exception, on account of its unique and highly identifiable location (where the Tensas, Ouachita, and Little [Catahoula] rivers join to form the Black). The main value of early accounts of the Mississippi valley is ethnological (e.g., Adair 1775; Bourne 1922; Dumont de Montigny 1753; DuPratz 1758; de la Vega 1986 [1722]; Jeffreys 1760; Joutel 1998 [1713]).

By the beginning of the nineteenth century, mention of archaeological phenomena becomes more frequent (e.g., Brackenridge 1814; Bringier 1821; Dunbar 1832; Nuttall 1980 [1819]; Stoddard 1812) and virtually every traveler notes the presence of mounds. This does not seem to represent increased interest, but simply the frequency of literate travelers in the region. Indeed, with rare exceptions, the character of the reports is little changed. Abandoned, aboveground, aboriginal architecture—mounds and earthworks—remain the sole subjects of explorers' and travelers' reports. Typically, still only the largest and most accessible structures are reported (Berry et al. 2006).

Accessibility, given the environment of the valley, was largely a matter of navigable waterways. This was to continue its pernicious effect in at least parts of the study area until well into the twentieth century (e.g., Dunnell 1998). The Mississippi River itself was easily navigable, though with strong currents, as was the Black-Ouachita (Anonymous 1897). In moving around through its valley, the Mississippi had destroyed many mounds, leaving relatively few that could be observed from the river itself. The banks were still almost entirely forested through the early twentieth century, preventing direct observation of even very large structures (Moore 1911:368).[3] Many other waterways, like the Red River, were obstructed to traffic, greatly impeding their use (Anonymous 1897). Thus, by the mid-nineteenth century, only a handful of sites in this vast region, now known for its spectacular remains, had become part of a "professional" database (Figure 3.1).

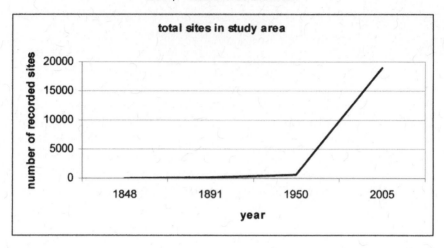

Figure 3.1. Number of sites recorded in study area (see Chapter 1, Figure 1.1; see Table 3.1 for data by state).

Early nineteenth-century travelers' reports are, like their predecessors, mostly useless for any modern purpose—dimensions are exaggerated, descriptions forced into stilted templates, interpretation is highly ethnocentric and frequently merged with description (e.g., something is called a "fort" and the label alone stands for a description). Locations are often erroneous. Indeed, in many cases, it is not clear that the travelers knew where they were with any precision, let alone things they saw or were reported to them. When coupled with the fact that observation and publication often were separated by years and based on unremarked secondhand accounts, it is little wonder that a small industry could be set up (as in the case of the "de Soto chronicles"[4]) just by figuring out what these reports describe with no threat of definitive resolution. But then there was no real motivation to provide accurate accounts in the early nineteenth century. Few readers would ever have the opportunity to gainsay erroneous accounts; still fewer would be done an injury by sloppy, even fanciful description. Curiosity and the desire to entertain, i.e., commercial motivation, are the principal, if not sole, motivations in evidence.

A notable exception is Henry Marie Brackenridge (1786–1871), whose *Views of Louisiana* (1814) is of signal importance in understanding not only early perception of the archaeological record but attitudes toward it by the sequent scholarly tradition. Although clearly incidental to his main purposes, Brackenridge devotes a chapter (pages 166–187) to "Antiquities in the Valley of the Mississippi," apart from their occasional mention elsewhere. Typifying the times, he is short on facts and long on speculation. He describes only three actual locations (McKee's Rocks in Pennsylvania, Cahokia in Illinois, and Troyville in

Louisiana), and mentions a few others (e.g., Marietta, St. Louis) already de-scribed in detail by others. The bulk of the chapter is spent on speculations of his own and others on the origin(s) of the monuments seen. Brackenridge is clearly well read and a logical thinker. He spends much time dismissing the Welsh as the authors of American earthworks, using arguments as easily ap-preciated today as then.

Crucial to his contribution is his friendship with Thomas Jefferson (Brack-enridge 1848) and his familiarity with *Notes on the State of Virginia,* in which Jefferson describes his own excavation of a burial mound on his Potomac es-tate (Jefferson 1801:143–147). Drawing upon his vastly broader knowledge of antiquities, Brackenridge distinguishes three classes of works: 1) fortifications, which he regards as of general occurrence; 2) "barrows," using, as did Jefferson, the English term for analogous structures in the Old World, meaning burial mounds, and to which he assigns Jefferson's mound; and 3) "pyramids," which he took to be foundation mounds for temples or other buildings and/or monu-ments to great men. Contrary to the received wisdom about early-nineteenth-century writers, Brackenridge seems to have had no more doubt than Jefferson about the Indian origin of at least some of the burial mounds or barrows. The pyramids, on the other hand, he regarded as too numerous, and in many cases too large, to have been constructed by the Indians as they were known to him; the traces exceeded the population necessary for their construction. Without making clear his reasoning, he correctly identifies the two kinds of mounds as being of different ages, but reverses the order. The pyramids are earliest, and this allows him to link the pyramid-builders to Mexico as ancestors to those peoples. In a letter to Jefferson, Brackenridge makes an astoundingly modern deduction from what was known to him at the time: "From some cause or other (and we know that there are enough which suffice to effect it) the population had been astonishly diminished immediately before we became acquainted with them" (Brackenridge 1848:153). He seemingly attributes the general lack of knowledge of the authorship of the mounds among American Indians to this event, foreshadowing use of the concept of "founder's effects" or drift by nearly two centuries in this context (Dunnell 1991).

Building a Database

The first general survey published that covers our target area is Squier and Davis' *Ancient Monuments of the Mississippi Valley* (1998 [1848]). The Missis-sippi River was a major artery into the center of the continent, but Squier and Davis enumerated only six archaeological monuments in our LMV study area. Although regarded as a monument in its own right, Squier and Davis' *opus* is of marginal direct significance from a modern perspective. For one, they breathed new life into the moundbuilder-as-a-separate-race hypothesis that had been rejected by educated people as a serious alternative since Morton's day (1839). Touted as scientific because of the supposed exactitude of its surveys, this precision was more than a little exaggerated (Holmes 1892). While they saw themselves as motivated by scientific aims, some of their scientific contemporaries rejected this claim rather vitriolicly (e.g., *Scientific American* 1848).

The most important positive legacy of *Ancient Monuments* may well be the national interest it created in reporting archaeological phenomena and in identifying a place to which they might be reported: the Smithsonian Institution.[5] Thus Squier and Davis' work was supplemented by a steady trickle of reports through the rest of the century, often in the *Annual Report to the Board of Regents of the Smithsonian Institution*. Although these ad hoc citizen reports of antiquities came to the Smithsonian regularly thereafter, a decision was made in 1878 to exploit this source of information and develop it into a national database. This was accomplished by the publication and distribution of *Circular 316* (Mason 1878a) on February 1 of that year over the signature of the Secretary, Joseph Henry. The objective was to obtain "from every available source whatever is now known, or can be ascertained by special investigation, of the antiquities of North America" (Mason 1878a:1). Information was sought about the size, shape, location, details of construction of mounds, earthworks, and other "traces of aboriginal engineering," as well as newspaper clippings and other published notices of the discovery and exploration of such structures and the locations and owners of collections of artifacts. To regularize the reports insofar as possible, short of using a form, reporting was to be guided by a series of 86 questions, employing a set of standard symbols published three years earlier in the *Annual Report of the Board of Trustees of the Smithsonian Institution* (reproduced in *Circular 316*). Thorough spatial coverage was the clear objective, as Mason emphasizes: "It is designed by the Institution . . . to have no blank spaces whatever; but to be able to give an intelligent account of every county and even every township in the United States" (Mason 1881:441). He even recognizes the importance of negative evidence: "Very few persons realize the preciousness of such a statement as 'There are no ancient remains whatever in my county'" (Mason 1881:441). Indeed, he received just such reports (e.g., Barton 1880:428–429). The need to differentiate "missing data" from zero, which depends on a statement of where one has looked, not just a statement of where what was found is located, would be lost on most archaeologists until comparatively modern times. New archaeological notices continued to be published in other venues, of course. The Knapp Mounds (Toltec Mounds), for example, were reported in *Harper's Weekly* along with several others, some of which are surely in the core study area (Du Pre 1875:346–351).

Although the planned exhaustive catalogue contained the germ of a scientific database, and Smithsonian personnel certainly thought of themselves as scientists, exactly why it was undertaken is by no means clear. Conservation of the resource was recognized as essential at least by 1820 (Atwater 1833), but to what end? The lack of any rationale for conservation continues to haunt the discipline. It explains how Mason's broadsides could actually encourage destructive digging in mounds. The exhaustive catalogue of American antiquities never came into being, of course. Neither Mason, Thomas, nor President Nixon (Executive Order 11593, May 13, 1971, 36 CFR.8921, Sec. 2a) had a clue as to the scope of the archaeological record in North America or any part of it. As close as the Smithsonian got was Cyrus Thomas' *Catalogue of Prehistoric Works East of the Rocky Mountains* (1891), compiled as a direct consequence of *Circular 316*. This is a precursor to Thomas' *Report of the Mound Explorations of the Bureau of Ethnology* (1985 [1894]). Not only did *Circular 316* activity provide the list of places to be investigated, but some of the reporters volunteering archaeological information to the *Annual Reports*, like Edward Palmer, turn out to be Thomas' field investigators in our study area (see also Jeter, ed. 1990; Jeter 2001). Although displaying none of the detail of Thomas' 1894 tour de force, his *Catalogue* provides a better measure of the growth of knowledge about the archaeological record by the end of the nineteenth century because it includes kinds of remains other than mounds (e.g., shell heaps, petroglyphs, and even localities with remains but no monuments) (Figure 3.1).

Thus, by the concluding years of the nineteenth century, the federal government, through the agency of the Smithsonian Institution, had become the keeper of site files, a central repository for archaeological information. Monuments, sites in modern terms, were still the focus of the Smithsonian, but the Institution received large numbers of artifacts as well. Specimens were, for the most part, warehoused; however, Charles Rau (1876), followed by Thomas Wilson (1899), did try to construct the first formal classifications of artifacts. Holmes' path-breaking ceramics studies (Holmes 1886a, 1886b) drew heavily upon private collections[6] as well as Smithsonian resources. With the exception of the mound survey directed by Thomas, however, federal funds were not expended in generating archaeological data; rather, the public at large was solicited as observers, investigators, collectors, and reporters. Professionals did not conduct field surveys. Apparently no special expertise was deemed necessary. Much of early-twentieth-century professional efforts would be directed to reversing this action.

The "motivation" driving these efforts was clearly conservation of traces of the country's early inhabitants. Indeed, conservation was an important motivation for ethnologists as well. In the late nineteenth century, archaeology still constituted a major part of anthropology, and most anthropologists "did" or were interested in archaeology. Section H (Anthropology and Psychology) of the American Association for the Advancement of Science and the American Anthropological Association provided national-scale organizations not connected to the federal government, and their most important early accomplishment was passage of the federal Antiquities Act of 1906. Conservation of the record is thus clearly attested; what was lacking, and continues to be lacking, are pragmatic reasons for conservation.

Systematic Generation of Data

A major change in character, as well as quantity, of archaeological data took place with efforts to systematically discover such remains. All of the early reports, even those of the Smithsonian *Circular 316* data, are properly thought of as anecdotal. Discovery and reporting was an accident of encounter. Field surveys, i.e., intentional, systematic forays to discover and describe aboriginal remains, did begin in the latter part of the nineteenth century, however. These surveys (e.g., McLean 1879) were undertaken first by private individuals at their own expense. At least three early surveys include portions of the LMV, those of Jacob V. Brower (S. Neilsen, personal communication 2004), Theodore Lewis (Jeter 2001; Keyes 1925, 1928, 1930), and that of Lewis M. Bean and D. L. Hoffman (Houck 1908:41–42).[7] Like the Smithsonian work, they too usually concentrated on mounds and earthworks. Although styled as a "mound survey," the Bean and Hoffman survey was cast more broadly than mounds alone. Louis Houck, who funded this survey, writes of his purposes and achievements (1908:41):

> make some observations . . . on the character of such remains and relics as have been discovered and have escaped the wreck and storm of the ages, the more ruthless plowshare, and the ignorance of destroying man. My main object, however, has been to accurately and definitely locate every mound and settlement of these pre-historic denizens. . . . It is not asserted that they [Bean and Hoffman] found every existing mound, or discovered every pre-historic settlement, but it is reasonably certain that all the most conspicuous and remarkable mounds have been . . . located.

Houck's motivation is revealed in the first sentence—conservation of evidence of early occupation. His surveyors, however, had little knowledge of geomorphology, and mistook many natural features for artificial mounds, a problem that continued to plague intentional surveys into the modern era (e.g., Phillips et al. 2003 [1951]). Brower's survey and that of Lewis were similarly motivated and extended further south into Arkansas, and in the case of the latter, even Mississippi.

As much as it would be gratifying to claim these precocious efforts as the forerunners of modern surveys and site files, there is not much to support such a connection. None of the modern site files, for example, seems to have been built on the data generated by these gentlemen. Reference to them, even when recognized, is made only retroactively. The quality of all three, however, is such that important information may yet be gleaned from them (see Jeter 2001 and Keyes 1930 for Lewis).

The last of the great private survey efforts is that of Clarence B. Moore's expeditions, many of which included part of the study area (1908, 1909, 1910, 1911, 1912, 1916a, 1916b; see also Brookes 2001; Morse and Morse 1998; Wardle 1913, 1956). While Moore's work is by far the most sophisticated of the private surveys (e.g., he solicited specialists to describe skeletal remains [Hrdlička 1908, 1909, 1912], did some of the first chemical analyses to identify archaeological materials [Moore 1908:484–485], and cited the existing scholarly literature), his motivation was clearly the acquisition of specimens and knowledge about artifacts rather than conservation of sites. Even though excavation was his investigatory tool, one looks in vain to find diagrams of the internal structure of the mounds he was digging, information that had become de rigueur in this area since the work of Forshey (1845), Squier and Davis (1998 [1848]), Beyer (1895, 1897, 1900), and most especially Thomas (1985 [1894]).[8] That his motivation was artifacts per se is abundantly clear in his field decisions as well. He declined, for example, to expend any effort on the Toltec Mounds (Knapp Mounds) (Moore 1908:557), because this otherwise spectacular site "had no history of discovery of artifacts in the vicinity." The same attitude accounts for the short shrift he gave the Yazoo Basin (Moore 1908:564–592; see Brookes 2001). Even though he provided many maps, later workers (e.g., Brown 1992 [1926]; Morse and Morse 1998; Phillips 1970; Phillips et al. 2003 [1951]) had difficulty in relocating his sites with certainty. While site destruction undoubtedly played a part, in most cases inadequate descriptions and maps appear to be the culprits. Furthermore, Moore thought he had discovered all of the "important" remains of the areas he had covered:

> While all of that part of the Mississippi under description within three miles of the river was carefully searched by us, we believe that conditions north of Vicksburg are such as to facilitate a more successful quest [than south of Vicksburg] and that consequently few if any sites of importance on this part of the river were passed by us unnoticed. It is true that aboriginal sites are often well back from the present course of the river and are frequently screened from it by trees, but large mounds, singly and in groups, such as seem to be found along this part of the river, are as a rule, known for some distance around, and diligent inquiry, such as was made

by our agents, and later by ourselves, must, we believe, almost invariably have led to their discovery (Moore 1911:367–368).

From a modern perspective Moore inflicted horrendous damage on the archaeological record. Nonetheless, his highly visible, quickly reported, well-illustrated work presents a sharp contrast to typical private artifact collecting of the period, as does his effort to catalogue sites.

Artifact collecting, including digging into mounds and cemeteries for the purpose of collecting artifacts, came into its own in the latter part of the nineteenth century. Many archaeological or natural history "cabinets" were created during this era (e.g., Butler 1894). Captain C. W. Riggs, whose 1880s collecting expeditions to the St. Francis and Mississippi rivers may have served as a logistical model for Moore's expeditions, brought the "treasures" of the Mississippi valley to general notice at the World's Columbian Exposition in 1892 (Brose 1980). He might well have been regarded as another Moore were it not that his collections were dispersed in private commerce after the exposition closed and the field notes and photographs lost. Indeed, it is difficult to distinguish Riggs' "archaeology" from that of the Smithsonian in its mound survey, save for the eventual disposition of the materials and publication. Just north of the study area, in the Cairo lowlands of Southeast Missouri, excavation for artifacts reached industrial proportions (Thomas 1891:183). Many of these materials were dispersed, but a large number ended up in public institutions such as Harvard University and the American Museum of Natural History. Stephen Williams' undergraduate thesis (1949), for example, was based on one such collection purchased by G. G. McCurdy for the Yale Peabody Museum from Scott County, Missouri. Most of these "cabinet" artifacts have since passed into oblivion, either through outright destruction or the loss of provenience data, the latter now forming part of the basis of the still lively commercial trade in artifacts.[9]

On the Trail of a Systematic Database: State Sovereignty Asserted

Initially, the federal government, through the agency of the Smithsonian, had taken the lead in the systematic generation and recording of archaeological data. By the beginning of the twentieth century, however, there were increasing efforts in many parts of the country to organize what basically had been the *Circular 316* task at the state level. This kind of activity had been encouraged by the formation of many local scientific societies, particularly after the Civil War. They generated interest in field work and publication of results (O'Brien and Lyman 2001). State and local control was driven at least partly by political motives, as O'Brien and Lyman (2001:8) record: "It was certainly most discreditable that one had to resort to the Smithsonian Institute, the Peabody Museum, and the Blackmore Museum in Salisbury, England to find proper collections of our prehistoric remains . . . it [the Missouri Historical Society] . . . would be the agency to bring together a collection that would not only rival but surpass, any similar archaeological and historical collection (AIA Archives 1:23)". Archaeology, then as now, was seen as a kind of "science" that any person might do; indeed, that had been official policy in the federal government, as we have seen. Other fields, like physics or even entomology (another early favorite), slowly had become more difficult for the nonprofessional to penetrate.[10] Even while the Smithsonian was encouraging mound excavation, other professionals were mindful of the damage being done to the record and attempted to replace haphazard digging with more sophisticated programs (e.g., Putnam 1887). State surveys began to appear in the early twentieth century (Parker 1929); these were mostly repositories of information on the *Circular 316* model when not conceived as a finite, or even one-shot, task.

The real impetus for the establishment of state archaeological surveys came from the Committee on State Archaeological Surveys (CSAS) of the National Research Council. O'Brien and Lyman (2001; O'Brien and Lyman, ed. 2001) have recently analyzed this important development and reprinted the key documents, viz., *Report on the Conference on Midwestern Archaeology Held in St. Louis, Missouri, May 18, 1929* (Dunlap 1929); *Conference on Southern Pre-History* (National Research Council 1932); *Guide Leaflet for Amateur Archaeologists* (Guthe 1930); and *State Archaeological Surveys: Suggestions in Method and Technique* (Wissler et al. 1923). As was recognized at the time, the main problem was identifying a stable organization to carry out this task. The volunteer model growing out of the local scientific societies usually was thwarted by the dual motives of volunteers—some motivated by conservation for "science," some, the artifact collectors, by curiosity and/or commerce. Yet Ohio and, in our area, Missouri, remain shining exceptions. More generally successful were state-funded surveys, usually finding their initial homes in previously established geological surveys (e.g., Skinner and Schrabisch 1913).

In the study area, the first state surveys were set up in the 1930s, with varying degrees of formality, but mostly in consequence of initiatives of particular individuals. In Louisiana and Mississippi the connection to geological surveys is strong initially: James A. Ford's early papers were published by the Louisiana Geological Survey (Ford 1935a, 1935b, 1935c, 1936); Calvin Brown's pathbreaking *Archeology of Mississippi* (1992 [1926]) (see Ford 1987) was published by the Mississippi Geological Survey, although it did not beget the modern Mississippi state archaeological survey. Brown attended the 1929 St. Louis conference as "Archaeologist attached to the Geological Survey." James Ford was instrumental in getting the surveys in both states going (Rivet 1991).[11] Rivet dates the beginning of the Louisiana survey to 1933, but 1935, when the first formal site forms, apparently modeled on the NRC recommendations, came into use, seems a better start date. Louisiana State University became the home for the state survey. In Mississippi, Ford teamed with Moreau Chambers, not only in excavations but also in field surveys, to locate sites, and the first site survey forms date to this collaboration in the late 1920s (Baca and Giliberti 1995:54; Samuel McGahey, personal communication 2006). Unique in the region, the state survey in Mississippi was housed by the Mississippi Department of Archives and History (MDAH), where the survey remains to this day. Neither Ford nor Chambers had been part of the 1929 conference, but both participated in the Birmingham conference (Brown did not), Chambers representing MDAH and Ford as a private individual. Fred Kniffen represented Louisiana State University and its newly founded Department of Geography and Anthropology (National Research Council 1932). Unlike most state surveys that followed the *Circular 316* strategy of using amateurs to collect data, the fledgling Mississippi survey actually expended funds on locating and excavating sites (Chambers 1937; Chambers and Ford 1941), although most of the money was federal (National Research Council, later Works Progress Administration [WPA]).

The other states followed more or less on the Louisiana model. S. C. Dillinger, zoologist at the University of Arkansas and Curator of the University Museum, began the state files for Arkansas (Ann Early, personal communication 2006). The state survey remained in the museum under Dillinger's direction until the Arkansas Archeological Survey was established by the state legislature in 1967 (Davis 2002). Thus Arkansas went from what was undoubtedly the least well-organized survey in the LMV to the best almost overnight. Louisiana would subsequently remodel its own program on the Arkansas system. Although it did not show in the Arkansas organization, Dillinger had attended both the 1929 and 1932 conferences sponsored by the NRC. Jesse Wrench, a historian soon to be joined by Carl Chapman (both faculty members at the University of Missouri in Columbia), began the state survey within the framework of the Missouri Archaeological Society (Chapman 1953; O'Brien 1996b). Wrench did not attend either of the NRC-sponsored conferences, even though the first conference was held in Missouri and attended by many Missourians from the governor on down. The Missouri model, certainly envisioned as one route by the CSAS, is not the usual one taken. The Missouri Archaeological Society has been closely tied to the University of Missouri from the outset, but amateur archaeological societies have not usually proved stable enough to support ongoing state surveys. Today the Missouri Archaeological Survey is locked in mortal combat with the state historic preservation bureaucracy over who will manage the site files.

First at the federal scale, then at that of the state, the need to generate a sys-

tematic archaeological database that could support scientific research was recognized by virtually all interested parties by the beginning of the last century.
Over the course of the next three decades, all of the states in the study area had
created state surveys of one sort or another. They ran the gamut from active
efforts to locate and catalogue sites and preserve antiquities to passive repositories of ad hoc information. They were run by academic, bureaucratic, and
amateur organizations with varying degrees of professional input.

With such a varied history it is not surprising that the initial objectives of
creating state surveys have yet to be realized. Although the Committee on State
Archaeological Surveys recognized the need to generate representative data, to
differentiate missing data from zeros in modern parlance (O'Brien and Lyman
2001), just as Mason had done before, this basic requirement was quickly abandoned. No state survey, even the most active ones like Mississippi, ever made
an effort to create this kind of database. Rather, the expedient and least expensive route, ad hoc reports solicited or simply received from the interested
public, became the norm for generating new data, just as in Mason's day a hundred years before.[12] This would not change until the 1970s.

Also not surprising given this history, site surveys are not seamless data
fields from state to state. Although the Committee on State Archaeological
Surveys tried to impart some uniformity in terminology, classification, and
procedure, we have seen that the LMV states variously participated in NRC
conferences from the start; none actually had a representative on the committee itself. Procedures, meanings of basic terms such as "site," and what information is recorded vary from state to state and even from time to time within
the same state. Although we have a lot more "data" now than in 1900 (Table 3.1;
Figure 3.1), it is not clear that we are better off in any practical sense. Archaeological data still remain anecdotal.

The Academy Gets Involved: Paradise Lost

At the same time that museums and academic institutions were availing themselves of the miners' loot (e.g., Holmes 1886a; Willoughby 1897), they also began
to undertake investigations of their own. Most of the earliest are little different
than the amateur efforts (e.g., Putnam 1881 in re Curtis on the St. Francis) but
some of these (unfortunately not in the study area) are of considerable renown,
having played a formative role in the establishment of archaeological practice
and professionalism (e.g., Wyman 1863, 1875). Since the first university-level
course in archaeology was not offered until 1877 (Mason 1878b:274), and departments of anthropology were not common until well into the twentieth
century (Freeman 1965), museums, particularly the Peabody Museum, took
the lead.

Table 3.1. Number of sites in study area "known to science" (see Chapter 1, Figure 1.1).

	1848	1891	ca. 1950	ca. 2005
Arkansas	0	88*	128	9,214
Louisiana	2	6	103	2,425
Mississippi	4	19**	392	4,516
Missouri	0	2***	16	862***
Tennessee	0	1	23	1,965
Total:	6	138	640	18,982

* 1 site noted had already been destroyed by the river.
** 1 site, the infamous Claiborne "wall," omitted from this tabulation.
*** 1 site added, "County Line," listed as being in Stoddard County (out of the study area) but actually being about half in Dunklin County.

Data for 1848 are taken directly from Squier and Davis (1998 [1848]); 1891 is taken directly from Thomas (1891); 1950 is from Phillips et al. (2003 [1951]) supplemented by Ford (1936), Williams (1954), and Phillips (1970) for those parts of the study area not covered in Phillips et al. (2003 [1951]). The 2005 estimate is derived from current or near-current site-file data from the respective states; I acknowledge the assistance of Michael J. O'Brien, Lela Donat, Jan K. Simek, Keith Baca, and Joe Saunders in this surprisingly difficult task.

In the study area, this activity began with the two seasons of work by Charles Peabody (1904) in Coahoma County, Mississippi. Thus Harvard University initiated a long and productive association with the archaeology of the region that is still active today. Peabody's excavations into what are now recognized as the Dorr and Oliver sites are sometimes characterized as the "first professional excavations" (Weinstein et al. 1985:3–1), in spite of Holmes', Palmer's, and Thing's earlier excavations in support of Thomas' *Report on the Mound Explorations of the Bureau of Ethnology* (1985 [1894]). Contrasting with his innovative work in other regions (Peabody 1908; Peabody and Moorehead 1904), Peabody's Mississippi excavations are rather standard for the time. Although it does give the first modern look at the construction and function of Brackenridge's pyramids, Peabody's reporting still leaves a lot to be desired (Belmont 1961; Phillips 1970).

Federal interest continued, albeit at a reduced level. Most notable is the work of Henry B. Collins (1926, 1932) just to the east of the study area. Even more important than these publications is that Collins was responsible for attracting James A. Ford to archaeology and serving as his mentor (Baca 2002). As departments of anthropology began to be established in the 1930s and 1940s, local academics began to conduct and report on small-scale research projects (e.g., Dellinger and Dickinson 1940; Dellinger and Wakefield 1936; Kniffen 1936).

Harvard returned to the valley with Philip Phillips' (1939) doctoral dissertation on Mississippian pottery. While important in its own right, this volume is more important as a precursor to what would turn out to be the single most important publication in the history of the study area, Phillips, Ford, and Griffin's (2003 [1951]) *Archaeological Survey in the Lower Mississippi Alluvial Valley, 1940–1947* (hereafter PFG). There is little archaeology done after this that does not use this work or its methods, and its importance has been generally recognized (e.g., Dunnell 1985; Lyman et al. 1997; Rees 2001; Willey and Sabloff 1993; Williams, ed. 2003). It was problem-oriented: the authors wanted to work out the origins of the Mississippian, the pottery of which had been described for more than a hundred years. They used the problem to define an appropriate study area rather than picking arbitrary and/or convenient boundaries. They devised a system of survey and site location that delivered seamless data for the whole region (actually the use of 15-minute quads was suggested earlier by Robbins [1936]) rather than by political subdivisions. They identified the methods needed to deliver a chronology, seriation, and stratigraphy, and integrated these into a research design to solve their problem. They constructed a language of observation, a classification that was suited both to their problem and the physical materials to which it was to be applied. They set their problem in ethnographic and geological contexts that both aided in the solution of the problem and gave that solution much broader meaning. Importantly, they provided insight into the rationales for their decisions, including fields of disagreement, that could inform subsequent scholars.

This is not to say that PFG is perfect. In fact, it is deeply flawed. Their classification is primitive, a fact that led them to make errors in their chronology (see Dunnell, this volume, Chapter 4). Much of the virtue of the chronology was lost when they divided it into periods. They routinely underestimated error stemming from formation processes, sample size, and other sources. They lacked the quantitative skills to execute their plan. Their grasp of stratigraphy was primitive at best. They did not archive their materials so that some of these flaws could be corrected by later scholars. But for all of these problems, PFG is head-and-shoulders above anything else done at the time.

The 1951 volume was part of a still larger research plan. Conceived as a three-stage operation—survey, testing, and major excavation of selected sites once their significance was understood—PFG reported only on elements of the first two stages. Williams (1954) extended aerial coverage to the north and first applied the Willey and Phillips (2001 [1958]; Phillips and Willey 1953) phase concept. Phillips (1970) himself extended coverage to the southern Yazoo Basin, reporting his own work and that of Robert Greengo (1964). Phillips also used the phase, not only for the Yazoo Basin but also retroactively for the territory covered by PFG. He also introduced the type-variety classification as a replacement for the Ford classification of PFG. Unfortunately, both of these innovations were adopted in principal by subsequent workers. It is at this point that "culture history went awry," to paraphrase O'Brien's (1995) critique of the Morses' (1983) *Archaeology of the Central Mississippi Valley*, which was done using this same scheme. Vincas Steponaitis, Jeffrey Brain, and Ian Brown extended coverage still farther south on the east side of the river, but this has yet to be published in whole (many bits and pieces have) and lies outside our study area. Williams brought coverage on the west side of the river south to include the Tensas basin (Williams et al. 1966). The third stage of the plan initiated by PFG, the excavation of key sites, also has borne fruit, notably at the Lake George (Williams and Brain 1983) and Winterville (Brain 1989) sites. Both attempt to make improvements to the Phillips' (1970) classification, but they remain within the faulty framework.

One can appreciate the virtues of the plan even while deploring its frailties. One did not have to be part of the LMV survey to contribute to a cumulative database. Areal projects, single sites, or even studies of particular classes of artifacts could be seamlessly integrated into a genuinely scientific database. In fact, broad adoption of the Phillips' (1970) types and phases by virtually all workers, as has happened in the study area, clearly had that potential. But when Phillips eschewed the problem orientation of the original PFG opus in favor of divining the "truth," he ceased being a scientist and adopted an expert-witness mode of operation. Ah, to have been so close but yet so far away!

Second Federal Era

New Deal Archaeology. While the federal government never got out of the business of archaeology, the 1930s saw a reinvolvement, this time as funding agent. This second federal era was interrupted only briefly by World War II. The new era of federal archaeology actually began in the southern part of the study area with the Federal Emergency Relief Administration excavations at Marksville (Seltzer and Strong 1936; see also Haag 1985). This was the pilot project for the use of federal relief labor for archaeology, the bulk of which was carried out by the WPA. Most of the work done was large-scale excavation of single sites, although some funds were expended on surveys, though not in the study area (e.g., Adams 1942; Wauchope 1966, but see Chambers and Ford 1941). Remarkably, with the exception of Avoyelles Parish, where five sites were excavated (16AV1 [Marksville], 16AV2 [Greenhouse], 16AV4 [Nick Place], 16AV22 [Nick Farm] and 16AV25 [Baptiste]) (Neuman 1984; Rivet 1991), our study area missed out on this data bonanza. Adams had attempted to excavate at Langdon, the largest Mississippian site in our area in Southeast Missouri, but was denied access by the landowner (Dunnell 1998).

Depression-era relief archaeology, usually termed "New Deal Archaeology," has been examined at length elsewhere and need not be repeated here (e.g., Dye 1991; Haag 1985; Lyon 1996; see also Jennings 1986 for a candid evaluation of the product). A couple of observations are in order, however. First, the explosion of archaeology brought about by relief funding placed great strains on the rather haphazard way archaeology had been done. To cope with this, an elaborate series of forms were promulgated so that relatively inexperienced supervisors and untutored laborers could generate comparable data (William S. Webb, personal communication 1960). This had the effect of standardizing observations in a way that the old CSAS never did. Secondly, it produced a cadre of university-trained archaeologists, mostly University of Chicago, Fay-Cooper Cole students (Haag 1986:66) to replace an earlier generation of archaeologists who had come to the profession from various routes and backgrounds. The potential, at least, for generating useful scientific data appeared for the first time.

The National Park Service Takes Over. After the war the federal government did not pick up where it left off.[13] Because archaeological projects had been terminated abruptly with the outbreak of hostilities, most of the New Deal–era excavations and surveys went unanalyzed and unpublished. When new federal money became available to archaeology, a new strategy—pejoratively called "salvage archaeology"—dominated thinking. Thus many New Deal projects still remain unanalyzed and unpublished; generations now separate excavation and analysis, not a promising circumstance. In any case, these important potential data have yet to become part of archaeological knowledge in any meaningful sense.

As McGimsey has reported (2001; see also Keel [1988] and the papers therein, esp. Davis [1988], Peebles [1988], and Thorne [1988]) the post-war reestablishment of federal involvement was initiated by a spate of dam construction and the potential loss of resources when thousands of acres of land were flooded by new reservoirs. The first iteration of this program was administered by the National Park Service (NPS) but carried out by the Smithsonian Institution under the River Basin Survey and included both an identification and mitigation component (Jennings 1986). The 1966 National Historic Preservation Act expanded the scope of the salvage program and placed virtually all federal archaeological work under the NPS. Most archaeological work was now contracted to university programs. Client-patron relationships developed between NPS regions and particular university programs, promoting a certain level of stability not normally associated with contracting. These relationships supplied a badly needed source of funding at the very time that the baby-boomers were entering college. There would never again be a shortage of archaeologists.

Once again our particular study area largely missed the federal largesse. Being entirely low-lying, reservoirs were not built in the valley proper. There were no salvage projects. There were a couple of important exceptions, however: agricultural land-leveling and highway salvage. Agricultural land-leveling is one of those strange bureaucratic animals. On the one hand, the federal government was committed to preservation of the archaeological record, while on the other they (the Soil Conservation Service) were funding its destruction. While not within its mandate (Davis 1988), the NPS funded two studies of the effects of land-leveling on the archaeological record and the need to extend salvage beyond dams (Ford et al. 1972; J. Williams 1967, 1968). While laudable in intent, these studies did not stop land-leveling or provide for salvage prior to land-leveling, but simply withdrew federal funding from most leveling. With the expansion of rice as a central Mississippi valley crop in the last 20 years, leveling is both economical for agribusiness and the number-one cause of archaeological destruction.

The other exception, highway salvage, was engendered by the Federal Aid Highway Act of 1956 (Interstate Highway System) that funded survey and excavation within the right-of-way. These funds were not administered by the NPS but by the Bureau of Public Roads. The NPS had developed a modest infrastructure to support its archaeological activities; the Bureau of Public Roads had none. More importantly, it led to the involvement of state departments of transportation (DOTs) in archaeological survey and mitigation. Subsequently, with the passage of the National Environmental Protection Act of 1969 (NEPA) and the Archaeological and Historic Preservation Act (a.k.a. Moss-Bennett) of 1974 (AHPA), federal funding for non-Interstate roads became available to state DOTs.

Not much came of the NPS era of federal archaeology in the lower and central valley. Much good work was done elsewhere (e.g., the Tennessee valley), but reservoir projects were lacking for environmental reasons and the other kinds of projects were isolated, linear right-of-ways. Archaeological contracting, and in particular contracting with academic institutions, was a novel business in the 1960s, with the result that what today we term "quality-control" was lacking. Investigators pretty much determined what was good enough. They, on the other hand, had no control over where and when the work would be done. While the rationale might have been "science," actual motives were more venial—getting money to do archaeology, any archaeology. This era also began the creation of the so-called gray literature, reports to funding agencies that were not generally available and sometimes consisted of a one- or two-page letter.

The Real New Archaeology

The archaeological revolution of the 1960s and early seventies so quaintly self-characterized as the "New Archaeology" has had relatively little impact in the study area. In part, this is directly attributable to the success of PFG and the Harvard program generally (Dunnell 1990). The culture-history paradigm was, after all, largely worked out in the Mississippi valley. Fifty years later it has all but vanished. What really changed archaeology, and changed it forever, was the passage of AHPA in 1974. In combination with NEPA, the scope of protection afforded the archaeological record was unambiguously identified and expanded to any federally funded or permitted project. The last remaining questions about whether agencies other than the NPS were permitted to expend funds on archaeological survey and mitigation were removed. The amount that could be spent on archaeological work was established as a percentage of the total project funding, which *greatly* increased the available funds. Partnership requirements between the federal government and the several states required that every state develop an infrastructure in order to avail themselves of the federal dollars, creating state historic preservation offices and officers (SHPO). Most of the Mississippi valley states were well prepared with state archaeologists already in place and ready to take on the role of SHPO, but some, like Missouri, were not. Two parallel systems, a state-based infrastructure feeding on federal funds and a university/archaeological society infrastructure based on more limited resources, were engendered with considerable potential for conflict.

The amounts of money involved coupled with a shrinking academic market for new degrees saw the rapid evolution of private-sector contractors. Even more dramatically, archaeologists now had to deal with a variety of federal agencies, not just the laid-back, rather gentlemanly NPS. Real-world task masters like the United States Army Corps of Engineers (USACE) had established contracting procedures and had no intention of cutting archaeologists any slack, even if the task was not strictly an engineering one. Furthermore, unlike the NPS, where some real understanding of archaeology had guided decisions and policies, these new masters couldn't care less, particularly at the highest levels. They had legal requirements to meet and, in good, sound engineering tradition, set out to find the cheapest way to meet them. Archaeology, for its part, was about as poorly prepared for this set of conditions as could be imagined. There was no discipline-wide agreement on purpose (it would have been nice to have had a reason for preservation instead of slogans) and no uniform theoretical underpinnings; questions such as "how much is enough?" or "why this but not that?" could not really be answered archaeologically. As a result, CRM archaeology came to be "compliance" archaeology.

To no one's surprise, the early CRM work reflects a period of settling in, of working out solutions to these problems in the absence of any robust rationale. Reports, and the work they relate, are variable in quality and detail; by academic standards the methods employed were often unreliable or at least ill-considered. Management recommendations appeared to be more closely related to the contractor's perception of his chance of gaining further contracts than anything archaeological. The normal engineering constraints that weed out inferior products (like using cardboard rather than steel for a bridge) and prevent work always being awarded to the lowest bid were simply not operative because archaeology did not have a product, or even just a set of standards, against which results could be measured. So the only relevant measure became, "will this get us off the hook?" If it did, the product was, by definition, adequate.

Two archaeologies thus came into being: the traditional one that mumbles about science or anthropology and that generated the laws that created CRM, and a new underclass that was, and had to be to exist, openly governed by commercial motives. Most early CRM reports are truly awful. That is no longer the case, however. While not addressing the root cause of the problem, such things as the Society of Professional Archaeologists and its successor, the Register of Professional Archaeologists, have, by stipulating some minimum standards for archaeological work, identified and thus helped to eliminate some of the worst contractors. The lion's share of the credit, however, goes to the federal agencies funding the work. As their personnel have improved and the agencies as a whole have come to understand, if not embrace, that the point to doing archaeology goes beyond simply getting bureaucrats off their backs, the number of contractors has decreased and the quality of reports vastly improved. In some few cases, SHPOs have made critical contributions by rejecting work done as not complying with the intent of the law.

The U.S. Fish and Wildlife Service, the U.S. Forest Service, and the NPS all have some lands within the study area boundaries. As noted elsewhere, though a tiny fraction of the study area is in their hands, the Forest Service has done some of the most useful work (Lipo and Dunnell, this volume; Peacock 1994). In our case, however, the USACE is by far the dominant force. The study area falls mostly within two districts, Memphis (northern area and some levees south of Memphis) and Vicksburg (pretty much everything else). Surprisingly, the Corps' interest in archaeology predates AHPA. Colonel John L. Fordyce, identified as representing the USACE in Arkansas, attended the St. Louis Conference (Dunlap 1929, Appendix A). Archaeology even garners a brief mention and a couple pictures in the official history of the Vicksburg District (Mills 1978). Both districts hired in-house archaeologists as soon as the USACE believed it would be spending Corps money on archaeology, i.e., the early 1970s, anticipating or following AHPA. In both districts only minor projects are handled in-house; the rest of the survey, testing, and mitigation work is mostly done by private sector contractors today (though early there was a more even mix of academic and private contractors). The reports generated follow the pattern described above. Those written in the 1970s are highly variable in what is reported, how it is reported, and what is actually done. Those written in the last decade or so are uniformly of high quality, adequately reporting procedures and findings in most regards when judged against non-CRM archaeological reporting. Both districts have clearly weeded out poor performers in favor of firms that do work acceptable to a much wider range of potential users.

Are we there yet? Unfortunately, the answer is no. Perhaps the greatest problem is the limited distribution that USACE reports get. All are sent to the state but beyond that, they are not generally available, hence "gray literature." In fact, not even lists of projects done, reports received, or other documentation that would let potential users know what is available are routinely distributed either by the USACE or the several state SHPOs. The NPS did fund overviews (Davis 1988), but that is not part of the USACE's mission as they see it.

A second problem is the nature of the CRM beast itself. CRM is pursued project by project and, while particular projects may generate appropriate samples of properly archived materials, they cannot be fitted together into a seamless database. This failure cannot be laid at the door of the Corps, but is attributed to the failure of archaeology as a whole to get its act together on what it is doing and why it is doing it. What is hopeful, however, is that the infrastructure and attitudes needed to deliver a scientifically useful product have largely been put in place by the USACE in our area.

The end of the explosive growth of CRM is in sight. The number of new projects is declining (e.g., Davis 2002) as the backlog of resource inventorying has been slowly consumed. Once this backlog is eliminated, CRM will be strongly tied to economic cycles. A downturn in CRM employment is in the immediate future (Moore 2006).

Summary and Conclusions

Since the middle of the nineteenth century, when archaeology began to come of age as a field of endeavor, there have always been multiple contributors to what constitutes contemporary archaeological knowledge. The roles of different contributors have waxed and waned over time, but still recognizable are artifact collectors, amateur archaeologists, professional archaeologists of various stripes, including academics, resource managers, and archaeological contractors, and administrators. Motivation has varied as well. More different peoples, agencies, and organizations are doing archaeology for more different reasons than ever before. While this has increased the amount of archaeology done, it is not at all clear that archaeological knowledge has grown commensurately.

Factors

Curiosity has been a motive since the first artifact was found; commercial motives have been around since the finder sold it or a story about it. Both continue to motivate archaeological work but, in general, commercial motivation has been a persistent motive only among artifact collectors and archaeological contractors, and then only some of them. Political motives made their serious appearance with state sovereignty in the early twentieth century and then again with the appearance of the American Indian constituency. Here the impacts of motivation have been substantial and deleterious. As the amount of money involved in archaeology as an activity has increased, so have the number of professional archaeologists, either directly on the dole or as educators producing archaeologists who will be. Since the 1970s, when the amounts of money being spent became significant, there has been a need to generate a rationale for the expenditures, i.e., develop constituencies. Thus we now also have people interested in archaeology but who have little or no role in its generation (the general public, "native" Americans, etc.) and to which archaeology has become subservient to some degree, reshaping itself to meet the desires of the new constituencies. This amounts to saying that the purpose of archaeology is to employ archaeologists.

Funding has been equally various. Initially all archaeology was privately funded. Gradually state funding became a factor in some areas through the establishment of state surveys, and everywhere with the involvement of universities. Post-1966, the ultimate source of much of the state money was the federal government through the NPS, but universities still played a major role in how it was spent. The major infusions of funds have been, however, federal, first in the late 1930s and pre-war '40s and then post-1971–1974 and continuing today. Use of the initial federal funds was guided by political motives—providing work for the unemployed and often otherwise unemployable without competing with the private sector. The most recent funds have gone toward inventorying federal properties and mitigation of adverse impacts. More importantly, a new archaeology was created that is not driven by traditional archaeological motives. Most would still cite "conservation" as the motive, but conservation to what end? For "science," of course, but where is that science?

Again it sounds suspiciously like archaeologists making work for archaeologists. When one needs outreach programs to "educate" the public, chances are there is no recognizable product.

As for the conceptions about the nature of the archaeological record, much less can be said because much less has been written. Clearly there has been a move away from the acquisition of objects toward generating information. Instead of most of the budget going for getting stuff, a significant fraction is now consumed by "interpretations," interpretations that are transitory at best. Museums and depositories of the "stuff" of archaeological work hold great potential as the basis for generating useful archaeological knowledge once we get our act together. They have not, however, been exploited to a great degree. Most researchers prefer to acquire their own stuff. In part this stems from not being able to determine what kinds of objects and records exist that could be easily used for a particular research. As a result, the value of these repositories has not been evaluated. They remain a potential resource if they are properly managed, but even that potential value has been diminished greatly by such politically driven legislation as NAGPRA. The idea that one can study materials and then bury them undermines the whole rationale for conservation and preservation in the first place—to have access for restudy with new tools and new ideas.

The archaeological record has grown in scope as well. In its early years archaeology in the Mississippi valley was basically prehistoric archaeology. Today, anything 50 years old qualifies—largely for political reasons. This cut-off point is not rationalized by reference to problem, data requirements, or the archaeological record; it is simply bureaucratic. This is not to say that historic archaeology is without value, only that the explosion of interest and opportunity is a direct result of historic preservation being construed by the tax-paying public as Euroamerican history, not anybody's prehistory.

The scope of the record has increased in other ways. Well up into the culture historical era, the target population was what is today called the "diagnostics." Indeed, most artifacts encountered by PFG were never collected or were later discarded (Phillips 1970), practices that today border on the criminal. When time and space were the goals, only artifacts that allowed one to map these dimensions were critical. With the introduction of functionalism in the early 1960s, all kinds of materials that had largely been ignored were now of critical value. The new interest in functionalism brought with it new quantitative demands, both in terms of sample size and representativeness. So it is safe to say, again in an intuitive way at least, that our conception of the archaeological record has changed and changed for the better, but without offering any solace on our achievements.

Growth of Archaeological Knowledge

I share with Thorne (1988) trepidations about how one might measure the growth of knowledge. As a crude measure of our familiarity with the archaeological record, I have tracked the number of "sites" "known to science" as we have gone along (Figure 3.1). Not surprisingly, there is a general relationship between the amount of money being spent and the number of sites known. The same, however, could be said for the number of archaeologists, or the number of artifact collectors, or the population of the United States or the average income of midgets. Most things "correlate" with time. What is worth noting is that no asymptote seems to have been reached or is even suggested in these data. This means that our knowledge of the record is woefully incomplete. We have not yet reached a point of diminishing returns.

Thorne (1988) also suggested looking at the number of publications as a measure of the growth of knowledge. He did not do so because, even when he was writing, the task was daunting, if not impossible. It is even less feasible today. The number of entries in the Lower Mississippi Valley Survey online bibliography (Brain and Phillips 1979; http://www.tulane.edu/~kidder/lmsbib. html) provides a means, albeit crude, of gauging the rate of growth of archaeological publication. Figure 3.2 graphs these data at ten-year intervals for most of the twentieth century. It was not possible to compile data for the nineteenth century as those dates were not searchable and, in any case, the number of publications is too low to be reliable. In fact, the number is sufficiently small in the early years of the twentieth century that I used the mean of two years (e.g, 1900 and 1901, 1910 and 1911, etc.) to provide more reliable estimates for the twentieth century. No data were available for 2000 and later.

As pronounced as the recent increase seems, the actual picture is even more dramatic. The early years include many ethnographic references, thus over-estimating strictly archaeological knowledge, and the later years seem to have underrepresented contract reports. The Vicksburg Corps of Engineers alone lists over 800 reports since the early 1970s, most of which were generated for the study area. In Arkansas, some 2,166 CRM reports were submitted to the state office over the comparable period for the Mississippi lowland counties. No one even knows all that has been written about the archaeology of the LMV, let alone actually read any significant fraction of it. This was true 20 years ago (Thorne 1988) and even more so today. The technology exists to correct this, but there is little sign that such an effort will be made a top priority anytime soon.

Of course, the quality of what we know has changed, and changed for the better in some intuitive way. Site locations *are* more accurate and we *do* have more and more data texture (content). Yet for all of this, modern analyses can-

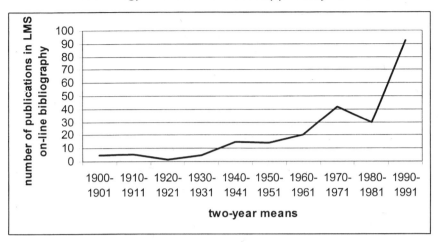

Figure 3.2. Number of publications listed in the Lower Mississippi Valley Survey online bibliography (http://www.tulane.edu/~kidder/lmsbib.html); two-year means at ten-year intervals. Standard deviations are: 1900–1901, 2.1; 1910–1911, 3.5; 1920–1921, 0.7; 1930–1931, 0.7; 1940–1941, 2.8; 1950–1951, 8.5; 1960–1961, 7.1; 1970–1971, 11.3; 1980–1981, 10.6; 1990–1991, 0.7.

not be performed using the accumulated database (see Lipo and Dunnell, this volume). Good work can and is done within the bounds of single projects, but beyond that, not really.

This is the lesson of our multi-stranded history. Archaeology, not just in the Mississippi valley but generally, has failed to coalesce around a general theory that could unify the field. Without that, the multifarious motivations, disparate funding sources, and various ideas about the archaeological record itself have precluded the creation of a unified and useful body of knowledge. Science, not just any kind of agreement on goals, is what is needed, because science, in insisting on an empirical epistemological standard, is the only cross-cultural basis for human endeavor.

Acknowledgments

A huge number of people have assisted me with this project, not all of them wittingly. Thanks are due to Keith Baca, Jim Barnett, Sam Brookes, Lela Donat, Ann Early, Diana Greenlee, Nancy Hawkins, Richard Kanaski, Mark Madsen, Sam McGahey, Jimmy McNeil, David Meltzer, Mike O'Brien, Robin Persons, Joe Saunders, Jan Simek, and Jim Wojtala. To those who find their names missing, failing memory and poor bookkeeping, not lack of appreciation, are the culprits. Most especially I want to thank Janet Rafferty and Evan Peacock for asking me to do this essay and then putting up with me until the bitter end. Lastly, my wife's encouragement and editorial talents were essential to its completion.

Notes

1. "Facts" do not exist outside the framework for their construction, be that framework the unanalyzed cultural background of a naïve observer or the explicit, constructed frameworks recognized as "theories." Analytic treatises that do not take this observation into account are necessarily done from within an unanalyzed framework.

2. By "scientific" is to be understood a sense-making system that uses an empirical epistemological standard to assess the correctness of its claims about the phenomenological world. This must be reiterated because, historically, being scientific has been used to rationalize and justify all manner of programs that there otherwise is no means to evaluate, often citing superficial elements like rigor, repeatability, quantification, or "objectivity."

3. Many of Moore's works (1908, 1910, 1911, 1916b) have recently been reprinted by the University of Alabama Press (Morse and Morse 1998). Only the original dates are given here for clarity.

4. The debate probably can be traced to the first map of De Soto's route produced in the Bradford Club edition (75 copies) of *Narratives of the Career of Hernando De Soto in the Conquest of Florida as Told by a Knight of Elvas and in a Relation by Luis Hernandez de Biedma, Factor of the Expedition* (Smith 1866). Enough public interest was excited as to engender a federal commission to work out the route (among other things) (Swanton 1985 [1939]). Debate continues unabated, with nearly everyone writing on LMV archaeology or ethnology having taken at least one whack at the issue.

5. Squier and Davis' work was not funded by the Smithsonian. They had sought funding from various private sources (unsuccessfully) but ended up paying for all of the surveying and excavation themselves. In fact, it is largely accidental that *Ancient Monuments* was published by the Smithsonian (see Meltzer 1998 for a thorough analysis of the context of *Ancient Monuments*).

6. Holmes' Mississippian ceramic data were derived from the Davenport Academy of Natural Sciences, Davenport, Iowa, which held vessels primarily from southeast Missouri and northeast Arkansas. Such "local" scientific societies played an important role in archaeology and other field sciences of the last half of the nineteenth and early twentieth centuries as attested in their memberships (e.g., such notables as A. Agassiz, S. F. Baird, L. Carr, E. S. Cope, J. D. Dana, F. V. Hayden, J. Leidy, L. Lesquereux, O. C. Marsh, O. T. Mason, L. H. Morgan, C. Rau, S. H. Scudder, and N. S. Shaler were corresponding members of the Davenport Academy

in 1877 [Preston 1877–80]). O'Brien and Lyman (2001) record a similar picture in St. Louis, where as many as three such societies existed at one time during this period. Archaeology was an early and important part of their agenda (e.g., Swallow 1857). These institutions both purchased collections of artifacts as well as sponsored and sometimes even funded archaeological expeditions, as did the Davenport Academy and, famously, the Academy of Natural Sciences of Philadelphia, which sponsored C. B. Moore's work. While a few, such as the reorganized Philadelphia Academy, would continue to have significance for many years to come, by and large these voluntary associations of professionals and scientifically inclined laymen would have their role usurped by academic institutions, some private, but more especially state-funded, in the early twentieth century.

7. Keyes (1930) and Jeter (ed. 1990) discuss the Lewis survey. The Brower survey remains unpublished, but the original notes and diagrams are held by the Minnesota State Historical Society, St. Paul. Houck (1908) published much of the Bean and Hoffman results, mostly as footnotes in Chapter 2; however, the original survey notes still exist and are held by Southeast Missouri State University, Cape Giradeau.

8. Moore's field notes often have many more details than do his published papers, although this generalization does not hold for the area in question.

9. This is also the fate of Moore's collections, many of which were sold to the Museum of the American Indian in Washington, D.C., or other public institutions, but some of which entered the commercial market. His field notes, fortunately, have been preserved by the Huntington Free Library (Davis 1987). These materials were transferred to Cornell University in 2004.

10. While the degree to which amateurs and local "scientific" societies, composed mainly of laymen, actually contribute to a field is sometimes taken to mark the maturation of an interest area into a real science, historical sciences like archaeology are exceptions to this rule. Because they address why things happen as well as how they work, there is no such thing as redundant data (*contra* the whole "determination of significance" approach to resource management). The uniqueness of observation required by these sciences means that "amateurs" can and should be an integral part of the field. Here again I distinguish amateurs from artifact collectors.

11. Ford's importance to the archaeology of the Mississippi alluvial valley can hardly be overestimated. Consequently a number of writers have analyzed his role in Southeastern and American archaeology as a whole (e.g, Brown 1978a; O'Brien and Lyman 1998, 1999a; O'Brien et al. 2000), relieving me of the necessity of doing so here.

12. Surveys were more systematic. Funkhouser and Webb (1932) used questionnaires mailed throughout their state (Kentucky) to try to insure uniform coverage. In Missouri, Chapman appointed county coordinators in the hope that this would

stimulate not only the amount of reporting but improve its distribution. Many states occasionally published county maps showing the number of recorded sites to engender something of a competition to the same ends.

13. The Tennessee Valley Authority is a major exception. It began archaeological work in 1934 and resumed this role after the Second World War, continuing to the present. Major William S. Webb directed the archaeology program for the TVA while he administered the WPA program in Kentucky at the same time; consequently both programs shared much in terms of procedure and aims.

4
Archaeological Things

Languages of Observation

Robert C. Dunnell

Introduction

There is nothing more fundamental to science than the categories used to perceive the external world. They are so fundamental that most people are completely unaware of the influence such structures exert on understanding. In some respects archaeologists, continually faced with unfamiliar objects and object parts, have proved more perspicacious than many "hard scientists" in these matters. "Typology" and "classification" are recurrent, if somewhat sporadic, concerns. The Lower Mississippi Valley (*sensu* this volume, hereafter LMV) has figured heavily in those considerations and has served as the testing ground for many new approaches throughout the twentieth century. Even so, the lack of familiar models in common sense (where these processes are necessarily cryptic) and the failure to recognize the role of theory or to reach a consensus on a particular theory have left us chasing our tails at the expense of the ever-diminishing archaeological record.

Here I explicate the role of classification in science generally and then in archaeology per se. A review of the history of "typological" constructs in the region precedes a critique of the dominant approaches today. I conclude by suggesting remedies.

Background

Language of Observation

Contrary to its popular use as a synonym for hypothesis, here I use the word "theory" to mean the assumptive structure necessary to construct a system of explanation (Dunnell 2002 [1971]; Guralnik and Friend 1968:1511). Thus, there is no "theory" that people first entered the New World through the Bering Strait land bridge, for example. Such a statement is a hypothesis. The theory comprises the assumptions that allow one to write the hypothesis and integrate it with others into a body of knowledge. There is no point to arguing about the words—theory *is* this or *is* that. Like any other word, "theory" is what it is defined as, nothing more or less. The point *is* that assumptions *are* made in writing the Bering Strait scenario, and those assumptions are the kind of constructions that are the target of the word "theory" here.

So conceived, theory has two components, a language of observation—what is often called classification—and a language of explanation. The former constructs the units of observation, things or kinds of things. The latter articulates observations into causal statements, explanations. All systems of explanation, sciences, religions, even cultures (common senses) can be shown to contain these two elements. And, despite what some writers contend (Binford 1977), they are not independent, but rather must be completely integrated, an iterative process well described in the sciences (e.g., Lewontin 1974a:8–12).

Science, as a particular kind of explanatory system, imposes special conditions on theory construction. First, to be subject to challenge, revision, and replacement, it must be explicit rather than cryptic. Secondly, it is distinguished by its reliance on an empirical epistemological standard, i.e., for a hypothesis to be regarded as an explanation it must have been empirically tested and not falsified. Following from this, and of particular concern to the language of observation, units in a scientific theory must be empirically sufficient (Lewontin 1974a:9), i.e., measurable in the empirical world, to generate empirically testable results. These units also have to be explicable, i.e., they must be the terms in the processes used in explanations. Hence the iterative nature of theory construction: trying to define units that can be measured and explained simultaneously. The failure of processualism as science can be laid to the lack of appreciation of this fundamental process, among other things. Explanations were typically cast in transactional terms (e.g., behavior) even though the archaeological record is distinguished from other human records by its non-transactional character. Consequently, none of the lofty efforts of processualists were empirically sufficient. Most of what passed as theory was, in point of fact, circumlocution designed to camouflage this insoluble problem—hence the focus on methods for "interpreting" or "inferring meaning," processes that converted archaeological units into those of common sense (our culture) and ethnology, either or both of which supplied the explanations. In this process, however, empirical sufficiency is lost because "inferences" and "interpretations" can never be tested in a scientific sense.

In the atheoretical condition of the discipline, archaeologists have frequently taken object-naming to be an act of classification. Thus chapters in substantive contributions labeled "classification" do not discuss the creation of the units used but the assignment of objects to existing classes of cryptic or traditional origin, a process called identification (Dunnell 2002 [1971]). This same conflation of naming also has led some of the more perceptive analysts to emphasize terminological issues (e.g., Clarke 1968; Krieger 1944). Conventional agreement on the meaning of terms is certainly a precondition to effective communication (i.e., language), but it in no way speaks to the origin of meaning, often deflecting concern away from the lack of theory and the process of classification itself.

These are complex issues deserving of extended treatment in their own right; however, this sketch should make the reader aware that the discussion that follows is not derived from ad hoc assumption, but rests on well-established epistemological analysis. Herein, the process of creating units of observation is termed "classification" (a broader usage than in Dunnell 2002 [1971]) and the products of that process are generically termed "classes." The term "identification" is used to designate the process of assigning objects to classes.

Archaeological Classification

As already noted, the unfamiliar, extracultural nature of archaeological subject matters almost compels recognition that kinds, or things, are created, not observed. The lack of an explanatory theory, however, has left this process largely uncontrolled and free-floating.

General History. Three different tacks on classification have emerged historically. One, which might be termed "cryptic empiricism," recognizes the process but claims and/or believes that its specifics are unimportant and exert no influence on the product. This is probably the dominant view, to judge from the ad hoc way in which archaeological classes of all sorts are created. Occasionally, this view is given frank expression (e.g., Cowgill 1972). A second, an explicit, empiricist approach, is aptly dubbed "systematic empiricism" (Willer and Willer 1973). This approach, particularly popular during the sway of processualism, was made explicit and rigorous through the efforts of the "number mechanics" to "discover" the correct units (e.g., Clarke 1968; Read 1977; Read and Russell 1996; Spaulding 1953; Whallon 1972; Whallon and Brown 1981). It may have looked like science (numbers) and smelled like science (numbers), but it is simply an explicit version of cryptic empiricism, which it was designed ostensibly to replace. Systematic empiricism found a salubrious home in 1960s programmatic archaeology because it had the appearance of doing away with the need for theory. Archaeology had no theory, but empiricism seemed to allow archaeology to be regarded as science anyway. Correctness was established by using the proper method, a ritualistic approach to epistemology. This is why processualism is dominated by methodological issues. This tack boiled down to the need to proclaim that units were correct because they were "real," i.e., discovered. The number-mechanic program had no practical impact, however. It is not possible to construct units in a theoretical vacuum; the only choice is whether the investigator is aware of the assumptive input or not.

Consequently, archaeology developed a literature of quantitative "classification methods" that are nowhere in actual use. The third option, a theoretically informed language of observation, has failed to emerge in archaeology simply because the discipline has yet to develop or embrace a general theory that could be used to start the process.

As I have argued elsewhere (Dunnell 1986b), however, during normal-science periods in archaeology as represented by culture history of the late 1930s–1950s (and most practice, though not program, in subsequent decades), agreement on an overriding problem, chronology, led to a quasi-scientific condition. Empirical testing of chronologies was possible. But a problem is not a theory. Not only was chronology unconnected to other issues (thus our history unfolded as a series of oppositions rather than ever-expanding constructions), but why chronological methods worked as they did was not understood (as witness Ford's feeble efforts [1954a, 1954b] to explain the type concept). The importance of explicit construction is nowhere more definitively manifest. Everybody thus regarded his or her own position as self-evident, so no one communicated with anyone who held a different view (e.g., Ford 1954a, 1954b; Spaulding 1953).

Contemporary languages of observation, classifications, thus actually date to the culture-history paradigm in terms of their structure, but they have undergone unsupervised, ad hoc revision for five decades or more, resulting in a jumbled mess even less useful than the original prototypes of the 1930s and 1940s. While we have certainly learned some things of value from their application, at least in the hands of the more rigorous and explicit practitioners, the structures themselves are clearly not salvageable for any modern purpose. To take this analysis further, additional analytic concepts are required.

As a particular science, archaeology imposes additional constraints on the construction of a language of observation. Archaeology is a historical science, i.e., we ask "why did it happen" questions, not just "how does it work" questions. "How does it work" questions can be answered in the here and now, as witness chemistry and physics. This obviates the need for the preservation, conservation, and management of an archaeological record altogether (an archaeological record is being continuously generated), again as witness physics and chemistry, which lack these concerns. Clearly ahistorical sciences like chemistry and physics are not appropriate models for historical sciences like archaeology. The central distinction between ahistorical and historical science is their conception of reality (see Dunnell 1982; Mayr 1959, 1982).

Materialism and essentialism. There are two different conceptions of the nature of reality broadly compatible with science, essentialism (Sober 1980) or "typological thinking" (Mayr 1959) and materialism (Lewontin 1974b; Sober 1980) or "population thinking" (Mayr 1982). In the first, the empirical world is conceived as being composed of a fixed set of things or kinds, which can be "discovered," and between which there can exist fixed relations (laws). Again, physics provides the archetype. In materialism, the empirical world is conceived as being in a state of becoming; things do not exist as fixed entities, and therefore there can be no fixed relations (laws). Evolutionary biology is the archetype here. In practice, materialist sciences incorporate essentialist sciences at lower levels in their structure (as, say, ecology and chemistry in evolution). I have examined these notions elsewhere in much greater detail (Dunnell 1982, 1986a, 1986b); what is important here are the implications for classification.

Materialist paradox. If classes are things or kinds of things, but the materialist ontology disallows the existence of things and kinds of things, then classification and historical science would appear to be totally incompatible. Both evolutionary biologists and archaeologists have solved this conundrum in similar ways—the creation of what might be called hyper-units. Unlike physics, where units (e.g., atoms, kinds of atoms, quarks, etc.) have fixed properties and thus are often talked about as if they existed in the empirical world, hyper-units are prescriptions that subtend the same kind of variability without specifying a fixed content. Thus, biology specifies genetic isolation, not a particular list of traits, to define species. Which particular traits mark genetic isolation needs to be determined empirically.

Similarly many archaeologists, beginning with the founders of culture history (Ford 1954a; Krieger 1944; Rouse 1939) appreciated that kinds, or "types," did not exist but were tools created by the archaeologist to do particular work (Dunnell 2002 [1971]; Jelinek 1976; Steward 1954). This is, of course, observationally true, but because culture history lacked explicit theory, this insight is lost in much of the subsequent methodological literature. What made culture history successful (i.e., able to produce empirically testable and tested results) to the extent it was, was a tacit agreement on the "particular work" (chronology), and unrelenting trial and error "testing" against that problem as so well described by Krieger (1944). When the discipline-wide agreement on purpose was lost in the 1960s, so was the utility of prior archaeological classifications as discipline-wide languages of observation.

Scale, Level, and Kind of Classification

One final set of concepts needs to be addressed for this review: that of scale and level. While both refer to inclusiveness, scale identifies inclusion relations in the empirical world and level identifies ideational inclusion (Dunnell 2002 [1971]; Ramenofsky and Steffen 1998). The relation between atom, molecule, mineral, rock, arrowhead is one of increasing scale. Atoms are part of molecules, contained within them. The relation between species, genus, family, order, class, etc., is one of increasing level. Rather than being different physical sizes, level varies inversely with the number of criteria necessary for membership (defining criteria). Thus the number of traits shared by members of a genus is fewer than, and a subset of, those shared by members of an included species. All, however, are kinds of the same thing—organisms, i.e., the Linnaean classification has many levels at the same scale.

Similarly, archaeological classifications attend several scales, but most commonly two: the scale of discrete object, or "artifact," and those sets of discrete objects commonly referred to as assemblages or occupations (Dunnell 2002 [1971]). There is nothing sacred about either. In the absence of a general theory, the use of these two scales is most likely a covert borrowing from everyday life and/or ethnography (which itself took them from everyday life). One can readily imagine smaller (e.g., attributes), intermediate (e.g., "features," households, etc.), or even larger (e.g., culture areas) scales. The fact remains, however, that only at the scale of discrete object and assemblage have classifications for general use been promulgated (e.g., Dunnell 2002 [1971]; Phillips 1970; Willey and Phillips 2001 [1958]). These are commonly referred to as "artifact types" and "phases."

Like biological classifications, archaeologists have also introduced multi-level classification, taxonomy (*sensu* Dunnell 2002 [1971]), at both scales: type-variety systems (Wheat et al. 1958) in the case of discrete objects, and the Midwestern Taxonomic Method (McKern 1939a) at the assemblage scale. At the type scale, variety is at a lower level than type and type is at a lower level than type-cluster or "ware." All, however, are kinds of potsherds or arrowheads or some other discrete object class and thus at the same scale. Furthermore, the number of potential members is controlled by level such that the potential membership of red-math-book ≤ red book ≤ book.

This rather straightforward set of concepts is not infrequently muddied by conflating difference arising from number of criteria (level) with difference arising from alternative criteria (different kinds of classification). Thus, for example, McKern (1939a) argued that the criteria for membership in high-level classes tended to be inferential and/or functional, while the lower levels (esp. foci, aspects) were defined by stylistic features. Culture historians had recognized by the middle 1950s (e.g., Rouse 1960; Steward 1954; see also Binford 1971) that different kinds of classification were possible or even essential (e.g., Jelinek 1976). As a consequence, not all parts of the "same" classification worked equally well and, over time, elements, usually the higher levels (in both archaeology and biology), fell into disuse.

Summary

I have not touched upon the mechanics of doing classification at all. Procedure is of critical importance to practice, but beyond the scope of this brief essay. Not only would its consideration have greatly lengthened this effort, but it would require taking a particular theoretical stance. Consequently the tack taken here is methodological—archaeology as science—rather than theoretical—archaeology as a particular kind of science. Nonetheless, this introduction should let the reader appreciate the gravity of a decision to do business as usual and of the necessity to take theory seriously.

Every time an archaeologist "describes" the record, classes are either used or created. Formal classifications, ones of which we are aware and borrowed for use from study to study, are pretty much limited to the two scales enumerated earlier. The remainder of the essay deals with classification at each of these scales in turn: types (discrete objects) and phases (aggregates of discrete objects).

The Type

Types, particularly pottery types, lie at the core of archaeological analysis in southeastern archaeology. They do serious work. It is by them that assemblages are attributed to whole cultural units, almost universally "phases," and these attributions usually establish the age of the assemblage and inferences about many behaviors. They are also used to construct chronologies and trace "influences"—trade, diffusion, ancestry and the like.

Historical*

In English, nouns are dominantly functional, i.e., a hammer is a hammer because of what it does; only secondarily are other things assigned to hammer because they "look like" hammers. Consequently, behavioral/functional discussion in archaeology is usually conducted in English, not in any special archaeological language. If the materials are really exotic, then an ethnographically informed "English" is deployed or the infamous problematical or ceremonial object is dragged out. Explicit archaeological types arose because they were asked to do different work, initially chronological work (e.g., Ford 1935a, 1936).

There were earlier efforts. Charles Rau (1876) and Thomas Wilson (1899) devised a geometrically grounded classification of "arrowheads and spear points" in the late nineteenth century, but this failed to find any general audience; even Wilson was disappointed when its application to the Smithsonian collections revealed no patterns. William Henry Holmes' (1886a; Meltzer and Dunnell 1992 [Holmes 1886c, 1903]) better-known efforts with pottery drew heavily upon the mound-survey samples being developed by Thomas (1985 [1894]) and the Davenport (Iowa) Academy of Natural Science's collections of LMV pottery. His focus was on whole pots and, while he had many important insights (e.g., distinguishing various tempers, realizing that shape was largely functional, that chronology was to be had in decoration) that informed, or should have informed, later analysts, he never undertook a formal classification. His "groups" were assemblage-scale, happenstance mixtures of time, space, form, function, style, and the unknown (to him) distribution of mortuary practices that included placement of ceramics with the dead (thus ensuring their preservation as whole or refitable objects).

Pottery Types

Thus it was that prior to the 1930s there was nothing that modern archaeologists would recognize as a pottery classification or pottery types. The Works Progress Administration and other federal archaeological programs provided the impetus to change this state of affairs. The Birmingham and Indianapolis National Research Council (NRC) conferences of 1932 and 1935 (see O'Brien and Lyman [2001; O'Brien and Lyman, ed. 2001] for excellent analyses of the impact of these conferences on southeastern archaeology) provided a set of guidelines that can still be seen in virtually every ceramic classification in use in the Southeast since (e.g., Brown 1998; Chase 1998; Phillips 1970; Phillips et al. 2003 [1951]; Thorne and Broyles 1968; Willey 1949). Even though these guidelines were confined to superficial, largely nomenclatural, matters, they are a glue that united attitudes toward pottery classification throughout the Southeast. Playing the primary role, however, has been the commonality of purpose, culture history, or "culture-historical integration," as Willey and Phillips (2001 [1958]) put it.

From this milieu a couple of forays into ceramic typology that, in retrospect, turned out to have important historical consequences, arose in our area. The first is James A. Ford's work in Louisiana and Mississippi beginning in the mid-1930s and recently and thoroughly explored by O'Brien and colleagues (O'Brien and Lyman 1998, 1999a; O'Brien et al. 2000). I note only four features of importance here. First, Ford's classification was for *sherds,* not pots. Secondly, following his mentor Henry Collins' lead (e.g., Collins 1927; see also Baca 2002), who in turn reached back to Holmes, Ford used *decoration* for defining types. Third, Ford's classification is strongly *dimensional* (*sensu* Dunnell 2002 [1971]), as revealed in his system of type designation. Finally, Ford made it clear that his classification was meant to deliver up *chronological* relationships and nothing else. Ford's seemingly arcane system of designation, which occasioned adverse comment quickly (e.g., Krieger 1944), was one of the first things to be discarded. While not structurally necessary, LMV ceramic types gradually lost their dimensionality without it.

The other early contributor was Philip Phillips, whose dissertation, *Introduction to the Archaeology of the Mississippi Valley* (1939), described most of the ceramic variability seen in the central and lower portions of the Mississippi valley. Phillips' concern lay with whole *pots,* not pieces, and while he, too, was concerned with decoration, this was mingled with considerations of form and thus function. Thus one is never quite sure in his later work whether he is talking about sherds or pots, or style, technology, or function (Phillips 1970). Phillips' early effort did not generate pottery types in the usual sense, but one can easily appreciate attitudes toward the formulation of kinds that would later manifest themselves in Phillips et al. (2003 [1951]) and find more complete and unfettered expression in his Yazoo Basin monograph (1970). *No purpose* is specified for pottery types. One is left with the impression that Phillip's intent is to discover the "true types," whatever that might mean. Lacking a purpose made the types impossible to evaluate empirically, and thereby set the stage for endless debate over their proper formulation and meaning, while insulating them from any factually based criticism. Indeed, it is hard to imagine two more different typologists: Ford, innovative, inarticulate, rigorous, and lacking in erudition; Phillips, conservative, articulate to the point of being glib, disorganized, and well-read. Ford was an untutored scientist in the making, Phillips the consummate humanist in the expert-witness mold.

These two disparate strings were brought together with the insights of the foremost ceramicist in the East, James B. Griffin, in the monumental *Archaeological Survey in the Lower Mississippi Alluvial Valley, 1940–1947* by Phillips, Ford, and Griffin (hereafter PFG) (2003 [1951]). The ceramic classification now in use in the Mississippi valley can be directly traced to this publication; indeed, many of the specific types created then are still in use today, even when their system *per se* is discarded in favor of more recent iterations (DeJarnette and Peebles 1970; Dunnell 1985; O'Brien 1994a). What makes this publication so important here (as well as, one hopes, accounting for its longevity as a basic reference; see Williams, ed. 2003) is the candid discussion of the type concept and the procedures employed in describing assemblages of sherds.

There is no doubt that they adopted the materialist position, a position clearly traceable to Ford (1935a, 1936, 1938; see also 1954a) and one with which Griffin, and especially Phillips, who later renounced it (1970), were uncomfortable. Although Phillips later claimed primary authorship of the types (1970), the original discussion and Ford's previous work belie this (I also have the original tabulations for the two northern subareas, courtesy of Jimmy Griffin, and they are in Ford's hand). Consequently, they see types as "created units of the ceramic continuum" (Phillips et al. 2003 [1951]:63) and as arbitrary "tools" created by the archaeologist, not inherent structures discovered in the data (Phillips et al. 2003 [1951]:61–63). But this commitment does not arise from understanding the relation between ontology, theory, and classification; rather, in the absence of explicit theory, it is derived from candid self-observation following Krieger's (1944) procedural insights. They knew types were arbitrary because they were aware that they made them up. They were right, but for the wrong reasons, or at least just by accident.

The lack of theory opens the door to ambiguity, mainly stemming from their own cultural background. Thus, we get statements like "Variations from the norm reflect the individual potter's interpretation of the prevailing styles" (Phillips et al. 2003 [1951]:62), where norm is clearly being substituted for "type," even when they had just told us that they made up the types themselves! Their statement is classic essentialism. Interestingly, when they make these lapses, they always do so when using contemporary cultural examples as rationales. The absence of theory compels them to use common sense to justify their decisions, and it gets them in trouble.

In a rather inarticulate way, considering cultural anthropological literature of the time (e.g., Driver and Kroeber 1932; Kroeber 1919, 1940), they distinguish between style, "determination of time and space relations" (Phillips et al. 2003 [1951]:61), and function (Dunnell 1978) "ideas and behavior of the people" (Phillips et al. 2003 [1951]:61) and clearly identify their goals with the former. They also recognize that these goals determine the choice of criteria used to define types. For example, they remark that the manner "of construction, paste, and surface finish . . . seem to mark vessels made for different purposes" (Phillips et al. 2003 [1951]:62), identifying these dimensions as functional. Given their averred goal of chronology, one would expect these dimensions to have played no role in type definitions. Quite to the contrary, some of these turn out to be of major importance in defining their types as well as a major source of difficulty in using them (see Galaty, this volume). What kept the whole enterprise, as vague and inconsistent at it was, on target was Krieger's test of historical significance, a necessary but unfortunately insufficient condition for insuring that the types were stylistic regardless of the particular choice of criteria (Dunnell 1986b).

The next major event in the ceramic classifications of the Mississippi valley was the introduction of the type-variety system by Phillips (1970). The PFG classification had approximated a paradigmatic classification (*sensu* Dunnell 2002 [1971]); Phillips' reworking created a taxonomy. Phillips had been a longtime advocate of the type-variety system (Phillips 1958) after its invention in the Southwest (Wheat et al. 1958). Indeed, as I have argued elsewhere (Dunnell 2002 [1971], 1986a), there was a legitimate problem with the Kriegerian type as espoused by PFG. One type might cover a large amount of time and/or space, while another type in the same system might cover a fraction of that time and/or space; in short, level was not controlled. To a certain extent, though hardly rigorously, this is what the introduction of type-variety did in other areas, especially Mesoamerica (e.g., Sabloff and Smith 1970; Smith et al. 1960).

In Phillips' (1970) hands, however, type-variety is an unmitigated disaster in the Mississippi valley. While Phillips did remove some of the dependency on temper (often functional), his intuitive, nonrigorous approach has turned the region's ceramic classification into a mystical structure understood and understandable only to the initiated. He takes both sides of most questions (essentialist vs. materialist), often in the same sentence. He disobeys his own injunctions (e.g., types should be sortable, but then under "sorting criteria" for specific types lists "none"). Nowhere does he discuss theory that might rationalize his decisions and partitions; they are treated rather much as a prophet's insight, truths obvious to him but obscure to common men. Perhaps most offensively, he makes light of the whole business by self-effacing humor, as if we are all constrained to be as confused and mystified as he is.

Others (e.g., Brown 1998; Williams and Brain 1983) have tried to sort out some of the worst messes, but even this otherwise laudable activity lends credibility to an undeserving scheme of ad hoc, intuitive kinds little different than those employed in pre–culture-history days—except for the great explosion in numbers. Anyone can, and nearly everyone does, create new varieties—all one needs is a plausibly novel observation and a few sherds from a new place. There are no tests anymore. The PFG types did have to work—they were designed to build chronologies and chronologies could be tested. Once seriation went out of vogue as a chronological tool, even this modest constraint was lost. Phillips' types and varieties, to the extent that they differ from PFG types, are linguistic conventions and nothing more. Lacking any justification, users are far more sensitive to criticism, and the now-useless types become more sacred than they ever have been before. You can be sure that it is always going to be blasphemy to study the sun among sun worshipers.

Projectile-Point Types

Comparable efforts at classification of common lithic artifacts, nowadays "bifaces" or "pointed bifaces," are more diverse in origin. While ceramic types have been almost exclusively the domain of professional archaeologists, projectile-point types, as noted earlier, predate the establishment of a real profession and have continued to be developed by artifact-collectors, amateurs, and professional archaeologists. Not surprisingly, there are two different trajectories, at least analytically. The artifact-collector tack has been to recognize intuitive groups of look-alikes, give them names, for communication purposes, supply a set of exemplars (pictures) to which others may compare their specimens and, since the late 1960s, attribute values to facilitate commerce. Since point form, like that of all other artifacts, is more or less continuously variable in a Fordian sense, such "typing" has inevitably led to expansion of the territory covered by any given name and much debate about the membership of marginal examples. Indeed, these problems are clear evidence of the poverty of the essentialist view. At their best, manuals tend to look like—and may even be modeled on—bird-watcher guides.

Amateur and professional attempts are just as uninformed. Instead of ad hoc groups of look-alikes, they tend to be constructed in a quasi-Kriegerian manner (but not always, as witness Bell [1958, 1960] and Perino [1968, 1971]). Stratigraphically associated sets of points are summarized in terms of common features (e.g., Broyles 1966; Coe 1964), and the temporal distribution of this set of features is then examined for temporal/spatial coherence. If this test is passed, then the type comes into use. There is, however, one serious complication to using this scheme with points. Pottery types are dominantly stylistic, initially skewed in this direction by the role given to decoration. But points are not "decorated" in the same sense. Consequently, object shape is the usual criterion employed to distinguish kinds. Yet since the nineteenth century it has been known that shape has a strong functional component—things look the way they do at least in part because of the work they do. This is doubly compounded because, as subtractive artifacts (artifacts made by breaking natural materials), the limitations placed on projectile-point form are so severe that recurrence of forms in different times and different places by chance alone is high. Some sophistication on the simple shape theme has occurred over time, most notably the recognition of the role of rejuvenation and reuse on shape (e.g., Thomas 1981, 1986). Still, the bumble-along, trial-and-error tack that served reasonably well in the development of ceramic classification has not proved efficacious with lithics.

These two approaches seem to have become wedded in a series of volumes by Justice (1987, 2002a, 2002b; Justice and Kudlaty 2001). The artifact-collector model seems to dominate, but they differ in being more rigorous in presentation, selective in inclusion of forms (reasonably clear chronological significance), and citation of precedents. Of course, they also lack the commercial-valuing component. Justice also introduces a hierarchic component with two levels of similarity, types, and clusters of types. But this is neither uniformly applied nor justified. Apparently it simply accommodates his intuitive sense of similarity among some types. Sales and citations seem to indicate these volumes have found an audience in all three groups. A similar approach has a long history in the Southeast (e.g., Cambron and Hulse 1990) and is taken by McGahey (2000) in the recent guide for the study area.

Almost unique to the LMV (Schambach 1970), the type-variety approach has been applied to projectile points by Williams and Brain (1983:221–239). Lacking the dimensional predecessor of the PFG ceramic sherd classification, this taxonomic classification is more obscure than its pottery counterpart. But they have clearly tried to draw similar kinds of distinctions among all types and all varieties. They also synonymize many of the obvious redundancies arising from earlier ad hoc naming. And it must be remembered that there had been no general effort to create classifications for projectile points in our study area. Just like the pottery version, however, there is no theoretical underpinning for the decisions embodied in the classification, no departure from shape as the main source of attributes, and no discussion, or even awareness, of the methodological literature on classification.

Summary

Artifact-scale classification is in a pretty sorry state in the LMV, as it is in Americanist archaeology generally. In fact, the only explanation for why something so utterly useless can persist is that it is not used to do anything of empirical import. No one dies because of this stuff. It does act as a jargon to establish professionals as an elite, but one suspects that only professionals are fooled. It does provide the terms for an endless discourse, endless because there is no way to tell when anyone is "right." To be sure this is an exaggeration, but only a modest one. Early on, ceramic classification, though far from scientific, did allow chronologies to be generated. Point classifications similarly have supplied some gross chronological order for the preceramic period, mostly by happenstance. What is probably most disturbing is the clear trend for these classifications to degenerate over time into less and less useful, less and less meaningful schemes of names.

Two horrors loom on the horizon that stem from the classification issues just raised. One is the effect that such a mess is having on the conservation, preservation, and utility of the archaeological record. If we get nothing else out of the last "new archaeology" it is the importance of problem to doing archaeology. Although there are good reasons not to treat resource management as research (Dunnell 1984), the investment in "state plans" insures that today's problems and language of observation will indelibly structure what can ever be known from the archaeological record.

The second horror is the impact that the mess will have on the development and subsequent use of electronic databases. Electronic databases must become a big hunk of the future of the discipline. As a historical science, archaeology is compelled to deal with truly enormous numbers of data, more than most archaeologists realize even today. But data are not "facts." Data are classes used to describe. The only good thing to be said on this score is that no one has yet invested the huge sums in a database that would prematurely freeze this arcane situation.

Suggestions for resolution are deferred to the end of this chapter after consideration of assemblage-scale classifications has been completed. But even in the absence of a solution, it should be clear that "business as usual" simply will not cut it anymore.

The Phase

The archaeological "phase" or its functional analogs (e.g., *a* culture, complex, people, ethnic unit, focus, etc.) is second only to type in terms of frequency of use among archaeological units. This remains the case in spite of it having been the subject of virtually no theoretical examination (exceptions are discussed later) or modification, while the discipline and its goals have undergone multiple, radical revisions. Much effort is devoted to assigning "sites," "components," and "assemblages" to their proper phases in Mississippi-valley archaeology.

History*

The phase concept is one of those archaeological rarities in which the origin of a concept is both well known and explicit. The phase was invented by Willey and Phillips in the 1950s (Phillips and Willey 1953; Willey and Phillips 1955, 2001[1958]). But similar constructs were already in existence and they, in turn, were efforts to regularize and rationalize informal, ad hoc, usages of still earlier vintage. Both the properties of the phase and its central place in archaeological, at least culture historical, thought require some consideration of these predecessors.

Units at the same scale as the modern phase made their appearance in the nineteenth century. The initial distinctions among associations of artifacts were linked to temporal differences (e.g., Worsaae 1849) recognized in stage and period kinds of constructions (e.g., the Stone Age, Bronze Age, Iron Age, the Paleolithic, Neolithic, subsequently Mesolithic; and the Reindeer Age, Mammoth Age, etc. [e.g., Lubbock 1872]). The recognition of regional differences soon followed, somewhat reluctantly for those with the strongest "evolutionary" leanings, the graphic representation of which produced the now-familiar time-space charts (e.g., Ford and Willey 1941; Johnson 1946; Setzler 1940). Although both temporal and spatial scales would be refined over time, the essential ingredients of what would become the archaeological phase were in place: time, space, and cultural form.

Because of the lack of anything that might be construed as theory at the time, the archaeological record had to be described in such a way that it made intuitive sense, i.e., was explicable using Western common sense (*sensu* Dunnell 2002 [1971]). Inasmuch as contemporary regional differences were also political and ethnic differences, these notions became a silent part of the baggage of all efforts to categorize assemblages early on. The European *Kulturkreise Lehre* of the 1920s was a partial exception, but its primary exposition in German and subsequent political events kept it from much influence on English-speaking countries, particularly the United States.

V. Gordon Childe (1936) is thus often credited as the father of the modern terminology, with his exposition of the concept of "culture," actually "a culture," as a term that had been in general anthropological use for 50 years. Childe's culture was simply a recurring, associated set of traits. While Childe's theoretical inclinations were virtually unique at the time, the culture notion did not flow from, or integrate with, his theoretical stance; rather it simply codified the existing intuitive notion of a group of people in an archaeological context.

About the same time Childe was formalizing his culture concept in Europe, a group of Midwestern archaeologists, led by W. C. McKern, was developing an analogous concept, the focus, as part of what came to be called the Midwestern Taxonomic Method (Fisher 1997; Kehoe 1990; Lyman 2003a; McKern 1939a, 1939b; O'Brien and Lyman, ed. 2001; Swartz 1996). Broadly similar to Childe's concept in that it erected units for assemblages based on "cultural" (meaning artificial) similarity, the McKern notion differed in that the focus was embedded in a larger hierarchical system of decreasing similarity (focus → aspect → phase → pattern → base). Also contrasting with the Childean culture defined by a set of shared traits, and thus a class (*sensu* Dunnell 2002 [1971]), the focus was a group (*sensu* Dunnell 2002 [1971]) of similar assemblages. This explains the mid-century fascination with trait lists; trait lists provided the basis for the intuitive assessment of similarity. It was, as I have observed elsewhere (Dunnell 1986a), a primitive, nonquantitative numerical taxonomy à la Sokal and Sneath (1963); indeed, contemporary observers (e.g., Kroeber 1940) pointed out the virtue of quantifying the system, but to deaf ears. Thus, archaeology missed an opportunity to beat biology to the punch once again, this time by nearly thirty years.

The focus was fundamentally flawed from the outset. Since foci were in effect lines drawn around a collection of assemblages, not sets of conditions for membership, they were groups. Consequently, accommodating new assemblages posed a problem. The whole classification would have to be redone whenever any new assemblage was added, because it might radically alter the patterns of similarity among assemblages by supplying links (commonalities) where none had been before. But the Midwestern Taxonomic Method did, at least at the focus and aspect levels, enjoy considerable currency and still does (though not in our area and not under its original name). One of the earliest and most faithful applications is James B. Griffin's (1941) *The Fort Ancient Aspect*.

Clearly some compromise had to have been reached for this success to be achieved. The compromise lay in McKern's enigmatic "determinants." He had characterized "traits" as linked, diagnostic, and determinant. Linked traits were those *shared* by units at any given level (e.g., focus); diagnostic traits were those contained *within* units at any given level. Given this account, all traits and any trait had to be either linked or diagnostic. There is no conceptual space for "determinants." They are clearly an add-on. They were defined as those traits common to all members of a focus and restricted to the focus. They, in effect, converted focus from a group to a class by providing a definition, a definition that would allow new material to be *assigned* to (identified with) existing foci. This means, however, that in terms of meaning and boundaries, existing foci were simply accidents of the order in which assemblages were discovered and reported. They did not, could not, reflect any structure of archaeological significance. Simply because everyone could now understand everyone else using the system did not mean that anything of value was being communicated— the fallacy of misplaced rigor, for want of a better name, and the plague of almost all archaeological efforts at classification.

McKern and his colleagues had definite goals in mind when proposing the Midwestern Taxonomic Method. They abhorred the willy-nilly way archaeologists had formulated "cultures" (e.g., Shetrone 1920) and wanted to regularize the process. Second, they realized that, despite all of the assumptions of ethnicity, age, and the like that drove people to recognize "cultures," the actual decisions were made on the basis of trait similarity and nothing more. Thus, the focus was explicitly conceived as based on what today would be called phenetic similarity. McKern (1939a) specifically denied that foci could be equated with ethnic units—indeed this was one of the evils he hoped his method would correct. He also specifically denied any chronological significance to these units (McKern 1939a). He spent, however, a good deal of effort trying to divorce these elements from applications of his approach by others (e.g., McKern 1939b, 1943; Praus 1945). In the space of another decade or so, the McKern system had rather much collapsed to the focus and aspect. The comparison of trait lists, still intuitive, was the only formal vestige of the method. Even the categories of traits had dropped out of common use. We were pretty much back to the vague, covertly created sets of assemblages in use long before either the McKern system or Childe's culture. And the vague ethnic inferences had crept back in, first as statements to the effect that "well they *might* represent sociopolitical or linguistic groups but further research was required," then as statements that made such linkages as matter-of-fact research results.

It is important to keep in mind that the Midwestern Taxonomic Method was not introduced as a tool in some larger theoretical system. Without theoretical justification, archaeologists lacked a rationale for making the critical decisions, like what constituted a trait or the effects of using some traits rather than others to assess similarity. Thus, what the units, the foci, meant was problematic. So it should not be surprising that the whole drifted back rather quickly toward the common-sense notion of quasi-ethnic-political units that could be observed in the modern world: "cultures."

The Phase

This, then, is the historical context for the invention of the archaeological "phase." An already degraded focus was the standard unit at the assemblage scale when there was any pretension to rigor. The concept was first proposed by Phillips and Willey (1953), and Phillips became its primary proponent (1970). The immediate predecessor to the invention again lay in the precocious and ambitious *An Archaeological Survey in the Lower Mississippi Alluvial Valley, 1940–1947* (Phillips et al. 2003 [1951]; see Dunnell 1985). Griffin, as a prominent proponent of the Midwestern Taxonomic Method, brought the McKern focus to the mix; however, unlike the Midwest, our area already had a chronology, so such a phenetic similarity scheme had little appeal. This is probably why the Midwestern Taxonomic Method never gained much of a foothold in the Southeast as a whole.

Ford took a different view (see Dunnell 1986a, 1986b; Lyman et al. 1997; O'Brien and Lyman 1998, 1999a), treating assemblages as samples of an ever-flowing culture stream (see esp. Ford 1954a). The most innovative element of this incredible monograph lay in Ford's seriations that provided a chronology (Phillips et al. 2003 [1951]:119–238). Neither Griffin nor Phillips understood this continuous view (Phillips et al. 2003 [1951]:417); again, this was the clash between materialist and essentialist ontologies. Because of the size of the area covered by their study and the spatial variability in its ceramic styles, Ford had to divide the LMV into a series of regions for his seriations to work. These were his local areas, and an independent seriation was created for each. This created a need to correlate the chronologies of the several local areas.

Their solution was to create a set of periods, "times," as they called them. They broke up the continuous strings represented by Ford's seriations using arbitrary ceramic-type frequencies (Phillips et al. 2003 [1951]:228–229). Inspection of Ford's diagrams and the authors' candid discussion quickly reveal that the divisions are accidents of the temporal density of data, error, and little else. For example, though each period was intended to represent the same hunk of time in all regions (Phillips et al. 2003 [1951]:229), the critical C line was drawn to more or less mark the point at which clay and shell tempers were about at equal frequency. Yet many of the assemblage frequencies reported were accidental averages of two or more distinctly different age components, while others might have been single occupations with roughly equivalent frequencies of the two tempers. Further, even though they were aware that frequencies changed through space as well as time, they assumed that this arbitrary event was synchronous throughout the area. Regardless of these obvious flaws, the intersection of local area and period provided the prototype for the phase. The subsequent history of the concept would be one of "refinement," i.e., sub-division of periods and areas (see esp. Phillips 1970) as well as incorporating additional regions beyond those of the initial study (e.g., Williams 1954). In fact, Williams' (1954) dissertation is the first real application of the phase con-cept anywhere. As the density of data grew over time, so did the number of phases.

Willey and Phillips (2001 [1958]:22) took the phase to be "in our opinion, the practicable and intelligible unit of archaeological study" and defined it as "an archaeological unit possessing traits sufficiently characteristic to distin-guish it from all other units similarly conceived, whether of the same or other cultures or civilizations, spatially limited to the order of magnitude of a lo-cality or region and chronologically limited to a relatively brief interval of time." Notice that, while they certainly tell us what a phase is, they do not say why it should be that way, i.e., no theory. Once again communication for the sake of communication is held out as the only purpose.

The acknowledged similarity to Kidder's discussion (Kidder et al. 1946), as well as the choice of name, identifies Willey's strong influence. Even though they see the focus as analogous (Willey and Phillips 2001 [1958]:21), the phase is, in fact, very different. First, it is a class, not a group: "an archaeological unit," a *conceptual construct* consisting of traits. In the McKern system, the focus was a group of *similar assemblages,* not a list of traits. Second, whereas the focus had been phenetic, simply formal similarity as assessed from traits, the phase had distinct temporal-spatial limits built in from the beginning, built in by the choice of traits. There is a subtle point here. On the one hand, the phase is a box with an age for a top and a bottom and a region (local area) for its sides, i.e., it is defined by time and space. In the 1950s, however, time was still largely a matter of cultural traits rather than independent measurement, so to get time, cultural traits, actually historical types, had to be used (Dunnell 1986b, 2002 [1971]) to define phases. Thus despite the acknowledged role of arbitrary deci-sions in creating all aspects of a phase, the phase itself came to have a certain aura of cultural reality, again drifting back toward the unanalyzed common-sense notion with which we started.

Although the term phase, representing either relabeled foci (mostly not in the Southeast, but see Phillips 1970:930) or the Willey and Phillips notion, completely dominates archaeological classification to the present at the assem-blage scale, there have been surprisingly few modifications and evaluations. For example, Phillips (1970), following Bordes (1952), introduced the use of ogives (his "cumulative type frequency patterns") as an "aid" to intuitive assessments of similarity. This gained at least modest currency in some quarters (e.g., Smith 1990). But these graphics changed nothing—the comparisons were not quantitative, they just looked that way. Indeed, one looks in vain for any definition of phase in any meaningful sense in Phillips (1970) or anything that might qualify as theory. If anything, Phillips' gentlemanly, self-effacing approach to "research" rather much glorified ambiguity as well as insulating his magnum opus from criticism. What can one do with statements like "Where cultural or chronological units not commensurate with the concept of phase have been formulated, I have taken the liberty of redefining them or setting up new phases, usually on inadequate grounds" (Phillips 1970:861)? Not only did he not provide instruction on how phases were to be formulated, he did not even define them, and then went on to cover himself anyway with the "inadequate grounds" clause.

The early criticisms of the phase all came from areas outside the Southeast (e.g., Abbott 1972; Olson 1962), but recently a few authors like Brown (this volume), Fox (1992, 1998), Johnson (2001), Mainfort (1999), and O'Brien (1993) have actually begun to investigate the meaning of phases by examining extant constructions. Mainfort actually does a quantitative analysis. He demonstrates that, while the assemblages assigned to some phases are more similar to one another than they are to those assigned to other phases, this is by no means true of all phases. This means that phases, whatever they are, are only occasionally, and apparently accidentally, groups (*sensu* Dunnell 2002 [1971]). In defense, one might claim that phases of the Willey and Phillips sort are not supposed to be groups, but rather classes, and that Mainfort's expectations would be fulfilled only where foci had been renamed phases. This is, of course, a charitable view. More likely, lacking any rationale, rules, or definition, phases have been erected on various grounds at various times and various places, for unremarked reasons.

Fox's (1992, 1998) examination is more complete and telling. Using the late phases of Southeast Missouri, he clearly demonstrates that the phases in use there are not groups. That is, the members of a phase are not necessarily more similar to each other than to members of other phases. He also demonstrates that they are not classes either; i.e., there does not exist any set of necessary and sufficient conditions, phrased as cultural traits, pottery types or whatever, for membership. In short, phases are just ad hoc names to which assemblages may arguably be assigned.

Once again the only thing that makes for any utility, even as a linguistic convention, is the Kriegerian test of historical significance: temporal-spatial contiguity. Spatial contiguity can be read from a map; temporal contiguity is entailed with the use of historical types, most especially pottery types. Now it should be apparent why, after years of criticism for overusing pottery, pottery remains the backbone of southeastern archaeology. It could not be otherwise.

Summary: The Functionality of Phase

Did the phase, or even its earlier analogs, ever do any work? Throughout, I have repeatedly noted that the lack of theory has been critical. Without any guiding theory, there has never been any rationale for doing anything in any particular way. Consequently, the principal function has been what archaeologists lovingly call "descriptive." All that is required to achieve this end is conventional agreement. When a new proposal turns up, there is no way to justify it either. The older traditional agreement is defended. The new guys chide the old ones for not being with it. Willey and Phillips did actually claim a purpose, "culture-historical integration" (2001 [1958]:5). Beyond time-space charts, which as we have seen have been around for a long time, it is by no means clear what this means, a situation not materially relieved by Willey and Phillips' own characterization of culture-historical integration as covering "almost everything that the archaeologist does." Phillips embraced this goal as well (Phillips 1970). No wonder that, time and again, the meaning of phase and its predecessor units has drifted back to the ur-notion of "people" or "cultural group" as a more or less discrete entity in both time and space, despite being drawn from our own cultural background with absolutely no relevance to the archaeological context. It satisfies some contemporary psychological need—no more, no less.

By giving the phase temporal and spatial boundaries, however, the Willey-Phillips phase did actually do some archaeological work. It is critical to remember that the early American chronologies were constructed by very few archaeologists (e.g., Coe 1964; Evans 1955; Ford 1935a, 1936; Kroeber 1916; MacNeish 1952; Mayer-Oakes 1955; Meggers 1957; Phillips et al. 2003 [1951]; South 2005; Spier 1917) even though those chronologies were used by whole generations. Phases provided access to those chronologies for archaeologists who could not or simply did not construct their own. This usage very much fueled the efforts to refine phases into ever smaller and finer units—you could date your assemblage more precisely (e.g., Brown 1985, esp. Table 1). While the *construction* of chronologies made serious data demands in terms of sample size, representativeness, description, and screening (even more serious demands than most of the chronologists realized), the *assignment* of an assemblage to a phase required no such rigor. Phases have become a poor man's dating machine.

As radiocarbon dates have become cheaper and the number of ways to obtain chronometric dates has increased, the phase should be out of work. It is now possible to assign virtually any assemblage to an independent time scale. The actual relations between data points can be studied instead of boxes of our own cryptic creation.

Resolution

My central theme has been the critical effect that the lack of a general theory has had on all archaeological classification. Without a theory there is no way to justify the decisions required in constructing classes: identifying the root of the classification, selecting the criteria to be used in dividing the root, and deciding on the number of criteria to be required. Of late, a particular scientific theory, evolutionary theory, has been gaining currency in some quarters. As a theory it has the requisite characteristics for archaeological application. It is a materialistic construction, able to cope with change and answer "why" questions. It is a scientific theory capable of generating empirically testable statements, and it certainly can provide the guidance required to construct an effective (i.e., able-to-explain) language of observation.

There are two primary mechanisms used by the theory, selection (a directed or biased mechanism) and drift (a probabilistic or unbiased mechanism). Please note that, contrary to some critics and proponents alike, there is more to evolution than selection! Keeping in mind that languages of observation have to be terms that can be explained by the guiding theory, this observation about mechanisms implies that two kinds of classifications are needed at a minimum, one that describes the record so that selection can be used to explain it, and another so that drift can be used. This is the basis of the function/style dichotomy (Dunnell 1978; see also Hurt and Rakita 2001 and the papers and references therein). One can easily recognize this intuitive distinction all the way back through PFG, Krieger, and even Holmes. Now, however, the difference can be formulated rigorously instead of intuitively (functional attributes are those that affect fitness; stylistic ones do not affect fitness), and thus tested (interactive vs. context-neutral). Neutral traits cannot be selected and, for that reason, under the terms "style" and "historical type," descriptions of artifacts written using neutral traits have consistently yielded chronology. Similarity displayed by such traits is due solely to transmission through space and time and, if space is held constant (e.g., Ford's "local area"), then time alone.

This has enormous potential to clarify existing problems, identify problems which have been hitherto undetected, and take us in new directions. For example, in the PFG classification, temper was used in type definitions with only a few exceptions. Temper, specifically shell temper as opposed to non-calcareous tempers, is known to be functional, i.e., to affect the fitness of its bearers through affecting production costs (including durability) and performance (Dunnell and Feathers 1991; Feathers and Scott 1989). Its inclusion as a criterion in PFG types means that they mistook functional change (everything changes) for style. Current research (Feathers, personal communication

2006) indicates that there is a relatively large fitness difference between shell and non-shell tempers in the Mississippi valley, which in turn means that the replacement of clay temper and sand temper by shell was fairly rapid where it happened. During this relatively brief period, during which shell temper increased from a small mutation frequency to fixation (100-percent less mutation rate), these types do deliver chronology, but they do so by accident. Functional change means that function is correlated with time. So what if PFG seriations are based on functional change—"as long as it changes, it can be used to tell time"? Not so. During the period of rapid functional change PFG types do deliver chronology as a result of the secondary correlation between function and time. But it also means that during the bulk of the period covered by these types, when clay or sand temper and shell temper approach fixation frequencies, the frequencies of these types are severely compromised by random variation. At best, the chronological resolution is highly variable from one part of the chronology to another; at worst it is wrong, save during the replacement period. There is a large undifferentiated early group of assemblages and a large undifferentiated group of late assemblages, separated by a few properly ordered assemblages.

Consider also the problems posed by late-pottery temper in our study area. The simple shell versus sand and/or grog dichotomy breaks down. Late potteries are sometimes tempered with one or the other or both, or still additional materials (e.g., Addis and Bell pastes). What they have in common is small temper-fragment size, and at small sizes, when shell particles are no longer plate-like but more or less spherical, much of their fitness difference is lost compared to sand or grog. When arrayed over selective environments (i.e., uses), a complex situation emerges where temper is sometimes functional, sometimes stylistic. Remember the injunction about not regarding things as universally one thing or another? Here it is played out graphically.

Another example from the northern part of the region demonstrates the role that theory can play in understanding the significance of variation. Prior to A.D. 800 or so, red-slipping is a minor decorative element on the sand-tempered, oxidized Barnes potteries. Likewise, mussel shell is encountered infrequently admixed with the sand (as is grog) or by itself. As Feathers and I have shown (Dunnell and Feathers 1991), even though shell is a superior temper to sand and occurs as a minor variation, it could never become fixed so long as the firing regime was uncontrolled, because shell becomes an unstable material above 800°C or so. Its rehydration destroys the pot upon cooling. Thus, only if and when lower temperatures were routinely used could shell become an important temper. Simple efforts to save fuel costs might have led to such a change. In any case, in the new selective environment, shell tempering increased fitness, whereas in the old it had had just the opposite effect.

Stronger—much stronger—lighter, and more flexible (in terms of form) pots were the result.

Concurrent with the rapid shift in temper is a rise in the frequency of red-slipping from less than 1 percent to over 80 percent. Why? Standard scenarios (the shell-tempered people replaced the sand-tempered people) aside, the very same mechanisms that explain the temper shift explain the slipping frequencies. The new shell-tempered paste is much more permeable, often more than twice as permeable, than the sand-tempered predecessor. Slipping reduces the permeability. This also explains why the early red-slipped shell-tempered pottery is most frequently slipped on the inside or both sides, rather than just on the outside of jars. And it is not a just-so-story. When Mississippian firing technology changes to a well-controlled reducing regime, it produces a much less permeable fabric, and red-slipping drops back to its earlier minor role as a decorative, i.e., stylistic, element. There is one exception to this change. Red-slipping continues at relatively high levels on one form, the "salt pan." If salt pans really are evaporating vessels for making salt, and there are good reasons for believing so, red-slipping may continue to be functional in this selective environment, reducing vessel damage by limiting the recrystallization of salt in the ceramic fabric.

Lipo's (2001a) recent work in the Mississippi valley shows some more of the potential that can be expected from theoretically informed ceramic classification. As his study shows, it looks like it may be possible, by tracking the rate of stylistic trait flow, to document how people were organized on the ground within what Ford had envisioned as a continuous, ever-flowing cultural stream. Even relatively simple methods of analysis, when coupled with informed classification, can yield robust structural information about past populations (e.g., Lipo et al. 1997). For the first time, a genuine, scientific theory is actually gaining some currency in the discipline that could lead to the formulation of assemblage scale units that actually mean something and are testable.

While the history of classification is rather checkered, indeed, downright embarrassing in many respects, one can expect to see genuinely new classifications that are more than just hoary convention emerge in the near future. This will require more than experience and intuition, the stock-in-trade of the expert. It will require serious, costly, time-consuming physical studies of archaeological materials, their frequencies, and distributions, the hallmarks of the scientist. Given the strong humanistic history of Mississippi valley archaeology, this may be an optimistic forecast. Pluralism (you can do it your way if you let me do it mine) and gradualism (we are already headed that way, and others as well, without any need for intellectual rationale) characterize humanistic approaches governed by cultural values rather than by testable results, and can effectively preclude the development of any scientific theory. Thus it remains to be seen whether the discipline will get its act together before the reasons for doing so disappear from the face of the earth. The LMV might even regain the intellectual lead it once had in Americanist archaeology.

Note

* Here and in the section on the phase, I have drawn heavily upon Dunnell (1986a and 1986b) as well as Lyman et al. (1997) and O'Brien and Lyman (ed. 2001). For more extended discussions of the historical development of Americanist classification, as well as more detailed references, the reader is referred to those articles.

5

Paleoenvironmental Modeling in the Central and Lower Mississippi River Valley

Past and Future Approaches

Evan Peacock

There can be no doubt that paleoclimatic reconstruction is a developing science and very much in its infancy with regard to the Lower Mississippi Valley.

Saucier 1994:42

Introduction

At first glance, the wide expanses of bottomland making up the Lower Mississippi Alluvial Valley (LMV) might seem to present a picture of homogenous environmental conditions. This perception is strengthened by synthetic environmental works in which the LMV is characterized as "southern floodplain forest" or some other broad term (e.g., Küchler 1964). While the general picture of a hardwood-dominated forest with relatively few major tree associations (H. Delcourt et al. 1981; P. Delcourt et al. 1999; Holloway and Valastro 1983a; Kidder 2002:67; Morse and Morse 1983:Table 1.1; Thorne and Curry 1983) is correct at one scale, that scale is of limited value in archaeological investigations (cf. McNutt 1996; Schuldenrein 1996:10–11). At finer scales, the daunting environmental complexity of the LMV is revealed (Lafferty 1998:139; O'Brien and Dunnell 1998:10; Saucier 1981, 1994). The area has been continually shaped by processes related to a variety of geologic, climatic, and structural controls. These processes are time- and space-transgressive, meaning that environmental changes took place at different times in different places (Table 5.1). For example, rising sea levels in the Early Holocene contributed to the establishment of a meandering river regime in the LMV, but it took about six thousand years of this transgressive process for a fully developed meandering regime to reach the latitude of Memphis, Tennessee (Saucier 1994). The effects of some climatic and geomorphologic processes proceeded from north to south, others from south to north (e.g., Saucier 1994:39). The I-69 project area in Mississippi lies in the middle, meaning that paleogeographical correlations with other parts of the Southeast cannot be taken for granted. The situation becomes even more daunting when post-depositional alteration of the archaeological record, including the impacts of modern land use, is considered. Environmental conditions at the local scale, and environmental changes at a variety of scales, have shaped the archaeological record of the LMV to an extent probably unmatched anywhere in the region (Johnson 1986:9; Kidder 2002:67).

Archaeologists must operate at these finer scales to understand human-nature relationships that played out over millennia in one of the richest and most dynamic environmental zones in North America (Saucier 1994:214, 2004; Thorne and Curry 1983). Here, I briefly describe the accomplishments and limitations of previous paleoenvironmental work in the LMV. I then suggest a range of alternative data sources that should be tapped for paleoenvironmental analysis. Because these alternative data must be derived almost exclusively from archaeological contexts, many potential biases must be acknowledged and, to the extent possible, accounted for before different data sets can be combined. A model is offered for linking the winnowed paleoenvironmental data to the archaeological record in such a way that change through time in both records can be viewed as a continuum. This can be done without recourse to arbitrary culture-historical units and without confining environmental data to use in a backdrop fashion, as is still commonly done in the Southeast (Reitz 1993). The need for more focused problem-orientation in environmental archaeology is illustrated by a brief exploration of mosaic climatic conditions during the Mid-Holocene.

Theoretical Considerations

In the Southeast, the paleoenvironment is often treated in terms of periods (or intervals, or optimums)—i.e., a backdrop approach (cf. Dincauze 1996:422–423). Although it has been empirically demonstrated that climatic conditions during periods such as the Little Ice Age and the Medieval Warm Epoch were highly variable (Blanton 2004; Fitzgerald 2001:45; Gunn 1996; Kutzbach and Webb 1991; Stahle and Cleaveland 1992, 1994; Stahle et al. 1985), this has yet to be widely incorporated into the general explanatory frameworks of southeastern archaeology. As King and Graham (1981:137) put it, "Because environmental and climatic change have been poorly known in the past, such changes have generally been ignored in producing human adaptation models. Thus, the assumption of stability has generally been more of a problem than overestimations of change." The "periodization" of the paleoenvironment is directly

Table 5.1. Selected Holocene time/space-transgressive geological processes and biotic responses in the LMV and adjacent uplands.[1,2]

Physical Process	Geomorphological Result	Biotic Response[3]	Direction	Response Time	References
Sea level rise and fall	Downcutting and entrenchment of streams, landscape stabilization and soil development during regressions; evolution of meandering regimes, aggradation of fluvial deposits during transgressions; marine limit plateau reached at ca. 6000–5000 B.P.; eastward progradation of Mississippi River Delta; continued slow sea level rise for ca. 1,500 years; small (1–3 m) fluctuations in last 3,000 years; coastal subsidence continuing	Development of mature forests/grasslands/chenier communities during regressions; bioturbation on stable landforms; more disturbance-favored/early successional communities during transgressions	Generally south to north; entrenchment of main stem of Mississippi River limited to near the Gulf of Mexico	Slow	Gibson 1982; Pirazzoli 1991; Saucier 1974, 1981, 1994; Schuldenrein 1996; Tanner 1991
Climate change	Landscape stabilization and soil weathering in dry periods; increased erosion/fluvial action during wet periods, with growth of alluvial fans/colluvial aprons along valley walls: OR, greater	Varied: different species react at different rates and scales depending on scale/duration of climate change; expansion of oak-hickory in Early- to Mid-Holocene; expansion of pine on lower Coastal Plain	South to north for increased Gulf Storm activity; variable in plant communities across the South-	Slow: rate variable for different species (e.g., up to 3,000 years for full replacement of dominant forest type)	Connaway 1988; P. Delcourt et al. 1980; H. Delcourt et al. 1997; P. Delcourt et al. 1999; Grissinger et al.

Continued on the next page

Table 5.1. *Continued*

Physical Process	Geomorphological Result	Biotic Response3	Direction	Response Time	References
	erosion during dry periods due to less stabilizing vegetation, with consequent growth of alluvial fans/colluvial aprons. Development of diagnostic landscape features (channel widths, meander wavelengths, terrace development) uncertain in LMV; probably increased storm and lightning activity during early Holocene (ca. 10,000 B.P.) and Mid-Holocene; lowered water tables and consequent drying out of lakes and swamps and channel stabilization during Mid-Holocene; lower-order streams became ephemeral in Mid-Holocene, return to perennial state in Late Holocene; increased variation in rainfall during Medieval Warm Epoch and Little Ice Age	beginning in Mid-Holocene, continuing in Late Holocene; decrease in tree cover with concomitant increase in grasses and herbs during Mid-Holocene; poor or no modern analogs for Early and Mid-Holocene vegetation communities; increased forest cover in Late Holocene with "modern" characteristics, including a decrease in the relative abundance of oak and an increase in mesic and hydric taxa such as bald cypress, willow, ash, elm, sycamore, and locust	east due to different limiting factors (e.g., pine increases from north to south along Atlantic Coastal Plain; prairie expansion from west to east along western edge of upper Mississippi alluvial valley)		1982; Gunn 1996, 1997; Joyce 1988; King 1981; King and Allen 1977; Morse and Morse 1983; Royall et al. 1991; Saucier 1994, 1997; Schuldenrein 1996; Sheehan et al. 1985; Stahle and Cleaveland 1994; Watts 1980; Watts et al. 1996; Whitehead and Sheehan 1985

| Development of Holocene meander belts | Creation of natural levees, backswamps, ridge-and-swale topography; continuous deposition of alluvial sediments in bottomlands; new lakes created via channel and chute cutoffs; older lakes and abandoned channels gradually silted in; minor periods of degradation resulting from knickpoint incision or temporary base-level changes (over-steepening) due to stream-course shortening; subsequent downstream deposition of newly contributed sediment as alluvium; lateral gradation of tributary streams as main meandering stream moves closer | Development of characteristic plant communities on different landforms relative to proximity to meandering stream (e.g., oak-hickory on levees, Tupelo gum-cypress in swamps, willow-cane along active river channels) | North to south in upper part of the alluvial valley with Late Pleistocene/Early Holocene decrease in meltwater; south to north from lower alluvial valley with change in base level associated with sea-level rise; consequent headward change along tributary streams; cutoff formation and meandering rates higher in upper part of LMV | Rapid transition to meandering regime in upper part of alluvial valley with Early Holocene decrease in discharge and change in bedload; otherwise slow (e.g., ca. 6,000 years for meandering regime to evolve from latitude of Baton Rouge to latitude of Memphis); centuries to millennia for development of new channel courses; different trunk channels and distributary belts formed at different rates; periods of alluviation in LMV not necessarily mirrored in adjacent uplands | P. Delcourt et al. 1999; Lafferty 1998; O'Brien and Dunnell 1998; Kesel and Yodis 1992; Kesel et al. 1992; Saucier 1974, 1981, 1994, 2001, 2004, n.d.; Schuldenrein 1996; Thorne and Curry 1983; Yerkes 1987 |

Continued on the next page

Table 5.1. *Continued*

Physical Process	Geomorphological Result	Biotic Response[3]	Direction	Response Time	References
Terrace formation via fluvial action (or lacustrine action early in the Holocene as glacial outwash impounded rivers); also lake formation when distributaries intersect or merge with valley walls and affect runoff patterns	Relatively flat, elevated landforms that may have different facies; soil pedogenesis following terrace stabilization with sufficient elevation above floodplain	Development of mature plant communities on stabilized terrace systems	Generally north to south; lacustrine terraces in uplands flanking northern part of LMV	Varied depending on origin; contrary to conventional thinking, terrace formation can be time-transgressive and hence terraces cannot be treated a priori as chrono-stratigraphic units	Keller and Campbell 1983; Saucier 1981, 1994, 2002
Diversion of Mississippi River flow into several major distributaries (e.g., the	Unequal development of abandoned channels (cutoffs); e.g., the older Yazoo Basin meander belts contain relatively few cutoffs; synchronous development	Fewer oxbow lake plant and animal communities than previously believed, as many channel systems continued to carry appreciable flow; increased rate of levee for-	Unclear	Unclear; larger distributaries may have functioned for centuries	Saucier 1994, 2002, 2004

Yazoo, Bear Creek, and Tensas meander belts)?[4]

of natural levees and other meander-regime features along distributary channels

mation, even along distal ends of distributary systems

1. Structural controls (e.g., earthquakes, faulting) and tectonic controls (e.g., uplift) not included.
2. Terminal Pleistocene/transitional Early Holocene processes related to glacial melting (e.g., valley-train deposition, braided-stream scouring) not included except for sea-level rise and fall and its effects on terrace formation.
3. Based on research within the LMV and in other parts of the Southeast.
4. A new model proposed by Saucier (1994) based on differences in cutoff densities within meander belts.

analogous to the practice of culture history in archaeology, with the same difficulties for explaining change through time:

> periodization . . . creates a set of internally homogeneous units that can be described, interpreted, and explained exactly as we describe, interpret, and explain the world around us. Differences among such units are treated like differences among contemporaneous units; the only difference is terminological. Differences between units of various ages are called "change"; those between contemporaneous units are called "difference." In effect, all of the "change" is squeezed out, and must be assumed to be lodged in the lines that separate periods on time/space charts (Dunnell 1982:13).

The environmental backdrop approach has long been criticized for a lack of precision (e.g., Phillips et al. 2003 [1951]:36), but its underlying problems are more fundamental. It is theoretically informed almost exclusively by an ecological (functionalist, adaptationist) viewpoint (cf. Winterhalder and Goland 1999). In essence, it is a systems approach in which change is seen as a change in state resulting from external (climatic) or internal (social) forces exceeding the system's tolerance limits (Baden 1987; Butzer 1982; Moran 1990). In recent years, models of long-term radiation and atmospheric cycles (Blanton 2004; Gunn 1994, 1997; Joyce 1988:200–204; Stahle and Cleaveland 1992), ecological succession, and cultural evolution have merged in an elaborated systems theory labeled "panarchy" (e.g., P. Delcourt and H. Delcourt 2004; Gunderson and Holling 2002; Redman 2005). Although panarchy claims to be evolutionary (see papers in Gunderson and Holling 2002), it retains large elements of classical systems theory, such as excessive external stimuli (negative feedback, in older terms) causing a system to "flip into another state" (Holling et al. 2002). Panarchy is further burdened with the baggage of progressive cultural evolution and the special pleading of human intentionality or the emergent properties of culture (P. Delcourt and H. Delcourt 2004:20–21; Redman 2005:71, 74). It also incorporates "cycling" in cultural and natural systems, a notion that is difficult to separate from circular reasoning even if the circle is twisted into a figure eight (Gunderson and Holling 2002; Redman 2005:Fig. 1; P. Delcourt and H. Delcourt 2004:Fig. 3.1). Panarchy was developed to be a "theory of adaptive change" (Holling et al. 2002), but it is unclear what advantages it has over current evolutionary theory in this regard.

An evolutionary perspective highlights another problem with an environmental backdrop approach, which is that cultural configurations are viewed as adaptations to coeval environmental conditions (e.g., when Middle Archaic cultural patterns are discussed as in relation to the Hypsithermal). As Neff and

Larson (1997:79) have pointed out, "adaptations must be understood . . . not as perfect solutions to present environmental conditions but as products of natural selection acting in past environments." In other words, cultural configurations at any given point in time are to some extent the result of selection acting on earlier cultural configurations within a *different* environmental context. Adaptation is not itself a process; it is the result of a process, or set of processes, that we label evolution (Rindos 1984). This is explicitly recognized by some evolutionary ecologists (e.g., Winterhalder 1994) but remains poorly understood by many archaeologists. Cultural traits, like biological traits, are cumulative; they may be adaptive, maladaptive, or neutral at any given point in time, and the selective value of any particular trait may change as the environment changes. This is why a long-term (evolutionary) as opposed to a synchronic (ecological) view is necessary in environmental archaeology.

Synchronic "environmental reconstruction" as traditionally practiced also suffers from the weaknesses of analogy. Analogous models in archaeology are expressed through what is labeled behavioral or cultural reconstruction. Behavioral reconstruction suffers from two major shortcomings. The first is that it consists of inferences about archaeological phenomena, so that the inferences, rather than the phenomena themselves, tend to become the subject of explanation (Dunnell 1989:43). That is, we conflate what we are ostensibly trying to explain with the concepts we create for the purposes of explanation. This makes falsification impossible (Dunnell 1989:43). The other problem with reconstruction is that it assumes invariate relationships:

> To create a behavioral reconstruction, one has to associate certain behaviors with the time-transgressive objects and their locations that constitute the contemporary archaeological record. This is formally recognized in "actualistic research" and ethnoarchaeology (Binford 1980a). Relations between behavior and material must be invariant if they are to serve as timeless, spaceless rules for reconstruction. This amounts to an assertion that behavior cannot change. Behavioral change, however, is precisely what archaeologists hope to describe and explain. In the last analysis, reconstruction employs an essentialist or typological metaphysic that is inimical to explaining change because it eliminates change (Dunnell 1989:43–44).

Do these same problems affect environmental reconstruction? Absolutely. One advantage environmental reconstructionists have had over behavioral reconstructionists is that the set of "facts" assembled is at least based on the same theory generally used to explain those facts; i.e., ecological theory. Environmental reconstruction assumes that the ecological relationships observable today existed in the past. But this approach is still tautological and ignores the frequent warnings by many researchers that no modern analogs exist for environmental conditions that prevailed in particular segments of space/time in the past (e.g., H. Delcourt and P. Delcourt 1974; P. Delcourt and H. Delcourt 2004:29; Dincauze 1996:422; Gunn 1997; Watts 1980:388–389; Watts et al. 1996). It also ignores the fact that human actions alter the evolutionary pathways of innumerable plant and animal species, mostly unintentionally and in most cases at temporal scales beyond the level of individual human awareness. Assuming invariant relationships ignores equifinality (e.g., does an increase in charcoal in sediment cores represent higher human population density or a climatically driven increase in lightning strikes? [Patterson and Sassaman 1988]). This is why it is absolutely critical for environmental archaeologists to employ multiple data sets (cf. Ford 1988:215–216). At very long time scales, even the use of species as the standard analytical unit of environmental archaeology must be called into question because species, of course, are not immutable. Because of these concerns, I consider "paleoenvironmental modeling" to be a more accurate and useful term than "environmental reconstruction" (cf. Peacock and Reese 2003).

From an evolutionary perspective, spans of relative environmental stasis are as important to identify as periods of relative instability. Any cultural changes that occurred between the beginning and end of a period of relative stasis might arguably be understood as the result of selection pressures deriving from those particular environmental conditions. The material expression of those changes—shifts in settlement patterns, house construction methods, subsistence practices, artifact types—might persist or vanish with subsequent environmental change, depending upon whether they have any adaptive value within the context of the new environment (Butzer 1996) or whether they have become widespread enough to persist over the long term even if their selective value becomes neutral. If, on the other hand, environmental conditions become unstable and change rapidly and unpredictably over time, then much accumulated cultural behavior would cease to have any positive adaptive value, or indeed might become maladaptive. Cultural changes that take place during periods of unpredictable environmental conditions are likely *not* related to those environmental conditions in a direct, functional sense (i.e., as "adaptations"); rather, existing cultural configurations are put under considerable stress, and failure rates should increase in ways that are visible archaeologically. Cultural changes might be attributable to rapidly shifting environmental conditions if those changes represent the diversion of energy into channels that dampen population growth, e.g., into the construction of monumental architecture, as suggested in Dunnell's "waste hypothesis" (Dunnell 1989; Dunnell and Greenlee 1999). To test this hypothesis, or any others that seek to relate the archaeological record to past environmental conditions, greater precision in paleoenvironmental research is obviously needed.

Scale is a fundamental consideration in environmental archaeology (cf. Butzer 1982; Kidder 1996a; Lyman 2003b; McGlade 1995; Stein and Linse 1993). From an evolutionary perspective, the scale of selection can shift depending on the selective pressures involved and other factors (Michod 1999). Whatever the theoretical approach being taken, analytical scale should be problem-oriented and relevant to the phenomena being investigated. Insects, for example, can respond very quickly to environmental changes brought about by human landscape modification (e.g., burning), while mature forest stands might take centuries to respond in a way that would be measurable using current paleoenvironmental methods. Both insect remains and wood charcoal can be examined to test hypotheses about the effects of human actions, but the differing scales of response have to be borne in mind, especially if comparisons between the two data sets are to be attempted. This is a critical point, as some practitioners of historical ecology, to give one example, have advocated a purely inductive approach to scale (Crumley 1994:9, 11). Such an inductive approach is theoretically sterile and needlessly sacrifices one of the few components of paleoenvironmental (or archaeological) investigation that can be controlled by the investigator (cf. Lyman 2003b).

Evolutionary archaeology provides a way forward in all these regards. In an evolutionary approach, a detailed, fine-scaled understanding of paleoenvironmental conditions is critical because the environment is arguably the main source of selective pressures acting to cause change in the human behavioral phenotype over time. This approach escapes determinism by focusing primarily on variability, not sameness (Dunnell 1989). If variability in the paleoenvironmental record can be recognized and robustly linked to the variability present in the archaeological record so that both records can be viewed as continua, then we will move beyond simple deterministic models or backdrop scenarios and develop much more sophisticated ideas about culture/nature interplay in the LMV and elsewhere.

Previous Environmental Work

Geomorphology and Palynology

Paleoenvironmental work in the LMV has been dominated by geomorphological investigations since Fisk's classic monograph (Fisk 1944). As Roger Saucier noted (2002:55), Fisk's work was both "a blessing and a curse" where archaeology is concerned. Its appeal lay in its apparent ability to provide precise chronological control for archaeological assemblages in the era before radiocarbon dating. Subsequent research has demonstrated that Fisk's chronology for landscape features in the LMV is badly erroneous in an absolute sense (Saucier 1981, 2001, 2002) and, while a case can be made that it still holds in relative terms (e.g., Gibson 1982:53; Johnson 1980; Lafferty 1998:127–128; Saucier 1981:15; 2002:52), there is considerable opinion to the contrary (O'Brien and Dunnell 1998:5; Saucier n.d., 1994:5, 253). The "curse" that Saucier referred to is the bias that Fisk's work conferred upon archaeological interpretations and even fieldwork results in the LMV (Kidder 1996a; Saucier 1981, 2001:64–65), especially at the survey level (e.g., an expectation that no Early Holocene occupations would be found). This is certainly a cautionary tale worth the telling (cf. Lewis 1996:53).

Another cautionary tale is provided by the continuing overreliance on geomorphological data in the LMV and subsidiary drainage basins, at least as it conditions whether and how archaeologists investigate other aspects of the paleoenvironmental record. This might seem like an odd statement, given that virtually all archaeologists, quite reasonably, make admirable attempts to understand the geomorphological contexts of sites they investigate in this active fluvial setting. There are scales at which geomorphological considerations must take precedence in a research design, one example being the focus on Pleistocene valley train surfaces in the search for Paleo-Indian sites (Brain 1970; Connaway 1988; Connaway and McGahey 1996; Hillman 1990; McGahey 1987). At the local scale, too, much remains to be learned, as evidenced by conflicting interpretations regarding site formation processes at the Short #3 site (22PA750) in Panola County, Mississippi (McGahey 2002) and the unexplained presence of shoals in the Sunflower River adjacent to the Oliver site in Coahoma County (Saucier n.d.). As Saucier (1994:21) stated, geomorphological considerations are an essential starting point for "understanding man/land relationships."[1] My contention is that we seldom get past this "starting point" in the LMV.

This contention is supported by a review of the archaeological literature. Beginning with another classic monograph, that of Phillips et al. (2003 [1951]), most research articles and virtually all CRM reports generated in the LMV and subsidiary basins contain a section on geomorphology. The problem is that most contain nothing else where the paleoenvironment is concerned. One possible reason is that efforts to employ other standard methods, such as palynology, have met with little success (see discussion of human impact below). Good, long-term pollen sites are relatively rare in the Southeast in general (Watts 1980:Fig. 1) and in the Central Mississippi Valley (CMV) and LMV in particular (P. Delcourt and H. Delcourt 1977; H. Delcourt et al. 1997; P. Delcourt et al. 1980:111; P. Delcourt et al. 1999; King and Allen 1977:308; Watts 1980: Fig. 1). Lakes and swales dry out, are recaptured or silted in (Saucier 2001:70), bottom sediments are affected by bioturbation, sedimentation rates have varied greatly, and so on (King and Allen 1977:308; Royall et al. 1991:161; Watts 1980:405; Watts et al. 1996:29). Attempts to extract meaningful pollen data from dry-land samples in the LMV and adjacent areas have been frustrated by poor preservation (e.g., Brown et al. 1994; Gremillion 1995a; Heartfield, Price and Greene, Inc. 1987:2.5–11; Holloway 1983; Holloway and Valastro 1983a, 1983b; Hunter et al. 1995:99; Morgan and Raspet 1979; Perrault and Saucier 2000:76–77; G. Smith 1978:66; Spencer and Perry 1978; Ward 1999). As a result, vegetation regimes characterized using pollen data are discussed in terms of periods of up to five thousand years (e.g., Thorne and Curry 1983), a classic backdrop approach. Add to these problems concerns over the translocation of pollen in soils (Bunting and Tipping 2000; Kelso 1994; Kelso et al. 2000) and it becomes evident why archaeologists have relied so heavily on geomorphology in paleoenvironmental research in the LMV. Palynology is discussed again below in relation to human environmental impact.

Geomorphological analysis has been applied in various ways in the LMV and in the lower Gulf Coastal Plain in general. For example, attempts have been made to link archaeologically dated fluvial landscape features with paleoclimatic events. Alford and Holmes (1985) employed this method in southwestern Louisiana with surprising results. The wavelengths of some Late-Holocene meanders in the Sabine River system indicate "an annual discharge that was only 5 percent of the present" (Alford and Holmes 1985:401). They attribute this to markedly decreased rainfall during the Little Ice Age, arguing that the cooler temperatures would have resulted in fewer storms originating in the Gulf of Mexico. Similarly they argue, based on bight size in meander-cut terraces, that increased temperatures during the Mid-Holocene led to increased storm activity and elevated levels of precipitation over the lower Southeast (cf. Gunn 1997:137), creating much larger meanders in some parts of the Sabine system than those found today (Alford and Holmes 1985:400–401; cf. Knox 1983; Royall et al. 1991). These ideas are an interesting contrast to traditional conceptions of paleoclimatic "periods" (e.g., Morse and Morse 1983:99–101; Whitehead and Sheehan 1985) such as the Hypsithermal having been a period of warmer, drier conditions while the Little Ice Age was cooler and wetter. A correlation between channel size and the Mid-Holocene Hypsithermal interval has been suggested for some parts of the CMV (P. Delcourt et al. 1999:20; Saucier 1974, 1985), including small channels on the alluvial fan of the Current River in the Western Lowlands (Price and Price 1981; Saucier 1994:45). In general, however, Saucier found no convincing correlation between channel size and paleoclimatic episodes in the LMV (Saucier 1994:43–46, 123–125). It must be kept in mind that archaeological materials provide a *minimum* age estimate for any given landform (Royall et al. 1991:159; Saucier 1994:14) and that, of course, not all archaeological materials have been found and/or dated (Saucier

2001:67). Alford and Holmes' model, while intriguing, must be tested in their study area by independent means before it can be applied to the LMV with any confidence.

Geomorphological considerations have provided testable hypotheses concerning settlement pattern changes at the local scale. One idea, for example, is that settlements shifted laterally along the banks of oxbow lakes as old channels silted in over time (Connaway et al. 1977; Kidder 1996a; Saucier 1977; Weinstein 1981a; Weinstein et al. 1979). At a grosser level, it is often assumed that prehistoric habitation must have focused on relatively stable landforms—e.g., levees fronting relict channels—rather than on active levees or other landforms subject to disturbance in a dynamic fluvial environment (Heinrich 1991; Kidder 1996a:313; Marshall 1986; Phillips et al. 2003 [1951]:297–300; Weinstein et al. 1979). While such observations make intuitive sense, and indeed may explain much regarding prehistoric settlement patterns in the LMV, we should continue to treat them as hypotheses and devise multiple ways of testing them to avoid the pitfalls of equifinality.

Perhaps geomorphology's most direct application at the moment lies in telling us why sites of certain ages are not found in certain areas. It has long been recognized that fluvial action in the Mississippi alluvial valley has buried or obliterated significant portions of the archaeological record over time (McGimsey and Davis 1968; Phillips et al. 2003 [1951]:299–300). Sites likely are buried under layers of alluvium of varying thicknesses (Arco et al. 2006; Connaway 1988; Kidder 2006; Lafferty 1998:139; Lafferty and Price 1996; O'Brien 1994b; Saucier 1974, 1978, 1981:10, 1994:124, n.d.), by backswamp deposits, alluvial fans and aprons (Connaway 1988; O'Brien and Dunnell 1998:10; Saucier 1981:15, 1994:91–92), and possibly by sand dunes (Saucier 1974:9, 1978:39) and eolian silts (Saucier 1981:9). They are destroyed by river meandering (House 1987:51; Lafferty 1998:132, 139; McGimsey 1996:5; O'Brien 1994b; O'Brien and Dunnell 1998:4–5; Saucier 1977, n.d.), and continually modified by bioturbation (McGahey 2002; Saucier 1994:188). In addition, sites are buried under the "postsettlement alluvium" (Saucier 1994:182), especially near the valley walls, and have been impacted by Historic-period farming (Barnhardt 1988; Saucier 1994:71–72) and modern land-use practices such as land-leveling and catfish-pond construction (Connaway and McGahey 1971:1–2, 1996; Morse 1986; Saucier 1994:36; Thorne and Curry 1983). Settlement pattern studies, in particular, must acknowledge these biases and try to account for them to the extent possible.

As noted earlier, our understanding of the chronology of landscape development in the LMV is nowhere near as precise as Fisk claimed sixty years ago. Indeed, Saucier came to believe that that level of precision may never be possible (Saucier 1981:8; 1994:214, 253; 2002:60), and the relative dates of some of his mapped meander-belt segments have recently been questioned (Arco et al. 2006). However, optically stimulated luminescence (OSL) dating of sediments has recently proved successful in the northern LMV (Rittenour et al. 2003) and elsewhere in the Southeast (Ivester et al. 2001). The method has the potential to absolutely date fluvial landforms with a high degree of precision (Feathers, this volume) and can be used on individual sand grains as little as 100 years old (Duller 1996; Wintle 1996). Targeted dating of landforms coupled with seriation of artifact assemblages (Rafferty, this volume) could radically improve the precision of landform chronologies and the understanding of archaeological settlement pattern shifts in the LMV.

Archaeologists should, of course, continue to conduct geoarchaeological analyses at the site level, but the focus could profitably expand beyond relative dating and local environmental context to include more problem-oriented research. A good example at problem-oriented, site-level analysis is provided by Arco et al. (2006), who cored and trenched across the Nolan site (16MA201) in northeastern Louisiana. Beyond establishing a specific geomorphological context and site developmental history, a Middle Archaic assignment for four mounds and an earthen ridge was demonstrated. The application of geoarchaeology to the question of Archaic mounds (e.g., Saunders and Allen 1994; Saunders et al. 1994; Saunders et al. 2005) has in general been one of the most important breakthroughs in southeastern archaeology in recent times. At a broader scale, problem-oriented geoarchaeology can contribute enormously to our understanding of prehistoric settlement and subsistence patterns. For example, Kidder (2006) combines geoarchaeological, paleoclimatological, oceanographical, and archaeological data to make a strong argument that increased flooding led to Late Archaic abandonment of the Tensas Basin, with repopulation not occurring until Early Woodland times (ca. 2500 cal B.P.) when a series of crevasse-splay surfaces on the east side of Joes Bayou were occupied. He further suggests that the LMV in general experienced greatly increased flood frequencies between 3000 and 2600 cal B.P. Such flooding could have led to significant avulsion, disruption of long-distance trade patterns, and a decrease in the availability of fish (Kidder 2006). Kidder's hypothesis is arguably supported by settlement pattern data from the hill belts east of the LMV; for example, Peacock (1997) notes a significant increase in site numbers during the Tchula (Early Woodland) period in the North Central Hills of Mississippi. Kidder's work shows the positive results of landscape-scale analysis, combining data from several disciplines to "arrive at a better understanding of how humans have interacted with and have been influenced by their environment" (Kidder 2006:222).

Historical Records

Analysis of historical records on environmental conditions in the LMV has revealed some surprising things. For example, Holloway and Valastro (1983a) note that walnut was widespread and very important economically in the mid-nineteenth century in the LMV, yet walnut pollen is "extremely rare" in pollen samples. Thorne and Curry (1983) compiled historical data to construct a paleoenvironmental model for the Yazoo Basin, characterizing floral communities in terms of associations with particular landform types. Their model, which is essentially an optimal foraging theory construct,[2] is an important work, especially in its considerations of scale and its incorporation of general land office (GLO) survey data. Their innovative grouping of trees by flood-tolerance levels showed that some parts of the LMV were drier than expected in the early nineteenth century (Thorne and Curry 1983:42–48). GLO notes can reveal the locations of relict channels and other landscape features in alluvial settings (e.g., Buchner 2001a:52–53, 2001b:67–69; Buchner and Albertson 2003), once recorder biases have been accounted for (Bourdo 1956; Whitney and DeCant 2001). Foster et al. (2004) recently employed catchment analysis using GLO notes to show vegetation differences between Historic Creek towns and uninhabited control areas in east-central Alabama. GLO data have also been used to document late prehistoric human environmental impact in Arkansas (G. Williams 1993). Cluster analysis is a relatively straightforward way to analyze GLO data in a way that provides fine-scale community classification (e.g., Barone 2005a; Whitney and DeCant 2001). Other records, such as Mississippi River Commission Charts (Buchner 2001c), exist that may show past environmental features. Anecdotal accounts such as traveler's diaries are more heavily biased and therefore less reliable as formal data sources (Edmonds 2001). All historical records are biased to some extent, a caveat that applies particularly to the earliest records for the study area (Galloway 1993). Galloway (1993) has called for greater attention to the methods of modern historiography, and her assessment of the biasing effects of the Direct Historical Approach à la Swanton (Galloway 1993:92–98; cf. Peacock 2001) holds value as a lesson for archaeologists who would too freely apply synthetic environmental works such as that of Küchler (1964), which are based on modern conditions, to the past.

Macrobotanical Remains

Wood charcoal and other plant remains have been used to examine the effects of prehistoric land clearance, agriculture, and other activities on local environments (e.g., Lopinot and Woods 1993). Gail Wagner (2005:229), for example, used macrobotanical remains to describe "deliberate but low-level management of the woods" around the Carlston Annis site in western Kentucky. Such remains have been underused in this regard in the LMV and adjacent areas, where only general statements about environmental conditions or past human impact based on plant remains are given (e.g., Shea 1999). Archaeobotanical data are usually discussed almost solely in terms of prehistoric subsistence practices (e.g., Brown et al. 1994; Byrd and Neuman 1978; Fritz and Kidder 1993; Kidder and Fritz 1993; McNutt 2003; Roberts 2004; Ryan 1995:51–54; Ryan and Roberts 2003; Ward 1998) or a simple list of taxa is given (e.g., Heartfield, Price and Greene 1987:2.5–11).

The few exceptions suggest that plant remains can yield interesting data on paleoenvironmental conditions and cultural practices in the LMV. For example, Connaway and McGahey (1971:16) present wood charcoal data from the Woodland-period Boyd site in Tunica County, Mississippi. Baldcypress, willow, and tupelogum were absent in the earlier Zone I but present in the later Zone II, suggesting either a change to wetter local environmental conditions (cf. the modern species recorded at Powers Fort Swale in the CMV; Royall et al. 1991:160; H. Delcourt et al. 1997) or "a change of preference in wood-use." Some of the species represented at Boyd, such as eastern redcedar and hackberry, are favored by disturbed-ground conditions. Connaway (1982a) had wood charcoal from a number of Mississippian house features in the northern Yazoo Basin identified. Species included baldcypress, pecan group, white and red oak groups, ash (including green ash), hickory and elm (including American elm, cedar elm, and probable winged elm). Interestingly, cultural bias in the selection of species for "strength and flexibility" in house construction is suggested (Connaway 1982a:21), a pattern noted in other areas of the Eastern Woodlands during the Mississippian period (Harvey 1977:276). Specifically, baldcypress seems to have been favored for large center posts and interior support posts, while hickory and species of the white oak and red oak groups were favored for wall posts (Connaway 1984; cf. Childress et al. 1995; Connaway 1982b; Starr 2003:29–30).

In the American Bottom, wood in Mississippian structures may reflect social status and ceremonial symbolism in addition to functional properties, as evidenced by association of red cedar with "ritual artifacts" such as figurines (Simon 2002). Interestingly, Early (2000) found no patterns in species use in a well-preserved Caddoan structure in the Ouachita Mountains of Arkansas. Such variability may be the result of the availability of different tree species, which can be affected by the duration and intensity of human pressure on local environments.

Cutler and Blake (1985 [1970]) note the presence of butternut (*Juglans cinerea*) shell at the Bonds site in Tunica County and the Denton Site in Quitman County, Mississippi, at the southern limit for the species. Similarly, black walnut (*Juglans nigra*) is found at Denton and at the Noe site in Coahoma

County, Mississippi, south of its known historical range in the LMV (Connaway 1977; Cutler and Blake 1985 [1970]). Red and white oak also seem to be more common in archaeological contexts than expected based on historical records—something that could be due to cultural importation or environmental change over time (Cutler and Blake 1985 [1970]). Fritz (this volume) has questioned the butternut identifications, and a reexamination of existing archeobotanical collections from the LMV would be a good first step in updating our knowledge of paleoenvironments and plant use in the area.

Dendroclimatology

Correlations between dendrological and archaeological data in the Southeast have thus far been relatively broad due to the subtleties of interpretation (see Kipfmueller and Swetnam 2001) and a lack of precision in dating archaeological occupations (Anderson et al. 1995), but there is great promise for further application of the method. Recent compilations have demonstrated decadal cycles of drought and wetness (Fye et al. 2003; Stahle et al. 1988), and some "megadroughts" have been identified, including one that lasted from A.D. 1570 to 1587 (Fye et al. 2003; Stahle et al. 2000). Such droughts, and indeed the intervening pluvials, must have had dramatic effects on the failure or success of agricultural societies in the Southeast (Anderson et al. 1995). Radial-growth anomalies detected in the annual rings of baldcypress trees in Reelfoot Lake, Tennessee, have been correlated with the New Madrid earthquakes of 1811–1812 (Stahle et al. 1992), and it has been suggested that the development of "sunk lands" such as the St. Francis Sunk Lands of Arkansas may be datable by this method if suitable specimens can be identified (Stahle et al. 1992). The tree-ring record of the LMV can potentially be pushed back several centuries into the prehistoric period (Stahle et al. 1992), factoring in the effects of ageing and competition on tree growth (Helama et al. 2005), and comparison with the archaeological record can be more precise using fine-grained chronological sequences derived via seriation (Rafferty, this volume).

Documenting Prehistoric Human Environmental Impact

Research over the last few decades has demonstrated conclusively that native societies transformed the landscapes they inhabited (Denevan 1992; Doolittle 1992; Krech 1999; Peacock 1998a, 1998b; Redman 1999; Vale 2002; G. Williams 1993). The prehistoric Eastern Woodlands of North America were once considered to be an exception in this regard, providing model "pristine" ecosystems against which modern anthropogenic impacts could be measured (Marquardt 1994:206; Russell 1997:240; Stahl 1996). Recent work has shown that prehistoric human impacts did occur in eastern North America (Kidder 1998; Peacock 1998b), with evidence from the Southeast and the American Bottom being especially strong (Chapman and Shea 1981; Chapman et al. 1982; H. Delcourt 1987; H. Delcourt and P. Delcourt 1997; P. Delcourt and H. Delcourt 1987:167, 2004; P. Delcourt et al. 1986; P. Delcourt et al. 1998; Early 1993; Fritz 1993:51; Johannessen 1988; Lopinot and Woods 1993; Scarry and Scarry 2005; Watson 1985). Impact is here defined as any action by a biological agent that reduces the productive potential of a given area for a period of time longer than the life span of that biological agent. Productive potential can be characterized as the capability for biomass production (e.g., Simmons 1989:13–14). This definition qualitatively differentiates impact from low-level environmental change that can result from innumerable human actions such as simple trampling along trails (Peacock 1998a) and from actions that actually increase the productivity of an area, such as burning and pruning (Doolittle 1992; King and Graham 1981). It also implies that measurable traces will be left in the archaeological/paleoecological records. By this definition, impact is change that is detrimental at some measurable scale. In theory, any human actions that physically depleted the topsoil in a given area would qualify as impact (e.g., Butzer 1992:349, 1996; Deevey et al. 1979; P. Delcourt et al. 1986; Newsom 1993; O'Hara et al. 1993; Thornes 1985; Tivy 1990; Woods and Holley 1991). In practice, we are often forced to rely upon proxies to try to recognize and quantify prehistoric human impacts.

The most familiar proxy for impact is an increase in disturbance-favored taxa in pollen diagrams. As noted above, good, long-term pollen sequences are rare in the CMV and LMV; however, the limited data available do suggest substantial human impacts, at least in the late prehistoric period. Ragweed percentages reached a peak similar to modern levels around 600 B.P., coincident with the appearance of abundant maize pollen in wetland cores (H. Delcourt et al. 1997:120; Royall et al. 1991:169). Paul Delcourt et al. (1999) designated a "Ragweed-Grass Old Field vegetation type" to "characterize a cumulative mosaic of secondary succession on anthropogenically disturbed landscapes" in the CMV. Thorne and Curry (1983) noted "prairies" in the GLO data from the LMV (cf. Thorne 1977:12) but, contrary to the suggestions of earlier researchers (Smith 1963), they believed that such open areas were too big to be anthropogenic features. Further GLO work has shown that such features were fairly common in the Mississippi Delta, especially near its eastern margins in Leflore, Carroll, Holmes, and Yazoo counties (Barone 2005b). These "alluvial prairies" average about 68 ha in area (Barone 2005b:Table 1). This is not at all out-of-line with the scale of prehistoric human disturbance suggested for the CMV and LMV by the Delcourts (H. Delcourt 2002; H. Delcourt and P. Delcourt 1991; H. Delcourt et al. 1997; P. Delcourt and H. Delcourt 2004; P. Delcourt et al. 1999) or with historical accounts of Southeastern Indian agriculture (e.g., Foster 2003; Scarry 1993:78). For example, Foster et al. (2004) note that Creek fields in east-central Alabama averaged about 33 ha in size, while Baden (1987) compiled ethnohistoric data from eastern North America and calculated field sizes of up to 1.5 acres per person (cf. Gremillion 1995b). Given the environmental constraints on field locations in the LMV, amalgamations of field systems over time could easily produce and maintain open areas the size of the "prairies." Better documentation of weed seeds from archaeological contexts will be useful in this regard, as it has been noted that up to 40 percent of the seed assemblages at early Historic-period Indian sites is comprised of weedy species, a finding attributable to land clearance (Gremillion 1995b). The need for further studies of prehistoric human impact in the Southeast has been noted several times in recent years (e.g., Gremillion 2002) and clearly will be an interesting avenue of research in the LMV.

The use and management of Delta land must have declined considerably with Protohistoric and early Historic-period declines in American Indian populations (see Brown, this volume). The scale of human impact then increased dramatically in the Historic period, as widespread forest clearance took place and bottomlands were converted into cotton fields (Saikku 2005). These efforts initially focused along the edges of major watercourses, especially where Indian old fields were still discernible, but later expanded into the wide expanses of bottomland hardwood forest. Massive increases in population followed the Civil War: in the ten "core counties" of the Delta (Bolivar, Coahoma, Humphreys, Issaquena, Leflore, Quitman, Sharkey, Sunflower, Tunica, and Washington), for example, populations grew from 48,705 in 1870 to 382,435 in 1930 (Saikku 2005:Table 1). Mechanized clearing and farming methods, combined with the spread of settlement, with improved flood control, onto previously marginal lands (Vance 1935), had a catastrophic effect on the area's flora and fauna (Saikku 2005). As noted earlier, it also contributed to greatly increased erosion, masking to some extent the environmental signatures of earlier cultures in the Delta.

Alternative Data Sources

Because of the dynamic nature of the LMV and because environmental processes are time- and space-transgressive, gaining a better understanding of environmental conditions at the local scale must be a major focus for archaeologists working in the region. Because of the limitations and biases of the paleoenvironmental record and the need for increased precision across different scales of investigation, it is necessary to access multiple sources of paleoenvironmental data, some of which have only rarely been employed in the Southeast.

Daub

A particular kind of archaeobotanical record is preserved as plant impressions in daub. Connaway (1984) suggested that such impressions could be used for paleoenvironmental work in the LMV, and work in the Tombigbee River drainage has demonstrated the potential of the method (Peacock 1993; Peacock and Reese 2003). Daub with plant impressions is quite common in the Delta (e.g., Connaway 1981b, 1984; Starr 1997). Among other things, daub impressions can be used to investigate environmental changes caused by field clearance and other human activities, by noting the presence/frequency of disturbance-favored species such as cocklebur (Caddell 1982; Connaway 1984; Starr 1997:95). It can also be used to account for biases in other data sets. For example, pollen obtained from the Yarborough site (22CL814) in Clay County, Mississippi, is probably modern based on comparison with daub impressions and charred seeds (Peacock and Reese 2003). As noted earlier, wood charcoal may reflect cultural selection in plant use, and archaeological context is usually the main point of argument in this regard (Smart and Hoffman 1988). If one assumes that the impressions of plants other than grass temper or construction members—e.g., leaves, cockleburs, nuts, and seeds—represent incidental inclusions, then a comparison of daub to the charcoal record can be used to assess cultural bias in the selection of wood for fuel or other purposes (cf. Ford 1988:219). Such an analysis is currently underway at the Lyon's Bluff site (22OK520) in Oktibbeha County, Mississippi (Seltzer 2005) and should provide a useful pilot study for the method. In addition, the size and form of plant impressions in daub (e.g., capped versus uncapped acorns, stiff spines on cockleburs, grass and frond inflorescences) can provide very precise estimates of the season of house construction (Caddell 1982; Connaway 1984; Peacock and Reese 2003:78; Seltzer 2005; Solis and Walling 1982). Connaway (1984) has made the interesting observation that an abundance of grass temper in daub implies open areas for grass growth; this in turn implies intentional management for a useful resource. Perhaps the main limitations of daub are its relatively short temporal duration (from ca. A.D. 900 to Contact-period times) and the limited area that may be represented by the plant impressions from any particular daub fall (Peacock and Reese 2003).

Phytoliths

A review of the literature and conversations with several scholars indicates that phytolith work is essentially nonexistent in the LMV. Although there is still an enormous amount of methodological work to be done, phytolith analysis continues to grow in importance in environmental archaeology because of the durable nature of the remains (Fredlund 2001; Pearsall 1989; Piperno 1988; Rovner 1983). Beyond further development of analytical techniques, one problem that presents itself is contextual. It has been demonstrated that, in sandy soils, macroartifacts can be vertically displaced to a significant extent by bioturbation (e.g., Peacock and Fant 2002). Microartifacts and other small objects such as phytoliths undoubtedly are moved downward as well (Piperno 1988:110–111). OSL may provide a relatively secure means for dating phytoliths in association with geological strata, but great care will need to be taken to insure that meaningful contexts are sampled at archaeological sites.

Small Mammal Remains

Although the analysis of faunal remains in the LMV and adjacent drainages has concentrated on subsistence issues (e.g., Breitburg 1999; Brown et al. 1994; Jackson, this volume; Jackson and Scott 2001), some environmental work has been done using small mammal remains. For example, Coxe and Kelley (2004) relate the prevalence of swamp rabbits over cottontails at the Hedgeland site (16CT19) in Catahoula Parish, Louisiana, to a lack of cleared areas such as agricultural fields in the vicinity of the site. This suggestion was bolstered by the presence of Eastern gray squirrel and the absence of fox squirrel. These same types of analyses have been conducted at sites in eastern Mississippi and western Alabama (Hogue 2003a; Scott 1983), where they seem to show the effects of prehistoric land clearance. Clearly this method could and should continue to be developed in the LMV (cf. Whyte 1991). Large mammals can also be used for paleoenvironmental modeling, e.g., through size analysis, but equifinality is a larger issue where such remains are concerned (Wolverton 2005).

Mollusks

Freshwater mussel species currently listed as extinct or endangered (i.e., those most sensitive to siltation and other forms of water pollution) began to decline in abundance in the Southeast ca. 5,000 years ago, coincident with the beginning of Indian horticulture. The rate of decline increased with the advent of maize agriculture ca. 1,000 years ago (Peacock 1998a; Peacock, Haag, and Warren 2005). Changes in species proportions can arguably be used as a proxy for measuring relative levels of prehistoric human environmental impact through time (Peacock, Haag, and Warren 2005). This method, which should have widespread applicability in eastern North America, may be relatively difficult in the lower Gulf Coastal Plain because most of the species found there are adapted to relatively turbid conditions (e.g., Kesel et al. 1992). However, recent work with archaeological shell assemblages has revealed the presence of species extirpated from the LMV and subsidiary basins early in Historic times, and which may serve as suitable indicator species for prehistoric, human-induced erosion. These include *Cyprogenia aberti* and *Plethobasus cyphyus*, found in sites along the eastern tributaries of the Mississippi River in Mississippi (Bogan 1987; Peacock and James 2002) and along the Tensas and other rivers in northeastern Louisiana (Coxe and Kelley 2004; Peacock and Chapman 2001; Saunders et al. 2005; Vidrine 1993, 1997). Stream flow and substrate characteristics may be characterized by adapting Warren's UNIO program (Warren 1990, 1991; Peacock n.d.).

Human pressure on the local environment resulting from population growth and territorial constraint may be addressed with mussel assemblages. Research in the Tombigbee and Tennessee River valleys has shown that, during the Woodland period, mussels were only gathered from areas immediately adjacent to the sites where the shell was deposited. This was demonstrated via correspondence analysis: shell assemblages fell along the major axes in ordination diagrams in the same order that the sites producing the assemblages occurred along waterways. In other words, site location was the primary determining factor in the makeup of the shell assemblages (Peacock 2002). For the Tombigbee River valley, this phenomenon was argued to be the result of population pressure rather than simple availability, because metric analysis showed no selection bias—mussels of all species and sizes were being consumed, including very small individuals—and because other data sets (botanical remains, faunal remains, skeletal indicators of nutritional stress and increased warfare) also implied intense pressure on the local environments (Blitz 1993; Futato 1987:226–238; Jenkins 1982:143–144; Peacock 2002:459; Welch 1990). Freshwater mussel shell is a common constituent of archaeological sites in the Delta, and paleoenvironmental and biogeographic studies employing shellfish remains should be a prime consideration for future research.

Land snails are another paleoenvironmental data source that has not been tapped in the LMV. Dramatic changes in the proportions of different groups can take place as a result of human land clearance. Research in the Mississippi Black Prairie, for example, shows that many species of Pupillidae are favored by disturbed-ground conditions (Peacock and Melsheimer 2003; Peacock and Gerber 2008) and can serve as indicators of land clearance. Land snails can also be quite valuable in investigating formation processes at archaeological sites. For example, Peacock, Rafferty, and Hogue (2005) report modern land snails throughout the matrix of what appeared to be undisturbed pit features at sites in the Black Prairie and discuss the implications of this finding for interpreting other classes of remains (cf. Whyte 1991). One problem with using land snails for paleoenvironmental modeling is that they most directly represent site-specific conditions. With the compilation of data from a number of occupations over a wide area, however, land snail data from archaeological contexts can also be used to characterize regional environmental conditions (e.g., Baerreis 2005; Klippel and Turner 1991), especially when correspondence analysis or other multidimensional analytical techniques are used (e.g., Peacock and Gerber 2008). Different sizes of shells are recovered from macroscreening, fine screening, and flotation, and determination of community characteristics depends upon obtaining a representative sample of snails using different recovery methods.

Both terrestrial and aquatic (salt and freshwater) mollusk shells can be subjected to oxygen-isotope analysis, which may yield information on past temperature regimes. Changes in shell size and shape over time may also be linked to changes in environmental conditions (Baerreis 1980; Barber 1988; Peacock 2005a; Rollins et al. 1990). Baerreis (2005), for example, was able to distinguish three distinct periods of alternate dry and moist conditions using snail size and assemblage composition at the Archaic-period Carlston Annis shell mound in western Kentucky. Combining morphometric and isotopic analysis can provide a powerful proxy for past climatic conditions, using materials commonly found at archaeological sites in the Southeast (Peacock 2005a).

Other Sources

In addition to these alternative data sources from archaeological sites, a number of methods can be employed in purely geological contexts. Space limitations prevent a thorough review, but a few examples can be mentioned. Salt-water mollusks may be used to investigate changes in Mississippi River discharge rates, as community characteristics and isotope levels can vary based on salinity, bottom type, turbidity, and current (Parker 1956). With careful consideration of reservoir (old carbon) effects, mollusks from near-shore environments in the Gulf of Mexico can be radiocarbon dated and analyzed in these regards. Cores taken from wetland areas like the Atchafalaya Basin are visibly homogenous, but methods like X-ray diffraction and X-ray diffusion reveal subtle stratigraphic differences most likely due to changes in environmental conditions (Coleman 1966; Scull et al. 1966). Pedogenesis rates are directly related to climatic factors, and provide a landscape-scale signature of periods of relative stability when significant soil development is apparent (Holliday 1990; Schuldenrein 1996).

A Model for Linking Archaeological and Paleoenvironmental Data

Environmental data derived from archaeological contexts have been characterized as being too "soft" for rigorous paleoenvironmental modeling (e.g., Knox 1976; cf. Crumley 1994:4–5) and indeed they can be very difficult to work with. Regardless of the biases attending such data, however, we must make greater use of them because in many cases they're all we have, they can be analyzed at scales commensurate with analyses of the archaeological record itself, and they can be directly linked to the archaeological record so that change through time can be viewed as a continuum, rather than as changes in state over a series of arbitrary periods. One way to do this is to move away from the traditional fixation on archaeological components and to focus on an actual material phenomenon that is measurable in space, time, and form: the occupation. Dunnell (2002 [1971]) defined an occupation as a spatial cluster of discrete objects that can reasonably be assumed to be the product of a single group of people at a particular locality and deposited there over a period of continuous residence. Rafferty (2001, this volume) has operationalized this definition by linking the concept of occupation to the concept of artifact lineages, so that occupations are artifacts at the scale of assemblage showing coherence in space, time, and form (Rafferty 2001, this volume). Different occupations can be linked using seriation (Rafferty, this volume), a method that provides the chronological precision, unobtainable by other means, but critically important for assessing "rates of change or synchroneity of different [environmental] data sets" (Dincauze 1996:423).

Figure 5.1 presents a model for linking archaeological and paleoenvironmental data through time. The unit of analysis is the occupation. Occupations can be of any size or duration, and can be arbitrarily subdivided if one wishes to investigate change through time within a given occupation. Artifact assemblages from occupations are ordered through time via seriation. Duration of occupations can be established through absolute dating of target assemblages. The biotic data recovered from individual occupations can then be examined for change through time without reference to arbitrary culture-historical boundaries; i.e., variability can be expressed, not compressed. With enough occupations linked into a temporal sequence, change through time in the environmental record can be viewed as a continuum, at whatever scale is appropriate to the particular question being asked. To account for the effects of cultural and natural biases, sampling error, and equifinality, it is necessary to employ multiple data sets derived from different types of biotic and physical materials (cf. Burgi and Russell 2001); this includes the incorporation of off-site data, if such are available, up to the landscape scale.[3] The biases affecting each of these data sets must be considered and adjustments made prior to synchronic and diachronic syntheses.

Problem-Orientation in Environmental Archaeology: Investigating the Hypsithermal Mosaic

Moving away from an environmental backdrop approach will entail more formalized problem-orientation in environmental archaeology, and the I-69 project represents an excellent opportunity in this regard. The addition of alternate

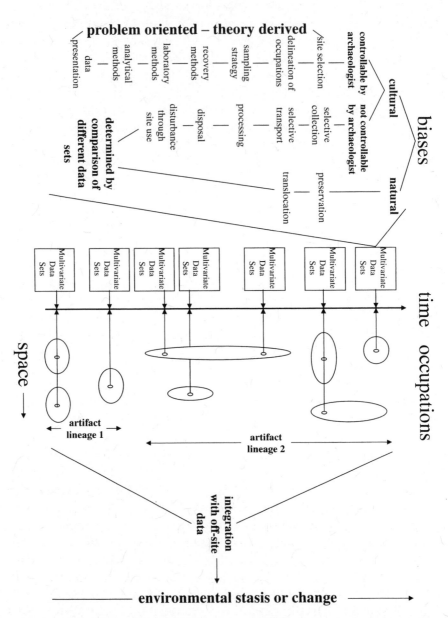

Figure 5.1. A model for linking paleoenvironmental and archaeological data through the use of occupations.

data sources as suggested here will allow us to more fully investigate paleoenvironmental variability and its implications for understanding the archaeology of the Southeast. For example, one traditional association between paleoclimate and culture has been the equation of Middle Archaic cultures with the Mid-Holocene Hypsithermal climatic optimum (Anderson 1995:152; Morse and Morse 1983). According to this traditional model, warmer, drier conditions had a profound effect upon the landscape; for example, less vegetation leading to destabilized conditions with consequent increases in slope erosion (e.g., Gunn 1997:145; King and King 1996:80; Saucier 1994:43; Schuldenrein 1996:3). It has been suggested that such erosion may have caused the silting-over of gravel bars, causing changes in lithic raw material procurement (e.g., McGahey 1999:7–8; but see Bense 1987). It also has been suggested that mussel beds became more accessible due to lower stream levels, leading to an increase in the use of this resource (Anderson 1995:156; Smith 1986). These ideas are clearly contradictory—if gravel bars were silted over to the degree necessary to prevent raw material acquisition, then mussels would have been smothered or otherwise unavailable. Unfortunately, both our archaeological and our paleoenvironmental data have been too coarse-grained to allow for the testing of such ideas, which remain largely within the realm of supposition.

New data indicate that the effects of the Hypsithermal were quite variable across space and time (Kutzbach and Webb 1991:187; Otvos 2005; Saucier 1994:45; Schuldenrein 1996). In particular, information from different data sources suggests that many parts of the eastern United States actually saw increased precipitation and consequent growth in stream size due to increased storm activity over the Gulf of Mexico during the Mid-Holocene (Watts et al. 1996:36). The geomorphological work of Alford and Holmes (1985) in Louisiana has already been mentioned. Rovner (2001, personal communication 2005) has recently described phytolith evidence for increased wetness in the Susquehanna River valley, Pennsylvania, during the Mid-Holocene, a finding in accordance with the paleo-monsoons modeled for the Atlantic Coastal Plain by Kutzbach (1987; cf. Gunn 1997). Goman and Leigh (2004) present pollen evidence for a Mid-Holocene wet phase in coastal North Carolina. Conversely, Otvos (2005) has discussed evidence for aridity along the Gulf Coastal Plain at that time. I recently analyzed freshwater mussel shells from the Vaughn Mound site (22LO538) in Lowndes County, Mississippi, which contains distinct Middle Archaic and Late Woodland shell-bearing strata. Valves in the Middle Archaic stratum displayed significantly less surface sculpture, a phenotypic indicator that suggests that the Tombigbee River was larger during the Mid-Holocene than in later times (Peacock 2005a). Isotopic and chemical analyses are underway to further test this finding.

The integration of these disparate data sets suggests a mosaic of precipitation patterns during the Hypsithermal rather than blanket warm/dry conditions (cf. Schuldenrein 1996), with increased precipitation and consequent increased stream size where storm systems would have been channeled during the Mid-Holocene, and smaller stream sizes outside those storm channels. Testable hypotheses can be generated as the influence of topography on past storm-tracks is better understood. For example, white-tailed deer should be larger in areas receiving enhanced precipitation (suggested here for the LMV) than in those areas that were drier during the Hypsithermal (Purdue 1991). Jackson and Scott (2001) note that the use of aquatic resources increased in importance in the major river valleys of Louisiana during the Middle Archaic. They suggest that the valleys may have acted as refugia for mast trees and associated faunal populations as southern pine forests expanded. It would be interesting to revisit such data with the idea of increased Mid-Holocene stream size in mind.

Conclusions

In sum, Saucier (2001:64–65) described how geomorphological expectations biased our understanding of the archaeological record of the LMV for quite some time. I would argue that the same type of tunnel vision continues to affect how we approach the paleoenvironmental record. In a typical CRM report, a very detailed and usually quite excellent chapter on geomorphology is given, after which paleoenvironmental considerations are only rarely raised. This bias has led to unfortunate practices such as discarding daub, mussel shell, and other valuable sources of paleoenvironmental data. Because entire plant and animal communities need to be considered, and because indicator species for disturbed conditions may be relatively rare, taking a sample of such remains is simply not adequate; what we retrieve from archaeological sites is already a sample and should be retained as such. Paleoenvironmental data are valuable; indeed, one could argue that they are particularly valuable in the LMV, given the dynamic nature of environmental conditions there over time. We need to quit throwing those data away, and we need to consider how to best recover and analyze other materials such as land snails and phytoliths. Such data are critical for an evolutionary approach, and indeed should be integral to any theoretical approach in which the interplay between humans and their environments is considered important. Site-level data are also important because, due to anthropogenic influence, sites were unique environments in their own right, something that affected later vegetation growth (Kidder 1998) and aboriginal land-use choices (Waselkov 1997).

Not only do we need environmental data from archaeological sites, but we need data that represent a range of occupation types, from short-term to long-term. Schuldenrein's (1996:4) criterion for landscape-scale analysis was that "landscape sequences include only those preserving linked and stratified prehistoric and geological successions." While that was appropriate for his work, from a holistic standpoint it is problematical: using only stratified sites to look at change through time introduces a systematic bias into the results, as long-term occupations are precisely those most likely to reflect human-modified, as opposed to "natural," environments. Moran (1990:23) has argued that "From an analytic perspective, one cannot confidently use site-specific studies as a basis for macro-ecosystem models." I disagree with this assertion. With careful assessments of cultural and preservation biases, environmental data retrieved from individual archaeological sites can be woven together to investigate a range of questions at a range of scales (cf. Nicholas 1988). As Gunn (1996:420) has stated, "site-specific conditions are a part of the global ecological context. . . . While it is true that every site has a unique set of ecological parameters, those parameters are, in part, a unique function of the greater world climate system." From the standpoint of evolutionary archaeology—indeed, from any theoretical standpoint—the need for greater precision and fuller incorporation of paleoenvironmental data is paramount. Efforts should be made to recover and analyze a full range of paleoenvironmental data from a full range of archaeological and geological contexts when opportunities like the I-69 project are presented.

Notes

1. We must be careful, however, not to let geomorphological assumptions over-condition our reasoning. As an example, Connaway (1988:49) states that rim-swamps "may be eliminated . . . as potential sources of early sites within their confines, since they are flood-prone swamplands where no cultural remains would be expected." What is rimswamp today might have had a very different character during, say, the Early Holocene, when conditions were appreciably drier than today (Schuldenrein 1996:10; Watts 1980:403; Watts et al. 1996:38—see Gunn's [1996] discussion of the "Worley Episode"). It is also certain that American Indians exploited those environments (e.g., for cypress trees used in palisades and canoe manufacture—McGahey 1986; Lafferty 1977). While the material traces of that exploitation might be quite hard to detect, the lands under question have arguably seen the least modification in modern times; hence, any archaeological remains found there could be some of the most well-preserved in the region. Saucier (2004:90) noted that the potential for buried sites is highest within backswamp environments in the Yazoo Basin.

2. E.g., "[prehistoric] habitation locales were generally selected so that distance from the home site to as great a diversity of resources as possible at any given time was minimized" (Thorne and Curry 1983:50).

3. Following the definition given in P. Delcourt and H. Delcourt (2004:53), landscape scale is "intermediate between an organism's normal home range and its regional distribution."

6
Settlement Patterns, Occupations, and Field Methods

Janet Rafferty

Introduction: Yazoo Basin Settlement Patterns

Settlement pattern analysis is dependent on well-thought-out delineation of occupations, following the understanding that occupations should be basic units, along with individual artifacts and features, for studying both variability and change in landscape use. In turn, occupation delineation is dependent on employing field methods that accurately record the three-dimensional location of artifact samples at all scales, from assemblages to mounds to microartifacts. In order to support use of methods that have the greatest potential to provide appropriate data, it is important to examine recent field practices in the Lower Mississippi Valley (LMV) and suggest ways they can be improved.

Much of our understanding of settlement patterning in the LMV, and especially in the Yazoo Basin, is based on data recovered by the Lower Mississippi Survey (LMS) in the 1940s and 1950s (Phillips 1970; Phillips et al. 2003 [1951]). The Survey recovered artifacts from 383 sites in 1940–1947 (Phillips et al. 2003 [1951]:219) and made a number of other collections, some from the same sites and some from newly recorded ones, in 1949–1955 (Phillips 1970:241–242), for a total of 899 sites (Phillips 1970:961). The emphasis in collecting and analysis was on pottery. Aceramic assemblages, aside from those containing Poverty Point objects, were not prominent in the LMS collections. Projectile points were relatively rarely found (Phillips 1970:247–248; Phillips et al. 2003 [1951]:45) and neither Ford, in the 1951 volume, nor Phillips (1970) made an attempt to use them to order materials through time. Carr (this volume) comments on this issue.

Ford's settlement pattern analysis consisted largely of a study of different kinds of mound sites using seriation-based periods and five regions (Phillips et al. 2003 [1951]:309–344). Few villages without mounds, and no hamlet-sized or smaller habitation sites, were included in the study. This meant that the main distinctions Ford could make were between places with conical or flat-topped mounds, plus those based on mound number and orientation. The result (2003 [1951]:335–344) is more a summary of the history of mound-building than of settlement patterns (see also Lipo and Dunnell, this volume).

This situation, with little control of the larger settlement context (for mound sites in particular) largely still holds true in the Delta. This is partly because of a paucity of new large-scale survey. The survey work done since the mid-1950s mostly has been cultural resource management (CRM)–related, with many surveys covering small areas or following narrow linear tracts for projects involving highways (Gray 1996; Gray et al. 1997; Hyatt 1990, 1991, 1992; Wells and Hahn 2005) and stabilization or channelization of waterways (Chapman et al. 1994, 1995a, 1995b, 1995c; Walling and Roemer 1993; Weinstein 1991; Weinstein et al. 1979; Weinstein et al. 1985). One exception is a survey of braided stream areas in the north Delta (Connaway 1988), which identified a series of predominantly pre-Mississippian components.

Since Phillips et al. (2003 [1951]), the display of settlement pattern data has been done using culture history–based units. Phillips (1970:7) undertook a division of Yazoo Basin materials into 13 phases, each conceived as a bounded entity manifested at sites as components. Eighty-five or so such phases were identified for the entire LMV survey area (1970:869–964). Phillips reified these phases, treating them as entities rather than analytic constructs (see Dunnell, Chapter 4, this volume). This resulted in strict presence/absence use of diagnostic artifact types to assign components. For instance, at Kinlock (22SU526), two sherds of Marksville Stamped *var. Manny* were recovered in an assemblage of nearly 8,000 sherds and are treated as follows: they "are absolutely typical of this late Issaquena variety. . . . I should prefer to assume the presence of a late Issaquena component somewhere on the premises rather than entertain the possibility of a late Issaquena intrusion into the Deasonville occupation of the site" (Phillips 1970:439). Kinlock is thus shown on both maps, of sites with Issaquena and with Deasonville phase components (1970:543, 548), disallowing the possibility that this variety could be accounted for in the assemblage by its decline to low frequency by the time Deasonville markers became common.

For the work reported in 1951 (Phillips et al. 2003 [1951]), Ford had removed only six of 273 assemblages (2 percent) from his seriations on the basis that they represented very long duration or discontinuous site use. In contrast, Phillips (1970:961–962) states that 135 of the 899 sites (15 percent) in the complete survey sample were occupied in non-sequent periods. This difference arises partly from how assemblages were collected and used. A number of the assemblages analyzed by Ford were collected in different parts of the same sites to attempt to make it more likely that each assemblage came from one occupation (Phillips et al. 2003 [1951]:43). In contrast, Phillips combined all artifacts from a given site (1970:961, footnote 73), using the site rather than the occupation as the basic unit. This, along with dividing the material among a larger number of periods and phases, had the effect of creating more assemblages with sherds from non-sequent periods.

Phillips states that the main interest of the potsherds collected by the surveys "lies in the extent to which they reflect the succession of occupations in the sites. The aim is to discover the clustering of such occupations, or components as I shall term them, in time and area, and thereby to delimit the archaeological phases" (1970:241). This makes it plain that he conflated occupations with components (although later in the book [1970:523], he seems to treat them as conceptually different) and that he treated phases as discovered ("delimited"), not constructed, by the archaeologist.

Since Phillips took this approach in 1970, the small amount of settlement pattern analysis based on Yazoo Basin data has been done by plotting the locations of components of phases (cf. Brain 1971, 1978a; Connaway 1977; Starr 1984). Usually, the phases have been treated as non-arbitrary spatial and temporal units, with the implication that they mark actual breaks in the distribution of phenomena through time or space rather than arbitrary divisions of a continuum.

How phases are defined and used has been critiqued for the Mississippi valley (Brown, this volume; Dunnell, Chapter 4, this volume; Fox 1998; Mainfort 1999, 2003b, 2005; O'Brien 1995). The brunt of the criticism is that phase definitions originally were based on particular assemblages grouped together because they were observed to be similar. In order to turn these groups of assemblages into phases, it should have been necessary to devise definitions for them, composed of the necessary and sufficient conditions that an assemblage must display in order to be identified as a member of the phase (cf. Dunnell 2002 [1971]). Such defining criteria often equate with diagnostic artifact classes. This step presumably was taken for the phases proposed by Phillips and others for the LMV, as components have been identified with them. However, because the list of required diagnostics for any given phase is largely implicit, it is difficult to discern whether definitions exist or are merely intuitive assessments of assemblage similarity (see Brown, this volume, for examples). In either case, the result is much the same: the phase definition is subject to adjustment every time a new component is added. This method of phase formation has led to inconsistencies in application and to phases that are congeries of traits that are not problem oriented and that lack coherence in time or space (cf. Fox 1998; Mainfort 1999, 2003b, 2005). It becomes increasingly difficult to credit that such units have any place in settlement pattern analysis.

Occupation Delineation

One reason that traditional phases continue to be used in this unproductive way is that archaeologists don't know what kinds of units to employ in their stead. Can artifact distributions and cultural change be addressed without using classes at the assemblage scale? The answer is clearly no—such classes are needed because they allow artifacts at smaller scales to be associated in meaningful assemblages. But they should be formulated with three goals in mind: attentiveness to variability and change, problem orientation, and more careful conceptualization of the phenomenological unit represented by classified assemblages. The resulting classes can be called phases, following the definition given by Robert C. Dunnell (2002 [1971]:202): a phase is "a paradigmatic class of occupations defined by types and/or modes." But most will not be the kind of culture-historical phases used by Phillips (1970), Toth (1988), and others, and primarily for chronological control. Rather, they will be units that allow various kinds of occupations—for example, mound groups, shell middens, and small pottery scatters—to be associated formally for synchronic analysis or to examine spatial variability (cf. Lipo 2001a).

Before problem-oriented phases can be employed routinely in settlement pattern analysis, it is necessary to have ways to meet the other two goals. The first requirement is for a valid empirical unit at the assemblage scale. This provides a warrant for treating the artifacts in an assemblage as parts of the same phenomenon. An assemblage-scale empirical unit suited to this kind of analysis is the occupation (Dunnell 2002 [1971]; Rafferty 2001). When archaeologists refer to the number of occupations at a site, or to occupation span or occupational history, they presumably are referring to such a unit. This has not prevented confusion. Occupations frequently are treated as synonymous with components (e.g., Fagan 2000:48), as the quote from Phillips' 1970 work (above) demonstrates. One reason for this is a difficulty in understanding that occupations are phenomena. An occupation is a spatially, temporally, and formally associated set of artifacts (Dunnell 2002 [1971]; Rafferty 2001). It is, therefore, itself an artifact, composed of individual discrete artifacts (features and/or portable artifacts) at smaller scales. Artifact assemblages can be recognized at many scales (see Lipo and Dunnell, this volume), but the occupation is the basic artifact scale used in settlement pattern analysis.

Sites also frequently are treated as archaeological phenomena and used interchangeably with occupations (e.g., Thompson 1956:36; see Dunnell, this volume). This is not defensible, as a site can accumulate artifacts from many different, unrelated uses—for example, artifacts from a camp used 10,000 years ago may occur in the same place as those from a midden resulting from events occurring 1,500 years ago. I suspect that site and occupation are conflated primarily in cases where there is only one occupation apparent at the site. But that does not excuse the practice. A site is merely a place where an artifact or, more usually, a cluster of artifacts, has been found. Sites are arbitrary divisions of space (Dunnell 1992), so it is possible to bound them in any way that suits the particular project and situation. This is not true of occupations, which have non-arbitrary, phenomenological (if sometimes hard to detect), boundaries at a particular scale.

A component is the manifestation of a phase at a particular site (Willey and Phillips 2001 [1958]:21–22), so the component boundaries are determined by the definition of the phase. If phases are classes at the scale of occupation, components are occupations that have been classified. Components do not provide a way to recognize bounded phenomena, but merely to classify those (i.e., occupations or parts of occupations) that already have been identified.

Spatial Boundaries of Occupations

The archaeologist's success in delineating occupations depends largely on the field methods employed. Proveniencing methods are of primary importance in being able to demonstrate that individual discrete artifacts, including features and their contents, are associated, forming part of one occupation. Spatial association is argued primarily via contiguity. Ideally, each artifact should be piece-plotted and thus have a unique three-dimensional provenience from which spatial association can be identified (Dunnell 1988; Dunnell and Dancey 1983). This is an especially pertinent issue with reference to surface collections, as it is common practice to obtain only site-level provenience, using the general surface collection (GSC) method, for surface artifacts. As noted above, sites are tactical units and as such may be places where many occupations occurred. If all the artifacts on the surface of a site are given one provenience, the diagnostic artifacts recognized can be sorted out (by component, not by occupation) but the non-diagnostic ones cannot. The GSC method often is chosen by culture historians, as it has the potential rapidly to yield large collections in which diagnostic artifact classes are more likely to be present. It also makes record keeping easier for CRM purposes, for which assemblages are organized by site number. Sole use of this practice, while perhaps convenient if component assignment is the main goal, often results in much loss of information about how many occupations were present and how site use changed through time, exactly the kind of information that is most crucial in settlement pattern analysis.

Controlled surface collection (CSC) is a well-tried method for obtaining more precise provenience information for artifacts on the surface. It can be done in the initial survey process, when it is called siteless or non-site survey (Dancey 1981; Dunnell and Dancey 1983), or on a previously recorded site that already has been subjected to general surface collection. Proveniencing can be done by recording individual artifact locations or by using grid-based collection units. CSC is advantageous for obtaining spatial information that can be used to examine the internal structure of an occupation or to help delineate different occupations. In many cases it will allow non-diagnostic artifacts in an artifact cluster to be associated, through spatial contiguity, with the occupation from which they came. Processual and evolutionary archaeologists have made considerable use of the method due to their interest in problems such as community layout (Binford et al. 1970) and variability across space (Lipo 2001a; Lipo et al. 1997).

It has long been known that artifacts on the surface of a cultivated field do not, as a result of cultivation, become randomized in configuration relative to their original locations (Binford et al. 1970; Lewarch and O'Brien 1981; Odell and Cowan 1987). In areas where land has been in cultivation, only a fraction (less than 10 percent: Lewarch and O'Brien 1981:45) of the artifacts in the plowzone is on the surface at any one time, so CSCs are possible even though GSCs have been done previously at the sites. It also may be instructive to repeat CSCs after recultivation so that more detailed and reliable spatial data can be recovered (cf. Dunnell 1988).

Sampling is important at the landscape scale, to attempt to assure that information on the entire range of occupations has been acquired. This consideration primarily affects survey methods; it is important that methods be used that can detect small as well as large artifact clusters, in vegetated areas and those that might have buried cultural deposits as well as in cultivated fields. Lithic scatters should be given as much attention as places producing ceramics; historic occupations must be recorded so that land uses not represented in written sources can be detected (see Young, this volume).

Temporal Boundaries of Occupations

Stratigraphic excavation provides another way to control for spatial contiguity, as artifacts in the same occupation may be expected to be associated in a depositional layer. Excavation by visible layers also has an important role in providing data from which arguments for coherence through time can be made. Following the law of superposition, in a set of superimposed strata, each of which represents a depositional event, the strata can be ordered through time relative to one another, from most recent at the top to oldest at the bottom (Rowe 1961). The artifacts in each zone, after consideration of formation processes that may have displaced or mixed artifacts from separate depositional strata, often can be treated as part of the same depositional event as the stratum. Then each depositional event must be associated with the archaeological event of interest, usually the artifacts' discard, after which the artifacts in a stratum may be held to be part of the same occupation. Not every depositional event results in a clear record of stratification, so a stratum may contain more than one occupation. Also, a stratum representing an occupation may be composed of many individual lenses, each representing shorter depositional events.

The importance of stratigraphy in delineating the spatio-temporal association of artifacts emphasizes how crucial it is to excavate by natural zones rather than arbitrary levels that crosscut zones (Praetzellis 1993). A host of other relative and absolute dating methods is available to aid in temporal association of artifacts, including those from surface assemblages.

Lineages

The third aspect of delineating occupations is arguing that the artifacts represent a continuous segment of a single lineage or cultural tradition, i.e., that their traits reflect relatedness (Dunnell 2006). Seriations of assemblages can be used expediently to establish lineage continuity (O'Brien and Lyman 1999b:65–66) because they display overlapping replacement of types or modes. This aspect of seriation adheres to the requirement that the assemblages in any given seriation be from the same cultural tradition (Dunnell 1970). If they are not, the assemblages will fail to seriate together. This is not the only reason for such failure, but a successful seriation does demonstrate that the assemblages are part of the same lineage (O'Brien and Lyman 1999b).

The power of seriation, if properly applied, to vet assemblages as coherent lineage segments is very attractive in dealing with GSCs. If the collections include artifacts that are non-sequent through time as measured by the classes used to order them, such assemblages will not seriate together with those that represent single continuous occupations, and must be removed from the seriation. The multiple occupations likely present at such sites would deserve further work to differentiate them.

Seriation also establishes the sequence of change in the historical classes used to order the assemblages within an area. Thus, to test whether a newly recovered assemblage forms a coherent part of an established lineage, an attempt can be made to add it to an existing seriation or to match it with the expected contents of a segment of the lineage. If there are no existing seriations, they can be devised. Both lineage composition and the use of seriation to verify that assemblages represent continuous lineage segments are dependent on the particular artifact classes used to define the lineage. Types generally have smaller spatio-temporal distributions than modes, so a set of assemblages might belong to the same lineage if defined by modes but to different, though closely related, ones if defined by types (Lipo 2001a:195–196; Lipo et al. 1997). The decision whether to employ types or modes must be made in view of the kinds of information available and the archaeological problem being addressed.

Both stylistic and functional classes change distribution through time, so either can be used to detect lineage continuity through time via seriation; however, functional classes stabilize their frequencies because they are under selection, while styles, being selectively neutral, do not (see Dunnell, Chapter 4, this volume). This means that assemblages formed in periods when functional traits are stable cannot be ordered relative to one another through time by classes based on those traits. Styles also vary through space and, when time is held constant, can be used to assess assemblage relatedness (cf. Lipo 2001a). Functional traits vary through space also, but with relation to environmental factors, not lineages (Dunnell 1978), so their spatial distribution cannot be used to put occupations into the same lineage.

Summary

Plainly, any given artifact assemblage does not necessarily represent one occupation, nor can all occupations be readily delimited. Despite these difficulties and the undertheorized nature of artifacts at this scale, archaeologists often recognize occupations. Especially commonly denoted are short-term occupations, in cases where well-defined surface artifact clusters and/or stratigraphic associations are present. Long-term occupations have been more troublesome: they usually either are subdivided arbitrarily into components or are treated as mixed and therefore uninterpretable. But this difficulty with long-duration occupations is not an insurmountable problem once it is understood what occupations are, as it then becomes plain that occupations can vary in duration. Assemblages that are removed from a seriation because they disrupt curves may represent occupations that differ in duration from the ones included on the seriation (Dunnell 1970). They may be ordered among themselves on that basis (cf. Rafferty 1994).

It is increasingly agreed that, if archaeologists wish to explain the phenomena they study, they will need to pay more attention to how the artifact classes vary through space and change through time. Use of seriation in settlement pattern analysis provides a way to order assemblages chronologically without using periods. This allows a move away from synchronic analyses and toward a view of past landscape use that is attentive to artifact variability and thus to cultural continuity and change. When enough appropriate artifacts, such as potsherds, are present, frequency seriation allows the finest temporal discrimination. Occurrence seriation can be used when artifact numbers are lower. Other relative dating methods, such as stratigraphy and fluoride dating (Schurr 1989), are site specific and so are not very useful for settlement pattern studies. Absolute dating methods (discussed by Feathers, this volume), are indispensable but require many dated samples from many occupations in order to be most useful in the study of settlement pattern change and variability. If contemporaneity can be established, the distribution of occupations through space can be studied to understand how settlement patterns were organized. Current data often leave us far from realizing either goal.

Assessment of Artifact Recovery Methods

Choosing appropriate methods involves being able to justify them, in terms of damage done to the archaeological record and of the problems being addressed. To make plainer why precise proveniencing, stratigraphic excavation, and sampling strategies are important in occupation delineation, it is instructive to review some examples of questionable practice from the Yazoo Basin. The main difficulty exhibited in many of these cases is that the field methods employed did not allow detailed information on artifact associations to be retained in the data or such information to be used to make later preservation or recovery decisions.

Site-based general surface/shovel test collecting is the most common kind used during archaeological survey. This method is most suitable if large areas are to be covered, as it is the fastest and thus least expensive. Examples from the LMV include much of the work reported in Phillips et al. (2003 [1951]) and Phillips (1970), as well as most CRM surveys (i.e., Chapman et al. 1994, 1995a, 1995b; Ryan et al. 2004; Walling and Chapman 1999; Walling and Roemer 1993). GSC has sometimes been poorly applied, leading to biased collections. Prime examples from the Yazoo Basin are many of the assemblages reported by Phillips (1970). Anthony's Fork (22YZ588) was collected during the course of repeated visits, resulting in an assemblage including 193 sherds. All 99 Baytown Plain sherds shown in the tabulation are rims (Phillips 1970:382), so it is apparent that plain grog-tempered body sherds were not collected or were not recorded. In contrast, a collection made during the course of the earlier LMV survey, from Paxton (22HU540) (Phillips 1970:400), contained 3,214 Baytown Plain sherds, of which 614 were rims, from a total sherd count of 3,337. Failing to collect the plain body sherds has permanently biased these data. This matters because the frequency of Baytown Plain, while apparently subject to stabilizing selection, did change through time, as indicated by Ford's seriations (Phillips et al 2003 [1951]) and mine (below).

An important alternative is controlled surface/shovel-test collection. Several main problems can be identified in applications of CSC in the Delta. The first is that the method is underused, often with the implicit rationale that huge quantities of artifacts will be collected, creating an analytic and curation problem. While large sites can produce large surface collections, the amount of information gained about the spatial dimensions of occupations, as well as about differing functional areas within occupations (cf. Mainfort and Moore 1998), can be argued to far outweigh the costs. Controlled surface collections often provide information that differs from that acquired through geophysics or excavation. Also, sites that might not have features or intact subsurface deposits often yield useful information at the scale of occupation via a CSC (cf. Teltser 1998).

Plainly, geophysical methods can be powerful complements to CSC in determining site structure (cf. Kvamme et al. 2006). Being nondestructive, they should be used commonly as another way to obtain broad areal coverage of sites, focused on identifying anomalies that might represent features (see Johnson, this volume). Sole reliance on geophysics, however, is dangerous, as it tends to foster a rigid equation of features with significance (Peacock and Rafferty 2007; cf. Johnson and Haley 2006). Understanding settlement patterns requires that occupations without preserved features—whether the occupations are small, early, or special-purpose in nature—to be included in data recovery so they can be included in analysis.

In addition to providing much information in their own right, surface artifacts can allow occupations to be subjected to more sensible excavation-based recovery through stratified sampling. This can result in much time and effort being saved. The same archaeologists who resist CSC, on the grounds that large collections will result, often will retrieve and curate masses of excavated artifacts without ever questioning their value.

Another problem in implementing CSCs is choosing an overly large grid-unit size, obscuring the phenomena being investigated. Odell and Cowan (1987:481) have argued, based on experimental data, that spurious artifact concentrations can be created by using small surface collection units, such as 2 x 2 or 3 x 3 meters. However, this appears to be a false conclusion, a result of the method they used to tabulate concentrations in their experimental data. A more convincing experiment concerning unit size (Lewarch and O'Brien 1981:45) concluded that "the smallest practical provenience unit" should be collected, as larger units blur and obscure any fine-grained patterns that might be present in artifact clusters. Units 4 x 4 to 10 x 10 m in size have been used profitably in the LMV (Dye and Buchner 1988; Teltser 1998).

A third difficulty arises when artifact collection in CSC is biased beyond the inevitable artifact size biases, most commonly by setting a time limit for collecting. Dye and Buchner (1988:67–68) provide an example, in which a five-minute limit was set for collecting each surface grid. This kind of procedure may create differences in artifact density data that arise not from differences on the ground but from collecting strategies. The main effect is to obscure the areas of highest artifact density, so that a moderate gain in time spent in the field may result in sacrifice of considerable distributional detail.

A fourth weakness may arise in analysis of the CSC, especially when artifacts are counted but styles that indicate lineage affiliation (often synonymous with diagnostics) are not identified (Johnson and Haley 2006; Kuttruff et al. 1995:38). This method is rationalized as a way to decide where to excavate, but by using artifact concentrations only. Because the procedure ignores the usefulness of identifying occupations, it is dubious. The problem can be corrected, as the artifacts can be analyzed later using stylistic and functional types or modes. But it seems plain that this step is most advantageously taken as part of the original analysis, so that the knowledge gained about occupations can help guide excavation.

Excavation by visible strata is a preferred archaeological method, including in CRM (cf. King 2005), as combining materials from two or more depositional layers may mix artifacts from more than one occupation. As a matter of expediency, however, test units often are dug using arbitrary levels (e.g., Kuttruff et al. 1995) and extensive excavations also may be carried out this way (e.g., Connaway and McGahey 1971; Greengo 1964; Heartfield, Price, and Greene 1987). In Phase III excavations at the Milner site (22YZ515), 28 m² of excavation was done using arbitrary levels and 55 m² was excavated using natural zones, sometimes subdivided by arbitrary levels (Heartfield, Price, and Greene 1987:2.2-8–2.2-9). Despite the predominant use of natural zones in recovery, the pottery and lithic distributions were reported only by arbitrary levels (1987:2.6-2–2.6-5). Given this and the failure to report the results of a partial CSC, it is hard to determine how many occupations were present at this site.

If arbitrary levels are employed throughout an excavation, attempts are sometimes made to reconstruct the association between the artifacts and depositional strata recorded on the walls of units; this kind of effort is tedious and inaccurate. For example, Phillips (1970:583) presents a correlation table for three zones in seven trenches excavated using arbitrary levels at the Thornton site (22IS507). In order to determine which sherds were deposited together, information from this table must be combined with the pottery tabulations (Phillips 1970:584–585) to assign sherds from the levels to strata. If the original excavation had been done without cross-cutting the strata, this kind of reconstruction would be unnecessary. Phillips (1970:583) says that "The midden layers that were responsible for most if not all of the pottery in these zones are very thin, reasonably level, and well separated by loaded zones." Digging by arbitrary levels that combined parts of different natural zones thus appears unjustifiable.

Investigating a representative sample of a site's area has rarely been an explicit issue in archaeology done in the LMV, especially in CRM. This latter is partly because only portions of sites, in a highway right-of-way, for example, may be endangered and require mitigation. This makes it harder to determine population parameters and thus decide how to choose a random sample of units. The imperative to recover as much information as possible from sites due to be destroyed also operates against sampling. Complete coverage often is preferred in such cases and is most commonly achieved for the surface, if cultivated, by the use of CSC and for features by stripping the plowzone and digging all the features. In the latter circumstance, strata and large features such as mounds may be sampled at very low percentages and often without employing formal random sampling. Use of partial CSCs is possible, but uncommon (cf. Dunnell 1998; Lauro and Lehmann 1982); employing simple or stratified random sampling is even less usual, although a combination of geophysics and surface inspection of artifacts before collection might make this more feasible.

Sampling all artifact sizes is an issue that also has been neglected. It is increasingly common (but not a universal practice; see Fritz, this volume, and Jackson, this volume) for archaeologists to take a sample of dirt from each provenience for flotation to recover small faunal and floral materials. Retaining part of each sample for purposes such as soil chemistry and microartifact analysis is undoubtedly rare, judging by the low frequency with which such results are reported. Such practices can be applied in the course of CSC, also, with informative results (cf. Dunnell 1998).

Settlement Pattern Analysis: An Example

With appropriate units and an appropriate way to order them chronologically, it becomes possible to analyze artifact distributions over space and through time to elucidate change. In order to show that an approach to the data without traditional phases or periods is productive, I attempted a demonstration seriation of ceramic assemblages from sites in the Yazoo Basin. This method has rarely been used in the valley since Ford's work (Phillips et al. 2003 [1951]), Lipo's (2001a) spatial analyses of Memphis-area assemblages being a major exception. I used assemblages for which I could find pottery tabulations, drawn from many sources (Table 6.1), including Phillips (1970), Mississippi Department of Transportation reports (Gray et al. 1997; Hyatt 1992), the Big and Little Sunflower surveys (Chapman et al. 1994, 1995a, 1995b; Walling and Roemer 1993), the McNight and Rock Levee site excavations (Walling and Chapman 1999; Weinstein et al. 1995), Johnson's work at Batesville Mounds (Johnson 2001; Johnson et al. 2002), Peacock's Holly Springs surveys (Peacock 1996, 1997), and others (Brookes 1985; Brown 1978b; Connaway and McGahey 1971; Jackson 1998; Kuttruff et al. 1995; Morgan 1988; Penman 1977; Toth and Brookes 1977).

I first used assemblages that contained 400 or more sherds, the rationale being to attempt to identify details of stylistic change in ceramics through time

Table 6.1. Data on seriated ceramic assemblages from the Yazoo Basin.

Site Number	Provenience	Site Name	Source of Data	Total	Non-Plain Sherd Total	Order on Seriation* (N-north, S-south)
Assemblages with ≥400 sherds:						
22CO560	surface/excavation	McNight	Walling and Chapman 1999	7,922	6,045	N6
22IS506	surface	Manny	Phillips 1970	2,184	548	S2
22IS507	Area G surface	Thornton	Phillips 1970	1,774	292	S1
22LF505	surface	Shell Bluff	Phillips 1970	753	495	N5
22LF513	surface	McLean	Phillips 1970	848	165	N5
22LF516	surface	Palusha Creek	Phillips 1970	1,013	100	N4
22LF519	surface	Nichols	Phillips 1970	6,136	253	N3
22SH500	Cut A	Spanish Fort	Phillips 1970	508	78	S4
22SH501	surface	Magee (Deer Creek)	Phillips 1970	1,290	138	S10
22TL501	test excavations	Buford	Marshall 1988	992	417	N5
22TL501	surface	Buford	Marshall 1988	4,842	3,341	N5
22TU531	Zone II	Boyd	Connaway and McGahey 1971	9,454	5,447	N5
22TU531	Zone I	Boyd	Connaway and McGahey 1971	1,793	773	N2
22TU533	Test units 1 and 2	Martin #1	Toth and Brookes 1977	2,546	647	N1
22WS508	surface	Refuge	Phillips 1970	747	49	S9
22WS512	surface	Hollyknowe	Phillips 1970	736	33	S8
22WS516	surface	Arcola	Phillips 1970	2,760	180	S9
22WS542	excavation	Kirk	Kuttruff et al. 1995	45,461	5,074	S6
22WS552	excavation	Granicus Bayou	Kuttruff et al. 1995	6970	302	S5

Continued on the next page

Table 6.1. *Continued*

Site Number	Provenience	Site Name	Source of Data	Total	Non-Plain Sherd Total	Order on Seriation* (N-north, S-south)
22WS627	excavation	Campbell	Kuttruff et al. 1995	1,197	107	S7
22YZ587	surface	Mabin	Phillips 1970	4,805†	1,916	S3

Assemblages with ≥20 sherds, including plain surfaces:

Site Number	Provenience	Site Name	Source of Data	Total	Non-Plain Sherd Total	Order on Seriation* (N-north, S-south)
22BO584	surface	Tibbs	Hyatt 1992	200	n/a	N4
22BO584	test units	Tibbs	Hyatt 1992	218	n/a	N3
22CO535	surface	Bobo	Potts and Brookes 1981	574	n/a	N12
22CO551	surface	Bramlett	Brown 1978b	507	n/a	N11
22CO560	surface/excavation	McNight	Walling and Chapman 1999	7,922	n/a	N10
22CO657	excavation	Pee Dee	Brookes 1985	87	n/a	N7
22CO775	surface		Gray et al. 1997	51	n/a	N8
22CO778	surface		Gray et al. 1997	139	n/a	N5
22HU500	surface of midden	Belzoni	Phillips 1970	72	n/a	S7
22HU508	surface	Golson	Phillips 1970	241	n/a	S6
22HU525	Mound A surface	Gooden Lake	Chapman et al. 1995a	59	n/a	S8
22HU539	surface	Simmons	Phillips 1970	1,644	n/a	S5
22HU676	surface		Chapman et al. 1995a	47	n/a	S6
22HU685	surface	Big Callao	Chapman et al. 1995a	157	n/a	S6
22IS507	Zone II	Thornton	Phillips 1970	144	n/a	S3
22IS507	Zone I	Thornton	Phillips 1970	112	n/a	S2
22LF516	surface	Palusha Creek	Phillips 1970	1,013	n/a	N6
22LF519	surface	Nichols	Phillips 1970	6,136	n/a	S6
22SH501	surface	Magee (Deer Creek)	Phillips 1970	1,290	n/a	S14

Site	Context	Site Name	Reference	Count		Phase*
22SH502	surface	Panther Burn	Phillips 1970	124	n/a	S14
22SH511	bank, surface	Lowery	Chapman et al. 1994	64	n/a	S4
22SH522	embankment excavation	Little Spanish Fort	Jackson 1998	28	n/a	S1
22SU526	north of Mound F, surface	Kinlock	Chapman et al. 1995b	75	n/a	S13
22SU526	surface	Kinlock	Phillips 1970	7,975	n/a	S12
22SU530	surface	Failing	Phillips 1970	382	n/a	S14
22SU531	surface	Lake Dawson	Phillips 1970	831	n/a	S10
22TU531	Zone II	Boyd	Connaway and McGahey 1971	9,454	n/a	N9
22TU531	Zone I	Boyd	Connaway and McGahey 1971	1,793	n/a	N2
22TU533	Test units 1 & 2	Martin #1	Toth and Brookes 1977	2,546	n/a	N1
22WS501	surface	Leland	Phillips 1970	8,395	n/a	S14
22WS506	surface	Metcalfe	Phillips 1970	262	n/a	S13
22WS507	surface	Ireland	Phillips 1970	365	n/a	S5
22WS508	surface	Refuge	Phillips 1970	747	n/a	S13
22WS510	surface	Sheldon	Phillips 1970	166	n/a	S14
22WS512	surface	Hollyknowe	Phillips 1970	736	n/a	S5
22WS513	surface	Arcola School	Phillips 1970	227	n/a	S9
22WS516	surface	Arcola	Phillips 1970	2,760	n/a	S13
22WS542	excavation	Kirk	Kuttruff et al. 1995	45,461	n/a	S5
22WS552	excavation	Granicus Bayou	Kuttruff et al. 1995	6,970	n/a	S5
22WS626	excavation	Abide Airport	Kuttruff et al. 1995	96	n/a	S5
22WS627	excavation	Campbell	Kuttruff et al. 1995	1,197	n/a	S5
22YZ557	surface	Lake George	Phillips 1970	9,195	n/a	S11

*from oldest (1) to most recent; temporally indistinguishable assemblages were given the same number

† plain sherds other than rims not collected

by focusing on pottery decoration. As most of the assemblages are dominated by plain pottery, large samples must be used in order to obtain a fair representation of non-plain surface finishes (Lipo 2001a). I disregarded information on temper and plain pottery, as well as collections that contained fewer than 20 decorated sherds. This left 49 assemblages of decorated sherds, including some collections reported in Phillips (1970), in which plain pottery, with the exception of rims, had not been collected. The seriation macro in Excel devised by Tim Hunt and Carl Lipo (Lipo 2001a:269–280) was used to display the data, with 5-percent error bars chosen; groups were moved until mode frequencies formed unimodal curves. Deterministic seriations, ones that conform to this requirement (Lipo et al. 1997), only came close to being possible after separating the assemblages geographically, into ones from northern and southern counties within the Yazoo Basin (Figures 6.1–6.2).

Of the 49 assemblages, 21 were successfully included in the two seriations. This included 10 from Bolivar, Coahoma, Leflore, Tallahatchie, and Tunica counties in the north (Figure 6.1), and 11 southern assemblages, from sites in Humphries, Issaquena, Sharkey, Sunflower, Washington, and Yazoo counties (Figure 6.2). The remaining 28 assemblages, eight from the north and 20 from the south, could not be included in the seriations without disturbing the curves. Only one of the assemblages reported in Phillips (1970) from the 1949–1955 survey, the one from Mabin (22YZ587), was included; the others noted as coming from Phillips (1970) in Table 6.1 are from collections made in 1940–1947. This is a result of the later collections not including 400 or more sherds.

Modes fell into unimodal curves on both decoration-based seriations in accord with existing knowledge about how pottery decoration changes through time in the Yazoo Basin (Figures 6.1–6.2). For example, in the southern area several modes associated with the Marksville period, including broad-line incised and stamped/incised combinations, especially incised dentate rocker-stamped (Marksville Stamped *vars. Marksville, Manny,* and *Newsome*), fell into acceptable curves (Figure 6.2). These played an insignificant role in ordering assemblages from the northern area because of their rarity (Figure 6.1). Zoned punctation (Evansville Punctated), as well as plain and dentate rocker stamping without associated incised lines (Indian Bay Stamped), appear to be concentrated slightly later in time (Figure 6.2). Another difference in decorated pottery frequencies in the northern and southern areas includes high frequencies of fine-line incised pottery in the south but only negligible amounts in the north (Figures 6.1–6.2). The fine-line incised types would fall mostly but not exclusively into the Coles Creek period.

Fabric marking was important in the northern area and cord marking in both areas. In the northern part of the basin, once cord marking replaced fabric marking, it remained dominant over the span of the remainder of the assemblages (Figure 6.1). This kind of distribution, in which there is little change

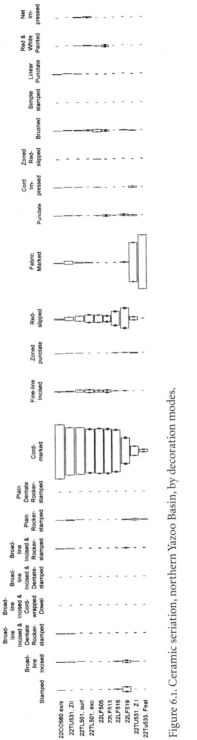

Figure 6.1. Ceramic seriation, northern Yazoo Basin, by decoration modes.

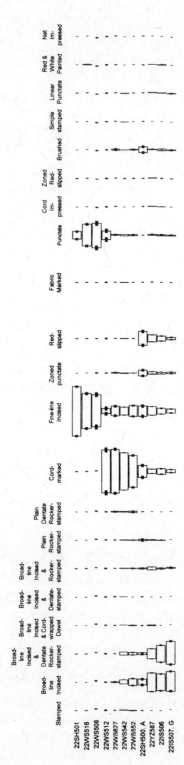

Figure 6.2. Ceramic seriation, southern Yazoo Basin, by decoration modes.

except for small nondirectional variation, often marks functional traits that are under stabilizing selection (Dunnell, Ch. 4, this volume). Thus, all-over surface treatment in this case may represent a functional rather than a stylistic trait, with different kinds of treatments (cord marking, fabric marking, brushing) arguably being functionally equivalent and so usefully treated as styles. This exercise shows how seriation can be useful in examining the structure of change through time to help discern likely stylistic, as well as functional, traits; for example, continuities in red-slipping, punctation, and incising are apparent across the likely functional change from grog to shell temper (cf. Dunnell and Feathers 1991).

I also attempted a seriation that included smaller assemblages (with fewer than 400 total sherds), using the plain as well as the decorated pottery, combining decoration/surface treatment with temper to form types. Given the smaller sample sizes, I collapsed many type-variety categories, which are most commonly used to classify the pottery in the area, into simpler types. These types are similar in structure to those used in Phillips et al. (2003 [1951]) but are more general. For example, instead of including zoned rocker-stamped, plain rocker-stamped, and dentate-stamped as separate grog-tempered types, I combined them to form one type, grog-tempered stamped. Similarly, I collapsed Phillips' 14 types and varieties of Baytown Plain, (excluding Tchefuncte Plain, which is untempered [see Galaty, this volume]), many of which are unsortable except on rim sherds (Phillips 1970:47–48), into one type.

Using these types, I successfully seriated 42 assemblages, dividing them into northern and southern groups as with the decoration-based seriations (Figures 6.3–6.4). Some of the assemblages included on these seriations also appear on the ones based on decoration/surface finish and serve to help confirm the order achieved. The assemblages were ordered on the basis of nine types. The grog-tempered types are plain, stamped, broad-line incised, fine-line incised, and cord-marked, with fabric-marked also useful in the northern area. The mussel shell-tempered types are plain and incised, with the punctate mode also used in the south. Other types, specifically grog-tempered zoned punctate, grog-tempered red-slipped, and grog-tempered brushed, form coherent curves but are present at very low frequencies.

Grog-tempered plain pottery forms a single unimodal curve on each of the seriations (Figures 6.3–6.4). The paste traits that were used by Phillips (1970) and others to differentiate some varieties of grog-tempered plain (i.e., Addis, Bowie, Little River) overlap considerably, making them unsortable using paste. Attempts to test paste-based grog-tempered varieties have repeatedly shown them to be meaningless as chronological indicators (Phillips 1970:47; Mainfort and Chapman 1994; Walling and Chapman 1999:172–174; Weaver 1963), as they seem primarily to reflect the clay the vessel was made from rather than any consistent change through time in either style or function (see Galaty, this

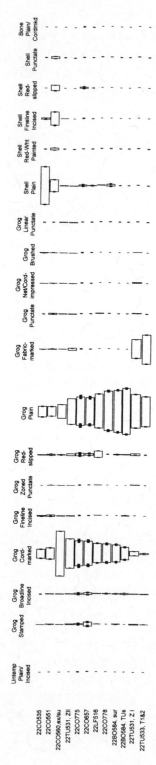

Figure 6.3. Ceramic seriation, northern Yazoo Basin, by temper-surface finish types.

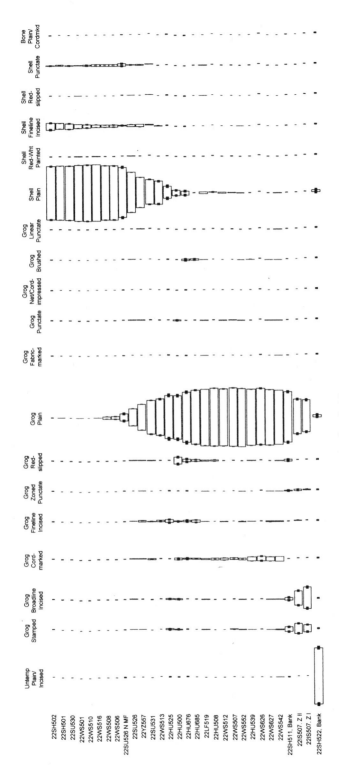

Figure 6.4. Ceramic seriation, southern Yazoo Basin, by temper-surface finish types.

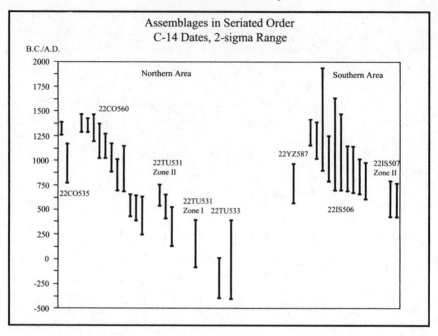

Figure 6.5. Radiocarbon dates associated with seriated ceramic assemblages.

volume). Whether there are any appropriate chronological uses for these plain grog-tempered varieties is questionable.

As above, one could argue that most of the temper-surface finish types, which play a large role in establishing the orders, reflect functional, not stylistic, changes. For instance, it might well be argued that the replacement of grog temper by mussel shell temper is due to selection (Dunnell and Feathers 1991). This does not mean such changes are useless for chronological purposes, as they can be used to order assemblages in sections of the seriations where frequencies have not yet stabilized.

I have not verified the seriated orders as chronological by doing other seriations of the same assemblages using independent classes, but I did tabulate available radiocarbon dates from the sites (Connaway and Sims 1997). The dates (Figure 6.5) tend to be more or less in accord with the seriated orders, while providing evidence that some of the sites were occupied over fairly long times. The ability of seriation to order assemblages chronologically is more powerful than that of individual absolute dates, as seriation takes into account the entirety of the ordered assemblage.

One stratified site, Thornton, 22IS507 (Phillips 1970:576–598), contributed two assemblages to the seriation of southern collections. The pottery groups from the zones appear on the seriation in correct stratigraphic order (Figure 6.4). Some other sites are represented by two or more surface collections or collections from different areas. Sometimes, as in the case of Kinlock, 22SU526 (Chapman et al. 1995b), these fall close to one another on the seriation (Figure 6.4). This presumably indicates that the various collection areas may represent one occupation. In other cases, such as Boyd, 22TU531 (Connaway and McGahey 1971) in the seriation for the northern area (Figure 6.3), they are far separated and composed of quite different type frequencies. This latter fact may indicate that the assemblages represent two temporally distinct occupations.

Each assemblage successfully included on these four seriations may be said to represent either a single occupation or a series of sequent occupations: groups of artifacts that cohere in space, time, and form. Additionally, assemblages must be of comparable duration in order to seriate together (Dunnell 1970), so that must hold true for these assemblages, given the types and modes used to order them.

This gives a more defensible basis for examining the spatial distribution of the sites represented on the seriations. Because so few sites have produced large assemblages, I display site locations only for the assemblages ordered by temper-surface finish types (Figure 6.6). The assemblages that show essentially the same type frequencies have been grouped together. For example, in the southern area, assemblages from 22WS510, 22WS501, 22SU530, 22SH501, and 22SH502 all have high percentages of shell-tempered plain pottery, similar frequencies of shell-tempered fine-line incised, and very small amounts of shell-tempered punctate (Figure 6.4). These five assemblages thus were held to be temporally indistinguishable and were grouped together under the same number (14) for map display (Table 6.1).

The map shows that the earliest occupations occur in the southernmost part of the southern area (along the Yazoo River) and in the north part of the northern area (near where the Coldwater River enters the Delta). In the south, those in groups 5 (mostly on Deer Creek) and 6 (on the lower Sunflower) show little overlap in their spatial distribution, while later assemblages (13 and 14) came from sites located in both of these areas. Given the vagaries of the data, it is uncertain whether these spatial patterns mean anything.

The need for larger, more carefully collected pottery assemblages from a much larger group of occupations seems plain. Without them, we must rely on extensive absolute dating, making it much more difficult to address ceramic-period settlement pattern change except in the largest-scale terms (see Lipo and Dunnell, this volume). Change during pre-ceramic periods is even harder to determine, and absolute dates may have to play a larger role in this endeavor.

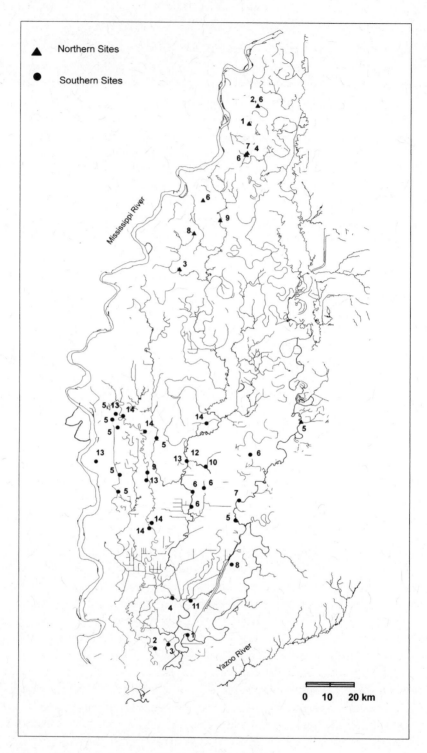

Figure 6.6. Site locations in seriated order, Yazoo Basin.

Conclusions

The above exercise shows how important adequate collection strategies are in producing assemblages that can be used for settlement pattern studies. It is plain that the assemblages collected in the earlier LMV survey (Phillips et al. 2003 [1951]) are more useful for seriation than those collected in the later one (Phillips 1970), particularly in the many cases where decorated sherds were rare. In the later collections, the representation of plain sherds often was biased by collecting only rims, a method not used in the earlier work. Problems also were created by Phillips' decision to combine all collections from a site, made in different areas, into a single assemblage; this very likely obscured spatially separate occupations.

Because much of the work was informant-based or consisted of finding sites by driving the roads (Phillips et al. 2003 [1951]), one of the marked deficiencies in the LMS data concerns the record of dispersed sedentary settlement. As the habitation sites in such settlement patterns are small (hamlet- or homestead-sized, encompassing space for one to several houses), they require intensive survey to be identified reliably. Despite protestations to the contrary (Phillips 1970:967), it seems unlikely that such sites, if they exist in the area, would have been found consistently. For ceramic periods, dispersed sedentary patterns appear to be represented in the LMS work only by those mound sites that had little or no habitation debris except on the mounds. Although Ford says that many of the small and large ceremonial centers were of this kind, the focus was on sites that produced enough pottery to allow dating via seriation, whether that was from a mound or a habitation area (Phillips et al. 2003 [1951]:315–316, 365). Given this, the settlement data that can be extracted for areas not on mounds mostly represent ceramic-period nucleated sedentary patterns. The other problem, more explicitly discussed (Phillips et al. 2003 [1951]:335), was that mounds may not be accurately dated by village debris, as any mound might predate or postdate the village; artifacts from mound surfaces also potentially suffer from this problem. Another deficiency caused by the survey methods used is that lithic scatters without pottery rarely were identified. With the exception of some Poverty Point occupations, the entire record of Paleo-Indian and Archaic use of the survey area is underrepresented in these data. Subsequent survey efforts focused on braided stream surfaces (Connaway 1988) have remedied this only partially.

This chapter is a demonstration of a set of methods for analyzing data, not an attempt to explain ceramic-period settlement patterns in the Yazoo Basin. These methods, based on identifying occupations, ordering assemblages from them continuously through time, and displaying their locations without using culture-historical phases, are powerful tools for examining a variety of settlement pattern questions. These could include changes in mound function, size, and number; changes in habitation site size (nucleation versus dispersion); population increase and decrease; duration of site use; and many others. Such settlement pattern questions can frame the way we look at excavated data and help us learn more about how and why occupations and settlement patterns differ and change.

7

Prehistoric Settlement in the Lower Mississippi Valley

A Critical Review

Carl P. Lipo and Robert C. Dunnell

Introduction

Although explicit and systematic analyses of the spatial aspects of the archaeological record were added rather late in the discipline's history, regional differences in the content, architecture, and occurrence of archaeological phenomena were recognized almost as soon as American archaeologists became aware of the interior of the continent (e.g., Atwater 1820). By the end of the nineteenth century and beginning of the twentieth century, there were numerous regional accounts (e.g., Brown 1992 [1926]; Bushnell 1919; Jones 1999 [1873]; Lapham 1855; Moore 1910; Thruston 1890) where the spatial element was supplied primarily by modern political boundaries or physiographic factors. William Henry Holmes (Meltzer and Dunnell 1992 [Holmes 1903]) developed the first archaeologically defined spatial units (cf. Holmes 1886a, 1886b) that had lasting impact. By mid-century (Griffin 1952; Martin et al. 1947; Willey and Phillips 2001[1958]) archaeologically (sometimes construed as ethnically) driven spatial units were de rigueur, even if modern political and geographic criteria still had surreptitious influence (e.g., Chapman and Chapman 1972; Willey 1949). Thus, by the mid-twentieth century, archaeological use of space was largely confined to providing the horizontal axes in the ubiquitous time-space charts of the culture historians.

Two events were of particular importance to the development of *analytic* approaches to archaeological space from earlier approaches. The first was the recognition that archaeological assemblages have emergent properties beyond the scale of the artifact; i.e., they have properties greater than the sum of their parts, including how things are arranged and related. Although there were precedents (e.g., Smith 1910), the Works Progress Administration (WPA) projects of the late 1930s and early 1940s provided the first major step toward the analysis of spatial variability (Fagette 1996; Lyon 1996). The Mississippi River valley was the site of the first of these federal efforts (Setzler and Strong 1936). While a concentration on mounds and the excavation of their contents continued unabated, a number of these large-scale studies systematically exposed large living areas (e.g., Webb 1951), providing comprehensive views of what were considered to be prehistoric communities in the eastern United States. The results of this work sparked interest in the internal structure of sites beyond stratigraphy and led researchers to view deposits as more than just places to generate sufficient numbers of artifacts for chronology. In turn, the new attitude toward deposits provided a fertile ground for the functionalist approaches of processualism in which a large, sophisticated literature developed, focused primarily on "site structure" (e.g., Carr 1985; Clarke 1977; Hietala and Larson 1984; Hietala and Stevens 1977). At its height, processualism fostered obsessive but purposeless quantification of artifact distributions. The effort was led by "number mechanics" who championed statistics as a means for searching for site structure where none was evident (e.g., Dacey 1973; Whallon 1973).

Fortunately, like many of the excesses of the New Archaeology, this particular vice did not find a home in the Southeast (Dunnell 1990). The cost of excavation required to investigate the massive deposits and archaeological features of the Mississippi River valley limited researchers' ability to generate adequate information about whole deposits. Thus, intrasite spatial analyses tended to focus on simple hunter-gatherer remains in the period after World War II, as they still do today. There are, however, notable exceptions that constitute some of the most valuable recent field work bearing on site structure in the Mississippi valley (e.g., Benn 1998; Price and Griffin 1979).

The second event that contributed to the development of analytic approaches to archaeological space was the recognition that archaeological sites existed in a variable space populated with other sites and physical properties (e.g., geography, topography, hydrology, geology). Researchers also began to incorporate the recognition that sites—or what they represented—once previously interacted with one another along economic dimensions. This interest in functional interaction was distinct from earlier culture historical efforts that tended to focus solely on measuring homologous similarity as a way of estimating the degree of social "influence" between spatially disparate populations (Lyman et al. 1997). Although the study of functional interaction is largely associated with the emergence of processualism in the 1960s and 1970s (O'Brien et al. 2005), Willey is rightly credited (Vogt 2004) with this innovation in his famous Virú Valley study (Willey 1953). It is from this publication (Willey 1953:1) that the term "settlement pattern" was first introduced and given its initial meaning.

> The term "settlement patterns" is defined here as the way in which man disposed himself over the landscape. . . . It refers to dwellings, to their

arrangement, and to the nature and disposition of other buildings. . . . These settlements reflect the natural environment, the level of technology on which the builders operated, and various institutions of social interaction and control that the culture maintained. Because settlement patterns are, to a large extent, directly shaped by widely held cultural needs, they offer a strategic starting point for the functional interpretation of archaeological cultures.

With roots in chronology-focused regional studies (e.g., Ford 1936; Phillips et al. 2003 [1951]; Webb 1938; Webb and DeJarnette 1942), the Mississippi valley saw early application of settlement pattern studies using the Willey formulation (e.g., Williams 1963). Settlement pattern analysis, however, gradually took an increasingly functionalist position and set the stage for the rise of processualism (O'Brien et al. 2005:86). With processualism, settlement pattern was reworked into subsistence-settlement *system,* on the assumption that subsistence was the primary articulation between environment and settlement location (e.g., Struever 1968). Of course, many researchers continued to treat settlement patterns as static notions while relabeling them "settlement systems," so as to partake of modernity without committing to its substance. In this mode, settlement pattern is treated as an attribute of a phase, focus, or culture (e.g., Phillips 1970), assuming that the distribution of sites constitutes the material remains of a once-existing behavioral and cultural system (e.g., Parsons 1972).

One group of processualists turned to method development as a way of building a science around the study of settlement patterns. Following the same strategy as those researchers investigating intra-site variability, "number mechanics" began to adopt quantitative methods that purportedly "discovered," described, and explained patterns in virtually every field of analysis (e.g., Read 1982; Spaulding 1953; Whallon 1973). Although lacking explicit archaeological theory development, the movement to analyze settlement patterns was more grounded than most fields, as archaeologists borrowed developed methods from the Scandinavian quantitative geographers (e.g., Haggett 1965) and home-grown plant geographers and ecologists (Clark and Evans 1954; Greig-Smith 1952; Thompson 1956). The introduction of these approaches from other disciplines led to the application of such concepts as central-place theory (e.g., Johnson 1972), site-catchment (e.g., Higgs and Vita-Finzi 1972), distance-decay models (e.g., Renfrew 1977), and various locational models (e.g., Plog 1976; see Hietala and Stevens 1977; Hodder and Orton 1976 for reviews).

By the 1980s, however, the quantification craze was largely over, and along with it, quantitative modeling of settlement studies. The decline of quantitative approaches to spatial variability occurred even in the parent disciplines and, in the case of geography, nearly brought the house down with it (Barnes

2004). Quantitative approaches became viewed as over-simplifications (Aldenderfer 1987; Ammerman 1992; Gaffney and van Leusen 1995; Lock 1995). Archaeologists also began to appreciate the circularity involved in quantitative approaches that lacked theoretical foundation. For example, many noted the inability to measure independent variables such as "site function" and proposed the substitution of the dependent variable "site size" in their place (e.g., Crumley 1979; G. Johnson 1980; Pearson 1980). As a result, quantitative approaches to settlements remained largely descriptive, using variables with no clear link to explanatory models.

In recent decades, settlement pattern studies have not been the focus of much excitement. For the most part, Willey-type applications that attend to the description of patterns of artifact distributions dominate contemporary archaeological field research when regions are explored as units of analysis. There have been occasional exceptions. Dewar and McBride's (1992) effort to retool the settlement pattern concept in light of formation processes, for example, introduces the important notion that surface age and artifact representativeness must be considered when accounting for artifact distributions. In addition, high-resolution satellite images are now involved in generating systematic information across large areas (e.g., Clark et al. 1998; Madry and Crumley 1990; Philip et al. 2002). Generally, however, these studies follow the basic framework provided by the Willey approach.

The point to this brief history of settlement pattern studies is to call attention to the ad hoc manner in which the idea of settlement pattern and settlement pattern studies has grown. In this respect, settlement pattern studies are not different from other archaeological fields because there is not yet any broad consensus on the purpose and practice of archaeology. Even critical terms such as "site" (cf. Dunnell 1992) and "settlement" (cf. Chang 1968) remain undefined and without consensus on usage. The lack of definitions is an all-too-predictable consequence of operating in a theoretical vacuum. Consequently, in order to address settlement patterns in the Mississippi River valley, we must define our terms carefully and do so in reference to a particular theoretic position, lest we do nothing more than add to the morass of terms, assertions, and tradition that characterizes current studies of settlement patterns.

Theoretical Background

Today, the notion of settlement pattern is composed of four radically different ideas, as laid out in Table 7.1. While representing divergent concepts, all conform to Willey's initial but unfortunately ad hoc formulation. On the one hand, the term is used to indicate the internal horizontal structure of archaeological deposits (i.e., intra-site variability). On the other hand, it indi-

Table 7.1. Four approaches to settlement patterns.

		Scale	
		Intra-Site	*Inter-Site*
Context	*Systemic*	I	II
	Archaeological	III	IV

cates the placement of such deposits in the environment and/or in relation to each other (i.e., inter-site variability). This distinction is a contrast in *scale*. In addition to divisions in scale, archaeologists also discuss settlement patterns in terms of *context*. Unfortunately, the distinction in context is often unremarked, and the choice of context represents a habit of willy-nilly combination of systemic and/or archaeological contexts (Schiffer 1972, 1988). At the intra-site scale, terms like "domestic site," "quarry," or "cemetery" imply a systemic context, as there is a reference to behavior and/or function. In contrast, things like "mounds," "lithic scatters," and the like generally fall into archaeological contexts, i.e., are descriptions of artifact composition. Terms like settlement-subsistence system (systemic context) and settlement pattern à la Willey (archaeological context) represent the same contrast at the higher scale (i.e., inter-site variability). This set of distinctions provides four combinations with which one could discuss settlement patterns. The potential for confusion is substantial, and too often the various contrasts are haphazardly mixed together (e.g., Bechtel and Strothers 1993; Yerkes 1989). Clearly, for progress to be made or even to facilitate communication, terms have to be defined.

The lack of a theoretical consensus in the discipline requires us to limit our discussion to the *archaeological* context, where descriptions of physical phenomena in the archaeological record, formation processes, and physical theories can serve as our structuring principles. Inasmuch as settlement pattern is routinely used for both intra- and inter-site scales, we consider both insofar as is possible.

The Notion Site

As is apparent from the foregoing, the cornerstone of all settlement-pattern studies is the notion of "site." Sites are often used as fundamental units of observation when settlements are discussed. For example, patterns of sites vis-à-vis each other or the environment and/or landscape or both, and patterns within sites—site structure—all require the concept *site*. Despite being treated as having properties of empirical entities, sites do not exist in any fundamental way (Dunnell 1992). This statement means that sites are *archaeological* rather than systemic in nature, even though they are often inadvertently, but unjustifiably, imbued with systemic significance. They are constructs of the archaeologist, consciously or not. Every archaeologist knows this because every archaeologist makes them up him/herself through observation and delineation. How they are made in terms of procedures and criteria, however, usually remains cryptic and variable. Thus, a large but unknown fraction of the variability observed in the archaeological record of sites, their structure, content, and relations is due to how sites have been recognized, defined, and conceived and *not* due to the structure of the archaeological record. Simply being explicit about how one made the decision about site definition, while a virtue, is insufficient to solve the problem. In fact, the inconsistencies in these definitions, though explicit, are partly responsible for the situation apparent today— different people use different ideas (e.g., Klinger 1976:55; MacCord 1988; May 1988; Plog et al. 1978; Zeidler 1995; see also Lyman 1985; O'Brien et al. 1982). Some go so far as to recommend that the definition of site be made on an entirely ad hoc basis (e.g., Chase et al. 1988). As a result, comparisons are difficult if not impossible to make between projects and researchers. As Ebert (1992:69–70) points out:

> the greatest impediment to methodological consistency within site-based survey . . . is the concept of the site itself. Consistency can never be reached, due to the very nature of the concept. Sites are never discovered during survey; it is always artifacts, features, and other individual, physically real materials that we find. Bounded sites and statements about their contents are abstracted—that is, essentially made up—by looking at individual artifacts, and usually if not always by looking at only a portion of those making up the site abstraction.

In the case of the Mississippi River valley, different definitions for "site" have been used by the organizations and authors who have investigated the valley. In some cases, a single artifact constitutes a site; in others a particular density threshold is required. More often than not, no record of how the decision was made is provided. In recent years, Anglo-American artifacts have come to be included in what was once exclusively limited to Native American material. To make matters worse, areas *not* containing entities marked as sites are entirely ambiguous, as it is often unclear whether the area was searched, how it was searched, what criteria were used, and what archaeological remains, if any, are unaccounted for simply by not meeting whatever definition was in place at the time of the study.

Our recognition of this problem came quickly. As we began to wade through site descriptions recorded in publications and in state files—there are over

18,000 "sites" in the study area now recorded (see Dunnell, this volume, Chapter 3)—it immediately became apparent that any effort at comparative analyses was a lost cause because of the unremarked variability in what constituted a "site" and how these entities were described. In the absence of a theoretical consensus, one cannot specify how sites should be defined or if they should be recognized at all. There are no reasons to prefer one definition over another unless a purpose can be stipulated. State-managed databases of site records provide no relief to this problem. Management of the archaeological record is *not* a purpose in itself; management itself requires one or more purposes to justify its own decisions. With respect to legal obligations for the documentation of the record, conventions taken to constitute "compliance" are without meaning in themselves and do not generate archaeologically useful information about the structure of the archaeological record.

Limitations of Existing Observations

We also recognized that whatever data existed would have to be examined from a skeptical point of view. From the beginning of this project, we were aware that our knowledge of the archaeological record, with which we could study settlement variability through the prehistory of the Mississippi valley, was going to be limited to the largest classes of artifacts: generally large deposits, earthworks, and mounds. Our own experience in southeastern Missouri and northeastern Arkansas has shown us that we cannot rely on current knowledge to meaningfully discuss the record of smaller artifact classes and the low-density record that covers most of the region. In a rejected NSF proposal submitted by Dunnell in the early 1970s to conduct a detailed transect survey of the region, one of the reviewers remarked that there was no need for the project, since "the farmers know where all the stuff is." This comment prompted Dunnell to seek out a location in his study area in which *no* evidence of archaeological remains had ever been reported by archaeologists, local collectors, or farmers: an 80-acre cotton field known locally as "Cold Water Farm." Over a period of three seasons of systematic surface collection, Dunnell established that not only does the field contain isolated materials that represent artifact losses outside of domestic contexts, but also stable, low-density clusters of artifacts that would be called "sites" in most contexts (Dunnell 1986c). The first implication of this study is that any claims about the absence of the record in a region are greatly exaggerated. Second, an implication of this study is that, even when we have information from surface inspection under the most ideal of conditions, single-surface collections may grossly underestimate the number of "sites," particularly in low-density situations (see also Shott 1995).

The underrepresentation of the record, when based on single periods of observation, also impacts our understanding of larger and denser deposits. Ford

(1936) found when he recollected surfaces for ceramics in locations in the Mississippi valley, for example, that multiple and large samples are required in order to generate reliable numbers. There is no guarantee that a single collection will produce values, even in presence/absence terms, that accurately reflect the archaeological record. This effect is largely related to the size of the sample: the larger the sample, the more likely it can be used to estimate the structure and composition of the archaeological record. Although the need to generate large collections was recognized by some of the pioneers of Mississippi valley archaeology (e.g., Phillips et al. 2003 [1951]), numerous later studies do not attend to such issues (e.g., Phillips 1970). The use of small samples can result in observations that are biased toward the most abundant material and/or can underestimate the importance of rare elements. Reliable estimates of the abundance of rare classes require substantial samples (Lipo 2001b; Lipo et al. 1997). Without careful consideration of formation processes and the effects of sampling, there is no guarantee that collections from even the largest deposits reflect anything beyond who made the collections, how the collections were obtained, and the size of the collections (Lipo 2001a).

Our understanding of the limitations of the existing descriptions of the record in the Mississippi valley grew even greater when we began to plot locations for known "sites" as recorded in publications (e.g., Phillips 1970; Phillips et al. 2003 [1951]; Williams 1954) and in state site records. We did this using topographic maps and high-resolution aerial and satellite images. Online public databases such as Terraserver (i.e., U.S. Geological Survey orthophotos and topographic maps, http://www.terraserver.com) and Google Earth (i.e., Digital Globe and Keyhole satellite imagery, http://earth.google.com) provide a rich and comprehensive base map for studying the landscape of the Mississippi River valley at virtually no cost. With resolutions of less than a meter, images in these databases provide a means of directly studying archaeological features, including the form, shape, and distribution of prehistoric deposits.

Using these public sources of images and maps, we identified the location of previously recorded prehistoric deposits as closely as possible, given the available documentation. Much to our surprise, in the process we identified approximately 100 undocumented and potential locations that appear to be mounds or other kinds of earthworks (Figure 7.1). These locations are either marked as "Indian Mound(s)" on the U.S. Geological Survey quadrangles and/or are characterized by distinct topographic structures that appear on the quadrangles and aerial photographs. Among these potential features are earthen mounds (e.g., Figure 7.2) and shell middens (e.g., Figure 7.3). In addition, we located at least three large semicircular ditches and earthwork deposits (Figures 7.4–7.6). The first ditch feature consists of a semicircular structure that circumscribes Taylor (25-I-1) and Boothe Landing (24-I-4) (Figure

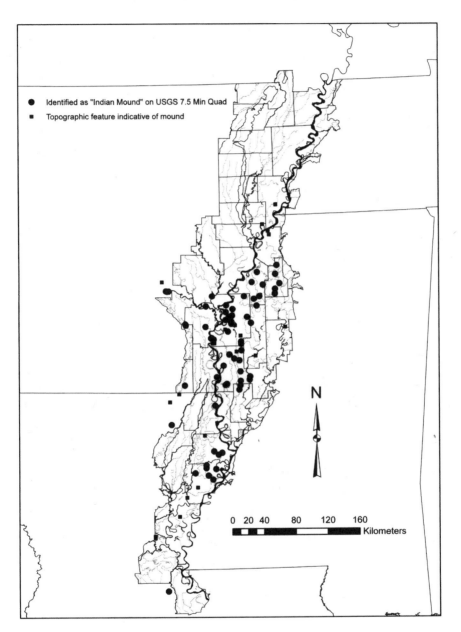

Figure 7.1. Locations identified as potential archaeological deposits on the basis of the inspection of aerial photographs and 7.5′ U.S. Geological Survey quadrangles.

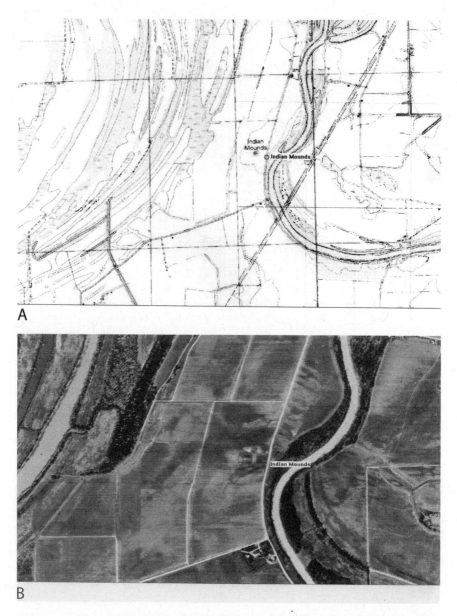

Figure 7.2. Archaeological location identified as "Indian Mounds" on a 7.5′ U.S. Geological Survey quadrangle near the Sunflower River in Mississippi and the aerial photograph from http://www.terraserver.com (B) showing mound features.

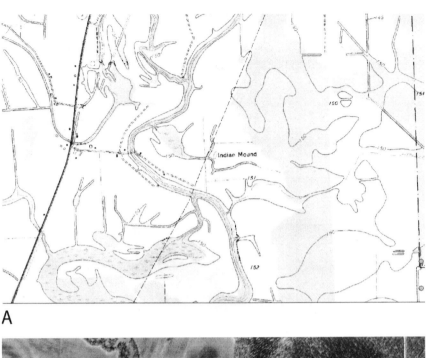

A

B

Figure 7.3. Archaeological location identified as "Indian Mound" on a 7.5′ U.S. Geological Survey quadrangle (A) along Opossum Bayou in Quitman County, Mississippi, and the aerial photograph from http://www.terraserver.com (B) showing what appears to be a shell midden ring.

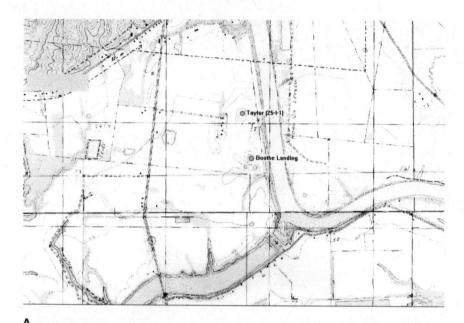

A

B

Figure 7.4. Locations of Taylor (25-I-1) and Boothe Landing (24-I-4) on a 7.5′ U.S. Geological Survey quadrangle (A) along the Ouachita River in Louisiana and the aerial photograph of the same location from http://www.terraserver.com (B) showing a semicircular ring earthwork feature that surrounds both locations.

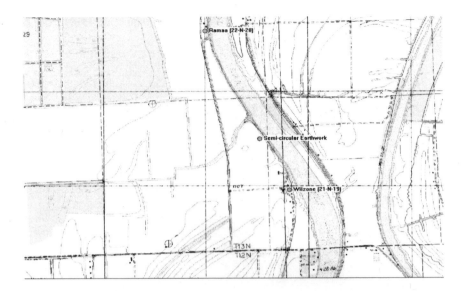

A

B

Figure 7.5. Location of a semicircular earthwork feature on a 7.5′ U.S. Geological Survey quadrangle (A) along Wolf Lake in Humphreys County, Mississippi, and the aerial photograph of the same location from http://www.terraserver.com (B) showing a semicircular earthwork feature.

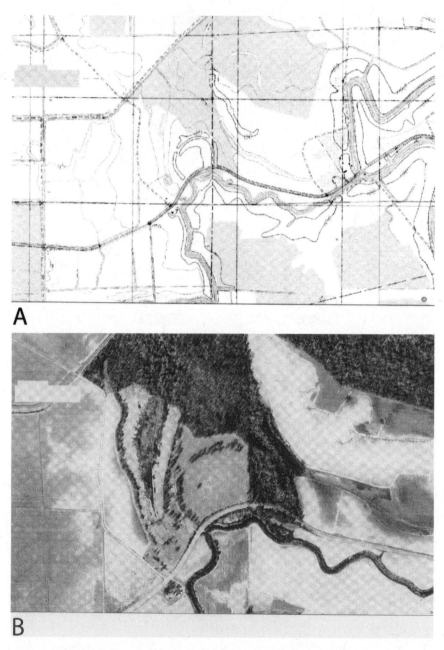

Figure 7.6. Location of a semicircular earthwork feature on a 7.5′ U.S. Geological Survey (A) along Black Bayou in Issaquena County, Mississippi, the aerial photograph of the same location from http://www.terraserver.com, (B) showing a circular earthwork feature, and (C) a ground-level photo of wall feature.

C

Figure 7.6. *Continued*

7.4) in Concordia Parish, Louisiana (Phillips et al. 2003 [1951]). It is likely these two deposits were described separately, as the division between LMS quadrangles 24-I and 25-I falls directly in between two sets of mounds. The ditch feature, however, was missed completely. After ground reconnaissance, two ditch features were found at other sites (Figures 7.5 and 7.6). These consist of unrecorded, large (ca. 500 meters in diameter) semicircular ditches and, in the case of a location on the Black Bayou in Issaquena County, Mississippi, walls (Figure 7.6C). Given that the inspection of the aerial photographs was extremely limited and nonsystematic, the results to-date and the identification of previously undocumented earthworks suggest that a comprehensive search through available imagery data sources (Historic and contemporary) will produce a wealth of new information about settlement variability in the region.

Strategy

Based on these sets of observations and conclusions, we quickly recognized that no meaningful quantitative analysis can be done across the valley as a whole. This is not the venue to resolve this matter, because there is nothing in our tool box that we can use to change the history of archaeological field work. It is important to note, however, that some degree of resolution is possible, provided that we approach the problem with a framework based on some fundamental aspects of formation processes. Ideally, in our analyses *the unit of recording should approximate the unit of deposition*. By generating units of measurement that approximate the unit of deposition, we have a means of making meaningful comparisons. There are, of course, complications. Some units of deposition degrade in the archaeological context. For example, arrows become projectile points, i.e., one object becomes a different object. In addition, spear throwers become weights, hooks, and handles, and pots or big sherds become small sherds, i.e., one object can become several or many objects. Still others disappear in any form recognizable to the human eye but leave their presence recorded in small particles and ions that require instrumentation for detection, documentation, and description. Some are reflected only in variability in electromagnetic spectra, such as magnetic signatures caused by heating or organic decomposition. Some few units of deposition probably leach away completely.

In spite of this, whenever we observe individual objects at any scale—the "artifact"—we come as close to the target variable as is possible. The implication is that archaeological surveys should be artifact surveys, not "site surveys," regardless of the "practical" issues that might be raised (Dunnell and Dancey 1983; Ebert 1992).[1] Sites, if needed, can thus be manufactured to suit any research purpose by any subsequent investigator without embedding those purposes in the basic unit of observation. This approach conceives fieldwork simply as the documentation of the distribution of artifacts at whatever scale they occur on the landscape. Ultimately, this position is the most conservative: regardless of theoretical persuasion, formation processes physically limit what can be known.

One might object that all we have done is shift attention away from the indeterminacy of "site" and move to a focus that encompasses similar ambiguity about the meaning of "artifact." Artifacts, however, pose different kinds of problems for identification. An artifact is taken to be anything that owes any attribute to human activity (Dunnell 2002 [1971]; see also Spaulding 1968). The crux of the matter is clearly seen to be the manner in which "attributes due to human activity" (i.e., artificial attributes) are identified. These attributes can consist of formal *and* locational properties. Since location is one of the attributes of an object that is potentially artificial, a standard means by which we can operationalize artifact identification can be created. The key to applying this notion of artifact is the recognition that identification is an empirical operation and therefore error-ridden. In a research context that focuses on explanations of the archaeological record, one wants to be certain that everything included as data actually is what is claimed, i.e., that artifacts are the set of things with artificial attributes. In this context, one would want to minimize Type-I errors (i.e., falsely identifying something as an artifact when it is not). In the conservation-management context, however, the reverse is true. One would want to minimize Type-II errors and ensure that nothing artificial is excluded. Thus, in a conservation-management mode, we would rewrite the definition of artificial so as to include "any attribute *not known* to be the product of natural processes." In this case, as knowledge grows about natural processes, one can become more efficient in identification. This strategy eliminates the chance that, at some future point, one would realize that something should have been recorded or collected but was not. Although such a strategy is rarely taken, logic dictates that *all* definitions of archaeological concepts that have empirical referents *must be* given definitions that minimize Type-II errors in the conservation-management context (see Dunnell 1984 for a more extensive discussion of these issues).

Compounding this problem of site-based approaches is the nature of the databases that have been compiled to document archaeological materials across the Mississippi valley. In general, databases maintained by state agencies and tabulations in most of the existing reports are themselves anecdotal (see Dunnell, this volume, Chapter 3). When available, documentation consists of a list of localities where artifacts have been reported and/or above-ground monuments, mostly mounds, have been noted. Because these lists (i.e., site-survey files) have multiple origins and are the aggregate product of a century of research projects, local informants, ad hoc observations, and historical lore, they cannot be treated as representative samples by any means. This presents a substantial problem for any attempt to characterize Mississippi valley settlement patterns. Since the information we currently have is not the product of a directed, rationalized effort, there is no clear remedy.

The lack of a remedy, however, does not warrant ignoring the consequences: we cannot simply proceed as if current site lists are unambiguously related to the archaeological record and not the myriad of effects of observation, site definition, and identification problems. The absence of statistically representative samples ultimately means that *no* quantitative analyses of associations between sites—however defined—and environmental variables are possible. Of course, the numbers can be crunched and reported, but they utterly lack an empirical warrant. While a tough conclusion to accept, we cannot pretend that our current data are anything other than what they are: cryptic and ad hoc observations.[2]

As discussed above, however, we can explore the distribution of measurements made that are as close to the unit of deposition as possible, the *artifact*. In the Lower Mississippi Valley (LMV) (see Fig 1.1), no large-scale research has been undertaken from artifact-as-unit-of-recording perspective, with a couple of exceptions. In the Delta area, U.S. Forest Service work in Mississippi, although still tied to sites, approaches this target closely (Sam Brookes, U.S. Forest Service, personal communication to Dunnell, 2005) by carefully documenting the area searched *and* the mode of the search, not just the location of positive findings. Since a relatively small area has been covered and the Forest Service holdings represent a distinctly biased sample in terms of environment, the empirical findings are too limited to generalize for the valley as a whole. The approach, however, provides a useful model for how we might address the problem of observation in future work.

Further north, Dunnell has been engaged in a somewhat simplified version of this kind of program on the Early Holocene surfaces of the Malden Plain in Dunklin and adjacent counties in Missouri. These data have not yet been published save for some methical methodological papers (e.g., Dunnell 1988, 1992; Dunnell and Feathers 1994; Dunnell and Stein 1989) and partial summaries (Morse and Morse 1983:184–185). Treating the artifact as the unit of deposition leads to conceiving of "sites" as clusters of artifacts, with a variety of different processes potentially responsible for the observed clustering, not all of which are compatible with the general assumption underlying site-based approaches: that spatial proximity equals relatedness. For example, most whole projectile points found within "sites" that display a broad spectrum of debris have no culture-historical connection to those clusters; they are just accidental associations. Points are presumably lost-in-use hunting products since the density of whole, finished points appears to be determined by environmental variables but is independent of the density of domestic debris such as potsherds. Since potsherds do not have comparable distributional properties (a sherd implies the presence of other culture-historically related artifacts, if only the rest of the vessel), this observation goes a long way to explain why "site" assemblages frequently show consistent ceramic assemblages but a broad range of point types. As a result, duration calculations based on descriptions of ceramic and projectile point types will often greatly differ. This example also serves to point out two bits of information beyond location that are essential to settlement pattern analyses: (1) a functional (*sensu* Dunnell 1978) description of individual data points, and (2) the time of deposition.[3] These classes of information are usually within easy reach of modern technology, despite traditional wisdom and customary practice to the contrary.

Because the southeastern Missouri data provide the best approximation to the data appropriate to settlement and subsistence pattern studies, they are employed as exemplars in the discussion that follows. Sites as points or sites as undefined or ill-defined areas bounded by the ubiquitous dotted lines are useless in this endeavor. Relying so heavily on a small, marginal part of a study area for insight is doubly damning because, as we will show, there are important differences between north and south in settlement type as well as settlement pattern, even if we do not know precisely what they are or how they came about.

Settlement

With this preamble, we are in a position to rephrase the indefensible "site" as artifact cluster and to lay out, with theoretical justification, how to define and identify clusters appropriate to the target embodied in the Willey notion of settlement. The model for the idea is clearly ethnographic (e.g., Chang 1968). However, rather than "inferring" what a settlement is archaeologically and thereby committing to a course with untestable results, we can build our measures around the properties that are important to settlement in traditional archaeological thought and use them to create a minimal *archaeological* unit.

From an archaeological perspective, there are more than just two potential scales of units—the discrete object and the aggregate. There is a continuum of organizational relationships, from the artifact to aggregates of objects to features within houses to sets of settlements within a region, each of which must be defined and identified. Figure 7.7 shows a hierarchy of possible organizational levels and units.

Our interest here is in a particular kind of aggregate unit—the *settlement*. In our research, we define settlement as the redundant set of nodes (functions or activities) along with unique communal structures or areas (such as burial mounds, plazas, cemeteries, walls, ditches). Note that this is an *archaeological* rather than a behavioral unit. Archaeologically, the settlement is identified as a corporate unit by the presence of a cohesive stylistic assemblage from one or more deposits (Fuller 1981:188). In terms of scale of observation, settlements are necessarily aggregate-type entities.

While the scale of the community is an aggregate scale, the configuration of the entities that compose the aggregate can vary in terms of space and time. The Neolithic farming village, in which all individuals in a community reside in the same location year-round (seasonality) for substantial periods of time (permanence), is often conceived as the prototypical (and common-sense) settlement (e.g., Chang 1968; Willey 1953). The terms "site," settlement, and community, however, more often than not are used synonymously. In practice, this equivalency of site, settlement, and community does not hold. Seasonally mobile populations, for example, leave several stylistically identical but functionally disparate "sites" over the course of a single year. Depending upon the stability of the pattern (permanence), some or all of these "sites" may be ephemeral lithic/sherd scatters or deep middens. Even when seasonality is not an issue, a single community (*sensu* Chang 1968) may leave multiple sites, as in the case of swidden agriculturalists. Such "sites" would be similar in both

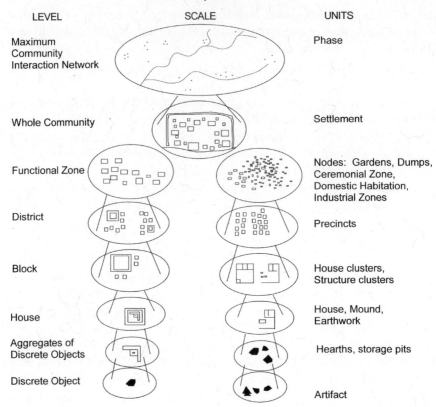

Figure 7.7. A hierarchy of organizational units for the study of settlement patterns.

stylistic and functional terms. Dispersed settlements, in which the individuals who constitute a community do not reside together, introduce further complications. One must measure stylistic structure across spatially disparate aggregates of artifacts to identify a community (Fuller 1981). This recognition is particularly important in the Mississippi River valley, as much of the settlement history may be characterized by dispersed settlements.

Settlement Structure

The simplest settlement is a single spatial node, an undifferentiated cluster of artifacts and/or features, depending on the kinds of data available. The relation of such settlements to other nodes is a matter of settlement pattern, at least in initial stages of analysis. While such settlements may well be the most numerous in the LMV, one is hard-pressed to identify examples. Such settlements are the easiest to overlook, least interesting to excavate, and least rewarding in terms of artifacts. While rare in terms of our records, such settlements have been documented in southeastern Missouri (Dunnell 1988; Dunnell and Feathers 1991), where they may be typical of the earlier Late Woodland Barnes phase (as defined by Dunnell and Feathers 1991). Single nodes also occur in the Late Archaic/Early Woodland (e.g., Dunnell and Whittaker 1990) and in the Mississippian (e.g., House 1995).

By definition, then, settlement structure applies to multi-nodal clusters and can be defined as the relation between nodes. Physical geometry plays a key role because it plays a determinant role in energetic costs (see Leeds 1979). Several simple forms may be defined that can be recognized in existing data, albeit not equally easily.

Mapped-on. In the first form, settlement structure may map onto environmental features such as levees, point bars, and even earlier occupations. With environment-driven structure, distance between nodes is less important than distance to the environmental feature boundaries or some other environmental constraint (e.g., in the valley, within a drainage) that takes precedence over social interaction. Consequently, functional structure may be patterned in a homogeneous fashion across the environment or arrayed parallel to the environmental grain. In addition, in this form, variability along mapped-on forms will feature stylistic similarity caused by the frequency of social interaction as a function of distance alone. Such settlements, though simple in structure, may be quite large and limited only by the space available. Importantly, these kinds of settlement structures can consist of artifacts at different scales: from discrete objects such as projectile points lost-in-use to aggregate sets of complex residential units.

In southeastern Missouri, middle- and late-period (*sensu* Morse and Morse 1983), finished whole Mississippian projectile points display this kind of distribution, in that they are found adjacent to water courses, whereas other point styles display no such pattern. Presumably, this represents hunting from boats and may be connected to the introduction of the bow around this time. An example of the mapping-on pattern at the residential scale in southeast Missouri is Robards (Morse and Morse 1983), which is latest Late Woodland to earliest Early Mississippian. When such localities have been excavated elsewhere, the community consists of houses arranged along a section of natural levee (Kelly et. al. 1990). Here, they also characterize the latest Late Woodland (Dunnell and Feathers 1991). The same may be true of northeast Arkansas, where the same kind of material (Big Lake–phase) occurs widely in the same situations. Even though there have been major excavations in this area (e.g., Zebree [Morse and Morse 1980]), settlement structure at this location is unclear.

Circular. A second commonly encountered pattern is a circular arrangement of nodes. Functional structure of these settlements is radial and consists of a series of concentric rings, where social interaction is structured by distance around the circumference (Dunnell 1983). Circular settlement structures, however, may represent two different factors at work: the minimization of internal distances or the minimization of the perimeter. In the latter case, defense may be the primary concern. Palisades, ditches, and walls are often indicators of a defensive explanation. In the former circumstance, the presence of a central facility along with the absence of a hardened perimeter may be taken as indicative of minimizing internal distances. Equivalent access to such facilities is often taken as indicative of egalitarian societies, but such is not necessarily the case, as is seen in the concentric structures of some Maya settlements (Arnold and Ford 1980).

Circular patterns have not been identified in the southeast Missouri data. They are, however, well documented in the Mississippi Delta in the form of shell rings, the so-called Tchula Lake settlement type (Phillips 1970). The high visibility of shell under some field conditions from the ground and the air accounts for the existence of settlement structure information in records that generally lack such data. Phillips took these settlements to be characteristic of the Deasonville phase (Late Woodland). By dating the shells and artifacts independently, more recent investigation has shown that at least two, and probably most, if not all, of the Yazoo shell rings are latest Archaic in age (Feathers, this volume). Subsequently, the rings attracted occupation as environmental features favorable for settlement. Each shell ring investigated has a different sequence of later occupation that uses only part of the ring, usually the part nearest a watercourse. The association with Deasonville has apparently arisen by the ubiquity of Deasonville usage and the absence or near-absence of any later use of the rings. This suggests that Deasonville settlements, as well as those of other Woodland units, may be wholly or partly of the mapped-on type just previously discussed.

Semicircular. A third frequently seen form of settlement is a semicircle or "c-shaped" structure. This format represents a compromise between environmental factors and social interaction, and in much of the study area of the Mississippi valley is the settlement structure most often associated with ditches and/or walls (Gibson and Shenkel 1988; Jackson 1998; Jones and Kuttruff 1998; McGimsey 2003; Thunen 1988; Toth 1988). While some (e.g., Savory [Phillips 1970]) are clearly domestic, others may well be specialized structures with limited or no domestic function (e.g., Jackson 1998). All of the factors driving the mapped-on environmental settlement form and the circular settlement forms may be at work in these structures.

Rectangular. A fourth settlement form is the rectangular settlement. Such settlements always place some occupants further away from common facilities. They are also more costly to defend and fortify, having a larger perimeter-to-area ratio. This settlement form seems to be driven by social interaction more strongly than environment (internal partitioning is limited to this form in the valley [Price and Griffin 1979], although most still seem to have a roughly concentric functional structure); changes in defensive technology (i.e., bow and arrow [Nassaney and Pyle 1999]) may also be at work. Because of the size of most of these settlements, remarkably little is actually known of their internal structure (see Dunnell 1998; Lipo et al. 2004 for discussion on the study of these kinds of settlements).

Settlement Structure History

Given the problems described above about the nature of "sites" and existing information about composition and distribution of the archaeological record, putting together a history of settlement structure in the Mississippi valley is not really possible. Not enough descriptions of settlement structure that also have detailed chronological information exist to begin to talk about the history of even these simple settlement forms. Only the crudest possible sketch can be suggested using typological dating means (i.e., phases, marker types), Saucier's (1974, 1994) geomorphic chronology (Figure 7.8), and published site descriptions in the counties that comprise the study area (Table 7.2).

In this study, we compiled a list of "sites" drawn from the literature, particularly the large regional surveys (e.g., Ford 1936; Phillips 1970; Phillips et al. 2003 [1951]; Redfield 1971; Williams 1954), summaries (e.g., Byrd 1991; Connaway 1984; Ford and Quimby 1945; Ford and Willey 1940; Gibson 1973; Gibson and Shenkel 1988; House 1991; Jackson 1981, 1986; Jones and Kuttruff 1998; Klinger 1975; Lehmann 1991; Morse 1981; Morse and Morse 1983; O'Brien 2001; Toth 1988; Webb 1982, 1991; Williams and Brain 1983), historical references (e.g., Beckwith 1887; Brown 1992 [1926]; Bushnell 1919; Moore 1910; Putnam 1875a) and site files from the Arkansas Archeological Survey, the Mississippi Department of Archives and History, and the Archaeological Survey of Missouri. We also gathered information from the Paleoindian Database of the Americas (Anderson 1990) and, as described above, added new information as we identified deposits on aerial photographs and topographic maps. Primary requirements for inclusion into the database included specifiable location and description that included composition and structure of the deposit. For the most part these locations were limited to various kinds of earthworks, as other kinds of deposits are even more poorly known and less well described. We entered all descriptions into a GIS database that ultimately included 1,345 discrete locations (Figure 7.9). Using information about the chronology of these deposits (primarily from culture-historical types), these data became the basis for evaluating the history of settlement structure for the Mississippi River valley.

The earliest settlements of the valley present their own problems. Effec-

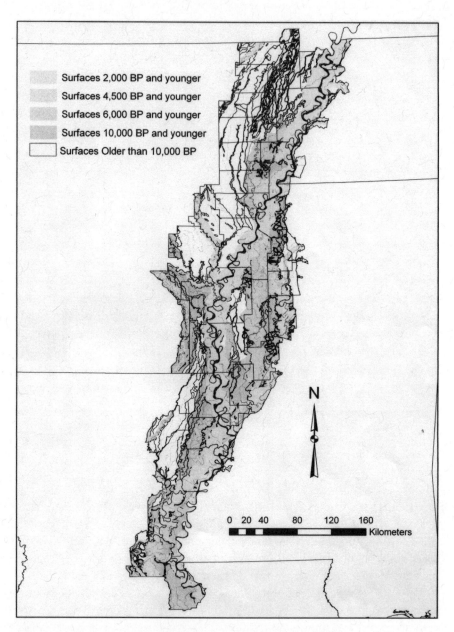

Figure 7.8. Surface ages of the Mississippi valley based on Saucier (1994).

Surfaces 2,000 BP and younger
Surfaces 4,500 BP and younger
Surfaces 6,000 BP and younger
Surfaces 10,000 BP and younger
Surfaces Older than 10,000 BP

N

0 20 40   80   120   160
Kilometers

Table 7.2. Counties and parishes included in the Mississippi valley study area.

State	County
Arkansas	Arkansas, Ashley, Chicot, Clay, Craighead, Crittenden, Cross, Desha, Drew, Greene, Lee, Lincoln, Mississippi, Monroe, Phillips, Poinsett, St. Francis
Louisiana	Avoyelles, Catahoula, Concordia, East Carroll, Franklin, Madison, Pointe Coupee, Richland, Tensas, West Carroll, West Feliciana
Mississippi	Bolivar, Claiborne, Coahoma, Copiah, DeSoto, Hinds, Humphreys, Issaquena, Leflore, Panola, Quitman, Sharkey, Sunflower, Tallahatchie, Tate, Tunica, Warren, Washington, Yazoo
Missouri	Dunklin, Pemiscot
Tennessee	Crockett, Dyer, Fayette, Gibson, Haywood, Lake, Lauderdale, Obion, Shelby, Tipton

tively, too few "sites" of any sort are securely known before Late Archaic times to begin examining settlement structure. Certainly by Dalton times there were functionally distinct sites being produced (Goodyear 1995 [1974]; Morse 1997), but the proposed settlement systems are plainly speculative (e.g., McGahey 1987; Morse 1971, 1973, 1975, 1977; Schiffer 1975a, 1975b). The distinctiveness of some early lithic types (e.g., Clovis and Dalton), however, does afford an opportunity to look at distributions with respect to the environment (Figures 7.10, 7.11). Other variants of early lithic types are too few to make meaningful comparisons across space. Not unexpectedly, the dominant feature that determines the distribution of Clovis and Dalton is the exposure of surfaces old enough to contain these elements. In the case of Dalton (Figure 7.11), however, it appears that, unlike the earlier Clovis occupation, these elements are largely restricted to only the western side of the Mississippi (802 west-side instances versus 55 east-side instances). Given the change from the previous Clovis distributions, which are more or less evenly associated with old surfaces regardless of the side of the Mississippi, this pattern may indicate the emergence of stylistic differences due to differential population interaction across the valley from east to west. Alternatively, this pattern may mean that Dalton "points" had little role to play in the eastern valley economy. On a smaller scale, this pattern is repeated. McGahey (1996; cf. Connaway 1988:43–69) notes that within the Yazoo Basin, the eastern side of the basin has substantially fewer Dalton points (N=10) recorded than the western surface (N=45). Additional studies about potential functional difference, detailed analyses with

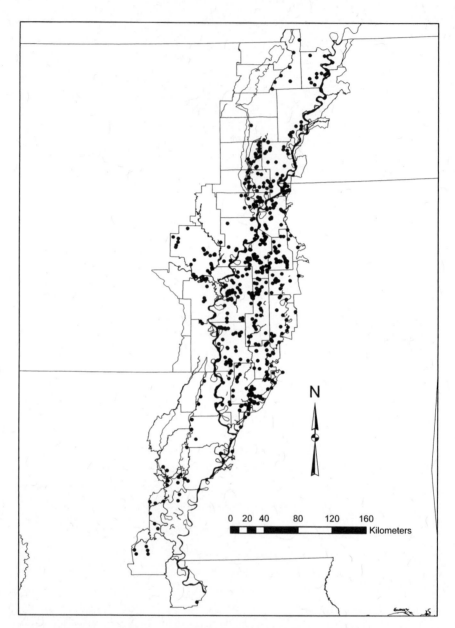

Figure 7.9. All 1,345 recorded locations in the Mississippi River valley study area.

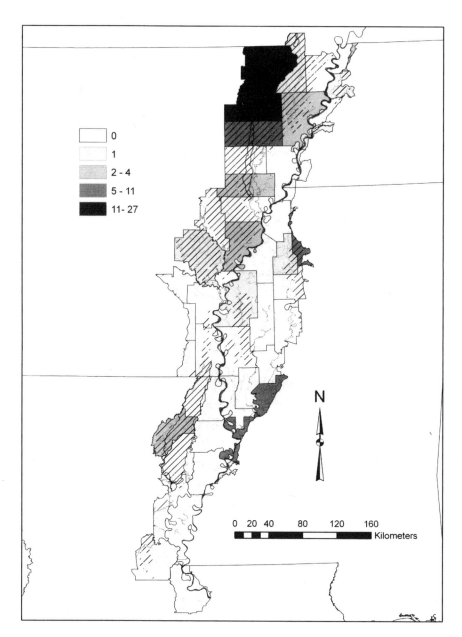

Figure 7.10. Counts of Clovis lithics by county in the survey area.

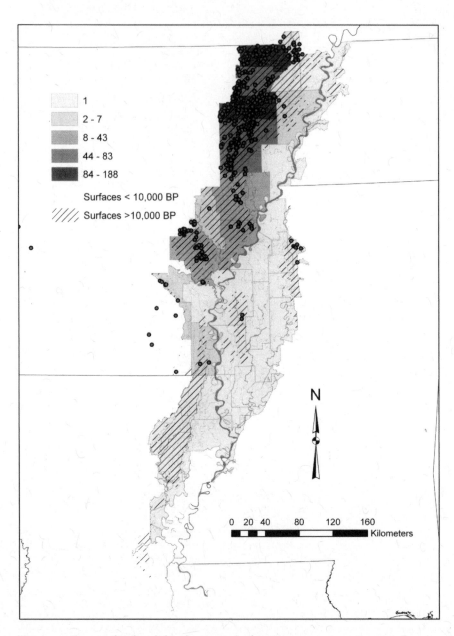

Figure 7.11. Counts of Dalton lithics by county in the survey area.

larger, representative samples, as well as identification of other, contemporaneous stylistic lithic types are required to evaluate this explanation further.

The Early and Middle Archaic is even more poorly known than the earliest occupation of the valley. Although there are hints of regional diversification of style among bifaces in the valley (McGahey 1996:362), Archaic lithics have not generated the same level of interest among archaeologists as have Paleoindian remains (e.g., there are no point censuses). Consequently, point typologies are more ambiguous and their application more haphazard, in spite of persistent attempts to correct the problems (e.g., McGahey 2000; Whatley 2002; Williams and Brain 1983:221–239). As a result, point distributions cannot be consistently compared across the valley for these periods.

It is during the Archaic, however, that we have the beginning of functional differentiation among nodes, where not all locations contain equivalent kinds of materials (Alvey 2005; Brain 1970). It is at this point, for example, that earthworks (mounds) begin to appear (Figure 7.12; Saunders et al. 1994; Saunders et al. 2005). The structure of these settlements appears to take two forms: mapped-on and semicircular. Both of these forms appear in much larger numbers later in the region. The small numbers early on may simply reflect population size, formation processes, cultural factors, or combinations of all three; but, lacking a representative sample, these alternatives cannot be differentiated at present.

Beginning in the Late Archaic, we begin to see a wide array of settlement forms with greater degrees of differentiation (Figure 7.13; Byrd 1991; Fogelman 1991; Ford et al. 1955; Gibson 1973; Jackson 1986; Kidder 1996b; Lehmann 1991; Ramenofsky 1991; Usner 1983; Webb 1991). These forms include circular, semicircular, linear, and irregular arrangements. It is at this point, however, where our poor understanding of what "sites" represent in terms of composition and chronology overwhelms our ability to tease out useful comparative information. For example, Lilbourn (Chapman 1977) and Lake George (Williams and Brain 1983), both settlements with a rectangular form, are thought to have Archaic components due to the presence of clay balls (i.e., Poverty Point objects). There are two problems with these assertions. First, we have no evidence to relate the final form of the settlement to occupation at that time. Second, the presence of clay balls is no guarantee of chronology, since clay balls are functional rather than purely stylistic types (*sensu* Dunnell 1978; see also Pierce 1998).

We also have to question whether Archaic deposits are systematically underrepresented in analyses. For example, Phillips' assignment of Tchula Lake, a circular shell midden in the Yazoo Basin, as a Late Woodland settlement confuses the last episode of occupation with the occupation responsible for the form and shape of the deposit (Dunnell et al. 2002). Other deposits (e.g., Palu-

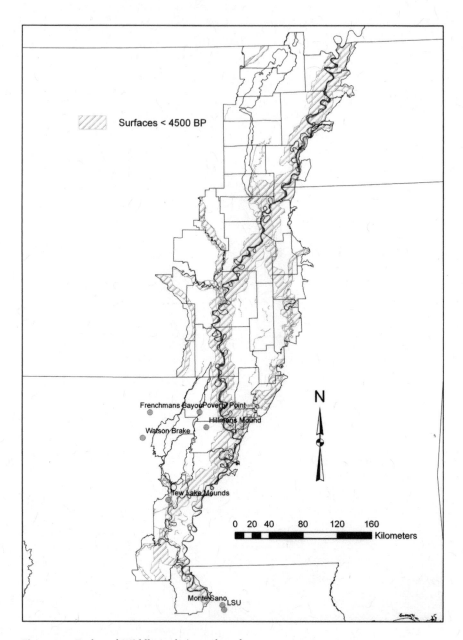

Figure 7.12. Early and Middle Archaic earthworks.

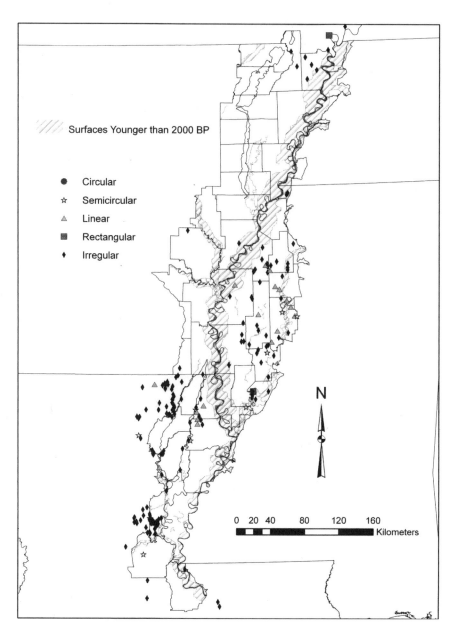

Figure 7.13 Distribution of Late Archaic settlement forms.

sha Creek, Barry, Shellwood) may well suffer from the same kinds of problems of chronology. Far better understanding of site-formation processes and chronology is required to sort out this problem. In addition, we must consider what kinds of deposits we may be systematically missing, especially in these earliest periods: how many Archaic shell middens are missing from existing records due to lack of systematic observation? Indeed, even our cursory examination of the valley using online aerial photographs turned up several middens (e.g., Figure 7.3).

Consequently, at this point we can only conduct a study of settlement structure without taking into consideration the chronological history of deposits. We simply have no way of making meaningful comparisons that consider chronology in addition to structural variability. We can, for example, examine the distribution of particular classes of settlements such as shell middens. From Figure 7.14, it is clear that the distribution of shell middens in the valley is primarily in the eastern margins of the Yazoo Basin, and here we find irregular, linear, circular, and semicircular forms. These circular/semicircular forms are unique to this area of the valley and, lacking defensive perimeters, are likely indicative of group organization and the minimization of internal distances.

We have only a single example in the northern part of the study area (i.e., Grey Horse Lake [Dunnell 1986c]) of a deep midden that is mapped on to a high point on the landscape. Based on Dunnell's own research, such arrangements seem to be typical for the Late Woodland in southeast Missouri and northeast Arkansas during the Barnes phase, when every high spot in the poorly drained terrain is occupied. Larger linear features, principally levees, thus give rise to linear settlements (Dunnell and Feathers 1991; Morse and Morse 1983). In southeast Missouri, over time, the smallest occupied areas were abandoned in favor of denser occupation of the larger contiguous features (Dunnell and Feathers 1991) in the latest phase of the Late Woodland (Barnes phase) and earliest Mississippian (Big Lake phase).

In addition to chronological limitations, inter-settlement relationships are not accessible from the existing database, nor can the relations between settlement and environmental parameters be addressed save in a nominal way. We are limited to studying the distributions of form only at the scale of the valley as a whole. One examination we can make is the distribution of overall settlement form when it takes regular (i.e., non–environmentally determined) shapes. As shown in Figure 7.15, rectangular settlements are largely restricted to the northern parts of the valley, while there are only a couple of instances in the south. Rectangular forms are usually present with defensive structures but are strongly related to internal social interaction (see above). Thus, clustering of these forms along the St. Francis is consistent with an explanation

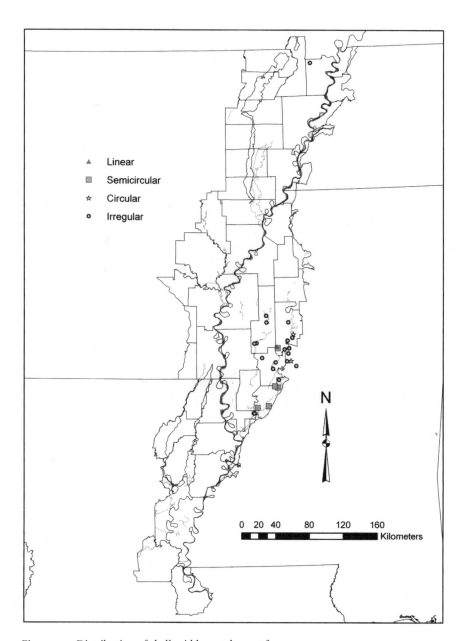

Figure 7.14. Distribution of shell midden settlement forms.

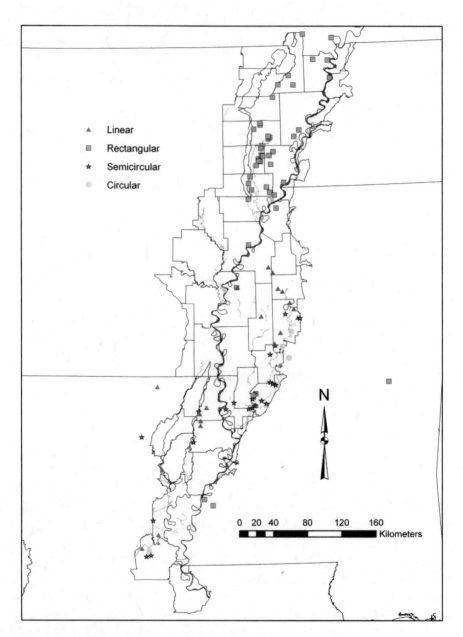

Figure 7.15. Distribution of overall settlement forms.

of a dense, highly interactive, and competitive set of populations (Lipo 2001a; Morse and Morse 1983). In the southern parts of the valley we find linear as well as circular and semicircular forms.

An examination of earthworks (i.e., ditches and earthen embankments) shows patterns similar to that of the overall settlement shape (Figure 7.16). Earthworks in the northern parts of the valley are dominated by rectangular-shaped ditches and embankments. One point of interest here is that these earthworks appear in the northern extent of the rectangular-form settlements seen in Figure 7.15. This pattern might suggest that only in the northernmost parts of the study area is the rectangular form largely related to defense. In the St. Francis area, the rectangular forms may be better explained as the result of social interaction than the hardening of perimeters. As in the overall settlement form, the earthworks of the southern reaches of the study area are primarily semicircular, with one "intruder" (i.e., Lake George [Williams and Brain 1983]).

Although the Mississippi River valley boasts the greatest density of earthen mounds in North America, and these data potentially provide an extraordinary data set for studying settlement variability, they are one of the most problematic of artifact classes with which to make comparisons. As others have noted (e.g., Stout 1991), the label "mounds" has been haphazardly applied to many kinds of features that form a rise in the land surface, including sand blows, levee remnants, clay plugs, middens, house remains, and earthen constructions. Consequently, the data on mounds, particularly the smallest classes, are notoriously unreliable, and only nominal analyses can be conducted. We can, for example, examine the distribution of the numbers of mounds recorded at individual locations (Figure 7.17). This provides a rough overall measure of mound density across the valley. Given inconsistent definition and identification of mounds, however, this information may be telling us more about the process of observation than about archaeological differences.

Figure 7.18 shows the ratio of mound height to estimated base area. This measure provides a means of examining the relative sizes of mounds through the study area. In general the largest mounds are located in the southern end of the Yazoo Basin. Of course, one problem with estimating mound height and basal area is the effects of post-depositional land-leveling and farming. Many mounds were likely much larger in prehistory, and what we see now reflects the actions of European farmers more than archaeologically meaningful variability.

Finally, we can examine the distribution of two relatively distinctive mound forms: conicals and flattops. Although plowing may dramatically alter the shape of mounds, the relative difference between these two forms is usually well maintained. Flattop mounds are low and wide. Conicals tend to be high

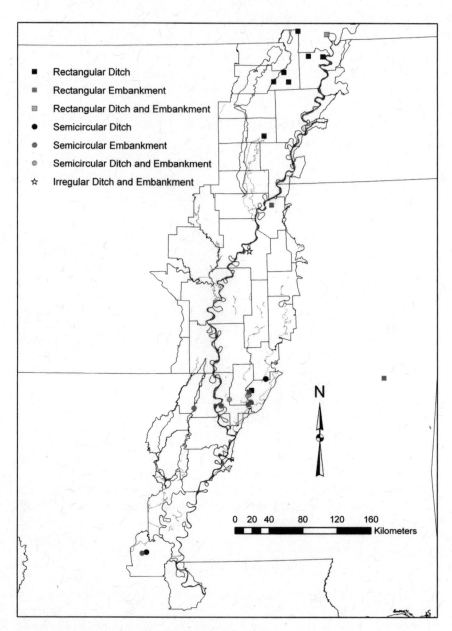

Figure 7.16. Distribution of earthworks forms.

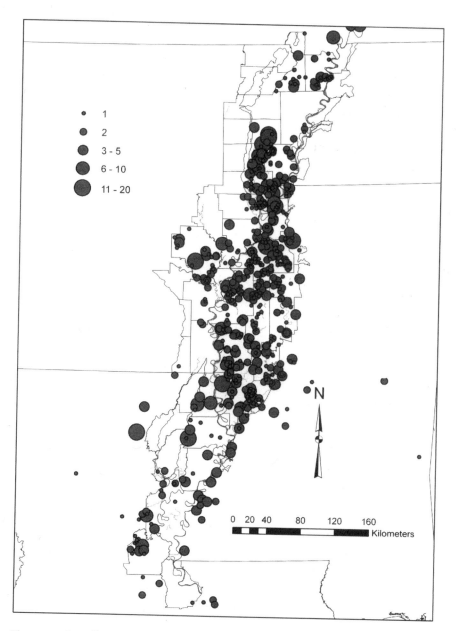

Figure 7.17. Overall numbers of mounds in the study area per location.

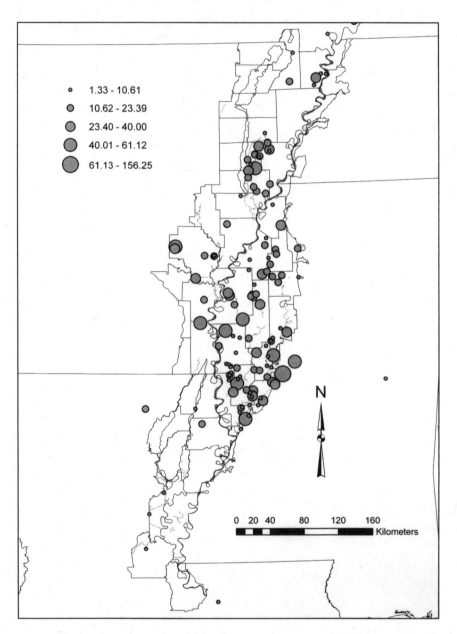

Figure 7.18. Distribution of mound sizes as measured by the ratio of height to basal area.

relative to their bases. The steepness of these mounds usually means that they are either avoided by farmers or knocked down completely. Thus, their presence in the data set is largely secure, though we may be missing many in our observations. Figure 7.19 shows the distribution of conicals and flattops in the study area. There is a marked gradient in the ratio between flattops and conicals as one travels from south to north in the valley. By and large, the northern area is dominated by flattops, while conicals are more common in the south.

The difference here might be explained by the different functions that the mounds served in the regions of the valley. In the north, mounds may be architecturally related to organization and served as the basis of structures. This is consistent with the rectangular and fortified settlements indicative of social interaction and, in the case of the farthest northern areas, defense. In the south, on the other hand, mounds may have been more commonly part of dispersed settlements, with seasonal activities taking place in empty mound centers. Obviously, these are critical questions to answer, as they speak directly to the reason we are interested in settlement patterns in the first place: understanding the stylistic and functional structure of the archaeological record. Until we generate more reliable, comprehensive, and theoretically meaningful data sets that can speak to chronology of deposition as well as to the functional and stylistic classes of artifacts, however, we are limited to these constrained and speculative examinations.

Conclusions

The situation in which we currently find ourselves in the study of prehistoric settlement patterns strongly echoes the realization that Saucier came to in his 1994 summary of Mississippi River valley geology and geomorphology. Following the publication of Fisk's monumental delineation of the history of meander belts across the span of the Mississippi valley in 1944, it was naturally assumed by many that our current knowledge would be only that much more improved at a point 50 years later. Instead, Saucier (1994:250–253) laments:

it is feared that many readers will be strongly disappointed that so little can be stated with certainty about the chronology of Holocene Mississippi River meander belts. After the detailed reconstructions of meander belt and abandoned channel ages by Fisk (1944), it is difficult if not even embarrassing for geologists to admit that during the past 50 years, we have taken *apparent* major steps backward rather than forward. The logical high expectations for even greater advances and more detail as a result of 50 years of more work cannot be met.

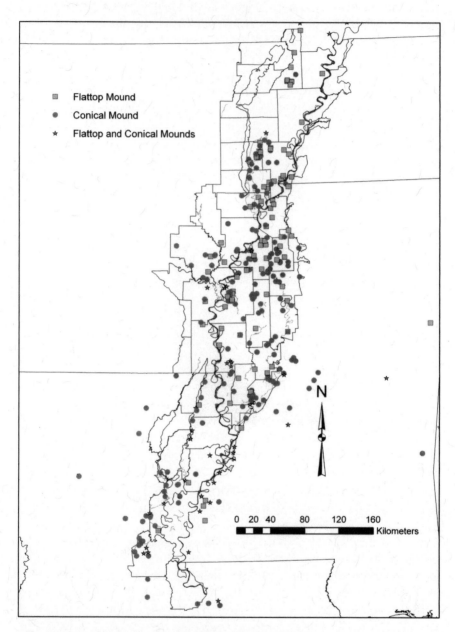

Figure 7.19. Distribution of conical and flattop earthen mounds.

In many ways, our current status is much the same as that confronting Saucier in his summary. Given the early interest in the prehistory of the region (e.g., Brown 1992 [1926]; Bushnell 1919; Holmes 1886b; Moore 1910), the quality of work that was conducted by the Lower Mississippi Valley Survey project in the 1930s and 1940s (e.g., Ford 1936; Phillips et al. 2003 [1951]; see Dunnell 1985; Lipo 2001a; O'Brien 1995 for further discussion), and the subsequent regional-scale work conducted by researchers (e.g., House 1991; Morse 1981; Phillips 1970; Webb 1982) and through cultural resource-management projects (e.g., Buchner et al. 1996; Chapman et al. 1995c; Connaway and McGahey 1970; see also Dunnell, Chapter 3, this volume), one might express the same disappointment that we do not have a better understanding of the basic structure of the archaeological record than we currently do. There is certainly warrant for such sentiment. Given the ad hoc nature of description and the inconsistent use of the term "site," what we know is vastly less than what we do not know.

The situation in which we find ourselves also mirrors Saucier's (1994) conclusions in another way. What we know about the prehistory of the Mississippi River valley is largely a product of increases in our understanding of site-formation processes and the nature of archaeological description. Saucier (1994:253) remarks:

> the interpretations presented below, which may ultimately prove to be no more correct than those of Fisk, do involve factors that were not previously considered. For example, 50 years ago, the chronological reconstructions were influenced by a knowledge of meander belt processes (such as cutoff formation) but not by why, when and where whole meander belts formed. While meander belt relationships are equivocal, thought *has* been given for the first time to the probable influences of preexisting topography and local drainage. Readers are cautioned that the reconstructions are also heavily biased by untested concepts of this writer as to why certain meander belts are apparently less than full-flow channels.

Saucier's comments are remarkably analogous to our current knowledge of the archaeological record of the Mississippi River valley. One could simply replace the subject "meander belts" with "archaeological deposits" and the author "Fisk" with "Phillips, Ford, and Griffin (2003 [1951])" and the result would closely resemble the current situation in archaeology. Given the amount of work that has taken place in the valley over the last 100 years, it would be easy to think we really understand something about the prehistory. As it turns out, the more we probe, the less we find we actually know. Ultimately, it is likely that some of our beliefs will hold up to future scrutiny, especially observations related to units of deposition, classes of pointed bifaces, and earthworks. Much of what we think we know may not hold up due to the lack of theoretically informed observation, the nonsystematic nature of studies, and inconsistent descriptions.

Despite this conclusion, however, we can acknowledge that the extent to which we know something about the archaeological record is a product of an emerging explanatory basis that allows us to frame observations of deposition and landscapes in terms of formation processes. As Saucier points out in his comments, the positive message in this analysis is that we are beginning to generate explanations of processes by which the record is formed. This understanding is the foundation upon which we must build future work and generate new observations of the record. Consistent descriptions about the deposits of the Mississippi River valley will allow us to generate representative and statistically meaningful samples. We need to know about areas where we currently have *no* data: are gaps in our knowledge due to the absence of prehistoric occupation, ages of depositional surfaces, or the lack of observation? We need consistent information about the internal structure and composition of deposits. We need better, high-precision chronological information about land surfaces and depositional units in order to determine the history of occupation for the archaeological record. We also require knowledge about the distribution of small artifact classes that provide functional information.

This information is certainly *possible* to generate. We have developed increasingly better models for comparing chronological variability and have the means for directly determining chronology of depositional events (Lipo et al. 2005; see also Feathers, this volume). With the availability of high-resolution aerial and satellite images and near-surface remote sensing techniques (Lipo et al. 2004; see also Johnson, this volume), we are able to study the record on larger scales and with greater precision than ever before. In this sense, the future of archaeology in the Mississippi River valley is more exciting than ever.

Primary documentation of prehistoric settlement patterns in the Mississippi valley is urgently needed. Since the nineteenth century, the deposits of the region have been mined for ceramic vessels (Beckwith 1887; Croswell 1878; Evers 1880; Foster 1864; Potter 1880; Putnam 1875a, 1875b; Rust 1877). This destruction has continued unabated. Despite the enactment of laws in the 1970s to prohibit looting, urban expansion and twentieth-century farming efforts have had a dramatic impact on the integrity of deposits in the Mississippi valley (Medford 1972; O'Brien and Wood 1998:229; J. Williams 1967:1, 1968, 1972). McGimsey and Davis (1968) estimate that by the 1960s, 25 percent of the archaeological deposits in the Arkansas portion of the valley had been destroyed due to land-leveling. Changes in agricultural practice, particularly with growth of rice production (requiring land to be bulldozed and leveled), continue to threaten the sites of the region. As Phillips (1970:974) has argued, "if, as I believe, putting the data of archaeology into a framework of historical reality is prerequisite to the formulation of 'general truths,' we in the Southeast are faced by the . . . danger that all the sites will have disappeared before that primary task has been achieved." Given the spectacular nature of the archaeological record in the Mississippi River valley and the degree to which our knowledge is incomplete, it is vital to develop primary information about these deposits. We must capitalize on our opportunities and act quickly.

Notes

1. In fields that produce empirical products, such issues never arise. One could not object to the use of steel in bridge construction because of its cost as compared to cardboard, or the difficulties of construction as compared with papier-mâché, because those bridges would not function, i.e., they would be worthless, rendering the savings envisioned in such considerations ridiculous. In archaeology, the lack of theoretical consensus makes such judgments impossible, and so students and professionals alike feel perfectly free to claim too little time, money, or other resources as a legitimate reason for action (or more usually inaction). Taking a formation-process stance within a conservation-rationalized context does, however, allow decisions to be made that minimize the impact of decision making on the use to which the subsequent record may be put.

2. Sadly, while the poor quality of archaeological data for the Mississippi valley is well known among field workers, the fact does little to prevent researchers from making empirical claims that suppose otherwise (e.g., Brain 1978a; Marshall 1987; Smith 1978; Webb 1970; Weinstein 1981a).

3. Complex objects may have more than one function that plays a role in the life history of an object and that results in the generation of functional attributes, either serially or simultaneously. In addition, the time of manufacture(s) may differ substantially from the time of deposition and must be identified to avoid systematic error. The location of an object pertains, of course, only to time of deposition and its last function. Thus, a Dalton point reworked to a drill had locational information relevant only to the drill's function and so might be found on a surface much younger than the age associated with the "Daltonness" of the object. Again, resolving these issues is usually easily done, but in this venue must be left unexplored.

8
Absolute Dating in the Mississippi Delta

James K. Feathers

Construction of chronology in the Mississippi Delta has relied primarily on stratigraphy and ceramic cross-dating. Seriation was employed early on (Phillips et al. 2003 [1951]), but once the basic sequence was worked out, the chronology was broken into a series of groupings called phases, extensionally defined by a diagnostic set of ceramics (Phillips 1970, Williams and Brain 1983). Radiocarbon dating and, rarely, some other ratio-scale chronometric methods, have been employed to complement phase construction, by anchoring the sequence in real time.

This chapter reviews the use of chronometric methods, particularly radiocarbon, in the Mississippi Delta. It evaluates radiocarbon from two perspectives, the limitations of the method itself and the framework in which radiocarbon dates have been interpreted. I make the argument that some temporal problems can be better addressed by other chronometric methods, particularly luminescence dating, and that archaeological research designs need to incorporate better the full range of methods available. While critical of radiocarbon, I do not dispute the important contributions it has made and will continue to make. It has been particularly useful at sites where a large suite of radiocarbon dates has identified clear temporal patterns, a good example being Poverty Point, where dozens of dates have constrained the time of the main occupation (Gibson 1987a, 1987b, 1994a). Radiocarbon has important strengths, not the least of which is high precision at relatively low analytical costs, and there is no doubt that radiocarbon in the foreseeable future will and should continue as the most widely used chronometric dating method in Southeast archaeology. The problem is that radiocarbon has been used to the near-exclusion of other methods, often uncritically, and even where other methods are more appropriate. Early applications of luminescence dating (to clay balls at Poverty Point [Huxtable et al. 1972]), for example, were never followed up by further work until very recently.

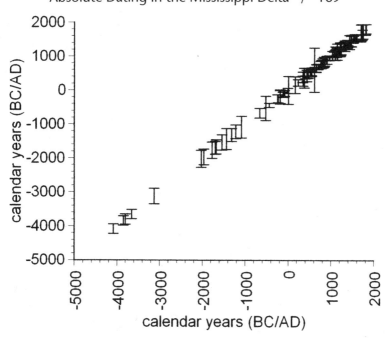

Figure 8.1. Radiocarbon dates from the Mississippi Delta.

Radiocarbon Dating and Its Limitations

Figure 8.1 shows all radiocarbon dates reported for the Mississippi Delta as tabulated by Sims and Connaway (2000). The dates are shown as one-sigma calibrated ranges, plotted against range midpoint. Not surprisingly, most of the dates fall in the post-A.D. 0 period. Except for a flurry of dates around the Poverty Point period (1200–2000 B.C.), the Archaic and Early Woodland are poorly represented and their detailed chronology poorly known. Four first-millennium B.C. dates from Jaketown (22HU500) were processed in the 1950s, when modern pretreatment procedures were not available, and have since been shown to be underestimates (Saunders and Allen 2003). Moving those four dates back into the Poverty Point period, one finds almost no dates immediately before or after Poverty Point. Exceptions are a few earlier dates at Teoc Creek (22CR504), which, however, is also dated to the Poverty Point period by thermoluminescence (TL) of clay balls (Connaway et al. 1977). The prelude and aftermath of Poverty Point is not well documented to begin with, and its regional manifestation not well defined. Having little chronological data either before or after makes Poverty Point all the more difficult to understand.

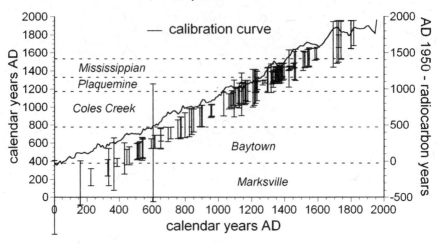

Figure 8.2. Post-0 A.D. radiocarbon dates from the Mississippi Delta (Sims and Connaway 2000), plotted as one-sigma calibrated ranges against the midpoint of the range.

Figure 8.2 shows only the post-A.D. 0 dates. The vertical scale is divided into generalized Lower Mississippi Valley (LMV) phases (after Williams and Brain 1983). Like the Archaic and Early Woodland, the Marksville period is poorly represented (Jackson 1998). Radiocarbon chronology for the Mississippi Delta is therefore mainly a post-Marksville affair. But how well is even this post-A.D. 400 period known chronologically? Superimposed over the dates is the radiocarbon calibration curve (Stuiver et al. 1998). For many time spans, A.D. 800–1000, A.D. 1100–1200, A.D. 1300–1400, A.D. 1500–1600 and A.D. 1700–1800, the curve is relatively flat, meaning that the precision of calendar dates drawn from radiocarbon determinations is typically 200 to 400 years, making fine-scale resolution difficult (e.g., Johnson et al. 2000). It is no surprise that the highest-precision dates fall where the curve is the steepest. For comparison, the one-sigma analytical precision of luminescence dates generated recently by the University of Washington (UW) laboratory for the LMV averages 11.2 ± 3.4 percent, which translates to a one-sigma range of 100–200 years, for a date of A.D. 1300.

For the later prehistoric period, both Phillips (1970) and Williams and Brain (1983) admitted that spatial and temporal differences among occupations were difficult to distinguish, a condition that still appears to hold (Mainfort 1996). While stratigraphy has helped understand the sequence in particular places, one must remember that at the scale of the Yazoo drainage, stratigraphic relations are strictly a local matter, and what may be sequential in one place may be contemporary in another. While multiple dates can increase precision, only seven sites have more than five dates, and these tend to have such a wide range

Table 8.1. Calibrated radiocarbon data from Yazoo Basin sites.

Site	# ^{14}C dates	1-σ age range
Rock Levee	8	3352 B.C.–A.D. 1297
Teoc Creek	9	2277 B.C.–1013 B.C.
Manny	11	887 B.C.–A.D. 1460
Batesville Mounds	7	381 B.C.–A.D. 685
Lake George	13	A.D. 263–A.D. 1656
McNight	11	A.D. 361–A.D. 1439
Hollywood	7	A.D. 1282–A.D. 1656

that averaging, which requires estimated dates of the same or closely related events, is not feasible (Table 8.1). These sites represent very broad occupation spans.

The calibration problems of radiocarbon are well known, and so is a second limitation of radiocarbon dating, although little has been done to overcome it. The cultural evolution of the Mississippi Delta has largely been framed in terms of changes in ceramics, but radiocarbon, except in rare circumstances, does not date ceramics. It dates the isolation of carbon from the global carbon cycle, usually the death of some organism. Bridging arguments are required to link radiocarbon dates to ceramics, arguments that usually rely on unproven associations based on spatial proximity. While such arguments can have some justification at sites that represent single, short-lived occupations, problems occur when they are applied to more complicated assemblages, even when different occupations can be recognized. Events that brought things together are not always the same events responsible for the manufacture or cultural affiliation of those things (Johnson et al. 2002).

A case in point is the Late Woodland–period Deasonville phase, a unit remarked by Phillips (1970) to be one of the best defined and best known in the Delta. He particularly underscored the apparent association of Deasonville-aged ceramics with shell middens, a rather remarkable circumstance given that use of shell does not appear nearly so important either immediately before or after Deasonville. As a prime example of a single-component Deasonville site, he highlighted Tchula Lake, in the upper-Yazoo drainage, based on collections he made in the 1950s. Robert Dunnell returned to the site in 2000 and noticed that the ceramics seemed to represent a greater time-span than Deasonville. He found Marksville and even earlier diagnostics. Why these ceramics were not recognized by Phillips will not be explored here, but the possibility that the ceramics are not all the same age calls into question the affiliation of the shells. Our laboratory employed luminescence to date several of the ceramics and

Table 8.2. Luminescence dates on pottery and calibrated radiocarbon dates on shells and human bone from Tchula Lake and Belzoni Cemetery sites, western Mississippi, in relation to age range of the Deasonville phase (Williams and Brain 1983). Errors are one-sigma.

Radiocarbon dates (calibrated 1σ range, years B.C./ A.D.)		Luminescence dates on pottery (years B.C./A.D.)	
Tchula Lake			
material	*date*	*Traditional type*	*date*
Shell-*Quadrula*	B.C. 590–900	Baytown Plain	B.C. 140 ± 278
Shell-*Fusconaia*	B.C. 820–920	Cormorant Cord-impressed	B.C. 41 ± 261
Shell-*Pleurobema*	B.C. 860–1010	Tchefuncte (?)	A.D. 227 ± 277
Shell-*Amblema*	B.C. 830–1050	Baytown Plain	A.D. 549 ± 204
Shell-*Pleurobema*	B.C. 900–1050	Baytown Plain	A.D. 645 ± 121
Shell-*Fusconaia*	B.C. 970–1190	Baytown Plain	A.D. 745 ± 104
Shell-*Amblema*	B.C. 930–1260	Baytown Plain	A.D. 780 ± 254
Shell-*Fusconaia*	B.C.1000–1220	Baytown Plain	A.D. 1084 ± 106
Shell-*Quadrula*	B.C.1050–1310		
Shell-*Pleurobema*	B.C.1120–1370		
Shell-*Quadrula*	B.C.1210–1400		
Belzoni Cemetery			
Human bone	A.D. 680–810		
Shell-*Amblema*	B.C. 940–1130		
Bold dates consistent with Deasonville Phase (A.D. 350-650)			

arranged for radiocarbon dating of the shells. Because of concern for freshwater reservoir effects on the carbon dates, we dated four different genera of shells with different eating habits (*Quadrula, Fusconaia, Pleurobema,* and *Amblema*) and have noted that no limestone bedrock is present in the drainage. The results are given in Table 8.2. Not only do the ceramics range from Early Woodland to Coles Creek, but the shells are Archaic in age. We also arranged radiocarbon dating of one shell and some human skeleton remains at another shell-midden site, Belzoni Cemetery, in an adjacent county. This site at one time contained a couple of mounds, which Phillips (1970) interpreted as Mississippian in age, but he deduced from the ceramics that the shell midden was Deasonville. The radiocarbon dates show that the shell is the same age as those at Tchula Lake, while only the human remains are Deasonville in age.

To my knowledge, no one has ever attempted dating the shell at Deasonville sites before, all previous Deasonville dates being on charcoal or sometimes human bone. More shell needs to be dated, because at present there is no evidence that the shell middens are Deasonville in age anywhere. The distinct possibility remains that they represent a pervasive Archaic component previously unappreciated, although no known Archaic-aged diagnostic artifacts have been reported from these sites. The mixing of artifacts and shells of different ages has probably occurred because the middens, representing high ground in a swampy environment, provided a favorable location for subsequent occupations. Possible reservoir effects need to be explored further before the Archaic affiliation can be fully accepted. Locating modern shellfish in similar waters would be useful in this regard, although many species have been driven to extinction by overharvesting, increased sedimentation, and other changes to waterways, and pesticide runoff from agricultural practices (the U.S. Fish and Wildlife Service estimates that 70 percent of American freshwater mussels are extinct or endangered). So what about Deasonville? Something like Deasonville—small occupations with little artistic embellishment and dating to the Late Woodland—is probably present in the record, but it is, so far, neither well defined nor well known.

Other Benefits of Luminescence Dating

Small occupations in general have not received much attention from radiocarbon dating, probably because most appear as surface scatters with no associated carbon. Their lack of diagnostic ceramics, or the possibility that the ceramics differ from those at mound sites (Hunter et al. 1995), also means their age remains largely unknown. Of the 150 radiocarbon dates reported by Sims and Connaway (2000), at least 124 are from sites with mounds or large villages. Only 16 are from smaller sites without mounds. I could not determine from the information I had available the kind of site represented by the other 10 (from six sites). Small sites are underrepresented, yet they must be important for understanding population dispersal and land-use patterns, which are key considerations for understanding cultural development, particularly of the large multi-mound complexes characteristic of later times.

The UW laboratory has begun a program of dating small sites using luminescence of ceramics in other parts of the LMV. I present two examples of issues that can be addressed. In the St. Francis drainage, west of the Delta, the late prehistoric period (A.D. 1300–1500) is marked by the presence of large planned settlements, often with mounds. Surrounding these sites are numerous small sites, sometimes called "farmsteads," whose chronological relationship with the large sites is not known. Most of these small sites contain no diagnostic pottery, but the conventional wisdom is that they date earlier than the large sites, which therefore represent a population aggregation as the farm-

Table 8.3. Luminescence dates of various samples from the Parkin site and from one outlier, 3CS264, eastern Arkansas. Errors are one-sigma.

Material or type	Luminescence date (years A.D.)
Parkin	
Mississippi Plain	A.D. 954 ± 291
Burned floor	A.D. 1342 ± 140
Clay object	A.D. 1448 ± 35
Bowl – Bell Plain?	A.D. 1460 ± 90
Bowl – Bell Plain?	A.D. 1472 ± 44
Bell Plain	A.D. 1510 ± 57
Daub	A.D. 1611 ± 33
Parkin Punctated	A.D. 1704 ± 62
3CS264	
Mississippi Plain	A.D. 898 ± 106
Baytown Plain	A.D. 969 ± 166
Varney Red?	A.D. 1087 ± 103

steads were abandoned, perhaps for defensive reasons (Morse 1990). Our laboratory tested this hypothesis in two locations. Table 8.3 gives luminescence dates from the large site of Parkin and one of its small outliers, 3CS264. This one outlier indeed dates earlier than Parkin. Farther downsteam is a late prehistoric manifestation known as the Kent Phase. Table 8.4 gives luminescence and C-14 dates from three farmsteads and two large settlements, Kent and Clay Hill, as well as a luminescence and a C-14 date from the latest use of Mound Cemetery, an isolated mound with no associated domestic debris. The farmsteads do date earlier, and some may be coeval with Mound Cemetery, which apparently was abandoned shortly before occupation of the large sites. Both these examples support the conventional wisdom of population aggregation at the later large centers, but obviously many more dates will have to be obtained before the chronological relationship between large and small sites can be clarified.

The nature of settlement systems and how they changed is also an issue during the Mississippian period in southeast Missouri. A long-debated hypothesis here and elsewhere is whether the region was abandoned sometime around A.D. 1400–1450, resulting in a so-called "vacant quarter" (Williams 1990), or whether later settlement is just not as visible in the record. Particularly puzzling is the presence of pottery types that are diagnostic for later periods further south. Are these just early appearances of these types in Missouri, or do

Table 8.4. Luminescence and calibrated radiocarbon dates from various sites in the Lower St. Francis drainage of eastern Arkansas. Errors are one-sigma.

Radiocarbon dates (calibrated years A.D.)		Luminescence dates (years A.D.)		
site	1-sigma range	site	material	date
		Fortified Village Middens		
Kent	1289–1435	Kent	Shell-tempered pottery	1516 ± 55
	1472–1666			
Clay Hill	1647–1953			
	1515–1955			
	1448–1621			
		Vacant Mound Center		
Mound Cemetery	1309–1409	Mound Cemetery	Grog/shell-tempered pottery	1403 ± 43
		"farmsteads"		
Brickeys Prison	1164–1276	North Alligator Bayou 3	daub	1415 ± 54
		North Alligator Bayou 4	Grog/shell-tempered pottery	1394 ± 54
		Troublesome Lake B	Grog/shell-tempered pottery	1378 ± 76
		Troublesome Lake B	Grog/shell-tempered pottery	1266 ± 78
		North Alligator Bayou 3	Bell Plain	1252 ± 70
		North Alligator Bayou 5	Grog/shell-tempered pottery	1170 ± 92
		North Alligator Bayou 10	Grog/shell-tempered pottery	1154 ± 94
		North Alligator Bayou 8	Grog/shell-tempered pottery	1075 ± 81

Radiocarbon dates provided by John House, Arkansas Archeological Survey

Table 8.5. Luminescence dates for coarse shell-tempered pottery (Mississippi Plain) and various fine shell-tempered pottery from the Rich Woods site, southeastern Missouri. Errors are one-sigma.

Ceramic Type	Luminescence date (years A.D.)
Old Town Red	1452 ± 57
Mississippi Plain	1439 ± 79
Old Town Red	1399 ± 42
Mississippi Plain	1396 ± 87
Bell Plain	1376 ± 83
Bell Plain	1375 ± 87
Bell Plain	1332 ± 59
Bell Plain	1326 ± 49
Carson Red-on-Buff	1326 ± 72
Bell Plain	1322 ± 73
Carson Red-on-Buff	1301 ± 57
Mississippi Plain	1285 ± 59
Nodena Red-and-White	1283 ± 88
Mississippi Plain	1236 ± 90
Mississippi Plain	1227 ± 92

they represent later occupation? Our laboratory has looked at this issue at the Rich Woods site, a large, mainly Middle Mississippian, village that contains some of this pottery (Table 8.5). Strong chronological overlap is apparent between the Mississippian-Plain samples and the fine-tempered diagnostics, and the latter, except one, are consistent with a pre-1400 age. The vacant-quarter hypothesis is not falsified by these data, which support the counter-hypothesis of relatively early dates for the fine-tempered diagnostics.

While radiocarbon has been used more or less successfully to date general occupations at mound sites, construction of individual mounds has proven more difficult to date particularly due to lack of clear association between any charcoal or ceramics within the mound and the building of the mound itself (Gibson 1994a). Saunders and colleagues have carefully studied pedogenesis within mounds and associated organic matter to clarify the radiocarbon dating of several Archaic-aged mounds in northern Louisiana (Saunders and Allen 1994; Saunders et al. 1994; Saunders et al. 1997; Saunders et al. 2001; Saunders et al. 2005) and at Jaketown in the Delta (Saunders and Allen 2003). Beginning as undifferentiated parent material, mound fill begins to develop a soil, first producing an A horizon as organic matter accumulates on the surface, and then a B horizon with the eluviation of clay and other minerals. The

B horizon further develops from a cambric to an argillic horizon as clay continues to translocate, eventually forming a depleted clay layer, called an E horizon, between the A and B (Saunders and Allen 1994). These stages in soil development allow a relative chronology of mounds, and the presence of argillic and E horizons alerted Saunders and Allen to the possibility of Archaic-aged mounds. This hypothesis was confirmed by a series of radiocarbon dates on both charcoal (presumably cultural) and soil humates from several mounds. Charcoal in mounds could be redeposited from earlier midden material, and humates are prone to contamination, but dates in correct stratigraphic order at sites such as Watson Brake minimize either of these possibilities (Saunders et al. 1997).

As a complement to this program, the UW laboratory has demonstrated that luminescence dating also can contribute to dating mounds. Luminescence dating of sediments addresses the last exposure to light, or a burial event. Because turbation processes in soils continually bring grains to the surface, where exposure to daylight occurs, luminescence can date A horizons to their burial (Bush and Feathers 2003). If these soils are preserved below or within mounds, the pile-up of sediments above them (the mound construction) can be dated. Because all grains are not fully exposed, it is necessary to isolate the ones most likely to have been exposed, a procedure possible with single-grain dating and with various statistical methods to identify the youngest grains. Table 8.6 gives results from various mounds in northeastern Louisiana. The procedure has been applied to only one mound in Mississippi, the Deathly Silent Mound on Camp Shelby in southern Mississippi, identifying a mound of uncertain affiliation to the Woodland period. Radiocarbon dating of Middle Woodland–aged mounds in western Tennessee and northern Mississippi is also beginning to clarify the chronological relationship of these mounds with each other and with Marksville and Hopewell, with implications for possibly early Middle Woodland mounds in the Yazoo, such as the Dorr Mound (Mainfort and McNutt 2004). Luminescence dating could complement this work.

Luminescence dating of sediments has other potential uses in the valley as well, particularly in dating the various meander belts and other fluvial forms that have always been important in constraining the dates of archaeological materials appearing on them, as well as in understanding geomorphic settings of occupations. Radiocarbon is used with difficulty to date these sediments, because organic material is sparse or contaminated (see Guccione 1987 for an example of using radiocarbon to date these features), or because the radiocarbon often dates a different event than the depositional event (Dunnell and Readhead 1989). Luminescence, on the other hand, dates either quartz or feldspar, both ubiquitous minerals in these sediments, and dates directly the depositional event. A combination of radiocarbon, luminescence of ceramics, and

Table 8.6. Optically stimulated luminescence (OSL) sediment dates from mound sites in the study area and adjacent areas.

Sample	# aliquots	OSL age (ka)	Expected Age	Reference
Watson Brake Mound B	580 (sg)	0.01±0.007	0	Modern topsoil
Watson Brake Mound C	84 (sa)	4.9±1.5	4.9±0.1	[14]C
Watson Brake Mound K	126 (sg)	4.7±0.5		
Watson Brake Ridge JK	90 (sg)	3.7±0.5		
Poverty Point Ridge 3	33 (sg)	3.4±0.7	3.1	Composite [14]C
Bush Mounds Mound A	298 (sg)	0.9±0.6	<1.1	Ceramics
Bush Mounds Mound C	15 (sg)	4.4±0.6		
Hedgepeth Mounds Mound B	17 (sg)	8.7±0.9		
Deathly Silent Mound	155 (sg)	1.8±0.2		

sg = single grain, sa = single aliquot, multi-grain

luminescence of sediments can sort out complex relationships between geological depositions and site occupations (e.g., Mueller 1981).

As one example, luminescence dating of quartz on a series of braided channel belts in southeastern Missouri produced dates in correct stratigraphic sequence of 19.7–17.8 ka, 16.1–15.0 ka, and 12.5–12.1 ka, suggesting formation during periods of high discharge of glacial meltwater (Rittenour et al. 2003). There was no evidence of partial bleaching of the sediments, despite turbulent currents typical of glacial outwash.

Applications of Other Dating Methods

Mention needs to be made of other available dating methods besides luminescence, which is my own field. Oxidizable carbon ratio (OCR) dating has become popular and controversial in the Southeast. The method is based on the biodegradation of carbon (as charcoal or soil humate) through time, expressed as a ratio between oxidizable carbon (measured by wet oxidation methods) and total carbon (measured by loss on ignition). It has been applied to five sites in the Delta, but not without difficulties in interpretation (e.g., Johnson et al. 2002; McGahey 2002; Walling and Chapman 1999), particularly in terms of agreement with other data. An exchange between Killick et al. and Frink in the SAA Bulletin (Frink 1999; Killick et al. 1999) centered on the scientific validity of the method. Without dwelling on the particulars of that debate, I think two things are worth noting. First, while OCR dates a burning event, rather than a death event, and therefore gets around some radiocarbon problems such as old wood (Frink 1994), it still, when applied to artifacts, has the same problems of association, as does radiocarbon (Johnson et al. 2002). Second, the history of dating techniques based on weathering—particularly the lessons from obsidian hydration dating and amino acid racemization—suggests that models based on chemical changes through time are more complicated than originally put forth, especially if the original formulation is empirically derived as is the case for OCR (Frink 1992). I think the problem with OCR dating is not the lack of science (this was not the problem of early attempts at hydration and racemization either), but lack of development and knowledge that can only come about with additional research into the technique. If the technique is to survive, other laboratories must take it up (Doug Frink so far is carrying the flag on his own), and archaeologists need to adopt a more critical and cautionary approach—advice that applies to any dating method, including radiocarbon and luminescence.

Archaeomagnetic dating has been applied sparingly in the Southeast. Early work by Dubois in the 1970s and Wolfman in the 1980s has recently been supplemented and summarized by Lengyel (2004; Lengyel et al. 1999). A master secular variation curve, based on 365 samples, has now been constructed encompassing most of the prehistoric era, although with the best resolution confined to the most recent period (Lengyel 2004). Fifteen of the samples were collected from Mississippi, although none from the Delta. The curve representing 850–75 B.P. has sufficient data points that new archaeomagnetic samples can be dated against it, although additional points are desired to increase resolution. The 2528–850 B.P. segment has fewer data points, but can be used with caution. No archaeomagnetic data are available for 4650–2528 B.P. period, and the 9755–4650 B.P. segment has poor resolution and should be used for general temporal placement only (Lengyel 2004).

Archaeomagnetic dating addresses a heating event (burning of a hearth or a structure) that is of direct interest to archaeologists. Recent applications include the evaluation of the temporal overlap of structure use at two adjacent mound sites in Southeast Missouri, concluding that the two sites are contemporary, not sequential, in time, and determination of the chronological sequence of features at a single Historic-period site in Tennessee (Lengyel 2004). Similar kinds of applications are particularly promising for Delta archaeology. Archaeomagnetism might also be used for dating consolidated sediments in the Mississippi valley, using depositional remanent magnetism (DRM).

Interpretation of Radiocarbon Dates

While Delta archaeologists should be aware of the limitations of radiocarbon, there is no question, as already mentioned, that it has contributed a great deal in applying real time to the ceramic sequence. But the interpretation of radiocarbon dates has suffered from the periodization fostered by phase construction. The implication of Phillips' (1970) and Williams and Brain's (1983) summation of Delta cultural history is that different blocks of time can be identified by a suite of diagnostic ceramics (or their frequencies) and other artifacts. This approach stresses the similarities within phases and the dissimilarities between them, suppressing contrary variation, and is "colored by a preference for (the) discontinuity" (Phillips 1970:568). Whether the cultural development at any time in the Delta can best be described as continuous or discontinuous should not be presumed by the chronological method used to describe it, yet Phillips' treatment of the radiocarbon dates available to him from the lower valley does precisely this by attempting to square the radiocarbon dates with the phase sequence. He confronts the problem of associating radiocarbon dates with ceramics by rejecting 24 of 85 available dates (and half of those from the Yazoo Basin) because of uncertain association. The 61 dates he does accept provide a generally reasonable order, but did not match, to his satisfaction, the phase sequence as he had developed it based on ceramics. Whether Mississippian phases, in particular, were sequential or contemporary could not be established. The radiocarbon dates, moreover, suggest two alternative time scenarios, neither of which he finds fully acceptable, but the third alternative, that they both might be right, reflecting strong geographic variation, to him is "too horrible to contemplate" (Phillips 1970:961). He acknowledges that, once more dates are available and the radiocarbon method better developed, the picture could change. Even with the last summation in the northern part of the Delta (McNutt 1996), the Woodland chronology remains fuzzy, and how contemporary the various Mississippian phases are remains unclear (e.g., Lumb and McNutt 1988; Mainfort 1996).

It has been appreciated for a long time (Dunnell 1970) that seriation only provides an order, and whether that order is temporal or not is a hypothesis that requires further information. That the LMV seriations contained a spatial component was apparent to Phillips et al. (2003 [1951]), who, because of that, divided the valley into regions. Only recently have methods been developed to detect spatial variation at a smaller scale and to assess statistical error (Lipo et al. 1997; Lipo 2001a). Yet too often radiocarbon dates are questioned because they do not fit into the regional ceramic sequence developed in some nearby area (e.g., Hunter et al. 1995; Johnson et al. 2002; Mainfort 1994; Toth and Brookes 1977; Walling and Chapman 1999). Evaluations of radiocarbon dates often consist of a comparison of the received dates with the expected dates based on the ceramic data. If the comparison is unfavorable, the radiocarbon dates are either rejected outright or dismissed as reflecting bad associations or contamination; rarely, an acknowledgement is made of some geographic variation (Cusick et al. 1995). By this practice, radiocarbon dates are not being used as a test of the ceramic ordering, but rather as a crutch in support of it. If the crutch does not achieve its goals, it is discarded.

While thoughtful evaluations of radiocarbon dates in the Delta are present in terms of discrepancies between the radiocarbon results and other dating information, e.g., Connaway (1977, 1984); Connaway and McGahey (1971); and Johnson et al. (2000, 2002), too often these are inductive in nature. In general, not enough thought during the research design is given to (1) the goals of the dating, (2) how best to achieve those aims, by radiocarbon (of what material) or through other methods, and (3) based on other information, the expectations. This would provide a deductive framework in which the results, including unexpected ones, can be evaluated. It also allows a way to deal with outliers, treating them in terms of probabilities rather than rejecting them outright.

The radiocarbon dating community has already taken the lead in providing statistical modeling, based in Bayesian statistics, for interpreting dating information. These are available in online calibration programs such as Ox-Cal and BCal, which go beyond simple calibration by providing frameworks for integrating dates with other chronological information (Buck et al. 1994). Such modeling not only improves resolution, but also informs on sampling design. Field strategies can be geared to obtain the optimal number and kind of samples to get the best resolution for the problem being addressed within the budget available (Buck and Christen 1998). While archaeologists will continue to rely on chance encounters of datable materials, a more systematic approach to sampling will lend more confidence in the interpretation of dating results and reduce the puzzlement about what a particular date might mean. These modeling programs have also been expanded to include luminescence and other dating methods (e.g., Millard 2006; Rhodes et al. 2003).

If such a systematic strategy is adopted, and as more absolute dates (from radiocarbon, luminescence and other methods) accumulate, the traditional phases, as Dunnell notes elsewhere in this volume, may simply become too cumbersome to be of use. Trying to force dates into preconceived notions should then be replaced by understanding the temporal relationships among the actual data. A much more dynamic understanding of Mississippi Delta cultural evolution might then be achievable.

Acknowledgments

The luminescence dating reported in this chapter was funded by the National Science Foundation and the National Park Service.

9

Bioarchaeology in the Mississippi Delta

S. Homes Hogue

Introduction to Bioarchaeology

Over the past several decades, bioarchaeology has risen to the forefront in understanding and interpreting human behavior from archaeological skeletal series. Introduced in the mid-1970s, bioarchaeology represents an explanatory framework that recognizes the correlation between biological, cultural, and environmental variables (Blakely 1977; Buikstra 1976; Smith 1993). The bioarchaeology paradigm is a consequence of the "New Archaeology" revolution of the 1960s. New approaches to archaeological research were being realized, and the development of methods useful in understanding subsistence strategies, settlement patterns, and ecological adaptations were beginning to replace the traditional culture-history approach dominated by tool typologies and ceramic sequences (Smith 1993). Smith (1993) provides a detailed synopsis of the history of physical anthropology in southeastern archaeology. Several main points from her overview are expanded upon in the following paragraphs.

Prior to the bioarchaeological focus, typological classifications of human populations, like tool typologies and ceramic sequences, were not uncommon among physical anthropologists studying skeletal populations in the southeastern United States. Underlying this typological approach was the premise that human phenotypes and measurements could be reduced to unique types or races resulting from evolutionary selection (Smith 1993). Cranial measurements and shapes were used much like lithic and pottery types to document population movement and stability, culture contact, and miscegenation. The classification of southeastern crania is best exemplified by the work of Georg Neumann (1952, 1959). Neumann's interest in the regional diversity of physical appearances was founded in evolutionary principles. While discussing human antiquity in the New World, he states: "The increase in time-depth allows for a much greater possibility of such factors as genetic drift and selection in the adaptation to different environmental conditions to become operative in the racial differentiation of populations in various geographical areas" (Neumann

1959:66). Using cranial types and associated temporal distinctions, Neumann and others addressed questions related to population migration and culture change. Although Neumann considered cranial variation as a response to environmental and geographical differences, he did not adequately answer how these factors affected cranial shape (Rose and Harmon 1989). Neumann's work (1952) was well publicized in Griffin's edited volume *Archaeology of Eastern United States* (Griffin, ed. 1952), a text likely read by anyone studying southeastern archaeology during the 1950s and '60s. Unfortunately, Neumann's efforts may have led many scholars to conclude that research on human skeletal remains had little to offer the archaeological discipline (Rose and Harmon 1989).

It is noteworthy that biological/physical anthropologists recognized early on that cranial typologies provided little if any help in reconstructing and explaining the past. This acknowledgement may illuminate why a typological research focus was soon abandoned in favor of methods involving more detailed osteological analysis of populations rather than individual skull shapes (Smith 1993). This switch would result in founding an important database useful in addressing future questions posed by bioarchaeologists. In contrast to the much-needed methodological shift by physical/biological anthropologists working with human skeletal collections, many archaeologists continue to use a typological approach to analysis (e.g., Mooney et al. 2004; Toth 1988; Walling and Chapman 1999; Weinstein et al. 1995).

Salvage archaeological projects began to increase in the 1930s, and with this, so did the number of skeletal collections in need of analysis. Although considered to be peripheral to archaeological problem solving, the archaeological projects of the New Deal (WPA, TVA, NPS) produced numerous skeletal collections that ultimately led to the expansion of biological anthropology in the Southeast (Smith 1993). In addition to craniometry, general osteological investigations involving morphological and metrical analyses led to increased accuracy in the determination of age, sex, and stature, with many methods still in use today (Bass 1995; Buikstra and Ubelaker 1994; Krogman 1978; Steinbock 1976; Stewart 1979; Ubelaker 1978). More descriptive information on pathology data also began to be recorded. Unfortunately, the overall descriptive nature of the analyses provided little information in reconstructing the archaeological past, and most skeletal reports were consigned to the appendices (Smith 1993:65). Many of the largest skeletal collections analyzed more recently in the Southeast are described in CRM reports (Hill 1981; Powell 1983) and research reports of the Arkansas Archeological Survey Research Series. These more detailed descriptions and inventories have allowed researchers access to relatively large collections for use in their work on paleodemography, mortuary practices, and paleopathology.

Finally, in the 1970s and 1980s, the bioarchaeological approach, a field integrating biological and archaeological research, broadened the reference base of osteology studies (Smith 1993:70). The bioarchaeological contributions usually fall into five major research categories: biological distance studies (Buikstra 1976; Droessler 1981), paleodemography (Buikstra 1976; Ubelaker 1978; Verano and Ubelaker 1992; Weiss 1973), biosocial dimensions of mortuary behavior (Goldstein 1980; Powell 1988; Powell et al. 1991; O'Shea 1984), nutritional/pathology studies (Lambert 2000; Ortner and Putschar 1985; Powell et al. 1991; Wing and Brown 1979), and biomechanical and structural adaptation (Bridges 1991; Bridges et al. 2000; Larsen 1997; Ruff and Larsen 1990; Ruff et al. 1984). Now, instead of demonstrating cultural similarities and migration based on human cranial shapes, bioarchaeologists are answering questions pertaining to prehistoric health, disease, diet, status, and sexual division of labor, to name a few research areas.

With the 1990 implementation of the Native American Graves Protection and Repatriation Act (NAGPRA) came inventories of skeletal collections that had once been confined to backroom shelves. Despite the efforts of archaeologists and bioarchaeologists to properly document these collections at universities and museums around the state, there is no central repository in Mississippi (such as the Mississippi Department of Archives and History [MDAH]) where these data can be accessed. One other important aspect of NAGPRA is that burial collections may be repatriated. A major consequence of reburial is that collections will not be available for future study, and knowledge gained from them will be limited to the methods available at the time of analysis. Over the last twenty or so years, bioarchaeological research has incorporated methods from the biological and chemical sciences. These include the implementation of DNA studies to determine genetic associations, isotope and trace-element analysis for diet reconstruction and population movement, AMS and fluoride dating of human bone for more accurate burial dating (e.g., Hogue 2006), and the increased use of computed tomography (CT) scans and X-rays to document skeletal morphology.

General Overview of Burials in and around the Research Area

The four Mississippi counties where highway construction will likely have the greatest impact on burials are Boliver, Coahoma, Tunica, and Sunflower. The MDAH website (www.mdah.state.ms.us/hpres), accessed on May 28, 2004, documents archaeological sites in these counties that are on the National Register of Historic Places. Sixteen are recorded for Coahoma County, one for Sunflower County, seven for Tunica, and none for Boliver County other than a

Historic-period battle site location. Among these 24 sites, those with published documentation of human skeletal remains include three sites located in Coahoma County (Dickerson [22CO502] [Weinstein 2004a], Oliver [22CO503] [Ross-Stallings 1992, 1995, 2002; Weinstein 2004a], and Salomon [22CO504]), and four sites located in Tunica County (Beaverdam [22TU513] [Weinstein 2004a], Dundee [22TU501] [Weinstein 2004a], Hollywood [22TU500] [Stallings and Ross-Stallings 1996; Weinstein 2004a], and the Johnson Cemetery site [22TU516] [Weinstein 2004a]).

An inventory of Mississippi sites with known human remains located in counties within the northern Yazoo Basin is provided in Table 9.1. Based on previous site surveys and descriptions by Brown (1992 [1926]), Moore (1911), Phillips (1970), Phillips et al. (2003 [1951]), Starr (1984), Thomas (1985 [1894]), and Toth (1988), Weinstein (2004a) provides invaluable descriptions of over 121 archaeological sites located in counties within or adjacent to the I-69 project corridor. These summaries indicate that human skeletal remains have been positively identified for about 20 of these sites, but most of the site descriptions (over 100) do not mention the presence of human remains or burials. These latter sites are often described as village or mound sites containing numerous artifacts as well as daub (see Weinstein 2004a:Tables 3–1 to 3–7). Based on these descriptions, which suggest year-round occupancy by a relatively large populace, these sites may very well have associated burials and cemeteries yet to be located.

Over the last 15 years, Nancy Ross-Stallings has analyzed or included burial data in publications and presentations from many of the Woodland and Mississippian Delta sites documented by Weinstein (2004a). These sites include Oliver (22CO503), Bobo (22CO535), Barner (22CO542), Austin (22TU549), Bonds (22TU530), and Dogwood Ridge Village (22DS511). Using these data, Ross-Stallings has tackled several important research questions such as documenting treponemal syndrome in Mississippi (Ross-Stallings 1989, 1997), recording evidence for warfare and interpersonal conflict during the Mississippian period (Ross-Stallings 1995, 2002), dietary reconstruction (Ross-Stallings 1992, 2002), and Mississippian mortuary practices (Ross-Stallings 2003). Chronological placement for the burials used in her research is based on radiocarbon dates obtained from organic materials (presumably charcoal) associated with house structures or feature fill rather than the burials themselves (Ross-Stallings 1992, 1997). More direct dating of the burials was possible in several instances where Historic artifacts were present in the graves (Ross-Stallings 2002). Separation of burials into customary culture periods was also based on ceramic temper and decoration (Ross-Stallings 1992, 1997, 2003).

At the McNight site (22CO560), excavated in 1998 by Walling and Chapman (1999), human skeletal remains were found in five features. In one case,

Table 9.1. Sites with burials identified in the project area. References for data are: (*) Weinstein 2004a; (1) Stallings and Ross-Stallings 1996; (2) Weinstein 2004a; (3) Brown 1992 [1926]; (4) Phillips 1970; (5) Phillips et al. 2003 [1951]; (6) Starr 1984; (7) Morse and Morse 1998 [Moore 1911]; (8) Connaway 1981b; (9) Ross-Stallings 1989; (10) Ross-Stallings 1992; (11) Ross-Stallings 1997; (12) Ross-Stallings 2003; (13) Ross-Stallings 1995; (14) Toth 1988; (15) Connaway and McGahey 1971; (16) Thomas 1985 [1894]; (17) Ross-Stallings 2002; (18) Chapman and Walling 1988; (19) Mooney et al. 2004.

County/Site Name	Site Number	Date/Cultural Period	Number Burials	Preservation/Comments	References
Tunica					
Hollywood*	22TU500	Late Mississippian	Unknown**		1, 2, 3, 4, 5
Dundee*	22TU501	Helena, Coahoma, Parchman phases	Unknown**		2, 3, 4, 6
Commerce	22TU504	Early Mississippian	Unknown**		2, 3, 4, 5, 7
Beaverdam*	22TU513	Early Mississippian	Unknown**	White cemetery	2, 3, 4, 5
Johnson Place/Perry Site*	22TU514	Kent phase	4**		2, 4, 7
Johnson Cemetery*	22TU516	Kent phase	Unknown**	Black cemetery	2, 3, 4
Oakwood Cemetery*	22TU517	Helena phase	Unknown**		2,4
Flowers	22TU518	Mississippian	14	Poor (disturbed)	8
Austin	22TU549	Late Woodland/Mississippian	147		9, 10, 11, 12
Bonds*	22TU530	Late Woodland/Transitional Mississippian	15		4, 10, 12, 13, 14
Boyd*	22TU531	Tchula, Marksville, Baytown	1	Good (disturbed)	2, 8, 14, 15
Coahoma					
Dickerson Mounds*	22CO502	Dorr, Coahoma, Peabody, Parchman phases	100+**		2, 4, 5, 6, 14, 16
Oliver*	22CO503	Middle Woodland	Unknown		2, 3, 4, 5, 10, 13, 14, 16, 17

Site	Site Number	Cultural Period / Dates	No. of Burials	Condition	References
Salomon*	22CO504	Middle Mississippian through Historic	91	Recent Burials	2, 3, 4, 5, 6, 14
Station	22CO518	Middle Baytown through Early Mississippian	Unknown**		2, 3
Bobo*	22CO535	Unknown	3?	Poor (disturbed)	2, 4, 5, 6, 8, 10
Barner	22CO542	Late Woodland/Mississippian	1?	Poor (disturbed)	11
McNight	22CO560	A.D. 735–1156 (calibrated 2-sigma)	5?	Poor (disturbed)	18
Brahan #2	22CO573/773	Unknown	4	Poor	2, 14, 19
Maddox	22CO586	A.D. 40–1640	1	Fair (disturbed)	8
Clarksdale Works*	22CO669	A.D. 500–800	Numerous**	Poor	2, 16
	22CO778	A.D. 780–1220	3	Poor	19
Bolivar					
Mound Near Neblett Landing*	22BO503	Late Baytown and Early Mississippian	3+	???	2, 7
Cook*	22BO533	Late Baytown	Unknown**		2, 5
Sunflower					
Boyer*	22SU507	Early Baytown	Unknown**		2, 4, 5
Marlow	22SU517	Early Mississippian	Unknown**		2, 5
Marlow Cemetery	22SU518	Unknown	Unknown**		2, 14

*Site within or immediately adjacent to I-69 corridor (Weinstein 2004a).

**No published analysis.

Feature 22, a subadult was well represented by over 19 skeletal elements and likely represents a burial that was not identified during the excavation of the feature. An inventory was presented for the burial elements and the elements aged when preservation permitted (Berryman 1999). No dates were discussed for the burials in the human remains chapter (Berryman 1999:251–253).

Connaway (1981b) also has reported sites with burials located within the research area in MDAH reports. For Coahoma County, burial descriptions are provided for the Maddox (22CO586) and Bobo (22CO535) sites. Two other sites, Shady Grove (22QU525) and Flowers (22TU518), contained secondary bundle burials (Connaway 1981b; see Brown, this volume). Both multiple- and single-bundle burials are associated with the Protohistoric period in east-central Mississippi (Hogue 2000).

Many brief descriptions of burials recovered near the research area during salvage or amateur excavations can be found in MDAH publications. These burials are associated with sites in Quitman (Johnson 1985), Grenada (—22GR36 Anonymous 1985), Leflore (Hony 1985), Warren (22WR537—Howell 1985), and Tunica (22TU531—Connaway and McGahey 1971) counties. Other MDAH reports provide minimal descriptions of in situ burials while providing details on the grave accompaniments (Brown 1985). Few reports provide tables listing each burial, with estimates on age and sex, along with information on burial behavior (Brain 1989; Lumb and McNutt 1988).

Mooney et al. (2004) recovered a minimum number of four individuals from site 22CO573/773 and three individuals from site 22CO778 during the Phase III mitigation of the Coahoma Welcome Center. In addition to an inventory of the recovered remains the materials were analyzed for age and sex, with these data presented in tables (Mooney et al. 2004:Tables 14.1 and 14.2). Ceramic chronology is used to date the individual burials, which are affiliated with the Woodland period (Mooney et al. 2004:468).

At several sites tested in or near the research area, burial pits were rarely observed (Anonymous 1985; Brain 1989; Connaway and McGahey 1971; Hony 1985; Lumb and McNutt 1988). One interpretation is that individuals were placed on top of midden deposits of old mound surfaces and then covered over (Brain 1989). At the Leflore site, based on the absence of a burial pit, an infant was believed to have been the victim of a collapsed burning daub house (Anonymous 1985). No evidence for burning was identified on the bones, however.

The overview of the collections already documented from the area show a major gap in the burial representation through time (Table 9.1). To date, no Archaic burials have been recovered in the research area; Woodland sites are scarcely represented, and little information is available on the burials recovered. These sites have few burials (Boyd Site, 22TU531, n=1) or the number recovered is currently unknown (Cook Site, 22BO533 and Boyer Site, 22SU507; Oliver, 22CO503). Transitional Woodland/ Mississippian sites with burials do exist (Bonds, 22TU530, n=15; Salomon, 22CO504, n =?; Bobo, 22CO535, n =3?; Neblett Landing, 22BO503, n=3), but only 21 known burials have been recovered. No attempts have been made to distinguish exact temporal placement of these burials.

Burials recovered from Mississippian mound and village components are the most common, totaling 195 individuals from three of the eight sites; Perry site, 22TU514 (n =3), Dickerson Mounds, 22CO502 (n = 100+), and Oliver site, 22CO503 (n = 91). Mention of burials, some Historic, are given for the Hollywood (22TU500), Dundee (22TU501), Beaverdam (22TU513), Johnson Cemetery (22TU616), and Oakwood Cemetery (22TU517) (Weinstein 2004a).

Important Research Elsewhere

As this discussion clearly demonstrates, the northern Yazoo Basin has yielded little in the way of systematic studies on bioarchaeological populations. For the Mississippi Delta region only two publications (Ross-Stallings 1989, 1997), which document treponemal infections from the Barner and Austin sites, are available. Because of the lack of burial data for most culture periods and absence of systematic research on larger representative burial series, the bioarchaeology of the area is virtually unknown.

In contrast, archaeological skeletal collections recovered from the adjacent LMV over the last two decades have been studied extensively, especially as concerns nutrition and paleopathology (Harmon and Rose 1989; Mitchell 1977; Rose 1999; Rose and Harmon 1986, 1989; Rose and Marks 1985; Rose et al. 1984; Rose et al. 1985; Rose et al. 1991). A brief overview of several major research contributions in this area follows below.

Probably the most significant bioarchaeological research in the LMV is the work by Rose and associates (Harmon and Rose 1989; Rose and Harmon 1986, 1989; Rose and Marks 1985; Rose et al. 1984; Rose et al. 1985; Rose et al. 1991). One of the most important contributions tested two archaeological premises about maize use in three culture areas, the LMV west of the Mississippi River, the Central Mississippi Valley (CMV), and Caddoan areas (Rose et al. 1984). The first test considers whether agriculture was a necessary adaptation to feed a growing population that had exceeded the carrying capacity of the environment, while the second examines whether maize agriculture was detrimental to human health (Rose et al. 1984:415). Using skeletal analyses done over a span of more than 80 years, the authors created a standardized system for extracting relevant pathology data from published site reports, osteological appendices,

Table 9.2. Cultural-period affiliation of sites with burials in or near the I-69 corridor.

Cultural Period	Site Name	Site Number	Burials
Archaic	None	n/a	0
Total Burials			**0**
Woodland	Boyd	22TU531	1
	Cook	22BO533	Unknown
	Boyer	22SU507	Unknown
	Oliver	22CO503	Unknown
Total Burials			**1+**
Transitional Woodland/ Mississippian	Bonds	22TU530	15
	Salomon	22CO504	Unknown
	Bobo	22CO535	3?
	Mound Near Neblett Landing	22BO503	3+
Total Burials			**21+**
Mississippian	Hollywood	22TU500	Unknown
	Dundee	22TU501	Unknown
	Beaverdam	22TU513	Unknown
	Johnson Place/Perry Site	22TU514	4
	Johnson Cemetery	22TU516	Unknown
	Oakwood Cemetery	22TU517	Unknown
	Dickerson Mounds	22CO502	100+
	Oliver	22CO503	91
Total Burials			**195+**

and skeletal collections from the three culture areas (Rose et al. 1984:394). They observed changes in pathology frequencies in agricultural populations when compared to preagricultural predecessors. One important aspect of the study is the authors' examination of variability among cultural units in ecology, demography, settlement patterns, and technology and the cumulative effects of each on the adoption of agriculture (Rose et al. 1984:393–394). The results show that maize adoption in the LMV was not the result of circumscription and dietary needs (i.e., the carrying capacity of the environment was well above population density; there was a reliable food base of natural resources that produced a surplus), but that maize may have been consumed as a status food in imitation of Caddo neighbors to the west and populous centers in the CMV to the north. Adequate naturally available dietary sources for the LMV inhabitants are confirmed in part by low frequencies of porotic hyperostosis and the lack of archaeological data showing maize dependency (Rose et al. 1984:417).

In 1989 the Arkansas Archeological Survey published *Archeology and Bioarcheology of the Lower Mississippi Valley and Trans-Mississippi South in Arkansas and Louisiana* (Jeter et al. 1989). In one chapter, Rose and Harmon (1989) take on a major task, an extensive overview and inventory of recovered skeletal collections from Louisiana and Arkansas. One result of this exhaustive study was the observed lack of collections that dated before the Mississippian period. The authors appropriately suggest that new methods be employed in cultural-resource-management site survey and testing in order to identify small habitation sites, not just village and mortuary complexes (Rose and Harmon 1989:322). In another chapter the authors (Harmon and Rose 1989) provide 16 sets of osteological data categories relevant to testing hypotheses in the Louisiana and Arkansas study area. The data categories are accepted by most bioarchaeologists as providing the standard basis of any analysis (Harmon and Rose 1989:353–354). In conjunction with archaeologists (Jeter et al. 1989), ten adaptation types and their subdivisions are identified for the research area. These types are based on the available records and include information on environment, subsistence and settlement, and bioarchaeology. A discussion of missing information for each adaptation type is presented to aid in developing future research questions (Jeter et al. 1989:355–378). One advantage of this model is that it offers the researcher a means for recognizing alternative and variable human behaviors in different environments. Similar and equally exhaustive bioarchaeological projects were accomplished for the Gulf Coastal Plain (Story et al. 1990) and south-central United States (Rose 1999). The latter volume provides an excellent source for comparative data for bioarchaeology of the Yazoo Basin, specifically the chapter on Louisiana and south and eastern Arkansas (Rose 1999:35–82).

In another study, Rose and his associates use bioarchaeological data to interpret available archaeological information from the lower portions of the Mississippi valley in order to examine subsistence change over time. One major focus of this research is to identify the transition to maize dependency (Rose et al. 1991). Using paleopathology data, carbon isotope analysis, and archaeological information, the authors observe changes in subsistence patterns for the CMV/LMV regions. They conclude that shifts in subsistence patterns are extremely complex and difficult to understand, and that such changes had variable effects on human health and culture. The authors provide a hypothesis for the adoption of maize agriculture in the research area, but are cautious in stating that there are other equally plausible alternatives. They argue that maize dependency did not occur until well after A.D. 1200, when population nucleation (Morse and Morse 1983) had depleted natural resources, and therefore "Mississippianization" and maize dependency were not contemporaneous in some areas within the Mississippi valley. Their sound methodology allows for further testing of the results (Rose et al. 1991).

Diana Greenlee (1998) also conducted research on maize diet in the CMV using carbon and nitrogen-stable isotope data from human bone. Her study samples represent a range of sites associated with different temporal placement and settlement patterns. Although her results were inconclusive, Greenlee did document variability in maize diet among the groups, a finding that may correspond with natural resource use by local inhabitants.

The research accomplished in the LMV region by Rose and others provides an excellent model for future research in the Mississippi Delta. These researchers have organized and reorganized information to provide a reliable bioarchaeology data set, produced research standards and models for the area, developed working hypotheses for future research in the area, and integrated ecological and cultural variables as part of their research agenda. Their work is theory-driven, with continuous testing and retesting of hypotheses. In more recent studies (Rose 1999; Rose et al. 1984; Rose et al. 1991), their recognition of variability in subsistence patterns and their examination of associated biological and cultural responses through time indicate their interest in evolutionary change as a means of explaining human adaptation in the LMV, although it is never explicitly presented this way.

Problems to Be Resolved

The I-69 project provides an excellent opportunity to develop or adopt models for the future recovery and interpretation of human skeletal remains in the area similar to those designed for the LMV and Trans-Mississippi South in Arkansas and Louisiana. Before systematic research can take place, several recommendations are discussed to ensure proper recovery and analysis of the burial materials. These recommendations are based on archaeological reports available for the research area and adjacent areas.

Archaeological Field Methods

The origin, testing, and modification of a significant hypothesis require extensive analyses of representative and temporally documented samples (Rose and Harmon 1999). Since no published information is currently available providing demographic profiles of the already excavated burials, age and sex representation for the two largest burial collections from Oliver and Dickerson Mounds is unknown. The other burial series are too small to be representative samples. Efforts to study these already existing collections should be paramount. But, more importantly, to ensure that large representative series are available, mitigation plans for sites containing a mortuary component must require excavation and analysis of all burials.

Archaeological recovery methods have affected burial preservation and accurate burial recording in the study area. In many instances, burial excavation resulted from developers and land-levelers uncovering graves and cemeteries (Brown 1985; Connaway 1981b), unaware that an archaeological site was present. The use of heavy machinery to expose site features can have negative effects on skeletal preservation. As one scholar pronounces, "given the use of heavy machinery in their discovery, all of the burials were damaged and incompletely recovered" (House 1982:29). Although time is a major consideration in archaeological recovery, the use of heavy machinery should be avoided whenever possible. Instead, time and labor costs factored for field recovery should ensure the adoption of less destructive field methods. The past history of burial destruction by heavy machinery warrants the use of less destructive stripping methods, such as hand excavation, for the research area.

In the absence of well-defined burial pits, it is recommended that field osteologists be on site to quickly identify human remains. Feature excavation where human remains are not readily recognized (Walling and Chapman 1999) can lead to inaccurate recording of possible burials and increase the destruction of delicate skeletal remains. Osteologists present in the field can readily identify, excavate, and record human bones in the instances where burial pits are not discernible and where burials were placed on middens or refuse pits and then covered. The inclusion of field osteologists will reduce the likelihood of improper excavation and recording of these burials. Also, failing to record pit-origin points presents problems when attempting to understand chronology and mortuary practices at multi-component sites.

The overwhelming majority of sites identified in the area are described as large village or mound sites (Weinstein 2004a). When research questions are addressed, large village and mound burial populations (100 individuals is often used as a minimum sample size for acceptable representation) naturally provide more reliable results (Ubelaker 1978). But such a focus on larger village or mound-site populations limits interpretations of prehistoric lifeways to those types of settlements, while ignoring others that are equally important (Hogue and Peacock 1995). Burial collections associated with settlements such as farmsteads or hamlets are often considered unrepresentative because of their small size, and are rarely included in studies outside of CRM reports (see Hogue 2003b; Hogue and Erwin 1993; Hogue and Peacock 1995). Farmstead occupants may have served to provision the elite inhabitants of Mississippian mound sites (Jackson and Scott 1995), supporting the hypothesis of a two- or three-tiered Mississippian hierarchy (Blitz 1993; Lorenz 1990, 1996; Peebles 1983). One source of data important for understanding intersite dynamics of this nature would be the comparison of health profiles of population occupying smaller habitation sites and those associated with larger mound/village sites. Conditions often associated with the higher population density present at village and mound sites include parasite contamination created by unsanitary conditions related to long-term occupancy of an area, increased competition for food, and greater disease transmission. Site survey must include methods for identifying small farmsteads and hamlets so that comparisons of this nature are possible, and some such sites must be considered eligible for the National Register of Historic Places to forward this type of research.

Problems with Recording Burial Information

As mentioned earlier in this paper, few reports provide detailed information on demographic profiles and mortuary behavior for the burials already recovered from the study area (Brain 1989; Lumb and McNutt 1988). All existing collections should be reexamined and included in a final I-69 report. To ensure comparative data recovery, standard osteological methods, such as those outlined by Buikstra and Ubelaker (1994), should be used in field and laboratory analyses of all burials. Standardized forms are needed for comparable burial recovery. Forms designed for osteological analysis prior to removal of bones from the ground should minimally include recording of skeletal preservation, age at death, sex of adults, osteometric measurements of skeletal elements, and observable lesions associated with trauma, degenerative disease, and infections. Poor skeletal preservation and posthumous disturbance yield laboratory specimens that cannot be accurately reconstructed. In situ analysis of burials, especially those that are poorly preserved, will provide data that could otherwise be lost after burial removal. Likewise, efforts should include recording in situ burials using digital and standard photography and scale drawings.

Research Methods and Questions

The I-69 project provides an excellent opportunity to measure biological adjustments of these past populations from an evolutionary perspective. Based on the previous discussion, the following research questions should be considered.

When were native and tropical cultigens integrated into the diet? Was this dietary shift a response to local circumstances or part of a wider phenomenon observed elsewhere? Dental caries, dental microwear analysis, and isotope assays can provide relevant bioarchaeological information.

How does adaptive efficiency change, through time and specifically with the adoption of native and tropical cultigens during the prehistoric period?

Adaptive efficiency is an approximate measure of a group's adaptation to their environment (Rose and Harmon 1999:68). Demographic analysis is considered the most informative for evaluation but frequencies of stress indicators such as infection rates (especially porotic hyperostosis) and linear enamel hypoplasia are also used to access efficiency (Rose and Harmon 1999). Other nutritional stress indicators are Harris lines (observable via radiographs), neural canal size (Larsen 1997), and long bone-lengths relative to dental age (Rose and Harmon 1999:81).

How do individual workloads compare among prehistoric preagricultural, prehistoric agricultural, Historic agricultural, and African-American slave populations? Osteoarthritis of the joints and back can progress more rapidly in populations with heavier workloads. Biomechanical analysis, including long-bone robusticity and symmetry, should be included to access the effects of different work-related forces on the skeletal system.

What effects do settlement patterns have on adaptive efficiency? Population nucleation and growth have been shown to have adverse affects on health by increased morbidity and mortality (Bogdan and Weaver 1992; Powell 1992). For the LMV, population density, rather than a decrease in dietary quality, is used to explain increased frequencies of infections during the Late Mississippian period (Rose et al. 1991). Maize was introduced as a food source during the Middle Mississippian period, but it wasn't until population nucleation depleted natural resources that maize dependency was later required. The questions not directly addressed are, did population density change because of nucleation of smaller villages, as the archaeological data suggest (Morse and Morse 1983), or was the increase due to growth associated with maize use, or were both factors possibly involved?

How do trauma frequencies related to warfare and interpersonal conflict differ through time and by settlement pattern? Bioarchaeological evidence for interpersonal warfare is identified through embedded projectile points, mutilation, scalping, and cranial depressions and parry fractures.

What are the genetic relationships, migration patterns, and biosocial interactions (exogamy versus endogamy) of the populations?

Is there an increase in Old World diseases and general decrease in life expectancy in Contact period populations? During Historic times, epidemic diseases played a major role in decreasing health, but other factors such as population density, soil depletion (Baden 1987), increased use of dietary carbohydrates and reduced nutrition (Rose and Harmon 1999), and social disruption (Larsen et al. 1992) were also important. By comparing demographic profiles through time, health changes can be assessed.

Are there differences in the overall health and diet of rural and urban slaves? Among rural slaves, are there perceived dietary and health differences between field and house slaves? Does African-American health improve during the Reconstruction period (Young, this volume)?

In all cases age at death and sex determination should be made where preservation permits, as these analyses provide the basis for demographic studies. Documentation of health should include, but not be limited to, recording evidence of infections, degenerative disease, trauma (whether they are related to environmental conditions or interpersonal conflict), and general physiological stress responses such as enamel hypoplasia, Harris lines, osteoporosis, and neural canal size. Minimally, standard indicators for dietary stress, dental caries, periodontal disease, and premortem tooth loss should be recorded.

Bioarchaeological research elsewhere in the Southeast has demonstrated an increase in birthrate during the adoption and intensification of maize use, a possible consequence of earlier weaning onto soft, easily digestible foods (Buikstra et al. 1986). A similar study for the research area would prove useful in understanding changes in population density through time. Variability and change in disease frequencies are commonly used to assess the effects of maize agriculture and settlement patterns on population health (Rose et al. 1984; Rose et al. 1991). If a skeletal series represents the amalgamation of different populations from other areas, then it seems probable that variability in disease frequencies may not reflect biological responses to conditions present at the "archaeological site." Instead, they could reflect biological responses to the surroundings experienced prior to village nucleation.

The integration of dental microwear analysis (DMA) and stable carbon and nitrogen isotope analyses in dietary reconstruction would complement the skeletal pathology evidence and provide a data set necessary for comparing similarities and differences in diets both temporally and spatially. Researchers have successfully used DMA to understand changes in diet by measuring the sizes and frequencies of microwear features (Rose 1984; Rose and Marks 1985; Rose et al. 1991; Schmidt 2001; Teaford 1991; Ungar 1994; Ungar and Spencer 1999). These features are identified as pits and scratches on dental enamel. Hard, abrasive foods such as nuts and food processing involving stone implements lead to higher frequencies of pits, while softer foods create longer and more frequent scratches (Grine 1987; Schmidt 2001; Teaford 1988a, 1988b; Ungar and Spencer 1999; Ungar and Teaford 1996). Rose et al. (1991) found a major reduction in large striations and an increase in smooth, polished enamel with the adoption of maize agriculture in the CMV.

Stable isotope analysis should include assays of carbon and nitrogen. Stable isotopes may be the only means for directly identifying the use of certain foods (maize, marine resources) and the quantities eaten. Carbon isotopes discriminate between two terrestrial plant classes known as C_3 and C_4. C_3 plants include such temperate grasses as wheat and rice, in addition to nuts, fruits, and root crops. Tropical grasses like maize are classified as C4 plants, and through human management have successfully adapted to temperate climates (Ambrose 1987:94–95). In the southeastern United States and elsewhere, carbon isotopes, measured as δ 13C values in human bone collagen, have been used to document dietary maize. In nonagricultural groups δ 13C values typically measure below –19 parts per mil (‰). With maize agriculture the δ 13C signature falls between –19 ‰ to –7.5 ‰ (Chisolm 1989:34). Less negative δ 13C values will be observed in human bone collagen where more C4 plants, such as maize, have been consumed (Buikstra 1992; Buikstra and Milner 1991; Larsen 1997; Lynott et al. 1986; Rose et al. 1991). Integrating carbon isotope studies would provide invaluable documentation on the adoption of maize agriculture and dependence on maize by prehistoric people living in the Delta.

Nitrogen has two stable isotopes, ^{14}N and [15]N. The ^{15}N values in animal tissue are positively correlated with values in the diet. In terrestrial environments, vertebrates typically have ^{15}N values that are 4 ‰ lower than marine vertebrates (Larsen 1997), and therefore terrestrial and marine systems should not be compared directly (Schoeninger 1995:84; Schoeninger and DeNiro 1984). As an organism moves up the trophic level, ^{15}N values increase (Schoeninger 1984, 1995). Carnivorous fish appear to have higher ^{15}N values than bottom feeders (Katzenberg 1989): studies conducted in the Great Lakes region (Katzenberg 1989) and at Moundville in Alabama (Schoeninger and Schurr 1998) document fish having diagnostic ^{15}N values higher than terrestrial browsers and omnivores.

Although destructive, little bone, around 5 grams, is necessary for conventional isotope assays. More recently, laser ablation, a nondestructive method, has been successfully used for isotope analysis (Sponheimer et al. 2006). Archaeological sites in northeastern Mississippi, where stable isotopes have been integrated into the research to better understand prehistoric diets, include Lyon's Bluff (22OK520) and other Protohistoric sites (22OK593, 22OK595, 22OK904, 22OK905) (Hogue 2000; Hogue and Dongarra 2002; Hogue et al. 1995; Hogue et al. 1996), the Josey Farm site (22OK793) (Hogue 2003b), and the South Farm site (22OK534) (Hogue and Peacock 1995). Several conclusions found in these studies include the continued use of maize in northeastern Mississippi during the Protohistoric period and less dependence on maize in farmsteads when compared with the Lyon's Bluff mound site. Additional comparative isotope data may be found in Rose's (1999) edited volume, *Bioarchaeology of the South Central United States.* If human bone cannot be used for isotope assays, domestic dogs have been found to provide useful data, especially when considering carbon-isotope levels (Hogue 2003b).

Biomechanics is an important means of analyzing and understanding skeletal morphology within the context of the environment. Studies of cross-sectional geometric properties can address a range of issues dealing with activities and behaviors associated with subsistence strategies, sex differences in dietary adaptation, and skeletal growth and development in response to environmental and subsistence change. The basic premise supporting biomechanical research is Wolff's law, which proposes that bone growth and remodeling result from stresses and demands placed on the skeletal system during activities (Larsen 1997). Hogue and Dongarra (2002) used biomechanical research to document changes in skeletal robusticity and symmetry among preagricultural and agricultural populations in northeast Mississippi and northwest Alabama. Recently Wolff's law has been challenged by evidence that age plays an important factor in skeletal remodeling. Young mammals exhibit strong bone remodeling to loading, while old adults exhibit little or no change (Pearson and Lieberman 2004).

Questions related to biodistance studies can be tackled using nonmetric discrete traits outlined in Buikstra and Ubelaker (1994). DNA studies could be attempted, but certain environmental factors are crucial for good preservation. Samples recovered from environments with dry conditions, cooler temperatures, and soils with neutral or slightly alkaline pH provide the best results (Stone 2000). The likelihood of these conditions existing in the Mississippi Delta is very low.

Before any of these research areas can be properly investigated, more precise dating of individual burials is needed to better understand biological adaptation in the research area. Related to this are questions that consider how changes in pathology frequencies and mortality patterns vary among people living in different settlement patterns through time. Instead of using transitional markers such as maize agriculture and European contact as fundamental causes for health change, an approach that considers population variation (pathology/nutrition, demography, biomechanical stress, biological distance, and biosocial dimensions of mortuary practices) along a temporal continuum would seem a more sensitive method for identifying evolutionary change and disruptions brought on by environmental (climatic and culturally induced) and cultural change (agriculture, European contact, etc). More precise dating of individual burials would allow researchers to examine gradual, less obvious adjustments in human biological adaptation. In turn this method could lead to a better understanding of physiological and biological reactions to maize dependency, population growth, or European contact.

One recommended starting point could be the 500-year span of the Mississippian period. Often, skeletal collections are placed in general cultural periods such as Early, Middle, or Late Mississippian, with little knowledge of whether a particular burial dates during the early or late part of a sequence. This means that a skeletal series may represent 200 years or more of continuous occupation, which could represent ten or more generations, or 200 years of gene flow, or both of these factors. Absolute dating could include AMS or standard radiocarbon dating, but these methods are often costly and require at least 7–10 grams of bone. Another method for dating the burials is fluoride dating. Fluoride dating is much less expensive than radiocarbon dating, and requires a small sample size of 5 mg. Fluoride content in prehistoric bone has been used for relative dating with some success in the southeastern United States (Haddy and Hanson 1981, 1982; Hogue 2006) and elsewhere (Callaghan 1986; Ezzo 1992; Oakley and Hoskins 1950). This method is based on the amassing of fluoride ions in bone. Other sources of relative dating include seriations of burial pots and handle sizes (Steponaitis 1983) and historic grave goods. Unfortunately, for either method to be worthwhile, all burials must contain similar types of grave goods.

Conclusions

Bioarchaeological data are, in effect, absent for the research area. No systematic studies on sites already excavated in or near the research area have been published. Much work in bioarchaeology is needed to match research and data sets already compiled in the adjacent LMV and Trans-Mississippi South in Arkansas and Louisiana. Familiarity with this research, specifically works by Rose and others, is critical in developing and implementing a research plan for the Yazoo Basin. Before any systematic research can go forward, several problems must be resolved. Already existing burial series from sites to be impacted or located near the research area should be included in the bioarchaeological data set. This will entail locating and reanalyzing the collections. Mitigation must also require excavation of all burials from the portions of sites to be impacted. Integrating already existing burial series with new ones will ensure that larger, more representative series will be available for research. Larger burial series will improve the reliability of the study results. A centralized repository for the bioarchaeology data and collections at MDAH or one of the major Mississippi universities would allow future accessibility by interested scholars. More attention needs to be given to the smaller, less represented series associated with small settlements, such as farmsteads, hamlets, or seasonal occupations, in order to identify alternative, but equally important, biological and adaptive responses present in the region.

Field recovery and laboratory analysis should integrate standardized methods to ensure comparability among skeletal collections in the research area and elsewhere. The use of heavy machinery to locate burials should be avoided at all costs, and a field osteologist should be on site during the duration of the excavation.

Bioarchaeologists must be willing to divorce skeletal series from tradition-ally used "social units" or "culture periods" and integrate more precise methods for dating individual burials, such as AMS and fluoride dating. Knowledge of individual burial dates is critical for documenting evolutionary change.

Finally, archaeologists and bioarchaeologists must work closely with Native American groups under NAGPRA guidelines and make every effort to deter-mine tribal affiliation. Mitochondrial DNA studies should be conducted if de-structive analysis is allowed, and skeletal samples archived for future studies.

10
Through the Lens of the Lithic Analyst

The Organization of Mississippi Delta Chipped-Stone Technologies

Philip J. Carr

Lithic analysis will never replace baseball as a spectator sport, but in the last couple of decades it has become a lot more fun than it used to be. What has made it fun is that its practitioners have achieved sound procedures for analysis and have added substantially to knowledge about the past; the research is rewarding.

Collins 1993:92

When thinking of the Mississippi Delta, the blues, catfish, and barbecue come to mind, and if you are an archaeologist, then mounds and pottery are probably on the list too, but not lithics. While there are reasons for this, both archaeological and historical, lithics nevertheless have played a role in our understanding of the prehistory of the Delta, especially for certain time periods and for particular types of prehistoric activities. Arguably, the limited availability of materials suitable for chipped-stone tool manufacture makes the Delta an interesting environmental situation from the perspective of a lithic analyst. Prehistoric populations used chipped-stone tools, but often lacked ready access to raw materials. This undoubtedly had a profound effect on how these peoples organized their technology to meet their social and economic needs. Therefore, Mississippi Delta lithics have great potential to provide significant information about the past and can serve as a critical line of evidence when developing and testing hypotheses concerning prehistoric behavior.

For the past fifteen years I have worked to develop methods to increase the information we can obtain from chipped-stone assemblages. Here, I will discuss theoretical and methodological approaches that could prove fruitful for investigating the prehistoric lithic assemblages of the Mississippi Delta. These approaches will be highlighted with examples using archaeological lithic assemblages from the Yazoo Basin, which is that portion of the Delta of particular interest in the context of impending development. McNutt (1996) has previously discussed the prehistory of the Yazoo Basin and Weinstein (2004a) has completed an overview of archaeological research in the Mississippi section of the I-69 corridor. The discussion presented here will draw upon these sources as well as others, but in an attempt to avoid redundancy this examination is purposefully conducted through the colored lens of the lithic analyst.

Looking Back: Delta Lithic Studies in Historical Context

In delving into the various sources of information concerning Mississippi Delta archaeology, I have had the opportunity of reading the works of some truly distinguished archaeologists. The scholarship of Jay Johnson has influenced my overall thinking for this project more than any other, and not only his publications concerning lithics. In the preface to the excellent edited volume, *The Development of Southeastern Archaeology,* he states, "In the past few years I have become interested in the history of the development of archaeology, how what was done and published in 1970 affects us today and how that is a response to what was done and published in 1940 and so on" (Johnson 1993a:ix). If the history of archaeology in the Mississippi Delta is examined from the perspective of a lithic analyst, one cannot help but be struck by the powerful—and largely negative—influence of past studies. Put simply, for many years lithic analysis was not a significant part of the archaeology of the Mississippi Delta.

In his general history of Mississippi archaeology, Johnson (2002) describes several major developments, from the search for museum pieces by Calvin Brown to modern cultural resource management (CRM). From the perspective of lithics and the Mississippi Delta, Calvin S. Brown in *Archeology of Mississippi* (1992 [1926]) did an adequate job documenting some of the range of variability in lithic tool types. His Chapter II, "Arrow-Heads, Spear-Heads, and Perforators," shows his geologic background in that he describes not only tools, but available raw materials. "The commonest material used in the western and central part of the state was the pebbles or gravels found all along the bluff which runs north and south thru the western part of the state paralleling the Mississippi River. These pebbles vary in size from that of a small shot or pea to four or five inches in length and even longer" (Brown 1992 [1926]:126). Subsequent statements regarding raw material availability in the Mississippi Delta do not include much greater detail, and this lack of material-source investigation remains problematic for lithic studies today.

Jumping ahead 25 years to the publication of *Archaeological Survey in the Lower Mississippi Alluvial Valley, 1940–1947* by Phillips et al. (2003 [1951]), we see that an interest in lithics had greatly waned. This is an excellent report by all standards, except perhaps of those who have an interest in lithics of the

region. These scholars provide significant discussions of the geographic setting including details of the physiography, climate, soils, vegetation, fauna, and
even flood conditions, but no mention of the types or locations of stone raw
materials is made. Additionally, recovered prehistoric stone tools were simply
ignored. "In this report the word 'collection' may be read 'potsherds.' Generations of small boys and collectors have seen to it that very few stone artifacts
are left on the sites. Local cultures are, understandably, poor in stone anyhow"
(Phillips et al. 2003 [1951]:45). They go on to say, "This sounds like the familiar
excuse of the ceramist for neglecting other categories of material, but at the
present we do not feel apologetic for it." Culture history was the paradigm of
choice and the potsherd the artifact du jour. Lithic analysts today may not appreciate their lack of an apology, but the position of Phillips et al. is made
more reasonable considering the huge quantities of pottery recovered in their
work and the relatively small assemblages of lithic materials. Further, Johnson
notes that "Stone tools, by their nature, are not as useful for chronology as ceramics, a point which is well documented by the relatively late contribution of
lithic analysis to culture history studies" (Johnson 1993b:51).

This is not to say that Delta lithics have never been discussed, but this early
study and others set the stage for the kinds of sites investigated and the important questions to be asked. For example, Kidder (2002:66–67), in a recent review of Woodland-period archaeology of the Lower Mississippi Valley (LMV),
like Phillips et al. (2003 [1951]), discusses the geographic setting in some detail, but fails to include a discussion of lithic resource availability. To be fair,
Kidder (2002) does provide a short overview of lithic use for each time period.
For example, it is suggested that the Tchula-period projectile points are similar
to those of Poverty Point times; that there is little use of nonlocal materials;
and that lithic reduction included flake tool and core tool strategies (Kidder
2002:70). However, the discussion is more a cultural-historical trait list, and the
lithic data do not play the same role that ceramics, mounds, and burials have
in the discussions of prehistoric lifeways for any given time period that is discussed. For prehistoric cultures that produced pottery, the lithic assemblage in
the Mississippi Delta remains underused.

The investigation of the Jaketown site in 1951 also certainly inspired later
studies, and in this report there is an excellent description of stone tools, particularly the "microflint industry" (Ford et al. 1955). However, this seems to
have been accomplished somewhat reluctantly, as the authors remark on the
lack of bone and shell, such that the trait list is limited, and that this "makes it
necessary to place greater emphasis on imperishable artifacts such as chipped
stone" (Ford et al. 1955:126). Projectile points are classified and very fine illustrations of various types are provided. The microflint industry is described in
detail and the duplication of such an industry at Poverty Point is emphasized.

The technique used to produce blades is well described, with an in-depth examination of the cores and resulting blades. For example, the platform angle for cores averages 55 degrees, and unmodified blades range in length from 20 to 50 mm. Blades are divided into various "functional" types, including end-scrapers, sidescrapers, and Jaketown perforators. These type descriptions are relatively detailed, but the similarity between types suggests it would be difficult for other researchers to accurately replicate the classification scheme. Further, equating artifact form with function is problematic. Overall, this study demonstrated that lithic assemblages in the Delta from certain time periods were worthy of study.

In an interesting twist, Sam Brookes (1999) has argued that Jaketown and the Poverty Point Interaction Sphere may have had too significant an impact on professional archaeologists in Mississippi, especially those unfamiliar with lithic-material identification. He reports that cores and blades of Burlington chert recovered at a site were identified as the "Jaketown microlith industry" despite the presence of Mississippian mounds, shell-tempered pottery, and "little white Cahokia arrowpoints" (Brookes 1999:93). Perhaps the general lack of detailed consideration of lithic assemblages in the Mississippi Delta has resulted in a certain naiveté when it comes to this artifact class.

Salvage archaeology and cultural resource management of the 1970s ushered in a new phase of archaeological research in the Mississippi Delta. There was an increase in the amount of work, and more lithic data are provided in these reports. This was likely due to a growing awareness of what could be learned from stone tool assemblages as well as fulfilling a coverage need for technical site reports. Here, select reports are used to highlight the manner in which lithic assemblages were treated over the past 35 years.

In 1971, salvage archaeology was undertaken by staff from the Mississippi Department of Archives and History (MDAH) at the Boyd Site in Tunica County. The site was to be destroyed through land-leveling, and excavations were planned to investigate the possibility of Baytown house remains (Connaway and McGahey 1971:5). Unsurprisingly, given the previous discussion, much of the report is devoted to assigning the recovered pottery to types and varieties, while a brief overview of the recovered lithic materials is provided. The four-and-a-half-page discussion includes low-quality plates of lithic artifacts and limited descriptions of artifact classes such as projectile point, flake scraper, core, perforator, ground celt, chopper, and miscellaneous broken bifaces, among others. It is interesting that the authors note with regard to the lithic artifact class "projectile points" that "little has been done toward classifying them and sorting out their cultural connections" (Connaway and McGahey 1971:56). Lithic material is not systematically discussed but is mentioned in the case of limonite gorgets and choppers of "gravel of a type which is available on gravel bars in the Misssissippi River today" (Connaway and McGahey 1971:57). Additionally, three of the lamellar blades are described as "of an excellent quality of blue-gray flint which is rarely found in this area . . . and is referred to by James A. Ford as Harrison County Indiana Flint" (Connaway and McGahey 1971:56). The rest of the discussion is limited to various observations relating to artifact morphology. No artifact counts are provided nor are metric measurements, and flake debris is not mentioned. The report conclusion focuses on the contribution made regarding the ceramic sequence for the region and associated date ranges.

Also part of archaeological salvage excavations in the Delta, the Wilsford site was investigated in 1969, but the full report of these investigations was not published until 1984. Though the lithic assemblage was particularly sparse (n=42), more detail is provided including metric measurements, lithic material descriptions, whether utilized, and flake counts (Connaway 1984). Flakes are not only enumerated, but also classified as primary decortication, secondary decortication, or thinning (Connaway 1984:Table 24b). Lithic materials are described as either "local yellow/tan gravel chert" or chert of some other color such as gray or banded; one piece of gray quartzite was recovered. While the greater detail is appreciated, without descriptions of how flake types and utilization were determined the data are impossible to assess or use in comparisons with other assemblages. This is a recurrent problem, and one that has stymied my attempts at making meaningful comparisons between reported lithic assemblages from the Delta.

An MDAH report of survey work in Mississippi, including the Delta, was authored by John Penman (1977), who recognized the lack of lithic data generally available. He states that "the heavy emphasis placed upon the illustration of lithic materials within this report has been an attempt to counterbalance the lack of discussion of lithic assemblages by previous authors" (Penman 1977:5). Penman provides an overview of lithic materials and a general discussion of lithic terminology. Lithic material categories include chert, quartzite, and sandstone, but these are generally only further designated by color. While "yellow" chert is described as occurring in the "upland areas of northern Mississippi" and "on modern Mississippi River gravel bars," little discussion of cherts of other colors is provided. Flake categories include primary decortication, secondary decortication, thinning flakes, block flakes, and undesignated. Unfortunately, these data play no specific and clear role in site interpretation. However, the illustrations of stone tools and the attempt at providing a range of lithic data are welcome, but are perhaps due in part to the fact that the pottery sherds were "finger-nail sized" due to "efficient farming machinery" (Penman 1977:5). That is, as with Ford et al. (1955) working with the Jaketown assemblage, the focus on lithics is at least partially because of the lack of other artifact classes for study. It is interesting that in each case the authors are compelled to discuss why they spent so much time on the lithics.

The Mississippi Department of Transportation (MDOT) has conducted a number of surveys in the Yazoo Basin over the past 30 years, and recently sites have been tested and large-scale excavations completed. Survey reports as recently as the 1990s provided only limited lithic data, such as dividing flakes into primary, secondary, or interior categories, and general morphological classes for bifaces (e.g., Gray 1996; Hyatt 1990, 1991, 1992). Further, lithic materials are not discussed, and lithics play essentially no role in site interpretations. However, Carr et al. (1998), in discussing four sites located in Coahoma County, conduct a more detailed study of the lithic assemblages, as is particularly evident in the analysis of flake debris using classification schemes shown to be accurate with experimental assemblages outside the region. Importantly, explicit definitions of flake types are provided. Lithic materials are mainly classified as "local," but petrified wood, Mill Creek chert, and quartzite are also identified in the site assemblages. Little site interpretation is offered in this report other than making cultural-historical designations. Overall, MDOT survey reports are generally lacking in lithic data; this is not surprising, given the history of investigations in the area.

MDOT-sponsored site testing and large-scale excavation of sites in the Yazoo Basin vary in the attention paid to lithic assemblages. Greater consideration of lithic assemblages in more recent reports is directly due to MDOT archaeologists requiring lithic analyses, as specified in requests for proposals. Unsurprisingly, such requirements are due to individual MDOT archaeologists, who themselves had research interest in lithics. Importantly, these more recent studies benefited from modern CRM lab budgets, such that financing was less of an issue than it was in previous salvage and CRM work.

In an MDOT-sponsored project, Walling and Chapman (1999) provide little analysis and discussion of the admittedly limited lithic assemblage from the archaeological data recovery investigations at the McNight Site (22CO560). Specific lithic-material types are reported and trade is inferred to explain the variety of materials present such as novaculite, Burlington chert, and Fort Payne chert. A more nuanced discussion of direct versus indirect procurement would have been possible with a flake-debris classification system other than one based on primary, secondary, and tertiary (PST) categories and by providing raw-material data in tables with specific lithic categories, as opposed to a general discussion of raw materials. The PST categories had been shown by Bradbury and Carr (1995) to be no more accurate than a random guess in assigning flakes to a reduction stage. With regard to raw materials, a number of researchers (e.g., Andrefsky 1994; Ingbar 1994) had clearly argued the importance of providing raw material data for lithic studies. One limited aspect of this report is the attention paid to chert pebbles. The authors suggest that these pebbles are "probably the result of historic activity at the site," but account for a fair share of the reported data and presumably extra time in order to make tabulations such as "Count w/o pebbles" and "Weight w/o pebbles," which indicates that the previously presented counts included pebbles (Walling and Chapman 1999:Tables 9.1, 9.2, 9.3). These pebble data do not take us very far in examining prehistoric lifeways.

George et al. (2001) provide a much more detailed examination of the lithic assemblage and provide some inferences regarding prehistoric lifeways based on their study of nine Coahoma County sites. While raw material and lithic data are clearly articulated, the lack of definition of specific lithic categories is disappointing. That is, definitions for artifact categories such as early stage biface, bipolar flakes, and prismatic flakes are not provided. This makes comparisons with other assemblages impossible. Of particular interest is the determination of expedient tool function (George et al. 2001:Table 59), but again failure to specify how such determinations were made calls into question the utility of these data. In all, the lithic assemblage was treated in greater detail, but confidence in the analysis would have been strengthened by a thorough discussion of methods. Finally, while the raw material data are provided in a useful way, designating a "chalcedony/agate" category is surprising. It is suggested that "it likely was obtained from distant quarries such as the Citronelle deposits situated to the east," but one wonders if this material is not novaculite from Arkansas. Artifact photos are not in color or of sufficient quality that a definite determination can be made, but the "Chalcedony/agate Gary var. *Gary* projectile point/knife" shown in George et al. (2001:Figure 99) appears to be novaculite.

The final MDOT-sponsored CRM report reviewed here, Mooney et al. (2004) was based on large-scale excavations at two sites initially tested by George et al. (2001). As observed for others, this report has strengths and weaknesses in terms of lithic analysis. The clear strength is the effort put into describing and classifying lithics in terms of raw material. Not only are the physical characteristics of each type listed, but the source locations are provided. Perhaps unsurprisingly, no chalcedony/agate was identified, which is in contrast to the findings of George et al. (2001) at the same sites. What is surprising in this regard is the low amount of novaculite. That is, if what George et al. (2001) called chalcedony/agate was in actuality novaculite, then novaculite should have been identified by Mooney et al. (2004) in a similar proportion to chalcedony/agate in the earlier report. Perhaps this brings forth a significant underlying problem with regard to interobserver errors in lithic-material identification.

While the lithic material discussion is generally to be applauded, material types are presented by total counts and not by artifact type (Mooney et al. 2004:Table 11.5). This severely restricts the utility of the lithic data for comparative purposes and for assessing interpretations. The major weakness of the lithic analysis is the continued use of the PST classification system for flake debris and the lack of awareness of current trends in lithic analysis. Such observations could be made about much of the work in the Delta, but it is particularly glaring in such a recent report and for a situation in which agency archaeologists were attempting to have contractors take a more sophisticated approach to lithic analysis. The statement that "little information can be obtained from flake fragments" (Mooney et al. 2004:400) is simply incorrect, as there are analytical methods that do use flake fragments, including aggregate analyses (e.g., Ahler 1989) and individual flake analysis (e.g., Magne 1985; Sullivan and Rozen 1985). The fact that the flake fragment category is second only to shatter by count in the assemblage from one of the sites (Mooney et al. 2004:11.3) calls into question inferences drawn from the categories used. Finally, while a few interpretive statements based on lithic data are provided, such as "much of the initial reduction took place at areas of procurement" and "such economizing behavior is common in areas poor in lithic resources" (Mooney et al. 2004:400), more substantive statements might have been possible through the use of current theoretical approaches and methods.

This is not a complete overview of lithic studies from the Delta, but it does convey some sense of common approaches and methods. While some level of identification of raw materials is obvious in most recent studies, the extent to which it has dominated questions concerning lithics in the Delta might not be as obvious. This point is driven home by the more comprehensive study of lithic materials in the Delta and surrounding region by Gibson (1994b), discussed below as part of a specific examination of raw material procurement. Another area of previous study of Delta lithics that must be mentioned here is stone bead manufacture. John Connaway's (1977) study of the Denton lapidary industry stands as a classic, and his discussion of zoomorphic stone beads as "fetishes" and the manufacture of these beads by craft specialists inspires contemporary researchers (e.g., Carr and Hadley 2005; Crawford 2004; Gibson 2005). This discussion will be expanded in a later section concerning culture lifeways.

In sum, the history of the investigation of Mississippi Delta lithics is not as simple as it first appears. On the one hand, analysis of prehistoric pottery has far outpaced that of lithics. On the other hand, there are significant and arguably unique lithic assemblages in the Delta that have garnered the interest of archaeologists, specifically exotic raw materials and stone beads. Further, greater investigation of lithic assemblages corresponds with the salvage archaeology of the 1970s and subsequent CRM studies, and there are excellent discussions of specific aspects of lithic analysis, especially prehistoric exchange and lapidary industries. Yet, lithic studies common in other regions of the Southeast, such as detailed production-trajectory models involving a range of products and byproducts (e.g., Koldehoff 1990) and settlement pattern models based on stone-tool assemblages (Anderson and Hanson 1988; Bradbury 1998; Carr 1994) are absent in the Delta. This is saying something, considering that Carr and Bradbury (2000), in a review of the current state of lithic analyses from the Southeast, argue that lithic data are not used to their full potential in the region despite a current expansion of lithic analysis nationwide. Mississippi Delta lithic analysis lags behind the Southeast, which is arguably behind other major regions of the United States and beyond.

Nearly twenty years ago, Watson (1990) discussed trends and traditions in southeastern archaeology. The number-one tradition was pottery typology and pottery chronology (Watson 1990:43), and lithics failed to make the top-ten list. In this matter, Mississippi Delta archaeology and that of the Southeast region are congruent. Also considering overarching trends, Dunnell (1990:19) discusses the conservative nature of southeastern archaeology and points out that archaeologists in the region played "virtually no role" in the development of processual archaeology and seem "to be ignoring the post-processual faddish fluff as well." Specifically, Johnson (1993b:52) notes the lag time between the introduction of the processual approach in the discipline and the adoption of the paradigm by some lithic analysts in the Southeast. It is possible that the focus on pottery and the conservatism of archaeologists in the Southeast have combined to limit the general acceptance of advances in lithic analysis. While caution is understandable, continued reliance on outdated and demonstrably unreliable methods in the analysis of lithics is unacceptable and inhibits continued growth of the discipline. Carr and Bradbury (2000) discuss seven fundamental problems with the manner in which lithic analysis is generally conducted in the Southeast: providing only generic lithic data; uncritical acceptance of analytical methods; lack of knowledge of the recent literature; lack of testing of new methods/theory building; failure to integrate tool and flake data; and not interpreting lithic data in relation to other artifact classes. These same problems are evident and in some cases magnified in lithic studies from the Delta. For example, one archaeologist with considerable local expertise recently mentioned that he had not heard of an organization-of-technology approach. This is somewhat surprising, given its prominence in lithic studies for the past fifteen years, and given that it continues to be used and expanded by some southeastern archaeologists (e.g., Bradbury 1998; Carr and Stewart 2004; Cobb 2000).

Goals of Archaeology

While previous investigations affect the trajectory of research in a region, an individual's course of study and experiences affects the trajectory of their personal research. Despite significant theoretical debate over the past two decades, I remain committed to the three goals outlined in my undergraduate archaeological method and theory text. David Hurst Thomas (1979) outlined those goals as constructing culture histories, inferring past lifeways, and understanding culture change. The first goal involving culture history is about answering questions concerning who was where and when. The second goal of lifeways addresses questions of what and how. The final of these goals involves why things have changed. Since that time many archaeologists have added a fourth goal of informing the public, which involves answering a wide variety of questions (cf. Peacock 2005b), including, "did you"; that is, "did you find any gold?"

Here, I will examine how chipped-stone tool assemblages from the Delta can aid in achieving these goals. I do not suggest that these goals can be attained by lithic analysis alone; rather, the use of multiple lines of evidence is critical for this endeavor. If appropriate methods are used, lithics can serve as one of these lines of evidence and play a significant role in archaeological studies.

Culture History

The archaeological investigation of culture history involves placing sites and artifacts in space and time. Hafted bifaces are the type of stone tool most commonly considered diagnostic of a period or a space-time unit such as a phase. The Mississippi Delta was one of the regions where the cultural-historical paradigm was developed and tested. As previously discussed, stone tools essentially played no role in the archaeological investigations of the region; this holds true for cultural-historical units until more recent archaeological investigations.

Sam McGahey (2000) has written the most comprehensive examination of diagnostic hafted bifaces for the state of Mississippi. This work discusses each type in chronological order and provides a map of the state with indications of those counties where a particular type has been found. Therefore, with a little work one can determine which types occur in the Yazoo Basin. For McGahey (2000:x), each type "is understood to represent a group of people within a certain area during a certain period." However, he recognizes that this publication does not represent the "final word" on types for the state, due to continuing research and the lack of understanding of variation in any particular type. It is this latter point that is critical, and one with which every publication addressing cultural-historical types must wrestle: that is, attempting to illustrate the range of variability within any particular type. This is not only a problem for publication, but also a theoretical issue that involves definitions of type and an understanding of why types change. To his credit, McGahey (2000:xii) has made "a conscientious effort in that direction, illustrating every known stage of each point type."

It is critical for researchers to heed McGahey's (2000:xiii) warning that "works such as this can never be complete." Instead of using this "guide" as providing the end point for cultural-historical research, archaeologists must test the cultural-historical inferences for specific regions. As an alternative to classifying hafted bifaces according to the types present in this guide, archaeologists must specifically determine whether, for example, Cache River points from the Yazoo Basin in fact date between 9500 and 9000 B.P. (McGahey 2000:45). Might the adoption of this form of hafted biface have occurred earlier than in other regions, or continued later? The majority of examples in McGahey's guide comes from private collections; therefore, contextual data are minimal. Absolute dating and stratigraphic context from sites in Mississippi are unavailable for many of these types. Therefore, date ranges and relationships to other types are often based on speculation or occurrences outside Mississippi.

In an article concerning the Cape Dorset culture on Baffin Island that may not be widely read by many archaeologists working in the Delta, Odess (1998) examines prehistoric interactions based on stylistic changes in artifacts as compared to interactions based on the occurrences of certain materials. Odess (1998:421) suggests that

in regions such as the Arctic, where local cultural histories of many areas are still poorly understood and many assemblages insufficiently dated, attempts to use style as an indicator of interaction run the risk of relying too heavily on typology-based chronologies derived from other areas to meet with success. Implicit in such chronologies is an assumption of homogeneity in the regional distribution of stylistic forms, which runs risks of obscuring significant spatiotemporal variation in the emergence and spread of particular tool forms. The outcome is a conflation of style and chronology that results in difficulty in recognizing situations in which artifact style in one area is decidedly out of step with what is occurring in other places. Under these circumstances, when age and style are conflated, radiocarbon dates that do not accord with the expectations derived from typology-based chronologies are likely to be seen as anomalous or bad.

Using "multiple and independent lines of evidence," Odess (1998:431) is able to develop a convincing cultural-historical framework as well as inferring a variety of interactions that would not have been identifiable otherwise. Lessons from this study are many and varied, but perhaps most important is that types are not distinct pigeonholes, but vary in time through space. By examining such variation, significant insight can be gained into cultural lifeways and culture process.

Culture Lifeways

One approach found useful for investigating cultural lifeways using prehistoric lithic assemblages is technological organization. This approach is not particularly new, except perhaps for explicit application to lithic assemblages from the Delta. Nelson (1991:57) effectively defined the organization of technology as "the study of the selection and integration of strategies for making, using, transporting, and discarding tools and the materials needed for their manufacture and maintenance." In an early example, Robert Kelly (1988) examined "the three sides of a biface" in conjunction with raw-material distributions in the Carson Sink of Nevada and suggested that a shift from the use of bifaces as cores to the infrequent use of bifaces as tools is indicative of the prehistoric occupants having changed from a logistical settlement strategy to short-term residential use of the area. Carr (1994:1) suggests that "adopting an organization approach to technology provides a framework for assessing variability within and among archaeological chipped stone assemblages," which "can be related to the functional requirements of tool use as well as the organization of the overall cultural system." An organization-of-technology approach has been widely applied (e.g., Andrefsky 1994; Carr and Stewart 2004; Shott 1989), but is not without its critics (e.g., Simek 1994; Torrence 1994). In particular, Clark (1999:126) has criticized the use of an organization-of-technology approach as dehumanizing and offers praxis theory as an alternative. Other analysts, who also recognize the need for examining the human agent and situating lithic analyses in a historical framework, are working to extend an organization-of-technology approach to include these elements (e.g., Cobb 2000).

While an organization-of-technology approach continues to be developed, lithic analysts are successfully employing it to understand the relationships among technology, economic/social strategies, and the environment. A simple model presented as a diagram outlining the basic tenets of this approach was developed by Margaret Nelson (1991:59). In the diagram, the environment sets the stage for social and economic strategies, which affect tool design and activity distribution, which in turn affect tool morphology and tool distribution, respectively. Archaeologists, then, can work from both ends of the diagram in an attempt to get at social and economic strategies. While this model has proved an important conceptual tool for lithic analysts examining prehistoric technological organization, it fails to include an important component of chipped-stone assemblages, flake debris. In place of Nelson's narrow focus on stone tools, a greater consideration of flake debris would allow better understanding of activities at specific sites and more accurate inferences concerning prehistoric behavior. In addition to tool design affecting tool morphology, it affects the morphology of flakes. Likewise, activity distribution affects both tool distribution and the distribution of flake debris. Expanding Nelson's model in this manner addresses one of the problems noted by Carr and Bradbury (2000) as evident in lithic studies in the Southeast, namely the lack of integration of flake and tool data.

Importantly, an organizational approach to technology emphasizes raw material acquisition, production, use, reuse, and discard as each plays a significant role in understanding the formation of lithic assemblages. With a comprehensive understanding of the types and accessibility of lithic raw materials, significant behavioral information can be derived from the analysis of lithic-assemblage variation. Detailed analysis of the entire lithic assemblage (i.e., tools, cores, and flake debris) and comparative analysis of the distribution of various assemblage types can provide insight into trade and mobility patterns as well as other aspects of culture. For example, it would be useful to know if the lithic assemblage at a mound center contained nonlocal materials and whether these materials were treated differently than locally available sources. One would want to insure that those materials identified as nonlocal to the region were not available as secondary deposits in the gravel bars of the Mississippi River. Also, it would be of use to know if the flake debris of nonlocal materials represented only tool resharpening or whether all stages of manufacture are present. Many other potential examples come to mind, but the important point is that Mississippi Delta lithics have the potential to provide an additional line of evidence for the investigation of prehistoric behavior that is on par with and complements other artifact classes.

Other than Jay Johnson's work, a technological organization approach remains largely unused in the Mississippi Delta. While he did not explicitly tie his study (Johnson 1993c) of Poverty Point–period quartz crystal drill bits, microliths, and social organization in the Yazoo Basin to such an approach, the tenets are readily seen. For example, he states: "I think that it is clear that technological systems, when modeled with enough detail, can shed light on things other than technology and function" (Johnson 1993c:63). He presents a range of blade core data for the Jaketown, Paxton Brake, and Slate sites, including: number of platforms, platform orientation, scar counts per platform, and percent of platform circumference showing blade removal. Additionally, he presents "needle" measurement data and discusses raw material use. He asks the question (Johnson 1993c:63), "if the sites were part of the same chiefdom-based economic system, should we expect uniformity in technology as well as style and raw material?" He answers affirmatively and, finding differences in the three Yazoo Basin sites states, "it is evident that chiefdom-level organization had not been achieved at this time in this region of the Southeast" (1993c:63). While discussions could ensue regarding the linkage of specific technological attributes to the concept of technological style and the relation of technology to political organization, it is clear that much is to be gained from looking at lithic artifact form and distribution to answer larger social and economic questions. Here, a brief examination of raw material acquisition, production, use, reuse, and discard is used to highlight the potential of a technological organization approach for employing Delta lithic assemblages in addressing questions of prehistoric lifeways.

Raw Material Procurement

There is considerable agreement about one aspect of lithic raw materials in the Mississippi Delta. Charles McNutt, Sr., (1996:159) sums it up this way for the Upper Yazoo Basin: "The major deficiency was stone, which had to be obtained by trade, from the beds of rivers draining the loess hills, or from gravel bars in the Mississippi River." There is debate amongst professionals concerning the variety of cherts available in the gravel bars of the Mississippi River, such that many of the presumed exotic cherts are thought by some to be in the gravels. However, Penman (1977:4) suggests that "most of the gravels on the modern Mississippi River gravel bars are yellow chert," though the empirical evidence for this claim is lacking. Gibson (1994b:132) has effectively argued against the assertion that what are commonly considered exotic cherts in the LMV, such as Fort Payne, Dover, Burlington, and Ste. Genevieve, were actually acquired from gravel bars of the Mississippi River. A similar argument is made by Carr and Stewart (2004), specifically concerning exotic materials from the Poverty Point site, and their use of regional lithic experts outside the LMV may prove a valuable model for future studies of Delta lithics.

An excellent beginning into the investigation of an available local lithic material, Citronelle gravel, on the periphery of the Mississippi Alluvial Valley was accomplished by Richard Stallings (1989). He provides a quantitative description of the macroscopic characteristics of chert samples collected from the Loess Bluffs of northwestern Mississippi in both their natural and thermally altered condition. This important lithic resource needs further investigation, and Stallings' study provides a foundation for future research.

More often, raw-material data are not available in Delta lithic studies. Here, two studies at different scales, region versus site-specific, are discussed. Jon Gibson (1994b) has provided an empirical characterization of exchange systems in LMV prehistory. One must appreciate the data he amassed from various studies, which largely represent chipped-stone artifacts. He suggests that "the most salient point of this comparison is that, except for the Late Archaic Denton site and most Poverty Point components, local lithic resources make up over 90 percent of the industrial materials. At Denton, local gravels constitute over three-quarters of the stock, and among Poverty Point components they drop as low as 18.6 percent" (Gibson 1994b:153). He characterizes Late Archaic and Tchula as examples of "ad hoc exchange" (1994b:168) due to the small volume of materials. In contrast, Poverty Point exchange is the "most vigorous and far-reaching system to operate in the area" and "the Poverty Point site came to dominate management of the whole exchange network" (Gibson 1994b:168). Finally, Gibson describes Marksville exchange as "the last really extensive system to visibly affect Lower Mississippi prehistoric development," but characterizes it as composed of "ad hoc trading contacts" (Gibson 1994b:169). Such big-picture comparisons are extremely important for our understanding of prehistory and providing contexts for viewing specific sites, but detailed consideration of particular sites can in turn refine data for the big picture.

Looking at raw-material acquisition at a single site in the Delta, Teoc Creek, a Poverty Point site in Carroll County, Mississippi, reported by Connaway et al. (1977), can show the difficulty of making large-scale comparisons without considering other aspects of technological organization. The chipped-stone assemblage at Teoc Creek is characterized as "bifacial and unifacial tools made almost entirely from pebble or cobble cores" (Connaway et al. 1977:34). Sixteen raw-material categories are listed, of which the first nine are all obtainable within a few miles of the site. Collapsing the data, 96 percent of the assemblage is local materials and only 4 percent nonlocal. But, the fact that any nonlocal material at all is present suggests something in need of explanation. The question arises, were the nonlocal materials acquired by direct or indirect acquisition? Just looking at the variety of raw materials originally listed, one would think direct acquisition is unlikely. This is because of the widely different geographic areas involved, but the question remains whether one of the materials could represent direct acquisition. Addressing these questions essentially causes one to consider aspects of behavior other than raw material acquisition, such as tool design, rates of curation, etc. The nonlocal materials at Teoc Creek could all have originated from a portable, curated tool kit. Finished points, bifacial cores, and drills are generally considered curated tools. The small number of flakes and blades resulting from reduction further supports the idea that there was little production of tools at the site, and activities were mainly oriented to the maintenance of curated tools. The lack of blade cores of exotic materials in the Teoc Creek assemblage may point to the curated nature of this artifact type. Further, the fact that 14 percent of the hafted bifaces are of nonlocal material, over three times that of the entire assemblage, is indicative of the sensitivity of raw-material percentages to tool type. This makes clear that a more accurate understanding of raw-material usage is gained from consideration of different artifact classes and comparisons between those classes. This is because each likely played a different, but related, role in how prehistoric people solved the problem of using stone tools to carry out certain tasks, but without always having raw materials easily available. One last comment: if we start with the supposition that Fort Payne chert was acquired directly by Teoc Creek peoples as part of their seasonal round, then this impacts the manner in which we think about the inhabitants' participation in exchange systems. That is, detailed study of each raw material present in an assemblage and consideration of how it was acquired will impact the way we characterize regional exchange. Obviously, raw-material data are best employed when considered in the context of other aspects of technological organization.

Much more could be written concerning raw materials in the Mississippi Delta. Interesting patterning in the use of raw materials has been explained for individual site assemblages and at region-wide scales. Here, I would simply echo Ingbar (1994:50):

> Thus, we are presented with a seeming Gordian knot: a causal arrow cannot be said to generally point one way or the other. Raw material acquisition and stone tool production, use, and discard are two sides of the same coin: technological organization. Interpretation of raw material source presence in an assemblage is most effective and probably most accurate, when it is linked with studies of tool production, discard, use, and maintenance.

Production

Technological organizational studies involve not only considerations of raw material, but also aspects of design and technological strategies such as curated and expedient. Flake debris has played an increasing role in understanding production activities at particular sites because flakes are rarely curated, in contrast to most stone tools. An examination of stone-tool production in the Mississippi Delta is difficult due to the lack of study of flake debris. For example, the Teoc Creek study involved simply sorting flake debris by raw material and providing counts, as was common for the time. However, even these basic data demonstrate differences in the reduction of local and nonlocal materials. Excluding the blade industry, for nonlocal materials there is almost an equal number of flakes and nonflakes, that is, cores and tools, but for the local materials there are over two-and-a-half times as many flakes as nonflakes.

If flakes were classified by reduction stage, we could further explore patterning between flakes and other components of the lithic assemblage.

Jay Johnson (1993b:46) has suggested that analysis of flake debris shows a certain level of maturity in lithic analysis. An article entitled "Delta Debitage," by Johnson and Raspet (1980), develops a flake-debris classification scheme. It is a two-dimensional paradigm employing amount of dorsal cortex and platform morphology. It is argued that these two attributes "reflect the technological expectations of bifacial reduction in a gravel based industry" (Johnson and Raspet 1980:4). While this classification may well provide the kind of data the researchers intend, experiments with other raw materials have called into question the relationship of cortex to reduction stage (Bradbury and Carr 1995; Magne 1985). The merits of the classification scheme could be debated, but categories are well defined, and the failure of subsequent researchers to use this scheme or other methods that are equally unambiguous remains problematic.

In a study of production-trajectory modeling in Mississippi, which includes three assemblages from the Yazoo Basin, Johnson (1989) uses the aforementioned flake-debris scheme and a biface classification key to make inferences concerning prehistoric behavior and the influence of distance from raw material sources. While interesting patterns emerge from the aggregate data, that distance from raw-materials sources is the determinant of the patterning is assumed rather than tested. This is evident in the manner that exceptions are explained away. For example, Johnson (1989:124) expects that there should be a negative correlation between distance from source and biface rejects, but his Yalobusha sample from the Delta stands as an exception. He explains that this is due to heavy collection by nonarchaeologists at a particular site in the sample, such that finished bifaces are underrepresented. This suggests that greater discussion of this particular bias should be included for each assemblage and the patterning reassessed. While I might disagree with the way data are presented and interpreted, I heartily agree with his conclusions that comprehensive production-trajectory modeling can play an important role in detecting patterns and that a basic research strategy would begin with a consideration of raw material sources.

No discussion of Mississippi Delta production involving lithics would be complete without mention of stone-bead manufacture and the question of craft specialization. Are craft specialists involved in the production of certain special items such as chert beads at the Denton site? John Connaway (1977), the leading authority on the lapidary industry of the Mississippi Delta, has effectively argued so. In a recent presentation, Connaway (2004:1) argued that "concerning stone zoomorphic beads, pendants, and certain other effigies, it is my opinion that they were created both psychologically and physically by specialists who were trained in their spiritual interpretations, their uses, and various manufacturing techniques." Production techniques for stone beads have been discussed in a general manner by Connaway (1977, 1982c, 2004). Johnson (2000) develops a production sequence for chert-bead manufacture, but does not see evidence for specialists in the manufacturing technique. The question of whether craft specialists manufactured stone beads is an important one, as it bears on questions of increasing cultural complexity that continue to be discussed for Archaic cultures in the Southeast (see Gibson and Carr 2004).

Use

Use-wear studies of stone tools are rare in the Southeast and even rarer in the Mississippi Delta. A continuing problem is the linking of functional terms to morphological types and treating such types as indicative of specific activities. Unfortunately, this situation means that little can be said concerning stone-tool use. Use-wear data can aid in determining whether stone tools are curated or expedient (Odell 1996a) and play a key role in helping to infer prehistoric activities and occupation types (Odell 1996b).

An artifact class from the Delta that deserves special attention with regard to use is a particular biface category. Referred to in the literature variably as choppers, celts, adzes, crude bifaces, and thin bifaces, these artifacts are not particularly restricted in time, but are certainly ubiquitous at some sites that date to the Middle and Late Archaic. "Delta" choppers or adzes may or may not exhibit polish, and due to vagaries in defining this artifact class it would be impossible to make comparisons between site assemblages. Use-wear analysis would provide information on tool function, and this would undoubtedly aid in making interpretations.

Great potential for investigating tool use exists in other avenues, including the recording of tool-failure types and examining the amount of retouch. By recording failure types, it can often be determined if a tool was broken in production or use. New methods are being developed and tested to measure the amount of resharpening (e.g., Bradbury and Carr 2005; Clarkson 2002). Both tool-failure types and resharpening provide information concerning tool-use life, and the point in its use life at which a tool was discarded can provide further insight into the organization of technology.

Discard

The final aspect of technological organization examined here is discard. Curiously, this has been given little attention by archaeologists, but obviously is a key to assemblage formation. Why are so many complete points found in the archaeological record? Prehistoric choice as to what and when to discard can provide important insights into prehistoric technological strategies. The

Denton assemblage includes 63 adzes and 174 choppers, as well as 153 broken bifaces (Connaway 1977). As previously mentioned, knowledge of the use of choppers and adzes is critical for accurate understanding of prehistoric activities, but the quantity discarded at the site needs careful consideration. Does the amount indicate year-long occupation or a particularly intensive engagement in a "chopper"-using activity? Such questions are most fruitfully addressed in the context of the entire lithic assemblage and other site characteristics.

Flake debris also can play an important role in understanding discard patterns. For example, at Teoc Creek exotic cream-colored chert was only identified in the blade and flake categories. This suggests that perhaps blade cores and tools of this material, from which the flakes were removed, were curated and discarded at another location. As with other aspects of technological organization, it is difficult to investigate discard patterns due to a lack of published information such as number of broken tools, failure types, and flake debris stages.

Culture Process

There is little I can say about culture process, described here as the third goal of archaeology, and the presence of lithics in the Delta. Others have described some general trends (e.g. McNutt 1996), and I do not believe I could go much further. This is not because, as Philip Phillips (1970) would likely argue, I am getting ahead of myself with trying to examine culture lifeways and culture process before constructing solid culture histories. My reasoning behind not trying to examine culture process in the Delta using lithic data is due to the kinds of data available. Rather than seeing Thomas' goals as separate, I would argue that the best results are achieved when working on all three goals simultaneously. In order to accurately interpret variation in stone tool form through space and time, we must also understand how that tool was part of a prehistoric technology, as well as how and why technologies change.

In order to address cultural process, archaeologists will need to insure that adequate samples of lithics are obtained from sites investigated. The usual scenario for work in the Delta is obtaining a reasonable sample of lithics from the surface and then very small samples of lithics, mostly flakes, from subsurface investigations. While there are only limited studies that could be conducted of surface assemblages of mixed time periods, the fine-screening of subsurface deposits would insure retrieval of small-flake debris and tools; broken drill-bit ends are often the size of a rice grain. At certain sites in the Delta, it may be that the majority of the chipped-stone assemblage is a result of the resharpening of stone tools. This resharpening will most often produce no flakes caught in a quarter-inch screen, but could be retrieved in a sixteenth-inch screen. Insuring that such samples are routinely recovered, and keeping in mind that even a small assemblage is providing information about technological organization, will go a long way in allowing us to examine change through time.

Public Education

Engaging the public in archaeology should be a significant concern of all archaeologists today. The public is interested in both the scientific methods employed in archaeology and the human past these methods reveal. In studying artifacts, it is important not to forget the individual person who manufactured, used, and discarded the artifact for both humanistic and scientific reasons. It is an interest in our shared past and what can be learned from traveling down "Time's River" that makes archaeology worthwhile. Involving native peoples will add richness to these endeavors and have a variety of benefits.

Perhaps surprisingly, stone tools can serve as a potential bridge between archaeologists and the general public. Collecting stone tools is a longtime tradition in the Delta, as elsewhere, and many of the better-known stone artifacts, such as stone beads, are in private hands. Much can be learned from working with private collections that have provenience. For example, the Slate site is argued to represent a Poverty Point occupation that shows intensive production of beads from an exotic material (Lauro and Lehman 1982), and Johnson (1993c) used cores, blades, and retouched bladelets from private collections of Slate-site materials to argue against the occupants being part of a chiefdom. Currently, Cliff Jenkins (personal communication) is working toward recording additional artifacts in private hands from the Slate site. Reaching out to the public, developing educational programs, and providing ways for people to get involved in archaeology will aid in recording, researching, and preserving the archaeological record of the Delta.

Conclusions

When I accepted the invitation to write an overview of Mississippi Delta lithics, this is not the study I thought I would conduct. I started out gathering tables of data from various sites and attempted to make raw-material categories and artifact classes comparable. Instead of resulting in something I could use, the data were both generic and suspect.

Interobserver error has not always been a major concern for archaeologists, but it undoubtedly impacts the science of archaeology (Beck and Jones 1989). Odell (1989) has argued for a 95-percent level of congruence between lithic analysts, and this has been achieved by lithic analysts for certain flake attributes (see also Bradbury and Carr 1995). The problem of interobserver error and comparability of data is one of the largest stumbling blocks for lithic analysts working in the Mississippi Delta and beyond. Two brief remedies will be discussed here.

Obviously, raw materials are an important consideration for studies of lithics in general, and this has been one area of focus for Delta lithic analysts. The question arises as to whether different lithic analysts would agree on the classification of a given piece of stone. A comprehensive study of raw material availability in the Mississippi Delta, building on previous research (i.e., Stallings 1989), is critical and must include gravel bars, especially those of the Mississippi River itself. This study must address questions of the range of variability in a given source as well as the density. This study should also attempt to identify potential look-alikes between local and nonlocal sources. One strategy would be to take stone from the Delta to lithic analysts outside the region and see if they can distinguish it from materials available in their region. While visiting these lithic analysts, it would be of use to obtain samples of lithics from their areas and for comparative collections that could be housed at various locations in the state, including MDAH.

A second improvement in method I will briefly discuss is in production, specifically flake-debris analysis. Comparability is a problem here due to classifying flake debris using undefined or disparate variables. Shott (1994) has argued for a minimal set of flake attributes specifically to address the problem of comparability between site assemblages. While recording these attributes is a good start, conducting experiments with gravel cherts from the Delta and determining which attributes best define reduction stages is an even better method. The development of a standard classification for bifaces and other chipped-stone tools would also go far in providing data for intersite comparisons.

This overview did not include a discussion of all lithic data available from the Mississippi Delta, but it is also apparent that existing data are unsuitable for answering many questions posed in contemporary lithic studies. A previous focus on pottery and the problem of those pesky boys picking up all the stone tools led some past researchers to downplay the importance of lithic studies. Here, I hope to have demonstrated that lithic analysis has the potential to provide significant information about prehistoric peoples of the Delta. Variation in access to lithic materials and variation in nonlocal materials in certain lithic assemblages make the Mississippi Delta a particularly fertile ground for investigating prehistoric technological organization. Perhaps Jay Johnson (1989:131) summed it up best in an article in a volume entitled *Alternative Approaches to Lithic Analysis*, in making the statement, "in Mississippi, as elsewhere, we still have a lot of work to do."

Acknowledgments

I would like to thank Janet Rafferty and Evan Peacock for asking me to participate in this project. My esteemed colleagues and friends, Janet and Evan, are the exemplars of do-it-all archaeologists. They are an inspiration because of their dedication to research, teaching, and service to the discipline. Their successes in these areas inspire me to work to become a better archaeologist. I would like to thank Sam Brookes for his enthusiasm for all things dealing with Mississippi archaeology, sharing his knowledge of the Delta, and comments on this paper. I would also like to thank T. R. Kidder for comments on this paper and for helping me to remember the person behind the stone tool.

It has been some time since I produced a sole-authored publication. The lack of additional names is not an indication that this work reflects only my thoughts. While a number of people have shaped my way of thinking about archaeology and lithics, Andrew Bradbury is the person from whom I have benefited most. I cannot wait until we attend the next lithics paper at a conference, chat about rocks over a beer, or e-mail pieces of our next co-authored paper back and forth. Thanks to all of these folks for making archaeology more fun than baseball!

11

Review of Ceramic Compositional Studies from In and Around the Mississippi Valley

Hector Neff

Introduction

This chapter summarizes published and unpublished ceramic compositional studies undertaken over the past half-century relevant to the archaeology of the Yazoo Basin and vicinity. In general terms, the objective of these studies has been to examine patterns of interaction among prehistoric populations, both within the Mississippi valley and between the valley and adjacent regions. Time periods addressed span the range from Late Archaic through Mississippian.

A number of projects have examined ceramic compositional variation in the Southeast and/or in the Lower Mississippi Valley (LMV). Perhaps the closest project directly relevant to the study area is a pilot project by Peacock and his colleagues (Peacock et al. 2003) examining the possibility that consistent differences in shell temper composition could be used to identify pottery that moved between drainages. Although preliminary results are promising, no conclusive data bearing on prehistoric interaction patterns have yet emerged from this project.

Aside from the shell temper characterization work of Peacock and colleagues, ceramic-characterization studies in the Mississippi valley can be categorized as either based on mineralogical characterization of paste inclusions or on elemental characterization of whole ceramic pastes (including both clay and nonplastic inclusions). The former approach typically relies heavily on optical petrography, whereas the latter has relied most heavily on instrumental neutron activation analysis (INAA). Because many more projects have been undertaken and many more samples have been analyzed via INAA, I devote most attention in this chapter to INAA studies. I present a brief summary of mineralogical studies first.

Mineralogical Characterization of Mississippi Valley Ceramics

Petrographic analysis of ceramic pastes has been used sporadically within the Mississippi valley since the 1950s. Elizabeth Weaver (1963) built on Anna Shepard's methods for texture analysis in a study of Tchula pottery from the LMV, concluding that the importance of natural as opposed to added inclusions of fiber and sand may have been underestimated. Shepard (1964) praised Weaver's study as an example of "balance at a time when interest is centered in physical methods of analysis that yield chemical data," initiating a spurious yet persistent opposition between petrographic and chemical approaches (e.g., Stoltman and Mainfort 2002). In another comment on Weaver's study, James Warren Porter (1964) describes his own observations and experiments with grog tempering, which lead him to doubt Weaver's conclusion that Tchula pottery is untempered. Galaty (this volume) further discusses this issue.

Bareis and Porter (1965) used mineralogical techniques to resolve questions about the source of an engraved, Caddoan-like bowl recovered from a burial at Cahokia. Porter studied the vessel paste both in thin section and crushed and mounted in refractive-index oils, and he had powder X-ray diffraction run to identify clay and nonplastic minerals. Comparisons with a larger collection of thin sections from Cahokia and nearby sites indicated that the vessel was nonlocal to the American Bottom, and assessment of the geology in surrounding regions pointed to the margins of the LMV as the most likely source. The basic methods employed in this study—comparing suspected imports to the range of variation in presumed local materials and considering geological characteristics of potential foreign sources—generalize quite easily to provenance investigations based on chemical characterization (e.g., Steponaitis et al. 1996). Stoltman (1989, 1991) has also used petrographic analysis in studies of Mississippi valley ceramics. He employs a point-counting technique that quantifies the amount of "grit," matrix, and sand in sherds, and assumes that shared textural characteristics imply a shared production location and tradition. Although he argues that elemental and petrographic techniques are complementary, Stoltman (1989:158) voices the traditional ceramic petrographer's defensiveness (e.g., Shepard 1964), when he states that petrography is "perhaps in jeopardy of being overlooked due to recent technological advances in elemental identification."

An alternative approach to quantifying texture characteristics involves image analysis of thin sections (e.g., Livingood 2003; Ortmann and Kidder 2004). In one study of ceramic fabrics from the LMV, Ortmann and Kidder (2004) address the question of whether the Poverty Point ceramic tradition, which includes untempered and fiber-tempered variants, was an indigenous development or comprised mainly imported pottery. Image analysis of thin sections and subsequent statistical analysis of the data suggested that most sherds were within the range of textural variation of local Poverty Point soils. One Weeden Island sherd from Florida was shown to fall outside the range of variation of Poverty Point specimens. The authors admit, however, that since potters in different locations might choose soils with similar characteristics, the textural approach alone cannot discriminate nonlocal from local pottery (Ortmann and Kidder 2004). In making this admission, Ortmann and Kidder expose the basic fallacy of Stoltman's (1989, 1991) assumption that textural groups correspond neatly to sources; whether quantified via image analysis or by Stoltman's laborious point-counting technique, ceramic texture arises out of an interaction between potters and the local ceramic environment (Arnold 1985), and thus cannot be assumed to provide a straightforward linkage of ceramics to source raw materials.

Petrographic analysis of ceramic thin sections, whether based on qualitative identification of nonlocal mineral assemblages or quantified textural characteristics, obviously has much to offer archaeology, as has been obvious since Shepard's (1956) time. Unfortunately, the polemical tone of several recent studies (Stoltman 1989, 1991; Stoltman and Mainfort 2002) has overshadowed substantive contributions, and such contributions have been few and far between in any case. Moreover, with the exception of Ortmann and Kidder's (2004) work, these studies have not addressed important methodological issues, such as how the depositional environment constrains the geographic resolution achievable with petrography-based provenance determination. For ceramic raw materials obtained within a river valley fed by a huge catchment like the Mississippi, where sediments are thoroughly mixed and remixed, such methodological issues are crucial.

INAA-based Ceramic Provenance Research

As mentioned previously, bulk-elemental characterization studies of pottery from in and around the Mississippi valley are dominated by INAA studies. INAA of Mississippian ceramics was initiated some time ago by Steponaitis and Blackman (1981) at the National Institute of Standards and Technology, but the vast majority of the work since approximately 1990 has been undertaken at the University of Missouri Research Reactor Center (MURR). Consequently, INAA procedures employed at MURR will be described briefly before summarizing the results of the various studies.

INAA is a highly reliable bulk-sample characterization technique that has been demonstrated repeatedly over the past 35 years to yield convincing information on the sources of inorganic archaeological materials (e.g., Bishop et al.

1982; Glascock 1992; Glascock and Neff 2003; Harbottle 1976; Neff 2000; Perlman and Asaro 1969, 1971). The MURR program has generated the vast majority of INAA data on ceramics, obsidian, and other archaeological materials since about 1989, when the current program was first funded by the National Science Foundation (NSF). The following paragraphs summarize standard sample preparation and analytical procedures as well as quantitative data-analysis techniques normally used at MURR, which were used in the INAA studies discussed below. More detailed descriptions can be found in a number of publications (e.g., Glascock 1992; Neff 2000, 2002; Neff and Glowacki 2002).

Sample Preparation

Pottery specimens were prepared for INAA by first removing surfaces and all adhering soil with a silicon carbide burr. Burred samples were then washed with deionized water and allowed to dry in air. Finally, the cleaned sherds were crushed in an agate mortar to yield a fine powder. Part of each specimen was retained, unpowdered, for the MURR archive of analyzed ceramic fabrics.

The powder samples were oven-dried at 100° C for 24 hours. Portions of approximately 200 mg were weighed and placed in small polyvials used for short irradiations. At the same time, another 200 mg of each sample were weighed into high-purity quartz vials used for long irradiations. Along with the unknown samples, reference standards of SRM-1633a (coal fly ash) and SRM-688 (basalt rock) were similarly prepared, as were quality-control samples (i.e., standards treated as unknowns) of SRM-278 (obsidian rock) and Ohio Red Clay.

Irradiation and Gamma-Ray Spectroscopy

Neutron-activation analysis of ceramics at MURR, which consists of two irradiations and a total of three gamma counts, constitutes a superset of the procedures used at most other laboratories (Glascock 1992; Neff 2000). In brief, a short irradiation is carried out through the pneumatic-tube irradiation system. Samples in the polyvials are sequentially irradiated, two at a time, for five seconds at a neutron flux of 8×10^{13} n/cm^2/s. The 720-second count yields gamma spectra containing peaks for the short-lived elements Al, Ba, Ca, Dy, K, Mn, Na, Ti, and V. The samples in quartz vials are subjected to a 24-hour irradiation at a neutron flux of 5×10^{13} n/cm^2/s. This long irradiation is analogous to the single irradiation used at most other laboratories. After the long irradiation, samples decay for seven days, then are counted for 2,000 seconds (the "middle count") on a high-resolution germanium detector coupled to an automatic sample changer. The middle count yields determinations of seven medium half-life elements, namely As, La, Lu, Nd, Sm, U, and Yb. After an additional three- or four-week decay, a final count of 10,000 seconds is carried out on each sample. The latter measurement yields the following 17 long–half-life elements: Ce, Co, Cr, Cs, Eu, Fe, Hf, Ni, Rb, Sb, Sc, Sr, Ta, Tb, Th, Zn, and Zr.

Elemental concentration data from the two irradiations and three counts (a total of 33 elements) are assembled into a single tabulation and stored in dBASE and Excel formats together with descriptive information available for each sample. All analytical data summarized in this chapter are archived in the MURR databank, and some of them are available publicly via the World Wide Web, at http://www.missouri.edu/~glascock/archlab.htm. Requests for results summarized here but not yet published elsewhere should be directed to Michael D. Glascock at MURR.

In some cases MURR data were combined with INAA data from the National Bureau of Standards (now the National Institute of Standards and Technology, or NIST) (Steponaitis et al. 1996). The NIST data were calibrated with MURR data using conversion factors obtained from multiple analyses of a homogeneous check standard (Ohio Red Clay) analyzed in both labs.

Quantitative Analysis of the Chemical Data

INAA of pottery at MURR produces elemental concentration values for 33 elements. Ni is usually below detection in a large number of specimens, and is therefore usually dropped from consideration.

A further complication in compositional studies of Southeastern and Mississippian ceramics is that these ceramics are often shell-tempered, and shell dramatically enriches concentrations of elements abundant in shell, especially calcium, strontium, and barium, making them unreliable for source analysis. Other elements are correspondingly diluted by this effect. Therefore, in several of the studies considered here, calcium, strontium, and barium are eliminated from consideration, and the dilution effect of shell temper on the other elements is removed by the following correction, originally suggested by Blackman (Steponaitis and Blackman 1981; Steponaitis et al. 1996; also see Cogswell et al. 1998):

$$e' = (10^6 e)/(10^6 - 2.5 Ca)$$

e' being the corrected (undiluted) concentration of the element of interest, e being the measured concentration in the shell-tempered sherd, and Ca being the concentration of calcium. Cogswell et al. (1998) show with pottery replicates that this correction very accurately reproduces the original chemical fingerprint of noncalcareous clay.

At MURR, analytical data are normally transformed to log base 10 values. This is done for two reasons. First, logging the data compensates for differences in magnitude between major elements, such as Al and Fe, on one hand, and trace elements, such as the rare earth or lanthanide elements, on the other hand. In addition, for highly skewed data, such as many of the trace elements, log-transformation yields a more nearly normal distribution.

The goal of quantitative analysis of the chemical data is to recognize compositionally homogeneous groups within the analytical database. Based on the "provenance postulate" (Weigand et al. 1977; Neff 2000), such groups are assumed to represent geographically restricted sources or source zones. The location of sources or source zones may be inferred by comparing the unknown groups to knowns (source raw materials), or by indirect means such as the "criterion of abundance" (Bishop et al. 1982) or arguments based on geological and sedimentological characteristics (e.g., Steponaitis et al. 1996).

Hypotheses about source-related subgroups in the compositional data can be derived from noncompositional information (e.g., archaeological context, decorative attributes, etc.) or from application of pattern-recognition techniques to the chemical data. In the former approach, ceramics from a single site or nearby sites or ceramics with similar form and/or decoration are hypothesized to derive from a single source or source zone. The latter approach involves searching four groups in the elemental data by means of principal components analysis (PCA), cluster analysis, or simply by examining bivariate elemental concentration plots (e.g., Baxter 1992; Neff 1994, 2002). In any case, the source-related group structure hypothesized to exist in the data needs to be verified.

The groups hypothesized to exist in the data can be evaluated by several means, the most straightforward of which is to inspect bivariate plots on which the specimens are identified as to presumed group affiliation; failure to find sets of elements that separate the hypothetical groups casts doubt on their validity. Hypothetical groups suggested by archaeological context and/or numerical pattern recognition can also be evaluated and refined with multivariate statistics based on Mahalanobis distance (Bieber et al. 1976; Bishop and Neff 1989; Harbottle 1976; Neff 2002; Sayre 1975). Mahalanobis distance (or generalized distance) is expressed as:

$$D^2_{y,X} = [y - \overline{X}]^t \, I \, x \, [y - \overline{X}]$$

where y is 1 x m array of logged elemental concentrations for the individual point of interest, X is the n x m data matrix of logged concentrations for the group to which the point is being compared with $\overline{X}$ being its 1 x m centroid, and I_x is the inverse of the m x m variance-covariance matrix of group X. Because Mahalanobis distance takes into account variances and covariances in the multivariate group, it is analogous to expressing distance from a univariate mean in standard deviation units. Like standard deviation units, Mahalanobis distances can be converted into probabilities of group membership for each individual specimen (e.g., Bieber et al. 1976; Bishop and Neff 1989; Harbottle

1976; Neff 2002; Sayre 1975). For relatively small sample sizes, it is appropriate to base probabilities on Hotelling's T^2, which is a multivariate extension of the univariate Student's t.

As is common in provenance research, specimen-to-variate ratios remain small for virtually all the reference groups considered. This causes Mahalanobis distance-based probabilities of group membership to fluctuate dramatically, depending on whether or not each specimen is assumed to be a member of the group to which it is being compared. Harbottle (1976) calls this phenomenon "stretchability." Cross-validation or "jackknifing," in which each specimen is removed from a group before calculating its probability of membership, helps counteract such inflated probabilities for small groups (Baxter 1994; Leese and Main 1994; Neff 2002), and is used in all the comparisons discussed below.

INAA-based Provenance Research Within and Adjacent to the Mississippi Valley

Chemistry-based ceramic-provenance studies within and adjacent to the Mississippi valley face methodological problems that arise from the fact that ceramic raw materials of the valley bottom are derived from weathering in a number of distinct drainage basins, which are mixed and remixed prior to their deposition in a particular location. Clay composition at a given location reflects the composition of sediments carried by upstream tributaries weighted by each tributary's relative contribution of sediment at that location. The most marked compositional shifts may be expected at major confluences, such as the Ohio and Arkansas rivers, where major new sediment inputs occur. The resulting compositional profile, however, may characterize clays for many miles to the south of the confluence, so that the concept of "clay source" may encompass a region of hundreds of square kilometers. On the other hand, east-west compositional variation is to be expected, as multiple upstream sources contribute to the sedimentary clays of the valley itself, whereas upland primary clays or sedimentary clays within small tributary drainages are derived from weathering of a much more restricted set of parent rocks. Even within the valley, compositional differences may be expected between the recent alluvial deposits along the modern river channel and older deposits near the valley margins. These characteristics of the Mississippi valley ceramic environment determine the geographic resolution achievable in ceramic provenance research.

The I-69 project area lies in Bolivar, Coahoma, and Sunflower counties, in northwestern Mississippi, just east of the Mississippi River. The surface of the entire corridor consists of quaternary alluvium, and an early soil survey (Logan 1907) identified clay-loam soils suitable for brickmaking and, presumably, earthenware pottery. Not far to the east, in Panola and Tallahatchie counties, is a band of loess containing clay-loam that is also suitable for earthenware pottery. With abundant local ceramic resources, one baseline expectation about the archaeological pottery of the project area is that much of it probably derived from local sources. Future composition-based investigation of interaction patterns involving northwestern Mississippi might include sampling and analysis of raw clays from the various soil types, in order to establish the range of variation in local ceramic raw materials. However, in keeping with the general remarks above, it must be borne in mind that "local" may refer to a region that may cover many hundreds of square kilometers.

Broad Regional Trends in Ceramic Composition

A pioneering study initiated by Steponaitis and Blackman (1981) employed INAA to characterize elemental variation in Mississippian pottery on a geographic scale encompassing the entire Southeast, from western Georgia to the Caddoan area of Oklahoma. Initially undertaken at NIST, the project was later expanded with additional analyses carried out at MURR (Steponaitis et al. 1996).

Ceramics from 21 regions (or site clusters) were found to subdivide into four broad compositional patterns. The western group subsumed ceramics from an area stretching from the Mississippi valley to western Louisiana and eastern Oklahoma. The northern group subsumed ceramics from western and central Tennessee. The eastern group subsumed western Georgia; the southern group subsumed most, but not all, sampling locales in Alabama. The four compositional patterns are discriminated from one another along a number of dimensions, the western group being relatively enriched in sodium, the eastern group being low in sodium and potassium, and the northern group being low in sodium but high in potassium. Considering that the ceramics assigned to each group come from multiple sites and multiple regions, the broad compositional similarities are plausibly attributed to broad similarities in geology and weathering.

Steponaitis et al. (1996) argue, in fact, that the compositional patterns discovered in the archaeological ceramics reflect underlying variation in the proportions of clay minerals present in sediments of the various regions. In effect, the four groups correspond to distinct clay-mineral provinces. High sodium in the western group, for instance, corresponds to the smectite-illite association of the Mississippi River and its western tributaries, whereas low sodium and potassium in the eastern group are consistent with the kaolinite-dominated clays of the Georgia piedmont and rivers that drain south from the piedmont toward the eastern Gulf of Mexico.

As a demonstration of the usefulness of the broad compositional patterns identified in their study, Steponaitis et al. (1996) compare sherds from Moundville, Alabama, that are stylistically similar to Plaquemine ceramics from the Mississippi valley to the four regional compositional groups. This comparison demonstrates that none of the sherds is local to Moundville and that they come from at least two other regions, one of which is certainly the LMV, the other likely being the low hills just to the east of the valley. This finding confirms the expectation that east-west movement of ceramics between the Mississippi valley and adjacent regions should be discernible based on bulk-paste analysis, a finding confirmed by subsequent additional sampling of Moundville ceramics, as discussed further below.

Ceramic Compositional Studies in Southeast Missouri

A series of studies synthesized by Lynott et al. (2000; also see Neff et al. 1995) focused on the northeastern corner of the "western zone" ceramic resource area delineated in the Steponaitis et al. (1996) study. The region lies within the bootheel region of southeast Missouri, and includes the eastern lowlands along the Mississippi River, the western Mississippi valley margin, and the adjacent eastern Ozark uplands. Clays on the floodplain of the modern river were deposited as clay plugs and backswamp deposits. Sediments lying west of Crowley's Ridge, in the western lowlands, were deposited by the Pleistocene-age Mississippi River and currently receive sediments from the St. Francis River, Black River, and other streams draining the Ozark uplands. Ceramic resources of the uplands themselves include primary clays developing on limestone and dolomite and alluvial clays in the valley bottoms.

The eastern lowlands composition was characterized in a study of Campbell Appliquéd pottery from sites near the Mississippi River in the southeast Missouri bootheel and across the river, in western Tennessee (O'Brien et al. 1995). The Campbell Appliquéd sherds were found to comprise a single compositional group, and clays collected near archaeological sites represented in the Campbell Appliquéd sample were found to lie within the range of variation of the pottery. Daub samples and two silty clays diverged from the main eastern lowland pattern. O'Brien et al. (1995) hypothesize that the modern alluvium of the Mississippi may comprise a single, relatively homogeneous source from the mouth of the Ohio River to the mouth of the Arkansas River. This would explain the lack of compositional differentiation observed in their ceramic/clay sample. In partial agreement with this hypothesis, pottery from the American Bottom analyzed subsequently for a project initiated by Greg Wilson and Vin Steponaitis has been found to overlap with Campbell Appliquéd pottery. If borne out by future work, this inference would obviously limit the resolution with which north-south movement of pottery can be identified within this part of the Mississippi valley.

Lynott et al. (2000) identified multiple compositional profiles for the western lowlands region and for adjacent upland zones lying to the west of the

Ozark escarpment, all of which diverge from the profile of the alluvium deposited by the Mississippi along its modern course. The various upland and western lowland groups are all linked to raw-material source zones by numerous raw materials that fall within the ranges of variation of the groups, and the lowland versus upland dichotomy is exceptionally well-defined chemically, there being virtually no overlap in multivariate space. In sum, it is very easy to identify east-west movement of ceramics between uplands and lowlands in southeast Missouri.

Because the uplands versus lowlands discrimination is so reliable, Lynott et al. (2000) draw some secure inferences about prehistoric interaction patterns in southeast Missouri and how they changed over time. Specifically, among the Varney complex and Emergent Mississippian ceramics from the Ozark uplands are a sizeable proportion that are made of alluvial soils of the western lowlands. Thus, during the five centuries or so prior to A.D. 1200, there was persistent, relatively frequent movement of pots (and presumably people) out of the western lowlands up the Current River, Black River, and other drainages. A few Barnes complex sherds from Upland drainages, but chemically linked to lowland clays, suggest that the lowland-upland interaction may date as early A.D. 400. This interaction disappears abruptly with the appearance of the Powers phase, around A.D. 1300.

Cogswell (1998) documented chemical variation due to sand temper in ceramics made from alluvial clays in southeast Missouri in his study of Late Woodland Barnes–tradition pottery from the region. Since sand temper contains a high proportion of quartz, sand temper acts as an inert diluent for elements other than silicon, reducing their concentrations in sand-tempered ceramics relative to their concentrations in raw clays. Thus, sand-tempered pottery is also expected to show lower concentrations of most elements compared to untempered or grog-tempered pottery from the same region (or shell-tempered pottery "undiluted" using the shell-temper correction described previously). Cogswell's results indicate that all sand-tempered ceramics from west of Crowley's ridge (including both Malden Plain and modern alluvium) form a single compositional group that is, as expected, diluted in many elements relative to untempered clays and ceramics from the region. Elements that are exceptions to this generalization are those that sometimes occur in accessory minerals in sands, such as sodium (in feldspars).

Ceramic Compositional Studies in Arkansas, Northeast Texas, and Louisiana

Several studies, some unpublished or only partially published, have generated analyses of ceramics and raw materials from locations west of the Yazoo Basin, in Arkansas, northeastern Texas, and Louisiana. These regions lie within the "western" compositional zone identified in the Steponaitis et al. (1996) study. Not surprisingly, the augmented sample of ceramics and raw materials has revealed additional geographic patterning in ceramic compositions.

Of direct relevance to the present overview, an unpublished study in southeastern Arkansas conceived by Marvin Jeter focused on ceramics from the Baytown (A.D. 400–700), Marksville (A.D. 100–400), and Coles Creek (A.D. 700–1200) periods (Neff, Cogswell, and Glascock 1996). Three of the sampled archaeological sites (Taylor Mounds, Possum Trap, and Powell Canal) are within the LMV region of southeastern Arkansas; Taylor Mounds has Marksville, Baytown, and Coles Creek occupations; Possum Trap has Marksville and Baytown occupations; and Powell Canal is mainly middle-to-late Baytown. Eagle Lake, a site in the Felsenthal archaeological region to the west of the Mississippi valley, has Marksville, Baytown, and Coles Creek occupation.

Three distinct sedimentary environments are represented in the analyzed southeast Arkansas sample. Seventy-six pottery samples and 12 raw clays come from the vicinity of Taylor Mounds and Possum Trap, both of which lie along the Bayou Bartholomew, an abandoned meander belt of the Arkansas River at the extreme western margin of the LMV physiographic province. Both sites are within about 30 km of the I-69 project's south end, at the Great River Bridge. Closer to the modern Mississippi River, on Bayou Macon, is the Powell Canal site, from which five ceramics and one clay were obtained. The Powell Canal location is about 60 km downstream from the I-69 project's southern terminus. The Eagle Lake site, which is represented by four ceramics and three raw clays, lies within the West Gulf Coastal Plain physiographic province, in the Saline-Ouachita drainage. This project's working hypothesis was that the three distinct sedimentary environments sampled would show three distinct elemental profiles.

In fact, the southeastern Arkansas pottery analyses fall into three distinct groups. As expected, given the sampling emphases, the largest compositional group includes the majority of specimens from Taylor Mounds and all but two specimens from the nearby site of Possum Trap. The four specimens from Eagle Lake and the five from Powell Canal make up two additional compositional groups. Thus, as hypothesized, pottery from archaeological sites situated in three distinct sedimentary environments manifests three distinct compositional profiles.

Comparison of the southeast Arkansas pottery groups with sampled raw clays strengthens the case for local production. As in the southeast Missouri study (e.g., O'Brien et al. 1995), a few raw clays diverge from the pottery along a "siltiness" dimension that mainly expresses variation in concentrations of Hf and Zr, elements that are enriched by higher proportions of the chemically resistant mineral zircon in siltier sediments. However, other raw clay samples from the Taylor Mounds–Possum Trap vicinity, especially one Portland series clay, approximate the compositional profile of the Taylor Mounds group, thus leaving little room for doubt that the group consists of pottery made from sedimentary clays deposited by the Arkansas River. Powell Canal clay and pottery, meanwhile, show a distinct local profile that appears to be characteristic of the modern Mississippi alluvium shared with the Campbell Appliquéd pottery of southeast Missouri discussed previously. Farther west, the three clays from near the Eagle Lake site show low sodium and potassium along with other characteristics of the Eagle Lake pottery, which confirms that pottery in the Eagle Lake group was produced locally in the Saline-Ouachita drainage.

Another fairly sizable INAA database pertinent to the study area includes analyses of Caddoan pottery from northeast Texas and surrounding regions undertaken for Timothy K. Perttula (2002) and his collaborators. As yet, there has been no effort to sample raw materials. However, systematic trends in ceramic composition across northeast Texas and adjacent Louisiana and Oklahoma have permitted recognition of nine reference groups that are inferred to represent ceramic resource zones of varying size (Neff, Cogswell, and Glascock 1996; Neff and Glascock 2000; Perttula 2002). The largest reference group is centered on Titus County and surrounding counties in the northeastern corner of Texas. Caddoan pottery with different chemical fingerprints was also made in the Red River valley and to the south of Titus County. There is a general north-to-south trend of gradual decrease in potassium and rubidium that is plausibly attributed to intensity of chemical weathering of residual clays as rainfall increases closer to the Gulf Coast (Neff and Glascock 2000).

A major substantive finding of Perttula's (2002) Caddoan pottery study is the secure attribution of Caddoan pottery from distant sites to production centers in the Caddo heartland. One Holly Fine-Engraved sherd from the Illinois River valley was found to have been made in northeast Texas, as were several samples of Caddoan pottery from late prehistoric contexts in south central Kansas (Walnut Focus, A.D. 1400–1720). A single Holly Fine-Engraved sherd from Taylor Mounds analyzed on the Jeter project also has a northeast Texas composition. Interestingly, however, a group of Holly Fine-Engraved specimens from Moundville, Alabama, analyzed for Vin Steponaitis shows an extremely anomalous composition unlike any other ceramics or clays yet sampled in the Southeast, Midwest, or Mississippi valley (Neff, Cogswell, and Glascock 1996; Neff, Glascock, and Stryker 1996).

One other project (Glascock, personal communication 2004) further augments the range of elemental diversity documented in ceramics and ceramic raw materials from the region lying west of the Yazoo Basin. The sample comes from a single site in Independence County, north-central Arkansas, and remains unpublished.

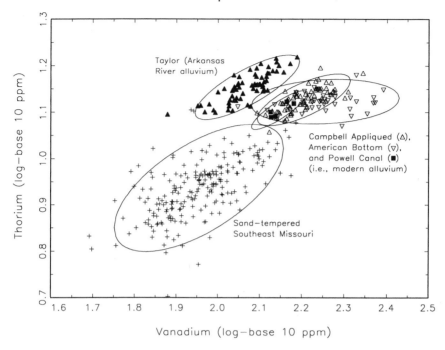

Figure 11.1. Plot of logged elemental concentrations of vanadium and thorium in ceramics derived from alluvial clays of the LMV. Ellipses represent 90-percent confidence level for membership in the groups.

Overview of Ceramic Compositional Patterns
Relevant to the I-69 Project

The above projects provide a baseline of information about the diversity of ceramic compositions that might be found within the I-69 corridor (Figures 11.1–11.4). One key finding is that the modern Mississippi alluvium appears to be relatively uniform in composition throughout the region of interest here, at least from the Powell Canal site in southern Arkansas north to the American Bottom region near present-day St. Louis. Powell Canal pottery and raw materials fall within the range of variation of the Campbell Appliquéd group (O'Brien et al. 1995) and the American Bottom group on numerous bivariate projections of the data (e.g., Figure 11.1), and Mahalanobis-distance calculations confirm that the similarity extends into multivariate space. Addition of sizeable proportions of sand temper to the Mississippi alluvium dilutes most elements, changing the Mississippi alluvial clay composition into a composition like that of the "sand-tempered group" shown in Figure 11.1 (i.e., sliding the data down and to the left). Thus, somewhat surprisingly, there

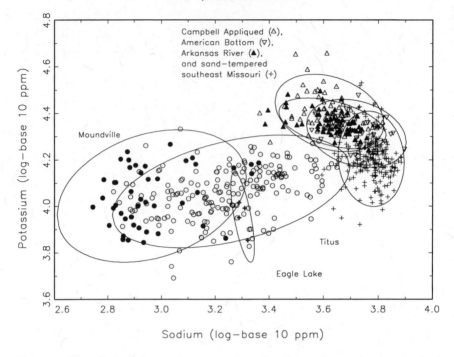

Figure 11.2. Plot of logged elemental concentrations of sodium and potassium in ceramics derived from alluvial clays of the LMV and extra-valley locations to the east (Moundville) and west (Titus, Eagle Lake). Ellipses represent 90-percent confidence level for membership in the groups.

already exists sufficient data to estimate what the composition of local pottery made within the I-69 corridor would look like: the Campbell Appliquéd and American Bottom groups can be considered reasonable approximations of grog-tempered, untempered, or shell-tempered (and corrected) compositions, whereas the southeast Missouri sand-tempered group can be considered a reasonable approximation of what the local sand-tempered compositions would look like.

Although it is gratifying that available data provide a baseline for discriminating local from nonlocal pottery within the I-69 project area, it is unfortunate that the "local" composition represents such a large portion of the Mississippi valley. In effect, since Powell Canal samples fall within the range of variation of American Bottom pottery, the Mississippi alluvium represents a single source at least from the vicinity of St. Louis to southern Arkansas. The lower Yazoo Basin sample of Steponaitis et al. (1996) also fits this general compositional pattern, so the chemical profile actually extends even further south. Finding compositional similarity over such a long stretch of the Mississippi

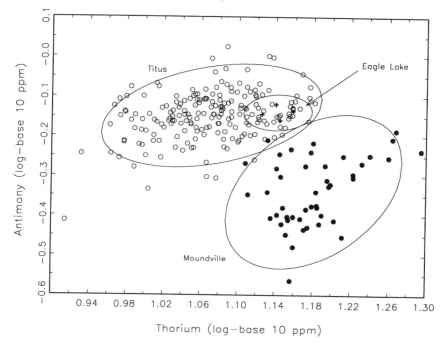

Figure 11.3. Plot of logged elemental concentrations of thorium and antimony in the Moundville, Titus, and Eagle Lake reference groups. Ellipses represent 90-percent confidence level for membership in the groups.

valley dramatically attenuates the geographic resolution possible for tracing north-south movement of ceramics among prehistoric groups who lived along the Mississippi River.

The prospects for identifying east-west movement of ceramics are more promising. At the western edge of the valley, sediments deposited by western tributaries are distinct from the modern alluvium, as O'Brien et al. (1995) showed for southeast Missouri. Similarly, the Arkansas River sediments sampled at Taylor Mounds and Possum Trap have a distinct compositional profile discernible on several bivariate projections (the "Taylor group" in Figure 11.1). Beyond the Mississippi valley, both to the east and to the west, clays tend to be low in sodium and potassium (Figure 11.2), an indication of intense chemical weathering and a clay-mineral assemblage dominated by kaolinite and illite (Potter et al. 1975; Steponaitis et al. 1996). This extra-valley compositional profile shows minimal overlap with the profile of Arkansas River alluvium or with the profile of Mississippi valley alluvium or sand-tempered variants thereof (Figure 11.2). Low-sodium, low-potassium compositions are found in the Ozark uplands of southeast Missouri (not shown in Figure 11.2, but see Ly-

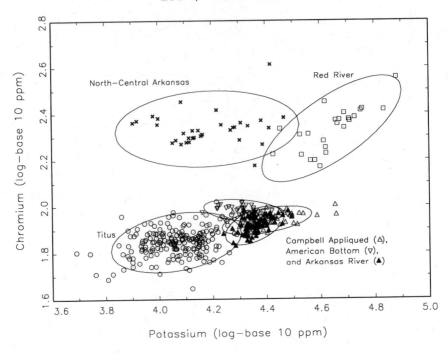

Figure 11.4. Plot of logged elemental concentrations of potassium and chromium in ceramics derived from alluvial clays of the LMV, northeast Texas (Titus), north-central Arkansas, and the Red River valley of northeast Texas and southern Oklahoma. Ellipses represent 90-percent confidence level for membership in the groups.

nott et al. 2000); at Eagle Lake, in the Ouachita-Saline drainage; farther west, in northeast Texas and adjacent northwest Louisiana (the Titus group in Figure 11.2); and to the east of the Mississippi valley, at Moundville, Alabama (the Moundville group in Figure 11.2). Although Moundville pottery shares low sodium and low potassium with pottery from west of the Mississippi valley, the similarity disappears on many other projections (e.g., Figure 11.3). These observations demonstrate that movement of prehistoric ceramics along an east-west axis from Alabama, across the Mississippi valley, and west into Arkansas, Texas, Louisiana, and Oklahoma should be discernible.

The low-sodium, low-potassium composition may also characterize alluvial sediments downstream from the Arkansas River confluence. In the Steponaitis et al. (1996) study, eight specimens from the Natchez region, near the confluence of the Red, Ouachita, and Mississippi rivers, show low-sodium and -potassium concentrations (they would fall within the range of variation of the Titus group in Figure 11.2). If these Natchez specimens are locally made, their composition may indicate that clays from the Natchez region show a greater contribution from western tributaries that drain areas of more highly weathered, high-kaolinite, high-illite clays, like those in the Ouachita drainage (Eagle Lake) or farther west, in western Louisiana and eastern Texas. The Natchez specimens also span the gap in vanadium and thorium concentrations between Mississippi alluvium and Arkansas River alluvium (i.e., they would be intermediate in composition if plotted in Figure 11.1). Thus, not only may sodium and potassium decrease downstream along the Mississippi, but the vanadium-thorium difference, which discriminates Arkansas River from modern Mississippi alluvium, may also become attenuated downstream, as the contribution from the Arkansas River and other western-tributary streams to the Mississippi alluvium increases. The possibility that Mississippi alluvium changes systematically downstream raises the possibility that ceramic imports from the south would be recognizable in Yazoo Basin collections by compositional analysis.

Finally, other ceramic samples analyzed by INAA from the region west of the Mississippi valley reveal additional compositional diversity in the region's ceramic resources (Figure 11.4). Elevated chromium concentrations clearly discriminate the Red River and north-central Arkansas groups from all other ceramics yet sampled in midcontinental North America. Considering that these elevated chromium concentrations are found in assemblages from the Ouachita-Ozark clay mineral province (Steponaitis et al. 1996), a plausible hypothesis is that they reflect procurement of high-chlorite clays more common in this province than elsewhere (Potter et al. 1975): clinochlore, a chlorite, includes a high-chromium variant called kaemmererite. High chromium, if found in ceramics from the northern Yazoo Basin, would unambiguously indicate derivation of ceramics from the uplands or plains west of the Mississippi valley.

To summarize, local ceramics of the Mississippi valley from St. Louis to the Arkansas River, including the northern Yazoo Basin, manifest the smectite/illite-derived, high-potassium, high-sodium chemical profile designated the "western" profile by Steponaitis et al. (1996). Addition of sand temper creates another chemical profile, found most commonly in Woodland sand-tempered pottery (Cogswell 1998), which is marked by dilution of most elements measured by INAA. Along the western margins of the valley, clays are still high in sodium and potassium, but distinctive trace-element profiles are found in sediments with major contributions from western tributaries, such as the Black, Little Black, St. Francis, and Current rivers in southeast Missouri and the Arkansas River in southern Arkansas. Outside the valley, both to the east (Moundville) and to the west, intense chemical weathering and high kaolinite in clays generate chemical profiles marked by lower potassium and sodium. Despite the similarity in major-element composition between extra-valley regions lying east and west of the Mississippi, trace elements unambiguously discriminate the regions, the Moundville area, for instance, showing a distinctive low-antimony high-thorium profile. Some regions lying west of the valley show a high chromium composition that probably originates in procurement of high-chlorite clays. The unusual chemical profile of a few samples from the Natchez region hints that alluvial clays in southern Mississippi and Louisiana may be distinct from those within the I-69 project area, but this hypothesis requires further testing.

Conclusion

Both petrographic (Bareis and Porter 1965) and chemical analysis are capable of distinguishing ceramics made within the LMV from those made in surrounding regions. I have focused on chemical analysis in this review because a number of INAA projects have been undertaken over the past decade-and-a-half within the LMV and surrounding regions, and these provide an increasingly complete picture of how Mississippi alluvial materials differ chemically from extra-valley materials, and of the diversity of compositions found outside the valley. Petrography is discussed elsewhere in this volume by Galaty. Moreover, since the INAA projects have been funded largely by NSF, most of the data are already in the public domain and available for comparison. Future projects, such as ceramic-provenance research associated with the I-69 project, thus will not have to start from the beginning, sampling potential source regions, to identify the directions and volumes of imported ceramics.

Within the LMV itself, ceramic provenance investigations face inherent limitations on geographic resolution imposed by the thorough mixing that sediments undergo as they are moved into and within the valley. Identifying ceramics moved within the valley is highly problematic because of the resulting widespread uniformity in raw-material composition. Subgroups are created by technological practices (e.g., addition of sand temper), and the alluvium along the western margins of the valley tends to differ from the modern alluvium, but north-south differences in the composition of the modern alluvium are at best highly attenuated. The one possible exception is the downstream variation suggested by the fact that Natchez-region ceramics sampled by Steponaitis et al. (1996) show a low-potassium, low-sodium composition that contrasts with compositions from north of the Arkansas River confluence.

Despite the lack of previous ceramic provenance investigation within the I-69 project area, a "local" elemental signature can already be inferred based on the relative uniformity of ceramics made from modern Mississippi alluvium in several neighboring regions. Nonetheless, sampling of ceramics and raw materials within the project area would still be desirable. The modern alluvium itself should be sampled intensively enough to test the hypothesis that it remains undifferentiated across the project area. East of the project area, clays within the loess band and farther east, in the uplands bordering the valley, should be sampled in order to document how they differ from the modern alluvial clays. The Steponaitis et al. (1996) study tentatively identified imports to Moundville from the hills east of the Mississippi valley in southern Mississippi, but as yet there are no raw-material or ceramic analyses from this region to support such an attribution.

Sampling of ceramics in the I-69 project area will presumably be driven largely by the nature of sites encountered and mitigated by the project. There is a high likelihood that imports from extra valley locations both west (e.g., the Caddo area) and east (e.g., Moundville, Alabama) could be identified by compositional means. Likewise, imports from the Delta region of southern Mississippi and Louisiana may be identifiable, although this hypothesis remains to be tested. Northern imports, however, for instance from the American Bottom near Cahokia, would likely not be distinguishable chemically from locally made pottery.

Little mention has been made so far of new instrumental technologies and what they might bring to the investigation of ceramic movement within the LMV. In particular, it is now possible with laser ablation-ICP-MS to target and to analyze small inclusions or patches of pigment or slips on ceramics (e.g., Speakman and Neff 2005). Although bulk paste composition does not vary sufficiently to permit identification of north-south movement over long distances within the valley, the possibility that special material exploited for pigments or slips might be diagnostic of localized ceramic-production centers remains to be explored. Likewise, Peacock's investigation of shell-temper variation may yet yield a means for determining ceramic provenance within modern Mississippi alluvial settings.

Acknowledgments

The INAA data summarized here were generated mainly at MURR, with a series of grants from the National Science Foundation (especially DBS-9102016). The combination of stable funding from NSF and stable direction by Mike Glascock, Director of the Archaeometry Lab at MURR, has created a unique resource for archaeologists interested in the investigation of prehistoric interaction. I am especially grateful to Dr. Glascock for twelve years of direct support and collaboration at MURR, as well as ongoing productive collaboration. I also thank several individuals who submitted ceramics and raw materials to MURR for analysis over the past 15 years, and whose work is cited above. These include Vin Steponaitis, Mark Lynott, Tim Perttula, Jim Cogswell, Greg Wilson, and, especially, Marvin Jeter, whose unpublished data from southern Arkansas are most directly relevant to the I-69 project.

12

Ceramic Petrography and the Classification of Mississippi's Archaeological Pottery by Fabric

A GIS Approach

Michael L. Galaty

Introduction

In this chapter I review the petrographic analyses applied to archaeological ceramics from the state of Mississippi, with a specific focus on the Yazoo Basin. I argue that the traditional southeastern type-variety system—which is particularly complex in its application to artifacts from the Lower Mississippi Valley (LMV)—fails to account fully for differences in the materials, such as clays and tempers, used in the manufacture of prehistoric pottery. Whereas the type-variety system systematically tracks components of ceramic style, such as so-called "decorative ideas," surface finishes (e.g., "plain" versus "stamped"), and form (i.e. "vessel modes") (Phillips 1970:27), it does not encourage careful and consistent recording of pertinent fabric characteristics. As a result, ceramic types and varieties often crosscut fabric categories, thereby confounding efforts to explain the spatial and temporal distributions of pottery (Connaway 1980; Mainfort 1994; Metcalf 1992; Rafferty and Galaty 2002). This problem could be solved in one of two ways: 1) by adding more meaningful fabric descriptions to the established system of types and varieties, which would likely require lumping together some types and varieties and splitting others; or 2) by creating a parallel system designed to handle southeastern fabrics specifically. Option two seems to me the better long-term solution. It preserves the traditional type-variety system intact and ensures that existing ideas about fabric would not compromise new fabric categories as they are tested.

Building a new, parallel system of classification based on fabrics will require that meaningful fabric categories be described. Whereas developing such a system from scratch is beyond the scope of this chapter, I will present in outline form the steps necessary to its eventual creation. Defining meaningful fabric categories will depend upon the systematic sampling of clays and tempers throughout the state of Mississippi and the careful comparison of these clays and tempers in various combinations to a wide range of archaeological ceramics. Comparison will require a program of thin-sectioning and petrographic analysis (which could also be integrated with chemical-compositional analyses; see Neff, this volume). To date, very little petrography has taken place in Mississippi (which is odd, given the great potential for petrographic analysis in the state). The petrographic projects that have taken place, reviewed below, were all of a preliminary nature; none of them developed into a large-scale program of resource survey and ceramic analysis.

I further suggest that the theoretical framework of "ceramic ecology," developed by Frederick Matson, be deployed in order to guide the study of Mississippi's prehistoric ceramics. Matson's (1965) framework, rarely used in the Southeast but put to good use elsewhere, provides an array of middle-range bridging theories that serve to connect the archaeological remains of pots to the behavior of the people who made them. Matson, who conducted ethnographic research with living potters, realized that what kind of pot a potter makes is dictated at least in part by the resources available (clay, water, temper, fuel, etc.), as well as by additional external factors, such as climate and economy. Matson's predictions have been tested and refined in a wide variety of ethnographic settings, and "ceramic ecology" can do much to help us construct plausible models of prehistoric Mississippi's ceramic production and distribution systems.

The ceramic-ecological approach depends to a great degree on a detailed understanding of a region's geology and paleo-environment. For Mississippi, there are fairly good data on surface geology, especially that of the LMV (e.g., Saucier 1994). Clearly, though, the environment of the Yazoo Basin has been altered since European contact. As a result, what paleo-environmental data exist for the Southeast must also be drawn into the model.

One excellent means of integrating these various kinds of data is through use of a Geographic Information System (GIS). For this chapter, I have managed to combine layers of data representing Mississippi's surface geology, hydro-systems, and physiography (provided by the Mississippi Automated Resource Information System, or MARIS), with archaeological site data supplied by the Mississippi Department of Archives and History (MDAH). In the last section of this chapter, I employ GIS to test some of the implications of the proposed ceramic-ecological model, and the results of these tests are used to refine the draft system of classification based on fabrics.

The Type-Variety System: Style Versus Fabric

The type-variety system was adopted in the mid-twentieth century to support the cultural-historical goals of southeastern archaeologists (Gibson 1993). It was thought that ceramic types represented in some fashion prehistoric ethnic groups, which, it was further thought, must have been similar in scale and organization to the Protohistoric and Historic tribes known for the region. To some degree southeastern archaeologists sought to support this connection using the direct historical approach, working back through time from extant tribal groups to prehistoric, presumably ancestral, ones. Eventually, the direct historical approach was abandoned, replaced by methods of stratigraphic seriation and radiocarbon dating (Gibson 1993:31). However, though the direct historical *approach* to culture history (i.e. cultural chronology and space-time systematics) was largely abandoned, the *idea* that pottery types represented ancient groups of people was not.

The type-variety system reached its zenith in the work of Phillips (1970), in which 77 types and 197 varieties were defined for the LMV (Gibson 1993:28). In his discussions of ceramic "phases," Phillips (1970:5–8, 969) argues that large-scale artifact distributions represent, in some form, archaeological "traditions" or "cultures," and that settlement patterns constructed based on phase data must somehow indicate where certain groups of people were living at certain times in the past (a form of paleo-"demography" Phillips 1970:962). The question is whether or not the chronological distributions of ceramic types and varieties, and their spatial correlates, phases, were in reality produced through the movements and interactions of different culture groups.

It has been demonstrated that for many tribal peoples, style, decoration in particular, may indeed signal cultural affiliation (among many others, Hegmon 1995; Hodder 1982; Stark 1998; Voss and Young 1995; Wobst 1977). In addition, ceramic-design elements may be associated with particular villages or groups of allied villages (Parkinson 1999:399–401). However, in societies that practice a domestic mode of production—in which pottery is made in the household primarily for the household's use—design elements more often represent clans, family groups, or individual potters. Importantly, when pots move in such societies, it is typically not as the result of trade between members of different culture groups; rather, potters may carry pottery between villages when visiting kin. It seems likely that for much of Mississippi's past, a domestic mode of pottery production was practiced, and pots were made by people who visited one another, carrying pottery when they did so. As a result, ceramic phases probably represent, at least in some periods, the interactions of domestic kin groups.

As opposed to style, descriptions of fabrics or "wares" by Phillips (1970) are relatively imprecise (Connaway 1980). "Pastes" are often described using subjective terms such as "chalky," "lumpy," or "lamellar." Temper types are few—e.g., sand, "grit," bone, "grog," and shell—and amounts of temper are rarely quantified (beyond simple, relative measurements of the "more or less," "presence-absence" variety). Many varieties receive no fabric description at all.

Given the LMV's ceramic ecology, and that of Mississippi in general, it is not difficult to understand why fabric descriptions are so very limited, whereas style descriptions are so complex. The materials potters had to work with, while abundantly available, are seemingly rather restricted in their distinguishing characteristics. When studied macroscopically, pastes and tempers cannot be described in more detail than Phillips, and his many adherents, have managed. Thus, many varieties contain "sand," and so using "sand" as a distinguishing characteristic is useless, except to say that sand "tempering" was in general preceded chronologically by "grog" tempering and followed by "shell" tempering. It is apparent that the many potters who lived and worked in Mississippi gathered similar sorts of resources in making their pottery. As a result, in the type-variety system fabrics crosscut phases, confounding attempts to use (or replicate) the system when fabric is one of the defining characteristics of a particular variety (Connaway 1980; Mainfort 1994; Metcalf 1992; Rafferty and Galaty 2002). The solution to this conundrum, it seems, would be to treat style and fabric as two fully separate and separable dimensions, each of which evolved independently and each of which must be classified along different axes of change (Klemptner and Johnson 1985; O'Brien et al. 1994:264–265).

Theoretically, the range of design motifs available to prehistoric potters in Mississippi was infinite, or at least very wide. Motifs could be combined and recombined in any number of ways. Furthermore, although styles may seem relatively stable over time, especially in small-scale societies, in fact independent potters have more room to experiment than do potters who mass-produce pottery, for whom experimentation is a much greater risk. It is likely that children learning from their elders how to make pots had a certain degree of freedom to develop their own particular style. Thus, style evolved in a branching ("dendritic") fashion (as people learned to pot, passed on their knowledge to others, and then died), thereby creating the so-called "battleship" curves that work so well in seriating southeastern pottery. Given that it responds to behavioral choices, style can be used to track "culture history" in the sense southeastern archaeologists intend, if what they are interested in are the decisions and interactions of potters, each of whom did indeed bear allegiance to a family, village, and culture, or tradition, writ large.

As compared to style, technological choices (the "*chaîne opératoire*") are more constrained, and therefore more conservative, and people had less choice when it came to what materials to use when making a pot. Unlike decorative motifs, paste recipes, also passed down, did not easily change, and therefore span the more frequent shifts in style (McNutt 1996). When paste recipes did change, change was less often dictated by the maker's choice than it was imposed from the outside. For example, a clay source that had been mined for generations might be exhausted, entailing a shift in the type of clay used. Or, a technological innovation (e.g., using shell as temper) might be introduced. As a result, fabrics changed in fits and starts. Long periods of adaptive "equilibria" were "punctuated" by the appearance of new fabric traits. Whereas style may be studied in order to understand the social interactions of groups of people, the study of fabrics more often leads to a better understanding of the technology and economy of pottery production and distribution, including, but not limited to, studies of production provenance and trade.

Fabric Classification

Given that we might want to learn more about the technology and economy of prehistoric ceramic systems, and bearing in mind the foregoing discussion, a parallel system for classifying Mississippi's pottery based on fabrics is clearly needed. Ideally, the attributes defined for classification in the system should function both for the petrographer and for the archaeologist working macroscopically.

It is often the case that ceramic-fabric differences that are very apparent in thin section are not easily recognized in hand sample. For example, using petrography I have identified four different fabric types from a small Middle Woodland (Miller I-II) site in Oktibbeha County, the Cork site (Galaty 2001; Rafferty and Galaty 2002). One of these, a sandy, micaceous ware, had not been previously identified macroscopically, but once isolated under the microscope was easy to spot on the sorting table. The key to sorting pottery by fabric is to employ various methods of petrographic analysis first, and then use the results of petrography to define recognizable, objective criteria for classifying larger numbers of sherds (Rafferty and Galaty 2002). Fabric groups defined based on petrography can also be used to "check" chemical compositional groups, and vice versa; the two approaches are not in any way mutually exclusive (see Neff, this volume).

In the past, I have found it useful to classify pottery by fabric based on the collection of both qualitative and quantitative forms of data. Qualitative analysis begins with identification and description of the mineral inclusions (e.g., quartz, feldspar, mica) visible in a ceramic thin section. Next, a pot's ground mass can be analyzed and described. I have used the system developed by Whitbread (1995), based on sedimentary petrology, for describing the qualitative attributes of a pot's ground mass.

Most of the fabric characteristics defined by Whitbread (1995) result from differences in clay type and preparation. For example, different clays may become different colors when fired to the same temperature. Some clays have many natural inclusions, while others do not. Clays that are wedged thoroughly before being formed into a pot tend to have fewer pores. Rarely are such characteristics controlled by the potter as a matter of style; rather, if anything, they relate more closely to the potter's technical knowledge and the types of resources available.

Importantly, most of Whitbread's (1995) fabric characteristics are visible macroscopically, though often their importance is not apparent until they have been defined in thin section. For example, a fabric that is highly porous in thin section may seem "friable" to the analyst. A fabric that has a preferred orientation under the microscope (at which the most light passes through the thin section) may have been smoothed or burnished. An optically inactive fabric may have been fired at high enough temperatures to cause vitrification of the clay paste, rendering it "hard, smooth, and glassy," whereas a low-fired, optically active paste will seem "chalky." Clay pellets (often the result of incomplete wedging) may be confused with grog, but once identified in thin section, their size and frequency may distinguish different fabric classes (di Caprio and Vaughn 1993). A fabric with many opaque minerals (such as hematite) may appear "speckled" in hand sample. A sherd with many crystalline concentration features (such as may result when calcium carbonate is redeposited in pores) may seem to "sparkle." Finally, clays change colors depending on firing temperature and atmosphere. Generally speaking, most prehistoric potters could not easily control fabric characteristics like porosity and color well enough to produce consistently a desired effect, though this could be done by controlling aspects of clay preparation and firing atmosphere (as when a pot is "smudged"). As a result, the utility and meaning of these characteristics as sorting criteria are often unclear at the outset. If they are thought to be meaningful, experimental reconstructions may become necessary as an aid to interpretation (cf. Gertjejansen et al. 1983). For example, if original clay color is thought to vary meaningfully, sherds should be refired in a kiln at high temperature in an oxidizing atmosphere. Refiring will produce a sherd's "true" color, thereby allowing color classification.

Qualitative analysis makes an excellent starting point in the classification of ceramic fabrics, but quantitative analysis, such as point-counting, provides a powerful means of further defining fabric differences and distinguishing additional, important fabric characteristics, such as intentional tempers from natural inclusions. I have found the methods developed by Stoltman (1989, 1991) to be particularly efficient and effective.

Stoltman (1989, 1991) makes an important distinction between clay "paste" and "body." Paste refers to the natural materials from which a vessel was made, to which temper might be added to produce the vessel's body (Stoltman 1991: 109–110). It is often impossible to distinguish temper (material intentionally added to a paste by a potter) in hand sample, but there are means of doing so in thin section. For example, much of what southeastern archaeologists call "grog" (defined as pieces of ground, fired clay intentionally added to a paste as temper) are in reality clay pellets (Whitbread's [1995] TCFs, "textural con-centration features") or ARFs, i.e. argillaceous rock fragments (more about this contentious issue below). Once a sherd is under the microscope, identi-fying true grog is possible, though not always easy (di Caprio and Vaughn 1993); it is typically much more angular than are TCFs and may itself be tem-pered and slipped, whereas TCFs are not. Grog possesses an aligned internal microstructure, parallel internal fractures, and is evenly distributed as com-pared to ARFs (di Caprio and Vaughn 1993:38). It is also very difficult to deter-mine when sand has been added to clay as a temper, but this can sometimes be done microscopically. For instance, a bi-modal distribution of sand sizes (e.g., fine versus coarse) may indicate the addition of (usually coarse) sand. Once tempering has been positively identified, temper can serve as a distinguishing characteristic in fabric classification. If natural inclusions are mistakenly re-ferred to as temper, and the presence/absence of temper is used to sort ceramic types, the system of classification can become hopelessly confused. It is for this reason that isolating true tempers is absolutely key to a system of fabric classifi-cation.

Stoltman's (1989, 1991) method depends on the practice of point-counting thin sections; a slide is moved (usually with a mechanical stage) under the mi-croscope at fixed intervals and the pot's composition is determined. At each stop, the material—clay matrix, void space, mineral inclusion, etc.—in the mi-croscope's crosshairs is counted. Inclusions, such as sand and rock grit, are mea-sured. Point-counting, while tedious, provides hard data useful in separating a ceramic assemblage into various fabric classes. Once fabric classes have been determined, they are usually reproducible macroscopically.

One final, key step in the process of fabric classification is collecting and de-scribing locally available ceramic resources, such as clays and tempers (Neff et al. 1992; Talbott 1984). Once collected, these should be mixed in various combinations and fired, and viewed in thin section as well. If local clays were used to make pots, this is usually very evident when they are compared to ar-chaeological pottery in thin section. For example, much of the pottery I ana-lyzed from the Cork site matched local clay samples (Galaty 2001; Rafferty and Galaty 2002). A ceramic-resources survey can help tremendously when fabric characteristics are being defined, not least by helping determine which pots were perhaps imported. It also provides the data necessary to construct ceramic-ecological models.

Review of Previous Research

To some degree, both qualitative and quantitative petrography and ceramic-resources surveys have been attempted in Mississippi (see also Neff, this vol-ume), but rarely in combination. Whereas the work of Anna Shepard (1956), first conducted in the 1940s, was recognized in the Southeast, very few archaeologists followed her prescriptions for ceramic classification based on technological analyses (Gibson 1993: 34). The earliest example of petrographic analysis of LMV pottery, along the lines outlined by Shepard (1956), is that of Weaver (1963), who studied Tchula period pottery from the Jaketown site. In a quirky, sometimes rambling article, Weaver (1963) argues that Tchula pots were not intentionally tempered with grog and fiber. What was thought to be grog were in fact clay pellets, according to Weaver, and fibers arrived in clay pastes by accident. Several archaeologists responded to Weaver, including Shepard (1964), who seems largely to have approved of the paper and its conclusions, and James Porter (1964), who was very critical of Weaver's approach. To this day, southeastern specialists have continued to debate the presence or absence of grog in Tchula ceramics (e.g., Mainfort 1994).

Weaver also made several general points about ceramic characterization, two of which foreshadowed arguments made in this chapter. First, she quickly realized that replicating pottery classifications based on the "texture" of pastes in hand sample is difficult, if not impossible, to do (Weaver 1963:49). Having also studied thin sections of the pottery, she declared Tchula pastes to be "woefully untidy" (Weaver 1963:53). As it turned out, the "clay-tempered" Tchula pots could only be meaningfully sorted based on the amounts of silt and fine sand in the paste, which was derived from local clays (Weaver 1963:53, 54). This conclusion flew in the face of the received system of classification (based on Phillips et al. 2003 [1951]; see also Phillips 1970:891, who had doubts about the original classification), which considered clay-tempered wares to be local (and chronologically later) and sandy wares to be imported (the so-called "Alexander" series; see Brookes and Taylor 1986) and/or earlier (perhaps Early versus Middle Woodland; see Johnson et al. 2002:68). Second, she argued that since there was no clay tempering (clay pellets arrived in the paste as a function of clay preparation), the presence or absence of "grog" was not a meaningful sorting attribute. Neither were pots fiber-tempered, so fiber, too, was a meaningless attribute. According to Weaver (1963:53):

> If the paste variations arose from deliberate additions on the part of the potter, then one would expect to find a correlation between paste varieties and surface decoration within the types forming the Tchula complex. No such correlation has been found, and this lack has strengthened the suspicion that Tchula pottery was untempered.

Weaver's conclusions make sense if indeed, as I have already asserted above, style and fabric evolved along different lines of descent. Right from the start, petrographic analysis revealed the deep flaws in the type-variety system, but Weaver's warnings went unheeded.

To the north of Mississippi, at the Cahokia site in Illinois, petrographic analysis was applied to pottery by Porter (1962). Building on his research, Bareis and Porter (1965) used petrography to establish the southern origin of a decorated, possibly grog-tempered, vessel from a Cahokian burial. Macroscopic and comparative analysis could do no more than link the pot to a variety of forms common throughout the Southeast, from Arkansas to Florida. Thin-section analysis confirmed the presence of fine, shell- and grog-tempered grog (which itself was red-slipped) in the paste, but also shell temper, which had undergone chemical replacement by a mineral called "collophane" and therefore was not identified in hand sample (Bareis and Porter 1965:98). There were also small shards of volcanic glass. Comparison to other thin sections indicated that the vessel was not made of locally available, American Bottom clays. Bareis and Porter (1965:100) concluded that the clay used to make the pot was perhaps "obtained from a weathered tertiary shale or clays (such as Porter's Creek) which crop out along the margins of the bluffs in the Lower Mississippi Valley."

Whereas Porter and others continued through the 1960s and 1970s to perform petrographic research in the American Bottom (Porter, who died in August 2003, eventually amassed a collection of several thousand Midwestern thin sections), none was conducted again in the LMV until the 1980s, by Maher (1983). Before turning to Maher (1983), however, I will review the important work undertaken by Gertjejansen et al. (1983), who returned to the issue of Early Woodland pottery, publishing a paper on Tchefuncte ceramics from the Pontchartrain Basin. While Lake Pontchartrain is quite a bit south of the Yazoo Basin and Gertjejansen et al. (1983) do not employ petrography, the results of their study are still pertinent.

Gertjejansen et al. (1983:37) begin by acknowledging that Tchefuncte pottery is, by all accounts, poorly made: "soft, poorly fired, poorly finished, and made from poorly prepared clays." Weaver's (1963) assessment of Tchula ceramics from Jaketown, also Late Archaic–Early Woodland but located farther to the north, is similar: Tchula pottery is also poorly made. But, unlike Gertjejansen et al. (1983), she concludes that the Jaketown potters were inexperienced, unable or unwilling to find good clay, and therefore produced sub-par pots (Weaver 1963:56). Gertjejansen et al. (1983:37) argue that the problem was a lack of good clay in the LMV, generally. Without mentioning Matson (1965), Gertjejansen et al. (1983) take a strongly "ceramic-ecological" approach to the issue, conducting clay-resources surveys and replication experiments. Using local clays, they replicated the "poor" Tchefuncte pottery with great success. Drawing on the work of marine and surface geologists (e.g., Potter et al. 1975), they conclude that because the LMV is largely dominated by the clay mineral smectite, a "three-layer, swelling" clay that holds water and does not fire well, potters in western Mississippi were limited in their ability to manufacture high-quality pottery (Gertjejansen et al. 1983:39–40). Finally, they also note the decreasing presence of available sand as one moves south along the Mississippi River (Gertjejansen et al. 1983:Figure 3, p. 43, adapted from Potter et al. 1975; possibly sand-tempered wares do not appear until the end of the Woodland and more commonly in the far northern LMV, the so-called Baldwin series; see Mainfort 1994; Smith 1979:75–78). A lack of sand for tempering made using the local smectite clays that much more difficult, as the logical solution to expansion and cracking, in the absence of high-temperature kilns, is the addition of temper. Lacking sand, potters turned to clay pellets, as Weaver (1963) had argued, and eventually, grog. According to Gertjejansen et al. (1983:46), true grog was not added to Tchefuncte ceramics until the very end of the Tchefuncte period.

Gertjejansen et al.'s (1983) conclusions about Tchefuncte pottery are borne out by Fullen (2005), who studied "laminated" and "contorted-paste" sherds from the Sara Peralta and Bayou Jasmine sites in Louisiana. Fullen (2005) demonstrates that Tchefuncte pottery-production methods improved through time, presumably as potters learned how to work with the region's poor clays. Furthermore, the Tchefuncte pottery from Bayou Jasmine is of higher quality earlier than that from Sara Peralta. Fullen (2005:2) argues that Bayou Jasmine "was more fully integrated into the Gulf Tradition of pottery manufacture" and that this might explain the better quality of pottery from the site, but it might also be the case that the quality of clay varied regionally (Fullen 2005:106).

In the case of the LMV's Early Woodland pottery, it was an ecological approach that explained the key fabric characteristics of the ceramic type, which seemingly were not determined by choices relating to style. Furthermore, the ecological approach taken by Gertjejansen et al. (1983) reveals the primary determining factor in the manufacture of pottery in Mississippi: the availability of good versus poor clay. This theme is reinforced in the work of Maher (1983), who applied petrographic analysis to a suite of southeastern clays, tempers (intentional and non-), and ceramics, mostly from Mississippi, thereby proving that the paste recipe (clays plus natural inclusions) is the main distinguishing factor when it comes to classifying pottery based on fabric differences.

Maher's (1983) research for his Master's thesis represents the best attempt to date to apply a holistic approach to Mississippi's archaeological ceramics, combining ceramic ecology (again, without citing Matson [1965]), including a clay- and temper-resources survey, with various scientific and statistical analyses. The material he studied from the LMV (from Natchez, Tunica, and Natchitoches sites) dates primarily to the Protohistoric and Early Contact periods. Smaller samples from Moundville and the Tennessee River valley were also analyzed. Maher (1983:24–30) first reviews the surface geology of the Southeast and, again based on Potter et al. (1975), comes to much the same conclusion as Gertjejansen et al. (1983): western Mississippi is dominated by smectite alluvial clays, which are difficult to work, and eastern Mississippi is dominated by illite and, to a lesser degree, kaolinite (sometimes called "potter's clay" because of its excellent potting qualities). However, as Maher (1983:25–30) further points out, marine clays, often montmorillinite or kaolinite, also crop up throughout Mississippi (in particular in the bluffs along the eastern edge of the Yazoo Basin), so that even in the LMV, potters could have exploited good clay. Certainly by Historic times, native potters had located and were mining marine clays; for example, Maher (1983:22) cites French accounts of Natchez potters using "potter's clay" from the bluffs, the so-called "Encore Blanc." Almost certainly, these sources were also exploited during Mississippian times, if not earlier. Thus, there is good evidence for a shift away from alluvial clays, used in earlier prehistoric periods, to marine clays, determined largely, if not wholly, by geological conditions and techno-functional needs and know-how.

Maher (1983) employed three analytical approaches: X-ray diffraction, petrography (point-counting), and heavy-mineral analysis. Of the three, heavy mineral-analysis proved the most useful to determine provenance and possible trade of pottery between sites in the LMV. X-ray diffraction did not work (Maher 1983:52). Petrographic point-counting was difficult due to the small numbers of inclusions in the pottery—only quartz, opaques, and the occasional detrital mineral grain (Maher 1983:52, 64). These do not represent intentional tempering. Most of the pottery was tempered with shell and, more occasionally, grog and bone, which Maher (1983:52) did not attempt to analyze. The heavy minerals, such as kyanite, rutile, epidote, tourmaline, etc., arrived in the pottery depending on the original geological source of the clay from which it was made. Heavy mineral analysis worked especially well to distinguish pottery from the three different regions: LMV, Moundville, and Tennessee River valley (Maher 1983:107). It less clearly distinguished sites in the LMV, which share a similar geological environment (Maher 1983:122). Interestingly, different named types shared similar fabrics, so that fabric differences, such as seemingly different temper types and amounts, did not allow or aid classification by type. As discussed above, fabric differences do not always or often correspond to differences in style, thereby confounding the type-variety system.

Taking a moment to summarize, ceramic-ecological and petrographic research conducted in Mississippi prior to 1990 had determined that: 1) pottery from various periods did indeed vary by fabric, but rarely did fabric differences align themselves with traditional types and varieties; 2) fabric differences were strongly determined by surface geology, in particular as it dictated access to clays and tempers; and 3) clay and temper availability varied across the state, in particular west to east. In the 1990s and 2000s, petrography has been employed occasionally, but often the goal was to explain ceramic variation in a single period or from a single site. As of yet, no one has tackled the systematic analysis of numbers 1–3, above.

In 1992, Metcalf analyzed a sample of sand-tempered pottery from northeast Mississippi. She focused on the sand itself, measuring the amount present in thin section and calculating average grain size. Studying Gulf Formational, Middle Woodland, and Protohistoric pottery, she sought to determine whether sand could be used to distinguish types from the different periods, noting, as had Connaway (1980) previously, that "there is significant overlap in most or all the sorting criteria used" to distinguish them (Metcalf 1992:19–20). Metcalf (1992:22–24) also tried sorting the pottery by Munsell-determined colors, only to discover that contrary to the expectations of the type-variety system, there was no systematic color variation by type. Likewise, texture and wall thickness varied unsystematically (Metcalf 1992:24–25). Disaggregation of sherds and analysis of sand-grain size proved more profitable. Metcalf (1992:25, 27) found that sherds of different type and from different periods did not vary meaningfully in sand size, but that sherds from different sites were distinguishable, despite type or period. Clearly, an "environmental bias" was in operation (Metcalf 1992:27); variations in the amount of sand in the various fabrics studied by Metcalf were apparently the result of variations in the amount of naturally-occurring sand in the clays available to potters.

Metcalf (1992) also employed petrographic point-counting, following Stoltman's procedures (see above). According to Metcalf (1992:31, 37–38), the results of point-counting appear to indicate that broadly different paste recipes, possibly using different clays and sands, were employed in each of the three different periods (Late Gulf Formational, Middle Woodland, and Protohistoric) studied. This is perhaps to be expected given the very long stretch of time under investigation. However, the ternary diagrams of the point-counting data do not clearly distinguish three separate fabrics (Metcalf 1992:38–39, Figures 14–15), and by Metcalf's own admission her reasons for separating the fabrics by period were largely subjective (1992:31). Nevertheless, in my estimation Metcalf's (1992) petrographic study represents one of the most comprehensive of those conducted to date in Mississippi.

Petrographic analysis of Middle Woodland ceramics from the Cork site conducted by Rafferty and Galaty (also described above) largely reinforces those conclusions drawn in all previous petrographic studies performed in Mississippi. According to Rafferty and Galaty (2002)—based on the petrographic analysis of 60 Miller I-II sherds and eight local clay samples, and the stylistic analysis of 416 rim sherds—there is no one-to-one correspondence between style and function, on the one hand, and fabric, on the other. Instead, style and functional attributes evolved independently from fabric attributes throughout the course of the Middle Woodland period at the Cork site:

> All decorations and surface finishes are found on sherds of both fabrics, another indication that fabric change is not stylistic. . . . The two fabrics were not used to make different kinds of vessels. . . . Neither the undirected force of drift nor selection working on functional attributes has much to offer in explaining the data so far obtained. The results presented here do provide somewhat of a cautionary tale for southeastern archaeologists, who often act as though slight variations in pottery paste or body, whether sortable or, often, not, are warrants for naming a new type or variety. The Cork site data provide a good example to the contrary (Rafferty and Galaty 2002: 5).

It is hoped that future, expanded studies of regional ceramics and clays will help to distinguish the range of paste recipes employed by potters in northeast Mississippi and that eventually, the intraregional exchange of pots during the Middle Woodland period—a time of many small villages and, we can surmise, household pottery production—can be substantiated, something not yet managed in the LMV (cf. Maher 1983).

As the new millennium dawned, Ortmann and Kidder (2004) again turned to the issue of "temperless" pottery from the LMV. They argue that pottery from the Poverty Point site is indistinguishable from Early Woodland Tchefuncte pottery. As a result, it seems quite likely that "temperless" pottery represents a ceramic tradition with some time-depth in the LMV, not an imported technology. Whereas various scholars have argued that Poverty Point and other sites in the LMV imported pottery from points farther east (*contra* Crusoe 1971:111, who performed petrographic analysis on a small sample of Baytown sherds), Ortmann and Kidder's (2004) work supports the idea that most pots were in fact locally produced, beginning during the Late Archaic. It is still not clear, however, that pottery was made at the Poverty Point site itself; Gibson and Melancon (2004:172) say yes, Hays and Weinstein (2000:79–82, 2004:163–164) say no, and Stoltman (2004), based on petrographic analysis of 16 soil samples, pottery, and Poverty Point objects, says maybe some Wheeler, but not Tchefuncte. According to Sassaman (1993), pottery manufacture began slowly during Poverty Point times due to elite support of the lucrative stone-bowl trade, an idea that Ortmann and Kidder (2004:208) reject. Be that as it may, by the Early Woodland pottery production had become a fixture of life in the LMV. What is more, there is good evidence that similar paste recipes were maintained in the LMV through later periods of the Early Woodland and into the Middle Woodland (if not later; see Rolingson 1985 regarding "clay-tempered" pottery from Mississippian times). For example, Toth and Brookes (1977:10) have noted that at the Martin site, located in Tunica County, Marksville decorations were applied to Tchefuncte-type fabrics. According to Toth and Brookes (1977:10), "the ceramics fit perfectly a situation in which a resident population (one making soft, badly tempered—or unconsciously tempered—pottery) adopts new decorative treatments to which it has been exposed."

One of Ortmann and Kidder's (2004:194) stated goals was to test methods of "digital image analysis" (DIA), in which digital photos are taken of a thin section and then subjected to computer-aided image analysis. Often, archaeologists turn to DIA as a means of saving time and money, but the approach has several inherent weaknesses. First of all, it allows counting and measurement of inclusions, but does not encourage the many other analyses, outlined above, typically undertaken by a trained petrographer. Second of all, it cannot distinguish very different particles if they are similarly shaped. Thus, in Ortmann and Kidder's (2004:204) study the software confused sponge spicules in St. John's ware with silt in local loess soils and Poverty Point objects. Finally, without the careful scanning of a thin section encouraged by point counting, important detrital minerals—those key to studies of provenance (cf. Maher 1983)—may be missed.

Recent research by Livingood (2003), applied to Plaquemine pottery from sites along the middle Pearl River in Lawrence County, also employed "digital image analysis." As noted by Livingood (2003:1) with regard to applications of the type-variety system, "many assemblages contain provocative mixtures of shell and grog tempering that make the type-variety system a challenge to apply." Some types, such as Addis, are downright messy, containing all kinds of organic and inorganic inclusions. Livingood's (2003:2–3, 4–6) goals, then, were to "reconstruct the paste recipes of the original potters"—Did they change through time and from region to region? Were different paste recipes particular to different communities?—and to test "Computer-Assisted Petrographic Analysis" (CAPA; i.e., DIA) as a means of recovering paste recipes.

As for the latter goal, my concerns regarding CAPA and Livingood's (2003) work are the same as those I have outlined regarding DIA and Ortmann and Kidder's (2004) research. In fact, many of the same difficulties experienced by Ortmann and Kidder were matched by Livingood (2003:6). For example, the software could not distinguish grog from all other "non-plastic inclusions that did not fit the criteria for other particle types" (Livingood 2003:6). The term "grog" became a catch-all for all inclusions that did not fit the other defined particle categories. This is, of course, a serious problem if indeed the goal is to reconstruct paste recipes. To Livingood's credit, he is working with petrographer Ann Cordell to improve CAPA's accuracy and expects that many of the identification problems experienced by the digital imaging software can be corrected (Cordell and Livingood 2004; Livingood 2004).

As for the main goal of Livingood's (2003) research—to reconstruct "paste" recipes—some of the preliminary results are quite interesting. In what has by now become a standard, oft-repeated theme in this chapter, there was no "100% correspondence" between microscopic and macroscopic ceramic categories, though this may have been due to deficiencies in the analytical methods employed (Livingood 2003:8). However, Livingood (2003:8) did find that differences in the amount of intentional temper used could be accounted for by function; utilitarian pots, such as cooking and storage pots, had more temper than did serving wares. (Sand appears to have occurred naturally in the clays used [Livingood 2003:9]). This stands to reason, but using the terminology of Stoltman (1989, 1991), Livingood (2003) has reconstructed *body* recipes, not *paste* recipes, which should be distinguished and studied separately. New temper types can be shared from potter to potter living in different communities without necessarily affecting paste recipes, i.e., the clays and associated naturally-occurring inclusions mixed in order to make pots. It seems that CAPA is perhaps best applied to studies of clearly defined tempers, such as shell.

In a very interesting twist, Livingood (2003:7) also found that shell and "grog" tempers were present together in almost all the sherds studied (see also Million 1975:202–203). As I discuss below, this may be a result of the cultural environment in which the middle Pearl River sites operated, right at the boundary between western and eastern Mississippi.

The "Ceramic-ecological" Setting: An Embarrassment of Riches?

Mississippi is rich in the primary resources needed to manufacture pottery: clay, water, fuel, and temper. Prehistoric potters had readily at hand all they needed to produce good pots. However, while abundant, these resources are not equally distributed throughout the landscape, nor are they of identical quality (Logan 1907, 1908, 1909). In the case of clays, some, kaolinites and illites, were better than others, such as smectites, for making pottery. The geographic variability in Mississippi's clays is reflected in the variable quality and distribution of the many types of prehistoric pottery. We might presume that through time experienced potters always chose to exploit the best of these clays, but such was not the case. Sometimes potters did not have access to the best clays, or collecting and working good clay was not convenient, and so they settled for clays that were sub-par. As a result, archaeological ceramics demonstrate real and meaningful fabric differences, the sources of which were dictated by geography (where potters lived versus where clay could be found) as well as by the decisions of individual potters (whether and what clays to use, and in what combinations).

Water

In the LMV, potters were never far from sources of water with which to wet their clay. In general, sites in all periods appear to follow river courses (though, admittedly this pattern may be the result of a "discovery" bias) (see Figure 12.1, below). In fact, the problem in Mississippi in some seasons may have been too much water and high humidity, during which "green" pots did not easily dry to the "leather hard" stage necessary for surface treatment, such as burnishing, to take place, nor to the "bone hard" stage necessary to firing (see discussions in Arnold 1985; see also Gertjejansen et al. 1983:38–39, 54–55). In other seasons, when the sun shone day after day and the temperature became very hot, the opposite problem existed; pots dried too quickly. Million (1975:207) has suggested that during the summer prehistoric potters may have used so-called "wet boxes" to diminish rapid drying and cracking of newly made pots.

Fuel

As was true for water, potters probably had plenty of available fuel for pit-firing pottery. According to Logan (1907:124), modern potters in Mississippi preferred various slow-, hot-, clean-burning hardwoods, such as oak and hickory. Both oak and hickory were available for use as a fuel in the Yazoo Basin in prehistoric times (Connaway 1982a:Table 1). Of course, many of the tree species available in the past in the LMV have recently disappeared (Connaway 1982a:Table 2). Million (1975:207) conducted experimental firings with corn cobs, corn stalks, bark, wood, cane, and thatch, all of which would have been available to Mississippi potters. Dried cane and thatch worked best, in his opinion, and represent a low-cost alternative to hardwoods.

Clay

In some parts of Mississippi, particularly in north-central and northeast Mississippi and in some secondary river drainages, potters had access to kaolinite or mixed-layer clays that included substantial amounts of kaolinite (Gertjejansen et al. 1983:39–41; Logan 1909; Potter et al. 1975:Figures 7 and 8; Reynolds 1991). In fact, in a report to the Mississippi State Geological Survey, Logan (1909:105–106) says that the very best potting clays in Mississippi are to be found in the northeast, associated with the "Tuscaloosa"/Eutaw and Wilcox formations. Prehistoric potters working in the northeast had a distinct advantage as compared to potters working in the LMV, who had—at least at first—to contend with poor clays and a general lack of suitable tempering materials.

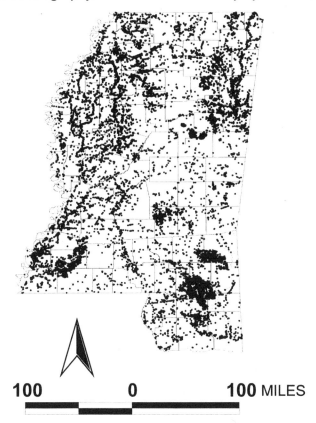

Figure 12.1. Map of all sites in the MDAH site file.

Interestingly, Steponaitis et al. (1996) have demonstrated that pan-regional variation in clays, as derived from different geological source materials (Griffin 1962; Neiheisel and Weaver 1967; Potter et al. 1975; Reynolds 1991), is reflected in the variable chemical composition of archaeological ceramics (see also Neff, this volume). Thus, as was found by Maher (1983), it should be possible to characterize *inter*-regional differences in southeastern fabrics. Whether or not *intra*-regional characterization is possible, however, remains to be seen. For example, Stoltman and Mainfort (2002) had great difficulty reproducing through petrographic analysis the results of an intra-regional, chemical-compositional study of sherds from Pinson Mounds and associated sites conducted by Mainfort et al. (1997). It appears likely that for intra-regional studies of ceramic fabrics to work, both chemical and petrographic analyses will need to be employed, and local clays surveyed, collected, and analyzed as well. A "ceramic-ecological" approach is, it seems, unavoidable.

Gertjejansen et al. (1983:42) found that whenever possible most potters working in the Pontchartrain Basin exploited pure "back bay" clays, those clays trapped behind natural river levees (Million's [1975:201] so-called "back-swamp" clays; see also Fullen 2005; Walling and Chapman 1999:173). Most, if not all, of these alluvial clays are without doubt smectites, the so-called "expanding layer" clays described above, which have high "shrink-swell ratios" and crack when drying (Gertjejansen et al. 1983:41–42; Million 1975:201). There are advantages to using these clays, however, which in a cost-benefit analysis may have outweighed problems with cracking (provided the cracking could be controlled): they are ubiquitous, highly plastic, need little preparation, and can be fired at low temperatures. The logical, most simple solution to problems with shrink-swell is the addition of tempers just large enough to bind expanding clay layers together (Gertjejansen et al. 1983:40; Million 1975:201).

Temper

As has been discussed already in this chapter, there still exists some disagreement as to whether or not prehistoric potters in the LMV consciously tempered their pottery, in particular in early periods. Certainly, in some periods and for some types, potters consciously chose to temper their pottery, most probably in order to solve technical problems caused by the clays used, such as the aforementioned problem with shrinking and swelling.

Some clays contain coarse natural inclusions, like sand, that automatically solve this problem, but most clays in the LMV contain only very fine sand (Weaver 1963:54). According to Gertjejansen et al. (1983:40), the last 200 miles of the Mississippi channel contains only fine sand, unsuitable as a tempering agent. At first, LMV potters "solved" the problem, perhaps unintentionally, by only partially pulverizing their clay, thereby leaving clay chunks behind that could act as a tempering agent (Gertjejansen et al. 1983:46; Weaver 1963:55). However, poorly wedged clay makes for "friable," weak pots (Gertjejansen et al. 1983:46). A better solution is to add grog, which serves the same purpose as clay chunks, but encourages more complete wedging, and has the added benefit, because it is made from already-fired potsherds, of reducing thermal shock (Million 1975:203). As discussed above, by the end of the Tchefuncte period, potters appear to have preferred grog. The other more costly option available to LMV potters was to search out better clays, those that did not suffer problems with shrinking, such as the rare (probably 15 percent or less; Gertjejansen et al. 1983:40) kaolinites. As described above, this probably did happen over time, as beds of marine clay were found and mined.

In northeastern Mississippi, where sand was more readily available for tempering or existed naturally in the clays used, grog was less often employed as a temper. As compared to LMV potters, potters in the north and east had better clays and a wider array of tempers available to them. Eventually, however, a "technological revolution" swept the Southeast: shell tempering (Million 1975:202). Unlike grog and sand, burned, crushed shell produces an electro-chemical reaction ("flocculation") when added to clay, allowing small, negatively charged clay particles to "clump" together, producing much better ceramic working qualities (Million 1975:202). Addition of shell to LMV smectites would have been particularly effective in overcoming problems with shrink-swell and would have allowed construction of larger vessels with more pronounced rim curvatures (Cogswell and O'Brien 1998:43–45). Burned bone, like shell also a carbonate of calcium and sometimes added to Mississippi pottery as temper, produces a similar effect when added to clay, as does ash and limestone (Cogswell and O'Brien 1998:43–45). In evolutionary terms, shell tempering was such an advantageous behavioral trait that it swept through the potting population unchecked.

By Mississippian times, all potters used at least some shell in their pottery, and the playing field in terms of ceramic ecology had been leveled. The stage was set for larger-scale, non-DMP manufacturing of pottery, which also may have been encouraged by intensive farming, surplus production of maize, and economic specialization. Whereas this scenario has been substantiated for Mississippian regions to the north (Emerson and Lewis 2000; Pauketat 1998), it can be assumed for the LMV but has yet to be fully documented. Careful studies of the pottery made in the Yazoo Basin during Mississippian times—employing a ceramic-ecological approach, accompanied by the chemical and petrographic characterization of pottery fabrics—may be able to distinguish specialized production and the subsequent distribution of pottery.

GIS Investigations of Mississippi's Ceramic Ecology

In order to illustrate some of the conclusions drawn in this chapter regarding Mississippi's pottery fabrics and ceramic ecology, and in order to further refine the suggested framework and methodology for fabric characterization, I have constructed a Geographic Information Systems project that combines archaeological data from MDAH site files with maps of the state (county boundaries, rivers, physiographic units, surface geology, soils, etc.) from MARIS.

The MDAH files record information, including location, regarding over 30,000 archaeological sites of all types and periods. I imported the site files into a database program called FileMaker, which could be easily searched for keywords. Once a sub-set of files had been created using a keyword search, the sub-set was imported into ArcView and mapped against the MARIS map layers.

This approach to mapping the site-file data is not without problems. First of all, only a small percentage of the site files have been checked for accuracy, their UTM coordinates in particular (Cliff Jenkins, personal communication). Second, sites have been described in the files in varying degrees of detail; some files are wonderfully complete, whereas others contain almost no information. Third, the terminology used in the site files is not standardized, making key-word searches suspect. For example, pottery types and varieties present on-site may be abbreviated in any number of ways, each of which needed to be first identified and then searched for separately. The data are therefore not exhaustive, by any means: a search for sites with "shell-tempered pottery" will not reveal all sites with Mississippian components. With these disclaimers in mind, I do believe, however, that the approach taken worked well enough to allow the identification of several broad regional patterns relevant to the foregoing discussion of Mississippi's ceramic ecology.

Turning to Figure 12.1, a map of all sites in the MDAH site file, it is clear that sites do tend to follow river courses. In addition, there do seem to be parts of the state which were more heavily settled than others during ceramic periods. For instance, eastern and western Mississippi were fairly densely settled, whereas central portions of the state were less so. This pattern is, at least in part, the result of different amounts of survey and site identification in different counties and national forests, but equally possible and testable is the hypothesis that the environment played a determining role in settlement choice. In fact, the overall settlement pattern fits well the ceramic ecology. The potting resources in the west are dense, yet of variable quality, while those in the east are excellent, though perhaps not as readily available (a "patchy" resource). The central portions of the state are dominated by the loess hills physiographic zone. As it turns out, silty loess is an exceedingly poor potting material (Snowden and Priddy 1968:15, Figure 1 and 195–200) and is typically lacking in good tempering agents (di Caprio and Vaughn 1993:25). However, the large rivers that drain this region, in particular the Pearl and Pascagoula, which have their sources to the north, carry heavy loads of kaolinite, thereby providing some good potting clay (Griffin 1962:749). In central Mississippi, the riverine settlement focus is especially pronounced, perhaps in small part because that is where good clay might be found.

As alluded to above, this east-west divide in Mississippi is visible in terms of tempering and temper resources, as well. Indeed, when site files reporting grog-tempered pottery (using the word "grog" or some variant thereof) are mapped, they are found to be numerous in both the east and the west (though not in far northeast Mississippi; see Figure 12.2). When site files reporting sand-tempered pottery (using the word "sand" or some variant thereof) are mapped, they are rarely found in the Delta region (Figure 12.2). In between, in central Mississippi, there are fewer sites and identified pottery types reported,

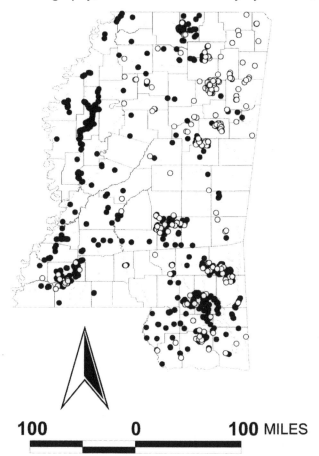

Figure 12.2. Map of sites in the MDAH site file that report "grog"-tempered pottery (filled circles) and "sand"-tempered pottery (open circles).

and those sites mapped indicate overlapping temper preferences. As discovered by Livingood (2003) for his middle Pearl River sites, temper constituents in this region are mixed, defying easy characterization. To some degree the pattern I have just described may be an artifact of the traditional biases of Mississippi's archaeologists: grog belongs in the west and so is primarily found and reported there, whereas sand is expected to the north and east. But I think the pattern exists in reality, as most Mississippi archaeologists have intuitively recognized (see Haag 1952:18; "It [the Grenada Reservoir] also lies in a zone that is transitional between clay-grit tempering to the west in the Mississippi Delta and sand-tempering to the north and east in North Mississippi and Alabama"), and can be explained with reference to Mississippi's ceramic ecology (see above). There is less sand tempering in the west because there is less sand to be found there. And, there is less grog tempering in the east because it was not needed.

Though MDAH site files that report pottery using the type-variety system are few, it is possible to catch glimpses of several interesting patterns when they are mapped through time. Early Woodland types that are traditionally characterized as grog-tempered, such as Tchefuncte, are confined to the southern and western portions of the state, while a sand-tempered type, like Middle Woodland Miller, is firmly, though not exclusively, situated in the northeast (Figure 12.3). Again, the state's ceramic ecology may have played a role here, as might have the biases of Mississippi's archaeologists, but it might also be that by the Middle Woodland period, ceramics are being traded more often on a much wider scale. Sand-tempered Miller pots make their way into the Delta, and in fact, grog-tempered Middle Woodland Marksville pots are found in the northeast (Peacock 2003:48–50).

In order to investigate the aforementioned biases and/or patterns more fully, I have compiled data from excavation and surface-survey reports of 62 sites in the LMV (Table 12.1). I only included in the analysis data from site reports in which the writers present specific and detailed descriptions of fabric/temper characteristics used to classify pottery (and, of course, raw artifact counts), and I have conflated various types, varieties, and periods in order to increase the sample size. Whereas most LMV archaeologists have employed in their reports the type-variety system following and referencing Phillips (1970), and so further fabric descriptions were deemed unnecessary, some LMV archaeologists have recognized problems with the system, in particular in its application to pottery containing multiple temper types. Those who have recognized problems typically make explicit their sorting criteria. For instance, in Haag's report of his survey of the Grenada Reservoir (in which he refers to southeastern pottery types generally as "artificial" and "arbitrary" groupings, and therefore difficult to apply [Haag 1952:19]), Baldwin Plain is referred to as a "sand-tempered, sandy-paste ceramic" (Haag 1952:19); Baytown Plain is "clay- or sherd-tempered, smooth, and hard" (Haag 1952:20); and Tishomingo Plain is "distinguishable from Baldwin and Baytown by the combination of sandy paste and clay or sherd tempering" (Haag 1952:20). The cord-marked type of Tishomingo is Tishomingo Cord-marked, whereas the cord-marked type of Baytown is Mulberry Creek Cord-marked; both are clay- or sherd-tempered (Haag 1952:21). All fabric-impressed pottery had a "sandier paste than typical Baytown but with all other Baytown characteristics" (i.e. clay- or sherd-tempered) and so was classified as Withers Fabric-impressed (a.k.a. Withers Fabric-marked) (Haag 1952:22–23). Using this "lumping" approach, Haag

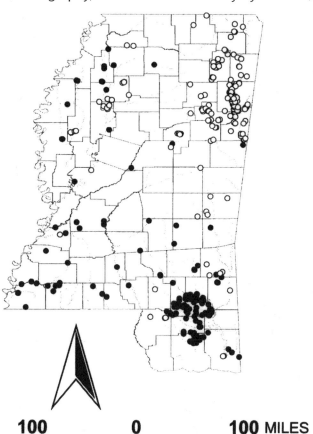

Figure 12.3. Map of sites in the MDAH site file that report Early Woodland types traditionally characterized as grog-tempered (filled circles) and the Middle Woodland Miller type traditionally characterized as sand-tempered (open circles).

(1952:24, Summary Table) identified 1,287 pieces of pottery from 48 sites. Of these, 1,100 were clay- or sherd-tempered and 185 were sand-tempered (i.e. Baldwin Plain); two sherds were shell-tempered (see Table 12.1).

A GIS analysis of Haag's (1952) sites indicates very little spatial patterning by temper type. Sand and grog tempering are not spatially segregated, often being found together at the same site. In fact, Haag's (1952) various types often are found together at the same site. This may indicate, for instance, that although potters used several different clays and/or paste recipes, the potters and/or the pots moved around, or that potting resources (various clays and

Table 12.1. Ceramic data from Mississippi sites. HPG: Heartfield, Price and Greene, Inc.

Site No.	AKA	Name	Source	Total Pottery	Fiber	Grog	Sand	Shell	Limestone	Bone
HU505		Jaketown	Lehmann 1982:47	6	6					
LF649		Palusha Creek 2	Brown et al. 1994:3	1,037		1,037				
JE543		O'Quinn	Brown 1985:192	99		18		38		
AD547		Rice	Brown 1985:192	111		34		29		
AD521		Fatherland	Brown 1985:192	97		24		65		
CR504		Teoc Creek	Connaway et al. 1977:87–89	211	43	70	91			
QU522		Denton	Connaway 1977:129–131	168	2	123	32	11		
YZ624		O'Neil Creek	HPG, Inc. 1987	11,524		11,509		15		
WS776		Swan Lake	Fuller 1992:19–24	114		49		65		
CO511		Parchman	Connaway 1985	1					1	
AD824		Lake George	Gibson 1985:76–78	71		71				
CB522		Grand Gulf	Brookes 1976	91		91				
TL501		Buford	Marshall 1988:Table 8	996		476		520		
PA1014		Batesville Mounds	Johnson et al. 2002	10,935		6,662	3,259			774
WS500		Winterville	Brain 1989:70–164	28,870		8,663	2	20,896		
CO560		McNight	Walling and Chapman 1999:171	34,380		34,396	2	425		
YA500	Ya 1	Womack Mound	Haag 1952	12		10	2			
YA501	Ya 2	County Line	Haag 1952	2		2				
YA502	Ya 3	Cypress Creek	Haag 1952	2		1	1			
YA503	Ya 4	Gums Village	Haag 1952	3		3				
YA504	Ya 5	Railroad	Haag 1952	1			1			
YA505	Ya 6	Dirt Road	Haag 1952	3		3				

Catalog	Site	Name	Reference				
YA506	Ya 7	Bryant Junction	Haag 1952			72	72
YA507	Ya 8	Muddy Creek	Haag 1952			2	2
YA508	Ya 9	Turkey Creek	Haag 1952			11	11
YA509	Ya 10	Hwy. 7	Haag 1952			13	13
YA510	Ya 11	Terrence	Haag 1952			9	9
YA511	Ya 12	Turkey Creek	Haag 1952			4	4
YA512	Ya 13	Turkey Creek	Haag 1952			8	8
YA513	Ya 14	Turkey Creek	Haag 1952			3	3
YA514	Ya 15	Bryant	Haag 1952	1	10	34	45
YA515	Ya 16	Terrence	Haag 1952			1	1
YA516	Ya 17	Gums #2	Haag 1952		11		11
YA517	Ya 18	Gums #3	Haag 1952			5	5
YA518	Ya 19	Bryant	Haag 1952		1		1
YA519	Ya 20		Haag 1952		1		1
CA502	Ca 1	West Mound	Haag 1952			9	9
CA503	Ca 2	Denton Village	Haag 1952		2	3	5
CA504	Ca 3	Crossing	Haag 1952			2	2
CA505	Ca 4	Hillock	Haag 1952			13	13
CA506	Ca 5	Sabougla	Haag 1952			11	11
GR505	Gr 2	Martin	Haag 1952			3	3
GR506	Gr 3	Cabin	Haag 1952		56	618	676
GR507	Gr 4	Kirkman	Haag 1952		7	62	69
GR508	Gr 5	Kirkman	Haag 1952		1	16	17
GR509	Gr 6	Kirkman	Haag 1952			7	7
GR510	Gr 7	Meager	Haag 1952			4	4
GR511	Gr 8	Perry Creek	Haag 1952			3	3

Continued on the next page

Table 12.1. *Continued*

Site No.	AKA	Name	Source	Total Pottery	Fiber	Grog	Sand	Shell	Limestone	Bone
GR512	Gr 9	Perry Creek	Haag 1952	2		2				
GR513	Gr 10	Jimmy	Haag 1952	4		3	1			
GR514	Gr 11	Church	Haag 1952	15		8	7			
GR515	Gr 12	Graysport	Haag 1952	12		12				
GR516	Gr 13	Lane	Haag 1952	30		20	10			
GR521	Gr 18	Brush Creek	Haag 1952	37		26	11			
GR522	Gr 19	Dirt Road V	Haag 1952	46		20	26			
GR523	Gr 20	Sparse Village	Haag 1952	17		17				
GR524	Gr 21	Grass Village	Haag 1952	4		4				
GR526	Gr 23	Torrence	Haag 1952	37		31	6			
GR527	Gr 24	Stream	Haag 1952	7		7				
GR528	Gr 25	Champion	Haag 1952	6		3	3			
GR529	Gr 26	Pasture	Haag 1952	10		7	3			
GR530	Gr 27	McCormick	Haag 1952	11		1	9			

tempers) were available on a regional scale, so that any potter at any site could make any type of pot so desired. In the absence of clay and temper surveys and a ceramic-ecological analysis of the Grenada Reservoir region, it is difficult to distinguish between these two, and other, possibilities. For his part, Haag (1952:20) assumed that the three types were "coeval and but regional variants of one pottery tradition." However, one pattern that is evident concerns Baytown (clay-tempered, no sand) and Tishomingo (clay-tempered, sandy paste) pottery. These two, whether cord-marked or not, are rarely found at the same site (though the pattern is not regionalized; e.g., Baytown in one river catchment, Tishomingo in the other). Again, it is difficult to evaluate the meaning of this pattern in the absence of ceramic-ecological data, but it may be that Baytown is earlier chronologically than Tishomingo, or vice versa. Given this scenario, choice of temper remained constant, but potters switched to sandier clay sources. Finally, Withers Fabric-marked is only found along the Yalobusha River, never along the Skuna. The effect here also may be chronological, as fabric marking is thought to be an early form of surface treatment.

In an effort to determine whether or not sand tempering really did precede grog tempering, Johnson et al. (2002) analyzed pottery from the Batesville Mounds, classifying it using criteria similar to those used by Haag (1952). In Johnson et al.'s (2002:43–57) scheme, Baytown Plain, *var. Thomas* is sandy with some grog temper, Baytown Plain, *var. unspecified* is grog-tempered with a clean paste and very little sand, Mulberry Creek Cord-marked, *var. Blue Lake* is sandy with some grog temper, whereas Mulberry Creek Cord-Marked, *var. unspecified* is still somewhat sandy but certainly grog-tempered, and Withers Fabric-marked *var. Withers* is grog-tempered whereas Withers Fabric-marked *var. Twin Lakes* is sandy with some grog temper. Using these criteria, Johnson et al. (2002:68, Table 4.5) separated all excavated pottery into categories: cord-marked versus fabric-marked; and grog, grog/sand, sparse grog/sand, versus sand-tempered. The results of this sorting were then compared against the excavation records, indicating that, generally speaking, sand tempering becomes more prevalent later, in the Middle Woodland, and that fabric marking is almost exclusively associated with grog tempering, and thus precedes cord marking. These results match those of Peacock (1996, 1997), who argued, based on work in the Holly Springs National Forest, that sand replaces grog tempering about the time cord marking replaces fabric marking.

Returning to Haag (1952), it would seem, based on Johnson et al.'s (2002) results, that the spatial patterning evident in his data is the result of broad temporal shifts reflecting changes in paste recipes through time (and perhaps intra-regional trade of pots as well). Thus, in site-specific (as at Batesville and the Cork site) and micro-regional (as at Grenada Reservoir and Holly Springs) analyses of fabrics we reach an impasse: without further scientific characterization (i.e. petrography and/or chemistry) combined with ceramic-ecological surveys, fabrics (whether pastes generally, or tempers specifically) are unlikely to serve, especially as currently operationalized within the type-variety system, as objective markers of spatial and/or temporal change in anything other than a very gross sense. But what of broader regional analyses based on fabric, such as of the whole LMV?

When pottery from the remaining 15 sites in my sample (see Table 12.1) is mapped in terms of the presence or absence of sand (Figure 12.4), it becomes clear that local, sand-tempered pottery is found only in the north. Four sites produced sand-tempered pottery and all four are confined to the northern half of the Delta. Based on research conducted in Arkansas, Morse and Morse (1980) argue for the mutual spatial exclusivity of grog and sand pastes, in particular during the Baytown period. According to Morse (1986:79), "It is a distinct possibility that these two pastes relate to major tribal differences in the Baytown period." As I have argued above, different paste recipes could mark tribal differences, but may also be the result of regional variation in clay and temper resources available to potters. In the Mississippi Delta, the divide between grog and sand tempering is likely to have been dictated not by cultural differences, but rather by the availability of sand suitable for use as temper (though chronology could also play a role), the southern half of the LMV being devoid of medium-coarse sand (Gertjejansen et al. 1983:40). As with site-specific and micro-regional analyses of pastes, given the current state of our knowledge we are unlikely to be able to say much more about pottery-fabric distributions until such time as more intensive, targeted research takes place.

As might be expected, a map of MDAH site files mentioning shell and shell-tempering transgresses the east-west divide, being found in many parts of the state, including the Delta (Figure 12.5). As with grog and sand, there is perhaps a degree of bias at work here, too. My impression is that archaeologists filling out site cards mention shell tempering less often because it is easily identifiable and Mississippian pottery types by definition contain shell, and are therefore more easily named. Sand and grog tempering are more difficult to identify and therefore are more often mentioned in the files, in particular when sherds were absent decoration and a type-variety designation could not be made. If the site files were more complete, it might be possible to map the spread of shell tempering through Mississippi, but at present this cannot be done.

Conclusions

To conclude, the GIS research conducted for this chapter indicates that when mapped by site, pottery-fabric distributions may reflect in part the state's complex ceramic ecology. Furthermore, there are indications that pottery fabric

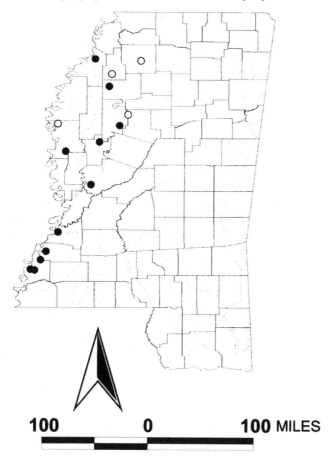

Figure 12.4. Sites in the LMV from Table 12.1 (excluding Haag 1952). Open circles mark those that produced sand-tempered pottery.

characteristics did indeed change systematically through time. I do not believe that distributional patterns are merely the result of discovery and/or classification biases, though these do have an effect. I expect that implementation of a parallel system of classification based on fabric, relying on petrographic analyses of ceramic thin sections, as described above, would, if further combined with clay and temper resources surveys, produce new insights into the manufacture and distribution of Mississippi's pottery. A good place to start would be in the LMV in association with MDOT- or other agency-funded mitigation projects.

Should intensive analysis of fabrics be attempted on a large scale in the I-69 corridor, I would suggest that:

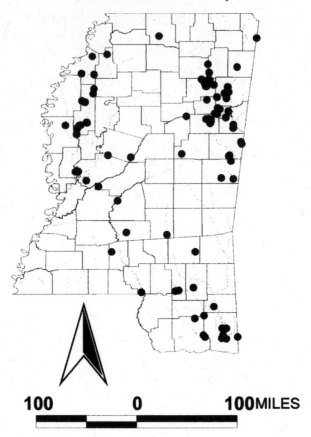

Figure 12.5. Map of sites in the MDAH site file that report
"shell"-tempered pottery. The paucity of data points reflects
the difficulty of using category-specific site-card data.

1. clay and temper samples be taken throughout the I-69 corridor;
2. clay/temper and a small but representative number of pottery samples be analyzed using the qualitative and quantitative petrographic methods outlined above; if necessary, digital imaging analysis and/or chemical characterization (see Neff, this volume) be used to refine and/or augment fabric classification based on petrography by increasing the number of samples analyzed and analyzing clay chemical constituents, respectively;
3. a fabric-type system be created that can be reproduced and employed macroscopically; and
4. the fabric-type system be systematically compared to the traditional type-variety system, which will perhaps help solve various, outstanding problems with the system.

If implemented as part of I-69 or other mitigation projects, these steps should pay large dividends, quickly, and at relatively low cost.

Acknowledgments

I would like to thank Janet Rafferty and Evan Peacock for inviting me to contribute to this volume, and for sharing ideas and information with me regarding Mississippi's pottery. Jeffrey Alvey of the Cobb Institute of Archaeology at Mississippi State University was a tremendous help in creating the GIS project. I owe a debt of gratitude to Cliff Jenkins for making available to me data from the MDAH site files. Map layers from the Mississippi Automated Resource Information System are available free of charge at *http://www.maris.state.ms.us/index.html*. Research for this chapter was conducted with the generous support of the Hearin Foundation, through a grant from the Millsaps College Faculty Development Committee.

13
Faunal Research in the Yazoo Basin and Lower Mississippi Valley

Setting Parameters for Future Research in the I-69 Corridor, Mississippi

H. Edwin Jackson

Introduction

Recovery and analysis of faunal materials have become integral aspects of archaeological research designs, providing valuable information regarding subsistence practices, site seasonality, impacts of human exploitation on animal populations, changes in procurement strategies due to environmental change, changing human demographics, and the gradual shift from hunting and gathering to horticulture to intensive agriculture. In addition, zooarchaeological remains have the potential for providing insights into socially defined variability in resource access, and even symbolic aspects of prehistoric cultures. This chapter reviews and synthesizes available zooarchaeological data from the Mississippi Delta region and, more broadly, from the Lower Mississippi Valley (LMV), to produce a baseline for anticipated data recovery as a result of mitigation efforts in the I-69 corridor in northeast Mississippi. Following a general discussion of environmental parameters affecting prehistoric procurement patterns, this chapter summarizes existing analyses of archaeologically recovered faunal collections from sites located in that portion of the LMV referred to as the Yazoo Basin (northwest Mississippi). It then augments these data with information from other sites excavated in adjacent states to examine and define broader temporal and spatial trends in prehistoric faunal use. This will help to better define current gaps in our understanding and thus guide further research.

The Role of Zooarchaeology in Archaeological Research

Archaeologically recovered faunal remains provide data for reconstructing the character of subsistence pursuits, including the species of animals used, the mix and relative contributions of these species, how procurement activities varied seasonally, and how they may have changed over time. Choices made by hunter-fishers in expending procurement efforts are conditioned by a matrix of variables. These include seasonal variability in prey condition and availability and ease of procurement, all of which affect relative procurement costs and thus the subsistence strategies employed. The prey available in a specific site locale also responded to longer-term patterns of biogeographic distributions, distributions affected by the dynamic alluvial valley environment that is the LMV. There were also the impacts of cultural practices such as farming on local plant and animal communities, conflicts with other necessary activities (for instance, crop harvesting), and the cultural rules that governed aspects of food sharing and consumption. Demographic characteristics of both local and regional human population also played a role in determining the range and relative contributions of resources used. For instance, increasing population density in a single locale may increase the range of resources used, since more people are hunting and collecting close to a settlement. Finally, social and political variables may play a role in subsistence pursuits. For instance, endemic intersocietal conflict may increase the risks of long-distance hunting, resulting in more localized pursuits (e.g., Keck 1997; see below).

There are a number of challenges to making cultural sense of the zooarchaeological record. First, archaeological faunal assemblages are rarely a perfect representation of the range of hunting, trapping, and fishing activities of a people. The length and purpose (residential, short-term, task-specific) of an occupation play a role in what is discarded and how. Season of the year affects not only the animals exploited, but how they are prepared and what becomes of the inedible skeletal parts. The remains from a site may represent a narrowly focused procurement effort at a particular point in the annual round, or be longer-term accumulations representing multiple decisions and consequent hunting and fishing efforts. Animals may be introduced to a site whole or, if cleaning or butchering occurs away from the habitation site, only in part. Preparation methods and patterns of refuse disposal affect the chances of bones being buried in a way that allows recovery by the archaeologist. A host of post-depositional taphonomic processes affect the likelihood that discarded bone will be recovered archaeologically. For instance, village dogs, rodents, and soil conditions (acidity, matrix texture, moisture, and temperature) all affect bone preservation. All of these figure into the composition of the faunal assemblage recovered through excavation. However, decisions made about how a site is excavated also affect the composition of the sample and its potential for accurately representing prehistoric subsistence patterns. The size of the excavation sample, the distribution of that sample, and the contexts—midden versus feature, for instance—all affect bone recovery. Finally, the skills possessed and the methods employed by the analyst also affect the translation of a sample of faunal material into inferences regarding prehistoric procurement and other subsistence-related behavior.

Environmental Parameters

Decisions about hunting and fishing are based in part on resource availability and the costs attached to procurement. On a broad scale, we can enumerate the many animals potentially available in the LMV that could have been resource targets. However, in order to begin to understand how the archaeofaunal assemblages reflect particular strategies employed by inhabitants of specific sites, we need a useful reconstruction of the site's environmental setting. Variation in the composition of assemblages, in addition to such contributing factors as changing seasonal availability of taxa and scheduling conflicts, is partially a function of the locally available subset of the total animal population. This is not a new idea, to be sure; it harkens back to catchment analysis paradigms of the 1970s. However, the task of identifying key potential resources in a particular site's catchment during a particular occupation of that site is made difficult in the LMV by the geomorphic dynamics of this large alluvial setting.

In addition to variation in environmental settings related to broad-scale climatic trends over the course of prehistory, the dynamic nature of the alluvial setting controlled by the Mississippi River and its tributaries produced both gradual and predictable geomorphic changes in the local environmental setting, as well as sometimes rapid and dramatic changes. These geomorphic processes can be expected to have produced an ever-changing patchwork of terrestrial and aquatic communities.

The surfaces on which prehistoric populations inhabited and made their livings are Quaternary in age, and the majority of land area in the Yazoo Basin was created during the Holocene era by alternating processes of erosion and deposition. With the exception of the extreme western edge of northern Mississippi, which is a part of the modern Mississippi River course, the Yazoo Basin is comprised of water courses that flow into the Yazoo River above its eventual confluence with the Mississippi in the vicinity of Vicksburg. However, much of the modern drainage pattern, as well as surface features, are a product of former Mississippi River meander belts (e.g. Saucier 1994). Once abandoned, these meander belts were occupied by local drainage systems.

Meander belt geomorphology has a significant role in the geographic and temporal distribution of food resources. In particular, the distribution of fish species is conditioned by the processes of stream channel evolution in the Yazoo Basin. Different species of fish are adapted to different combinations of aquatic environmental attributes, related to water temperature, current, substrate, turbidity, vegetation characteristics, and of course the complex array of predator-prey relationships among aquatic organisms. In any particular location the values of these variables will be altered over time as a consequence of the geomorphic processes at play.

Occupied river courses periodically flood, typically in winter and spring, and in the process build coarser-textured, slightly higher natural levees immediately adjacent to the river channel. Behind these levees, fine sediments (silts and clays) are carried by laterally flowing floodwaters, creating sometimes quite extensive low-lying and poorly drained backswamps. These may hold pockets of water for some time after river levels have receded. Differences in elevation, soil texture, and drainage create different forest communities, which in turn play a role in the variable distributions of animal populations and their availability for human exploitation.

Other geomorphic processes produce additional floodplain features. Channel migration, which is responsible for the sinuous channel shape of meandering river channels, erodes the bank edges on the outside concave side of the channel while depositing point bar sediments on the opposite side of the river. Extremely sinuous segments of the channel may breach the natural levees, shortening the course and causing abandonment of a segment of the river channel, forming oxbow lakes. These stillwater habitats support fish communities with different species composition than are found in the main channel and, while they are no longer permanently attached to the river, they are periodically reconnected to the active channel by floodwaters in subsequent years. The regularity of this reintegration is indicated by the movement of spawning river-channel species into oxbows and other slackwater areas created by flooding. Oxbow lakes undergo change over time, as sediments introduced by the flooding of subsequent years eventually reduce their depth, alter the substrate, and affect turbidity.

Eventually the process of overbank flooding and sediment deposition raises the elevations of the entire meander belt to the point that it is abandoned by the main river course for portions of the floodplain with lower elevation. Local watersheds are formed, with abandoned channels occupied by local underfit rivers. Ecological changes can be predicted in these different systems, associated with changes in species distributions.

Previous Synthetic Studies

A number of previous zooarchaeological studies are relevant to the present effort. Bruce Smith (1975) authored a now-classic examination of faunal exploitation during the Mississippian period. The study synthesized environmental parameters, as well as behavioral and reproductive characteristics of Mississippi valley faunal species and how these conditioned ecological relationships between late prehistoric human populations and the most commonly used taxa. Smith compiled data from seven Middle Mississippian sites representing four broad environmental settings, including but not limited to the Mississippi valley. Using meat-weight estimates based on Minimum Number of Individuals (MNI) data, Smith identified the 13 most important species or species groups. These included (in rank order): deer, raccoon, fish (collectively), migratory waterfowl (ducks, geese, etc.), turkey, beaver, opossum, rabbits (*Sylvilagus* sp.), snapping turtles (Chelydridae), dogs, squirrels (*Sciurus* sp.), bear, and elk. The contributions of these taxa varied among the sites according to geographic location and environmental setting. Using reproductive and behavioral characteristics, as well as archaeological seasonality indicators and limited ethnohistoric information, he predicted the seasons during which each taxon/taxon group would be most likely to make its greatest contribution to the diet. Greatest intersite differences related to the relative importance of fish (mainly a warm-season resource), as well as migratory waterfowl (mainly exploited in cooler months), with both of these significantly better represented in assemblages from sites in the meander belt setting. Secondarily, there were differences in the ratios of cottontail to swamp rabbits and of fox squirrels to gray squirrels, the latter in each case being more prominent in the meander belt–associated assemblages, compared to sites in upland settings.

Potentially relevant for the segment of the Mississippi valley under consideration here are analyses by Bonnie Styles and Emanuel Breitburg further upstream. Styles (1994), using combined data from 45 components at 10 sites in the lower Illinois River valley and the adjacent section of the Central Mississippi Valley (CMV), identified several trends. Simplifying her discussion somewhat, Styles identified for the Lower Illinois valley an initial increase in the representation of fish in assemblages during the late Middle Archaic. The proportion of fish peaked in assemblages from the late prehistoric time range (Middle Woodland through Mississippian). Other aquatic resources, including turtles, migratory birds, and aquatic mammals, also appear to increase in importance later in prehistory. Coincident with these trends is an apparent decline in the use of terrestrial resources. Data from the CMV are somewhat more complicated, though fish use is greatest during the late prehistoric time range, coinciding with somewhat less use of deer and terrestrial mammals. Aquatic bird use, however, appears to have been less than during the previous Archaic time range.

Breitburg (1992), in conjunction with zooarchaeological analysis of the Emergent Mississippian Petitt site in southern Illinois, compared twelve Mississippian assemblages, stretching from the American Bottoms south to Memphis, including the data provided in Smith's 1975 study. Without detailing the steps in his analysis, Breitburg used principal components analysis to discern two broad patterns of exploitation that correlate with the geographic proximity of sites. Sites analyzed by Smith, with the exception of the Lilbourn site located in the Missouri bootheel, reflected an apparent focal use of deer and forest-edge habitats. Lilbourn and sites further upriver, including data sets produced from excavations at Cahokia, displayed a more diffuse use of resources and broader use of a range of habitats. Notwithstanding the possibility of a bias toward the larger-sized elements representing deer in several of the assemblages due to the recovery methods of the excavators, especially at Banks and Chucalissa, the pattern identified by Breitburg's method is worthy of further evaluation, and may well reflect fundamental differences in floodplain exploitation in geographically different segments of the Mississippi valley. In a similar vein, Breitburg (1999) used data he analyzed from the McNight site (see below) to further explore variability in resource use in the region, detailed in the following section.

Finally, a study by this author and Susan Scott (Jackson and Scott 2002) is worth brief mention. In an examination of eleven Woodland period assemblages from the area under consideration in the present study (and considered further below), Jackson and Scott found that assemblages could be sorted into two groups, based on the dominance of either fish or deer, regardless of temporal context. The difference could reflect differences in site use (seasonality of occupation and thus different subsistence pursuits). However, contexts of recovery appear to play a central role in the composition of the faunal assemblages. Midden-derived faunal assemblages had significantly greater proportions of large mammal relative to fish, while those recovered mainly from pit contexts exhibited the opposite pattern. Jackson and Scott suggested that seasonal differences in patterns of refuse disposal (burial of refuse during warmer months, and less careful disposal in surface dumps during the cooler times of the year) might be responsible for the distinct pattern. This of course fails to address whether the different patterns of refuse disposal relate to the seasonality of occupations of different sites, or merely that selective excavation strategies produce spurious patterns created by a disproportionate emphasis on certain refuse-disposal contexts. In addition, it should be noted that Weinstein (2005) recently suggested that the poorer preservation potential of sheet midden contexts may be the cause of the significantly reduced representation of more fragile fish remains. Aside from the fish-deer dichotomy, other patterns disclosed by the study include an apparent increase over time in the combined contributions of less important taxa: reptiles, birds, and small mammals. In contrast to earlier Late Archaic and later Mississippian assemblages, the range of avian and mammalian taxa are narrower during the Woodland period (although, with some exceptions such as the Rock Levee site discussed below, sample sizes may be at the heart of this difference).

Faunal Research in the Yazoo Basin

Given the wealth of archaeological resources in the Mississippi Delta and more than a century of interest in the region, there are surprisingly few analyses of prehistoric faunal assemblages. Much of the available data are the product of CRM mitigation and testing (Figure 13.1).

Rock Levee

The most exhaustive analysis is that by Scott (1995) of faunal remains from the Rock Levee Site (22BO637), excavated by Coastal Environments, Inc., for the U.S. Army Corps of Engineers. More than 39,000 specimens were analyzed from an assemblage that was estimated to exceed 120,000 bone fragments. The assemblage, dating to the late Marksville–early Baytown and late Coles Creek periods, were recovered using ⅛-inch screen. Analyzed material was recovered from refuse-filled pits or other discrete features. All ¼-inch-sized material was analyzed (approximately 5,900 specimens) and 25-percent or 10-percent subsamples (by weight) of the less than ¼-inch material were identified (25 percent of well-dated contexts, 10 percent of mixed contexts). The remaining portions of the samples were scanned to detect taxa not represented in the identified subsamples.

More than 60 species were identified. Fish remains dominate the late Marksville–early Baytown features, ranging from 44 to 77 percent of bone weight. Seasonal indicators point to spring and summer season accumulations, the former characterized by slightly greater amounts of large mammal remains (mainly deer, but also bear in one feature). Large mammal contributes 1.4–7.7 percent of bone weight to summer season pits, and 11.1–15.5 to the spring season accumulations. Other small animals (small mammals, birds, turtles) variably contribute between 17 and 46 percent to summer refuse and 31–42 percent to spring refuse. In general, the faunal remains indicate heavy dependence on fishing during spring and summer, and a broader spectrum of subsistence targets during the spring. Whether the data point to a spring-summer occupation of Rock Levee during the late Marksville–early Baytown time range is unclear, given that only feature contexts produced significant faunal materials (Scott 1995:243). It is clear, however, that fishing was at the very core of spring-summer subsistence activities.

Late Coles Creek–period (late Baytown culture) features presented a somewhat different picture. Lower levels of these large bell- and spool-shaped pits

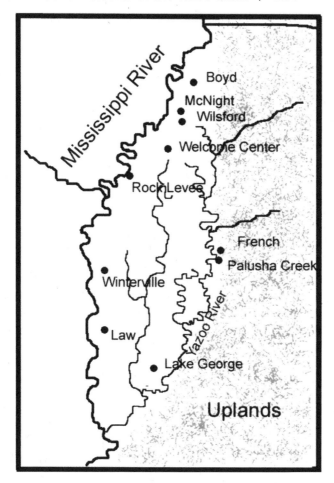

Figure 13.1. Sites in the Mississippi Delta with analyzed faunal
assemblages discussed in text.

appear to be in situ accumulations, while adjacent sheet midden may have
sloughed into the upper levels of the pits, augmenting the faunal contents.
Fishing continued to the central spring-summer subsistence pursuit, but deposits in the upper levels of the features appear to include remains from cool-
weather deer hunting.

Despite differences in seasonality, the samples from the two occupations
are remarkably similar, based on Number of Identified Specimens (NISP).
However, weight differences display greater use of large mammals in the Coles
Creek–period sample, presumably the consequence of the inclusion of cool-
weather refuse. There also appears to be less selectivity in fish exploitation dur-

ing the later occupation, with increases in shad, sucker, sunfish, and drum, and generally smaller fish sizes, a shift that Scott (1995:258) interprets as evidence for greater pressure on aquatic resources or else selection for individuals/taxa more amenable to preservation. Terrestrial fauna hints at more open habitats later, presumably a consequence of greater reliance on agriculture and consequent field clearing.

McNight (22CO560)

Excavations at the McNight site by Panamerican Consultants, Inc., for the Mississippi Department of Transportation produced an assemblage in excess of 7,000 specimens analyzed by Emanuel Breitburg (1999). The faunal remains were recovered from contexts dating to Prairie (Late Marksville), Coahoma (Baytown), and Peabody (late Coles Creek) phases and the Mississippian period. The vast majority of specimens and identified taxa represent Peabody-phase procurement (roughly 60 percent of the total sample). Thirty-three taxa were identified.

Deer and cottontail rabbits are the most frequently occurring mammal taxa, with deer likely the single most important species in the assemblage. Deer remains suggest that entire carcasses were returned to the site. Other mammalian taxa reflect forested and riparian environments of the Delta. Birds are dominated by ducks and geese, but also include turkey, quail, screech owl, grackle, and unidentified passerines. Mud/musk are the most commonly occurring turtle taxa, followed by snapping turtle. Nearly 57 percent of the NISP are fish remains. Gar, bowfin, channel-dwelling catfish, and drum are the most common taxa, suggesting exploitation of multiple aquatic habitats. Of interest is the identification of redhorse (*Moxostoma* sp.), a sucker and member of the family Catostomidae. The only commonly found redhorse in Mississippi in drainages that flow into the Mississippi River is *M. poecilurum,* the blacktail redhorse. Currently its distribution in north Mississippi is limited to the Yalabousha, Yocona, and Tallahatchie rivers, as it prefers less turbid waters than would be found in the meander belt (Ross 2001:292). It is possible that the redhorse was caught during the cool season, when it migrated downstream into deeper water.

Breitburg (1999:237) concludes that the assemblage reflects procurement strategies focusing on riparian/aquatic habitats and secondarily on forest-edge taxa. Year-round procurement activities are represented at the site. In a comparison that extends the work begun with the Petitt site, Breitburg notes the clear association of this pattern with sites within the Mississipi valley, in contrast to those on its margins which more heavily depended on deer and forest-edge terrestrial taxa. Data from the McNight site and the roughly contemporary late Coles Creek sample from Rock Levee are fairly comparable, particularly with respect to the contributions of fish and deer. The most striking difference is the significantly greater contribution of birds (both waterfowl and terrestrial species) to the McNight site collection and greater contribution of small and medium mammals to the sample from Rock Levee.

Palusha Creek 2

The Palusha Creek 2 site (22LF649) was the subject of test excavations by R. Christopher Goodwin & Associates for the U.S. Army Corps of Engineers (Brown et al. 1994:132–159). The site dates to the Deasonville phase of the Baytown period. Faunal remains consisted of 3,744 bone fragments (gar scales removed from totals), 118 gar scales, and nearly 3,400 scales of other species. The 3,400 fish scales were analyzed separately from the animal bone. This is a relatively small sample, subject to some degree of sampling error. This is particularly apparent when comparing the variable contributions of different taxa using different measures. Deer and large mammal, in particular, contribute only 3 percent of the NISP (this includes all unidentified mammal, since these were not differentiated by size of animal), yet represent 68 percent of bone weight. The low frequency of identified deer suggests that they were not as important to subsistence as the proportional weight would suggest. That said, deer was likely the single most important species.

In terms of overall composition, fish as a class comprise 88 percent of the NISP, followed by reptiles (mainly turtles) and amphibians, 5.9 peercent, large mammal, 3.3 percent, and birds and other mammals, 2.3 percent. The composition is very similar to that found for both the late Marksville–early Baytown and late Coles Creek components at Rock Levee.

With respect to the contributions of specific taxa, bowfin (36 percent) and centrarchids (37 percent), including largemouth and temperate basses as well as sunfish, make the greatest contribution to the fish fauna based on NISP (bluegills and crappie were identified by scale analysis). Catfish are also well represented (15 percent). Gar comprises 5.5 percent of the bone assemblage (scales removed from consideration) and drum, 1 percent. Although suckers are not represented in the bone sample, scale analysis indicates their use as well. Turtles include mud turtle, aquatic emydids, and box turtle. Ducks, turkey, and an unidentified warbler each are represented by single elements. Small mammals include opossum, raccoon, gray squirrel, and rabbit.

Welcome Center

The Welcome Center site (22CO573/773), excavated by Michael Baker Jr., Inc., for the Mississippi Department of Transportation, produced faunal samples from Middle and Late Woodland and Mississippian components. A total of 27,731 fragments were recovered from 137 feature contexts (Mooney et al. 2004).

Most of the assemblage represented early Middle Woodland Dorr Phase and Mississippian-period occupations. Twenty-two taxa were identified.

Assemblage composition appears to shift over time. To simplify analysis, the original data from Middle Woodland features, Late Woodland features, and Mississippian features are here lumped into three analytical units. There is a dramatic increase in the proportional contribution of fish, from 37 percent in the Middle Woodland and 58 percent in the Late Woodland, to 85 percent in the Mississippian sample. An associated decline can be seen in the contributions made by mammals as a class, from 37 percent in the Middle Woodland to 7 percent by Mississippian occupation. Large mammal (deer and unidentified large mammal combined) parallels the decline exhibited by mammals as a class, from 35 percent in Middle Woodland features to 4.3 percent in Mississippian contexts. At the later end of the time range, proportional contributions compare closely with that from Rock Levee. However, the two Middle Woodland samples diverge. As noted, Rock Levee was interpreted to represent a narrow range of warm-season procurement activities focused on fishing. However, Middle Woodland remains from 22CO573/773, also recovered from features, reflect a different subsistence strategy or, alternatively, the aggregation of both cool- and warm-weather strategies. If the latter is correct, the Middle Woodland residents of the site disposed of their refuse in pits during cooler as well as warmer months. The greater emphasis on terrestrial game reflected by the Middle Woodland sample is similar to penecontemporaneous samples from northeast Louisiana (Mariaca 1988), the seasonality of which was not determined. Moreover, the impact of either preservation or recovery methods on this comparison of site similarities and differences cannot be easily evaluated.

French Site

The French Site (22HO569) is an early Mississippian site located on the eastern margin of the Yazoo Basin. A trash-filled pit produced a rather sizable (vertebrate NISP=13,758) assemblage analyzed by Wilson (1987). Mammals (n=7,802, 56.7 percent) and fish (n=5,360, 38.9 percent) dominate the assemblage, followed by bird (3.1 percent), and reptiles/amphibians (1.2 percent). The most commonly identified mammal taxon is deer (54 percent of mammal specimens identified below the level of class). Of particular note is the large number of small-rodent remains (n=45 representing at least 4 species) from this single pit. Birds include both migratory waterfowl (ducks, geese, cranes), and other taxa (turkey, vulture, and crow). Another unusual aspect of the sample is the large number of snakes, which contribute 44 percent of the identified reptile specimens. Fish include bowfin, gar, and a large proportion of bullheads and sunfish, suggesting a backwater lake source. Seasonality indicators (deer dentition, shellfish growth rings, and presence of migratory fowl) suggest a late fall/early winter deposit.

The Law Site

The Law Site (22WS549) is a 2–3 mound Mississippian site, tested for National Register eligibility by Coastal Environments (Perrault et al. 1999). Excavations produced a small sample of fauna (n=2,972, NISP=1,804; Coxe 1999). Mammals, birds, reptiles, and fish contribute 13.6 percent, 1.5 percent, 17.6 percent, and 67.2 percent of the NISP, respectively. Deer comprises 1 percent of NISP. The Law site sample also produced a large number of small rodent remains (26, or nearly 46 percent of the mammal specimens identified below the level of class). The only identified bird is a member of family Picidae (woodpeckers). Drum, catfishes, and gar (presumably as a consequence of including scales) dominate the fish subsample.

Other Analyses

Several other studies deserve brief mention. Belmont and Barber (1983) reported on faunal remains retained during the 1958–1960 Harvard excavations of the Lake George site (Williams and Brain 1983). Unfortunately, much of the faunal material was discarded in the field, save large-mammal elements that preserved articular portions and an unknown portion of small-mammal remains. Much of the focus understandably is on deer-element representation, which shows relatively higher numbers of meat-bearing elements, a trend that increases over time. Since the material from Lake George largely derives from elite contexts (middens associated with or incorporated into pyramidal mounds), the pattern reported by Belmont is expectable. Nonetheless, given the variable survival potential of different elements, in the absence of systematic recovery and consideration of smaller fragments and unidentifiable large-mammal remains, it must be considered plausible rather than demonstrated. Among mammals, deer and rabbits increase over time relative to woodland taxa, such as raccoon, opossum, and squirrels (identified only as *Sciurus* sp.), a likely consequence of some combination of expansion of field agriculture and the associated shifts in biogeography and the social or ritual activities that occurred at the site. Increased intensity of deer hunting is suggested by age profiles based on dentition, with average age declining over time.

A meager sample (NISP=553) of fauna was recovered and retained from excavations by Brain (1989) at Winterville, identified by Stanley Olsen. Deer comprises 48 percent of the identified specimens, followed by swamp rabbit (26 percent). Other mammals identified include raccoon, opossum, cottontail, coyote, cougar, bobcat, and bear. Birds include geese, ducks, and turkey.

As a class, mammals contribute 90 percent to the sample, birds 7 percent, and turtles 3 percent. No fish are reported (although Brain mentions their presence), suggesting that the sample suffers from recovery bias.

Robert Wilson identified a small sample of fauna (n=122, including crawfish and mussels) from the Late Mississippian–period Wilsford site (22Co516) (Connaway 1984). Fish contribute 52 percent, birds 28 percent, and mammals 17 percent of the sample NISP.

Stanley Olsen (1971) identified a collection of fauna (NISP=1947) from the Early Woodland Boyd site (Connaway and McGahey 1971). Deer and reptiles/amphibians contributed roughly 18 percent of the NISP each, while other mammals, fish (excluding scales) and birds contributed 5 percent, 8 percent, and 6 percent, respectively. Unidentified mammal makes up 44 percent of the NISP. Aside from the taxa mentioned for most of the sites already summarized, one interesting identification is elk, which if accurate would indicate long-distance hunting.

Patterns of Resource Use in the Mississippi Valley

Beyond the patterns noted in earlier studies, what can be said about the subsistence systems of the LMV? One might expect that with the considerable CRM efforts in the region, sufficient data have been produced to reveal long-term trends in animal use. As part of this study, approximately 45 sites with faunal analyses were consulted. A number were eliminated due to small sample size, avowed poor preservation, or incomplete information, and several could be used for part, but not all, of the analysis. Not all sites are within the strict bounds of the main Mississippi valley. For instance, work on Plum Bayou sites in the Arkansas River valley is included, and, following Smith and Breitburg, some sites immediately adjacent to the Mississippi River valley were included as well. Sites from the Mississippi River deltaic plain at the extreme southern end of the Mississippi River valley were excluded because they clearly reflect a different adaptive pattern that included exploitation of estuarine and marsh habitats (e.g., Byrd 1994; Lewis 1997; Misner 1991; Springer 1980). Several authors assigned portions of the faunal assemblage to particular temporal components, and these are treated as separate samples. In a couple of cases, separate analyses from different excavations were combined to create suitable sample sizes, or samples from different phases were combined to represent a large sample size representing a particular period (for instance, different phase assignments of a particular period were combined for the Welcome Center material, as discussed above). Ultimately, only assemblages or sub-assemblage samples with a NISP of 1,000 specimens were included. For the discussion of fish, 100 specimens identified below the level of class were required for inclu-

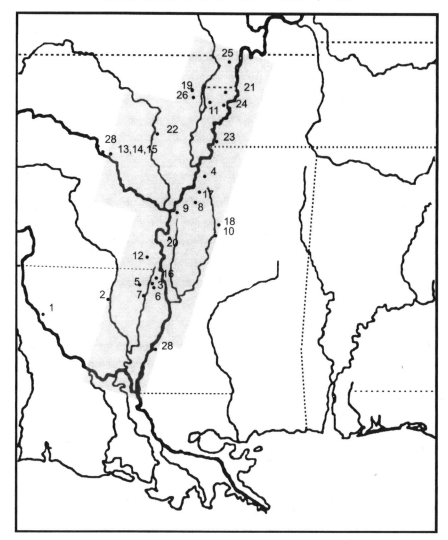

Figure 13.2. Sites with analyzed faunal assemblages used in regional analysis. Numbers refer to key in Table 13.1.

sion. Analyses from a total of thirty-eight sites were examined in the research. In the present discussion, 31 time-assigned samples from 28 sites are included (Figure 13.2; Table 13.1).

Except when they couldn't be extracted, ¼-inch samples were used in the analysis. This restriction certainly reduces the representation of small taxa such as fish, which are more effectively recovered by fine screening and flotation samples. However, variable approaches to sampling and the fact that many

Table 13.1. Sources for faunal data.

Site with NISP >1000	Site No.	State	Components Used	Reference
Conly	1	LA	Middle Archaic	Jackson and Scott 2001
Watson Brake	2	LA	Middle Archaic	Jackson and Scott 2001
J. W. Copes	3	LA	Late Archaic	Jackson 1989
Boyd	4	MS	Tchula	Olsen 1971
Stephenson	5	LA	Marksville	Mariaca 1988
Panther Lake	6	LA	Marksville	Mariaca 1988
Mansford	7	LA	Marksville	Mariaca 1988
Welcome Center	8	MS	Marksville, Mississippian	Mooney et al. 2004
Rock Levee	9	MS	Early Baytown, Coles Creek	Scott 1995
Palusha Creek	10	MS	Baytown	Brown et al. 1994
Roland	11	AR	Baytown	Butsch 1991
Powell Canal	12	AR	Baytown	Carr 1982
Ink Bayou	13	AR	Coles Creek	Colburn 1987
Faulkner Lake	14	AR	Coles Creek	Scott 1996
Toltec	15	AR	Coles Creek	Hoffman 1998; Kelly and Rolingson 2003
Lake Providence	16	LA	Coles Creek	Scott 2005
McNight	17	MS	Coles Creek	Breitburg 1999
French	18	MS	Coles Creek	Wilson 1987
Priestly	19	AR	Coles Creek	Kelly 1990
Law	20	MS	Mississippian	Coxe 1999
Zebree	21	AR	Mississippian	Guilday and Parmalee 1975
Parkin	22	AR	Mississippian	Keck 1997
Chucalissa	23	TN	Mississippian	Smith 1975
Banks Village	24	AR	Mississippian	Smith 1975
Lilbourn	25	MO	Mississippian	Smith 1975
Moon	26	AR	Mississippian	Kelly 1992
Goldsmith-Oliver	27	AR	Protohistoric	Scott and Jackson 1990
Fatherland	28	MS	Historic	Cleland 1965; Penman 1983

sites are only represented by ¼-inch recovered fauna made the incorporation of small-sized fractions too difficult.

In addition to looking at broad patterns of use by assessing taxonomic ubiquity, intersite comparisons and assessment of temporal trends rely primarily on the reported number of identified specimens, or NISP. There are some quantitative problems with this approach—variable fragmentation and variable conventions for dealing with material identified at more general taxonomic levels (for instance, whether mammal fragments were differentiated into large- and medium- to small-sized animals or simply lumped as "unidentified mammal"). However, weight is rarely reported, and methods of calculating Minimum Number of Individuals varied considerably from report to report (in some cases whole-site MNIs are reported, while in others feature-by-feature MNIs were calculated). In sum, NISP is the best-reported primary quantitative measure, and it has been used productively by Styles in her studies in the Midwest.

Assemblages vary widely in composition. First, there is great difference in taxonomic richness among samples, largely explained by sample size (Figure 13.3). The correlation between NISP size and the number of identified taxa is 0.79. However, it is clear that large samples of well-preserved fauna include a very large number of species. This reflects the taxonomic richness of the LMV, in particular the contributions made by fish and fowl.

There do appear to be some differences between periods that are not entirely accounted for by sample-size differences. Middle Woodland assemblages have a small range of species that is not greatly affected by the size of the sample. However, several of the samples were analyzed by a single individual who identified fish only to the level of family, thus reducing potential richness significantly. Preservation at all the Middle Woodland sites could be a factor. By contrast, Baytown-period sites include a greater number of taxa represented, even though several sample sizes are comparatively small. Differences in species representation in Mississippian and Archaic samples are closely related to the size of the samples.

The composition of assemblages according to major taxonomic groups is examined next. The categories used included large mammals, medium and small mammals, birds, reptiles and amphibians, and fish. These categories reflect in a general but useful way the different activities that comprise the overall subsistence pattern. Material identified only to class was included. Unfortunately, a number of reports provide NISP for unidentified mammal without indicating animal size. In these cases only material identified below the level of class is included in the tabulations, which depresses the overall representation of the mammal class. Commensal taxa are excluded from the calculations— mainly small rodents, frogs other than bullfrog, and toads; but for most sites,

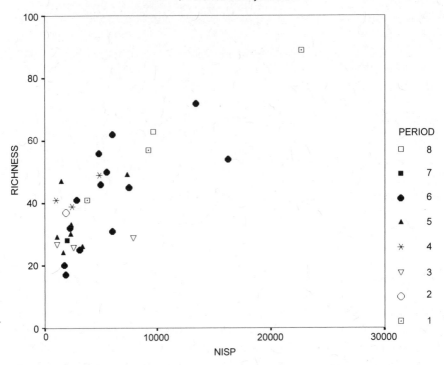

Figure 13.3. Relationship between sample size (NISP) and the number of identified species (richness) in samples included in present study. Sites labeled 1 are Archaic; 2, Tchula period; 3, Marksville period; 4, Baytown period; 5, Coles Creek and Emergent Mississippian periods; 6, Mississippian period; 7, Protohistoric; 8, Historic Native American.

none of these would have substantially changed the proportional contributions of larger taxonomic categories, were they to have been included.

In an attempt to discern patterning in the composition of the assemblages, they were grouped according to similarity using hierarchical cluster analysis performed in SPSS (Figure 13.4). Two broad groups were identified, based on dominance of deer or fish. Within these overarching groups, five groups of sites emerged. Groups 1 through 3 are dominated by fish, and distinguished either by a paucity of other taxa (Group 1), by relatively high representation of reptiles (Group 2), or by relatively high representation of small mammals and/ or birds (Group 3). Group 4 isolated the sites with moderate amounts of large mammal and fish, but a high—greater than 20 percent—number of reptile remains, mainly turtle. Group 5 consists of sites with high proportions of large mammal specimens relative to other major taxonomic categories. The Priestly site stands apart from other assemblages due to a uniquely high contribution

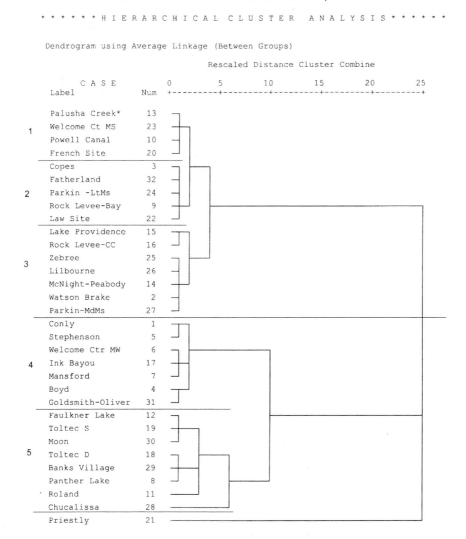

Figure 13.4. Assemblage groupings produced by cluster analysis. Numbers refer to discussion in text.

to the avian fauna by passenger pigeon (see below). The contrast between high large mammal (Group 5) and high fish (groups 1–3) was noted in an earlier examination of Woodland assemblages (Jackson and Scott 2002), and the larger sample examined here reflects the same dichotomous pattern. Whether this reflects persistent seasonality in site occupations, or else skewing of samples primarily represented by only one context, remains to be seen.

Looking at taxonomic composition of sites ordered chronologically (Figure 13.5), it is apparent that the variable contributions of fish versus deer are shared among sites within each period. Contributions of small and medium mammals, birds, and reptiles and amphibians also appear to be consistently variable over time, although combined appear to make consistently greater contributions over time.

One assemblage stands out from the rest in terms of uniquely high contribution made by birds. Lucretia Kelly (1990) reported on fauna from the Emergent Mississippian Priestly site in the St. Francis basin of northeast Arkansas. Nearly 60 percent of NISP is bird remains. A part of the bird fauna represents use of migratory waterfowl, but there is also a significant contribution made by passenger pigeon, which otherwise is rare among the samples examined. Breitburg (1994) reports a similarly high proportion of passenger pigeon from the Oliver site in western Tennessee, a site not included in the sample. These examples indicate that short-term events, such as the fortuitous exploitation of migratory fowl, may have a significant impact on the composition of the faunal assemblages of single sites (e.g., Jackson 2005), underscoring the importance of a regional-level perspective in the search for general patterns or trends.

Given the pivotal role of fishing, the fish fauna reported in the consulted zooarchaeological analyses were examined in hopes of discerning either temporal or other trends. Using NISP, relative contributions were assessed by the most commonly identified families (Lepisostidae—gar; Amiidae—bowfin; Catostomidae—suckers; Ictaluridae—catfish; Centrarchidae—bass and sunfish; and Scianidae—drum). A final combined category of all other taxa (pickeral, temperate basses, shad, and others) is included as well. Greater specificity would have been useful for teasing out possible differences related to ecological settings of fishing activities, but unfortunately much of the identified bone is at a gross taxonomic level.

No clear temporal (Figure 13.6) or, for that matter, spatial trends are evident in the data, suggesting that local fishing habitats rather than cultural selection had much to do with the composition of fish fauna. There appear to be a greater number of sites with large contributions by gar in the later prehistoric periods (after Baytown), and drum makes a significant contribution to a greater number of the later sites, but these observations are by no means uniform. It might be inferred that there was some greater emphasis on capturing larger individuals later in prehistory, since these species can be quite large and might require more substantial fishing infrastructure (technology, organization). Decline in the contribution of bowfin after the Baytown period may signal a shift to greater use of main-channel fish resources.

An average-link hierarchical cluster analysis was used to group fish assem-

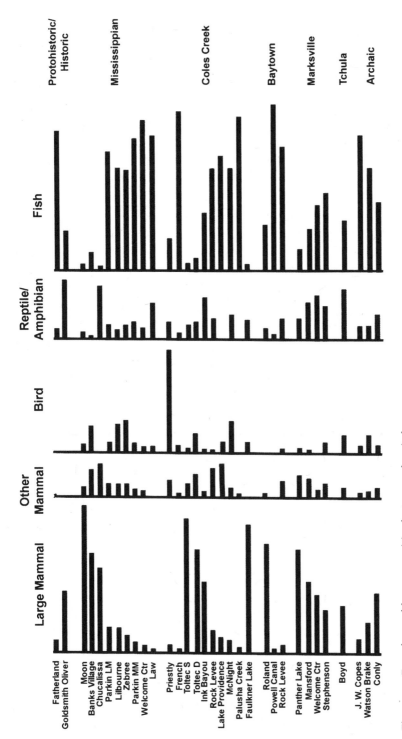

Figure 13.5. Faunal assemblage composition by temporal period.

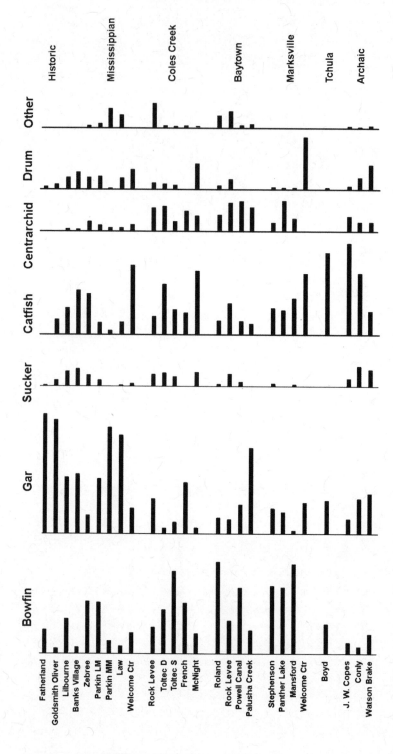

Figure 13.6. Fish subassemblage composition by temporal period.

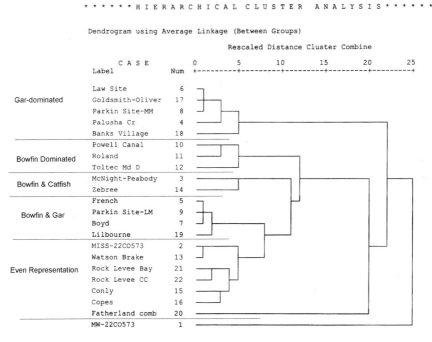

Figure 13.7. Fish subassemblage groupings produced by cluster analysis.

blages (Figure 13.7). It produced essentially four groups: sites in which bowfin exceeds 40 percent of the sample, sites with comparatively even contributions by each family, sites in which catfish contribution is most significant, and sites dominated by gar.

Spearman Rank Order correlation was applied to the fish subsets to see whether associations might reflect something about exploited aquatic environments. Gar is negatively correlated with both bowfin and bullheads, (p= .05), suggesting a distinction between either channel and lake exploitation or lake size and turbidity. Both bowfin and bullheads are more prevalent in smaller, murkier bodies of water than gar. One of the strongest positive correlations is between bullheads and small sunfish, again a probable reflection of exploitation of smaller lakes. There are also significant positive correlations among sunfish, bass, and temperate basses, which I take to reflect analyists' skill or the quality of available comparative material in differentiating perciform fish.

Some General Comments

Some of the most productive zooarchaeological work includes thoughtful consideration of the contexts, processes of deposition, and concern with associated archaeological evidence. For instance, Charlene Keck (1997) compared samples recovered from two houses at the Parkin site, one that dates to the Middle and the other to the Late Mississippian period. She found a shift away from large mammal use and toward greater fish exploitation. She hypothesizes greater emphasis on fishing in the moat that surrounded the fortified site, and interpreted the change in faunal composition as a shift in strategy resulting from increased intercommunity conflict in the region. Scott's analysis of fill sequences in light of seasonality at the Rock Levee site offers another example. Further, great care in assessing size distributions allowed Scott to consider the nature of fishing technology employed by Rock Levee inhabitants.

Since the overall aim of the participants in this volume is to help guide anticipated investigations in the northern Mississippi Delta, let me offer some preliminary suggestions that are intended to maximize the productivity of future zooarchaeological analyses. First, a number of general, as well as more chronologically specific, research questions come to mind. It is clear that, with few exceptions, the composition of faunal assemblages is dictated by the relative contributions of two inversely related resources, fish and deer. However, we have some problem with equifinality in attempting to explain this phenomenon. Either analyses have encountered samples reflecting seasonal variation in subsistence pursuits, or else taphonomic processes have had variable attritional effects on assemblages, perhaps as a function of the contexts sampled in excavations. If the former, then how seasonal subsistence pursuits relate to settlement pattern is an essential question. Despite an assumption that settlements were relatively stable, as late as the Baytown period there are indications that seasonally differentiated sites might have been occupied. This impression could of course be sampling error, but it points out how important excavation sampling might be for understanding the nature of settlement systems and how these might have changed over time. Thus, an obvious research goal for any future work is to examine seasonal patterns of resource use within the context of settlement function and duration.

A second research goal relates to how changes in other aspects of food procurement might have affected animal procurement, with respect to scheduling and changes in the local catchments with the intensification of agriculture. The most dramatic predictable changes in subsistence ought to be the shift to and intensification of maize production. While it may be there and I just haven't nailed it down, there don't presently seem to be clear indications to suggest major changes. I suspect that the kinds of changes to be expected will be best monitored at the level of single sites that span the critical transition—how intensification of maize production restructures local procurement efforts in the immediate site environments. The issue of garden hunting comes into play, and while there seems to be a diversification in the range of minor species, particularly small and medium mammals, reflected by the Mississippian samples, these are also some of the largest samples available. Attention to critical environmental indicators—the ratios of gray to fox squirrels, swamp rabbits to cottontails (e.g., Scott 1983), and the composition of small rodent fauna all may reflect the impact of land clearance on the local fauna (cf. Peacock, this volume).

Fishing was obviously an important component of Lower Valley adaptation. Careful identification and assessment of the fish fauna should provide useful information about aquatic settings in the vicinity of the site. However, fish identification is a difficult and often frustrating task. Distinguishing the species within certain taxonomic groups, Catostomidae or Centrarchidae, for instance, depends on subtle differences of a small number of elements. The fragile nature of fish remains makes them susceptible to a variety of destructive taphonomic processes, reducing the possibility of species-level identifications. That being said, the available data on fish assemblages from Lower Valley sites is on the whole disappointing, given the pivotal role this resource plays. Nearly all collections are dominated by two easily identifiable taxa, bowfin and gar. The role of gar is exaggerated in many of the collections by the inclusion of gar scales in the NISP, thousands of which are produced by a single individual. In several of the collections, gar comprised more than 80 percent of the NISP, though I am doubtful that this accurately reflects its importance relative to other taxa. Insufficient attention seems to be paid to identification below the family level in just those families where more specific identifications would provide much needed environmental data. Knowing whether the catfish were bullheads or their channel-dwelling brethren is a case in point. Further, there is little attempt to quantify size ranges, which affect assessments of the importance of fish and relative importance of different taxa, seasonality, and procurement technologies.

Excavation sampling must be carefully planned to maximize faunal recovery. If different contexts—pit versus midden, for instance—reflect different facies of the procurement system, then adequate representation of those contexts is critical. Fine-screen recovery to collect small, environmentally sensitive taxa is required. Decisions regarding how to subsample recovered remains can be made after the field work is completed.

The analyses of faunal remains will be crucial to furthering our understanding of the ecological and economic arrangements of the prehistoric societies inhabiting the Mississippi Delta. It goes without saying that there must be adequate sample sizes to maximize probabilities that assemblages will include the critical elements to differentiate species, and the rare taxa that will shed light on environmental or other parameters. Communication between zooarchaeologists and excavators and other analysts is critical for ensuring that the contexts of faunal samples and other artifactual remains guide the analysis and interpretations.

Let me say a brief word regarding quantification. One of the areas of weakness in zooarchaeological research is a lack of consensus on what quantitative approaches are most productive for interpretation. First, let me make a plea for identifying remains as specifically as is possible. A great portion of every faunal assemblage is relegated to general taxonomic categories, and necessarily so. However, often it is possible to use general categories that include useful information when broad patterns are considered. For instance, many analysts continue to lump unidentified mammal remains into a single category, when size of the animals ought to be considered. Differentiating unidentified large-mammal from small- and medium-mammal remains allows that material to be employed in a general assessment of the relative roles of those two categories.

Second, sensible and complete reporting of primary data is essential. Regardless of the analytical tack taken, basic information including counts and weights of bone by taxon is essential, including unidentified or only generally identified material. I was surprised at the number of reports that fail to include unidentified bone counts, or even material identified only to class. I would strongly urge that bone be weighed, so that meaningful comparison of broad taxonomic categories can be included without resorting to the distorting vagaries of NISP. Weight offers the means of describing quantities of bone without regard to the impact of fragmentation.

There is still much to document with respect to prehistoric hunting and fishing. Earlier periods are poorly represented in the current database. Seasonality issues will only be resolved with a sufficient number of roughly contemporaneous assemblages to afford intersite comparison. How Mississippian social and political trends, as well as agricultural intensification, affected hunting practices and the distribution of the meat from those efforts are still to be worked out. Effective procurement of adequate meat supplies was an essential aspect of the day-to-day lives of the prehistoric peoples of the region, and a thorough understanding of the strategies involved and changes therein are part of a comprehensive understanding of prehistoric life.

14

Paleoethnobotanical Information and Issues Relevant to the I-69 Overview Process, Northwest Mississippi

Gayle J. Fritz

Introduction

The overview process serves three broad purposes for dealing with paleoethnobotanical remains. First, it provides an opportunity to pull together information from previous reports, both in the immediate zone of potential impact and in the surrounding region. Second, based on this information, it makes it possible to assess relevant questions and issues. Third, it is a forum for making recommendations about future recovery and analysis of plant remains, framed within appropriate research domains. I begin by summarizing what we know—and things about which we would like to know more—in the realm of relationships between plants and people in northwest Mississippi and the wider south-Central and Lower Mississippi Valley (CMV/LMV). Throughout this discussion I suggest key questions that archaeologists might try to answer. I conclude with some suggestions for incorporating paleoethnobotanical research as an integral component of fieldwork and analysis during upcoming work in Mississippi.

As summarized in Table 14.1, macrobotanical remains have been reported from at least 73 archaeological components in northwest Mississippi, eastern Arkansas, extreme southeast Missouri, southwest Tennessee, and northeast Louisiana. The plants from 27 of these components, however, were recovered during hand excavations or routine dry screening, without the benefit of fine-mesh flotation or water screening. Therefore, few items other than corn cobs, nuts, or persimmon seeds were found at those sites. Tables 14.2 through 14.6 summarize the types of nutshell and seeds reported for various time periods, along with remains of corn and squash. These are not complete tabulations. Acorn nutmeat is not included, nor are most taxa that analysts were unsure about, or several seed types represented by only one or two specimens. The tables nevertheless reflect changing temporal trends in subsistence and spatial variations across the broader area of concern.

Table 14.1. Sites yielding macrobotanical remains, ordered by cultural period and by state.

Cultural Period	State	Site Name	Site No.	Reported By:	Year	Flotation	Water Screen
Middle Archaic							
	Mississippi	Denton	22QU522	Cutler and Blake	2001		
		Longstreet	22QU523	Cutler and Blake	2001		
Late Archaic							
	Mississippi	Teoc Creek	22CR504	Cutler and Blake	2001		
	Louisiana	Poverty Point, Peripheries		Shea	1978	Yes	
		Poverty Point, Ridge 1		Ward	1998	Yes	
		J. W. Copes	16MA47	Jackson	1989	Yes	
		Cowpen Slough	16CT147	Ramenofsky	1986	Yes	
Early Woodland							
	Louisiana	Raffman	16MA20	Trachtenberg	1999	Yes	
	Tennessee	Fulmer	40SY527	Shea	1999	Yes	Yes
Middle Woodland							
	Mississippi	McNight (Prairie phase)	22CO560	Shea	1999	Limited	Yes
		22CO573 (Prairie phase)	22CO573	Mooney et al.	2004	Yes	
		Boyd	22TU532	Connaway and McGahey	1971		
		Acree	22BO551	Cutler and Blake	2001		
	Louisiana	Marksville	16AV1	Roberts	1999b	Limited	Yes
		Reno Brake (Issaquena)	16TE93	Kidder and Fritz	1993	Yes	
		Osceola, Mound F (Issaquena)	16TE2	Kidder and Frtiz	1993	Yes	
		Raffman	16MA20	Trachtenberg	1999	Yes	

State	Site	Site number	Reference	Year		
Arkansas	Possum Trap (Late Marksville)	3DE37	Gardner	1982		Limited

Late Woodland, pre-dating A.D. 800/900

State	Site	Site number	Reference	Year		
Mississippi	McNight (Coahoma phase)	22CO560	Shea	1999	Limited	Yes
	Rock Levee (mixed Baytown)	22BO637	Scarry	1995	Yes	Yes
	22CO573	22CO573	Mooney et al.	2004	Yes	
	Oliver	22CO503	Fritz	1999b		Yes
	Noe	22CO587	Cutler and Blake	2001		
Arkansas	Powell Canal (Troyville)	3CH14	King	1982	Yes	
	Taylor Mounds (Troyville)	3DR2	Brown	1996	Yes	
	Zebree (Barnes component)	3MS20	Morse and Morse	1983	Yes	
	DeRossitt	3SF49	Cutler and Blake	2001		
Louisiana	Reno Brake (Troyville)	16TE93	Kidder and Fritz	1993	Yes	
	Hedgeland (Early Coles Creek)	16CT19	Roberts	2004	Yes	
	Osceola (Early Coles Creek, Mound B)	16TE2	Kidder and Fritz	1993	Yes	
	Richardson	16CT409	Fritz	1995	Yes	
Missouri	Hayti Bypass (Baytown)	23PM572	Lopinot	1995	Yes	

Terminal Late Woodland/Emergent Mississippian/Late Coles Creek

State	Site	Site number	Reference	Year		
Mississippi	Rock Levee	22BO573	Scarry	1995	Yes	Yes
	Palusha Creek 2	22LF649	Brown et al.	1994	Yes	
	McNight (Peabody phase)	22CO560	Shea	1999	Limited	
	22CO573 (Peabody phase)	22CO573	Mooney et al.	2004	Yes	
	Bonds	22CO556	Cutler and Blake	2001		
Arkansas	Priestly	3PO490	Pearsall and Hunter	1990	Yes	
	Mangrum	3CG636	Harris	1982		Yes
	Boydell Mound A	3AS58	Blake	1994	Yes	Yes
Missouri	Hayti Bypass (very early Mississippian)	23PM572	Lopinot	1995	Yes	Yes

Continued on the next page

Table 14.1. *Continued*

Cultural Period	State	Site Name	Site No.	Reported By:	Year	Flotation	Water Screen
	Louisiana	Blackwater	16TE101	Fritz	2007	Yes	
		Jolly	16TE103	Fritz	2007	Yes	
		Birds Creek	16CT416	Fritz	1997	Yes	
		Lake Providence	16CE6	Roberts	2005b	Yes	
	Tennessee	Oliver	40OB161	Shea and Mainfort	1994	Yes	
Mississippian							
	Mississippi	Rock Levee	22BO573	Scarry	1995		
		McNight	22CO560	Shea	1999		
		22CO573	22CO573	Mooney et al.	2004		
		Bobo	22CO535	Cutler and Blake	2001		
		Buford	22TL501	Cutler and Blake	2001		
		Craig	22CO566	Cutler and Blake	2001		
		Flowers No. 3	22TU518	Cutler and Blake	2001		
		Hays	22CO612	Cutler and Blake	2001		
		Humber	22CO601	Cutler and Blake	2001		
		Lafferty West	22CO636	Cutler and Blake	2001		
		Oliver	22CO503	Fritz	1999b		Yes
		Powell Bayou	22SU516	Cutler and Blake	2001		
		Wilsford	22CO516	Cutler and Blake	2001		
	Tennessee	Chucalissa	49SY1	Lumb and McNutt	1988		
		Fuller		Jones	1953		
	Arkansas	Moon	3PO488	Pearsall	1992	Yes	
		Brougham Lake	3CT98	Harris in Klinger et al.	1983	Yes	

Region	Site	Number	Reference	Year	
	Kochtitzky Ditch	3MS599	Lopinot and Thomas	2003	Yes
	Nodena	3MS4	Blake and Cutler	1979	
	Parkin	3CS29	M. Williams	1993	Yes
	Lawhorn	3CG - ??	Blake	1962	
	Banks	3CT13	Blake	1986	
	McDuffie		Blake	1986	
	Burris	3CG218	Blake	1989	
Louisiana	Klueppel (Sicily Island, Routh phase)		Roberts	1999a	Yes
	Emerson (A.D. 1400)	16TE104	Kidder et al.	1993	Yes
Historic					
Arkansas	Wallace Bottom (late 1600s to mid-1700s)	3AR179	Turner and Fritz	n.d.	Yes
	Zebree	3MS20	Morse and Morse	1983	Yes

Table 14.2. Nuts and seeds from Middle and Late Archaic sites.

	Denton	Longstreet	Teoc Creek	J.W. Copes	Poverty Point Peripheries	Poverty Point Ridge 1	Cowpen Slough
Thick Hickory	x	x					
Pecan ("Thin Hickory")		x			200	80% ubiquity	
Carya (Undifferentiated)				3,659	3,234		
Water Hickory							1.16 g
Juglandaceae						10% ubiquity	
Walnut	x	x			49		
Butternut?	x						
Walnut or Butternut			x				
Acorn Shell				440	7,764	22.5% ubiquity	0.06 g
Castanea sp.						2.5% ubiquity	
Gourd/Squash				15	possibly 3	22.5% ubiquity	
Persimmon	x	x		12	83	22.5% ubiquity	
Grape					41		
Honey Locust				1			
Hawthorn or Holly						5% ubiquity	
Plum				1			
Hackberry					1		
Black Gum					1		

Chenopodium sp.	1	1	12.5% ubiquity	x
Possible Maygrass			2.5% ubiquity	
Polygonum arifolium		1		
Little Barley			20% (39 seeds)	
Grass Family	1		2.5% ubiquity	
Wild Bean	possibly 1	1		
Sumpweed	1			
Aster Family		1		
Doveweed		37		
Spurge Family	1		5% ubiquity	
Purslane	1			
Possible Gromwell	1			

Table 14.3. Nuts and seeds from Early and Middle Woodland sites.

	Early Woodland					Middle Woodland					
	Raffman	Fulmer	22CO573	Acree	Boyd	McNight	Marksville	Raffman	Reno Brake	Osceola Mound F	Possum Trap
Thick Hickory	3	17		x	x	9.5 g	68				37.55 g
Thin Hickory/ Pecan				x	x	0.1 g	54	15	13	2	
Juglandaceae							296				
Walnut		4	12.8 g	x	x	4.3 g	1				
Hazelnut		3									
Acorn Shell	25		475.7 g	x	x	1.9 g	217	1,479	165	8	0.13 g
Undifferentiated Nutshell			19.7 g								
Persimmon	3		1	x	x	9	51	37	17	2	8
Palmetto							25		8		
Grape				x		2			9	1	
Plum					x						
Pawpaw				x							
Bramble (Rubus)									19		
Cucurbit Rind						2				1	
Sunflower						7					
Sumpweek				x		1			2		

Chenopod	36	x	7	
Knotweed	7	2		
Maygrass	33	4	1	1
Little Barley			1	
Amaranth	1		2	
Purslane	18		7	1
Grass Family	x	4	3	
Pokeweed	2		1	
Bean Family		2		
Bedstraw	x	4	3	
Water Lily			4	1
Carpetweed	1			
Wood Sorrel	x			
Copperleaf	x			
Tulip Poplar			1	

6

Table 14.4. Nuts and seeds from Late Woodland sites predating A.D. 800/900.

	McNight (Coahoma phase)	Rock Levee (flotation)	Rock Levee (water screen)	22CO573 (Coahoma phase)	Noe	Oliver (22CO503)	Reno Brake (Troyville)
Thick Hickory	13.5 g	15	78			1,940	
Pecan ("Thin Hickory")	0.1 g	68	449		x	116	23
Water Hickory						15	
Juglandaceae		1					
Walnut	0.1 g		6				
Acorn Shell	2.5 g	171	683	0.1 g	x	5,920	366
Hazelnut	9.9 g						
Undifferentiated Nutshell				0.1 g			
Persimmon Seed	4	80	303		x	21	6
Palmetto Seed	7	1					14
Grape Seed		1	1	1			7
Plum Seed	1	1	1				
Cherry Seed	1				x		
Hawthorn Seed							
Sumac Seed		2					
Blueberry Seed		1					
Bramble (Rubus)							
Hackberry Seed			1				
Cucurbit Rind						1	

	Corn	4 cupules, 4 kernels	1 cupule	12 cupules, 2 kernels	3 cupules, 1 kernel	
Corn	3	1				
Sunflower						
Sumpweed	1			1 (domesticated)	1 (domesticated)	2 (non-domesticated)
Chenopod		96		13	1	
Knotweed	10	30		1	12	
Maygrass		54		3	1	
Little Barley					1	
Type X Grass					40	
Giant Cane						
Amaranth						
Cheno-Am		19				
Purslane			2	2		1
Nightshade						
Barnyard Grass						
Crabgrass			7			
Grass Family	1					
Sedge Family	2					
Pokeweed						
Smartweed						
Prickley Sida						
Geranium					x	
Wild Bean		1	1		3	
Vetch-type					6	
Bean Family						

Continued on the next page

Table 14.4. Continued

	McNight (Coahoma phase)	Rock Levee (flotation)	Rock Levee (water screen)	22CO573 (Coahoma phase)	Noe	Oliver (22CO503)	Reno Brake (Troyville)
Aster Family							7
Bedstraw	1						
Water Lotus							
Water Lily							
Spurge Family							
Morning Glory							
Ampelopsis					x		

	Hedgeland (Early Coles Creek)	Osceola Mound B (Early Coles Creek)	Richardson (Early Coles Creek)	Powell Canal	Taylor Mounds	DeRossitt	Zebree (Barnes)	Oliver (22CO503)	Hayti Bypass (Barnes)
Thick Hickory	188		1,071	40.1 g	1,294	X	x	x	250
Pecan ("Thin Hickory")		224			5				
Water Hickory									
Juglandaceae					2				392
Walnut								x	22
Acorn Shell	850	2,493	97		2,425	X	x	x	
Hazelnut									102
Undifferentiated									

Continued on the next page

Nutshell								
Persimmon Seed	45	39	3	2	22	X	x	32
Palmetto Seed	18	197						
Grape Seed	12	5					x	6
Plum Seed								
Cherry Seed		5						
Hawthorn Seed								
Sumac Seed		4			6			14
Blueberry Seed	1							
Bramble (Rubus)								
Hackberry Seed								
Cucurbit Rind		36			40			
Corn			2 possible cupules		13			2 cupules
Sunflower	8 (domesticated)							
Sumpweed		45			2 (non-domesticated)			6 (domesticated) 7 (domesticated)
Chenopod	511	83		3	227	X		64 (non-domesticated)
Knotweed	5	17		1	45			22
Maygrass	62	206			109			177
Little Barley				1	9			2
Type X Grass					3			

Table 14.4. *Continued*

	Hedgeland (Early Coles Creek)	Osceola Mound B (Early Coles Creek)	Richardson (Early Coles Creek)	Powell Canal	Taylor Mounds	DeRossitt	Zebree (Barnes)	Hayti Bypass (Barnes)
Giant Cane		35						3
Amaranth	1	5			42			
Cheno-Am		76			61			
Purslane	4	14			210			1
Nightshade					10			
Barnyard Grass	291	84						
Crabgrass		20						
Grass Family	4	16			15			4
Sedge Family				1				
Pokeweed	5	2						
Smartweed								2
Prickley Sida								2
Geranium								3
Wild Bean							x	2
Vetch-type		15						
Bean Family		1						1
Aster Family		8						2
Bedstraw		2	1					5
Water Lotus				1				
Water Lily		48						
Spurge Family				1				2
Morning Glory					1			
Ampelopsis								1

Table 14.5. Nuts and seeds from Terminal Late Woodland, Emergent Mississippian, and late Coles Creek components.

	Rock Levee (flotation)	Rock Levee (water screen)	22CO573 (Peabody)	McNight (Peabody)	Palusha Creek 2	Bonds	Priestly	Mangrum	Boydell
Thick Hickory	2	40		27.2 g	40	x	2,959	8.29 g	3.8 ml
Pecan ("Thin Hickory")	11	48		2.1 g	10	x	139		
Juglandaceae							1,054		14
Undifferentiated Nut			5.7 g						
Walnut		1		9.2 g			15	1.30 g	3
Acorn Shell	48	302		5.5 g	461	x	2,608	0.31 g	21
Hazelnut				0.1 g					
Persimmon Seed			20	113	1	x	10	0.26 g	17
Palmetto Seed									
Honey Locust Seed				1					
Grape Seed			10	21	Possibly 1		3		
Plum Seed						x			
Cherry Seed									
Sumac Seed				1					
Blueberry Seed									
Bramble (Rubus)							5		
Cucurbita Rind		1	2						
Cucurbita Seed									
Bottle Gourd Rind							1		

Continued on the next page

Table 14.5. Continued

	Rock Levee (flotation)	Rock Levee (water screen)	22CO573 (Peabody)	McNight (Peabody)	Palusha Creek 2	Bonds	Priestly	Mangrum	Boydell
Corn Cobs					7	7	7		
Corn Cupule/Glume	12	43			12		502		
Corn Kernel	59	255			8		238		
Corn (undifferentiated)			5	112					
Common Bean?			10						
Sunflower	1			9					
Sumpweed	1			3			4		
Sunflower or Sumpweed									
Chenopod	4		6	x			148		
Knotweed	11		35				126		
Maygrass	1		31	30			755		
Little Barley							176		
Amaranth							137		
Cheno-Am	1						9		
Purslane	1		4				29		
Panic Grass							110		
Grass Family			41				174		
Aster Family			17						
Copperleaf			1						
Euphorbia spp.	1								
Spurge Family									
Wood Sorrel			2						

Bedstraw	1	
Vervain	1	
Pokeweed	1	
Barnyard Grass	1	
St. John's Wort	1	
Nightshade		46
Vetch (Vicia/Lathyrus)		
Wild Bean		
Bean Family		23
Yellow Star Grass		14
Smartweed Family		13
Rose Family		7
Silene sp.		5
Prickly Sida		
Pondweed		
Passion Flower		
Water Lily		
Morning Glory		
Bulrush		
Sedge (*Cyperus* sp.)		

Continued on the next page

Table 14.5. *Continued*

	Hayti Bypass, Early Mississippian	Blackwater	Jolly	Birds Creek	Oliver (40OB161) flotation	Oliver (40OB161) water screen	Lake Providence
Thick Hickory	265			956	11.1 g	120.4 g	47
Pecan ("Thin Hickory")	308	81	18	7	0.1 g	0.6 g	480
Juglandaceae		3					
Undifferentiated Nut							
Walnut	5				0.1 g	0.6 g	
Acorn Shell	77	7,152	79	230	0.2 g	1.6 g	5,564
Hazelnut					0.1 g	0.3 g	
Persimmon Seed	17	48	5	13		8	262
Palmetto Seed		19		1			1
Honey Locust Seed	10						
Grape Seed							67
Plum Seed							
Cherry Seed	1						
Sumac Seed	2					1	
Blueberry Seed	2						
Bramble (Rubus)	1	2					
Cucurbita Rind		25	1		2		12
Cucurbita Seed						3	
Bottle Gourd Rind							7
Corn Cobs							
Corn Cupule/Glume	10	38	4	7	2	28	2,231

Corn Kernel	25	6	3	1	3	19	851
Corn (undifferentiated)							
Common Bean?							
Sunflower	1 (domesticated)						
Sumpweed							
(domesticated)	1						
(undomesticated)	4 (undomesticated)	1 (undomesticated)				7	
Sunflower or Sumpweed	2						
Chenopod	944 (including thin)	1	2		23		106
Knotweed	106	1	1		8	145	111
Maygrass	534	3	8		48	2	32
Little Barley	33		1	1		1	1
Amaranth	27	6				1	1
Cheno-Am	3	1					34
Purslane	2	1	2				90
Panic Grass							
Grass Family	3	2			2		51
Aster Family							13
Copperleaf							36
Euphorbia spp.	13						16
Spurge Family							
Wood Sorrel							
Bedstraw	4	4		5			
Vervain							
Pokeweed	2	2					
Barnyard Grass							6

Continued on the next page

Table 14.5. Continued

	Hayti Bypass, Early Mississippian	Blackwater	Jolly	Birds Creek	Oliver (40OB161) flotation	Oliver (40OB161) water screen	Lake Providence
St. John's Wort							1
Nightshade	5	2	1				
Vetch (Vicia/Lathyrus)							205
Wild Bean	16				2	6	
Bean Family		11			3	35	20
Yellow Star Grass							33
Smartweed Family	3						
Rose Family							
Silene sp.					2		
Prickly Sida	16	9					
Pondweed	4						
Passion Flower							2
Water Lily		5					2
Morning Glory Family						89	12
Bulrush						6	
Sedge (Cyperus sp.)					2	3	

Table 14.6. Nuts and seeds from Mississippian-period sites.

	Rock Levee "Late Mississippian" flotation	McNight	22CO573	Oliver (22CO503)	Bobo	Craig	Flowers 3	Hays
Thick Hickory	2	2.3 g		224		x	x	x
Pecan	3	1.7 g		9		x	x	x
Juglandaceae								
Walnut		1.9 g						
Butternut								
Acorn Shell	11	1.3 g	209.4	38				
Hazelnut								
Undifferentiated Nutshell			136.9					
Persimmon Seed		13	143			x	x	x
Palmetto Seed								
Grape Seed			1			x		
Plum								
Cherry			1					
Honey Locust								
Hawthorn								
Bramble (Rubus)				1				
Sumac								
Pawpaw								

Continued on the next page

Table 14.6. *Continued*

	Rock Levee "Late Mississippian" flotation	McNight	22CO573	Oliver (22CO503)	Bobo	Craig	Flowers 3	Hays
Cucurbita Rind								
Bottle Gourd Rind								
Cucurbitaceae				1				
Corn	6 cupules, 14 kernels	23 cupules, 79 kernels	44 cupules, 41 kernels	3,053 cupules, 28 kernels	ca. 75 kernels	15 cobs	22 cobs	14 cobs
Common Bean			10 possible					
Tobacco							1	
Sunflower		1	5					
Sumpweed		3 (domesticated)	8					
Chenopod		x						
Knotweed			40					
Maygrass	3		6					
Little Barley			1					
Amaranth								
Cheno-Am								
Purslane			20					
Nightshade								
Barnyard Grass								
Panic Grass								
Grass Family			20					
Sedge Family							x	

	3	
Pokeweed		
Smartweed		
Prickly Sida		
Wild Bean		x
Vetch-type		
Bean Family		
Ragweed		
Aster Family		
Bedstraw		
Morning Glory		
Yellow Star Grass		
Euphorbia sp.		
Spurge Family		
Wood Sorrel		
Violet		
Carpetweed		
Verbena		

Continued on the next page

Table 14.6. *Continued*

	Humber	Lafferty West	Powell Bayou	Wilsford	Brougham Lake (Late Woodland/ Mississippian)	Moon	Kochtitzy Ditch
Thick Hickory					3,680		32
Pecan	x				1		101
Juglandaceae							17
Walnut					132		6
Butternut							
Acorn Shell					312		14
Hazelnut							
Undifferentiated Nutshell							
Persimmon Seed	x				27		27
Palmetto Seed							
Grape Seed					10		6
Plum							
Cherry							
Honey Locust							
Hawthorn					3		
Bramble (Rubus)							6
Sumac					342		8
Pawpaw							
Cucurbita Rind							x
Bottle Gourd Rind							
Cucurbitaceae					48		

Corn	9 cobs	1 cob	9 cobs	5 cobs	x cupules, 353 kernels	7,207 kernels, 1,155 cupules
Common Bean	x					
Tobacco	x (possible)			2		11
Sunflower					5	35
Sumpweed					11	
Chenopod					148	133
Knotweed					474	2
Maygrass					1,285	697
Little Barley						11
Amaranth					10	57
Cheno-Am						1
Purslane						639
Nightshade						140
Barnyard Grass						
Panic Grass						67
Grass Family					12	100
Sedge Family						
Pokeweed					1	20
Smartweed					29	56
Prickly Sida						41
Wild Bean					60	
Vetch-type						
Bean Family						19
Ragweed					5	22
Aster Family						4
Bedstraw						1

Continued on the next page

Table 14.6. *Continued*

	Humber	Lafferty West	Powell Bayou	Wilsford	Brougham Lake (Late Woodland/Mississippian)	Moon	Kochtitzy Ditch
Morning Glory					1		38
Yellow Star Grass							
Euphorbia sp.							42
Spurge Family					5		
Wood Sorrel							
Violet							45
Carpetweed							21
Verbena							10

	Nodena	Parkin	Burris	Klueppel	Emerson	Chucalissa	Fuller	Moon
Thick Hickory	x	75	x		19	x		x
Pecan	x	14		82	7	x		x
Juglandaceae		31		36	3		x	
Walnut	x		x	n13				
Butternut						x		
Acorn Shell		369	x	154	1,015			x
Hazelnut	x							
Undifferentiated Nutshell								
Persimmon Seed	x	45	x	36	13	>6	200	

Palmetto Seed							
Grape Seed			35		23	x	1
Plum							
Cherry	x						
Honey Locust							
Hawthorn							
Bramble (Rubus)							
Sumac							
Pawpaw		x					
Cucurbita Rind		170					
Bottle Gourd Rind							
Cucurbitaceae							
Corn	98 cobs	10,259 cupules, 5,532 kernels	64	199 cupules, 47 kernels	1,599	200+ cobs	36 cobs, 4 kernels
Common Bean	10	14					1
Tobacco						x	
Sunflower	262 (domesticated)	3 (undomesticated)		8 (undomesticated)		x	
Sumpweed	34				12		
Chenopod	6			1			
Knotweed					1		
Maygrass				1	11		
Little Barley	2						
Amaranth	15				4		
Cheno-Am	4				1		
Purslane		3			6		
Nightshade	14				2		

Continued on the next page

Table 14.6. Continued

	Nodena	Parkin	Burris	Klueppel	Emerson	Chucalissa	Fuller
Barnyard Grass		2					
Panic Grass							
Grass Family		44			5		
Sedge Family							
Pokeweed		1					
Smartweed		7					
Prickly Sida		2			1		
Wild Bean					1		
Vetch-type		2			7		
Bean Family		5	x				
Ragweed							
Aster Family		1					
Bedstraw							
Morning Glory							
Yellow Star Grass							
Euphorbia sp.		4			1		
Spurge Family							
Wood Sorrel				1			
Violet							
Carpetweed							
Verbena							

I could find no direct evidence for plant use by Paleoindians or Early Archaic peoples in this part of the Mississippi valley. Extrapolating from archaeobotanical remains from sites farther north and east such as Dust Cave in Alabama (Hollenbach 2005) and Icehouse Bottom in eastern Tennessee (Chapman and Shea 1981), it is likely that nuts were routinely harvested by the end of the Early Holocene and that wild seeds and fruits were used to some degree. Two Middle Archaic sites in northwest Mississippi—Denton (22QU522) and Longstreet (22QU523)—are included in the compilation by Cutler and Blake (2001:119) of "Plants from Archaeological Sites East of the Rockies." Both of these sites yielded persimmon seeds and hickory, walnut, and acorn shell (Table 14.2). Butternut is included in the list of plants from Denton, but this identification should be confirmed through reanalysis of the remains if at all possible, because shell fragments of walnut and butternut can overlap in morphology, and to my knowledge butternuts do not grow today in the Mississippi Delta (see, for example, Gunn et al. 1980). Pecan and possible wild bean (*Strophostyles* sp.) seeds also came from Longstreet. As riverine adaptations developed, bottomland taxa and aquatic plants probably became increasingly important.

The Middle Holocene was the time when native *Cucurbita pepo* ssp. *ovifera* gourds began to be used for multiple purposes and spread to groups living beyond their natural range (Decker-Walters et al. 1993; Fritz 1999a; Hart and Sidell 1997; King 1985). Wild *Cucurbita* gourds could have grown freely across Mississippi and adjoining states during this time, so fisher-hunter-gatherers in the Delta may well have participated in early stages of cultivation and domestication. Fine-mesh flotation is necessary to recover squash/gourd seeds and rind fragments from non-waterlogged, open sites, and even then it can be impossible to classify the remains as wild versus domesticated. Smith (2000) sets 2 mm as a useful rind thickness measurement for distinguishing between wild and domesticated *C. pepo*, because no wild or weedy pepo gourds have been found with rinds thicker than 2 mm. However, it does not follow that rind fragments thinner than 2 mm came from wild plants, because selection for edible squashes with sweet flesh resulted in many cultivars, such as those we eat today, that have extremely thin rind even when left on the vine to mature past their most succulent stage. This is an issue that needs much more attention, and upcoming archaeobotanical research for the Yazoo Basin has the potential to contribute key data.

Key Question 1:   How did people adapt to Early and Middle Holocene environments in this part of the Mississippi valley?

Key Question 2: Did these groups participate in use, cultivation, and/or spread of native *Cucurbita pepo* ssp. *ovifera* gourds?

Late Archaic (ca. 3000–800 B.C.)

Flotation-recovered assemblages are available from at least three Late Archaic sites in the broader zone of interest, all in Louisiana: Poverty Point, J. W. Copes, and Cowpen Slough. Archaeobotanical remains from Poverty Point are reported by both Andrea Shea (1978), who analyzed material from the site's peripheries, and Heather Ward (1998), who focused on material from Ridge 1. *Cucurbita pepo* was reported from both Poverty Point and J. W. Copes. There is no reason cultivation of native gourds could not have been practiced throughout the LMV by this time, but the fragmentary specimens from Louisiana have not been noted as differing morphologically from wild pepo gourds, so there is no evidence yet for cultivation or selection.

Nutshell is the most common category of food plant in flotation samples from all three Late Archaic sites, but proportions of acorn, pecan, and thick hickory differ (Table 14.2). At J. W. Copes, pecan (a thin-shelled hickory) is the most common nutshell type, using both ubiquity (percentage of samples in which an item is present) and total counts, with acorn coming in second. At Poverty Point, Shea (1978) reported more acorn fragments than pecan or hickory, but the 92-percent ubiquity of the combined thick- and thin-shelled hickories (genus *Carya*) exceeds the 63-percent ubiquity of acorn. Walnut shell (*Juglans* sp.) was present at Poverty Point, but uncommon (16-percent ubiquity). Ward (1998) reported considerably higher ubiquity of *Carya* sp. (80 percent) than *Quercus* sp. (22.5 percent), along with the occurrence of *Castanea* (probably chinquapin) in one sample (2.5 percent). The Cowpen Slough assemblage is unusual in being dominated by water hickory (*Carya aquatica*), followed by acorn (Ramenofsky 1986). The absence of either thick hickory or pecan at Cowpen Slough probably reflects the site's extreme bottomland location.

This variation seen among Late Archaic assemblages—and even *between* assemblages from the Poverty Point site—leads to two more key issues. Did use of nut taxa vary across the region primarily due to environmental factors affecting availability, or, as Jackson (1989) has suggested, did some Archaic people enjoy the option of harvesting first-line resources, especially pecans? Could Heather Ward's samples from Ridge 1 in Poverty Point's core area have differed from Andrea Shea's on the site's peripheries because of status or ritual concerns? Are inconsistencies in methods of recovery and/or analysis skewing the values?

Seeds from fruits, grasses, and other plants occur in these Late Archaic assemblages (with the exception of Cowpen Slough), but in relatively low amounts. Persimmon (*Diospyros virginiana*) had become the most ubiquitous fruit (18-percent ubiquity at the peripheries of Poverty Point; 22.5-percent ubiquity at Ridge 1; 7.1-percent ubiquity at J. W. Copes), followed by grape (*Vitis* sp.), and with a single honey locust (*Gleditsia triacanthos*) and a plum (*Prunus* sp.) at J. W. Copes. The highest number of nonfruit seeds from any site is 39 little barley seeds (*Hordeum pusillum*) from 20 percent of the samples reported by Ward. Wild-sized sumpweed (*Iva annua*) and possible maygrass (*Phalaris caroliniana*) show up as single occurrences at Copes and Poverty Point, respectively. Jackson (1989) and Shea (1978) each report one chenopod seed (*Chenopodium* sp.), whereas Ward (1998) reports it in 12.5 percent of her samples. With values this low and no indication of nonwild-type morphology, these and other archaeologists agree that there was no participation in pre-maize starchy seed cultivation or domestication in Louisiana at that time (Fritz and Kidder 1993; Russo 1996).

Other seed types reported from Late Archaic sites include wild bean (*Strophostyles*), a smartweed (*Polygonum arifolium*), blackgum (*Nyssa sylvatica*), doveweed (*Croton* sp.), spurge family (Euphorbiaceae), hackberry (*Celtis* sp.), aster family (Asteraceae), purslane (*Portulaca oleraceae),* possible dropseed grass (cf. *Sporobolus*), grass family (Poaceae), possible gromwell (cf. *Lithospermum*), and possible hawthorn or yaupon holly (cf. *Crataegus* or *Ilex*).

Cutler and Blake (2001:119) report plant remains from one Late Archaic site in northwest Mississippi—Teoc Creek (22CR504)—where flotation was not conducted. Only "black walnut or butternut" is listed for that site, underscoring the occasional difficulty of differentiating between the two species of *Juglans* when dealing with fragmentary archaeobotanical material.

Key Question 3: How can we explain different proportions of nut species across space and through time?

Key Question 4: Do the data reflect different/special plant use by participants in large-scale gatherings such as those at Poverty Point?

Early Woodland (ca. 800–200 B.C.)

Although Morton Shell Mound near the Gulf Coast in Louisiana is outside the area of concern here, it is important to note that both bottle gourd (*Lagenaria siceraria)* and a small-seeded pepo gourd were found there in Tchefuncte deposits (Byrd 1976). The pepo gourds might have been gathered from wild populations, since coastal Louisiana is well within the probable Holocene range of the native eastern *Cucurbita* gourd (*C. pepo* ssp. *texana*). The bottle gourds, however, were probably cultivated, as they are African natives that reproduce in North America only temporarily without human cultivation. Bottle gourds had arrived in Florida by 5000 B.C. Until recently, these were suspected of having been collected as drift gourds by Archaic people, including those who buried one of their dead with a gourd bowl in the Windover cemetery (Newsom 2002). New evidence derived from ancient DNA, however, indicates that bottle gourds came to the Americas via an Asian route, and that domesticated gourds conforming genetically to an Asian rather than African clade had arrived in Mexico very early in the Holocene (Erickson et al. 2005). This discovery forces more serious consideration of Archaic peoples as carriers and exchangers of gourds across broad regions, although it does not rule out drifting of gourds along rivers and intra-hemispheric coastal currents. Bottle gourds were used at least 4,000 years ago in western Missouri, as demonstrated by seeds from Phillips Spring (King 1985). Their spread across the Southeast, Midwest, and points northward had to involve human transport and exchange, with easily grown gourds fitting into the lifeways of both low-level food producers and foraging peoples who were not necessarily undergoing a transition to food production. I think it likely that both pepo squash/gourds and bottle gourds were being widely grown in the CMV/LMV by early Woodland times, primarily for use as containers and other implements.

One small Tchefuncte flotation assemblage (54.5 liters of soil floated; 6 sampled contexts) is available from the Raffman site (16MA20) in northeast Louisiana (Trachtenberg 1999), with food plants consisting of 25 pieces of acorn shell, 3 of pecan, 3 persimmon seed fragments, and 1 purslane seed (*Portulaca oleracea*) (Table 14.3). Flotation samples from five features and water-screened samples from nine features at the Fulmer site (ca. 400–100 B.C.) in Shelby County, Tennessee, yielded only 17 fragments of hickory nutshell, 4 fragments of walnut shell, and 3 of hazelnut shell, along with 6 charred tulip poplar seeds (*Liriodendron tulipifera*) (Shea 1996). Much more information is obviously needed from this period, but it appears that the Archaic pattern of heavy reliance on local nuts and fruits persisted.

Middle Woodland (ca. 200 B.C. to A.D. 300/400)

Between 4,000 and 2,000 years ago, people in parts of the Eastern Woodlands had begun to plant, and in some places rely more and more heavily upon, indigenous cultigens including sunflower (*Helianthus annuus* var. *macrocarpus*), marshelder or sumpweed (*Iva annua* var. *macrocarpa*), chenopod (*Chenopodium berlandieri* ssp. *jonesianum*), and erect knotweed (*Polygonum erectum*). Middle Woodland sites across the Midwest riverine area and upland south as far south as northern Alabama and the Arkansas Ozarks have yielded impressive quantities of these crop seeds, sometimes in storage contexts (Fritz 1986;

Smith 1985), indicating that food production, although still possibly practiced on a relatively small scale compared to later Mississippian farming, comprised a significant part of the subsistence economy. Bruce Smith's (1992) Floodplain Weed Theory focuses on river valleys as prime ecological settings for plant domestication to evolve, but except for the possibility of native squash cultivation, discussed above, Late Archaic and Early Woodland sites in the I-69 Project area lack evidence for production of Eastern Agricultural Complex (EAC) domesticates. A number of archaeologists have discussed possible factors contributing to the persistence of nonagricultural lifeways in the lower Southeast in spite of suitable soils, long growing seasons, and interactions with societies farther north (in northwestern Arkansas, central and eastern Tennessee, and elsewhere) practicing food production along with hunting and wild plant harvesting (Caldwell 1958; Fritz 1990; Johannessen 1993; Scarry 1993). These factors have recently been summarized by Gremillion (2002), who points out that the zone of developed pre-maize agriculture falls mostly north of an isotherm representing an average of 60 days or more in which frost occurs. As drawn by Gremillion (2002:447, Figure 22.4), this isotherm crosses the Mississippi River somewhere near Memphis, Tennessee. To the south is a band of "limited pre-maize agriculture" that falls between the 60-day and 40-day isotherms, below which is a zone where pre-maize agriculture has not been documented. These valuable insights highlight the importance of seasonal variability, closely associated with storage technology, in predicting the pace and intensity of early food production in the Central and Lower Mississippi Valley.

Key Question 5: When was the earliest pre-maize (Eastern Agricultural Complex) food production practiced in northwest Mississippi and in the broader zone of interest, and how did climatic, geomorphological, phytogeographical, and historical variables feed into the processes by which people either added food production to previously existing foraging economies or persisted in nonagricultural subsistence pursuits?

Production of domesticated sunflower and chenopod may have spread into northwest Mississippi by the end of the Middle Woodland, since both are present in features with mixed late Marksville and early Baytown ceramics at the Rock Levee site in Bolivar County (Scarry 1995). Sunflower (*Helianthus annuus*) and sumpweed (*Iva annua*)—too fragmentary to measure and therefore possibly not domesticated—came from Prairie Phase components (A.D. 200–400) contexts at the McNight site in Coahoma County, along with maygrass (*Phalaris caroliniana*) and knotweed (*Polygonum erectum*) seeds (Table 14.3) (Shea 1999). Two features assigned to the Prairie Phase at McNight also yielded corn (*Zea mays*), totaling 4 kernel fragments and 11 cupule fragments. Shea (1999:245) states, "If these assignments are correct, this would be evidence for some of the earliest of corn in the Upper Basin," pointing out that OCR and C-14 dates for one of the features, Feature 17, "suggest a fourth-to-fifth century A.D. date." Due to the importance of determining the onset of maize production, at least one of these maize fragments should be directly dated by the AMS method.

Middle Woodland flotation samples from 22CO573/773 in the Coahoma Welcome Center Project area yielded 36 chenopod (*Chenopodium* sp.), 33 maygrass, and 7 knotweed seeds, but the chenopod seeds are described as biconvex rather than truncate, with some specimens possibly being uncharred modern contaminants (Mooney et al. 2004:431). Therefore, although this assemblage (combined Dorr phase, Prairie phase, and undifferentiated Middle Woodland) might reflect some level of gardening, there is no solid morphological evidence for domestication, nor can the argument be made for cultivation of any species outside its natural range. Acorn is the most abundant type of nutshell, reported by weight, because of a concentration of acorn shell and nutmeat in Feature 111.

Archaeobotanical remains from Middle Woodland components in northeast Louisiana and southeast Arkansas lack evidence for pre-maize seed crops. An assemblage of 177 liters of soil from 18 samples from the Marksville site in Avoyelles Parish shows reliance on acorns (217 fragments), thick-shelled hickory nuts (68), pecans (54), walnut family (296; this includes all members of the genera *Carya* and *Juglans*), persimmons (51 fragments), and palmetto (*Sabal minor*) fruits (25), with no potential domesticates (Roberts 1999a). A smaller assemblage (84 liters of soil floated from eight contexts) from the late Marksville component at the Raffman site was dominated by acorn shell (1,479 fragments), with low frequencies of pecan shell (15) and persimmon seeds (37 fragments), along with 1 maygrass seed (Trachtenberg 1999). Maygrass grows across this region today and is not necessarily indicative of agriculture, especially when recovered infrequently and in isolation from other Eastern Agricultural Complex crops. A few *Cucurbita* rind fragments were recovered from Raffman, which also has a major Coles Creek occupation, but not from zones with clear stratigraphic integrity.

Small flotation assemblages dating to late Middle Woodland (Issaquena) times are available from the Reno Brake and Osceola sites in Tensas Parish. The one from Reno Brake consists of six samples (71 liters of soil matrix floated), and the one from nearby Osceola all came from one large feature under Mound F (76 liters floated). Acorn is the most abundant food plant at both sites, with pecan, grape (*Vitis* sp.), persimmon, and palmetto represented. Fruits constitute 60.9 percent of the Reno Brake seed assemblage. The same samples contain only 7 chenopod and 1 little barley seed, all of which look wild or weedy (9.2 percent "starchy seeds"). Only 6 seeds were identified in the Issaquena feature at Osceola, including 1 maygrass but no other starchy seeds.

Plant remains were recovered without flotation from two sites in northwest Mississippi, Acree and Boyd, which are listed by Cutler and Blake (2001:119) as having Middle Woodland components. The Marksville remains from Acree are noted as being mixed with Baytown deposits, and the late Marksville ones from Boyd are mixed with both earlier (Tchula) and later (early Baytown) ones. Both sites yielded hickory nut, pecan, acorn, and persimmon seeds. Boyd also yielded walnut, pawpaw (*Asimina triloba*), grape, chenopod, and sumpweed ("marshelder") seeds, but measurements for the sumpweed are not given. A nonflotation assemblage from the late Marksville Possum Trap site (3DE37) in southeast Arkansas contains only wood charcoal (58.54 g), thick hickory nutshell (37.55 g), acorn shell (0.13 g), persimmon seeds (8), and unidentified seeds (3) (Gardner 1982).

Although the amount of flotation-derived information available is less than ideal, current evidence points to a pattern of heavy acorn use across eastern Louisiana and western Mississippi by this time. Middle Woodland flotation assemblages differ from earlier Archaic ones by having higher ubiquities and densities of acorn than pecan shell, in spite of the fact that acorn shell is more fragile and considered by most paleoethnobotanists to be underrepresented in the archaeological record. Because it is necessary to remove bitter tannins from most acorns by the process of leaching, acorns are suspecting of having been less desirable than nuts that require no leachng. However, archaeologists might be guilty of applying a modern ethnocentric bias against a type of food not consumed by Euro-Americans. If in fact there was a trend toward heavier use of acorns at this time, we might infer that intensification accompanied population increase, territorial circumscription, and improvements in ceramic technology.

Key Question 6:   What are the implications of acorn intensification?

I found no reported Early or Middle Woodland flotation assemblages from northeast Arkansas or southeast Missouri, which is unfortunate because of the greater potential for sites in more northerly latitudes to reflect pre-maize food production by this time, and for sites on higher, better-drained soils such as Crowley's Ridge to reflect different proportions of nut use.

Late Woodland (A.D. 300/400–700/800)

Unmistakable signs of increased food production are manifested by Late Woodland plant remains from northwest Mississippi, eastern Arkansas, and southeast Missouri, but most of the crops produced during this time were members of the Eastern Agricultural Complex rather than corn. It remains unclear when native seed production became economically important and how the timing varied spatially. The general pattern is one of earlier and heavier use of native crops in regions closest to the Ozark Highlands, American Bottom, and lower Ohio River valley, where pre-maize agriculture had flourished since at least Middle Woodland times, and later, more sporadic, or no use of pre-maize agriculture in the LMV south of Vicksburg. There is no distinct boundary, but rather a general clinal transition, with intra-subregional variability indicating cultural, seasonal, activity-related, and/or environmental differentiation, along with inconsistency in recovery of plant remains.

Key Question 7: What factors account for first millennium A.D. variation across space and through time in degree of participation in pre-maize food production?

In the upper Yazoo Basin, archaeologists face the difficulty of distinguishing early Baytown ceramics of the Coahoma phase from those of the following Peabody phase, which leads to a major problem for assessing the rise and relative importance of food production. Plant remains from Baytown pits at both the Oliver and McNight sites, for example, indicate starchy seed crop production (knotweed, chenopod, and maygrass seeds), even though the fill was water-screened rather than floated, except for five one-liter flotation samples from McNight (Fritz 1999b; Shea 1999). The age of the material from Oliver, however, could fall anywhere between A.D. 400 and 1000. Archaeologists should apply every possible chronometric tool at sites that either span the phases or were occupied only during an otherwise indeterminate time within one or the other.

Corn was probably grown during the middle and late centuries of the first millennium A.D. in northwest Mississippi, having been reported from four Late Woodland components (Table 14.4), but absolute verification of this through direct AMS dating is needed. The earliest direct AMS date on corn from the immediate project area is 1060 +/– 60 B.P. (cal. A.D. 985 intercept), coming from Feature 12 at the Rock Levee site (Scarry 1995:281). Even at the one-sigma confidence interval, this might postdate A.D. 1000. Scarry cautiously withholds judgment on the antiquity of maize fragments from possibly older contexts due to the problem of mixed deposits at Rock Levee. Even if present relatively early, corn seems to have been a minor player in emerging food-producing economies of the Late Woodland period in the upper Yazoo Basin. No Late Woodland component has yielded more than 14 fragments of corn (Table 14.4). At McNight, Rock Levee, Oliver, Taylor Mounds, and Hayti Bypass, the corn is swamped out by nutshell, seeds of native crops, and wild fruits.

Key Question 8:   What was the timing and impact of the earliest corn in the
surrounding region?

The largest flotation-recovered archaeobotanical assemblage from early
Baytown contexts in northwest Mississippi is from Rock Levee, and it is supplemented by water-screened samples. Unfortunately, contents of most pits
with Baytown materials were mixed with earlier and sometimes later artifacts.
Scarry (1995) describes Baytown subsistence as a combination of foraging and
pre-maize seed production, with the latter being less important at Rock Levee
than at CMV sites to the north. Acorn was the most abundant nutshell type,
followed by pecan and thick hickory. Quantities of cultigen chenopod (96),
sunflower (1), maygrass (54), and erect knotweed (30) are sufficient to demonstrate that mid-first-millennium A.D. people at Rock Levee had garden plots,
but crops seem to have supplemented wild plant foods rather than dominated
the diet. Persimmon, as usual, is the most abundant wild plant seed.

Coahoma phase assemblages from the McNight site and 22Co573 both contain small amounts of corn (3 fragments from McNight and 14 from 22Co573)
and low numbers of maygrass (10 and 3, respectively) and sumpweed seeds (1
from each site) (Shea 1999; Mooney et al. 2004). Chenopod and knotweed are
also represented at 22CO573. Late Woodland plant remains have been recovered
from a third site in Coahoma County—Oliver—but salvage excavations during land-leveling operations made it impossible to separate Coahoma phase
from Peabody phase features. Water-screened material from 13 Late Woodland
pits is dominated by acorn shell (5,920 fragments, compared to 1,940 pieces of
thick hickory, 116 pieces of pecan, and 15 fragments of water hickory). Four
fragments of corn came from these features, along with 1 cultigen-sized sunflower, 1 cultigen-sized sumpweed, 12 knotweed, and single counts of maygrass, chenopod, and little barley (Fritz 1999b). The fact that any seeds at all
smaller than window-screen mesh size survived the water screening process
leads me to suspect that these features held many more chenopod, maygrass,
and little barley seeds that would have been recovered by flotation. The most
abundant seed type at Oliver is the large Toltec Type X grass (n=40), which
has not been reported from other sites in Mississippi but indicates close affiliation with the Plum Bayou culture immediately across the Mississippi River in
eastern Arkansas.

Key Question 9:   What signs of particular food preferences might indicate
cultural affiliation or interactions with centers such as Toltec
or regions such as the American Bottom?

Taylor Mounds in Drew County, Arkansas, is on Bayou Bartholomew at
about the same latitude as Rock Levee, and the Late Woodland flotation assem-

blages are similar in composition. At Taylor Mounds, acorn shell constitutes 65 percent of the nutshell remains by count and, as at Rock Levee, persimmon is the most abundant wild seed type. Starchy seeds from Taylor Mounds include chenopod (227), with many being notably thin-testa, maygrass (109), knotweed (45), and little barley (9). Malaina Brown (1996), who analyzed and reported the Taylor Mounds plant remains, sees a diversified strategy of wild plant harvesting and native seed crop production similar to that at Rock Levee, but notes that other sites in eastern Arkansas and especially those farther to the south display variability in the degree to which people deposited Eastern Agricultural Complex taxa. The contemporaneous Powell Canal site (3CH14) in Chicot County, Arkansas, yielded only 3 chenopod and 1 erect knotweed seed from 700 liters of soil floated (26 samples), and hickory was the only nutshell reported (King 1982).

The Baytown component at the Hayti Bypass site in the Missouri bootheel, dated by Lopinot (1995) to A.D. 400–800, reflects a classic CMV pattern with dominance of hickory nutshell followed by acorn and walnut (Table 14.4). The 26 Late Woodland flotation samples, from 179 liters of soil, yielded only two fragments (cupules) of corn as compared to 445 seeds, 73 percent of which were chenopod (64), maygrass (177), erect knotweed (22), and little barley (2). Six sunflower and seven sumpweed seeds were also present, which, after adjustment for shrinkage during charring, reflect small-seeded cultigen populations.

Moving south into Louisiana, we have very little information on Troyville (A.D. 400–700) plant use. A small flotation assemblage (42 liters) from the upper midden at Reno Brake has far more acorn (366) than pecan (23), no thick hickory nutshell, and few seeds other than persimmon (6), palmetto (14), and grape (7). The 2 chenopod seeds are not thin-testa and therefore there is no reason to infer any pre-maize seed production.

The work T. R. Kidder and I did at Osceola, Jolly, and Blackwater in the Tensas Basin led us to infer that LMV dwellers on the west side of the river engaged in little if any food production during early Coles Creek times (ca. A.D. 700–900) (Fritz and Kidder 1993; Kidder and Fritz 1993). Chenopod, maygrass, and sumpweed are well represented in the rich midden under Mound B at Osceola, but the chenopod seeds have thick seed coats, the sumpweed is wild-sized, and maygrass, as discussed above, could have been harvested from natural stands. Starchy seeds (chenopod, maygrass, and knotweed) comprise less than 40 percent of the total seed assemblage. The subsequently excavated Hedgeland site (Roberts 2004) has required modification to include recognition of at least spotty starchy seed gardening along the Tensas River at this time. At Hedgeland, more than 60 percent of the Sundown phase (A.D. 700–900) seeds were erect knotweed, maygrass, chenopod, and cultigen-sized sunflower, with many of the 511 chenopod seeds appearing to represent thin-testa cultigens (Roberts 2005a). Therefore, we now recognize both geographic variation, with a general transition from heavier manifestation of the Eastern Agricultural Complex to the north and far less to the south, and variation among assemblages belonging to the same cultural phase in any given county or parish.

Securely identified corn is absent so far from early Coles Creek components in northeast Louisiana, including Hedgeland and the Osceoa Mound B midden deposit. Nuts are extremely abundant, with acorn usually surpassing pecan. Native fruits are always common, led by persimmon and palmetto and followed by grape, bramble (*Rubus* sp.), hawthorn (*Crataegus* sp.), and blueberry (*Vaccinium* sp.).

Terminal Late Woodland/Emergent Mississippian/ Late Coles Creek (A.D. 800/900–1050/1200)

Corn increases in abundance across the region during the last centuries of the first millennium A.D. (Table 14.5). I include in this group the Peabody phase components at McNight and 22Co573 and the "Late Coles Creek" samples from Rock Levee. Cutler and Blake (2001:118) assign plants from the Bonds site, 22TU530, to Late Baytown and Early Mississippian, "ca. AD 800–900." If so, this small sample of 7 cobs with mean row number of 12.0 (two 10-row, three 12-row, and two 14-row) is the earliest for which row number counts are available, other than extrapolations from the angles of loose cupules. Mooney et al. (2004:434) include seven fragments of beans (*Phaseolus vulgaris*), in their Table 12.7, the tabulation of Peabody-phase plants from 22CO573, but do not discuss the implications of this surprisingly early occurrence. Because Hart et al. (2002) have recently revised the dating of the earliest domesticated beans in eastern North America to after A.D. 1250, the Coahoma Welcome Center specimens need further examination and direct AMS dating.

At the northern end of the broader area of concern, flotation at sites including Priestly in Pointsett County, Arkansas, Hayti Bypass in Pemiscot County, Missouri, and Oliver in Obion County, Tennessee, clearly shows that Emergent Mississippians or very early Mississippians in this part of the CMV resembled their neighbors in the American Bottom by producing corn, along with impressive amounts of native seed crops, at the end of the first millennium and beginning of the second millennium A.D. (Table 14.5) (Lopinot 1995; Shea and Mainfort 1994; Pearsall and Hunter 1990). At Priestly, maygrass, chenopod, and erect knotweed constitute 71.4 percent of the seed assemblage, with a combined count of 1,205 for those four taxa (Pearsall and Hunter 1990). The starchy seed count of 1,567 (constituting 73.1 percent of the seed assemblage) is even higher for the ca. A.D. 1020 component at Hayti Bypass, with thin seed coats and truncate margins demonstrating domesticated chenopod status (Lopinot 1995).

A recent report by Neal Lopinot and Gina Powell on plant remains from a large flotation assemblage (1,255 liters of floated sediment; 15 samples) from the Gary 2 site (22LF551) gives hard evidence for mixed maize and native seed crop agriculture at the end of the Peabody Phase, ca. A.D. 1100 (Lopinot and Powell 2003). More than 3,000 chenopod, erect knotweed, and maygrass seeds constitute roughly 50 percent of the seed assemblage. Tobacco seeds and clearly domesticated sunflower and sumpweed seeds were also represented. Corn came from 11 of the 15 samples, with 252 fragments counted. This type of composition is more typical of what has been found by paleoethnobotanists working on Emergent Mississippian and Early Mississippian material from north of the Arkansas/Mississippi River confluence, again showing that variation can exist within areas that may or may not otherwise display a clinal trend. The newly reported Lake Providence site in extreme northeast Louisiana also yielded a healthy mix of native crops and corn at the transition of Coles Creek and Mississippian-period times (Roberts 2005b).

South of Lake Providence, late Coles Creek components, including those at Blackwater, Jolly, and Birds Creek, have yielded modest amounts of corn, but nowhere near the numbers of native starchy seeds nor specimens displaying cultigen morphology as have been reported from sites farther north (Table 14.5). It appears that heavy use of acorns persisted in the bottomland floodplains, whereas people living on or near Pleistocene terraces (at Birds Creek, for example) also harvested the thick-shelled hickories that require better-drained soils (Fritz 1997).

Mississippian Period (ca. A.D. 1100 to Contact)

The immediate project area is wide open when it comes to discussing dynamics of late pre-Contact foodways and chiefdom-related economic issues involving agricultural production. Sites in the immediate I-69 project area where flotation and/or water screening have been conducted—McNight, Rock Levee, 22CO573, and Oliver—yielded smaller and less-rich assemblages from Mississippian period components than did the earlier features at those sites. Corn is well represented, obviously having become a staple across the region by A.D. 1100, possibly with a lag of one or two centuries in parts of eastern Louisiana. Plant remains have been reported by Cutler and Blake (2001) from eight late prehistoric sites in northwest Mississippi where flotation was not conducted, with a focus on row numbers and cupule widths of corn.

With the exception of sunflower and eastern squash, native crops eventually fell out of the system, but the persistence of cultigen chenopod and sumpweed until A.D. 1300 at the Gypsy Joint site in southeast Missouri makes it unwise to discount late appearances farther south (Wetterstrom 1978). Starchy seeds still comprise 45.1 percent of the total seed assemblage (331 out of 723) at the Moon site (3PO488), estimated to date between A.D. 1175 and 1300, where corn came from 92 percent of the features floated (Pearsall 1992). At the similarly corn-rich Kochtitzy Ditch site (3MS599, ca. A.D. 1200–1400), the cultivated starchy-seed category constitutes 37 percent of the identified seed assemblage, with an especially high number (697) of maygrass seeds (Lopinot and Thomas 2003). The Brougham Lake (3CT98) assemblage, also from northeast Arkansas, was reported with Late Woodland and Mississippian components lumped, making it impossible to determine if the large numbers of starchy seeds found there were being produced at the same time that maize was abundant (Harris 1983).

Key Question 10: Until what date were EAC crops grown, and what factors were associated with the demise of those that disappeared?

Maize-based economies developed across the broader zone of interest during late prehistory, with common beans probably incorporated fully at some point between A.D. 1200 and 1400. Securely pinning down the date of their arrival in the project area, as John Hart and colleagues (2002) have done in the Northeast, would be a significant contribution. Beans were reported from 10 of the Mississippian-period components included in Table 14.6, although never in large numbers.

Key Question 11: When were common beans (*Phaseolus vulgaris*) introduced and integrated into the agricultural systems?
Key Question 12: What kinds of corn were grown, what differences existed across space and through time, and what does this mean about Mississippian foodways and societies?

We still have poor understanding of intra-site diversity in corn assemblages, much less temporal and regional variation across the CMV/LMV, and need to move beyond speculations about an early (but hypothetical and probably non-existent) Tropical Flint race being replaced by "superior" corn such as Eastern Eight-row. Tropical Flint, also known as North American Pop, is mentioned by several authors discussing the transition to agricultural in northwest Mississippi (Brain 1971; McNutt 1996:175, 177; Potts and Brookes 1981:19). Citing Cutler and Blake (1985 [1970]) but interpreting the evidence in his own way,

Brain (1971:69–70) wrote: "By A.D. 1200, the Coles Creek Culture had reached its maximum extent. Although obviously successful, it was a very local culture which stayed within its zone of local adaptation, the lower half of the [Yazoo] valley. This may have been due to dependence upon a variety of tropical flint corn which required such an environment and did not do well outside it." Twelve-row corn from the Bobo site was interpreted by Potts and Brookes (1981) as conforming to Tropical Flint and therefore demonstrating that this variety could flourish in the Upper Yazoo as early as A.D. 1000. McNutt (1996:176), citing an unpublished paper by Brookes (1988), calls the Peabody phase affiliation of corn in the region into question due to the possibility that mixing of Terminal Woodland with later debris occurred. However, in discussing the Early Mississippian period (A.D. 1000–1250), McNutt (1996:177) wrote, "Tropical flint corn, probably from the Lower Yazoo . . . seems to be established."

As we have seen, it is unlikely that any type of corn spread from south to north before A.D. 1000, because serious corn agriculture was probably not practiced in the LMV until after that date. Furthermore, the case for Tropical Flint corn being represented by late prehistoric 12-rowed cobs in northwest Mississippi or elsewhere in eastern North America is very weak. The concept of Tropical Flint/North American Pop was based on a few cobs with high row numbers believed to date to the Early and Middle Woodland periods (Cutler and Blake 2001:96). These are now known to be considerably younger. Corn dated directly by AMS to Middle Woodland times is too fragmentary to allow reliable reconstruction of row number, much less size and shape. Archaeobotanists who have attempted to derive row number from loose Middle Woodland cupules do not see evidence that it belonged to a different race than later corn (Chapman and Crites 1987; Parker 1989). Because of these developments, Tropical Flint is no longer established as an early variety anywhere in North America (Wagner 1994), although some corn dating to Woodland times may well have conformed to the template constructed by Cutler in being small, cigar-shaped, and relatively high in row number.

The earliest corn in the Eastern Woodlands seems to have spread into the mid-continent across the Plains from the Southwest more than 2,000 years ago (Hart et al. 2007; Riley et al. 1994). It had been grown in the Greater Southwest since 2000 B.C. (Diehl 2005) and was well adapted to temperate latitudes. Early Eastern corn came from a gene pool with considerable biodiversity and a wide range of row numbers. A restricted population appears to have been passed into the Northeast, where a uniform, low row-numbered variety called Eastern Eight-row or Northern Flint was bred (Crawford et al. 1997). This corn spread across the northern Midwest and Atlantic seaboard, but it never strongly influenced the LMV. Most Mississippian assemblages from Mississippi, Arkansas, and Tennessee have predominantly 10- and 12- row cobs, although specimens with 8 and 14 rows are common, and 16-row cobs are sometimes included. These assemblages come under the umbrella of "Midwestern Twelve-row" but, as noted by Wagner (1994) and Leonard Blake (personal communication, 1995), this is not a clearly defined race, but rather a broad complex. It probably includes numerous varieties appreciated by the farmers but unrecognized so far by us. Local landraces undoubtedly varied by subregion and changed through time.

Other key questions about relationships between plants and Mississippian peoples involve: persisting or shifting patterns of wild plant harvesting and management (Fritz 2007; Scarry 2003); the role of agricultural surplus in complex political negotiations (Scarry and Steponaitis 1997; Welch 1991); possible signatures of differential social status; potential environmental impact caused by increased clearing for fields; changes (or continuity) in animal procurement patterns coinciding with intensified agriculture (Jackson, this volume); and responses to environmental stresses including drought (Scarry and Reitz 2005).

Contact, Protohistoric, and Historic Periods

I have found no reports on flotation-recovered plant remains from Protohistoric or Historic-period sites in the I-69 project area. One key question here concerns subsistence change as a response by Native Americans to disease, social reorganization, new exchange partners, and participation in the hide trade. Another issue deals with selective adoption of European crops, as discussed by Gremillion (1995b, 1996) for other parts of the Southeast.

Quapaw Indians gave Henri Joutel watermelons to eat in July 1687 (Joutel 1998 [1713]), and flotation samples from the Wallace Bottom site currently being analyzed at Washington University in St. Louis demonstrate that peaches were grown at the late-seventeenth-century Quapaw village of Osotouy. Subsistence at Osotouy—where the first Arkansas Post was built—was diverse, with corn, squash, pecan, hickory, walnut, acorn, and many native fruits and herbaceous seed plants well represented in most samples. When the analysis is finished, we will look for possible differences between this assemblage and earlier ones from eastern Arkansas and northwest Mississippi—both Protohistoric and pre-Contact—addressing the questions above, as well as the timing of Quapaw presence in this region.

Recommendations and Suggestions

1. It is important that paleoethnobotanists be among the top-level decision-makers from earliest stages, planning and implementing recovery systems,

working in the field and in the field lab during excavation, and involved in all discussions and communications up to final report publication.

2. Flotation should be as standardized as possible in order to insure comparability among assemblages recovered. Archaeologists and paleoethnobotanists should agree in advance about the following equipment and procedures:

   Type of flotation system

   Mesh sizes for light and heavy fractions

   Volumes of soil samples taken for flotation (these should be measured consistently and always recorded)

   Sampling strategy (see Pearsall 2000)

   Whether or not soil is sifted or dried prior to flotation

   Whether or not (and if so, how) the heavy fractions are refloated or otherwise processed

3. Plant remains from heavy fractions should be analyzed and reported along with those from light fractions.

4. Water screening can be supplemental to flotation, especially where soils are recalcitrant, but it is never a substitute.

5. Laboratory methods should be as comparable as possible:

   2 mm standard cut-off for total sorting

   Both counts and weights should be reported (except for small seeds, where counts are sufficient)

   Acorn and pecan shell should be sorted to 1.4 mm

   Seeds should be reported as both SNE (Seed Number Estimate) and fragment #

6. Measurements are needed for the following:

   a) *Cucurbita* rind thickness

   b) Sunflower and sumpweed achene size (both actual lengths and widths, and adjustments for shrinkage during carbonization)

   c) Seed coats (SEM needed for chenopod seed coat thicknesses)

Although absolute standardization of recovery and analytical methods is probably an unreasonable goal, especially if archaeologists from multiple institutions are involved, it is crucial to require that results be comparable. In the past, some analysts of plant remains reported results only as presence or absence of the various taxa, some used only counts, some used only weights, and in a few instances, only the volumes of material were reported. This is easy to remedy by recording and publishing both counts and weights of all material except seeds smaller than 2 mm, for which weights are unnecessary. Paleoethnobotanists are inconsistent in the cut-off point for sorting acorn and pecan shell fragments, which leads to lack of comparability between data sets, including those tabulated here. Some analysts today report seed quantities as Seed Number Estimates (SNE), whereas others report the number of fragments. Quantities of persimmon seeds presented in Tables 14.2–14.6 are not comparable for that reason. Again, if both the number of fragments and the SNE are reported, this problem will be avoided.

15
Archaeological Remote Sensing Research in the Yazoo Basin

A History and Evaluation

Jay K. Johnson

The following will be a broadly historical review of remote sensing applications in the archaeology of the Lower Mississippi Valley (LMV). By LMV, I mean the Mississippi River drainage from approximately the Missouri/Arkansas line south, although I will be a little flexible in this definition, particularly in the early period. By remote sensing, I mean to include any technique that allows the near-surface of the earth to be characterized at a distance. Most people think of satellites when you mention remote sensing, but sometimes, in the case of many geophysical techniques, the sensor is at, on, or intruded into the surface of the earth but still measuring soil features that are remote from the instrument. The goal of this summary is to provide a general understanding of the factors involved in the development of these techniques and a set of recommendations for future applications.

Beginnings

Remote sensing in archaeology got off to a precocious beginning in Mississippi as a result of a fortunate set of circumstances. Mark Williams, with a brand new undergraduate degree in anthropology and a background in electronics, was stationed at Keesler Air Force Base in Biloxi during the early 1970s. His job as an instructor allowed him a good deal of free time in the afternoons, which he spent volunteering on local archaeology projects (Mark Williams, personal communication 2004). This included John Connaway and Sam McGahey's search for Fort Maurepas in Ocean Springs. Mark and his father had been experimenting with building a soil-resistance meter suitable for archaeological prospection (Williams 1984) and Mark employed an early, two-probe version of the device in the Fort Maurepas project. The project was frustrated by the fact that the most likely location for the fort is along a waterfront bluff line in Ocean Springs that had become prime real estate, with big houses and manicured lawns. Not everyone allowed excavation. It is situations like this where the nondestructive aspects of remote sensing become important. At one location, "Although no excavations were allowed, the use of a resistivity meter in the area suggested the presence of many subsurface features" (Connaway 1981a:65). A recent attempt to find the fort using geophysical survey techniques discovered patterns that are likely to be French and could possibly be part of the fort (Held 2004) but, once again, the ground-truth excavations necessary to evaluate the structure are not likely to happen.

The first magnetometer survey in the Lower Valley was conducted in the Red River in 1975 in search of shipwrecks (GSRI 1975). There followed a large number of similar application as the Corps of Engineers funded dredging and bank stabilization throughout the region (Birchett and Pearson 1995; Irion et al. 1995; James 1994; Pearson et al. 1982; Pearson et al. 1992; Perrault et al. 1995; R. Christopher Goodwin and Associates 2000; Saltus 1977a, 1977b, 1979a, 1979b; Weinstein 1991). A progressive refinement of techniques is evident in these reports, most of which involve the use of more-and-more sophisticated locational devices, the addition of depth finders, and ultimately side-scan radar. Of course, these riverine surveys are not directly relevant to work focusing on terrestrial resources, even when that work is restricted to filled-in oxbows and the recordings are made by mounting the magnetometer on a staff and walking the survey area. This is due primarily to the nature of the archaeological resource targeted. Most of the shipwrecks in the rivers of the Lower Valley date to the nineteenth century and contain large amounts of metal. This means that relatively large deflections of the magnetic field can be expected, and the effects of drift and instrument height do not need to be considered. In fact, in terrestrial applications, the sensor was generally elevated up to 1.8 meters above ground surface in order to reduce the sensitivity to small and near-surface metal artifacts. On the survey that successfully located the wreck of the gunboat *U.S.S. Eastport,* the sensor head was suspended below a helicopter on a nylon ski rope (Birchett and Pearson 1995). The primary importance of these riverine surveys is that the same instruments were sometimes used to survey prehistoric and Historic sites on land.

At about the same time, another promising young archaeologist was experimenting with geophysical instruments on archaeological sites. Vincas Steponaitis, then a graduate student at Michigan, whose interests "include the archaeology of the Lower Mississippi Valley and the application of electronic techniques to field investigations" (Steponaitis and Brain 1976:463), was inspired by advances in geophysical prospection in Great Britain. Working with scientists from Rutgers and MIT, he developed one of the earliest magnetic gradiometers to be used in North American archaeology. The instrument, which was called a differential proton magnetometer, had the advantage of using simple circuitry and components that could be constructed from readily available material, estimated to cost less than $100 (Steponaitis and Brain 1976:455). It produced an audio signal that changed in a distinctive way when the magnetic field at one sensor differed from that of the other. The operator would note areas of localized magnetic differences as likely locations of burned structures, midden-filled pits, bricks, or metal. The primary drawback was the lack of a quantifiable output and consequent unsuitability in mapping variations in the magnetic field. It was used on several sites in the Lower Valley, including Poverty Point and the Trudeau site, but the results were never reported in any detail.

The Trudeau site also saw the first application of ground-penetrating radar in the Lower Valley. A substantial portion of the 1980 and 1981 seasons was spent conducting a ground-penetrating radar (GPR) survey of most of the site and ground truthing the results. The interpretation of the GPR results relied on hard copy, thermal-paper profiles. It was hoped that patterns in the profiles could be related to specific kinds of archaeological features. "Unfortunately, the radar did not live up to . . . expectations, although it was found to have a limited capability for distinguishing gross geological disconformities" (Brain 1988:111).

Jon Gibson (1989) included GPR survey in his 1988 field school research at Poverty Point with what must be viewed, in retrospect, as an unqualified success. At the time there was some disappointment that the technique was not successful in detecting individual artifacts other than a truck's hubcap, which was buried to calibrate the signal in terms of depth (Mayer 1989:217). However, as James Doolittle (1989:209) indicated, the nature of the soils at the site required the use of a low-frequency antenna whose wavelength is much too broad to detect things as small as artifacts. In fact, the experiment showed great promise in that the boundary between artificial fill and the original land surface was delineated in the southeast plaza (Mayer 1989).

Richard Weinstein (1981b) was the first to use a magnetometer to produce a digital map of the magnetic field on a prehistoric site in Mississippi. Although Moores Creek is not actually in the Lower Valley watershed, I have included its report because this was the project that set the trajectory for the application of the technology to several sites in the region in the years to follow. A controlled surface collection was followed by a magnetometer survey with one-meter reading density. Experiments with rod heights were conducted in order to determine the appropriate sensor-to-ground distance for the best noise-to-signal ratio. This was particularly important at this site because the soil was rich in iron minerals. Despite the interference, a general correlation between Middle Archaic pits and areas of high return was noted.

Weinstein and his colleagues at Coastal Environments, Inc., continued to get double service from their magnetometer during the 1980s and 1990s, using it both on underwater and terrestrial sites including prehistoric (Flores et al. 1991; Weinstein et al. 1985; Weinstein et al. 1995) and plantation (Hahn et al. 1994) site surveys. The magnetometer data were used as one more data layer in a strategic combination of controlled surface collection, auger testing, test pits, and block excavation. A general and occasionally specific correlation between concentrations of features and concentrations of high returns in the magnetometer data was noted. As recognized by Weinstein et al. (1995:20), there are inherent limitations in single-instrument applications of this sort. Although the elevated instrument height reduces the effect of metallic surface debris, it also limits the sensitivity of the survey. More importantly, variations in the Earth's magnetic field throughout the course of the day (diurnal drift), although small, often exceed the magnitude of the signature for subtle archaeological features such as earth-filled pits and ditches.

There are two solutions to the problem of diurnal drift. Two instruments can be used, one as a base station that records the general changes in the magnetic field at a stationary point throughout the course of the survey. These readings are used as a timed series to "zero" the readings made with the mobile instruments so that all that is left are the differences caused by local soil and cultural features. The second and more recent instrument configuration consists of two sensor heads mounted one above the other, so that what is recorded is the gradient between the two. Since both are affected about equally by temporal shifts in the magnetic field, and since magnetic anomalies in the soil directly below the instrument will have a stronger effect on the lower sensor than the upper sensor, the gradient between them is unaffected by diurnal drift.

Michael Kaczor reports on a base-station, mobile-sensor proton magnetometer survey done by John Weymouth at Toltec in 1980 (Kaczor and Weymouth 1981). Because of the greater sensitivity afforded by the configuration, several subtle features in the mound-construction sequence were suggested by the resulting plots. A number of these were tested and plausible interpretations, most of which were based on the difference in the magnetic susceptibility between midden, humus, and subsoil, were offered.

A second and even more successful application of the total field-base station configuration is only reported in a contract report with extremely limited distribution (Wadleigh and Thomson 1989). Linda Wadleigh and Kevin Thomson from Western Wyoming College surveyed several tracts within a large Mississippian-period site on the Eaker Air Force Base reservation in northeastern Arkansas. The results are remarkable in that they used an early, color spectrum–based mapping software that was a distinct improvement on the dot-density and contour-mapping techniques being employed by most people doing geophysics at the time. As good as the graphics are, the patterns they reveal are even more impressive. House floors show as red, high-return areas arranged along the edge of blue, low-return fortification trenches. Areas of midden and pit features were also designated. A reassuring number of these features were verified by means of test-pit excavation. Unfortunately, there was little immediate response to the success of the early applications of the two-instrument configuration, perhaps because the instruments and operators were affiliated with institutions located outside of the South.

Really Remote Sensing

A limited number of experiments in the application of satellite and airborne remote sensors was conducted during this same period of time. Many of these can be linked to the inspiration and support provided by Tom Sever, then with the NASA Science and Space Technology Laboratory at the John C. Stennis Space Center in Mississippi. It is fitting that the best-known of these applications was at Poverty Point, since this is the site of one of the earliest and most spectacular airborne discoveries when, in the early 1950s, James Ford discovered the concentric sets of ridges while examining aerial photographs (Ford 1954c; Ford and Webb 1956). Sever based his analysis on data collected using two airborne sensors, a thematic mapper simulator (TMS) and a thermal infrared multispectral scanner (TIMS) (Sever and Wiseman 1985:32–37). Although the ridges are readily evident in the classified imagery (Sever and Wiseman 1985:Plate 5), this is primarily because park managers at the site had planted the ridge tops in a different vegetation so they could be seen from the observation tower next to the visitors center. Other features, including a buried ramp and traces of nineteenth- and twentieth-century activity, were also evident (Gibson 1987b).

Working with Sever, I used Landsat TM satellite imagery in two large-scale survey projects starting in the late 1980s and continuing into the 1990s (Johnson 1991; Johnson et al. 1988). Although this relatively low-resolution imagery was useful in delineating broad-scale environmental zones and allowed us to refine our model for site location, it proved useless in terms of site discovery, much less the mapping of features within sites. Therefore, when we received funding from the Mississippi Department of Archives and History to conduct an assessment of the Hollywood Mounds, a mid-size Mississippian ceremonial center located in the Yazoo Basin not far from the proposed route of I-69, we included airborne remote sensing using ATLAS, a multispectral sensor flown out of Stennis Space Center (Johnson et al. 2000). A separate NASA grant also allowed us to experiment with high-resolution thermal imagery by suspending a sensor from a tethered blimp (Haley et al. 2002). Our initial assessment of the ATLAS data was not too promising. The thermal data proved to be easier to use in terms of locating known structures at the site. However, a reevaluation of the ATLAS imagery once we had conducted a thorough assessment of the site using geophysical survey techniques demonstrated that the images did contain information about the distribution of subsurface features; the data were just substantially more subtle than had been anticipated (Haley 2002).

A Geophysical Renaissance

In fact, it was while working at Hollywood that I first became aware of the remarkable research potential of geophysical survey techniques on this sort of site. It all began innocently enough when Rich Stallings told me that Berle Clay had an instrument that measured earth conductivity that he would like to try on a Mississippian-period site. The results were spectacular (Clay 2001), and I became a convert.

During the first decade of the twenty-first century, a number of factors have converged to make geophysical survey a "must-do" component of archaeological research in the Lower Valley. The first is a refinement in instrumentation. Berle brought a Geonics EM38 conductivity meter to Hollywood on his first visit and produced imagery that allowed us to test eight probable house locations. Six of these test pits encountered burned house floors just below the plowzone. The EM38 also revealed several enigmatic, donut-shaped patterns, one of which we trenched with a backhoe. This and later excavations demonstrated that these were the remnants of plowed-down mounds. On the next visit Berle brought along another instrument, a Geoscan FM36 gradiometer. Developed in Great Britain, where geophysical survey is a regular feature of archaeological research, this instrument has become the standard tool for magnetic surveys of archaeological sites. During that visit, Berle surveyed only four 20-meter squares, but they were centered on the location of a known house that we had found on the basis of the EM38 survey and had cross-trenched the following summer. The gradiometer image was even better than the conductivity image. We could see the outline of the house. Berle went on to survey most of the rest of the plaza and boundary mound area, and we extended the survey with our own FM36 once we found the money to buy one. As a result of the work that Berle started, in combination with a season of test-pit excavation guided with surgical precision by the remote imagery, we now know as much about the Hollywood site in terms of construction sequence as any other Mississippian site in the Yazoo Basin, and perhaps more (www.olemiss.edu/research/ anthropology/archaeology/).

Steve Jones also volunteered to visit Hollywood in 1998 and try his SIR 8 GPR system on the site. Although we ran the antenna across known features, including the filled-in backhoe trench and a steel culvert, the fine sediments at the site led to an attenuation of the signal so that the only part of the site where interpretable signals were recovered was along the front edge of the natural levee, where coarser sediments had been deposited (Johnson et al. 2000). Unfortunately, at the time, we had no information about the location of structures in that area. We returned to the site in 2001 with a SIR 2000 and, with the improved instrument, were able to record structures along the back slope of the levee (Peukert 2002).

However, another factor contributed significantly to our success. In 1998, Steve and almost everyone else using GPR relied on interpretations based on the line scans produced as the antenna was dragged across the site. These are essentially vertical slices of the sediments with areas of reflection marked by hyperbolic echoes. The greater the contrast, the stronger the reflection, the thicker the hyperbola. This traditional approach to reading GPR data is the same that was used at Trudeau in 1980. There is now a new suite of software that allows the data from several different, parallel vertical slices to be arranged side-by-side so that a three-dimensional matrix of data points is created. The software thereby provides horizontal slices through the data cube, providing plan-view images of the deposit. This procedure, known as time slicing because the vertical axis in the data cube is measured in the number of nanoseconds it takes for the signal to return to the antenna, was pioneered by archaeologists in the late 1900s (Conyers and Goodman 1997) and has revolutionized the use of GPR in archaeology. Similar advances have been made in the software used for integrating and interpreting the output from other geophysical instruments. So, the second major factor in the recent increase in the application of remote-sensing survey techniques to the archaeology of the Lower Valley has been a remarkable improvement in the software used to process and interpret remotely sensed data.

Excepting GPR, most of the innovations in technology and software in geophysical prospection in archaeology have taken place in Great Britain. Two recent reviews of remote sensing in that country (Clark 1996; Gaffney and Gater 2003) do an excellent job of presenting the innovations and making their implications for archaeological applications clear. However, as you might expect, the instruments and software are too complicated to be learned from a text. In this, the annual workshop on remote sensing and archaeology, sponsored by the Lincoln office of the National Park Service, has played an important role. Berle is a regular instructor at the workshop, as is Ken Kvamme, an archaeologist on the faculty at the University of Arkansas.

Although Ken's primary area of research is the Great Plains, he has done some work in the Lower Valley, most notably at Wallace Bottom, the likely site of the Arkansas Post, an early French trading post in Arkansas. He was joined in that project by John House, the station archaeologist at Pine Bluff, and Jamie Lockhart, who has assumed the geophysical remote-sensing responsibilities for the Arkansas Archeological Survey. In addition to the remarkable results that Jamie helped derive at Wallace Bottom, he has done surveys at a number of other sites in the Lower Valley, ranging from Middle Archaic mound sites, to major Mississippian mound centers, to Historic plantations. Although most of this research has occurred within the past three years and has not been published, the results clearly demonstrate the value of geophysical survey in Lower Valley archaeology (Lockhart and Green 2006).

Michael Hargrave, another regular at the NPS workshops, joined Tad Britt to conduct geophysical survey at Poverty Point (Britt et al. 2002). The ridges and borrow areas between them show up extremely well in the southwest quadrant in this imagery because humus was borrowed from the area between the ridges and redeposited on the ridges themselves, decreasing the magnetic susceptibility in one area and increasing it in the other. The imagery also suggests the location of possible pit features on the ridges.

Berle Clay also conducted geophysical survey of a portion of the Little Spanish Fort site, a Woodland-period earthwork in the lower Yazoo Basin (Clay 2001). At that site the gradiometer was relatively ineffective, but the conductivity data show the former location of the earthwork in a section of the field where it had been plowed down. Berle returned to Mississippi to join us in the gradiometer survey of the village site at the Parchman Place Mounds in the winter of 2002. Once again, the magnetic signatures of the burned Mississippian period houses allowed a detailed, comprehensive, composite picture of the layout of the village without digging a single test pit (Figure 15.1). Of course, geophysical survey, as it is currently applied, cannot control for chronology. Still, it may be possible to refine the use of magnetic data to allow burned features from different periods to be distinguished on the basis of the orientation of polarity, using the same principles that are fundamental to paleomagnetic dating (Bruce Bevan, personal communication 2001). There is also the challenge of detecting structures that have not been burned. For that, alternative measurements—resistivity for example—will have to be used. Still, the map of magnetic features at Parchman provides a remarkable starting point for exploring site structure using more traditional techniques.

However, ours is not the only gradiometer in Mississippi. Janet Rafferty and Evan Peacock at Mississippi State have used theirs to good advantage at Lyon's Bluff, a Mississippian mound center in the Tombigbee drainage of northeastern Mississippi (Rafferty et al. 2003). A more recent application focused on the Pocahontas Mounds, located in central Mississippi not far from the Ya-

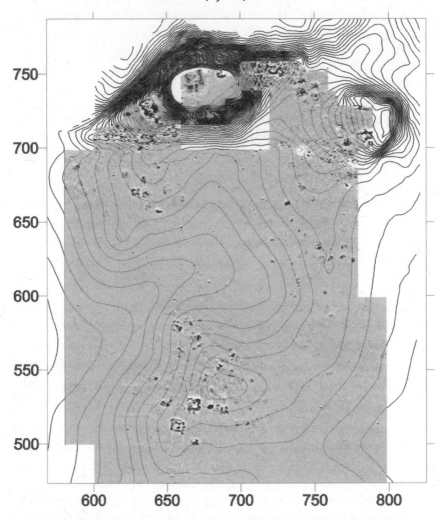

Figure 15.1. Gradiometer image of the Parchman Place Mounds (22CO511) with super-imposed contour map and 50-meter grid ticks. Surveyed with the assistance of Berle Clay.

zoo Basin. Their test excavations at that site indicate a Coles Creek through Plaquemine occupation with clear indication of intact, sub-plowzone deposits (Rafferty et al. 2005). However, the gradiometer image of the site fails to show the layout of houses we have come to expect on platform-mound sites. One of the markers for a Mississippian-period site in the Yazoo Basin is daub, and daub is not a regular feature of the test-pit assemblages from Pocahontas. That means that either the houses didn't burn or, more likely, the walls of the houses at Pocahontas were not plastered with clay. At any rate, the major factor making the Mississippian-period house in the Lower Valley accessible to magnetic detection is burned clay.

Recommendations

That is not to say that geophysical prospection is not going to be productive at sites without structures marked by massive daub falls. Rafferty and her coauthors (2005) identify probable features at Pocahontas, as did Kaczor and Weymouth (1981) at Toltec. It does mean that it will be necessary to approach the data in a different way. Much of the identification of cultural features in remotely sensed imagery has relied on shape recognition. If it looks like a Mississippian house or French fort in plan view, then it probably is. However, differentiating a small pit from a large tree root cannot be done on the basis of shape. We will have to rely on the "spectral" characteristics of the feature (Johnson 2006). That is, it will be necessary to use multiple techniques and carefully examine the way in which the feature is revealed or not revealed by the different instruments, to consider those data in light of what is known about the way that the various instruments respond to different ground characteristics, to test-excavate a large sample of potential features, and to develop a signature for pits, hearths, burned floors, and so on. Bryan Haley's work at the Walford site, a Yazoo Basin site on which most of the house remains have been stripped away by land planes, leaving only the pit features, indicates that this approach has a good deal of potential. Mike Hargrave (Hargrave 2006) has already done work along these lines, as has Ken Kvamme (Kvamme 2001, 2003a, 2003b; Kvamme, Johnson, and Haley 2006).

Once it has become possible to distinguish cultural features from natural features, it will become quite easy to determine site boundaries. This approach is particularly attractive in the Lower Valley, where the alluvial soils tend to be relatively quiet unless they are disturbed by human activity. Several years ago, Weinstein (1981b) observed that, while he couldn't always make a direct correlation between the magnetic imagery and specific excavated features, there was a clear correspondence between areas where there was a concentration of anomalies and areas where there was a concentration of features. This is likely to be because a magnetometer measures both remnant magnetism and magnetic susceptibility. On prehistoric sites in the LMV, remnant magnetism is generally restricted to areas of burned clay. Magnetic susceptibility, on the other hand, occurs as the result of natural pedogenic processes generally restricted to the A horizon, but which are significantly enhanced by the increase in organic content that results from human activity (Dalan 2006). Bryan Haley and I (Haley and Johnson 2006) have been working to distinguish these two components of the magnetic signature of archaeological features by using an

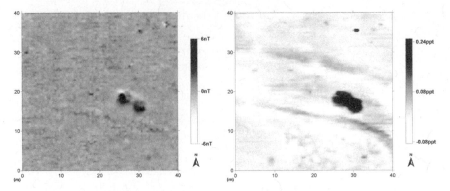

Figure 15.2. Gradiometer (left) and magnetic susceptibility (right) images of a portion of the Slope site (22LE1005) showing two intersecting, Contact-period Chickasaw midden pits as well as humic deposits at the edges of twentieth-century agricultural terraces.

EM38B electromagnetic conductivity meter in conjunction with a gradiometer. In addition to recording the soil conductivity, the EM38B also measures magnetic susceptibility. Although we have had remarkable success in detecting Contact-period pit features on a Chickasaw site (Figure 15.2), we have so far not been able to differentiate areas of sheet midden on prehistoric sites in the way that susceptibility has been used in Great Britain (Gaffney and Gater 2003:44). Still, there is the potential for being able to use geophysical survey in delineating site boundaries on sites that lack intact features.

The traditional approach to mapping out areas where sub-plowzone features are likely to be uncovered is to conduct a controlled surface collection. However, as a result of more than a century of cultivation, the distribution of artifacts on the surface of the site is likely to be much broader than the distribution of features. And, there is no guarantee that features are still preserved below the plowzone, even when there is a substantial concentration of artifacts on the surface. Finding the features once you map the surface concentrations requires either block excavations, mechanical stripping of the plowzone, or a large number of test pits. All of these activities, including controlled-surface collection, are expensive. A few years ago, Bryan Haley and I did a cost-benefit analysis contrasting controlled-surface collecting and remote sensing as a means to site characterization in preparation for a full-scale excavation (Johnson and Haley 2006). Discounting the initial investment in equipment and training, remote sensing is not only better, it is much cheaper. The simulation we used in this study was based on data recovered from the Parchman Place Mounds where, as I have indicated, the conditions for remote sensing were ideal. I believe, however, that once we have developed the expertise necessary to evaluate Woodland and Archaic sites, equivalent results will be possible.

As the editors pointed out in a comment on an earlier draft of this chapter, geophysical survey and controlled surface collection are complementary, not redundant. This is, of course, true. Given our current understanding of the spectral signatures of different kinds of archaeological features, unless the site being investigated includes features that can be distinguished on the basis of spatial patterning—Mississippian-period houses for example—a geophysical survey will tell you nothing about chronology. Moreover, if there are no intact features on the site, geophysical survey as it is currently applied will not provide guidance in locating areas of artifact concentration. However, as indicated above, a closer attention to magnetic susceptibility has the potential of resolving this problem. Still, even if susceptibility does not provide the answer in terms of mapping midden concentration on sites without features, I would argue that, in terms of cost-effectiveness, a geophysical survey should be the first step in site evaluation. If that survey fails, it should then be followed up with a controlled-surface collection or shovel-test survey, whichever is appropriate.

In all of the cases presented above, excepting airborne and satellite applications, remote sensing has been used to map features within the boundaries of known sites. North American attempts to locate sites using airborne sensors have not been particularly successful. That is not be say that site discovery is not possible using remote sensing. In Great Britain, not only is geophysical prospection a regular component of site characterization, but magnetometers are routinely used to search for sites (Gaffney and Gater 2003). However, since a much larger component of the archaeological record in that country is made up of sites containing metal and bricks, that approach is more likely to be productive there. Given our current instrumentation and level of expertise, I do not believe we are at the point where site-detection surveys using geophysical techniques would be cost-effective. Taking into account the variability in ground cover and relatively subtle nature of the archaeological record, I also have doubts about the future of airborne remote sensing used alone in detecting subsurface cultural resources. However, in a recent pilot study, Haley and I used structure locations delimited on the basis of geophysical survey as training fields for a multivariate analysis of airborne imagery with a surprising degree of success (Johnson and Haley 2004). Although the results were promising, we are still a long way from taking advantage of the broad-scale coverage available through the use of airborne sensors.

For the time being, remote sensing will continue to make its major contribution in intra-site mapping. As the results I have reviewed suggest, geophysical prospection as well as large-scale data recovery programs should be a mandatory part of site evaluation. This is not an idealistic goal. The benefits in terms of cost as well as results have already been demonstrated in the archaeology of the region.

Acknowledgments

I would like to thank several people who made possible the grey literature search that was fundamental to this review. I began with a list of relevant contract archaeology reports compiled by Nicole Palmer. It was an excellent starting point. From there I went to Jackson, Mississippi, and Baton Rouge, Louisiana, in order to read the actual documents. David Abbott at the Mississippi Department of Archives and History provided essential guidance through the filing system at Archives. Rich Weinstein and David Kelley made the considerable resources of Coastal Environments, Inc., available to me, and Rich guided me through the archives in Louisiana. I even got a free lunch out of the visit. Finally, I thank Evan and Janet for asking me to contribute to this volume and giving me the opportunity to read the literature produced by some of the pioneers in the application of remote sensing to archaeology. I also appreciate their patience as editors. I've been on the other side of the process often enough to know what it is like to deal with chapter authors who have committed too much of their time to too many other projects.

16
Culture Contact along the I-69 Corridor

Protohistoric and Historic Use of the Northern Yazoo Basin, Mississippi

Ian W. Brown

Introduction

One might think that it would be relatively easy to discuss the Protohistoric (A.D. 1541–1673) and Historic aboriginal (A.D. 1674–1730) occupations of the northern Yazoo Basin. After all, this is the time when Europeans were on the scene, either indirectly or directly, so there should be ample written documentation available to chart the life and movements of the indigenous inhabitants. That indeed would be the case had the region continued to experience use on the same level as it had prior to 1541, but that did not happen. A massive depopulation occurred in the region in the late sixteenth or early seventeenth centuries, probably brought about by the onset of disease (Ramenofsky 1987:42–71). Consequently, we know less about life processes during these two centuries than for any other time in the culture chronology of northwest Mississippi. The irony of the matter is that this region experienced an intensity of occupation during the Late Mississippian period, so much so that the participants of the de Soto Entrada have left us with far more information about the lifeways of Mississippian people in the northern Yazoo Basin than elsewhere. This region should be a perfect arena for a study of culture contact, if only we could find sites that existed during this dynamic time.

Culture contact implies the coming together of two peoples of different autonomous cultural traditions (SSRC 1954:974–975). It also suggests a degree of change and continuity as the less technologically inclined society attempts to maintain stability under the influences of newly introduced items and all the cultural baggage that comes with them. This is a topic that numerous people have wrestled with in adjacent regions to the south of the study area (Brain 1979, 1988; Brain et al. 1994; Brown 1979a, 1985; Neitzel 1965, 1983). The nature and effects of culture contact are difficult to deal with ethnographically, even when live people are available, so one might suppose that archaeology would be able to contribute little to the subject. However, one advantage that archaeology does have over ethnography is that the assemblages can be stacked in time. It is true that archaeologists are limited to artifacts and their contexts, but a study of such can yield very useful information about what kinds of things changed, both materially and culturally, and what remained the same when Europeans and Indians came together.

Although the case is not particularly good for the northern Yazoo Basin for the Protohistoric and Historic aboriginal occupations, there are bits of tantalizing data available that do indeed provide some insights as to what happened there between A.D. 1541 and 1730. But before anything substantial can be said regarding the effects of culture contact, it is necessary to examine the database (Figure 16.1). We must first ask which sites are definitely Protohistoric or Historic, which probably date to these times, and which are possible candidates. Naturally, the further we move down the line of questioning, the less confident we are of being able to say anything of note. The best way of knowing that we actually do have a Historic site is to have evidence of actual Historic European objects, i.e., trade goods. The next-best way is to have sites with Colono ware, or native copies of European artifacts. Without actual European objects or imitations of such, we enter into a fuzzy zone in attempting to determine whether or not specific contexts are Historic, Protohistoric, or of the Late Mississippian period. However, there are two situations wherein an argument can be made for Protohistoric or Historic dating. First, there are the native-made artifact associations. By this I mean aboriginal artifacts that have been found in direct association with Historic European artifacts at other sites and, hence, can be used for cross-dating purposes. The other situation deals with absolute dates. As will be discussed, I believe the latter to be the weakest measure of establishing Protohistoric or Historic occupation. After discussing each of the dating categories below, I will then consider what directions might be productive as regards the study of culture-contact archaeology in the twenty-first century.

Sites with Historic European Objects

If one makes an argument that a site is Protohistoric or Historic, it seems logical to expect that there should be evidence on that site for culture contact having taken place. And there is no better evidence for contact than the presence of European materials. Better yet is to have recovered these artifacts in well-defined contexts, such as on house floors or in burials. Of course there is no way of telling whether the actual contact was direct or indirect, but if Euro-

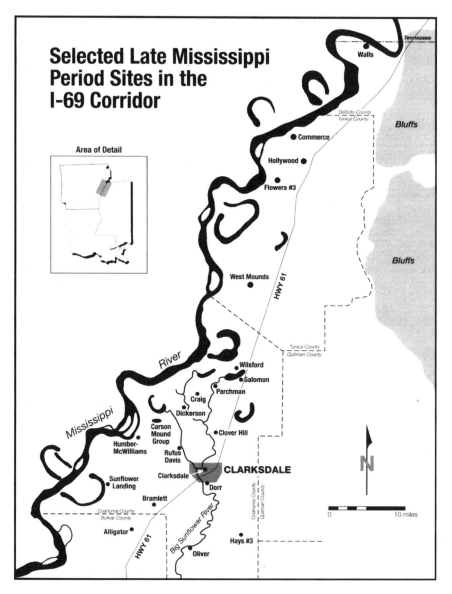

Figure 16.1. Sites in or near the I-69 Corridor that are mentioned in the text: Alligator (22BO500), Bramlett (22Co551), Carson Mound Group (22CO505/518), Clarksdale (22CO669), Clover Hill (22CO625), Commerce (22TU504), Craig (22CO566), Dickerson (22CO502), Dorr (22CO538), Flowers #3 (22TU518), Hays #3 (22CO612), Hollywood (22TU500), Humber-McWilliams (22CO601/605), Oliver (22CO503), Parchman (22CO511), Rufus Davis (22CO525), Salomon (22CO504), Sunflower Landing (22CO713), Walls (22DS500), West Mounds (22TU520), and Wilsford (22CO516).

pean objects are present we can at least say that peoples of the two autonomous cultural traditions had to have made some sort of contact, items were passed, and (perhaps) some aspect of Indian society or culture was impacted. There are only four sites in the northern Yazoo Basin that I know of which fit into this category: Oliver (22CO503), Humber-McWilliams (22CO601/605), Bramlett (22CO551) and Clover Hill (22CO625), and they will be discussed in turn.

Oliver (22CO503)

I first visited the Oliver site in September of 1977. I had just started work for the Peabody Museum at Harvard, and my initial task was to do a survey of Coahoma County, which was no small enterprise. L. B. Jones of Greenwood, who was both prime mover and patron for the Cottonlandia Museum, had been pushing for more professional work in the northern Yazoo Basin, and he came to the Peabody for help. Some years earlier Brain and his colleagues (Brain et al. 1974) had built a case for the de Soto expedition having passed through Coahoma County on its way to the Mississippi River, and they reasoned that the army visited some of the sites in which Jones was most interested (Brain et al. 1974). Being young, adventurous, and most importantly, available, I was sent by Stephen Williams and Jeffrey Brain to the northern Yazoo for a month of explorations. Half this time was to be spent surveying the bluffs around Greenwood (Brown 1978c) and the other half, which relates to the current topic, was to be devoted to Coahoma County (Brown 1978b). My objective for Coahoma County was to map and surface collect as many Late Mississippian sites as I could that had been proposed by Brain et al. (1974:255–262) as de Soto–age contenders. I was also to examine and photograph artifacts in private hands from related sites (Brown 1978d).

The Oliver site was one of the sites that I had the fortune of visiting in that hot and dusty autumn, but by the time I explored the site it was a mere shadow of what it had been a century earlier. Oliver is located on the south bank of the Big Sunflower River, about 26 km south of Clarksdale. At one time the site may have had as many as fourteen small conical mounds surrounding a large pyramidal mound (Brown 1992 [1926]:100–106, Figure 18; Peabody 1904:Plate 7), but by the time that Phillips et al. (2003 [1951]:Figures 28, 61) investigated Oliver there were only two extant mounds. Both of these mounds were still standing when I examined the site in 1977, but by that time its principal mound was only about 1.5 m tall, a far cry from the 26 ft (7.9 m) reported earlier (Phillips et al. 2003 [1951]:253–260, 322, Tables 1, 12, Figure 61).

Charles Peabody and his assistant W. C. Farabee were the first professional archaeologists to dig at Oliver (Peabody 1904) and, quite coincidentally, they were also employed by the Peabody Museum. Their excavations in 1901 and 1902 at Oliver and at the nearby Dorr site (22CO538) (Peabody 1904:23–25) were the first large-scale professional investigations in the northern Yazoo Basin. Most of their time at Oliver was spent on the western tumulus, which was dubbed the "Edwards Mound." They did dig in the smaller one, known as the "Cemetery Mound," but not to the same extent (Peabody 1904:28). As Weinstein (1985:8–11, 2004a) has already offered an excellent description of the extensive research conducted at Oliver over the past century and its many important contributions to regional archaeology, I will not repeat the information here. Rather, I will focus only on the site's Protohistoric/Historic component.

Oliver is, by far, the best Historic Indian site we have for the study area in northwest Mississippi, but even then, if one considers just how much digging has occurred at the site, it really cannot be judged a very impressive component. Its Historic collection consists of the following materials, as referenced in Peabody (1904:47–51):

Cemetery Mound

"A shell bead and a brass perforator were under a skull in the Cemetery Mound."

"A brass perforator was found with a skull in the Cemetery Mound."

Edwards Mound (arranged according to skeleton number)

Skeleton 4: "Two series of glass beads were found under the chin of Skeleton 4 (bundle burial). Position: 2′9″ down in the Edwards Mound."

Skeleton 5: "Beads of glass, a brass point and small shells were (all) found under the skull of Skeleton 5 (bundle burial). Position: 3′1″ down in the Edwards Mound."

"A brass point was found with Skeleton 5 under the skull, accompanied by glass beads and shells (a bundle burial). Position: 3′1″ down in the Edwards Mound."

Skeleton 7: "Eleven glass beads were found in a group with Skeleton 7 (bundle burial). Position: 3′4″ down in the Edwards Mound."

Skeleton 8: "A glass bead was found with Skeleton 8 (bundle burial). Position: 1′5″ down in the Edwards Mound."

Skeleton 14: "One brass bell was found with Skeleton 14, near, or in contact with the skull (a 'scissors-shaped' burial). Position: 1′2″ down in the Edwards Mound."

Skeleton 25: "One shell bead, two beads of quartz and a brass bell were found with Skeleton 25 (bundle burial and a child's skeleton). Position: 2′ down in the Edwards Mound."

"One brass bell was found under the left ear of Skeleton 25 (a bundle burial of a child). Position: 2′ down in the Edwards Mound."

Skeleton 28: "Glass beads were found under the left humerus of Skeleton 28 (a bundle burial). Position: 1′6″ down in the Edwards Mound."

Skeleton 31: "Glass beads were found with Skeleton 31 (a bundle burial). Position: 1'3" down in the Edwards Mound."

Skeleton 32: "Brass was found near the neck of Skeleton 32, the bone near it being discolored by the brass. Position: 2'3" down in the Edwards Mound."

Skeleton 137: "In addition to the beads mentioned over one hundred minute discoidal beads of turquoise were found with a child's skeleton (No. 137) in connection with the enamel of the teeth. Also a small turquoise pendant; the beads were some of them less than one-tenth of an inch in diameter, divided equally between the two sides and the perforation; the thickness was one forty-fifth of an inch or less. The pendant was half an inch long and half an inch broad, shaped like a section through a pot-shaped vase, with a round handle. The skeleton was not deeply buried and some glass beads were also found with it. The turquoise is the same as that used by the Pueblo Indians, and, as suggested by Professor Putnam, there is little doubt that it was obtained from some Pueblo Indians by trade in early white man's times."

Skeleton 151: "A long bead of brass was found inside the occiput of Skeleton 151 (a full length burial in an intrusion). Position: 1'6" down in the Edwards Mound."

Skeleton 157: "Two beads of brass were found with Skeleton 157 (a bundle burial of a child). Position: 11" down in the Edwards Mound."

Surface Collection: "Glass beads were also found on the surrounding surface near the Edwards Mound."

Peabody indicated that the greatest depth for any of the above Historic artifacts was no more than 3'4" below the surface of the Edwards Mound. Consequently, he felt that "There is no reason to believe, from the evidence of the articles found, that the lower part of the Edwards Mound was constructed or disturbed after white contact" (Peabody 1904:49). There are quite a few European items identified in the above tallies. From Peabody's report it is not possible to give a total number of the glass beads, but clearly there were many of them and they occurred in seven burial contexts (Skeletons 4, 5, 7, 8, 28, 31, and 137) as well as on the surface. They were described as follows: "The beads of glass are all globular; the smaller flattened, the larger elliptical; they are of iridescent blue color. The size varies from a diameter of $\frac{1}{10}''$ with a perforation $\frac{1}{30}''$ in diameter to $\frac{4}{10}''$ in diameter with a perforation of $\frac{1}{10}''$ in diameter" (Peabody 1904:49). Brass objects consisted of two bells (Skeletons 14 and 25), a brass point (Skeleton 5), three brass beads (151 and 157), a brass perforator (Cemetery Mound), and some unidentified brass (Skeleton 32). The bells from Oliver have had a high profile in the archaeological literature. Brain (1975:133,

Figure 1) classified these bells as the Clarksdale type, and made a strong case that they may have been distributed during the de Soto Entrada. Three additional Clarksdale bells from the region were once part of Charles W. Clark's collection. As Clark is known to have dug in the Cemetery Mound at Oliver prior to Peabody and Farabee's work, these three bells may have come from that context (Brown 1992 [1926]:358, Figure 352; Peabody 1904:27; Weinstein 2004a:3:8–9, 19–20). It is worth noting that Burial 25 in the Edwards Mound, which possessed one of the brass bells, was a bundle burial of a child. In fact, many of the interments that were made in the flanks of this mound were of children. According to Belmont (1961:147), who did a reanalysis of Peabody and Farabee's excavations as his Senior Honors Thesis at Harvard, these children may have held a somewhat special position in their society. He believed this was so because grave goods were more often associated with them than with adults.

Over the years, the Clarksdale bells from Oliver continued to be considered as solid de Soto Entrada markers by a number of archaeologists, myself included (Brain 1984:53, Figure 2; Brown 1977:76, 1979a:204; Weinstein 1985:9, 17–18), but not everyone agrees. Marvin Smith (1976:28, 34, 1977:156, 1987:43–47), for example, has insisted that their distribution occurred later than de Soto, primarily in the early seventeenth-century. Others, however, continue to be more sympathetic to a sixteenth-century attribution (Mitchem and McEwan 1988:47). Recently, John Connaway (2000) borrowed the two bells from the Peabody Museum as well as the three bells excavated by Charles Clark so that he could study them in tandem. One surprising interpretation he made is that one of the Peabody Museum specimens (Cat. No. 54370), the one that was found with Burial 25, is a Saturn-type bell. If true, this would make it part of the French trade sphere (Brown 1977:75–79, Figure 5, 1979a:202–203, 205). Having been involved in the original classificatory work, I find this hard to believe. Admittedly, I have not seen the bells since Connaway's reassessment, but from my own detailed notes and from the photograph of the bells in Brain (1975: Figure 1), there is no question in my mind that both specimens fit the Clarksdale definition.[1] An important result of Connaway's microscopic analysis of the bells was the discovery that four of the Clarksdale bells exhibit either a complete or partial fleur-de-lis impression on their surface, something that no investigator (myself included) had observed previously. He believes this mark represents a tax collector's export stamp (Connaway 2000:5), which might be true, but perhaps a more critical question with regard to culture contact is whether or not Spaniards also applied the fleur-de-lis symbol to their trade goods. Conversely, did the Spaniards ever trade French objects? Neither of these questions has been resolved as yet, but the de Soto Entrada linkage to the Oliver site certainly has weakened as a result of Connaway's research.

Connaway did some salvage excavations at Oliver in 1991, at which time forty complete or partially complete pots were recovered, as well as a number of European items. Mary E. Starr (1992) analyzed these materials and presented some interesting contextual information. One of the graves contained two individuals, one interred above the other. Two brass or copper coils were found near the head and elbow of the upper skeleton and a Nodena point occurred near its right hand. Interestingly enough, a hooded effigy bottle (probably an owl) on Bell Plain ware was also found in this grave (Starr 1992:48, 51, Figure 12; Weinstein 2004a:3:109). It is very strange for hooded vessels to last so late in time (Brown 2002), so I suspect that it may have been a curated vessel. Another grave uncovered in the 1991 excavations contained two children. There were no pottery vessels in this grave, but each skeleton did have European trade goods in association. One skeleton had four copper bracelets with it, while the other had five small glass beads that are either black or dark blue in color. Starr (1992:51, 53) concluded that these burials were of mid-seventeenth-century date, which seems reasonable.

Considering all the work that has been done at Oliver over the past century, the inventory of Historic European objects really is rather pitiful, and yet it is the best evidence that we have for culture contact having occurred in the region. Most of the items that were found, excepting perhaps the Clarksdale Bells, are more at home in a seventeenth-century context.

Humber-McWilliams (22CO601/605)

In early July of 1974, while I was working with Jeffrey Brain at the Haynes Bluff site (22WR501), our crew took some time off to visit other excavations. L. B. Jones had told Brain that he had hired a couple of archaeologists by the name of Louis Tesar and Donna Fichtner and that they were digging at a site called "Humber" in Coahoma County, so our crew headed north to see what they were finding. The site itself was singularly unimpressive to me, as I was far more accustomed to big mounds, trees, and most importantly, shade. As we ambled across what seemed to be an endless, flat, sun-baked field high in crops, I figured that we had certainly been led on a wild-goose chase. But once we stood upon the edge of a large square block and stared down into their excavations, I knew that this was a unique site. It certainly was a sight to behold, as I had never seen so many burials clustered together in one spot. Although I had no idea what any of it meant, I can still remember being suitably impressed.

Humber, or rather Humber-McWilliams, as it came to be called as a tribute to the different landowners, has long been recognized as a de Soto–period site. Considering the quantity and range of artifacts that have been found at this site over the years, the odds are extremely high that it was occupied during the mid-sixteenth century (Brain et al. 1974:261). Whether it was one of the villages the Spaniards actually visited in 1541 is another matter, because archaeology unfortunately is seldom so conclusive. Nevertheless, if we eventually do end up removing the Clarksdale bells from the Oliver site as de Soto time markers, Humber-McWilliams is the best candidate we have for yielding sixteenth-century European items. Unfortunately, the evidence is slim, as it consists of but two thin brass strips, as discussed below.

The Humber-McWilliams site is situated to the southeast of Island No. 63 of the Mississippi River, approximately 4 km due west of Farrell. Occupational debris occurs along the inside levee of an old Mississippi channel and stretches in a north-south fashion between 2.4 and 3.2 km. In other words, this is an enormous village site (Brown 1978a:14). At one time there seem to have been three large mounds at the northern extremity of the site, but these were destroyed in 1929 when a levee was built there. It was also at this time that collectors discovered Humber-McWilliams (Weinstein 2004a:3:58–60). For the next forty years, uncontrolled digging occurred over this vast stretch of land, with at least a thousand burials having been plundered—perhaps as many as two thousand. Most of the published exotic pottery vessels from "unidentified" Yazoo Basin sites probably came from Humber-McWilliams, had the various collectors been willing to provide location information (Dye and Wharey 1989; Hathcock 1976, 1983; Weinstein 2004a:3:99–100).

One of my main objectives in the 1977 survey I conducted in Coahoma County was to survey Humber-McWilliams and record the artifacts from it contained in various public and private collections. In addition to burning the midnight oil at the Carnegie Free Library in Clarksdale and the Cottonlandia Museum in Greenwood, I spent many hours photographing and measuring pots within the cramped quarters of Jimmy Humber's storage shed. I described and depicted forty-six vessels from Humber-McWilliams in my final report. I also made a sketch map of the site, conducted controlled-surface collections, and offered suggestions as to where future excavations would be most profitable (Brown 1978b:14–17, 46–59, Table 16). My research relied heavily on the field notes made by the late Glen Johnson, an amateur who kept meticulous records of his excavations. Most of Johnson's work at Humber-McWilliams was conducted to the west and northwest of the Zion Traveler Church on Gary McWilliams' property. Tesar and Fichtner's 1974 block excavation, on the other hand, was placed in the middle portion of the site, just south of the modern cemetery. As far as I could tell, the most undisturbed part of Humber-McWilliams, as of the late 1970s, was the land between the cemetery and the Humber residence to the south.

It is sad to say that, despite the obvious importance of Humber-McWilliams, the work done by Tesar and Fichtner remains the only professional excavations conducted at this site. And although there is an incredible amount of information contained within their reports of use to archaeologists (Tesar 1976; Tesar and Fichtner 1974), it should also be pointed out that their conclusions have come under severe criticism from later researchers. Their skeletal analysis, in particular, seems to be highly suspect (Mitchell 1977; Weinstein 2004a:3:70–71). Of greater interest here, in terms of the topic of culture contact, are some findings that were made by Glen Johnson and, later, reported by Jonathan Leader (1990). Two burials had three thin brass strips in association with them that constituted two artifacts. One of the strips was found with Burial 83, according to Johnson's numbering system. This grave contained three bundled burials, one of which, a subadult, had a triangular-shaped strip on its forehead. Presumably, this object was part of a headdress. There were three worn holes in the strip, and one of the holes still had the original twine within it (Leader 1990:Figure 1A). The other two brass strips came from Burial 102, a single bundle burial, and these, too, were found on the individual's forehead. The object in question is a rectangular band made out of two fragments of brass. They were attached by pushing metal tabs through chiseled slits and then bending them back to lock the pieces together. There were two holes at one end of the strip, a series of punched dots along the edges, and two sets of large embossed squares, which formed the principal decoration (Leader 1990: Figure 1B). Although the hammering techniques seem aboriginal, in that they are identical to marks on native copper artifacts from the Etowah site (9BR1) in Georgia and the Lake Jackson site (8LE1) in Florida, a metals analysis of these artifacts has revealed them to be brass. Both of the bands have copper, tin, and zinc in them, which is a three-part alloy of brass (Leader 1990:68). A sixteenth-century date is also supported by the many pottery vessels of late Mississippian vintage that were found in and around these particular burials (Weinstein 2004a:3:103–104).

Bramlett (22CO551)

The Bramlett site is located a little over .8 km west-northwest of Bobo. It is situated on the exterior levee of an old river channel called Annis Brake. Calvin Brown (1992 [1926]:106) first recorded Bramlett, and since then it has been referred to numerous times as a prime Late Mississippian site (Brain 1988: Figure 196; Brown 1978b:34–38; Phillips 1970:Figure 447; Phillips et al. 2003 [1951]:Table 1, Figures 19, 59). However, it should be stressed that this interpretation is based solely on surface collections. To my knowledge, there have never been any professional excavations at Bramlett beyond a core that Sam McGahey drilled near the edge of a field road in 1971. A 2.5 ft-(.8 m) midden deposit was observed in this core (Brown 1978b:34). Bramlett makes it into this section solely because of a "possibly sixteenth-century Spanish pendant" identified by Marvin Smith (in Morgan 1996:7, Table 1; see also Weinstein 2004a:3:133). Considering that the object is from a surface collection (I guess), it is rather flimsy evidence. On the other hand, Bramlett is certainly of the "right date" for a Protohistoric occupation with regard to its native ceramics, a point I shall return to later.

Clover Hill (22CO625)

The Clover Hill site is located between .4 and .8 km southwest of the community of this name, on the east bank of an old Mississippi River channel. It supported a small Mississippian village at one time, but it also seems to have had a relatively large mound on it. Only a remnant of that mound remains today. There are also several daub concentrations on the site indicative of former house locations. In 1973 the Mississippi Archaeological Survey (MAS) excavated the largest of the daub concentrations, the one that occurred on the eastern edge of the mound. Most of the house remains they uncovered were damaged, but the investigators did find a shallow refuse pit as well as a centrally located clay-lined hearth (Connaway 1981b:45–49, 83, Figure 7, Plates 27–30, 1982a; Weinstein 2004a:3:76).

I visited Clover Hill in the fall of 1977, but it was in very heavy cultivation at the time and I was not able to see much at all. However, in my survey report I did photograph and describe five vessels that were recovered in the MAS excavations (Connaway 1981b:Plate 30), and I also analyzed their sherd collection (Brown 1978b:24–26, 59, 61). The complete or near-complete pottery vessels associated with the house structure consisted of an Avenue Polychrome, *var. unspecified* bottle, a Bell Plain, *var. unspecified* bottle, a Bell Plain, *var. unspecified* bowl, a Mississippi Plain, *var. Neeley's Ferry* bottle and a Mississippi Plain, *var. Neeley's Ferry* jar, all consistent with a Late Mississippian occupation.

Clover Hill is significant for this chapter because of the surface discovery of a turquoise-colored glass bead of the type Itchtucknee Plain or Early Blue. It has been dated to the seventeenth century (Buchner 1996:86; Weinstein 2004a:3:130–131). Although this bead does reveal the existence of a Historic component at Clover Hill, it is doubtful that it dates the excavated structure. Three radiocarbon samples secured from this building have uncorrected dates of A.D. 1360 ± 65, 1510 ± 60, and 1525 ± 55 (Connaway 1981b:49, Appendix II; Connaway and Sims 1997:Table 2; Weinstein 2004a:3:76). John Connaway felt the latter two dates accurately date the structure, and if that is so, it could have been around when de Soto entered the region. Clover Hill certainly is an interesting site and it does deserves more work, but it requires a stretch of the imagination to expect that it will tell us much about European-Indian culture contact in the region.

Sites with Colono Ware,
Native Copies of European Artifacts

Actual European items are the best means to show that culture contact has occurred in a region, but in lieu of such materials, a close second are objects that were made in imitation of trade goods. Such objects have been referred to as Colono ware (Ewen 1991:75, 77; Ferguson 1978; Noël Hume 1962). The trouble with this category, however, is that it is not always clear that the native-manufactured objects were actually purposeful copies. For example, teapot-shaped vessels have been found on a number of Historic sites in the Lower Mississippi Valley (LMV), including Fatherland (22AD501) in the Natchez Bluffs region (Neitzel 1965:Figure 210) and Russell (22WR507) in the southern Yazoo Basin (Brain 1988:263, Figure 184b). The use of the "teapot" name to describe the form implies both function and European derivation (Holmes 1884:482, Figures 159, 160) and it has been suggested by some that the Indians who occupied these sites may have seen French settlers using teapots and simply copied the form (Quimby 1942:263). This argument falls apart, however, when it is realized that the teapot shape is also akin to bottle gourds, a form that was copied by potters long before Europeans entered the scene (Brown 2003; Phillips et al. 2003 [1951]:172–173, Table 9, Figure 113a–h). What complicates the matter is that teapot vessels have been found at Oliver (Peabody 1904:Plate 14) and other Late Mississippian sites in the northern Yazoo Basin that are also strong contenders for Protohistoric occupation. As an example, in my analysis of the vessels from the Humber-McWilliams site (22CO601/605), I counted eight vessels with the teapot form: one Avenue Polychrome, *var. Avenue,* five Bell Plain, *var. Bell,* one Mississippi Plain, *var. Neeley's Ferry,* and one Nodena Red and White, *var. Nodena* (Brown 1978b). I do believe it is extremely likely that these vessels were the products of Indians contemporary with de Soto, but I doubt very much that they copied his teapots, or even that he carried any!

The teapot serves as a prime example of why one should be very careful in attributing significance to similarities based on form, but having said this, there may be a few Colono-ware contenders at northern Yazoo Basin sites that merit mentioning, especially as the artifacts have been observed on sites that have also yielded European items. At the Oliver site, for example, a Mississippi Plain, *var. unspecified* bowl was found with a bundle burial during John Connaway's 1991 salvage excavations. Starr (1992:48, Figures 11, 16) reported it to be kettle-shaped, as it has a flat base, cylindrical sides, and perforated rim tabs like those found on European brass kettles (Weinstein 2004a:3:109). This is a much better case than teapot-shaped vessels, because not only is the form complex, but there is no comparable prehistoric prototype for the vessel. It would certainly have been nice if a trade item or two were found in association with the same burial, but that, perhaps, is too much to ask.

Another contender for Colono ware, which is not as strong, is a plate found at the Parchman site (22CO511). Parchman is an extremely important Late Mississippian site, which may also have been occupied when de Soto passed through the region (Brain et al. 1974:261). The site is located approximately 2.7 km to the southwest of Coahoma, and at one time had at least five mounds. Four additional rises have been noted that may also be mounds (Brown 1978b: 3–5). Parchman is now owned by the Archaeological Conservancy and has been under investigation by Jay Johnson of the University of Mississippi in recent years (Finger 2003a, 2003b; Weinstein 2004a:3:166). Of significance for the current discussion is a grog-tempered plate or shallow bowl found on the surface by a local collector and reported by Connaway (1985:Figure 1). Although the design of the vessel fits the Walls Engraved type description, its paste is Addis Plain, which is not "supposed" to happen in the world of archaeological sorting.[2] Another oddity is that the pot has a flared ring on its flat base. The ring has been notched, which is also atypical for the region. Although the plate form itself is not out of the ordinary prehistorically, the ring base is unusual and may represent an attempt to copy a European plate or bowl (Weinstein 2004a:3:91). Admittedly, this is a slender thread for evidence of culture contact, but the threads are at least starting to get stronger.

Sites with Native-made Artifact Associations

With this category of artifacts we are getting into even murkier waters, if that is possible. Sites with native-made artifact associations consist of objects or complexes of objects that have been found elsewhere in direct association with Historic European artifacts. Thus, if we know them to be of Protohistoric or Historic date at one site, the argument is that if they are found at other sites that lack European items, they can still be used to establish contemporaneity. This is the standard archaeological procedure of cross-dating. There are, of course, some problems with this reasoning, because often the artifacts or artifact complexes were around earlier. With that said, let us consider the possibilities, starting first with pottery.

Fatherland Incised is perhaps the best diagnostic type we have for Protohistoric or Historic occupation (Brain 1988:351–353; Brain et al. 1994; Brown 1983:3, Figure 4, 1985:64–68, Figures 35, 78–80; Neitzel 1965:Figures 19–20; Quimby 1942:263–264, Plates 13–14; Steponaitis et al. 1983:141), but admittedly the study area is far to the north of the range for this type. Consequently, we should not expect to find it with any frequency, and when it does occur it is probably indicative of trade from the Natchez region to the south.[3] It is comforting that the Oliver site (22CO503) has produced a Fatherland Incised vessel, and in good context as well. Burial 25, the same child burial that had with it one of the Clarksdale bells and two cut-quartz beads, also featured a Fatherland Incised vessel (Peabody 1904:59, Plate 14). This reinforces the Protohistoric/Historic connection (Brain 1975:133), but unfortunately, Fatherland Incised has not been found elsewhere in the study area to my knowledge. When I conducted my survey of Late Mississippian sites in Coahoma County in 1977 I saw large collections of pottery from many sites, but I never saw a single Fatherland Incised sherd. It certainly is a good marker for lateness, but if it is seldom found it is of little use.

Another marker that has been proposed for the assignment of Protohistoric dates is the Tunica pottery complex (Brain 1988:273, Figure 180). The Tunica Indians, who figured so prominently in eighteenth-century culture contact in the Yazoo Bluffs region of Mississippi and, later, in the Tunica Hills of Louisiana, are believed to have had their late prehistoric/Protohistoric roots in the northern Yazoo Basin (Brain 1979:Table 18, 1988:48–55; Brain et al. 1974:281, 283). The Yazoo 8 subset, which is the core of the Tunica pottery complex, consists of Barton Incised, *vars. Davion* and *Portland* and Owens Punctated, *var. Redwood*. These varieties were established on the basis of work that I did at Historic sites along the Yazoo Bluffs (Brown 1975, 1979b, 1983), as well as excavations undertaken by Brain (1988:196–248) at the Haynes Bluff site (22WR501). In the Yazoo Bluff region these varieties are considered good Historic markers, but in the northern Yazoo Basin Brain believes they are Protohistoric. In essence, they are thought to be ethnic identifiers for ancestral Tunica. In addition to the Yazoo 8 subset, Winterville Incised, *var. Tunica,* and the Tunica mode are also assigned to the Tunica pottery complex and are good indicators of the Parchman phase, according to Brain. He assigns the Parchman phase to Protohistoric times.

We will return to the Parchman phase shortly, but let us first look at sites where the Tunica-complex pottery has been found. Table 16.1 is a listing of some of the sites that I examined in my 1977 survey of Coahoma County. Being fresh from my doctoral experience along the Yazoo Bluffs, I was especially primed for detecting late pottery markers. Most of the sites that I went to were ones earmarked by Brain as potentially contemporary with the de Soto Entrada's appearance in the LMV. Unfortunately, my findings do not give much support for the Tunica pottery complex having been dominant. Out of a total of 12 sites that I studied that had Mississippian pottery, only two possessed Tunica pottery complex markers, the Carson Mound Group (22CO505 and 518)

Table 16.1. Representation of the Tunica pottery complex in the surface collections and private collections of twelve Mississippian-period sites in Coahoma County examined by Brown (1978b).

	var. Davion	var. Portland	var. Redwood	var. Tunica	Tunica mode	Other Mississippian-period sherds
Parchman						126
Carson Mound Group				12		418
Humber-McWilliams						162
d'Oyle						6
Larson #1						25
Oak Ridge						11
Clover Hill						3
Mullens						19
Salomon						99
Bramlett				7		284
Mattson						7
Crawford Lake						7
Total				19		1,167

and Bramlett (22CO551). Winterville Incised, *var. Tunica* is the only one of the markers that I recognized; there were a total of only 19 sherds of this variety. In contrast, I collected 1,167 Mississippian-period sherds that were not part of the complex. Although I had little luck detecting evidence for Proto-Tunicas in the northern Yazoo Basin, it should be stressed that my sample is small. Perhaps it has been recognized in greater numbers by other investigators, but if so I am unaware of these studies.

If we turn to lithic artifacts, a number of objects seem to fall within the category of native-made artifact associations. We have already seen that cut-quartz beads and turquoise beads are good candidates (see above), but as these objects have only been found at Oliver (22CO503) and Hollywood (22TU500) (Brown 1992 [1926]:191, 193), they have not yet lived up to their potential. Brain (1988:277–280, Figure 199) has defined the Oliver lithic complex as being a marker for the Historic Oliver phase in the northern Yazoo Basin. This complex consists of Nodena Lanceolate points, small snub-nosed end scrapers, triangular knives, and pipe drills. Brain believes the scrapers functioned in the deerskin trade that became dominant in the late seventeenth and early eighteenth centuries. He argues that the Quapaw or some closely related group, like the Ofo, were the manufacturers of the Oliver lithic complex. This interpretation has been questioned by Jeter (1990:149, 2002:200–201) who insists that the complex has significant time depth in the region and was also used by other groups (Weinstein 2004a:3:97–98, 165–166). Just for the record, it might be useful to mention that the Hollywood site (22TU500) in Tunica County has yielded two Nodena Lanceolate points, one each of *vars. Nodena* and *Russell*. If not Historic, we can at least say that a Protohistoric component probably exists at this site (Stallings 1994; Weinstein 2004a:3:117, 155).

Sites with Absolute Dates

We now come to the least reliable of the lot—sites with absolute dates. The problem with using absolute dates to determine whether or not a site is Historic has to do with the error factor. Although it may be cause for celebration when a date comes back from the lab as A.D. 1540 ± 50, we must remind ourselves that the double-sigma rule applies. This means that the item dated could just as easily be 1640 (Historic), 1540 (Protohistoric), 1440 (prehistoric), or anytime in between, which really does not help a great deal. Any archaeologist worth his or her salt should be able to figure out from the associated pottery that the site dates within a two hundred–year interval. However, because some folk do take great stock in the use of absolute dating, I will list here the sites that have been offered as Protohistoric/Historic contenders based on radiocarbon dates alone (cf. Feathers, this volume).

The Hays #3 site (22CO612), which is situated in Coahoma County but outside the I-69 corridor, has produced a Historic radiocarbon date. The site is either a Mississippian farmstead or a small hamlet, but what makes it very interesting is that it had at least one platform house similar to those observed at the Wilsford site (22CO516) (Connaway 1984; Connaway and McGahey 1970:9–12; Hill 1969). Raised structures such as these fit descriptions of buildings recorded in Garcilaso de la Vega's account of the de Soto expedition (Clayton et al. 1993, Vol. 2:411–412, 490–491). Leonard Blake (1986:Table 1.1) reported on corn from Mississippian contexts at Hays #3 that dated between A.D. 1000 and A.D. 1200. Another date for this site was secured from charcoal removed from the center post of the raised structure. It was reported to be A.D. 1705 ± 60 (Connaway 1981b:84; Connaway and Sims 1997:Table 2; Weinstein 2004a:3:43–44, 116, 130).

The Hollywood site (22TU500) is located in the northern portion of Tunica County along Mound Bayou, an abandoned channel of the Mississippi River. According to sketch maps drawn by Calvin Brown and Philip Phillips, a large pyramidal mound (A) about 20 ft high (6.1 m) sits in the middle of a large rectangular embankment. A smaller oval-shaped mound (B) occurs immediately to the southeast of the big mound, and between eight and fourteen low mounds once surrounded the edges of the embankment (Brown 1992 [1926]:120-122, 191, 193, Figure 24; Phillips 1970:938; Phillips et al. 2003 [1951]: Tables 1, 13, Figures 2, 20, 59; Stallings 1994:Figure 4; Weinstein 2004a:3:18, 26, 115–117).[4] Hollywood was purchased by the Mississippi Department of Archives and History in 1992 and has been the scene of several projects conducted by Jay Johnson and his University of Mississippi crews in the years since. Richard Stallings (1994) reported on the 1993 field season in which a number of absolute dates were secured. A test trench that sliced through the northern end of Mound B revealed three distinct house floors (Stallings 1994: Figures 5–6). The upper floor (house 1) had numerous maize cobs and kernels on it. A date of A.D. 1808 ± 147 was obtained on the maize, giving a one-sigma range of 1660–1955 (Stallings 1994:5). Some charcoal uncovered from midden beneath Mound B produced a date of A.D. 1420 ± 20 (Stallings 1994:6). A burial (No. 2) found in a unit to the north of Mound A had several slabs of cypress wood in it, and one of the slabs yielded a date of A.D. 1565 ± 85. It is certainly possible that Hollywood is a Protohistoric or Historic site, as Stallings believes (1994:12), but it is equally possible that its occupation is exclusively late prehistoric. The absence of European artifacts of any sort is troublesome. On the other hand, the quartz bead that was personally found by Calvin Brown (1992 [1926]:123, 191, 193) at the site is certainly suggestive of Protohistoric occupation.

The Flowers #3 site (22TU518), also located in Tunica County, is now destroyed, but it once consisted of a large village and an aboriginal cemetery. In 1974, John Connaway (1981b:50–55, Plates 31–38) opened up a 10 by 20 ft (3.0 by 6.1 m) block in the cemetery and discovered fourteen bundled individuals in ten burial pits. In the village area, which measured approximately 100 by 400 yards (90 by 365 m), portions of twenty-four house patterns were detected. Most of the buildings were of rectangular wall trench construction, but a circular wall trench structure 11 ft (3.4 m) in diameter was also detected (Connaway 1981b:Plate 31). Four dates were secured on charred material from different parts of the Flowers #3 site. The earliest date was A.D. 1380 ± 125. It came from charred cane and wood recovered from a firepit in the corner of a house. Another date of A.D. 1345 ± 90 came from charred cane found in a small pit associated with one of the houses. Charred corn removed from a wall trench belonging to another house gave a date of A.D. 1640 ± 70. And, finally, the latest date of A.D. 1705 ± 65 was associated with a burial pit (Connaway 1981b:Appendix II). In the initial report on this site, Connaway (1981b:55) felt that the rebuilding of the many houses and the vast differences in dates are indicative of a long period of occupation at Flowers #3. However, Weinstein (2004a:3:76–

78) questions the reliability of the charred cane, which produced the earliest dates, and says that a more reasonable approximation for site occupancy is A.D. 1600–1700. That may be so, but it does seem that we must have faith that the rejected dates actually deserve such a fate. Had a glass bead or two been found in association with the structures or burials, I would have far greater confidence in the seventeenth-century attribution.

The last candidate for the absolute date category is the West Mounds site (22TU520), which is also located in Tunica County (Phillips et al. 2003 [1951]: Table 12; Starr 1984:197–198). It consists of three mounds situated on a point-bar ridge on the inside of an old Mississippi River channel. This site was the focus of two Memphis State University field schools led by David Dye and Andrew Buchner in 1988 and 1989. From their work it was discovered that two of the mounds (A and B), at least, date to the Late Mississippian period. Mound A was built in two stages, while Mound B was built in one stage (Buchner 1989; Dye and Buchner 1988; Weinstein 2004a:3:98–99, 128–131). Although the investigators excavated a number of units in various parts of the site, the most interesting findings came from the top of Mound A. In particular, a burned wattle-and-daub structure was discovered on top of Stage 1. An interesting array of ceramic vessels occurred in association with this building. A total of fourteen whole or partial burned pots was recovered, including four bottles (Bell Plain, Mississippi Plain, Old Town Red, and Walls Engraved), five bowls (two of Bell Plain and one each of Anna Incised, Avenue Polychrome, and Mississippi Plain), a miniature effigy bowl (untyped), and four jars (three of Barton Incised and one a combination of Parkin Punctated and Ranch Incised) (Buchner 1996:Table 10.1, Figures 10.5, 10.7, 10.8, 10.10). The Avenue Polychrome bowl had within it pulverized, calcined mussel shells that may have been destined for use as pottery temper. Interestingly, the vessels found in association with this structure, presumably items that were used (and made?) by the elite, were rare in surface collections elsewhere on the site, plain pottery aside (Buchner 1996:84). The authors argued that the deposit of artifacts belonged to a "child's living area" because some of the vessels are miniatures and one of the associated objects is a clay doll-like human figure (Buchner 1996:81–82, Figure 10.7). There are, of course, other interpretations for why miniature vessels and "dolls" could be found in an elite context such as this. Just being small does not necessarily equate with age of the user. It should also be mentioned that an interesting collection of seven highly calcined bone pins was found on the lower building floor of Mound A. These objects occurred in association with a ferruginous sandstone abrader (Dye and Buchner 1988:73, Figure 8).

Of concern here are three radiocarbon dates secured from the West Mounds, all of which were taken on burned thatch woven out of big bluestem grass (*Andropogon gerardia*). One of the samples came from a unit on the top of Mound B (120 ± 70 B.P.), one came from the burned structure on top of Mound A's

Stage I, the structure that is described above (160 ± 50 B.P.), and one came from a stratigraphically younger structure placed on top of Mound A's Stage II (174 ± 89 B.P.) (Buchner 1996:85; Starr 1992:Table 1; Weinstein 2004a:3:130). As all three of these dates are reasonably close, the investigators are convinced that the West Mounds were in use in the latter half of the seventeenth century, possibly even into the early eighteenth century (ca. A.D. 1670–1750) (Buchner 1996:86). If one were to use dates alone, that is certainly a reasonable interpretation, but it is also appropriate to question why there should be a complete absence of European trade materials in what are presumably elite contexts, or anywhere else on the site, for that matter. Furthermore, unless there was a resurgence of Anna Incised in Historic times, one might wonder just how an Anna-phase marker (A.D. 1200–1350) from the Natchez Bluffs region bearing a Southern Cult motif, could have ended up in a late-seventeenth-century structure. But having said that, I must concede that all of the other vessels found in the structure do date to Late Mississippian times or later, so the Anna Incised bowl does require some explaining. Maybe it is a revival (Lord help us!), or perhaps it was curated. Whatever the case, I would be amazed if it actually does relate to a late-seventeenth-century occupation. And if this structure does date to this time, to what time does the structure that occurred above it date? This does not make sense to me.

In summary, the evidence for Protohistoric/Historic sites in and around the I-69 Corridor is bleak, to say the least. The site with the most clear-cut evidence for both Protohistoric and Historic occupancy is Oliver, but it took quite a bit of digging over the past century to yield that evidence. Humber-McWilliams is the next-best candidate because, like Oliver, European objects were found in direct association with skeletons. Bramlett and Clover Hill are also contenders for culture-contact sites, because each has yielded a Historic European object, though unfortunately without context. And now the evidence becomes weaker, if that is really possible. Sites that have possible to probable Colono ware include Oliver and Parchman. Sites that bear native-made artifacts found elsewhere with Historic European objects and that can be used for cross-dating include Oliver, the Carson Mound Group, Bramlett, and Hollywood. And, finally, sites with "correct" absolute dates include Hays #3, Flowers #3, and the West Mounds. Of all these sites, and there certainly are not many, the ones repeated most frequently for the various categories are Oliver, Humber-McWilliams, and Bramlett.

The Search for Quizquiz

Quizquiz has become the Holy Grail of Yazoo Basin archaeologists. When de Soto passed through the northern Yazoo Basin, little did he realize that his army's march would keep several generations of historians and anthropologists busy trying to figure out just where they went. De Soto himself did not have a clue as to where he was and, despite abundant efforts by numerous scholars over the years, we have not been able to help him much. It is recognized that the Entrada visited three Quizquiz villages before ultimately crossing the Mississippi River (Clayton et al. 1993, Vol. 1:299–300). Although there has been much studious thought devoted to where these villages were, and even more rampant and vocal speculation, we really have not made great progress in identifying them. The value of doing so is obvious. If we could establish which sites were visited, we would then be able to add "flesh to the bones." Contained in the various accounts are wonderful descriptions of what life was like in a Mississippian society that had arrived at its sociopolitical climax. Moreover, a correct identification of Quizquiz's location would provide the key for the rest of de Soto's explorations in the LMV. Once the crossing place is firmly anchored, the rest of the route has to fall into place; or that, at least, is the theory.

There are several reasons it is so difficult to determine the whereabouts of Quizquiz (Brain 1985:xxxiii–xxxvii). First, there are just too many Late Mississippian sites in the northern Yazoo Basin occupied in the sixteenth century, thus providing a cornucopia of choices. Second, many sites that were once located near the Mississippi River have either been destroyed by the actions of the river or have been ravaged by human activities. We know, for example, that some of these sites now beyond the realm of study once contained impressive pyramidal mounds, which is exactly what we would expect of Quizquiz. With these sites gone, the possibilities have been narrowed, to be sure, but we will never know if the missing sites "were the ones."

A third reason it is so difficult to pin down Quizquiz is that de Soto and his men seem to have doled out very few artifacts in their peregrinations. We know that the Entrada did distribute some objects in the southeastern U.S., or we would have very little to contribute archaeologically on the matter, but they certainly did not flood the market. And even had the Spaniards given lots of items as gifts or in exchange, there is no guarantee that the objects would have stayed close to the route. The best chance we have for discovering European artifacts distributed by early European explorers, of any nation or in any area, is to investigate burials. This is true because, in most cases, European objects were considered to be precious. In the LMV, for example, it was not unusual for such objects to end up in temples (Brown 1979c:115, 117; Swanton 1911:260, 269). The important point is that it is extremely unlikely that these items entered burial contexts soon after they were distributed. It is doubtful that they would have ended up in midden deposits, unless perhaps they were very small and were lost, like beads on a string. It is far more likely that the objects distributed by de Soto to the occupants of the Yazoo Basin were worn on their persons, perhaps for years, before entering the ground as grave goods. Consequently, there is no guarantee that the final possessors of these objects were buried at or near the place they received the objects. They may not even have been the original recipients, as in the case of the Oliver-site children who were buried with the Clarksdale bells. This is especially true considering the demographic turmoil brought about by epidemics following the Entrada. Depending upon one's stance, if one has one, it could just as easily be argued that the existence of a Spanish item on a site would infer considerable distance from the route (Ramenofsky 1990:35)! All of this is moot, of course, because we simply do not have the Spanish items in the Yazoo Basin to argue a case one way or the other. As discussed above, the Clarksdale bells at Oliver, the pendant at Bramlett, and the brass-strip headdress fragments at Humber-McWilliams are all we have in the way of Spanish objects—not a very good showing at all.

Even so, it is worthwhile to at least offer the major route possibilities given by past researchers. In the event that Spanish objects are ever found at designated sites in the future, at least some scholars will feel vindicated. The first major attempt to come to terms with de Soto's route through Mississippi was "A Symposium on the Place of Discovery of the Mississippi River by Hernando de Soto" (Rowland 1927). In that volume, Charles Barton (1927) offered a detailed topographical description of the region and concluded that the river crossing occurred in Tunica County, somewhere near Commerce Landing. In 1939, the de Soto Commission, led by John R. Swanton (1985 [1939]:227–228, 232–239), tackled the issue once more. Swanton argued that de Soto's army, after having spent the winter of 1540–41 among the ancestors of the Chickasaw, followed the Yocona River into the Yazoo Basin and into the province of Quizquiz. Contrary to Barton, Swanton (1985 [1939]:248) believed that the crossing was made at Sunflower Landing in the western part of Coahoma County.

Philip Phillips was the next scholar to tackle the Quizquiz issue. A major portion of his chapter on the "Identification of Sites from Documentary Sources" in the *Archaeological Survey in the Lower Mississippi Alluvial Valley* volume was devoted to tracking de Soto through the northern Yazoo Basin and into the state of Arkansas (Phillips et al. 2003 [1951]:348–391). After a masterful discussion of all the theories, Phillips sadly (and knowingly) ended with but a whimper. He himself favored a crossing near Commerce Landing, just below the Tennessee line, largely because of the impressive "Walls-Pecan Point"–complex sites that occur in that region, but he was wise enough to realize that the data could be argued in different ways (Phillips et al. 2003 [1951]:391).

By the early 1970s, enough archaeology had been done in the northern Yazoo Basin and in surrounding regions on both sides of the Mississippi River that the topic could be taken up again. Brain et al. (1974:235, Table 1, Figure 2) did an exhaustive study of the ceramic types and varieties believed to be of mid-sixteenth-century date and, using this information, they were able to plot the route by virtue of site clustering. It was possible to do so at this time because of major refinements that had taken place in dating pottery (Phillips 1970). The Brain et al. (1974:262–264, Figure 7) study resulted in yet another crossing for the Entrada, this time just to the south of Friars Point. This would put the Quizquiz villages somewhat farther to the south, in and around the city of Clarksdale. Prime candidates for the Quizquiz villages, according to the "Friars Point hypothesis," were the destroyed Clarksdale site (22CO669), which was thought to be the capital of the province, Rufus Davis (22CO525), and Montgomery (22CO518). The latter site is now considered part of the Carson Mound group (22CO505 and 518). The authors also felt that Dickerson (22CO502), Salomon (22CO504), Parchman (22CO511), Humber-McWilliams (22CO601/605), and Craig (22CO566) were part of the Quizquiz province (Brain et al. 1974:255–262; see also Brain 1984 and Weinstein 2004a:3:57–58).

In the 1980s, Dan and Phyllis Morse (1983:306, 308, Figure 13.2, 1996:129) and Charles Hudson (1985:3, Figure 1, 1987:6; Hudson et al. 1990:200–202) revived the Commerce Landing crossing (or points north), while Richard Weinstein (1985; Weinstein et al. 1985) resurrected the Sunflower Landing crossing. According to Weinstein, de Soto would have followed the Skuna and Yalobusha rivers from southern Chickasaw County or northern Pontotoc County. This would have brought the army a few miles northeast of Greenwood, where they would have looked down on the Yazoo Basin. The expedition would have then followed a Historic trail known as "Charley's Trace" (Atkinson 1987:68–69; Swanton 1985 [1939]:237; Weinstein 1985:15–16, Weinstein et al. 1985:7:1), which would have brought them to the general vicinity of the Oliver site (22CO503). This hypothesized route at least has the advantage of bringing the expedition to Oliver, the best Protohistoric/Historic site we have for the region. The Alligator site (22BO500) was considered to be the second Quizquiz village, while the third village was Sunflower Landing (22CO713) (Weinstein 1985:11–15, 19; Weinstein et al. 1985:6:33–57, 7:1–8). Kenneth Styer (1991) tested Weinstein's hypothesis by examining the above sites for the existence of diagnostics set forth by Brain (1988:264, 272–277, Figure 197) as mid-sixteenth-century markers. Styer reported little success in detecting such material at Alligator, Sunflower Landing, or Oliver, so concluded that these could not have been the villages of Quizquiz encountered by de Soto. Styer may indeed be right, but his reasoning is based on the premise that Brain is correct, and that may not be so. If Brain's premise is invalid, then Styer's test proves nothing. On the other hand, the Weinstein hypothesis could very well be wrong, but not for the reasons put forth by Styer (Weinstein 2004a:3:106–107).

In the late 1990s the Mississippi Department of Archives and History conducted a de Soto trail-mapping project, whose purpose was to plot the general course of the army through the state along existing roads and highways. David Morgan (1996:Appendix II) came up with a series of maps that plotted the possible routes through the northern part of the state, but he admitted that not much progress has been made in the past twenty years to either confirm or deny existing routes (Morgan 1996:8–9; Weinstein 2004a:3:132–133). We must either go back to the drawing board, or reassess the approach.

I believe that we do have to reassess the approach. Considering the quantity of sites in the northern Yazoo Basin that are contenders for Quizquiz based on their Late Mississippian–period ceramics, the only way we are going to be reasonably certain that a Quizquiz village is found is to discover confirmed Spanish artifacts (or European objects known to have been distributed by mid-sixteenth-century Spaniards) in well-defined contexts. Burials are not going to be of much help here because, as discussed earlier, European items were probably curated. In all likelihood they entered the sociopolitical system and were exchanged several times before getting into the ground. The best evidence would be to find Spanish artifacts in midden deposits, or perhaps pushed into the dirt floors of houses, because in these contexts it is more likely that the objects had a relatively short use-life, thus entering the archaeological record soon after they were distributed. This is how the de Soto winter camp of 1539–40 was identified at the Martin site (8LE853B) in Tallahassee, Florida (Ewen 1988, 1990:86–90), but the difference, of course, is that the army camped for some time at that particular location. Moreover, it was their own garbage. The odds are high that what was considered trash to the Spaniards, especially early on in the expedition's history, would have been valued much more highly by the Indians. As such, the likelihood of ever finding midden deposits containing de Soto–related materials in Yazoo Basin sites is very low; consequently, so is the probability of ever being able to come up with an argument that will convince the majority of people that Quizquiz has been located.

A Consideration of Phases

It might seem strange to have waded so far into this paper, if indeed the reader is still here, without encountering a discussion of phases. As a concept, the phase is a very powerful tool for archaeologists. It is a mechanism that brings together sites that were occupied at the same time, or at least that have contemporaneous components. In effect, phases are the prehistoric or Historic archaeological equivalent of ethnology's societies. It has long been recognized that many issues of anthropological significance really cannot be addressed unless well-defined phases are constructed. What good does it do, for example, to speak of a hierarchy of settlements unless one can be sure that they were all occupied at the same time? Similarly, conclusions about status based on mortuary behavior have far more value when it can be demonstrated that the burials under consideration are temporally equivalent. Refinements in pottery typology, especially the adoption of type-variety classification, have arguably led to more believable and useful phase definitions for the later periods of prehistory (Brain 1978a, 1978b; Phillips 1958; Wheat et al. 1958; Willey and Phillips 2001 [1958]:22–24]). The phase has become such an integral aspect of research in the LMV, largely as a result of Phillips' (1970) monumental study of the southern Yazoo Basin, that it is almost criminal to question its utility. As I have made great use of the phase in most aspects of my work over the past three decades, the reader should realize that if I come off sounding derogatory in this discussion, I am including myself as one of the targets.

A plethora of Mississippian-period phases have been set up for the northern Yazoo Basin, as well as for adjacent regions on the west side of the Mississippi River. Weinstein (2004a, 2004b) makes a valiant attempt at coming to terms with how these phases have been defined and used, especially with regard to the I-69 Corridor, but one senses an undercurrent of frustration in his writings as he wrestles with the various interpretations. The problem relates to motivating factors for either creating or changing phase terminology, because sometimes "States' Rights" seem to play more of a role than the acquisition of new data (Weinstein 2004b:4:35–36). Phases of the Mississippian period and later times mentioned most often for the northern Yazoo Basin are Commerce, Hollywood, Hushpuckena, Oliver, Parchman, and Walls. I list them alphabetically rather than chronologically or by region, because they have been juggled about to such an extent that if one wishes to know a definition, it is best first to ask "according to what author, and what year?" Weinstein (2004a, 2004b) deals with the various phases in great detail in his recent study, but it is worthwhile to present a little background here on the topic.

By virtue of his reanalysis of the Oliver site excavations, I believe that John Belmont (1961) was the first to use three of the phase names: Hushpuckena, Oliver, and Parchman. Phillips (1970:941–942) drew from Belmont's work in the Lower Yazoo Basin volume, but he was not overly happy with how the three phases stood up once neighboring regions were brought into the picture. The Parchman phase, which ended up covering the northern half of Coahoma County, the southern third of Tunica County, and the northwestern half of Quitman County (Starr 1984:165), was described by Phillips (1970:939–940) as being very similar to the Kent phase, located on the other side of the Mississippi River in Arkansas. Parchman is characterized by nearly even proportions of Bell Plain and Mississippi Plain, *var. Neeleys Ferry* and, as with the Kent phase, Barton Incised is much more common than Parkin Punctated. Parchman is different from Kent, however, in that it has far more Barton Incised, *var. Barton* than *var. Kent.* Phillips considered Walls Engraved, *var. Hull* to be a marker for the Parchman phase, and he also wrote that it was not unusual to see Owens Punctated and a scattering of "southern" ceramics such as Leland Incised on Parchman sites. Phillips was not at all content in distinguishing Hushpuckena- and Oliver-phase components, so he ended up including them as a hyphenated phase on his distribution map (Phillips 1970: Figure 447). Belmont, on the other hand, felt there were significant differences between these two phases and even suggested that the Oliver phase may represent a site-unit intrusion at the Oliver site (Belmont 1961:131–132). As a result of excavations that the LMS conducted at the Walls site (22DS500) (see Phillips et al. 2003 [1951]:243–248), Phillips believed there was a distinct possibility that the Parchman phase preceded the Walls phase in the Memphis region, but as he was not sure, he decided to leave them as phases with distinct geographical entities, with Walls to the north, Parchman to the south, and Hushpuckena-Oliver even farther south (Phillips 1970:940, Figure 447; Weinstein 2004a:3:53).

The next scholars to make an attempt to sort out the phases were Brain et al. (1974), as they tried to come to terms with de Soto's route through the Yazoo Basin. In this study, Hushpuckena and Parchman were combined in a newly hyphenated name, which they dated to Protohistoric times. They considered Oliver to be a culturally distinct Historic phase that, in line with Belmont, possibly represented an intrusion from a Quapaw-related group (Brain et al. 1974:283–284). Although Hushpuckena and Parchman were basically contemporary, there were some notable differences between the two, according to these scholars. Hushpuckena was set up on the basis of sites in the southern portion of Coahoma County, whereas Parchman was generally placed in the northern part of the county. In terms of pottery, Hushpuckena components tended to have higher amounts of Mississippi Plain, *var. Neeleys Ferry* relative to Bell Plain but, similar to the Parchman phase, Barton Incised took precedence over Parkin Punctated. Walls Engraved, *vars. Walls* and *Hull,* on the other hand, were reported to be quite rare in Hushpuckena. Painted wares had about the same level of frequency in the two phases, but Avenue Polychrome was even more typical of Hushpuckena. Also more common were Winterville Incised, *var. Winterville,* Wallace Incised, and other types found more commonly to the south.

In the Lake George site (22YZ557) report, both the Hushpuckena and Parchman phases were considered to be of Protohistoric vintage, contemporary with the Wasp Lake phase in the southern Yazoo Basin (Williams and Brain 1983:381–382, Figure 11.21), but by the late 1980s, Jeffrey Brain (1988:266–269) set up two subphases of Hushpuckena, both of which were prehistoric. That left the Parchman phase by itself in a Proto niche (Brain 1988:272–277). The Oliver phase continued to be defined as a purely Historic phase at the tail end of the sequence. In essence, Brain felt that the Parchman phase was ancestral Tunica, while the Oliver phase was Historic Quapaw (Brain 1988:277–280; Weinstein 2004a:3:93–94). The Parchman phase was said to have been characterized by the Tunica pottery complex (Brain 1988:273) but, as discussed earlier, the markers that Brain put forth really do not seem to be very common in the region. Plus, as pointed out by Weinstein (2004a:3:7), if only these particular diagnostics are considered, a great multitude of other types and varieties that could (and probably did) date to the mid-sixteenth century would not be considered Parchman-phase markers. The Wilsford site, for example, as well as most of the sites discussed by Starr (1984; Weinstein 2004a:3:Table 7), would not be included under the Parchman phase according to the criteria listed by Brain (1988:273). But if they are not Parchman, then what else could they be?

Archaeological syntheses written from the perspective of the Memphis region have offered some new insights, but unfortunately they have not clarified matters much. Gerald Smith (1990), for example, created a new Late Mississippian phase named after the Commerce site (22TU504), but it really does not seem to be all that different from earlier definitions for the Parchman phase. According to Smith, the Commerce phase includes sites in Tunica and northern Coahoma counties. Assemblages are characterized by a relatively large quantity of Mississippi Plain vs. Bell Plain, a good representation of Barton Incised, and small amounts of Parkin Punctated and Old Town Red (Smith 1990:147–151, Figure 8.9). Many of the sites listed by others as having Parchman components ended up as Commerce-phase components in Smith's study but, as Weinstein (2004a:3:102) points out, instead of the new Commerce phase "capturing" more southerly sites, one could just as easily have stretched Parchman north to include Commerce and related sites.

Charles McNutt (1996) has argued that the Commerce phase, as defined by Smith, covers too great a geographic range. McNutt set up a new phase to take its place, naming it after the Hollywood site (22TU500), which is also located in Tunica County. This newly defined phase includes the Kent-like phase sites that occur east of the Mississippi River as well as other Mississippian sites in the region that have slightly more Mississippi Plain than Bell Plain and good representations of the decorated types Barton Incised, Parkin Punctated, and Old Town Red, in order of frequency. Hollywood was set up as the type-site for this phase, and most of the sites Smith had earlier put in the Commerce phase were shifted to the Hollywood phase. McNutt continued to use the Parchman phase for sites to the south but, unlike Brain (1988), he believes it dates exclusively to prehistoric times (McNutt 1996:178–184).

Clearly, one is hard-pressed to get any two scholars to agree on just what the various phases mean. After much deliberation, Weinstein (2004b:4:35–36) did end up adopting Brain's (1988) interpretations in his recent synthesis of northern Yazoo Basin archaeology, but he admitted that "Although the current author (Weinstein) is not particularly tied to either point of view, and recognizes the very complex situation involved, he will favor Brain for now mainly because he feels that Brain's sequence is easier to understand and to follow chronologically (perhaps because it is too neat and clear-cut)." In 1978, upon completion of my survey of Coahoma County, I vented my own frustration in trying to come to terms with the identification of Late Mississippian/ Protohistoric phases in this region:

> While these phase distinctions appear to be true in an overall sense for the Mississippi period in Coahoma County, there are marked differences between sites which are clouded over if all sites are simply pigeon-holed into one or another phase. Phillips' units are useful in comparing the region to other contemporary peoples in the Lower Mississippi Valley, but they are of little use in arriving at ethnic distinctions within the Coahoma County area itself. Major differences are apparent *within* the Parchman phase, merely on the basis of surface collections made in this survey. (Brown 1978b:44)

As an example of the problem, it might be beneficial to consider four sites described in my survey for which the Mississippian pottery samples were reasonably good: Bramlett (22CO551), Carson Mound group (22CO505/518), Humber-McWilliams (22CO601/605), and Parchman (22CO511) (Table 16.2). In the case of Bramlett, the collection that I studied had been surface-collected by Burt Jaeger, a resident of Clarksdale (Brown 1978b:Table 12). Dr. Van Burnham, another local collector, is responsible for the Carson Mound group collection that I examined. He retrieved most of his material on and around Mound A (Brown 1978b:Table 3). The Humber-McWilliams material was gathered by me in nine different parts of the site (Brown 1978b:Table 4, Figure 4), while the Parchman material was collected in five discrete locations (Brown 1978b:Table 1, Figure 2). All of these sites have evidence for multiple occupations, but as the focus here is on the latest phases, only the pottery markers that relate to the Mississippian period are listed in Table 16.2.

Although decorated types are far more useful than plain pottery as phase markers, it is worth considering the latter, if only to ascertain the strength of the collections. Recorded in Table 16.3 are the numbers and percentages of decorated versus undecorated sherds at the four sites under consideration. It can easily be seen that there is a major difference between the ratios of decorated to undecorated sherds for the collections I made, when compared to those made by the two local collectors. Whereas Humber-McWilliams and Parchman yielded 88.3 percent and 73.8 percent of undecorated sherds respec-

Table 16.2. Representation of Mississippian-period pottery types and varieties in the surface collections and private collections at four Mississippian-period sites in Coahoma County that were examined by Brown (1978b).

	Bramlett	Carson Mound A	Humber-McWilliams	Parchman	Total
Decorated Pottery Types/Varieties					
Anna Incised, *var. unspecified*				1	1
Avenue Polychrome, *var. Avenue*	2	3			5
Barton Incised, *var. Barton*	29	99		16	144
Barton Incised, *var. Arcola*	3	2			5
Barton Incised, *var. Togo*	2	8		1	11
Barton Incised, *var. unspecified*		7			7
Carter Engraved, *var. Carter*		1			1
Grace Brushed, *var. Grace*				1	1
Hollyknowe Ridge Pinched, *var. Hollyknowe*		1			1
Hollywood White, *var. Hollywood*			2	1	3
Leland Incised, *var. Leland*	3	1			4
Leland Incised, *var. Blanchard*	1	2			3
Leland Incised, *var. Williams*	2				2
Mound Place Incised, *var. Mound Place*				1	1
Nodena Red and White, *var. Nodena*	16	2		2	20
Old Town Red, *var. Old Town*	2		4	1	7
Old Town Red, *var. Beaverdam*	43	9	6	3	61
Old Town Red, *var. St. Pierre*			1		1
Owens Punctated, *var. Owens*		6			6
Owens Puntated, *var. Menard*	4	1			5
Owens Punctated, *var. Widow Creek*	2	7			9

Owens Punctated, *var. unspecified*	6	8	1		15
Parkin Punctated, *var. Parkin*	4	19	4		27
Pouncey-Pinched, *var. Pouncey*		3		2	5
Wallace Incised, *var. Wallace*	2				2
Walls Engraved, *var. Hull*		9		3	12
Winterville Incised, *var. Winterville*	35	4	1		40
Winterville Incised, *var. Belzoni*	24				24
Winterville Incised, *var. Blum*	1	1			2
Winterville Incised, *var. Tunica*	7	12			19
Winterville Incised, *var. unspecified*				1	1
Unclassified Incised on Mississippi Plain, *var. Neeley's Ferry*	2	4			6
Subtotal	190	209	19	33	451
Undecorated Pottery Types/Varieties					
Addis Plain, *var. Greenville*			2		2
Addis Plain, *var. unspecified*			2		2
Bell Plain, *var. Bell*	14	46	3	9	72
Bell Plain, *var. unspecified*			10	8	18
Mississippi Plain, *var. Neeley's Ferry*	87	43	126	75	331
Mississippi Plain, *var. unspecified*				1	1
Subtotal	101	89	143	93	426
Total	291	298	162	126	877

Table 16.3. Comparison of the numbers and percentages of decorated and undecorated pottery at four Mississippian-period sites in Coahoma County that were examined by Brown (1978b).

	Bramlett	Carson Mound A	Humber-McWilliams	Parchman
Decorated Pottery Types/Varieties				
No. Sherds	190	209	19	33
Percentage	65.30%	70.10%	11.70%	26.20%
Undecorated Pottery Types/Varieties				
No. Sherds	101	89	143	93
Percentage	34.70%	29.90%	88.30%	73.80%
Total Sherds	291	298	162	126

tively, these percentages were much reduced at Bramlett (34.7 percent) and Carson Mound A (29.9 percent). What this suggests is that whereas I adopted a democratic principle and picked up every piece of pottery I saw lying on the ground, Mr. Jaeger and Dr. Van Burnham had far more discriminating tastes. Their strategy makes sense, however, because they returned to the sites on numerous occasions and decided (whether consciously or not) that decorated sherds were far more interesting than plain ones. I cannot blame them for this, but it does gum up the works if we are to base percentages on total counts.

Although I do believe there may be some utility in comparing decorated versus undecorated or Mississippi Plain versus Bell Plain at Humber-McWilliams and Parchman, for the reasons discussed above I doubt this will be a useful exercise for comparative studies that include Bramlett or Carson Mound A. It is for this reason that Table 16.4 lists only the decorated pottery collected at the four sites. Percentages for each site are calculated on the basis of decorated totals alone. Rafferty (this volume) uses a similar approach in seriating decorated assemblages. Presumably this approach will have a better chance of producing results that may have some validity. In Table 16.4 the pottery types and varieties are arranged alphabetically so that the percentage of each type/variety can be examined from site to site. These same numbers are rearranged by site in Table 16.5, with the most common type/variety listed first and the least common last.

Before looking at how these four sites stand up to established phase definitions, a summation is in order. It can be seen that Old Town Red, *var. Beaverdam*, is the most typical decorated type/variety at both Bramlett (22.63 per-

Table 16.4. Percentages of decorated pottery types and varieties at four Mississippian-period sites in Coahoma County examined by Brown (1978b).

	Bramlett	Carson Mound A	Humber-McWilliams	Parchman
Decorated Pottery Types/Varieties (%)				
Anna Incised, *var. unspecified*				3.03
Avenue Polychrome, *var. Avenue*	1.05	1.44		
Barton Incised, *var. Barton*	15.26	47.37		48.48
Barton Incised, *var. Arcola*	1.58	0.96		
Barton Incised, *var. Togo*	1.05	3.83		3.03
Barton Incised, *var. unspecified*		3.35		
Carter Engraved, *var. Carter*		0.48		
Grace Brushed, *var. Grace*				3.03
Hollyknowe Ridge Pinched, *var. Hollyknowe*		0.48		
Hollywood White, *var. Hollywood*			10.53	3.03
Leland Incised, *var. Leland*	1.58	0.48		
Leland Incised, *var. Blanchard*	0.53	0.96		
Leland Incised, *var. Williams*	1.05			
Mound Place Incised, *var. Mound Place*				3.03
Nodena Red and White, *var. Nodena*	8.42	0.96		6.06
Old Town Red, *var. Old Town*	1.05		21.05	3.03
Old Town Red, *var. Beaverdam*	22.63	4.31	31.58	9.09
Old Town Red, *var. St. Pierre*			5.26	
Owens Punctated, *var. Owens*		2.87		
Owens Punctated, *var. Menard*	2.11	0.48		
Owens Puncated, *var. Widow Creek*	1.05	3.35		
Owens Punctated, *var. unspecified*	3.16	3.83	5.26	
Parkin Punctated, *var. Parkin*	2.11	9.09	21.05	
Pouncey Pinched, *var. Pouncey*		1.44		6.06
Wallace Incised, *var. Wallace*	1.05			
Walls Engraved, *var. Hull*		4.31		9.09
Winterville Incised, *var. Winterville*	18.42	1.91	5.26	
Winterville Incised, *var. Belzoni*	12.63			
Winterville Incised, *var. Blum*	0.53	0.48		

Continued on the next page

Table 16.4. *Continued*

	Bramlett	Carson Mound A	Humber-McWilliams	Parchman
Winterville Incised, *var. Tunica*	3.68	5.74		
Winterville Incised, *var. unspecified*				3.03
Unclassified Incised on Mississippi Plain, *var. Neeley's Ferry*	1.05	1.91		
Total Decorated Sherds	190	209	19	33

cent) and Humber-McWilliams (31.58 percent). At Carson Mound A and Parchman, on the other hand, *Beaverdam* is only minimally represented. The most common decorated type/variety at these two sites is Barton Incised, *var. Barton,* which has an extremely high representation at both Carson Mound A (47.37 percent) and Parchman (48.48 percent). These percentages are amazingly close, but there is no consistency with regard to what comes next at the four sites in terms of frequency. At Bramlett the Winterville Incised type and its varieties have a good showing, with *var. Winterville* (18.42 precent), *var. Belzoni* (12.63 precent) and *var. Tunica* (3.68 precent) constituting more than one-third of the decorated sample. Little can be said of Humber-McWilliams, as the decorated sample is small, but Old Town Red, *var. Old Town* (21.05 precent), Parkin Punctated, *var. Parkin* (21.05 percent) and Hollywood White, *var. Hollywood* (10.53 precent) seem to be more than minimally represented. At Carson Mound A, Parkin Punctated, *var. Parkin* (9.09 percent) is a distant second to Barton Incised, *var. Barton,* whereas at the Parchman site Old Town Red, *var. Beaverdam* (9.09%) and Walls Engraved, *var. Hull* (9.09 precent) are tied for second place.

All of the sites clearly have a little bit of this and a little bit of that, so one is hard-pressed to make convincing groupings, but on the basis of the major markers the closest ties are between Bramlett and Humber-McWilliams on the one hand, and Carson Mound A and Parchman on the other. The irony is that all four sites are often grouped together, as on the Parchman phase map in Brain (1988:Figure 196). According to Phillips (1970:939–940), both Parchman and Carson are mentioned as being prime Parchman-phase markers. Although Bramlett was not discussed in the text, it was recorded on the Mississippian-period map as having a Hushpuckena-Oliver–phase component (Phillips 1970: Figure 447). Humber-McWilliams did not enter the synthesis, because not much was known about it at the time. As mentioned earlier, Phillips believed that Parchman-phase components had nearly even proportions of Bell Plain

Table 16.5. Decorated pottery types/varieties in descending order at four Mississippian-period sites in Coahoma County examined by Brown (1978b).

Bramlett	%
Old Town Red, *var. Beaverdam*	22.63
Winterville Incised, *var. Winterville*	18.42
Barton Incised, *var. Barton*	15.26
Winterville Incised, *var. Belzoni*	12.63
Nodena Red and White, *var. Nodena*	8.42
Winterville Incised, *var. Tunica*	3.68
Owens Punctated, *var. unspecified*	3.16
Owens Punctated, *var. Menard*	2.11
Parkin Punctated, *var. Parkin*	2.11
Barton Incised, *var. Arcola*	1.58
Leland Incised, *var. Leland*	1.58
Avenue Polychrome, *var. Avenue*	1.05
Barton Incised, *var. Togo*	1.05
Leland Incised, *var. Williams*	1.05
Old Town Red, *var. Old Town*	1.05
Owens Punctated, *var. Widow Creek*	1.05
Wallace Incised, *var. Wallace*	1.05
Leland Incised, *var. Blanchard*	0.53
Winterville Incised, *var. Blum*	0.53
Carson Mound A	
Barton Incised, *var. Barton*	47.37
Parkin Punctated, *var. Parkin*	9.09
Winterville Incised, *var. Tunica*	5.74
Walls Engraved, *var. Hull*	4.31
Old Town Red, *var. Beaverdam*	4.31
Barton Incised, *var. Togo*	3.83
Owens Punctated, *var. unspecified*	3.83
Owens Punctated, *var. Widow Creek*	3.35
Barton Incised, *var. unspecified*	3.35
Owens Punctated, *var. Owens*	2.87
Winterville Incised, *var. Winterville*	1.91
Avenue Polychrome, *var. Avenue*	1.44
Pouncey Pinched, *var. Pouncey*	1.44
Barton Incised, *var. Arcola*	0.96
Leland Incised, *var. Blanchard*	0.96
Nodena Red and White, *var. Nodena*	0.96
Carter Engraved, *var. Carter*	0.48
Hollyknowe Ridge Pinched, *var. Hollyknowe*	0.48

Continued on the next page

Table 16.5. *Continued*

Leland Incised, *var. Leland*	0.48
Owens Punctated, *var. Menard*	0.48
Winterville Incised, *var. Blum*	0.48
Humber-McWilliams	
Old Town Red, *var. Beaverdam*	31.58
Old Town Red, *var. Old Town*	21.05
Parkin Punctated, *var. Parkin*	21.05
Hollywood White, *var. Hollywood*	10.53
Old Town Red, *var. St. Pierre*	5.26
Owens Punctated, *var. unspecified*	5.26
Winterville Incised, *var. Winterville*	5.26
Parchman	
Barton Incised, *var. Barton*	48.48
Old Town Red, *var. Beaverdam*	9.09
Walls Engraved, *var. Hull*	9.09
Nodena Red and White, *var. Nodena*	6.06
Pouncey Pinched, *var. Pouncey*	6.06
Anna Incised, *var. unspecified*	3.03
Barton Incised, *var. Togo*	3.03
Grace Brushed, *var. Grace*	3.03
Hollywood White, *var. Hollywood*	3.03
Mound Place Incised, *var. Mound Place*	3.03
Old Town Red, *var. Old Town*	3.03
Winterville Incised, *var. unspecified*	3.03

and Mississippi Plain, *var. Neeleys Ferry.* This may be the case for burial contexts at Parchman-phase sites, but if we consider just the surface collections from the four sites I have presented, Mississippi Plain vastly outnumbers Bell Plain, whether these are considered Parchman phase or whatever. At Parchman and Humber-McWilliams, the two sites I personally collected, the Mississippi Plain to Bell Plain ratio is almost 5:1 and 10:1, respectively. Phillips also said that Barton Incised is much more common than Parkin Punctated in the Parchman phase, as compared to the Kent phase, its closest relative. That certainly is the case for all of the sites considered here, except for Humber-McWilliams, which curiously lacks Barton Incised altogether, at least in my surface collection.

Phillips also said that Barton Incised, *var. Barton* is more common than *var. Kent* in the Parchman phase, which fits the three sites here that have Barton Incised on them. None of them produced *var. Kent.* Phillips considered Walls Engraved, *var. Hull* to be a marker for the Parchman phase, but of the four sites discussed here, only Carson Mound A and Parchman have this variety, and it is indeed represented well. Finally, Phillips wrote that Owens Punctated and a scattering of "southern" ceramics such as Leland Incised occur on Parchman sites, and that is true of all but the Parchman site in the collections considered here.

I could continue by comparing each of the four sites listed in Tables 16.2–16.5 with other authors' phase definitions, but I think the point has been made. Some things surely fit, as some sites have the same basic percentages, at least for the major diagnostics, but there are always enough differences to raise doubts as to phase designation. There is too much background noise, if you will, and that should cause us to question whether or not any groupings make sense. The problem is that we rely very heavily on pottery in the fashioning of phases, which is certainly logical, because we have so much of it. Moreover, it has long been recognized that pottery is the best means we have for dividing the time sequence (at least for the latest stages of prehistory), so to ignore it would be ludicrous. Controlling for time and space is the prime advantage of pottery typology, but there always seems to be a monkey wrench thrown in that messes up the gears, and in this case the wrench is ethnicity. As we go about our work, most of us are very careful to offer the appropriate caveats about equating specific type/varieties with discrete groups, whether they are prehistoric or Historic. We either know or suspect that a Taensa, an Avoyel, a Koroa, or even a Tunica Indian was perfectly capable of making Fatherland Incised pots (Brain 1988:280–281; Jeter 1990:148, 2002:210; Kidder 1988; S. Williams 1967:9), and yet we more often than not attribute such pots to Natchez Indians (see above). To what, then, do we attribute the high incidence of Barton Incised, *var. Barton* on Carson Mound A and Parchman, as compared to the high incidence of Old Town Red, *var. Beaverdam* at Bramlett and Humber-McWilliams? Is it because the people of these sites represent two different ethnic groups, or did the groupings come about because two different times are represented? If the latter, is this a reasonable amount of change to have occurred in several decades, or is it more likely that pottery resulted from a couple or perhaps several Mississippian occupations at the same site? Unfortunately, there is absolutely no assurance that the materials from Bramlett, Carson Mound A, Humber-McWilliams, and Parchman that I have discussed here actually date to the same time, or were even dropped by the same people, and yet I have dealt with them as such. In our many valiant attempts to clarify the stream of prehistory by setting up phases, it is possible that we are making the waters even muddier. This is a depressing admission for someone who has done more than his share of slopping around in the mud, but who is now questioning whether or not high ground will ever be reached by this approach.

Conclusions and Recommendations

Depressing though it may sound, I have come to the conclusion that culture-contact archaeology does not have much of a future in the northern Yazoo Basin. I may be wrong in this prediction, but it is based on an analysis of a century of investigations that have failed to produce much of post–A.D. 1541 date. The real research value of the region rests in the Terminal Mississippian period, or rather the fifty or so years leading up to de Soto. Admittedly, we do not know which sites are Quizquiz, and perhaps will never know, but in lieu of that we have a pretty good understanding of which sites were occupied in the early sixteenth century. We also know that these people were living in the manner that is so richly detailed in the various de Soto accounts. That way of life, and most of the people, came to an abrupt end in the mid- to late sixteenth century. So drastic was the demise that we are forced to grasp at straws to come up with Protohistoric or Historic contenders. Although clearly traumatic for the people of that region, the almost total depopulation is distinctly advantageous for archaeologists who wish to study a Mississippian society at its climax. For that subject I would certainly go to the northern Yazoo Basin, because the abundant sites that were part of this society were affected only minimally afterward by Protohistoric or Historic occupation. I would not go to the northern Yazoo Basin with a prime interest being culture-contact studies, however. For that one needs survivors, and although there were some, there certainly were not many. Students of Historic Indians would be wise to go west or south in search of them.

Although I am pessimistic (cynical?) as to the future of culture-contact studies in the northern Yazoo Basin, I would be extremely surprised if Protohistoric or Historic period sites do not come to light every so often in the years ahead. They are out there, to be sure, but they are true "needles in haystacks," and their ethnic attributions will no doubt continue to be a focus of debate. In all probability, I will be involved in trying to figure out whether they represent Tunica, Quapaw, Ofo, or Koroa; but having said that, I do hope that the direction of research changes somewhat. We already have enough clues in the existing data as to what some of the research directions might be. From burials we have observed situations at Humber-McWilliams (22CO601/605) and Oliver (22CO503) that are extremely intriguing. The thin strips of brass found at Humber-McWilliams are interesting primarily because of where they are found. Their occurrence on the foreheads of skeletons is suggestive of headdresses, but how might such a use have affected the people of Humber-McWilliams? Was this something new added to the culture, or did the brass simply substitute for similar metals that existed earlier, like native copper? I suspect that the latter was the case and, if so, this particular introduction probably had little impact on the people. But what about the Oliver finds? Here we see a strong emphasis in placing grave goods with child burials, including rare and presumably precious Historic European and Southwest Indian objects. If these items really were valuable to the Indians, we must question why children were the recipients. Moreover, how come a hooded vessel, which seems oddly out of place in a Historic context, was found in association with these same children? Surely the burial remains at Oliver are an expression of sociocultural change for these people. Their children were dying, as were their hopes and their future. How the remnants of Yazoo Basin denizens came to terms with the collapse of their way of life is reflected in their mortuary patterns, but unfortunately we are only receiving snippets of such; we need to know more.

On another matter, if we are going to really gain an appreciation of the Late Mississippian period and its phases in the northern Yazoo Basin, we need far more fieldwork. I second Starr's (1984:202–203) call for more intensive survey, combined with detailed mapping of sites. Even though many sites have been destroyed, there is still much that can be learned from studying the landscapes of those that have survived. We have seen from excavations conducted at Clover Hill (22CO625) and the West Mounds (22TU520) that there is a wealth of information contained on the floors of structures, whether they relate to simple households, chiefs' houses, or temples. Midden excavations can certainly provide us with chronological information, but it is far more convincing to establish that artifacts are contemporaneous when they are found in sealed contexts with structures. The five pottery vessels of identifiable types/varieties found at Clover Hill were discovered sitting on the floor of a burned structure. There can be no argument that these pots were in use at the same time. Some of them may, of course, have been curated, but at the time the structure burned they formed a snapshot of the occupants' material repertoire. Both Clover Hill and the West Mounds have provided us with contemporaneous assemblages of this sort. The West Mounds excavations also serve to remind us that the pottery used on the summits of mounds is often very different from that which was used below. We perhaps know that intuitively, but we often tend to forget the importance of such when we gather pottery from a site to use for phase definitions. The Wilsford site (22CO516) has provided us with unusual platform houses that have made us question our understanding of Mississippian construction techniques, and I am certain that sites like Parchman (22CO511) and Hollywood (22TU500), both of which are under current investigation, will continue to surprise us as large areas are opened up.

Hopefully, the reader should recognize that I am not really saying anything new or particularly astonishing here. I am merely making a plea that large-scale excavations become the norm, not the exception. Archaeology is already at a disadvantage because of the passage of time, the lack of preservation, and the absence of people who can talk with us. But what we do have that other disciplines lack are the imprints that people made both on and in the ground. Unfortunately, sometimes we are so fearful of destroying (which is, of course, what we do every time we put a trowel in the ground) that we are very hesitant to move beyond the testing of a site. Archaeology is so time-consuming and so expensive that few projects have the resources to do more than test a site in a season or two. I am as guilty as the rest in this, but I have slowly come to the realization that if archaeology is really going to make significant contributions to understanding the past, we need to shift our strategy and open up large exposures. This is the only way we are going to be able to comprehend what the imprints might mean.

Notes

1. In my original paper on bells (Brown 1971:22–24, 50, Figure 12b), I referred to these specimens as the Oliver variety of Class C bells (lapped-edge construction, after Jelks 1966:87–89, Figure 42g). Brain (1975) changed the variety name to Clarksdale but, considering that all the northern Yazoo Basin bells appear to have come from the Oliver site, there has been a call from some scholars to revert to the Oliver name in order to recognize it as the type-site (Weinstein et al. 1985:7:3–4). I understand the reasoning, but I have no qualms with the Clarksdale name. It is a very nice city, after all.

2. Having said that, I should note that an unusual vessel with a Walls Engraved decoration and a Southern Cult motif also occurred on Addis Plain ware at the Anna site (22AD500) (Brown 1997:Figure 7). An analogous situation is the Anna Incised plate found at the West Mounds (22TU520); it too has a Southern Cult motif.

3. See Walthall (1992) for a comparable situation in the Illinois Country.

4. Brown referred to the site as the Bowdre Mounds but Charles Barton (1927: 85–86) called it the DeBe Voise Mounds after a former owner.

17

Sad Song in the Delta

The Potential for Historical Archaeology in the I-69 Corridor

Amy L. Young

Introduction

The Mississippi Delta has historically been, and continues to be, one of the most tormented regions in the South. John Emmerich, former editor and publisher of the *Greenwood Commonwealth,* noted in 1991 in a *Time* magazine article that the Delta has "the highest rate of everything bad, like teen pregnancy, and the lowest rate of everything good, like income" (Sidey 1991). In the 1960s, from Memphis to Vicksburg, this area was one of the deadliest battlegrounds in the Civil Rights movement, and one of the poorest and blackest parts of this country. Blacks who had not left Delta cotton plantations to migrate to Northern cities suffered horrible poverty and, in some cases, near-starvation. When Robert F. Kennedy visited the Delta in 1967, he expressed (cited in Sidey 1991) his shock at the living conditions there, saying, "My God, I didn't know this kind of thing existed. How can a country like this allow it?"

The poverty and harsh segregation that Kennedy witnessed were preceded by the oppression associated with the rise of King Cotton in the Delta. This chapter considers the historical archaeology that has been accomplished in the region, or more accurately, the near-lack of historical archaeology in the Delta, but most significantly, the potential that historical archaeology in this area has to address some critically important questions similar to the one asked by Bobby Kennedy: "How *could* a country like this allow it?" I am interested in examining the historical processes that led up to the characterization of the Delta today as having the most of everything bad and the least of everything good. In this, I unabashedly view the culture of the Delta in the Historic period as a consequence of blackness and so tend to emphasize African-American sites. But blackness is meaningless without whiteness, and so I do not advocate ignoring white sites. In fact, to fully understand the black experience, because it took place largely in the context of white hegemony we absolutely must examine planter homes, white-owned mercantile establishments, and towns where both whites and blacks lived, albeit in segregation, for most of the Historic period. Furthermore, since two cities just outside the Mississippi Delta, Memphis and Jackson, tended to dominate the area economically and politically, historical archaeologists must be aware of the important archaeological work conducted there. I think historical archaeology in the Delta, as well as in Jackson and Memphis, has a tremendous potential to help us understand the historical processes of the Delta.

A Brief Historical Sketch

The Delta was Indian territory until the 1830s; therefore, the archaeological material considered "Historic" for this region dates predominantly from after this period. European explorers visited the region earlier, though the precise locations of their stops and the nature of their interactions with Indian groups remain largely speculative (Brown, this volume). Therefore, prior to the Delta opening for European/American settlement in the 1820s and 1830s, it is much more fruitful, I think, for archaeologists working on the Protohistoric period to focus predominantly on the European impact on aboriginal societies.

For most of the Historic period between circa 1830 and circa 1960, the Delta was largely agricultural and focused primarily on cotton production driven by black labor. There is a common misperception that during the antebellum era, the Delta was the social capital of the Old South, a place of gracefully columned Greek Revival mansions and simpering Scarlett O'Hara–like belles in crinolines. In reality, as historian and novelist Shelby Foote (Sidey 1991) noted, those so-called mansions were not well furnished, and the Delta isn't really the Old South. A quick look at census data at 20-year intervals reveals population trends. It was not until *after* 1880 that the total population (black and white) topped 200,000 people and cotton plantations began to grow rapidly.

Antebellum plantations, though present in the Delta, were quite rare until the end of slavery times. One reason the Delta, with its incredibly rich soils, was slow to develop agriculturally is that it was Indian territory. Secondly, the region to the south, known as the Natchez District, also with incredibly rich soils suitable for cotton agriculture, had been settled since the mid-1700s and was ready for cotton plantations when the viable and hardy strains needed in this part of the South were finally developed in the 1830s (Scarborough 1973). It was only after the soils in the Natchez District were becoming exhausted and the district was already largely under cultivation that planters there began to expand into the Delta. Some Delta planters, however, came in from other states, especially Kentucky. For example, Brutus Clay, a planter who resided at his Bourbon County plantation of Auvergne in the heart of the Bluegrass, also had a plantation in Bolivar County, Mississippi, called Isole (Young and

Wolfe 1998). Others came from the Natchez District, shifting their properties north to the Delta. Stephen Duncan, who owned Saragossa Plantation just outside Natchez, also owned plantations in Issaquena County, Mississippi, in the southern part of the Delta. He began to shift his plantations slowly north in the 1830s (Brazy 1998). Maps showing the distribution of slave populations in Hilliard's (1984) *Atlas of Antebellum Southern Agriculture* illustrate the slow expansion of cotton production in the Delta. In 1820 there are virtually no slaves shown in the Delta. In 1830 there is some encroachment up the Yazoo River. The 1840 and 1850 maps show a scattering, but significant slave populations do not really appear in the Delta until 1860. Planters brought their slaves to the wilderness of the Delta to cut forests, uproot stumps, and plant cotton. Possibly because slaves outnumbered planters dozens to one and planters took steps to crush rebellion before it started, or perhaps because the labor of transforming the forests and swamps was so physically demanding, slaves across the South feared being sold "down the river" to Mississippi (Young 1997; Young et al. 2000).

The Civil War ended slavery, but the region remained cotton plantation country. Sharecropping replaced slavery as the next Delta institution. This form of exploitation is considered by some to be almost as severe as slavery. Blacks struggled as sharecroppers in a sociopolitical system that continued to terrorize, marginalize, and disenfranchise them. It was in this context that the Delta emerged after the Civil War as a major cotton region. By 1930, it was the South's principal plantation area and had the largest black population in the entire South (Aiken 1990:224). Also by this time, the typical experience was black sharecropper families living in shacks dispersed across Delta cotton fields (Aiken 1990; Hudson 1982; Vance 1935). Woodman (1997) suggests that many former slaves between 1880 and the 1930s were attempting to climb the agricultural ladder to farm ownership, but often at the expense of better incomes. The racialized agricultural system in the Southeast offered essentially two choices for most former slaves: working as croppers/wage laborers under close supervision of plantation owners that might yield more income; or tenancy/ownership of small farms, often with inferior land but avoiding close supervision. This latter option often meant that former slaves began the climb up the agricultural ladder without tools, work animals, or capital to invest in fertilizer or larger plots of land. Typically, the small plots of land they could afford could not support a family, so many had to have non-farm work or work as croppers to supplement income from their own farm. Modernization under these circumstances would have been quite difficult.

In the 1930s, as the Delta's black population approached its peak, the rural South began to be transformed through modernization in farming. The black population began to decline as farms were increasingly mechanized and reorganized, and blacks were forced to migrate to find jobs. In some instances, black sharecroppers and laborers were literally forced out of their homes by planters who no longer needed their labor.

Between 1940 and 1980, the Delta underwent another transformation, from a predominantly black rural population to a predominantly "municipal" population in 1980 (Aiken 1990:224–225). In 1930, 91 percent of the black population in the Delta was rural (Aiken 1990). But in 1980, 77 percent of the black population in the Delta was "municipal" and only 23 percent rural (Aiken 1987, 1990).

In sum, the history of the Delta can be divided into three distinct periods, the third of which encompassed the Civil Rights movement. First is the antebellum plantation period, dating from ca. 1830 until 1865 and characterized by cotton production and an arguably brutal slave system, meant to keep the black majority from staging revolts. The second period is characterized by cotton production and sharecropping, desperate poverty, and oppression that too often escalated to terrorism by white supremist groups like the Ku Klux Klan. This second period began just after the Civil War and ended with the peak in black population in the Delta about 1940. The third period, from 1940 to the present, is marked by the rise of municipalities, towns, and small cities, where most of the population, both black and white, had come to live. Oppression, poverty, and terrorist activities such as lynching continued and even escalated in this third period (McMillen 1989). Additionally, during this period, African Americans continued to migrate to Northern cities in huge numbers and drastically altered the demographics of the Delta. Within each of these periods, there are socially relevant questions that historical archaeology can address.

Historical Archaeology

Before moving to these specific questions and examining how archaeology can provide the data to address them, however, I want to spend a bit of time discussing the nature of historical archaeology itself, since there seem to be some misperceptions about the practice and the role of this important field within American archaeology in general and Mississippi archaeology specifically. The most common question I get, as an archaeologist primarily engaged in the investigation of the modern era (specifically on the late eighteenth through twentieth centuries), is why, when there are so many documents available, should we spend time and money when we already basically know everything? Shouldn't we focus our efforts on preserving the more fragile, older sites rather than waste time and money on resources that are not only abundant, but accessible through other means? The answer is simple, yet not so. Historical archaeology is not history, but anthropology. As anthropologists, we all know that the documents historians of this period use tend to portray the ideal rather than the real. Or, if some sort of social reality is portrayed, say in a personal diary, we have some difficulty making generalizations, but must also remember that for much of this period, from about 1780 until 1960, not everyone was leaving documents for us to read and not everyone was literate. Additionally, even with splendid documents that might apply to a single site, it is rare to find just the type of information we might be most interested in exploring—for example, information related to foodways. We may have period cookbooks, but not everyone had access to these, and certainly nobody uses all or even most of the recipes in any given cookbook. Another example might help make this point. We have some Sanborn maps of Jackson that provide important information, but for the most part, structures are not labeled. Can we look at a map and determine that in 1904 this lot was (or was not) an urban farmstead, and conclusively identify what the buildings were used for and what activities typically took place on the lot around the turn of the last century? Of course not. This does not mean that documents are not useful. Historical archaeologists make extensive use of documents in much the same way as historians. But we are not historians, and our questions tend to be different from our able colleagues in history.

Many outside of historical archaeology have a great deal of difficulty justifying the expenditure of time and money on very late sites. The failure to assign site numbers to sites dating after 1900 in Mississippi reflects this attitude. I have bitterly complained about this backwardness. However, I now understand that it is my job to help clarify the need for more consideration of relatively recent sites. Since the historical sites in the Delta date primarily between 1840 and the present, I will let the remainder of this presentation serve not only to outline some of the research questions we might address, but also to clarify what late sites can teach us.

Historical archaeology is not history. But it does fit comfortably within Americanist archaeology, which is predominantly prehistoric. Like their counterparts in prehistoric archaeology, historical archaeologists tend to focus on three broad questions: culture history, lifeways, and culture change (Young et al. 1997).

Culture history in historical archaeology tends to focus on identifying the particular occupants and events that occurred at any single site. Through using multiple lines of evidence, documentary, architectural, and archaeological, most studies in historical archaeology are able to satisfactorily address this important goal in modern archaeology. Often this type of historical archaeology is referred to as particularistic, as it is highly descriptive and tends to focus very little on comparisons with other sites or on placing a given site within a regional context. An excellent example of this type of historical archaeology is Charles Faulkner's study of the Weaver Pottery site in Tennessee (Faulkner 1981, 1982). Thorough historical documentary research, coupled with meticulous archaeological excavations, allowed Faulkner to reconstruct the Weaver pottery complex in great detail. However, many sites must be investigated before regional comparisons are possible. Thus, archaeology at most Historic sites in the Delta must take a particularistic approach and emphasize the reconstruction of culture history before we are in much of a position to address lifeways and culture change at a regional level.

Historical archaeologists also focus on reconstructing lifeways through studies that focus on foodways, architecture, or trade patterns. For example, Robert Genheimer (2000) examined trade interactions in a Kentucky city through examination of the origins of manufactured goods deposited in that Southern setting. He found that most manufactured goods had originated in the North rather than in the South. Larry McKee's studies of plantation housing (McKee 1992) and plantation foodways (McKee 1999) can serve as models for reconstructing lifeways. In a similar vein, my studies of slave housing at Saragossa Plantation in Natchez (Young 1999) and of risk management strategies in slave communities (Young 1997; Young et al. 2000) are additional examples of reconstructing past lifeways that can serve as models for historical archaeology in the Delta. These studies focus on how individuals and communities perceived and coped with dangers in their lives. One of the more surprising aspects of the archaeology of slavery and plantations is that it has revealed that some level of literacy is represented in the remains recovered around slave houses across the South (Young 2003a, 2003b).

Most studies (though they are few in the South) that focus on culture change have tended to take up modernization as the theoretical orientation (Orser 1996). Seminal among these studies is that of rural modernization in the Aiken Plateau of South Carolina (Cabak et al. 1999). This investigation highlighted how households from the eighteenth into the twentieth centuries gradually transformed from producers to consumers as rural families became increasingly accustomed to purchasing the latest and most popular mass-produced goods. As households became predominantly consumer-oriented, the architecture and household-level technology in rural settings remained static. New dwelling styles were adopted only by a minority of upper-wealth groups. Interestingly, macro-level structural change (in trash disposal, electrification, and telephone systems, for example) did not transpire until the 1950s in rural areas. This study should stand as an exemplar for historical archaeological investigations in the Delta.

Limited studies of culture change in Mississippi do exist. For example, work at Peachwood in Wayne County (Young 2000, 2002a; Young and Wright 2001) examined the transition from slavery to freedom on a modest slaveholding turned tenant farm in the Pine Hills of Mississippi. Testing at two African-American midwives' homes in the Pine Hills (Young 2002b) examined modernization in yards and midwife practices in the region. Additionally, I have begun to investigate the strategies adopted by African Americans after freedom in the many different types of communities established after the Civil War (Young 2004). Finally, archaeology at The Oaks, in Jackson (Young 2005), looks at the transition from urban farmstead to modern urban yard at a white middle-class houselot.

Historical archaeology in the Delta must also focus on addressing the three basic goals of archaeology. As in prehistoric archaeology, we must examine cultural processes at a regional level. Therefore, we must concentrate first on basic culture history and small-scale lifeways studies before we can begin to understand modernization processes that characterized the entire Delta and resulted in this area being viewed as having the most of everything bad and the least of everything good.

The Three Historic Periods in the Delta

Antebellum Cotton Plantations, 1830–1865

Between 1810 and 1830, the white population in Mississippi had increased from 38,925 to 70,443, and the black slave population had risen from 17,371 to 65,659. By 1836, the slave population had ballooned to 164,383. Many of the slaves were concentrated in the Natchez District, comprised of Warren, Claiborne, Jefferson, Adams, and Wilkinson counties. This period marked the beginning of the spread of plantations into the Mississippi Delta. Not all of the growth of plantations in the Delta came from the Natchez District, however. Mississippi continued throughout the antebellum period to rely on the importation of slaves from the Upper South.

The Delta is associated with the most brutal form of slavery. Since there was such an overwhelming majority of slaves to planters, Miller (1993) suggested that the fear of uprising and rebellion led planters to institute a particularly rigid and harsh system that would keep slaves in their places. Another equally compelling reason that slaves all across the South viewed the idea of being "sold south" with such fear is that the labor itself was more brutal than the regime of the planters and overseers.

The Delta during most of the antebellum period was a wilderness of swamps, sloughs, and forests—a frontier. As such, it presented a formidable challenge facing planters, and most especially their slaves. The slaves were faced with carving plantations from forests. This entailed cutting trees, grubbing out and burning stumps and underbrush, and rolling logs. William B. Beverly, a Virginia planter who moved to the Alabama frontier, reported that establishing a plantation in the wilderness required hard work that was not generally suitable to most slave women and children (Miller 1993:159). While the condition of the land and the size of the work force were factors, it has been estimated that an efficient slave man could, at best, clear approximately one-eighth acre per day, requiring about four months to clear 12 acres, sufficient for one man to cultivate (Miller 1993:158). Rather than occurring continuously all year long, such clearing on developing cotton plantations tended to be focused on the out-of-crop months of the planting cycle—roughly between early January and early March (Miller 1993:159).

With an emphasis on clearing land, Delta planters may have delayed planting at each agricultural cycle until the last possible moment, compressing the crop year and thus intensifying labor demands in the field, as was common on other frontier cotton planters in Mississippi and Alabama (Miller 1993:162). Prior to planting each year, typically two or three weeks beginning in mid-February were spent in clearing and fence building, but on a new plantation this activity would last four or five weeks. With such a late start in the season, planters and overseers had to push slaves quite hard in order to finish picking before rainy winters damaged the crop. Until enough land was cleared to employ all hands profitably, slaves were probably made to clear land at any slack time of the year (Miller 1993:162).

In the process of transforming forests and swamps to fields and making their plantations profitable, Delta planters likely made heavy labor demands on their slaves. Working days were lengthened. Normal lull times in the yearly planting cycle typically associated with mature cotton plantations were filled with the hard labor of clearing. For slaves newly arrived from tobacco plantations and grain fields of the Upper South, as many slaves in the Delta undoubtedly were, such heavy demands for labor must have been difficult both physically and psychologically. These slaves, however, were not totally without recourse. They could and did resist. According to Miller (1993:163), frontier planters "faced the problem of extracting prodigious amounts of labor from unwilling and unruly slaves while not completely demoralizing their hands or endangering their own precarious position atop the social order." Such slaves recently torn from their families and old work routines in the Upper South, no doubt, found few incentives to be obedient, faithful, and hard-working for their new masters. However, unless the strangers assembled at emerging Delta plantations quickly formed community bonds, resistance would have been quite difficult (Young 1997; Young et al. 2000).

Most cotton planters favored the gang system of organizing their slave labor (Miller 1993:163–164). On frontier plantations, such gangs tended to be small (Davis 1994). Nevertheless, slaves and planters struggled over the plantation labor system. Newly arrived slaves accustomed to different work routines on tobacco plantations and diversified farms were forced to adjust to new daily and seasonal work cycles. In addition to the heavy work required to clear forests, they had to learn new skills that the production of cotton required.

Excavations at slave quarters at a variety of plantations in the Delta can provide important information to help answer the question of why slaves feared being sold "down the river." Was it the brutal labor or the punishment meted out by overseers and planters? Animal bone from slave quarters can be used to ascertain the degree of hunting/fishing/gathering that slaves did to supplement rations, with the expectation that slaves driven hard in gang labor would have had little time to produce their own food (Klippel 2001). Another clue would be to focus excavations in areas around slave houses to detect how much activity might have taken place in yards. Were the slave quarters primarily places for sleeping? Or were they places to feed, nurture, and care for the slave family?

If whipping and other forms of physical punishment were prevalent in the Delta, it might be expected that this area would have a high frequency of items that we today consider to be charms for warding off evil. Such items have been identified on a variety of plantations in the Upper South (Young 1997), but not so much in the Lower Mississippi Valley. My excavations at Saragossa and Mount Locust revealed little that could be construed as items used to protect the individual and family.

Where there were slaves, there were also planters and/or overseers. Therefore, plantation studies in the Delta (and elsewhere) must also examine planter and overseer residences. These provide significant comparisons with basic material conditions and allow for a better reconstruction of past lifeways, as well as a full understanding of the culture history at that particular site. Also, it must be remembered that plantations were often complex landscapes that included a variety of activity areas and buildings such as cotton gins, blacksmith shops, barns, sheds, landing sites for loading cotton, and plantation stores, as well as fields for penning animals and areas for fowl and small livestock. Whenever possible, all such crucial components of antebellum plantations deserve thorough archaeological examinations. We are nowhere near approaching a good understanding of the complete organization of any type (e.g., cotton, rice, tobacco, large, small, wealthy, middling) of plantation in any region, including the Delta. We have access to Southern agricultural journals that describe the ideal, but not necessarily the real, conditions experienced by all occupants of the plantation landscape.

Because plantation records do exist, it may be possible to examine any differences from slave-quarter populations moved up from the Natchez District and those plantations associated with westward expansion from the Upper South. For example, Stephen Duncan's slaves from the Natchez District may have been quite accustomed to working in gangs raising cotton. They may have had the experience of carving a cotton plantation out of the wilderness there. The experience of slaves from the Upper South would have been quite different and not associated with cotton production. However, many plantations need to be examined before we can reliably distinguish differences in the material culture in these two rather distinct groups.

Postbellum Sharecropping and Singin' the Blues, 1865–1940

One of the most turbulent eras in the American South occurred between Emancipation and the 1930s (Foner 1988; Litwack 1979; Magdol 1977; Powdermaker 1993). During this period, newly freed African Americans were learning to navigate the unfamiliar and often treacherous terrain of freedom (Kolchin 1992; Litwack 1979; Magdol 1977; McMillen 1989; Orser 1988). Activities involved in mapping this terrain included assessing a variety of economic opportunities (sharecropping, timber industry, establishing small farms), avoiding attacks from terrorist vigilante groups like the Ku Klux Klan, fighting the extremely repressive black-code laws that attempted to return blacks to a virtual state of servitude, and searching for family members sold away during slavery (Katz-Fishman and Scott 2002; McMillen 1989). Many experts agree that Reconstruction largely failed to provide former slaves with real freedom and equality (Kolchin 1992:292; Magdol 1977), and the Freedman's Bureau actually facilitated, largely unwittingly, the restoration of power to former planters (Litwack 1979). As one former slave from South Carolina expressed in a WPA narrative, "The Master he says we are all free, but it don't mean we is white. And it don't mean we is equal" (cited in Litwack 1979:224). Blacks in the Delta were plagued by terrorist activities from secret societies while trying to live in an economic and political environment that seems almost impossible to cope with. It was this environment in the Delta that gave birth to the Blues.

Neil McMillen (1989) noted that lynchings in Mississippi between 1889 and 1945 were all too common. The heaviest concentrations are found in the Delta. The number of reported lynchings in Washington, Bolivar, Sunflower, Leflore, Coahoma, Quitman, and Tunica counties was particularly high.

Having few skills other than growing cotton and facing a multitude of terrors, many newly emancipated slaves and families continued to work for their former owners in the new system. One thing that tended to change was that sharecropper's cabins were dispersed in the cotton fields rather than nucleated near the planter's house.

Freedom for former slaves was fraught with danger and unfortunately presented few economic and very limited political opportunities. Documents, oral traditions, and WPA narratives are replete with information concerning the risks that African Americans faced during this period. Two major concerns emerge from these data. First, economic conditions were an important factor to newly freed slaves in the South. Second, secret societies terrorized Southern blacks. Both of these factors influenced newly emancipated African Americans to remain at the place of enslavement, living in much the same material conditions as suffered under slavery. The documents, oral traditions, and WPA narratives, however, provide few details about the specific material and economic conditions that African Americans also faced. Intensive excavations have the potential to provide this information and to help us piece together a more complete and accurate picture of how African Americans adapted to the risky and racist environment of freedom. Just as in slavery, conditions varied greatly from place to place, but no doubt there are overarching social structures and customs that influenced individual decisions. These overarching structures can only be identified and analyzed with data from many archaeological and historical investigations of sharecropper sites. The use of risk-management theory can allow us to focus on the many and complex factors that influenced the life choices of newly emancipated African Americans.

Former slaves faced a number of formidable challenges upon Emancipation. With white Southerners again in control soon after the Civil War, the African-American population must have felt there was going to be little substantial change from slavery times. The widely held belief of whites that former slaves should remain in their place at the bottom of the social, political, and economic hierarchy must also have contributed to the decisions of former slaves. With little or no financial resources and few market skills, the prospect of setting off with a family alone must have been daunting. Leaving the home where you were born and bred, where your family has roots, must also have been a challenge. Many families also faced the difficulty of finding members who years before had been sold away. Perhaps the first impulse for dispersed family members was to head for the old home place.

For a variety of reasons, many former slaves chose to continue to live where they had been previously enslaved. One study I conducted at Peachwood (Young and Wright 2001; Young 2000, 2002a, 2004) outside of State Line, Mississippi, suggests that this condition was temporary. Some remained a few years, some perhaps several decades, but eventually most set out on their own. What became clear in the analysis of the archaeological remains recovered during site testing was that material conditions had likely deteriorated during the postbellum occupation. There was little evidence of repairs or remodeling of the houses in which the black laborers lived. Few new ceramics entered the archaeological record. In economic terms, the conditions appear quite bad. The unchanging or deteriorating material and economic conditions at Peachwood after freedom may have contributed to the decisions of former slaves to leave. The reasons for staying and the reasons for going were complex, but rational decisions were taken to cope with the many dangers they faced after freedom. More than anything, Emancipation must have meant uncertainty for newly freed slaves. As Felix Haywood, a former slave from Texas, put it (cited in Rawick 1977), "We knowed freedom was on us, but we didn't know what was to come with it."

Diachronic studies of sharecropper houses will allow for a detailed examination of the material conditions experienced during this difficult period in the Delta. As during slavery, however, blacks individually and collectively developed strategies for coping with the brutality they experienced. This period was one of great transition as newly emancipated slaves began to explore the uncertain terrain of freedom.

The investigation of black sharecropper sites constitutes only one aspect of life in the Delta between 1865 and 1940. White planters continued to dominate the social and political development of the region, and their dwellings also deserve archaeological investigations. So, too, do ordinary farms owned by blacks and whites in the Delta in this period. In actuality, with a near-lack of archaeological investigations, such aspects as foodways, literacy, the rise of a consumer economy in the U.S., and community development remain largely unexplored.

Outmigration, Urbanization, and Civil Rights, 1940 to Present

The period after 1940 in the Delta was also one of dynamic changes characterized by the redistribution of the black and white populations. According to geographer Charles Aiken (1990), the black population that, during slavery and sharecropping times, had been dispersed across the agricultural landscape became nucleated in several types of places: black hamlets, the margins of municipalities that refused to annex black residential areas, and municipalities with predominantly black populations. The last kind of settlement was actually the result of white outmigration.

These settlements often led to an increase in segregation, a phenomenon that continues today. The movement of blacks from farms and plantations to nucleated settlements in the Delta was in response to both "push" and "pull" factors. Push factors encompassed imposition of federal acreage controls on crops and modernization of cotton production (especially mechanical harvesters and eventually herbicides for weed control) (Aiken 1990).

The municipalities of the Delta developed within an agrarian, central-place hierarchy as centers for retail and wholesale businesses and agricultural processing facilities that served a plantation economy and society (Aiken 1990). They were planned as segregated, biracial settlements, as blacks were needed as laborers in cotton gins, cotton-oil mills, cotton compresses and warehouses, and sawmills. Also, blacks were servants in white households, even in less affluent white households.

The black residential area was actually a territory to which blacks were confined by economic, social, and political constraints. Most of the dwellings were cheaply constructed and owned by whites. The infrastructure was minimal. There were typically no water and sewer lines, and frequently not even electrical power lines, years after electricity had come to the municipalities of the Delta (Aiken 1990).

Hortense Powdermaker (1993) and John Dollard (1937) each studied segregation and race relations in Indianola in the 1920s and 1930s. Both noted stark contrasts between conditions in the white and black residential areas. The boundaries between black and white were clearly marked. The black neighborhood, noted Powdermaker (1993), was essentially comprised of a few substantial houses among many shacks. This phenomenon begs archaeological investigation. How did the residents in black and white sections of these towns manage to cope with the material realities of their lives? While we can paint a picture in broad strokes based on historical documents and ethnographic studies like Powdermaker's and Dollard's, we do not know the details. As in archaeological studies of slave cabins, with discoveries of previously unknown sub-floor pit cellars and evidence of literacy that seem to be quite common, we may find ourselves quite surprised at what is discovered archaeologically from contexts that date to the period between 1940 and the present. This is the period that many feel does not deserve our attention. This is extraordinarily sad, since it was precisely in these contexts that the Civil Rights movement swept through the Delta. I think it is absolutely imperative that we commence archaeological studies on these very late sites, while we still have access to oral histories and standing structures that can all combine to form a synergistic base for research.

Excavations conducted at a site in the community of Turkey Creek (Young 2006, 2004) are an example of this type of research. Turkey Creek was a small, rural black community established just after the Civil War. However, it was soon associated with processes of industrialization and urbanization. Between 1870 and 1900, most families were small farmers. But after the turn of the century, most residents worked in naval stores, in the timber industry, for the railroad, or for a local creosote plant. Excavations at a single houselot dating from about 1900 to the 1970s illustrate a transition from an economy based on family-level production to one based on the family as a unit for consumption. The material record clearly illustrates the heavy dependence on mass-produced goods, while the documentary record shows that the residents all became laborers in local industry. As in the study by Cabak et al. (1999), Turkey

Creek residents were quick to adopt mass-produced goods and become families of consumers rather than producers, but slow to adopt new forms of architecture in the construction of their dwellings.

Previous Archaeological Studies: What We Already Know

Unfortunately, Historic sites in the area of the Delta, like other regions in Mississippi, have received little attention. In this respect, the entire state is woefully behind other states in terms of the number of major historical archaeology projects. In essence, only two sites have received more than passing attention from archaeologists: Mound Bayou and Doro Plantation.

Mound Bayou—Planned Community of Racial Uplift

Historical Sketch of Mound Bayou

Norman Crockett (1979:xii–xiii) indicates that between 1865 and 1915 at least sixty black towns were founded in America. Little is known about many of these communities, like Blackdom, New Mexico, or Hobson City, Alabama, except that they were part of a movement to create, through self-segregation, communities of residents who wanted to determine their own political and economic destiny. An example of this type of community is Mound Bayou in Bolivar County in the heart of the Delta.

Mound Bayou was established in 1887 by former slaves from the Davis Bend plantations near Vicksburg, owned by Joseph and Jefferson Davis. The most prominent of these early Mound Bayouans was Isaiah T. Montgomery, considered to be the primary force behind the founding of this famous all-black town (Hermann 1981; Hamilton 1991). Montgomery and his cousin from Davis Bend, Benjamin Green, established Mound Bayou to be a haven and self-sufficient black community in the midst of the white-controlled cotton kingdom of the Delta (Hermann 1979, 1981). The early pioneers wanted to create a refuge for blacks in the heart of plantation country. In the words of modern residents, "Mound Bayou was a place where a black man could run FOR sheriff instead of FROM the sheriff."

Isaiah T. Montgomery was born in slavery on May 21, 1847, to Ben and Mary Montgomery (Hamilton 1991). Ben Montgomery was one of Joseph Davis' favored slaves. Benjamin Montgomery had been sold "down the river" from his Loudon County, Virginia, home to Natchez, Mississippi, in 1836, where he was purchased by Joseph Davis (Hermann 1979:20). He learned special skills including farm management, reading, and writing, and managed to accumulate wealth (Hermann 1979:20–21). His son Isaiah Montgomery served as Joseph Davis' personal slave and secretary until Davis fled from the Union Army in

1862. He, too, learned special skills as a slave from a white tutor whom his enslaved father had hired (Hermann 1979:23).

After the war, Ben Montgomery purchased the Davis Bend plantations that had been owned by the Davis brothers (Hermann 1979, 1981). In other words, he owned the plantations where he and his family had been held in captivity. Because of financial setbacks, however, he lost the property in 1881. His son, Isaiah Montgomery, spent his life trying to bring his family back to their former state of wealth and comfort. Mound Bayou was one of the results of these efforts (Hermann 1979, 1981).

Benjamin Green also was born a slave in 1857 on the Davis Bend plantations. In 1886 he lived with his aunt, Mrs. Benjamin Montgomery (Isaiah's mother), and learned the mercantile business. Benjamin Green became the Montgomery's mercantile manager at Davis Bend.

Montgomery and Green convinced many other former slaves from the Davis Bend plantations to join them in their new settlement of Mound Bayou. They also attracted other black settlers as well. Modern Mound Bayou residents feel that the success of the early colony is a clear demonstration of the potential and abilities of peoples who had been held in slavery. Therefore, modern Mound Bayouans are not ashamed of their roots in slavery. Rather, they are proud of the accomplishments of their ancestors as former slaves.

Mound Bayou was developed as part of the extension of railroads into the Deep South, placed on the Louisville, New Orleans, and Texas line (Hermann 1979:309; Hamilton 1991:43). The Delta during the 1880s was still largely uninhabited and an untamed wilderness (Hermann 1979:311; Saikku 2005). Even in the twentieth century, there remained vast tracts of undeveloped land. "Poisonous snakes, wolves, panthers, and bears endangered adventurers ... and settlers" of Mound Bayou (Hamilton 1991:44). The earliest pioneers of Mound Bayou faced the tremendous challenge of carving a town and community out of the wilderness with little or no economic resources.

According to Hamilton (1991:50–51), the experiences of early colonist Simon Gaiter seem to typify those of the early settlers. Gaiter arrived in 1887 with $175. His family did not join him until the following year. Gaiter purchased a 40-acre tract, cleared a small part, and with the timber built a small log house for his family. After the down-payment of $40, the purchase of supplies, and the cost of transporting his family and possessions to Mound Bayou, Gaiter was left with only $10, not enough to make it through the first year. Gaiter's wife and children cleared five acres of the town for $4 per acre and picked cotton for $.50 per hundredweight on nearby white-owned plantations. Gaiter himself cut firewood for $6 per cord. Gaiter supplemented his family's diet with hunting and fishing, but recalled many weeks without meat.

In the 1890s and in the first years of the twentieth century, the population of the town and surrounding black colony grew (Hamilton 1991:53). Isaiah Montgomery, Benjamin Green, and other colonists not only spent time and energy on their own family pursuits, establishing businesses and farms, but also continued to contact people of means around the nation to invest in Mound Bayou, with the ultimate goal of making the town self-sufficient. In 1891, there were about 500 residents of the colony, living in the town and surrounding countryside. In 1893 there were 182 living in the town proper. By 1900, the town was home to 287 residents, with an additional 1,500 living in the surrounding hinterlands on farms (Hamilton 1991:53). Analysis of the 1900 United States Census for Mound Bayou shows 65 households in the town. Also, nearly 90 percent of the population could read. This is a very high percentage for any 1900 Mississippi town, black or white. It is apparent that Mound Bayouans placed a high priority on education, even in the early years of the colony, as pioneers struggled with conquering the wilderness and establishing farms and businesses. The 1900 census shows that there were two blacksmiths in Mound Bayou, as well as two general contractors, three ministers, three carpenters, a postmaster, a stenographer, a wheelwright, a barber, two teachers, one lawyer, and one physician.

Within the first three years of establishment, a school was begun in one of the rooms of Isaiah Montgomery's home. According to Hermann (1979:312), the pupils were only those whose families could afford to spare them from working in cotton fields.

In the first years of the twentieth century, a prominent black businessman, Charles Banks, arrived in the community and founded the Bank of Mound Bayou (Jackson 2000). By 1910, the pioneers of Mound Bayou had succeeded in transforming the little community into a thriving town of 500 people, with many more in the hinterlands. In 1912, Mound Bayou had a population of nearly 1,000, with another 8,000 in the periphery, and was the largest all-black town in the United States (Jackson 2000:272). There were numerous grocery and dry goods stores, several restaurants, a brick factory, a cotton oil mill, two gins, three schools, six churches, a train station, a telephone exchange, and a weekly newspaper. To residents of Mound Bayou today, the period between about 1900 and 1920 represents the peak of the development of the town. By this time, it appeared that the dream of Isaiah Montgomery and the other early settlers had been realized (Hermann 1981).

Today, Mound Bayouans understand that their unique history has also given them a unique perspective. Mound Bayou has always had black officials like mayors, sheriffs, school board members, aldermen, and police, and so residents have not had potentially threatening contact with their white counterparts. They recognize that the everyday oppression felt by many black Mississippians was not the norm for Mound Bayouans. Mound Bayou was a refuge from the terrorist activities. Nevertheless, they also feel that they have never been completely shielded from the harsh outside world.

Mound Bayouans feel that they have a special story to tell and that their town holds a special place in local, state, and national history. They believe that their town and the accomplishments of former slaves can be a source of pride for many black Americans, and they want to educate the larger American public about their history. They also strongly feel that their youth need to be better educated about their own history and culture, but because of encroaching economic conditions, this is becoming more and more difficult. Because Mound Bayouans do not want the dream of the early settlers to fade, a public archaeology project was designed to engage the youth, and investigate a site associated with the peak of Mound Bayou history. The project was entitled, "Digging for the Dream: Archaeology at Mound Bayou."

Archaeology at Mound Bayou

Archaeological testing was designed to investigate two important symbols of the progress and potential of the early town: the ca. 1904 Bank of Mound Bayou and the original lot of the ca. 1920 town hall and mayor's office. Historians had documented at least some of the numerous activities that took place in the bank building, a two-story brick structure that is being restored today. The first floor contained the bank, but the second story held other offices, including the offices of the Mound Bayou Oil Mill, the most prominent industry in the town, as well as a physician's office. The building also served as the headquarters of the Knights and Daughters of Tabor, a black fraternal organization. Charles Banks, who built the bank, was a significant lieutenant of Booker T. Washington (Jackson 2000); he organized the Mississippi Negro Business League as a chapter of Washington's national organization. The bank building occupies nearly the entire lot on which it stands, but the lot immediately behind was empty for nearly 20 years. That lot eventually became the site of the first town hall and mayor's office. That building was constructed by Benjamin A. Green, son of pioneer founder Benjamin Green and first child born in Mound Bayou. Benjamin A. Green served as mayor of Mound Bayou from 1920 until 1970. Green, a lawyer, housed his extensive law library in the building and is reported to have tutored white law students there. The original town hall was finally torn down in the late 1970s after a devastating fire, by which time the new town hall had been constructed. The first town hall, however, served other purposes after the new town hall was built.

Five 1 x 1 meter units were excavated in the lot in 10-cm arbitrary levels, unless cultural strata were observed. Archaeological data concerning five episodes of site use were recovered. First, the oldest cultural layer was composed of a thinly scattered stratum probably associated with trash from the bank building. The sample was quite small, unfortunately, but contained amethyst glass, a few broken dishes, and some soft-drink-bottle glass, some of which came from the local bottling company. No identifiable medicine bottles associated with the physician's office were recovered.

The next episode identified in the archaeological deposits was the construction of the first city hall. Artifacts and features confirm that this took place around 1920. The construction materials, which were the most abundant artifacts recovered, consisted of concrete block fragments used in the foundation, asbestos shingles used as siding, and, from firm evidence, material indicating that the building was plumbed and wired for electricity when it was originally constructed. One of the most telling features was the iron pipe that, with artifacts included in the builders' trench, dated the feature to around 1920.

The third episode, in the form of thinly scattered debris across the rear yard units, documents the use of the building. Unfortunately, the sample was quite small. The yard appears to have been kept quite clean during the years between 1920 and ca 1970.

Fourth, there was abundant evidence of the next use of the building—in the 1970s, before it burned and was razed. The building had been reused as a juke joint, as attested to by the second-most common artifacts recovered: beer cans and bottles.

The last episode visible in the archaeological record was the destruction of the building, in the form of architectural debris. Abundant nails, window glass, asbestos siding, and concrete block fragments formed a thick layer over the parts of the lot we investigated.

Interpretations at Mound Bayou

Archaeological testing in Mound Bayou illustrates how Mound Bayouans, during the peak of their town development, sought to present themselves to the public and to each other. A modern, concrete-block, asbestos-clad structure, plumbed and electrified, symbolized how citizens viewed themselves and their future. They saw themselves not as a small country village, but as a progressive, rising urban center where black residents could determine their own economic and political destiny. In some ways, the two-room town hall with rear shed addition resembles a dwelling that would have been perceived as comfortably middle-class and up-to-date, with modern conveniences. This contrasts with descriptions of farmhouses used at the time of the construction. Milburn Crowe, Mound Bayou resident and the moving force behind the restoration of the Bank and the preservation of town history and heritage, describes his early childhood home as a simple wooden structure with no indoor plumbing or electricity, and considers it typical for the period. When most folks in and around Mound Bayou were living in such modest vernacular structures, they built a thoroughly modern town hall with all the amenities. The town hall would also have served as a symbol of an attainable goal for comfortable housing in Mound Bayou.

Ideally, work on domestic sites in Mound Bayou would allow for an understanding of whether the model presented by the town hall was followed. Houses in the town proper, as well as in the surrounding hinterlands, need to be tested and compared to the town hall excavations. Moreover, work on domestic sites within the town boundaries would allow for a good comparison with excavations in Delta municipalities that arose in the 1940s.

Much remains to be done in the effort to recover and reconstruct the history and heritage of Mound Bayou, a rare and special example of an African-American town in Mississippi. Because of the fame of the town, it presents an excellent opportunity to educate Americans about the efforts of Mound Bayouans to attain freedom and equality. Mound Bayouans have always prized the unique and important contributions African Americans have made to American culture.

Historical and Archaeological Investigations of Doro Plantation

Archaeological and historical research at Doro Plantation was conducted by Coastal Environments, Inc., under the direction of Charles Pearson (Hahn et al. 1994). Three locations were investigated: Jacobs' Store, Doro big house, and Doro gin. Overall, 37 features were discovered and more than 50,000 historic artifacts recovered.

Doro Plantation was established in the 1840s and 1850s by Charles Clark and his wife, Anne Eliza Darden. Both were from the Natchez region of Mississippi. The plantation structures and activity areas identified through historic research and archaeological investigations included the big house, which was flooded, moved, and rebuilt, the slave quarters, also moved and rebuilt, a sawmill, Jacobs' stores, Clark's office, an overseer's house, levees, tenant houses, and several cotton gins. A landing existed on the Mississippi River, where bales of cotton were loaded onto steamboats and shipped to New Orleans. The rebuilt slave quarters were one or two rooms and whitewashed. In 1854, 53 slaves were valued at $51,700. In 1860, Clark owned 149 slaves. In addition to cotton, plantation workers also produced corn, oats, millet, barley, and spring and summer vegetables (peas, turnips, sweet potatoes, and Irish potatoes). A fruit orchard provided cherries, plums, apples, pears, peaches, and figs. The slaves had their own vegetable garden plots.

Jacobs' Stores

The first Jacobs' store was occupied from 1878 until 1895. The location is covered by the present levee. The establishment of the first Jacobs' store coincides with the conversion of Doro Plantation to a sharecropping system, and the predominant customers at the store were the plantation tenants. The second Jacobs' store was built about 1895 and occupied until 1912 or 1913.

Over 20,000 artifacts were recovered from excavations at the second Jacobs' store. Of these, 4,073 were identified as to function (domestic, personal, health, architecture, economic, group, and ritual). Most of the artifacts (approximately 70 percent) were classified as architecture and nearly 26 percent were identified as domestic.

Doro Big House

The Doro big house was originally constructed in 1852 and moved after a devastating flood that occurred in March 1854. The artifacts (n=25,990) predominantly represent the latter years of the house occupation, though the entire date range is represented in the assemblage. Most of the identifiable artifacts from the Doro big house consisted of architectural objects (approximately 56 percent), and over 36 percent were classified as domestic.

Doro Gin

The Doro Gin site had three major phases of use. From 1851 to 1853, the gin was mule-powered. The second phase is marked by a change to steam power, beginning in 1853; it lasted until 1859 or 1860, when a third gin was constructed (Hahn et al. 1994:170). The third gin burned in 1862, and the second gin was brought back into operation, marking the third phase of use. As expected, few artifacts (n=748) were recovered at the gin site, and most (nearly 93 percent) were architecture artifacts (Hahn et al. 1994:171–172).

Doro Interpretations

Faunal remains were not well preserved at Doro. From Jacobs' store, identified remains include pig, cow, squirrel, raccoon, catfish, gar, unidentified turtle, turkey, and unidentified bird. From the Doro big house, the faunal assemblage was much the same in terms of animals represented, except that a single horse bone was identified. Other than inclusions of wild species abundant in the region, little else can be said of the diet of residents of Doro at this time.

The excavations at Doro big house included heavier concentrations of both porcelain and wine bottle glass than the excavations at Jacobs' store. This likely reflects the status differences between the residents of the big house and the customers at the store.

The investigation by Coastal Environments, Inc., (Hahn et al. 1994) at Doro Plantation allowed for a partial reconstruction of some aspects of its culture history and culture lifeways. The culture history is defined in the combination of archaeological and historical data to date the uses and occupations of the structures that were investigated. The reconstruction of the landscape and settlement pattern provides some insights into culture lifeways. Before the Civil

War, plantation workers (slaves) were housed in nucleated slave quarters near the overseer's house. After the War, these houses continued to be used by plantation workers until about 1880. At this time, the settlement pattern shifted to housing of plantation workers in dispersed tenant houses. This suggests that the plantation workers between 1865 and 1880 led lives much as they did during slavery times. In 1880, Fred Clark, Charles Clark's son, instituted a tenant system where tenants paid rent but were supplied with tools and mules.

The archaeological and historical investigations at Doro Plantation highlight the complex cultural landscape that seems to have been typical for the Delta between the 1830s and the early decades of the twentieth century. However, only a very brief sketch is provided, and much more archaeology needs to be conducted on Delta plantations before we have even a basic understanding of what is typical and how much variability existed in plantation life there.

Memphis and Jackson: Keys to the Delta

The economic and political development of the Delta has been, and continues to be, closely tied to Jackson as the capital of Mississippi and to Memphis as a major commercial hub. Though the Delta remained predominantly rural until the 1940s, one might argue that true cities have never developed there. Therefore any discussion of the potential for historical archaeology in the Delta must be tied to the archaeology in those urban areas most closely associated with the region.

Jackson

Jackson is located near the center of Mississippi and just south of the Delta. It replaced Natchez as the state's capital. With the admission of Mississippi into the Union in 1817, an unprecedented period of growth was initiated for the new state. Settlers and slaves streamed into Mississippi from the east as lands ceded by the Choctaw Indians in the Treaty of Doak's Stand along the Mississippi, Yazoo, Big Black, and Pearl rivers were opened for white settlement. Geographic factionalism soon developed between the older, wealthy river districts such as Natchez and Greenville and the newly expanding areas of the state. As a result of this controversy, in January of 1821, the state General Assembly voted to provide for the location of a permanent capital near the geographic center of the state. Several spots were considered, including Columbia in Marion County, which was selected as a temporary capital. In November of 1821, a spot on the western side of the Pearl River at LeFleur's Bluff, a small trading post, was selected as the site of the permanent state capital of Mississippi (Young 2005).

Individuals commissioned by the state's General Assembly chose the site at LeFleur's Bluff carefully; the close proximity to the Pearl River and the Natchez Trace would allow for the transportation and shipping of goods necessitated by a political and commercial center, and the climate and soil of the area would appeal to those interested in participating in the state's growing plantation economy. On November 28, 1821, Thomas Hinds, William Lattimore, and Peter A. Van Dorn were commissioned to develop plans for the new capital, to be named in honor of General Andrew Jackson. Building soon began on the site of the new city. The General Assembly first met in the newly completed State House in Jackson in December of 1822 (Young 2005).

As government buildings went up, so did residences, storefronts, and offices in the new capital. By the 1830s, the bi-weekly newspaper, *The Mississippian,* was filled with advertisements and announcements. Jacksonian merchants advertised as jewelers, druggists, clothiers, lawyers, and land dealers. They advertised partnerships with other local businessmen, and the dissolution of these partnerships. Notices of financial scams, runaway slaves, and lost horses filled the pages of the small bi-weekly.[1]

These times, especially the mid-1830s, were known as the "Flush Times" in Mississippi. It was a time of population growth, a proliferation of business ventures, large-scale land speculation, and expanding frontier towns. However, Mississippi banks, like state banks across the United States, had loaned more money than their reserves could cover. In an attempt to remedy the situation, in 1836 President Andrew Jackson issued the Specie Circular, which mandated that payments for loans to purchase public lands be made only in gold or silver. The deflationary effect of the Specie Circular was at least partially responsible for the panic of 1837, which ended the Flush Times and left many Mississippians in especially difficult financial situations. A number of Mississippi planters avoided payment of their debts by abandoning their plantations and relocating entire households, often including large numbers of slaves, to Texas (Gonzales 1973). Others weathered the depression by switching to alternate crops and modifying their farming methods, both of which led to the greater sustainability of Mississippi's agricultural economy in later decades (Scarborough 1973; Young 2005).

The Railroad and Prosperity

Despite a long period of economic depression, Jackson's population continued to increase in the decades prior to the outbreak of the Civil War. So did the city's demand for reliable transportation-related services. When the site of Jackson was selected, the location was situated near a major waterway and the Natchez Trace. However, roads were very bad and proved to be a risky means of transporting goods to the Mississippi River or between waterways. When railroading reached the United States in the late 1820s, Mississippi was quick to jump on the bandwagon. The first functioning rail line in the state was

Table 17.1. Cities connected to Jackson by rail line, 1840–1927.

Location	Year
Vicksburg	1840
Canton	1856
New Orleans, LA	1858
Memphis, TN	1861
Meridian	1861
Natchez	1882
Yazoo City	1884
Gulfport	1900
New Orleans, LA (II)	1909
Union	1927

the West Feliciana Railroad, chartered in 1831 and operational by 1836, which bridged the gap between Woodville, Mississippi, and St. Francisville, Louisiana. A line connecting Vicksburg and Jackson was chartered in 1831 as the Vicksburg and Clinton Railroad Company, later rechartered as the Commercial and Railroad Bank of Vicksburg, and completed in 1840 (Gonzales 1973). Although rivers were still very important trade routes, railroads were so crucial to the economic prosperity of Mississippi that the framework of the state's modern rail system was already in place by 1861 (Moore 1973). By 1927, Jackson was directly connected by railroad to at least nine other cities in the region (Table 17.1) (McCain 1953).

Life in Antebellum Jackson

The antebellum social landscape of Jackson can be divided into a rough five-tiered hierarchy: elite society, the middle class, white laborers, free people of color, and slaves. The urban elite group in any Mississippi city was small in comparison with the general population. They were, however, significant property owners, perhaps politically connected to state or national government, and sufficiently financially secure to support a large household including family members and servants. Members of the large middle class in Jackson would have consisted of successful merchants, doctors, lawyers, and other skilled specialists who gained some degree of social prominence from their profession or public service. White laborers would have had less economic and social power than the Jackson middle class. Within the city, they would have held both supervisory and subordinate positions in construction, manufacturing, and with the railroad companies. Free persons of color were an extreme minority in Hinds County in the antebellum period. According to the U.S. Census, from 1830 to 1860, between fourteen and thirty-six free blacks were enumerated in Hinds County. These individuals may or may not have resided within the city of Jackson. Further information regarding the livelihood of free blacks in the Jackson area is not available at the current time.[2] Black slaves lived and worked both in the city of Jackson and the surrounding rural area, although many more lived outside the city. Slaves in Jackson, in addition to being domestic servants, often worked in the shops of local merchants, in manufacturing yards, or for railroad companies. Planters often traded slave labor for railroad stock, and slaves were often employed in laying railroad track or as brakemen (Moore 1973).

Jackson's entrepreneurs offered many amenities to citizens who could afford the price. As early as the 1830s, one could purchase fine silver, jewelry, clocks, clothing, and furniture in Jackson's shops.[3] Fraternal lodges were popular meeting places for men in Jackson's middle class. Hotels such as Jackson House and the Magnolia Cottage addressed the needs of visitors to the city. Restaurateurs promised patrons lavish meals of fresh wild game prepared in the European style at any time of day or night. At least two shops in antebellum Jackson offered imported ales, coffee, and chocolate. Ice and ice cream were available in Jackson in the late 1850s (McCain 1953).

By 1860, three newspapers were printed in Jackson: the *Eagle of the South,* the *Mississippian,* and *Mississippi Baptist,* a denominational newspaper. These were printed weekly, semi-weekly and, in the case of the *Mississippian,* daily when the legislature was in session.

Officials in the growing capital city sought to bring many distinguished visitors to Jackson as guests of the state in the years before the Civil War. These state visits were grand celebrations, accompanied by parades, parties, balls, speeches, and other festivities. These were possibly the most important social events in antebellum Jackson, with often thousands of people from surrounding areas crowding the streets to enjoy the festivities. Among distinguished visitors to Jackson was former president Andrew Jackson, presidential candidate Richard M. Johnson, and a famous Hungarian exile named Louis Kosuth.

As Jackson made the transition from a frontier town to a more urban environment, churches served a role of increasing importance in society. In an urban setting, churches and pastors tended to become more tolerant of moral shortcomings and more in touch with the secular interests of the people in their congregations. In addition to providing for matters of faith, the many churches in Jackson provided crucial social networks for men, women, and children (Pillar 1973).

War and Reconstruction

Soon after the election of Abraham Lincoln in the 1860 presidential election, events in Mississippi began to move rapidly in the direction of the state's secession from the Union. Many Mississippians believed that the very safety of the state was at stake and that the newly elected administration would, through the limitation of slavery as an institution, destroy the foundation of Mississippi's economy and social structure. The majority of white Mississippians considered slavery to be absolutely necessary, both as a labor system and as a means of maintaining social control over blacks. Thus, when a convention was convened to address the issue in Jackson in January of 1861, it had a clear secessionist majority. An ordinance to dissolve the union between Mississippi and the United States was drafted and accepted with a vote of eighty-four to fifteen.

News of the passed ordinance of secession was met with an outpouring of patriotism in the state. Jackson saw patriotic demonstrations, including cannon fire and the ringing of bells. A Jacksonian woman even made a flag for the new "nation" of Mississippi, a white star on a field of blue, which would come to be called "the Bonny Blue Flag."

Through the fanfare, the Jackson convention remained in session, revising the state constitution and making plans to attend a meeting in Montgomery, Alabama, for the purpose of organizing a confederacy of Southern states. The convention reconvened later that month to ratify the constitution of the Confederate States of America (Moore 1973). As the constitution was ratified, war fever spread throughout the South and, although Jackson itself did not feel battle until 1863, many of its citizens did, either directly as soldiers or indirectly through wartime shortages. As the war raged throughout the South, Jackson became a target of the Federal army in a campaign to divide the Confederacy, which included disabling towns such as Vicksburg, Port Gibson, and Raymond. By taking Jackson, the Federal troops would damage an important supply line of the Confederacy, the railroad line connecting Vicksburg to Jackson. When Jackson was taken, not only were the railroad lines disabled, but factories, shops, homes, hotels, farms, and churches were burned. The destruction of Jackson was so extensive that the pillaged capital became known as "Chimneyville," because charred chimneys were all that could be seen after the fires went out. Few pre–Civil War buildings remained intact (Bettersworth 1973).

The people of Jackson emerged from the Civil War defeated and poverty-stricken. Many livelihoods had been destroyed as the Southern agriculturally based infrastructure collapsed. Despite the diversified crops and labor-saving techniques that had come into practice after the panic of 1837, and the promise of high cotton prices, Mississippi's farmers struggled to recover from the war. However slowly, Mississippi's agricultural economy strengthened as the twentieth century approached. At the same time, former slaves were struggling to find employment and security. Many freedmen joined the Federal army and were stationed in Jackson for a time shortly after the war had ended. Others sought employment with former owners, often merchants or planters, but few formerly wealthy whites could afford to pay even low wages while the economy floundered.

Despite the challenges of recovery that lay ahead for Jackson, the state, and the region, the city continued to grow. The population of the city grew from roughly 1,800 people in 1850 to over 7,800 in 1900. Only a few years after the Civil War, citizens of Jackson were able to use natural gas provided by the Jackson Gas Light Company. In 1878, the same company was authorized to provide electricity within city limits. The Louisiana Telephone Company was granted permission in 1882 to locate a telephone in the mayor's office. Telephones may have been available to the general public as early as 1907. The Light, Heat and Water Company of Jackson was providing water services to the city by 1889 and sewer services by 1899. The city began paving the streets in 1903 (McCain 1953).

Urban Archaeology in Jackson

A search of the state site files at the Mississippi Department of Archives and History in Jackson indicates that virtually no urban archaeology has been conducted in Jackson, particularly archaeology geared toward understanding urbanization and urban processes (i.e., archaeology *of* the city rather than *in* the city). In the late 1970s, limited work at the Charles Manship house was conducted to aid in reconstruction of this museum home. This late-1850s house was originally in a rural setting outside of the town, but now is at the corner of a busy intersection in north Jackson, and therefore relates only in a limited way to the understanding of urban processes.

Limited work was conducted by James Lauro in the 1990s at the Civil War site of Battlefield Park in what is now the city of Jackson. This work was done in an effort to contribute to a management plan for the continued development of the park for public recreational use. While earlier work conducted in 1971 suggested the possibility of intact archaeological deposits, Lauro concluded that no cultural resources of any consequence remain at this site (Lauro 1993). The testing strategy was extraordinarily limited, and I do not believe that it is safe to write off this potentially important site.

Very limited work at the Old Capital has been conducted as part of Mississippi Archaeology Week and (later) Month, but no report of these investigations is available. This was done with the help of volunteers from the general public.

I conducted limited testing at The Oaks, the antebellum home of James Hervey Boyd, his wife Eliza Ellis Boyd, and their six children (Young 2005). The property was purchased in 1853, and curiously, only Eliza Boyd is listed on the deed as owner. James Hervey Boyd was a businessman and served as the mayor of Jackson during the antebellum era.

Archaeological and historical investigations indicate that the lot purchased by Eliza Boyd was unoccupied, and no buildings existed prior to the Boyds' occupation. Testing consisted of systematic auger testing of the side yard and excavation of 10 1x1 meter units and one 1 x ½-meter unit. The purpose was to evaluate the potential for archaeological data to illuminate the lives of the Boyds and middle-class urban Jacksonians.

Testing indicates that the preservation of outbuildings and activity areas is good to excellent. Further, the lot in the antebellum era is best classified as an urban farmstead (Stewart-Abernathy 1986), characteristic of a producing rather than a consuming economy. Since the Boyds occupied the property from 1853 until about 1960, the lot provides an excellent opportunity to investigate the transition and modernization from a traditional urban farmstead to a modern urban lot. Additional archaeology at The Oaks is planned for the future. Data from this site should prove to be interesting for comparison with archaeological data recovered in the Delta.

Obviously, much can and should have been done in the way of archaeological investigations in Jackson. In this case, the potential of the record itself has not been adequately assessed, though the history of the development of the pioneer town into a twentieth-century city hints that we can learn much from such investigations. Town residences of blacks and whites, of all classes, need to be investigated, as well as commercial and more government and possibly military sites. Jackson was more than just the state's capital. It was a cultural center, and possibly an important entrepot for people living in the southern portion of the Delta. Therefore, as more historical archaeology is conducted in Jackson, archaeologists in the Delta should carefully monitor the results.

Memphis

Memphis history may have begun with the de Soto expedition, although the original city plan was not laid out until 1819. As a port on the Mississippi River, the economy of Memphis was heavily dependent on commerce. By 1850, the city's population was approximately 22,000 (Garrow 2000; Weaver and Hopkins 1996). Garrow (2000) divides the history and development of Memphis into three broad periods. The first is 1541–1819, with temporary occupation by Spanish, French, and American military and traders. Little or no evidence of this first period has been found archaeologically. The second period dates from 1819 to 1879 and encompasses the period when Memphis developed as a city and the population was composed primarily of immigrants. The third period, from 1879 to the present, coincides with the emergence of Memphis as a modern city and includes the devastating effects of the yellow fever epidemic of the 1870s. It is these last two periods that should inform historical archaeology in the Delta.

Urban archaeology in Memphis was inaugurated in the early 1980s with Smith's (1982) attempt to locate the Spanish Fort San Fernando de las Barrancas, and with McNutt and Smith's (1982) salvage excavations in downtown Memphis. Since that early urban archaeology, quite a few major projects investigating urban, commercial, and industrial sites have been investigated (Table 17.2). Of particular interest are the commercial and industrial sites that may have been a source of employment as blacks left plantations during mechanization and migrated to urban areas for work.

The Peabody Place, AutoZone, and MATA projects were all major urban investigations conducted with explicit research designs and likely have the greatest potential to inform Delta archaeology. The Rum Boogie site (Garrow 1992; Weaver and Hopkins 1991) was the primary site investigated during the Peabody Place project. An icehouse, dating from the 1840s and abandoned by 1856, was excavated. A mill was established in the same building in 1866 but was not in operation from 1869 to 1881, when it reopened briefly before being destroyed by fire in 1882. The artifacts that accumulated around the icehouse cellar appear to have come primarily from "female boarding houses" located in the "Blue Light District" of Memphis near the site (Garrow 2000). The AutoZone project (Hopkins and Weaver 1993; Weaver, Hopkins, Weaver, Kowalewski, and Childress 1996) was focused on two wells. One well was dug around 1844 and then used for trash disposal beginning around 1866. The other well was dug around 1866 and began to be filled with refuse by 1872. The trash accumulated in these wells was likely associated with a saloon, a confectionery, and a boarding house (Garrow 2000). The MATA project (Garrow et al. 1998; Weaver and Hopkins 1996; Weaver et al. 1997) explored a block that contained features and deposits associated with the Memphis and Ohio (M&O) and Louisville and Nashville (L&N) Railroads. The deposits date between 1854, when the M&O Railroad began, and approximately 1912, when the depot was moved to Union Station in Memphis. Interestingly, one feature, Feature 39, was a cistern associated with the M&O Railroad. Animal bones and even ethnobotanical samples appear to be associated with the meals and snacks of passengers.

Table 17.2. Urban archaeology in Memphis (after Garrow 2000: Table 10.3).

Project	Site Function	Source	Level
Fort San Fernando	Military	Smith 1982	Phase II
Adams and Riverside	Domestic?	McNutt and Smith 1982	Salvage
Magevny House	Domestic	Weaver and Weaver 1985a	Phase III
Falls Building	Domestic	Weaver and Weaver 1985b	Feature
Navy Yard	Industrial	Council 1985	Phase I
Peabody Place	Mixed	Jolley 1984	Phase I
Peabody Place	Mixed	Joseph 1986	Phase II
Peabody Place	Mixed	Weaver 1988	Phase II
Peabody Place	Industrial and Domestic	Weaver and Hopkins 1991	Phase III
AutoZone	Commercial and Domestic	Hopkins and Weaver 1993; Weaver, Hopkins, Weaver, Kowalewski, and Childress 1996	Phase I, II, III
Memphis Landing	Commercial	Weaver et al. 1994; Weaver, Hopkins, Oats, and Patterson 1996	Phase I, II
MATA	Commercial and Domestic	Weaver and Hopkins 1996; Weaver et al. 1997; Garrow et al. 1998	Phase I, II, III

Conclusion: "How can this exist in our country?" The Social Relevance of Historical Archaeology in the Delta Region of Mississippi

Unfortunately, there has been tremendous resistance to historical archaeology in much of the state. This is particularly true concerning recent sites (Stewart-Abernathy 1998, 1999). All too often, archaeology has focused on the visible and predominantly elite sectors of societies, prehistoric and Historic, and thus has failed to place attention on sites that have the potential to really tell us about everyday life for everyday people and how those people shaped the historical processes that eventually led us to today's problems. We all know that the present is connected to the past (Leone et al. 2005). And in reality, even with the recent past, we really do not know how individuals and communities of the past were shaped by and helped shape those social processes. Thus we are often at a loss as to how to change the present. There are many questions we can address through historical archaeology in the Delta that will lead to a greater understanding of why this region is considered one of the poorest parts of the country. These include:

1. Were all antebellum cotton plantations very similar to one another, or was there variability in layout, types of structures, housing, foodways, and other material conditions?
2. Can we detect differences between plantations of transplanted Mississippians and transplants from the Upper South?
3. Was it the harshness of the planters and overseers or the labor that made being sold "down the river" to Mississippi such a dreadful fate?
4. What different strategies did black families adopt with Emancipation, knowing that equal access to employment, land, and the political process were denied them? Were coping strategies similar for rural blacks and town-dwelling blacks in the Delta? How did they cope with violence from secret societies like the KKK?
5. What were material conditions of white farmers and sharecroppers? Are differences apparent in the archaeological record?
6. The sharecropping black Delta was the birthplace of the Blues. What, precisely were the material, social, political, and economic conditions from Emancipation until modernization?
7. African Americans moved from farms and plantations to Delta municipalities. It was in this increasingly segregated environment that the Civil Rights movement occurred. What strategies were employed by blacks to create the solidarity needed for the success of the Civil Rights movement? How did white town residents cope with the stresses of urbanization and living in close proximity to blacks? What were the differences in town existence (housing, foodways, and other material conditions) between whites and blacks? If white sections of towns were electrified and plumbed earlier, why and how much earlier? How do yard layouts compare?
8. Through archaeology and oral history, can we trace the connections between people in the Delta and the cities of Jackson and Memphis? What kinds of relationships existed that may have made these connections possible? Did many Delta folk have family in Jackson and Memphis whom they relied on in times of stress?

These questions deserve answers, and many of the answers can come from intensive and extensive archaeological investigations at sites dating from the 1830s until the modern era. Then, perhaps, we can begin to understand why the Delta has been characterized as having the most of everything bad and the least of everything good.

Notes

1. *Mississippian*. Editions from 5 March 1835, 20 November 1835, and 12 January 1836. Microfilm, Mississippi Department of Archives and History, State Archives, Jackson, Mississippi (McCain 1953).

2. University of Virginia U.S. Census Database (http://www.fisher.lib.edu/collections /stats/histcencus/).

3. *Mississippian*. Editions from March 5, 1835, November 20, 1835, and January 12, 1836. Microfilm, Mississippi Department of Archives and History, State Archives, Jackson, Mississippi.

18
Fording the River

Concluding Comments

Janet Rafferty and Evan Peacock

Mississippi Valley archeology cannot exist half slave and half free, the upper half hog-tied but happy in their typological fetters, the lower half progressing step by step in determining the time relations of cultural manifestations in one area after another.

Letter from Henry B. Collins to James A. Ford,
April 11, 1941. (From Baca, 2002:154).

The authors in this book represent a considerable diversity of archaeological theories and a great degree of expertise in specialty areas. Despite these differences in theory and substantive approaches, there is general agreement on a number of points. This summary looks in a broad way at some commonalities among the chapters and, from them, draws conclusions about some ways forward. Much more detail is presented in each chapter, especially concerning the state of current knowledge. We urge readers to refer to the individual chapters for the specifics in each case.

Fieldwork

Recovery methods are a constant concern. Even though archaeologists might appear to agree on a number of standard field methods and their rationales, much of this accord may be sacrificed for the sake of expediency. One such precept is that every archaeological project should recover artifacts at all scales. Failures in this area have especially adverse effects on environmental, floral, and faunal data at one end of the scale and on settlement pattern data at the other. The theoretical and preservation-based arguments in support of this rule sometimes have been neglected. For example, screening excavated dirt through ¼-inch mesh is often chosen for practical reasons, such as clay-heavy soil or the short-term nature of the project. Without taking dirt samples from each provenience, fine-mesh and flotation recovery become impossible. Fish bones (Jackson), charred seeds (Fritz), and land snails (Peacock) are three kinds of small objects for which recovery will be biased without explicit thought given to using fine-screen and flotation methods. Recovering all artifacts at all scales is impossible, so it is necessary to carefully plan a strategy that will return a sample of each size class. Such sampling would assure that small artifacts and environmental indicators have a chance to be recovered for comparison with larger-scale objects. Another part of sampling is making sure that sample sizes are adequate. Without large enough samples, it is difficult to say anything decisive about the archeological record. This problem compromises existing data and has made summarizing harder for all the authors involved in this volume.

Another principle is the precise recording of provenience, with use of smaller rather than larger units being favored. Recovering a sample of large artifacts, especially occupations or settlements, is primarily a matter of using appropriate recording methods, as the spatial relationships of the individual artifacts that make up these large-scale agglomerations are crucial to delineating them. Lipo and Dunnell argue for recording artifacts in as close-as-possible association with the depositional event they represent. Fortunately, it is standard practice to follow this stricture with features, drawing them in plan and profile, excavating them by zones, and precisely recording their locations in three dimensions. With portable artifacts, this kind of detailed recording is less common. Nonetheless, in both surface-collection and excavation, smaller provenience units are preferable to larger ones (Rafferty). Understanding formation processes, functional variability within an occupation, and occupation boundaries all depend on detailed provenience records. In the end, the larger units of settlement analysis (Lipo and Dunnell) are built on appropriately recorded occupations.

Finally, sampling archaeological space in three dimensions, i.e., taking a spatially extensive approach, is necessary. Often, excavation has focused on the center of a site, or the most artifact-rich deposits, or the area within a right-of-way. A better practice is to sample each depositional stratum and feature, with the boundaries of each identified so that the sample can be related meaningfully to the whole. As shown by Jackson, what a faunal analyst can learn from bones in midden deposits and features may differ in important ways. Similarly, it is difficult to make arguments about the size and layout of an occupation without knowing its boundaries (Rafferty). Minimally destructive to nondestructive methods, such as geophysical survey, controlled surface collection, and augering, can provide much spatial information and may not require large additional expenditures of time. Johnson discusses the importance of using multiple geophysical methods, as they provide different kinds of data; this can be generalized to advocacy for multiple methods in all recovery. All of these minimally destructive methods are practically applied over entire sites, because they are more rapidly accomplished than excavation and because land-owner permission may be forthcoming more readily for them.

The chapter authors make a number of other observations on fieldwork methods. One recommendation that comes from several papers is to make less use of the most destructive methods, such as stripping and large-scale excavation. Stripping can destroy or damage burials, precluding adequate recording of them (Hogue). Such methods, admittedly, have their place, being invaluable in efficiently locating features, along with the artifacts, animal bones, and floral remains they contain. Large exposures can add much to our knowledge of settlement layout (Brown). By using heavy equipment such as Gradall excavators, which do not run over the area being stripped, damage to burials can be lessened. Nonetheless, these methods too often are used instead of, rather than in addition to, other informative methods, including those mentioned above—geophysics, controlled surface collection, and augering. Excavation often can be targeted based on the results of these less-destructive methods; stripping can then become one of the last steps in mitigation, not a substitute for other spatially extensive methods. The equation of features and significance, which has increasingly led to stripping at the Phase II level, also needs to be reevaluated (Peacock and Rafferty 2007).

Another theme is that fieldwork be done outside sites to collect environmental data to address specific archaeological problems. Systematically obtaining information on lithic and clay sources is recommended (Carr, Galaty, Neff). Routine collection of geomorphological, soil, land snail, and other on-site environmental data will also enhance our understanding of associated archaeological phenomena (Peacock). This leads to another concern, that specialists routinely be involved in fieldwork. This especially applies during excavation. The presence of bioarchaeologists would be immensely helpful in recognizing burials so they can be correctly recovered (Hogue). Fritz makes a similar argument that floral analysts should be included to design sampling and assure that flotation is carried out correctly.

Most chapter authors have concentrated on excavated data because those are the main data currently available or appropriate for their studies. It must, however, be plain that adequate historical background and environmental research is basic to archaeological understanding. These help put the other data in context and determine biases that may exist in them. A constant bias in settlement pattern analysis is that against recording or doing more intensive work at small, low-density, and Historic-period sites. (We use the term "site" here to refer to any place where artifacts have been found, however their proveniences were recorded: "site" as an analytic unit will be of limited utility in most cases [Dunnell, Chapter 4, Lipo and Dunnell, Rafferty], especially in areas like the Delta, where non-sequent occupations are common). Several authors (Peacock, Lipo and Dunnell, Rafferty, Young) discuss the deleterious effects that inadequate attention to certain kinds of phenomena in survey can have on archaeologists' ability to understand and explain the full record. Site-based provenience recording during survey not only makes the resulting artifact assemblages non-comparable as analytical units, but also introduces systematic bias at the survey level. Recent surveys suffer less from this problem, but much of the available survey data is old. This fundamental aspect of fieldwork must be subject to the same principles and best fieldwork practices discussed above for "within-site" investigations.

Analytic Methods

Just as it is important not to be led by rote methods in the field, so too is it important to break away from the use of "be-all" classes in artifact analysis. Archaeologists can agree that analysis should be problem-oriented. That being the case, unless we are always asking the same questions, there is no justification for always using the same categories for grouping our artifacts. To do so is a sure strategy for minimizing what we learn in return for the considerable resources invested in CRM. The assessment provided by this volume forces us to acknowledge, however, that this is precisely what most archaeologists are doing. Many automatically employ the type/variety system of pottery classification, for example, without regard for whether it is appropriate to the questions being asked (Galaty) and without acknowledgement of criticisms of the approach. Many automatically employ a primary-secondary-tertiary scheme for debitage analysis, despite similar drawbacks (Carr). This could be justified if one assumed that the only purpose of CRM was to obtain representative samples and provide descriptions of materials that could be used by other, research-focused, archaeologists. But there are two problems with this rationalization. The first is that it precludes short-term return on resources invested: the generation of knowledge from CRM-derived collections is delayed for some indeterminate amount of time. One implication is that CRM itself loses the benefit of knowledge generation, so that research designs quickly grow stale. (Such a philosophy also begs the question of why a research design is needed in the first place.) The second problem is that traditional classification schemes are inconsistent in nature (e.g., the loosely defined, largely descriptive, nonsortable[1] and nonexclusive, hierarchical classes of the type/variety system) and/or are inconsistently applied (e.g., how are "secondary flakes" defined?).

Fortunately, we live at a time when technological advances can be coupled with the most challenging theories to produce a much more robust scientific archaeology. No longer do hypotheses concerning trade, for example, have to rely on the analysis of stylistic attributes, an approach founded upon the fallacious notion that style can be directly equated with ethnicity and one which presupposes the answers (e.g., when "exotic" ceramics found at a site are assumed to be derived from elsewhere). Instead, sourcing studies using a variety of methods (INAA, LA-ICP-MS, XRF, petrography, etc.) can directly test such hypotheses (Neff, Galaty). The traditional styles recognized by archaeologists provide as good a starting point as any in this regard, so that the benefit of decades of culture-historical work is not discarded but is built upon. In certain situations, sourcing studies will be critically important. For example, artifacts thought to be indicative of early culture contact, such as "Clarksdale bells," potentially can be sourced using essentially nondestructive methods such as LA-ICP-MS. Such an approach presents at least a partial solution to the thorny problems plaguing culture-contact studies in the Delta (Brown).

Each time some new technology is employed, it provides an opportunity, not only to test a particular hypothesis at the local-to-regional scale, but also to help refine analytical techniques, thereby benefiting the discipline at the global scale. For example, the employment of multiple dating methods (standard radiometric and AMS radiocarbon, TL, OSL, OCR, etc.) not only can provide corroborative results but, in those cases where dates on the same or apparently associated materials differ, also provides an opportunity to explore why some dates are "bad." This is a critically important area of research, as new methods allow us to date things that otherwise are undatable (Feathers): landforms via OSL dating of sand grains, for example, or heat-treated lithics at pre-ceramic sites using TL; or to better develop less expensive methods, such as fluoride dating of bone at long-term occupations with anchors provided by targeted radiocarbon assays (cf. Hogue 2006). Comparative work confirming that the ^{14}C reservoir effect is negligible in the Delta will be very useful, as shell and shell-tempered pottery are common constituents of sites in the region. All of these absolute and relative dating methods can be linked with seriations to establish the temporal ordering of artifact assemblages, allowing us to view change through time along a continuum (Rafferty) rather than compressing variability into arbitrarily defined boxes (Dunnell, Chapter 4). This approach also should help us better understand duration, a key component of settlement-pattern studies (Rafferty, Lipo and Dunnell). Linking seriated assemblage orders with more robust paleoenvironmental data, derived from multiple sources, will allow a much better understanding of environment as selective force and will allow the exploration of particular research questions concerning, for example, the timing, nature, and scale of prehistoric human impact in the Delta (Peacock).

The same opportunities arise when the results of elemental sourcing studies seem to be in contradiction with the results of petrographic analysis. Detection plates don't lie: clay, stone, shell, pigments, and other materials have particular elemental make-ups that can be ascertained with a high level of precision (Neff). Yet such analyses cannot answer all questions. Petrographic analysis is extremely useful for understanding ceramic manufacturing processes and the selective factors underlying them, for example (Galaty). When mineralogical or fabric analysis and elemental analyses disagree where ceramic source areas are concerned, then clearly we have something important to learn.

It has already been noted that more consistency is needed in the retrieval of floral, faunal, and human skeletal remains. The same is true where analytic methods are concerned. More precise identifications of plant and animal remains are needed to address questions related to paleoenvironment, paleoeconomy, paleoecology, and cultural change through time (Jackson, Fritz). More standardized procedures, such as recording bone weights as well as counts, are needed (Jackson). Reanalysis of existing collections is needed to corroborate or dismiss range extensions and other earlier interpretations of biotic remains (Fritz). Reanalysis also will help objectify and broaden interpretations by providing an independent assessment of results, something that currently is lacking in human skeletal analysis, to give one example (Hogue).

Final Thoughts

A common theme throughout this volume is how little we actually know about one of the richest archaeological regions in North America. The Early and Middle Archaic periods, on one end of the temporal scale, and the Protohistoric and Historic periods, on the other end, are especially underinvestigated. There also are major substantive areas—paleoenvironment aside from geomorphology, as well as burial patterns/bioarchaeogical study—in which current data are glaringly inadequate. It will take increased attention to the entire range of archaeological materials to begin to remedy these deficiencies. It is perhaps not surprising that much of what *has* been learned in the last thirty-plus years has come through specialist analyses, especially faunal and floral studies. While both Jackson and Fritz point out the considerable gaps in our knowledge in these regards, they do marshal more substance in their overviews than most of the other authors were able to do. This is, of course, a testament to what archaeology can achieve when a materialist approach is taken. It is possible because the basic units of analysis in zooarchaeology and archaeobotany—species—transcend the particularistic conceptual boundaries imposed on the record by archaeologists. One result is that such things can be accomplished as devising zones for levels of pre-maize plant domestication that correlate well with continental-scale environmental factors, a finding that is satisfyingly robust in scientific terms. There is no theoretical reason other archaeological phenomena cannot be explained in similarly robust terms.

Plainly, the answer isn't just that more data are needed, but newly rethought methods as well. These cannot stand alone, but must be linked to and derived from explanatory theory. It will be necessary to go beyond explanations such as the common-sense ones used by culture historians and those grounded in ethnographic analogy that archaeologists have leaned on so heavily over the last forty years. The highly inductive, pseudo-ethnographic phase-based approach has had a dampening effect on innovation. Archaeologists working in the Delta tend to spend at least as much of their time "sorting out the phases" (Brown, this volume) as they do testing hypotheses derived from explicit theoretical stances. It is important to realize that we need not be bound by existing typological or time/space frameworks. As Dunnell and Feathers note, we do not need phases to control for time. As Dunnell (Chapter 4), Rafferty, Brown and others point out, the type-varieties and phases never worked that well in the first place, either as time or space units. The traditional remedy has been to work to "refine" the phases, but it is legitimate to question whether that endless game is worth the effort, or whether our time might be better spent focusing on the kinds of substantive questions raised in this volume. The methods for practicing archaeology without dependence on periodization are at hand. We hope that archaeologists will be encouraged by this volume to use them. This will be possible if we approach the phenomena from explicitly scientific, theory-driven viewpoints, and if we are attentive to the variability in the archaeological record, something that virtually all of the authors call for. The degree of precision and the amount of work needed in recovery and analysis in this regard are daunting, to say the least. But the rewards should be great, and given that archaeology is a destructive undertaking, we are obligated to try our hardest to move forward on such fronts.

Note

1. E.g., Phillips 1970: "The rest of these types [Troyville, Haynes Bluff, Addis, Fatherland, Coles Creek, Baytown], notwithstanding the long span of history they represent, cannot be reliably sorted"(47). *In re* varieties of Baytown Plain, there is "no way to abstract . . . the sorting criteria" for *var. Baytown* (48) and "no absolutely reliable criteria for sorting" *var. Addis* (49). The sorting criteria used, especially where varieties are concerned, are routinely inconsistent, non-comparable and subjective, including various mixes of paste and/or surface texture, sherd color, surface treatments, temper inclusions, decorative rim modes, etc. (cf. Rafferty 1986).

References Cited

AA Roads
  2004   Priority Corridors: Interstate 69 (Corridors 18 and 20). Electronic document, http://www.aaroads.com/high-priority/corr18.html, accessed September 1, 2004.

Abbott, David N.
  1972   The Utility of the Concept Phase in the Archaeology of the Southern Northwest Coast. *Syesis* 5:267–278.

Adair, James
  1775   *The History of the American Indians.* Edward and Charles Dilly, London.

Adams, Robert M.
  1942   Archaeological Surface Survey of New Madrid County, Missouri. *Missouri Archaeologist* 8:2. (whole issue)

Ahler, Stanley A.
  1989   Mass Analysis of Flaking Debris: Studying the Forest Rather Than the Trees. In *Alternative Approaches to Lithic Analysis,* edited by Donald O. Henry and George H. Odell, pp. 85–118. American Anthropological Association, Archaeological Papers 1.

Aiken, Charles S.
  1987   Race as a Factor in Municipal Underbounding. *Annals of the Association of American Geographers* 77:564–579.
  1990   A New Type of Black Ghetto in the Plantation South. *Annals of the Association of American Geographers* 80:223–246.

Aldenderfer, Mark S.
  1987   *Quantitative Research in Archaeology: Progress and Prospects.* Sage Publications, Newbury Park, California.

Alford, John L., and Joseph C. Holmes
  1985   Meander Scars as Evidence of Major Climate Change in Southwest Louisiana. *Annals of the Association of American Geographers* 75:395–403.

Alvey, Jeffrey S.
  2005   Middle Archaic Settlement Organization in the Upper Tombigbee Drainage: A View from the Uplands. *Southeastern Archaeology* 24:199–208.

Ambrose, Stanley H.

1987   Chemical and Isotope Techniques of Diet Reconstruction in Eastern North
        America. In *Emergent Horticultural Economies of the Eastern Woodlands, Occa-
        sional Papers 27*, edited by William F. Keegan, pp. 87–107. Center for Archaeo-
        logical Investigations, Carbondale, Illinois.

Ammerman, Albert J.

1992   Taking Stock of Quantitative Archaeology. *Annual Review of Anthropology*
        21:231–255.

Anderson, David G.

1990   A North American Paleoindian Projectile Point Database. *Current Research in the
        Pleistocene* 7:67–69.

1995   Recent Advances in Paleoindian and Archaic Period Research in the Southeastern
        United States. *Archaeology of Eastern North America* 23:145–176.

Anderson, David G., and Glen T. Hanson

1988   Early Archaic Settlement in the Southeastern United States: A Case Study from the
        Savannah River Valley. *American Antiquity* 53:262–286.

Anderson, David G., David W. Stahle, and Malcolm K. Cleaveland

1995   Paleoclimate and the Potential Food Reserves of Mississippian Societies: A Case
        Study from the Savannah River Valley. *American Antiquity* 60:258–286.

Andrefsky, William, Jr.

1994   Raw-Material Availability and the Organization of Technology. *American Antiq-
        uity* 59:21–34.

Anonymous

1897   The Climate of New Orleans, Louisiana. *Publications of the New Orleans Historical
        Society* 2(1):35–39.

Anonymous

1985   Archaeological Excavations at the LeFlore Site. In *Anthology of Mississippi Archae-
        ology 1966–1979*, edited by Patricia Galloway, pp. 109–112. Mississippi Department
        of Archives and History, Jackson.

Arco, Lee J., Katherine A. Adelsberger, Ling-yu Hung, and Tristram R. Kidder

2006   Alluvial Geoarchaeology of a Middle Archaic Mound Complex in the Lower Mis-
        sissippi Valley, U.S.A. *Geoarchaeology: An International Journal* 21:591–614.

Arnold, Dean E.

1985   *Ceramic Theory and Cultural Process.* Cambridge University Press, Cambridge.

Arnold, Jeanne E., and Anabel Ford

1980   A Statistical Examination of Settlement Patterns at Tikal, Guatemala. *American
        Antiquity* 45:713–726.

Atkinson, James R.

1987   The De Soto Expedition through North Mississippi in 1540–41. *Mississippi Archae-
        ology* 22(1):61–73.

Atwater, Caleb

1820   Description of the Antiquities of the State of Ohio and Other Western States. *Ar-
        chaeologia Americana* 1:105–247.

1833   *The Writings of Caleb Atwater.* Columbus. Published by the author.

Baca, Keith A. (editor)

2002   Correspondence between James A. Ford and Henry B. Collins: Selected Letters, 1927–1941. *Mississippi Archaeology* 37:99–158.

Baca, Keith A., and Joseph A. Giliberti

1995   The Utility and Potential of the Mississippi Archaeological Site File. In *Archaeological Site File Management: A Southeastern Perspective,* edited by David G. Anderson and Virginia Horak, pp. 54–61. Interagency Archeological Resource Division, Interagency Archeological Resource Protection Series No. 3, Atlanta.

Baden, William W.

1987   *A Dynamic Model of Stability and Change in Mississippian Agricultural Systems.* Doctoral dissertation, University of Tennessee, Knoxville. UMI Dissertation Services, Ann Arbor, Michigan.

Baerreis, David A.

1980   Habitat and Climatic Interpretation from Terrestrial Gastropods at the Cherokee Site. In *The Cherokee Excavations: Holocene Ecology and Human Adaptations in Northwestern Iowa,* edited by Duane C. Anderson and Holmes A. Semken, Jr., pp. 101–122. Academic Press, New York.

2005   Terrestrial Gastropods at the Carlston Annis Site (15Bt5): Their Habitat and Climatic Interpretations. In *Archaeology of the Middle Green River Region, Kentucky,* edited by William H. Marquardt and Patty Jo Watson, pp. 243–253. University of Florida, Institute of Archaeology and Paleoenvironmental Studies, Monograph No. 5, Gainesville.

Barber, Russell J.

1988   The Use of Land Snails from Prehistoric Sites for Paleoenvironmental Reconstruction. In *Holocene Human Ecology in Northeastern North America,* edited by George P. Nicholas, pp. 11–28. Plenum Press, New York.

Bareis, Charles J., and James Warren Porter

1965   Megascopic and Petrographic Analysis of a Foreign Pottery Vessel from the Cahokia Site. *American Antiquity* 31:95–101.

Barnes, Trevor J.

2004   The Rise (and Decline) of American Regional Science: Lessons for the New Economic Geography? *Journal of Economic Geography* 4:107–129.

Barnhardt, Michael L.

1988   Historical Sedimentation in West Tennessee Gullies. *Southeastern Geographer* 28(1):1–18.

Barone, John A.

2005a   Historical Presence and Distribution of Prairies in the Black Belt of Mississippi and Alabama. *Castanea* 79:170–183.

2005b   The Historical Distribution of Prairies in the Jackson Prairie Belt and in Western Mississippi. *Journal of the Mississippi Academy of Sciences* 50:144–148.

Barton, Charles A.

1927   Where Did De Soto Discover the Mississippi River? In *A Symposium on the Place of Discovery of the Mississippi River by Hernando De Soto*, edited by Dunber Rowland, pp. 52–96. Publications of the Mississippi Historical Society, Special Bulletin No. 1, Jackson.

Barton, Stephen

1880   Correspondence with the Smithsonian Institution. *Annual Report of the Board of Regents of the Smithsonian Institution for the Year 1879*, 428–429.

Bass, William M.

1995   *Human Osteology: A Laboratory and Field Manual.* Missouri Archaeological Society, Columbia.

Baxter, M. J.

1992   Archaeological Uses of the Biplot—a Neglected Technique? In *Computer Applications and Quantitative Methods in Archaeology 1991*, edited by Gary Lock and Jonathan Moffett, pp. 141–148. BAR International Series S577. Tempus Reparatum, Archaeological and Historical Associates, Oxford.

1994   Stepwise Discriminant Analysis in Archaeometry: A Critique. *Journal of Archaeological Science* 21:659–666.

Bechtel, Susan K., and David M. Strothers

1993   New Perspectives on the Settlement-Subsistence System of the Late Woodland Western Basin Tradition, ca. 500–1300 A.D.. *North American Archaeologist* 14:95–122.

Beck, Charlotte

1981   Prehistoric Settlement Patterns in the Lower Mississippi Valley during the Late Mississippian Period (A.D. 1200–1600). Paper presented at the 46th Annual Meeting of the Society for American Archaeology, San Diego.

Beck, Charlotte, and George T. Jones

1989   Bias and Archaeological Classification. *American Antiquity* 54:244–262.

Beckwith, T.

1887   Mounds in Missouri. *The American Antiquarian* 9:228–232.

Bell, Robert E.

1958   *Guide to the Identification of Certain American Indian Projectile Points.* Special Bulletin No. 1, Oklahoma Anthropological Society, Oklahoma City.

1960   *Guide to the Identification of Certain American Indian Projectile Points.* Special Bulletin No. 2, Oklahoma Anthropological Society, Oklahoma City.

Belmont, John S.

1961   *The Peabody Excavations, Coahoma County, Mississippi, 1901–1902.* Bachelor's Thesis, Department of Anthropology, Harvard University, Cambridge.

Belmont, John S., and Russell J. Barber

1983   Faunal Remains. In *Excavations at the Lake George Site, Yazoo County, Mississippi, 1958–1960*, by Stephen Williams and Jeffrey P. Brain, pp. 451–469. Cambridge: Papers of the Peabody Museum of Archaeology and Ethnology 74.

Benn, David W.

1998   Moon: A Fortified Mississippian-Period Village in Poinsett County, Arkansas. In *Changing Perspectives on the Archaeology of the Central Mississippi Valley*, edited by Michael J. O'Brien and Robert C. Dunnell, pp. 225–257. University of Alabama Press, Tuscaloosa.

Bense, Judith A.

1987   Summary of Results. In Judith A. Bense (editor), *The Midden Mound Project,* pp. 371–405. Report submitted to the U.S. Army Corps of Engineers, Mobile District, by the University of West Florida. University of West Florida, Office of Cultural and Archaeological Research, Report of Investigations 6.

Berry, Trey, Pam Beasley, and Jeanne Clements (editors)

2006   *The Forgotten Expedition, 1804–1805: The Louisiana Purchase Journals of Dunbar and Hunter.* Louisiana State University Press, Baton Rouge.

Berryman, Hugh

1999   Human Remains. In *Archaeological Data Recovery at the McNight Site (22Co560), Coahoma County, Mississippi,* by Richard Walling and Shawn Chapman, pp. 251–253. Report submitted to the Mississippi Department of Transportation, Jackson, by Panamerican Consultants, Inc., Memphis, Tennessee.

Bettersworth, John K.

1973   The Reawakening of Society and Cultural Life, 1865–1890. In *A History of Mississippi, Volume I,* edited by Richard A. McLemore, pp. 622–639. University and College Press of Mississippi, Jackson.

Beyer, George E.

1895   Mounds of Louisiana, I. *Publications of the Louisiana Historical Society* 1(4):12–32.

1897   Mounds of Louisiana, II. *Publications of the Louisiana Historical Society* 2(1):7–27.

1900   Mound Investigation at Lamar, La. *Publications of the Louisiana Historical Society* 2(3):28–34.

Bieber, A. M., Jr., D. W. Brooks, G. Harbottle, and E. V. Sayre

1976   Application of Multivariate Techniques to Analytical Data on Aegean Ceramics. *Archaeometry* 18:59–74.

Binford, Lewis R.

1977   *For Theory Building: Essays on Faunal Remains, Aquatic Resources, Spatial Analysis and Systems Modeling.* Academic Press, New York.

Binford, Lewis R., Sally R. Binford, Robert Whallon, and Margaret Ann Hardin

1970   *Archaeology at Hatchery West.* Society for American Archaeology, Memoirs 24.

Binford, Sally R.

1971   The Significance of Variability: A Minority Report. In *The Origins of* Homo sapiens, *Volume 3, Ecology and Conservation,* edited by François Bordes, pp. 199–210. Unesco, New York.

Birchett, Thomas C. C., and Charles E. Pearson

1995   *Historical Assessment and Magnetometer and Terrestrial Surveys of the Gunboat U.S.S. Eastport and Steamboat Edward F. Dix, Red River Waterway, Grant Parish, Louisiana.* Report submitted to the U.S. Army Corps of Engineers, Vicksburg District, by Coastal Environments, Inc., Baton Rouge, Louisiana.

Bishop, Ronald L., and Hector Neff

1989   Compositional Data Analysis in Archaeology. In *Archaeological Chemistry IV,* edited by Ralph O. Allen, pp. 576–586. Advances in Chemistry Series 220, American Chemical Society, Washington, D.C.

Bishop, Ronald L., Robert L. Rands, and George R. Holley

1982   Ceramic Compositional Analysis in Archaeological Perspective. In *Advances in Archaeological Method and Theory,* vol. 5, edited by Michael B. Schiffer, pp. 275–330. Academic Press, New York.

Blake, Leonard W.

1962   Analysis of Vegetal Remains from Lawhorn Site. Appendix in *The Lawhorn Site,* by John Moselage, pp. 97–98. *Missouri Archaeologist* 24.

1986   Corn and Other Plants from Prehistory into History in Eastern United States. In *The Protohistoric Period in the Mid-South: 1500–1700,* edited by David H. Dye and Ronald C. Brister, pp. 3–13. Mississippi Department of Archives and History, Archaeological Report No. 18, Jackson.

1989   Carbonized Plant Remains form the Burris Site (3CG18). In *The Burris Site and Beyond: Archaeological Survey and Testing Along a Pipeline Corridor and Excavations at a Mississippian Village, Northeast Arkansas,* edited by Marvin D. Jeter, pp. 140–146. Arkansas Archeological Survey Research Series No. 27, Fayetteville.

1994   Charred Floral Material. In Excavations at Boydell Mound A (3AS58), Southeast Arkansas, by John H. House and Marvin D. Jeter, pp. 72–73. *Arkansas Archeologist* 33 (for 1992):1–82.

Blake, Leonard W., and Hugh C. Cutler

1979   Plant Remains from the Upper Nodena Site (3MS4). *Arkansas Archeologist* 20:53–58.

Blakely, Robert L. (editor)

1977   Biocultural Adaptations in Prehistoric America. *Proceedings of the Southern Anthropological Society* No. 11. University of Georgia Press, Athens.

Blanton, Dennis B.

2004   The Climate Factor in Late Prehistoric and Post-Contact Human Affairs. In *Indians and European Contact in Context,* edited by Dennis B. Blanton and Julia A. King, pp. 6–21. University Press of Florida, Gainesville.

Blitz, John H.

1993   *Ancient Chiefdoms of the Tombigbee.* University of Alabama Press, Tuscaloosa.

Bogan, Arthur E.

1987   Molluscan Remains from the Milner Site (22YZ515) and the O'Neil Site (22YZ624), Yazoo County, Mississippi. Appendix D in Heartfield, Price and Greene, Inc., *Data Recovery at the Milner (22YZ515) and O'Neil Creek (22YZ624) Sites, Yazoo County, Mississippi,* pp. D-1-D-11. Report submitted to the U.S. Army Corps of Engineers, Vicksburg District, by Heartfield, Price and Greene, Inc., Monroe, Louisiana.

Bogdan, Georgieann, and David S. Weaver

1992   Columbian Treponematosis in Coastal North Carolina. In *Disease and Demography in America,* edited by John W. Verano and Douglas H. Ubelaker, pp. 155–163. Smithsonian Institution Press, Washington, D.C.

Bordes, François

1952 Stratigraphie du Loess et Evolution des Industries Paléolithiques dans l'Ouest du Basin de Paris. *L'Anthropologie* 56:405–452.

Bourdo, E. A., Jr.

1956 A Review of the General Land Office Survey and of Its Use in Quantitative Studies of Former Forests. *Ecology* 37:754–768.

Bourne, Edward G. (editor)

1922 *Narratives of the Career of Hernando de Soto in the Conquest of Florida as Told by a Knight of Elvas and in a Relation by Luis Hernandez de Biedma, Factor of the Expedition.* 2 vols. Allerton, New York.

Brackenridge, Henry Marie

1814 *Views of Louisiana; Together with a Journal of a Voyage up the Missouri River, in 1811.* Cramer, Spear, and Eichbaum, Pittsburgh.

1848 On the Population and Tumuli of the Aborigines of North America. In a letter from H. M. Brakenridge, Esq. to Thomas Jefferson (1818). *Transactions of the American Philosophical Society* 1:151–159.

Bradbury, Andrew P.

1998 The Examination of Lithic Artifacts from an Early Archaic Assemblage: Strengthening Inferences Through Multiple Lines of Evidence. *Midcontinental Journal of Archaeology* 23:263–288.

Bradbury, Andrew P., and Philip J. Carr

1995 Flake Typologies and Alternative Approaches: An Experimental Assessment. *Lithic Technology* 20(2):100–116.

2005 Material and Retouched Flakes: More Complicated Than We Thought. Paper presented at the 70th Annual Meeting of the Society for American Archaeology, Salt Lake City, Utah.

Brain, Jeffrey P.

1970 Early Archaic in the Lower Mississippi Alluvial Valley. *American Antiquity* 35:104–105.

1971 *The Lower Mississippi Valley in North American Prehistory.* Report submitted to the National Park Service, Southeast Region, by the Arkansas Archeological Survey, Fayetteville.

1975 Artifacts of the Adelantado. In *The Conference on Historic Site Archaeology Papers, 1973,* 8, edited by Stanley South, pp. 129–138. University of South Carolina, Institute of Archeology and Anthropology, Columbia.

1978a Late Prehistoric Settlement Patterning in the Yazoo Basin and Natchez Bluffs Regions of the Lower Mississippi Valley. In *Mississippian Settlement Patterns,* edited by Bruce D. Smith, pp. 331–368. Academic Press, New York.

1978b The Archaeological Phase: Ethnographic Fact or Fancy? In *Archaeological Essays in Honor of Irving B. Rouse,* edited by Robert C. Dunnell and Edwin S. Hall, pp. 311–318. Mouton Publishers, The Hague.

1979 *Tunica Treasure.* Papers of the Peabody Museum of Archaeology and Ethnology 71, Cambridge.

1984   The De Soto Entrada into the Lower Mississippi Valley. *Mississippi Archaeology* 19(2):48–58.

1985   Introduction: Update of De Soto Studies since the United States De Soto Expedition Commission Report. In *Final Report of the United States De Soto Expedition Commission,* by John R. Swanton, pp. xi–lxxii. Reprint of the 1939 publication. Smithsonian Institution Press, Washington, D.C.

1988   *Tunica Archaeology.* Papers of the Peabody Museum of Archaeology and Ethnology 78, Cambridge.

1989   *Winterville: Late Prehistoric Culture Contact in the Lower Mississippi Valley.* Mississippi Department of Archives and History, Archaeological Report 23, Jackson.

Brain, Jeffrey P., Ian W. Brown, and Vincas P. Steponaitis

1994   Archaeology of the Natchez Bluffs. Unpublished ms., Research Laboratories of Anthropology, University of North Carolina, Chapel Hill.

Brain, Jeffrey P., and Philip Phillips

1979   *Archaeological and Historical Bibliography of the Lower Mississippi Valley.* Lower Mississippi Valley Survey, Peabody Museum, Harvard University, Cambridge. Reissued as a Supplemental Revision by Jeffrey P. Brain, 1983. Updated and revised by Tristram R. Kidder (on-going); available online at http://www.tulane.edu/~kidder/lmsbib.html.

Brain, Jeffrey P., Alan Toth, and Antonio Rodriguez-Buckingham

1974   Ethnohistoric Archaeology and the De Soto Entrada into the Lower Mississippi Valley. In *The Conference on Historic Site Archaeology Papers, 1972, 7,* edited by Stanley South, pp. 232–289. Columbia: University of South Carolina, Institute of Archeology and Anthropology.

Brazy, Martha Jane

1998   *An American Planter: Slavery Entrepreneurship, and Identity in the Life of Stephen Duncan, 1787–1867.* Ph.D. dissertation, Department of History, Duke University.

Breitburg, Emanuel

1992   The Faunal Assemblage. In *The Petitt Site (11AX253), Alexander County, Illinois,* edited by Paul A. Webb, pp. 295–329. Research Paper No. 58, Center for Archaeological Investigations, Southern Illinois University, Carbondale.

1994   The Faunal Assemblage. In *Archaeological Investigations in the Obion River Drainage: The West Tennessee Tributaries Project,* edited by Robert C. Mainfort, pp 164–166. Tennessee Department of Environment and Conservation, Division of Archaeology, Nashville.

1999   Faunal Remains. In *Archaeological Data Recovery at the McNight Site (22Co560), Coahoma County, Mississippi,* by Richard Walling and Shawn Chapman, pp. 231–237. Report prepared for the Mississippi Department of Transportation, Jackson, by Panamerican Consultants, Inc., Memphis.

Bridges, Patricia S.

1991   Skeletal Evidence of Changes in Subsistence Activities Between the Archaic and Mississippian Time Periods in Northwestern Alabama. In *What Mean These Bones? Studies in Southeastern Bioarchaeology,* edited by Mary Lucas Powell,

Patricia S Bridges, and Ann Marie Mires, pp. 89–101. University of Alabama Press, Tuscaloosa.

Bridges, Patricia S., John H. Blitz, and Martin C. Solano

2000   Changes in Bone Diaphyseal Strength with Horticultural Intensification in West-Central Illinois. *American Journal of Physical Anthropology* 112(2):217–238.

Bringier, Louis

1821   Notices of the Geology, Mineralogy, Topography, Productions and Aboriginal Inhabitants of the Regions Around the Mississippi and its Confluent Waters. A Letter Communicated to Rev. Elias Cornelius. *American Journal of Science and Arts* 3: 15–46.

Britt, Tad, Michael L. Hargrave, and Janet Simms

2002   *Geophysical Archeological Survey at Poverty Point State Historic Site (16WC5) West Carroll Parish, Louisiana.* U.S. Army Engineer Research and Development Center, Construction Engineering Research Laboratory, Champaign, Illinois.

Brookes, Samuel O.

1976   *The Grand Gulf Mound: Salvage Excavation of an Early Marksville Burial Mound in Claiborne County, Mississippi.* Mississippi Department of Archives and History, Archaeological Report No. 1, Jackson.

1985   Two Issaquena Sites. In *Anthology of Mississippi Archaeology 1966–1979,* edited by Patricia Galloway, pp. 151–152. Mississippi Archaeological Association and Mississippi Department of Archives and History, Jackson.

1988   The Peabody Phase: Coles Creek in the Upper Sunflower Region. Paper presented at the 45th annual Southeastern Archaeological Conference, New Orleans, Louisiana.

1999   Prehistoric Exchange in Mississippi, 10,000 B.C.–A.D. 1600. In *Raw Materials and Exchange in the Mid-South: Proceedings of the 16th Annual Mid-South Archaeological Conference, Jackson, Mississippi, June 3 and 4, 1995,* edited by Evan Peacock and Samuel O. Brookes, pp. 86–94. Mississippi Department of Archives and History, Archaeological Report No. 29, Jackson.

2001   Clarence Bloomfield Moore: Some New Perspectives. In *Historical Perspectives on Midsouth Archaeology,* edited by Martha A. Rolingson, pp. 51–58. Arkansas Archeological Survey, Research Series 58, Fayetteville.

Brookes, Samuel O., and Cheryl Taylor

1986   Tchula-Period Ceramics in the Upper Sunflower Region. In *The Tchula Period in the Mid-South and Lower Mississippi Valley,* edited by David H. Dye and Ronald C. Brister, pp. 23–27. Mississippi Department of Archives and History, Archaeological Report No. 17, Jackson.

Brose, David

1980   How Captain Riggs Hunts for Moundbuilder's Relics: An Historical Investigation of Some Influences on C. B. Moore. *Southeastern Archaeological Conference Bulletin* 22:145–152.

Brown, Calvin S.

1992   *Archeology of Mississippi.* University Press of Mississippi, Jackson. Originally
[1926] published by the Mississippi Geological Survey, University, Mississippi.

Brown, Clifford, Thomas Fenn, Stephen Hinks, Paul V. Heinrich, Justine Woodard, and
William P. Athens

1994   *A Cultural Resources Assessment of the Palusha Creek 2 Site, 22LF649, Leflore County,*
        Mississippi. Report submitted to the U.S. Army Corps of Engineers, Vicksburg
        District, by R. Christopher Goodwin & Associates, Inc., New Orleans, Louisiana.

Brown, Ian W.

1971   Trade Bells of Mid-America. Unpublished Term Paper for Harvard College Course
        Anthropology 126, taught by Stephen Williams. Gulf Coast Survey Archives, Ala-
        bama Museum of Natural History, University of Alabama, Tuscaloosa.

1975   *Archaeological Investigations at the Historic Portland and St. Pierre Sites in the*
        Lower Yazoo Basin, Mississippi, 1974. Unpublished M.A. Thesis, Department of
        Anthropology, Brown University.

1977   Historic Trade Bells. *The Conference on Historic Site Archaeology Papers, 1975,* 10:
        69–82.

1978a   *James Alfred Ford: The Man and His Works.* Special Publication No. 4., Southeast-
        ern Archaeological Conference, Memphis.

1978b   An Archaeological Survey of Mississippi Period Sites in Coahoma County, Missis-
        sippi: Final Report. Unpublished ms., Cottonlandia Museum, Greenwood, Missis-
        sippi, and Lower Mississippi Survey, Peabody Museum, Harvard University, Cam-
        bridge.

1978c   An Archaeological Survey of the Tchula-Greenwood Bluffs Region, Missis-
        sippi: Final Report. Unpublished ms., Cottonlandia Museum, Greenwood, Mis-
        sissippi, and Lower Mississippi Survey, Peabody Museum, Harvard University,
        Cambridge.

1978d   The J. O. Wheeler Collection, West Helena, Arkansas: Pottery of the Kent and Old
        Town Phases of the Mississippi Period. Unpublished ms., Cottonlandia Museum,
        Greenwood, Mississippi, and Lower Mississippi Survey, Peabody Museum, Har-
        vard University, Cambridge.

1979a   Bells. In *Tunica Treasure,* by Jeffrey P. Brain, pp. 197–205. Papers of the Peabody
        Museum of Archaeology and Ethnology 71, Cambridge.

1979b   *Early 18th-Century French-Indian Culture Contact in the Yazoo Bluffs Region of the*
        Lower Mississippi Valley. Unpublished Ph.D. Dissertation, Department of Anthro-
        pology, Brown University.

1979c   Historic Artifacts and Sociocultural Change: Some Warnings from the Lower Mis-
        sissippi Valley. *The Conference on Historic Site Archaeology Papers, 1978,* 13:109–121.

1983   Historic Aboriginal Pottery from the Yazoo Bluffs Region, Mississippi. *Southeast-*
        ern Archaeological Conference Bulletin 21:1–17.

1985   *Natchez Indian Archaeology: Culture Change and Stability in the Lower Mississippi*
        Valley. Mississippi Department of Archives and History, Archaeological Report
        No. 15, Jackson.

1994   Recent Trends in the Archaeology of the Southeastern United States. *Journal of*
        Archaeological Research 2(1):45–111.

1998   *Decorated Pottery of the Lower Mississippi Valley: A Sorting Manual.* Mississippi
        Archaeological Association/Mississippi Department of Archives and History,
        Jackson.

2002 The Hunchbacks of Tennessee: Ceramic Human Effigy Vessels in the Collections of the Peabody Museum of Archaeology and Ethnology, Harvard University. Paper presented at the 59th Annual Meeting of the Southeastern Archaeological Conference, Biloxi, Mississippi.

2003 Mississippian Ceramic Effigy Vessels from Tennessee and Missouri: Hunchback Humans and Gourds. Paper presented at the 68th Annual Meeting of the Society for American Archaeology, Milwaukee, Wisconsin.

Brown, Ian W. (editor)

1997 *Excavations at the Anna Site (22AD500), Adams County, Mississippi: A Preliminary Report.* Gulf Coast Survey Archives, Alabama Museum of Natural History, University of Alabama, Tuscaloosa.

Brown, Malaina L.

1996 Plant Remains from the Taylor Mounds (3DR2) Site, Southeastern Arkansas. Paper presented to the Graduate School of Arts and Sciences of Washington University in St. Louis in partial fulfillment of the requirements of the degree of Master of Arts.

Broyles, Bettye J.

1966 Preliminary Report: The St. Albans Site (46 Ka 27), Kanawha County, West Virginia. *West Virginia Archaeologist* 19:1–43.

Buchner, C. Andrew

1989 Ceramic Collection from the West Mounds (22-Tu-520), Tunica County, Mississippi. Paper presented at the 24th Annual Meeting of the Southern Anthropological Society, Memphis.

1996 Mound A Excavations at the West Mounds Site, Tunica County, Mississippi. In *Mounds, Embankments, and Ceremonialism in the Midsouth,* edited by Robert C. Mainfort and Richard Walling, pp. 78–86. Arkansas Archeological Survey, Research Series No. 46, Fayetteville.

2001a *Cultural Resources Survey for the Ditch 2 Outlet Project, Craighead County, Arkansas.* Report submitted to the U.S. Army Corps of Engineers, Memphis District, by Panamerican Consultants, Inc., Memphis, Tennessee.

2001b *Cultural Resources Survey for the Big Slough Ditch Project, Craighead County, Arkansas.* Report submitted to the U.S. Army Corps of Engineers, Memphis District, by Panamerican Consultants, Inc., Memphis, Tennessee.

2001c *Cultural Resources Survey of the Blue Lake Project Area, Crittenden County, Arkansas.* Report submitted to the U.S. Army Corps of Engineers, Memphis District, by Panamerican Consultants, Inc., Memphis, Tennessee.

Buchner, C. Andrew, and Eric S. Albertson

2003 Modeling Mississippian Community & Settlement Patterns: An Example form the Little River Lowlands. In *Proceedings of the 19th Mid-South Archaeological Conference: Papers in Honor of Charles H. McNutt, Sr.,* edited by C. Andrew Buchner and David H. Dye, pp. 1–16. Panamerican Consultants, Inc., Special Publication No. 3, and University of Memphis, Anthropological Research Center, Occasional Paper No. 22, Memphis.

Buchner, C. Andrew, Richard Walling, and Terry Lolley

1996 *A Cultural Resources Inventory (Phase V Survey) of a Portion of Bogue Phalia, Bolivar and Washington Counties, Mississippi: Intensive Archaeological Survey within the Big Sunflower Watershed, Volume* 5. Panamerican Consultants, Inc., Memphis, Tennessee, Report of Investigations 42–20, submitted to Vicksburg District, U.S. Army Corps of Engineers.

Buck, C. E., W. G. Cavanagh, and C. D. Litton

1996 *Bayesian Approach to Interpreting Archaeological Data.* John Willey and Sons, Chichester.

Buck, C. E., and J. A. Christen

1998 A Novel Approach to Selecting Samples for Radiocarbon Dating. *Journal of Archaeological Science* 25:303–310.

Buck, C, E., C. D. Litton, and E. M. Scott

1994 Making the Most of Radiocarbon Dating: Some Statistical Considerations. *Antiquity* 68:252–263.

Buikstra, Jane E.

1976 *Hopewell in the Lower Illinois Valley: A Regional Study of Human Biological and Prehistoric Mortuary Behavior.* Scientific Papers No. 2. Northwestern University Archaeological Program, Evanston, Illinois.

1992 Diet and Disease in Late Prehistory. In *Disease and Demography in the Americas,* edited by John W. Verano and Douglas H. Ubelaker, pp. 87–101. Smithsonian Institution Press, Washington, D.C.

Buikstra, Jane E., Lyle W. Konigsberg, and Jill Bullington

1986 Fertility and the Development of Agriculture in the Prehistoric Midwest. *American Antiquity* 51:528–546.

Buikstra, Jane E., and George R. Milner

1991 Isotopic and Archaeological Investigations of Diet in the Central Mississippi Valley. *Journal ofArchaeological Science* 18: 319–329.

Buikstra, Jane E., and Douglas Ubelaker

1994 Standards for Data Collection from Human Skeletal Remains. Arkansas Archeological Survey *Research Series* No. 44, Fayetteville.

Bunting, M. J., and R. Tipping

2000 Sorting Dross from Data: Possible Indicators of Post-depositional Assemblage Biasing in Archaeological Palynology. In *Human Ecodynamics,* edited by Geoff Bailey, Ruth Charles, and Nick Winder, pp. 63–69. Symposia of the Association for Environmental Archaeology 19. Oxbow Books, Oxford.

Burgi, Matthias, and Emily W. B. Russell

2001 Integrative Methods to Study Landscape Change. *Land Use Policy* 18:9–16.

Bush, Daniel. A., and James K. Feathers

2003 Application of OSL Single-Aliquot and Single-Grain Dating to Quartz from Anthropogenic Soil Profiles in the SE United States. *Quaternary Science Reviews* 22:1153–1159.

Bushnell, David I., Jr.

1919 Native Villages and Village Sites East of the Mississippi. *Bureau of American Ethnology Bulletin* 69:1–109.

Butler, James Davis

1894 Prehistoric Pottery—Middle Mississippi Valley. *Proceedings of the State Historical Society of Wisconsin* 41:70–78.

Butsch, Elizabeth

1991   Vertebrate Faunal Remains from the Roland site (3AR30), Arkansas County, Arkansas. In Investigations at the Roland Site, by James A. Scholtz. *Arkansas Archeologist* 30:7–56.

Butzer, Karl W.

1982   *Archaeology as Human Ecology.* Cambridge University Press, Cambridge.

1992   The Americas Before and After 1492: An Introduction to Current Geographical Research. *Annals of the Association of American Geographers* 82:345–368.

1996   Ecology in the Long View: Settlement Histories, Agrosystemic Strategies, and Ecological Performances. *Journal of Field Archaeology* 23:141–150.

Byrd, Kathleen M.

1976   Tchefuncte Subsistence: Information Obtained from the Excavation of Morton Shell Mound. *Southeastern Archaeological Conference Bulletin* 9:70–75.

1994   Tchefuncte Subsistence Practices at the Morton Shell Mound, Iberia Parish, Louisiana. *Louisiana Archaeology* 16:1–128.

Byrd, Kathleen M. (editor)

1991   *The Poverty Point Culture: Local Manifestations, Subsistence Practices, and Trade Networks.* Geoscience and Man 29 (whole issue). Louisiana State University, Baton Rouge, Louisiana.

Byrd, Kathleen M., and Robert W. Neuman

1978   Archaeological Data Relative to Prehistoric Subsistence in the Lower Mississippi River Alluvial Valley. *Geoscience and Man* 19:9–21.

Cabak, Melanie A., Mark D. Groover, and Mary M. Inkrot

1999   Rural Modernization During the Recent Past: Farmstead Archaeology in the Aiken Plateau. *Historical Archaeology* 33(4):19–43.

Caddell, Gloria M.

1982   Plant Remains from the Yarborough Site. In Carlos Solis and Richard Walling, *Archaeological Investigations at the Yarborough Site (22C1814), Clay County, Mississippi,* pp. 134–140. Report of Investigations 30. Office of Archaeological Research, University of Alabama, Tuscaloosa.

Caldwell, Joseph R.

1958   *Trend and Tradition in the Prehistory of the Eastern United States.* American Anthropological Association, Memoir 88, Menasha, Wisconsin.

Callaghan, Richard T.

1986   Analysis of the Fluoride Content of Human Remains from the Gray Site, Saskatchewan. *Plains Anthropologist* 31:317–328.

Cambron, James W., and David C. Hulse

1990   *Handbook of Alabama Archaeology Part I: Point Types.* Alabama Archaeological Society, Huntsville.

Carr, Christopher

1985   Alternative Models, Alternative Techniques: Variable Approaches to Intrasite Spatial Analysis. In *For Concordance in Archaeological Analysis,* edited by Christopher Carr, pp. 302–473. Westport Publishers, Kansas City, Missouri.

Carr, Holly Ann

1982   Preliminary Analysis of the Faunal Remains. In *Powell Canal,* by John H.

House, pp. 66–71. Arkansas Archeological Survey, Research Series 19, Fayetteville.

Carr, Philip J.

1994 The Organization of Technology: Impact and Potential. In *The Organization of Prehistoric North American Chipped-Stone Tool Technologies,* edited by Philip J. Carr, pp. 1–8. International Monographs in Prehistory, Ann Arbor, Michigan.

Carr, Philip J., and Andrew P. Bradbury

2000 Contemporary Lithic Analysis and Southeastern Archaeology. *Southeastern Archaeology,* 19:120–134.

Carr, Philip J., Kevin L. Bruce, Cliff Jenkins, and Bruce Gray

1998 *Preliminary Report on Archaeological Investigations at 22Co670, 22Co749, 22Co750, and 22Co764. Supplement to: Cultural Resources Survey of Proposed Widening/Relocation of U.S. Highway 61 from the Bolivar-Coahoma County Line to U.S. Highway 49 (MDOT Project No. 98-0009-04-011-10), Coahoma County, Mississippi.* Environmental Division, Mississippi Department of Transportation, Jackson.

Carr, Philip J., and Alison Marie Hadley

2005 The John Forrest Site: Data and Supposition. Paper presented at the Mississippi Archaeological Association Annual Meeting, Vidalia, Louisiana.

Carr, Philip J., and Lee H. Stewart

2004 Poverty Point Chipped-Stone Raw Materials: Inferring Social and Economic Strategies. In *Big Mounds, Big Power: The Rise of Cultural Complexity in the Southeast,* edited by Jon L. Gibson and Philip J. Carr, pp.129–145. University of Alabama Press, Tuscaloosa.

Chambers, Moreau B.

1937 A Selected List of Significant Archaeological Sites in Various Counties of Mississippi, with Approximate Locations of All Sites Named. Manuscript on file, Mississippi Department of Archives and History, Jackson.

Chambers, Moreau B., and James A. Ford

1941 Indian Mounds and Sites in Mississippi. Works Progress Administration document prepared for the National Park Service. Manuscript on file, Mississippi Department of Archives and History, Jackson.

Chang, K. C.

1968 *Settlement Archaeology.* National Press, Palo Alto, California.

Chapman, Carl H.

1953 The Archaeological Survey of Missouri. *Missouri Archaeologist* 15(1–2):7–41.

Chapman, Carl H. (compiler)

1977 Investigation and Comparison of Two Fortified Mississippi Tradition Archaeological Sites in Southeast Missouri: A Preliminary Compilation. *The Missouri Archaeologist* 38 (whole issue).

Chapman, Carl H., and Eleanor F. Chapman

1972 *Indians and Archaeology of Missouri.* 2nd edition, revised. University of Missouri Press, Columbia.

Chapman, Jefferson, and Gary D. Crites

1987   Evidence for Early Maize (*Zea mays*) from the Icehouse Bottom Site, Tennessee. *American Antiquity* 52:352–354.

Chapman, Jefferson, Paul A. Delcourt, Patricia A. Cridlebaugh, Andrea B. Shea, and Hazel R. Delcourt

1982   Man-Land Interaction: 10,000 Years of American Indian Impact on Native Ecosystems in the Lower Little Tennessee River Valley, Eastern Tennessee. *Southeastern Archaeology* 1:115–121.

Chapman, Jefferson, and Andrea Brewer Shea

1981   The Archaeobotanical Record: Early Archaic Period to Contact in the Lower Little Tennessee River Valley. *Tennessee Anthropologist* 6(1):61–84.

Chapman, Joseph Shawn, Richard Walling, and Terry Lolley

1994   *A Cultural Resources Inventory (Phase II Survey) of Portions of the Big and Little Sunflower Rivers, Sharkey and Yazoo Counties, Mississippi.* Report submitted to U.S. Army Corps of Engineers, Vicksburg District by Panamerican Consultants, Inc., Memphis, Tennessee.

1995a   *A Cultural Resources Inventory (Phase III Survey) of a Portion of the Big Sunflower River, Humphreys, Sharkey, and Washington Counties, Mississippi.* Report submitted to U.S. Army Corps of Engineers, Vicksburg District by Panamerican Consultants, Inc., Memphis, Tennessee.

1995b   *A Cultural Resources Inventory (Phase IV Survey) of a Portion of the Big Sunflower River, Humphreys, Sunflower, and Washington Counties, Mississippi.* Report submitted to U.S. Army Corps of Engineers, Vicksburg District by Panamerican Consultants, Inc., Memphis, Tennessee.

1995c   *A Cultural Resources Inventory (Phase V Survey) of a Portion of the Big and Little Sunflower Rivers, Humphreys, Sunflower and Washington Counties, Mississippi.* Report submitted to U.S. Army Corps of Engineers, Vicksburg District, by Panamerican Consultants, Inc., Memphis, Tennessee.

Chase, David W.

1998   Prehistoric Pottery of Central Alabama. *Journal of Alabama Archaeology* 44:52–98.

Chase, J. E., J. L. Montgomery, and K. Landreth

1988   *Southeast Louisiana Cultural Resource Management Plan, Volume I, Cultural Resources Series, Report No. COELMN/PD-87/02.* U.S. Army Corps of Engineers, New Orleans District, New Orleans, Louisiana.

Childe, V. Gordon

1936   *Man Makes Himself.* Watts & Co., London.

Childress, Mitchell R., Guy G. Weaver, John L. Hopkins, and Marsha Oats

1995   *Cultural Resources Investigations at Mound City Plantation, Crittenden County, Arkansas.* Report submitted to the Promus Companies by Garrow and Associates, Inc., Memphis, Tennessee.

Chisolm, Brian S.

1989   Variation in Diet Reconstruction Based on Stable Carbon Isotope Evidence. In *The Chemistry of Prehistoric Human Bone*, edited by T. Douglas Price, pp. 10–37. Cambridge University Press, Cambridge.

Claassen, Cheryl

1991   Normative Thinking and Shell-Bearing Sites. In *Archaeological Method and Theory, Vol. III,* edited by Michael B. Schiffer, pp. 249–298. University of Arizona Press, Tucson.

Clark, Anthony J.

1996   *Seeing Beneath the Soil: Prospecting Methods in Archaeology.* New Edition. B. T. Batsford, Ltd, London.

Clark, C. D., S. M. Garrod, and M. P. Pearson

1998   Landscape Archaeology and Remote Sensing in Southern Madagascar. *International Journal of Remote Sensing* 19:1461–1477.

Clark, J.

1999   On *Stone Tools: Theoretical Insights into Human Prehistory,* by George Odell. *Lithic Technology* 24:126–135.

Clark, Philip J., and Francis C. Evans

1954   Distance to Nearest Neighbor as a Measure of Spatial Relationship in Populations. *Ecology* 34:445–453.

Clarke, David L.

1968   *Analytical Archaeology.* Metheun, London.

1977   *Spatial Archaeology.* Academic Press, New York.

Clarkson, Chris

2002   An Index of Invasiveness for the Measurement of Unifacial and Bifacial Retouch: Theoretical, Experimental, and Archaeological Verification. *Journal of Archaeological Science* 29:65–75.

Clay, R. Berle

2001   Complementary Geophysical Survey Techniques: Why Two Ways are Always Better than One. *Southeastern Archaeology* 20:31–43.

Clayton, Lawrence A., Vernon J. Knight, Jr., and Edward C. Moore (editors)

1993   *The De Soto Chronicles: The Expedition of Hernando de Soto to North America in 1539–1543,* 2 vols. University of Alabama Press, Tuscaloosa.

Cleland, Charles E.

1965   Analysis of the Faunal Remains of the Fatherland Site. Appendix 2 In *Archeology of the Fatherland Site: The Grand Village of the Natchez,* by Robert S. Neitzel, pp. 96–101. Anthropological Papers 51(1), American Museum of Natural History, New York.

Cobb, Charles R.

2000   *From Quarry to Cornfield: The Political Economy of Mississippian Hoe Production.* University of Alabama Press, Tuscaloosa.

Coe, Joffre L.

1964   *The Formative Cultures of the Carolina Piedmont.* Transactions of the American Philosophical Society 54(5) (whole issue), Philadelphia.

Cogswell, James W.

1998   *Late Woodland Sand-Tempered Pottery from Southeast Missouri.* Unpublished Ph.D. Thesis, Department of Anthropology, University of Missouri, Columbia.

Cogswell, James W., Hector Neff, and Michael D. Glascock

1998   Analysis of Shell-tempered Pottery Replicates: Implications for Provenance Studies. *American Antiquity* 63:63–72.

Cogswell, James W., and Michael J. O'Brien

1998   Analysis of Early Mississippian-Period Pottery from Kersey, Pemiscot County, Missouri. *Southeastern Archaeology* 17:39–52.

Colburn, Mona L.

1987   Faunal Exploitation at the Ink Bayou Site. In *Results of Final Testing for Significance at the Ink Bayou Site (3PU252), Pulaski County, Arkansas,* by David B. Waddell, John H. House, Francis B. King, Mona L. Colburn, and Murray K. Marks. Report submitted to the Arkansas Highway and Transportation Department by the Arkansas Archeological Survey, Fayetteville.

Coleman, J. M.

1966   Ecological Changes in a Massive Fresh-Water Clay Sequence. *Transactions of the Gulf Coast Association of Geological Societies* 16:159–174.

Collins, Henry B.

1926   Archaeological and Anthropometric Work in Mississippi. *Smithsonian Miscellaneous Collections* 78(1):89–93.

1927   Choctaw Sherds from Village Sites in Mississippi. *Journal of the Washington Academy of Sciences* 17:259–263.

1932   Excavation of a Prehistoric Indian Village Site in Mississippi. *United States National Museum Proceedings* 78(32):1–22.

Collins, Michael B.

1993   Comprehensive Lithic Studies: Context, Technology, Style, Attrition, Breakage, Use-wear and Organic Studies. *Lithic Technology* 18(1–2):87–94.

Connaway, John M.

1977   *The Denton Site: A Middle Archaic Occupation in the Northern Yazoo Basin, Mississippi.* Archaeological Report 4. Mississippi Department of Archives and History, Jackson.

1980   The Baldwin-O'Neal Dilemma. *Mississippi Archaeology* 15(1): 22–29.

1981a   Fort Maurepas Investigation. In *Archaeological Investigations in Mississippi 1969–1977,* by John M. Connaway, pp. 62–68. Archaeological Report 6. Mississippi Department of Archives and History, Jackson.

1981b   *Archaeological Investigations in Mississippi, 1969–1977.* Archaeological Report No. 6. Mississippi Department of Archives and History, Jackson.

1982a   Wood Identified from Mississippi Period Houses in the Northern Yazoo Basin. *Mississippi Archaeology* 17(1):17–22.

1982b   The Sturdivant Fishweir, Amite County, Mississippi. *Southeastern Archaeology* 1:138–163.

1982c   The Keenan Bead Cache: Lawrence County, Mississippi. *Louisiana Archaeology* 8:57–71.

1984   *The Wilsford Site (22-CO-516), Coahoma County, Mississippi: A Late Mississippi Period Settlement in the Northern Yazoo Basin of Mississippi.* Archaeological Report No. 14. Mississippi Department of Archives and History, Jackson.

1985   An Unusual Engraved Vessel Fragment from 22-CO-511. *Mississippi Archaeology* 20(2): 42–46.

1988   Remnant Braided Stream Surfaces in the Northern Yazoo Basin: Preliminary Observations. *Mississippi Archaeology* 23(1):43–69.

2000   New Discoveries Regarding the "Clarksdale Bells." *Field Notes: Newsletter of the Arkansas Archeological Society* No. 294, pp. 5–6. Fayetteville.

2004   The Enigma of the Specialist—Middle & Late Archaic—Zoomorphic Objects. Paper presented at the Enigma of the Specialist: Middle and Late Archaic Beads, Big Bifaces, and Caches in the Lower Mississippi Valley and Greater Southeast Conference, Poverty Point, Louisiana.

Connaway, John M., and Samuel O. McGahey

1970   *Archaeological Survey and Salvage in the Yazoo-Mississippi Delta and in Hinds County: November 1, 1968–December 31, 1969.* Mississippi Archaeological Survey, Preliminary Report, Mississippi Department of Archives and History, Jackson.

1971   *Archaeological Excavation at the Boyd Site, Tunica County, Mississippi.* Technical Report 1. Mississippi Department of Archives and History, Jackson.

1996   Archaeological Reconnaissance: Survey of Braided Stream Surfaces in the Western Central Yazoo Basin, Mississippi. *Mississippi Archaeology* 31(2):23–50.

Connaway, John M., Samuel O. McGahey, and Clarence H. Webb

1977   *Teoc Creek: A Poverty Point Site in Carroll County, Mississippi.* Archaeological Report 3. Mississippi Department of Archives and History, Jackson.

Connaway, John M., and Douglas C. Sims

1997   A Chronometric Database for Mississippi. *Mississippi Archaeology* 32(2):98–116.

Conyers, Lawrence B., and Dean Goodman

1997   *Ground-Penetrating Radar: An Introduction for Archaeologists.* Altamira Press, Walnut Creek, California.

Cordell, Ann S., and Patrick Livingood

2004   Point/Counter Point: The Accuracy and Feasibility of Digital Image Techniques in the Analysis of Ceramic Thin-Sections. Paper presented at the joint Southeastern Archaeological Conference/Midwestern Archaeological Conference, October 2004, St. Louis, Missouri.

Council, R. Bruce

1985   *Historic Documentation and Site Reconnaissance of the Memphis Navy Yard Archaeological Site, Memphis, Shelby County, Tennessee.* The Jeffrey L. Brown Institute of Archaeology, University of Tennessee, Chattanooga.

Cowgill, George

1972   Models, Methods and Techniques for Seriation. In *Models in Archaeology,* edited by David L. Clarke, pp 381–424. Metheun, London.

Cox, Wendell, and Jean Love

1996   *40 Years of the US Interstate Highway System: An Analysis—The Best Investment A Nation Ever Made: A Tribute to the Dwight D. Eisenhower System of Interstate & Defense Highways.* Prepared for American Highway Users Alliance. Electronic document, http://www.publicpurpose.com/freeway1.html, accessed July 27, 2004.

Coxe, Carey L.

1999   Vertebrate Faunal Analysis. In *Cultural Resources Inventory, Upper Steele Bayou Project, Swan Lake Mitigation Area, Washington County, Mississippi,* by Stephanie L. Perrault, Elizabeth L. Davoli, Carey L. Coxe, and William Cash, pp. 225–232. Report submitted to the U.S. Army Corps of Engineers, Vicksburg District, by Coastal Environments, Inc., Baton Rouge, Louisiana.

Coxe, Carey L., and David B. Kelley

2004   Faunal Remains. In *Data-Recovery Excavations at the Hedgeland Site (16CT19),Catahoula Parish, Louisiana,* edited by Joanne Ryan. Report submitted to the U.S. Army Corps of Engineers, Vicksburg District, by Coastal Environments, Inc., Baton Rouge, Louisiana.

Crawford, Gary D., David G. Smith, and Vandy Bowyer

1997   Dating the Entry of Corn (*Zea mays*) into the Lower Great Lakes Region. *American Antiquity* 62:112–119.

Crawford, Jessica F.

2004   *Archaic Effigy Beads: A New Look at Some Old Beads.* Unpublished M.A. Thesis, Department of Sociology and Anthropology, University of Mississippi.

Crockett, Norman L.

1979   *The Black Towns.* Regents Press of Kansas, Lawrence.

Croswell, C.

1878   Mound Explorations in Southeastern Missouri. *Transactions of the Academy of Science of St. Louis* 3:531–538.

Crumley, Carole L.

1979   Three Locational Models: An Epistemological Assessment for Anthropology and Archaeology. In *Advances in Archaeological Method and Theory,* edited by M. B. Schiffer, vol. 2, pp. 141–73. Academic Press, New York.

1994   Historical Ecology: A Multidimensional Ecological Orientation. In *Historical Ecology: Changing Knowledge and Cultural Landscapes,* edited by Carole L. Crumley, pp. 1–16. School of American Research Press, Santa Fe.

Crusoe, Daniel L.

1971   The Missing Half: The Analysis of Ceramic Fabric. *Southeastern Archaeological Conference Bulletin* 13:108–114.

Cusick, James G., Todd McKakin, Shannon Dawdy, and Jill-Karen Yakubik

1995   *Cultural Resources Documentation, Black River Bridge at Jonesville, Jct. LA 3037 to LA 565, Catahoula and Concordia Parishes, Route LA-US 84.* Report submitted to Frederic R. Harris, Inc., by Earth Search, Inc., New Orleans.

Cutler, Hugh C., and Leonard W. Blake

1985   Food Plant Remains from Eight Prehistoric Indian Sites in the Yazoo Delta Area of
[1970]   Mississippi. In *Anthology of Mississippi Archaeology 1966–1979,* edited by Patricia Galloway, pp. 114–122. Mississippi Department of Archives and History and Mississippi Archaeological Association, Jackson. Originally printed in the *Mississippi Archaeological Association Newsletter, Vol.* 5, No. 2, pp. 1–6.

2001   Plants from Archaeological Sites East of the Rockies. In Gayle J. Fritz and Patty

Jo Watson, editors, *Plants from the Past,* by Leonard W. Blake and Hugh C. Cutler, pp. 93–147. University of Alabama Press, Tuscaloosa.

Dacey, Michael F.

1973   Statistical Tests of Spatial Association in the Location of Tool Types. *American Antiquity* 38:320–328.

Dalan, Rinita A.

2006   Magnetic Susceptibility. In *Remote Sensing in Archaeology: An Explicitly North American Perspective,* edited by Jay K. Johnson, pp. 161–204. University of Alabama Press, Tuscaloosa.

Dancey, William S.

1981   *Archaeological Field Methods: An Introduction.* Burgess Publishing Company, Minneapolis.

Daniel, Glynn

1975   *A Hundred and Fifty Years of Archaeology.* Harvard University Press, Cambridge.

1981   *A Short History of Archaeology.* Thames and Hudson, London.

Davis, Hester A.

1988   Double the Work, Double the Treasure: Federal Archeology in Arkansas, 1966–1986. In *Advances in Southeastern Archaeology 1966–1986: Contributions of the Federal Archaeology Program,* edited by Bennie C. Keel, pp. 4–6. Southeastern Archaeological Conference Special Publication No. 6.

2002   Pot Hunters, Salvage, and Science in Arkansas, 1900–2000. In *Histories of Southeastern Archaeology,* edited by Shannon Tushingham, Jane Hill, and Charles H. McNutt, pp. 51–60. University of Alabama Press, Tuscaloosa.

Davis, Mary B.

1987   *In Search of C. B. Moore.* Huntington Free Library, New York.

Davis, Ronald L. F.

1994   *Black Experience in Natchez, 1720–1880.* Natchez National Historical Park, Natchez, Mississippi.

Decker-Walters, Deena S., Terrence W. Walters, C. Wesley Cowan, and Bruce D. Smith

1993   Isozymic Characterization of Wild Populations of *Cucurbita pepo. Journal of Ethnobiology* 13:55–72.

Deevey, E. S., Don S. Rice, Prudence M. Rice, H. H. Vaughan, Mark Brenner, and M. S. Flannery

1979   Mayan Urbanism: Impact on a Tropical Karst Environment. *Science* 206:298–306.

DeJarnette, David J., and Christopher S. Peebles

1970   The Development of Alabama Archaeology: The Snow's Bend Site. *Journal of Alabama Archaeology* 16:78–119.

de la Vega, Garcilaso (El Inca)

1986   *Florida del Inca.* Edited version printed in 1986, edited by Sylvia Hilton. Historia,
[1722]   Madrid.

Delcourt, Hazel R.

1987   The Impact of Prehistoric Agriculture and Land Occupation on Natural Vegetation. *Trends in Ecology and Evolution* 2:39–44.

2002   *Forests in Peril.* The McDonald and Woodward Publishing Company, Blacksburg, Virginia.

Delcourt, Hazel R., and Paul A. Delcourt

1974   Primeval Magnolia-Holly-Beech Climax in Louisiana. *Ecology* 55:638–644.

1991   *Quaternary Ecology: A Paleoecological Perspective.* Chapman and Hall, New York.

1997   Pre-Columbian Native American Use of Fire on Southern Appalachian Landscapes. *Conservation Biology* 11:1010–1014.

Delcourt, Hazel R., Paul A. Delcourt, and P. Daniel Royall

1997   Late Quaternary Vegetational History of the Western Lowlands. In Dan F. Morse, *Sloan: A Paleoindian Dalton Cemetery in Arkansas,* pp. 103–122. Smithsonian Institution Press, Washington, D.C.

Delcourt, Hazel R., Darrell C. West, and Paul A. Delcourt

1981   Forests of the Southeastern United States: Quantitative Maps for Aboveground Woody Biomass, Carbon, and Dominance of Major Tree Taxa. *Ecology* 62:879–887.

Delcourt, Paul A., and Hazel R. Delcourt

1977   The Tunica Hills, Louisiana-Mississippi: Late Glacial Locality for Spruce and Deciduous Forest Species. *Quaternary Research* 7:218–237.

1987   *Long-Term Forest Dynamics of the Temperate Zone.* Springer-Verlag, New York.

2004   *Prehistoric Native Americans and Ecological Change.* Cambridge University Press, Cambridge.

Delcourt, Paul A., Hazel R. Delcourt, Ronald C. Brister, and Laurence E. Lackey

1980   Quaternary Vegetation History of the Mississippi Embayment. *Quaternary Research* 13:111–132.

Delcourt, Paul A., Hazel R. Delcourt, Patricia A. Cridlebaugh, and Jefferson Chapman

1986   Holocene Ethnobotanical and Paleoecological Record of Human Impact in the Little Tennessee River Valley, Tennessee. *Quaternary Research* 25:330–349.

Delcourt, Paul A., Hazel R. Delcourt, Cecil R. Ison, William E. Sharp, and Kristen J. Gremillion

1998   Prehistoric Human Use of Fire, the Eastern Agricultural Complex, and Appalachian Oak-Chestnut Forests: Paleoecology of Cliff Palace Pond, Kentucky. *American Antiquity* 63:263–278.

Delcourt, Paul A., Hazel R. Delcourt, and Roger T. Saucier

1999   Late Quaternary Vegetation Dynamics in the Central Mississippi Valley. In *Arkansas Archaeology: Essays in Honor of Dan and Phyllis Morse,* edited by Robert C. Mainfort, Jr., and Marvin D. Jeter, pp. 15–30. University of Arkansas Press, Fayetteville.

Dellinger, Samuel C., and S. D. Dickinson

1940   Possible Antecedents of the Middle Mississippian Ceramic Complex in Northeastern Arkansas. *American Antiquity* 6:133–147.

Dellinger, Samuel C., and Elmer G. Wakefield

1936   Obstetric Effigies of the Mound Builders of Eastern Arkansas. *American Journal of Obstetrics and Gynecology* 31:683–684.

Denevan, William M.

1992   The Pristine Myth: The Landscape of the Americas in 1492. *Annals of the Association of American Geographers* 82:369–385.

Dewar, Robert E., and Kevin A. McBride

1992   Remnant Settlement Patterns. In *Space, Time and Archaeological Landscapes,* edited by Jacqueline Rossignol and LuAnn Wandsnider, pp. 227–255. Plenum Press, New York.

di Caprio, Ninina Cuomo, and Sarah Vaughn

1993   An Experimental Study in Distinguishing Grog (Chamotte) from Argillaceous Inclusions in Ceramic Thin Sections. *Archeomaterials* 7: 21–40.

Diehl, Michael W.

2005   Morphological Observations on Recently Recovered Early Agricultural Period Maize Cob Fragments from Southern Arizona. *American Antiquity* 70:361–375.

Dincauze, Dena F.

1996   Modeling Communities and Other Thankless Tasks. In *The Paleoindian and Early Archaic Southeast,* edited by David G. Anderson and Kenneth E. Sassaman, pp. 421–424. University of Alabama Press, Tuscaloosa.

Dollard, John

1937   *Caste and Class in a Southern Town.* Yale University Press, New Haven.

Doolittle, James A.

1989   Ground Penetrating Radar (GPR) Survey of the Poverty Point Site, Northern Louisiana. Appendix C In *Digging on the Dock of the Bay(ou): The 1988 Excavations at Poverty Point,* edited by Jon L. Gibson, pp. 207–210. Report No. 8, Center for Archaeological Studies, University of Southwestern Louisiana, Lafayette.

Doolittle, William E.

1992   Agriculture in North America on the Eve of Contact: A Reassessment. *Annals of the Association of American Geographers* 82:386–401.

Driver, Harold M., and Alfred. L. Kroeber

1932   Quantitative Expression of Cultural Relationships. *University of California Publications in Archaeology and Ethnology* 31:211–256.

Droessler, Judith

1981   *Craniometery and Biological Distance: Biocultural Continuity and Change at the Late-Woodland-Mississippian Interface.* Research Series Volume 1, Center for American Archaeology, Evanston, Illinois.

Duller, G. A. T.

1996   Recent Developments in Luminescence Dating of Quaternary Sediments. *Progress in Physical Geography* 20(2):127–145.

Dumont de Montigny, F.

1753   *Memoires Historiques sur la Louisiane* (2 vols). Bauche, Paris.

Dunbar, William

1832   A Description of the Washita River in Louisiana, and the Country Bordering Thereon. *American State Papers, Indian Affairs* 1:731–743.

Dunlap, Knight (editor/arranger)

1929   *Report on the Conference on Midwestern Archaeology, Held in St. Louis Mis-*

souri, May 18, 1929. Bulletin of the National Research Council, No. 74. Washington, D.C.

Dunnell, Robert C.

1970   Seriation Method and Its Evaluation. *American Antiquity* 35:305–319.

1978   Style and Function: A Fundamental Dichotomy. *American Antiquity* 43:192–202.

1982   Science, Social Science, and Common Sense: The Agonizing Dilemma of Modern Archaeology. *Journal of Anthropological Research* 38:1–25.

1983   Current Research, Missouri. *American Antiquity* 48:842.

1984   The Ethics of Archaeological Significance Decisions. In *Ethics and Values in Archaeology,* edited by Ernestene L. Green, pp. 62–74. The Free Press, New York

1985   Archaeological Survey in the Lower Mississippi Alluvial Valley, 1940–1947: A Landmark Study in American Archaeology. *American Antiquity* 50:297–300.

1986a   Five Decades of American Archaeology. In *American Archaeology: Past and Future,* edited by David J. Meltzer, Don Fowler and Jeremy A Sabloff, pp. 23–49. Smithsonian Institution Press, Washington, D.C.

1986b   Methodological Issues in Americanist Artifact Classification. In *Advances in Archaeological Method and Theory* 9, edited by Michael B. Schiffer, pp. 149–207. Academic Press, New York.

1986c   Current Research, Missouri. *American Antiquity* 51:858.

1988   Low-Density Archeological Records from Plowed Surfaces: Some Preliminary Considerations. *American Archeology* 7:29–38.

1989   Aspects of the Application of Evolutionary Theory in Archaeology. In *Archaeological Thought in America,* edited by C. C. Lamberg-Karlovsky, pp. 35–49. Cambridge University Press, Cambridge.

1990   The Role of the Southeast in American Archaeology. *Southeastern Archaeology* 9:11–22.

1991   Methodological Impacts of Catastrophic Depopulation on American Archaeology and Ethnology. In *Columbian Consequences III, The Spanish Borderlands in Pan-American Perspectives,* edited by David H. Thomas, pp. 561–580. Smithsonian Institution Press, Washington, D.C.

1992   The Notion Site. In *Space, Time, and Archaeological Landscapes,* edited by Jacqueline Rossignol and LuAnn Wandsnider, pp. 21–41. Plenum Press, New York.

1998   The Langdon Site, Dunklin County, Missouri. In *Changing Perspectives on the Archaeology of the Central Mississippi River Valley,* edited by Michael J. O'Brien and Robert C. Dunnell, pp. 200–224. University of Alabama Press, Tuscaloosa.

2002   *Systematics in Prehistory.* Blackburn Press, Caldwell, New Jersy. Originally pub-
[1971] lished by Free Press, New York.

2006   Measuring Relatedness. In *Mapping Our Ancestors,* edited by Carl P. Lipo, Michael J. O'Brien, Mark Collard, and Stephen J. Shennan, pp. 109–118. Aldine, New York.

Dunnell, Robert C., and William S. Dancey

1983   The Siteless Survey: A Regional Scale Data Collection Strategy. In *Advances in Archaeological Method and Theory, Vol. 6,* edited by Michael B. Schiffer, pp. 267–287. Academic Press, New York.

Dunnell, Robert C., and James K. Feathers

1991　Late Woodland Manifestations of the Malden Plain, Southeast Missouri. In *Stability, Transformation, and Variation: The Late Woodland Southeast,* edited by Michael S. Nassaney and Charles R. Cobb, pp. 21–45. Plenum Press, New York.

1994　Thermoluminescence Dating of Surficial Archaeological Material. In *Dating in Exposed and Surface Contexts,* edited by Charlotte Beck, pp. 115–137. University of New Mexico Press, Albuquerque.

Dunnell, Robert C., James K. Feathers, and Diana M. Greenlee

2002　Recent Surface Investigations at Tchula Lake (20-O-9): Tchula Lake, Deasonville, and Lower Mississippi Valley Prehistory. Paper presented at the 59th Annual Meeting of the Southeastern Archaeological Conference, Biloxi, Mississippi.

Dunnell, Robert C., and Diana M. Greenlee

1999　Late Woodland Period "Waste" Reduction in the Ohio River Valley. *Journal of Anthropological Archaeology* 18:376–395.

Dunnell, Robert C., and Mark L. Readhead

1989　The Relation of Dating and Chronology: Comments on Chatters and Hoover (1986) and Butler and Stein (1988). *Quaternary Research* 39:232–233.

Dunnell, Robert C., and Julie K. Stein

1989　Theoretical Issues in the Interpretation of Microartifacts. *Geoarchaeology* 4:31–42.

Dunnell, Robert C., and Fran Whittaker

1990　The Late Archaic of the Eastern Lowlands and Evidence of Trade. *Lousiana Archaeology* 17:13–36.

Du Pratz, Le Page Antoine Simon

1758　*Histoire de la Louisiane* (3 vols.). De Bure, Delaguette, Lambert, Paris.

Du Pre, L. J.

1875　Wonders of the Lowlands. *Harper's New Monthly Magazine* 50 (297):346–351.

Dye, David H.

1991　New Deal Archaeology in the Middle Tennessee Valley. *Louisiana Archaeology* 18:23–60.

Dye, David H., and C. Andrew Buchner

1988　Preliminary Archaeological Investigations of the West Mounds, 22-Tu-520: Tunica County, Mississippi. *Mississippi Archaeology* 23(2):64–75.

Dye, David H., and Camille Wharey

1989　Exhibition Catalogue. In *The Southeastern Ceremonial Complex: Artifacts and Analysis, the Cottonlandia Conference,* edited by Patricia Galloway, pp. 319–382. University of Nebraska Press, Lincoln.

Early, Ann M.

2000　The Caddo and the Forest. In *Forest Farmsteads,* edited by Ann M. Early, pp. 93–110. Arkansas Archeological Survey Research Series 57. Arkansas Archeological Survey, Fayetteville.

Early, Ann M. (editor)

1993　*Caddoan Saltmakers in the Ouachita Valley: The Hardaman Site.* Arkansas Archeological Survey Research Series No. 43. Arkansas Archeological Survey, Fayetteville.

Ebert, James I.

1992   *Distributional Archaeology.* University of New Mexico Press, Albuquerque.

Edmonds, Michael

2001   The Pleasures and Pitfalls of Written Records. In *The Historical Ecology Handbook,* edited by Dave Egan and Evelyn A. Howell, pp. 73–99. Washington, D.C.: Island Press.

Emerson, Thomas E., and R. Barry Lewis (editors)

2000   *Cahokia and the Hinterlands: Middle Mississippian Cultures of the Midwest.* University of Illinois Press, Urbana.

Erickson, David L., Bruce D. Smith, Andrew C. Clarke, Daniel H. Sandweiss, and Noreen Tuross

2005   An Asian Origin for a 10,000-Year-Old Domesticated Plant in the Americas. *Proceedings of the National Academy of Sciences* 102:18315–18320.

Evans, Clifford

1955   *A Ceramic Study of Virginia.* Bureau of American Ethnology, Bulletin 160. Washington, D.C.

Evers, E.

1880   The Ancient Pottery of Southeastern Missouri. In *Contributions to the Archaeology of Missouri, by the Archaeological Section of the St. Louis Academy of Science,* pp. 21–30. Part 1: Pottery. Bates, Salem, Mass.

Ewen, Charles R.

1988   *The Discovery of De Soto's First Winter Encampment in Florida.* De Soto Working Paper No. 7. University of Alabama, State Museum of Natural History, Tuscaloosa.

1990   Soldier of Fortune: Hernando de Soto in the Territory of the Apalachee, 1539–1540. In *Columbian Consequences, Vol. 2, Archaeological and Historical Perspectives on the Spanish Borderlands East,* edited by David Hurst Thomas, pp. 83–91. Smithsonian Institution Press, Washington, D.C.

1991   *From Spaniard to Creole: The Archaeology of Cultural Formation at Puerto Real, Haiti.* University of Alabama Press, Tuscaloosa.

Ezzo, Joseph A.

1992   A Refinement of the Adult Burial Chronology at Grasshopper Pueblo. *Journal of Archaeological Science* 19:445–458.

Fagan, Brian M.

2000   *Ancient North America.* Thames and Hudson, London.

Fagette, Paul

1996   *Digging for Dollars: American Archaeology and the New Deal.* University of New Mexico Press, Albuquerque.

Faulkner, Charles H.

1982   The Weaver Pottery: A Late-Nineteenth-Century Family Industry in a Southeastern Setting. In *Archaeology of Urban America: The Search for Pattern and Process,* edited by Roy S. Dickens, pp. 209–236. Academic Press, New York.

Faulkner, Charles H. (editor)

1981   *The Weaver Pottery Site: Industrial Archaeology in Knoxville, Tennessee.* Tennessee Department of Transportation Project #29001–1219–04. University of Tennessee, Department of Anthropology, Knoxville.

Feathers, James K., and W. D. Scott

1989   A Prehistoric Ceramic Composite from the Mississippi Valley. *American Ceramic Society Bulletin* 68:554–557.

Federal Highway Administration

2001   Interstate 69 Fact Sheet. Electronic document, http://www.nationalI-69.org, accessed September 14, 2004.

Ferguson, Leland

1978   Looking for the "Afro-" in Colono-Indian Pottery. *The Conference on Historic Site Archaeology Papers, 1977* 12: 68–86.

Finger, Michael

2003a   A Mississippian Ceremonial Center: An Investigation of Parchman Place Mounds Reveals the Expected and the Unexpected. *American Archaeology* 7(1):20–25.

2003b   Parasailing at Parchman Place. *American Archaeology* 7(1):23.

Fisher, Alton K.

1997   Origins of the Midwestern Taxonomic Method. *Midcontinental Journal of Archaeology* 22:117–122.

Fisk, Harold N.

1944   *Geological Investigations of the Alluvial Valley of the Lower Mississippi River.* U.S. Army Corps of Engineers, Mississippi River Commission, Publication 52, Vicksburg, Mississippi.

Fitzgerald, William R.

2001   Contact, Neutral Iroquoian Transformation, and the Little Ice Age. In *Societies in Eclipse: Archaeology of the Eastern Woodland Indians, A.D. 1400–1700*, edited by David S. Brose, C. Wesley Cowan, and Robert C. Mainfort, Jr., pp. 37–47. Smithsonian Institution Press, Washington, D.C.

Flores, William M., Thurston H. G. Hahn III, Sylvia Timmons Duay, and Richard A. Weinstein

1991   *Cultural Resources Survey and Testing of the Proposed Cornerstone Natural Gas Pipeline Route, Richland and Madison Parishes, Louisiana and Warren County, Mississippi.* Report submitted to Bio/West Inc., by Coastal Environments, Inc., Baton Rouge, Louisiana.

Fogleman, James A.

1991   The Avoyelles–St. Landry Area of South-Central Louisiana in Poverty Point Times. In *The Poverty Point Culture: Local Manifestations, Subsistence Practices, and Trade Networks*, edited by Kathleen M. Byrd, pp. 3–6. *Geosciences and Man.* vol. 29. Louisiana State University, Baton Rouge.

Foner, Eric

1988   *Nothing but Freedom: Emancipation and Its Legacy.* Louisiana State University Press, Baton Rouge.

Ford, James A.

1935a   *A Ceramic Decoration Sequence at an Old Indian Site near Sicily Island, Louisiana.* Anthropological Study No. 1. Louisiana Geological Survey, Department of Conservation, New Orleans.

1935b   An Introduction to Louisiana Archaeology. *Louisiana Conservation Review* 4:8–11.

1935c   Outline of Louisiana and Mississippi Pottery Horizons. *Louisiana Conservation Review* 4:32–38.

1936   *Analysis of Indian Village Site Collections from Louisiana and Mississippi.* Anthropological Study No. 2, Department of Conservation, Louisiana Geological Survey, New Orleans.

1938   A Chronological Method Applicable to the Southeast. *American Antiquity* 3:260–264.

1954a   The Type Concept Revisted. *American Anthropologist* 56:42–54.

1954b   Comment on A. C. Spaulding's "Statistical Techniques for the Discovery of Artifact Types." *American Antiquity* 19:390–391.

1954c   Additional Notes on the Poverty Point Site in Northeastern Louisiana. *American Antiquity* 19:282–285.

Ford, James A., Philip Phillips, and William G. Haag

1955   *The Jaketown Site in West-Central Mississippi.* Anthropological Papers Vol. 45, Pt. 1. American Museum of Natural History, New York.

Ford, James A., and George I. Quimby

1945   The Tchefuncte Culture, an Early Occupation of the Lower Mississippi Valley. *Society of American Archaeology, Memoirs* No. 2.

Ford, James A., and Clarence H. Webb

1956   *Poverty Point, a Late Archaic Site in Louisiana.* Anthropological Papers Vol. 46, Pt. 1. American Museum of Natural History, New York.

Ford, James A., and Gordon R. Willey

1940   Crooks Site, a Marksville Period Burial Mound in La Salle Parish Louisiana. *Louisiana Department of Conservation Anthropological Study* 3.

1941   An Interpretation of the Prehistory of the Eastern United States. *American Anthropologist* 43:325–363.

Ford, Janet L.

1987   Calvin Brown and the Archaeology of Mississippi. *Mississippi Archaeology* 22:63–70.

Ford, Janet L., Martha A. Rolingson, and Larry D. Medford

1972   *Site Destruction Due to Agricultural Practices.* Research Series No. 3:1–40. Arkansas Archeological Survey, Fayetteville.

Ford, Richard I.

1988   Commentary: Little Things Mean a Lot—Quantification and Qualification in Paleoethnobotany. In *Current Paleoethnobotany,* edited by Christine A. Hastorf and Virginia S. Popper, pp. 215–222. University of Chicago Press, Chicago.

Forshey, Caleb G.

1845   Description of Some Artificial Mounds on Prairie Jefferson, Louisiana. *American Journal of Science and Art* 49 (first series):38–42.

Foster, H. Thomas, III

2003   Dynamic Optimization of Horticulture among the Muscogee Creek Indians of the Southeastern United States. *Journal of Anthropological Archaeology* 22:411–424.

Foster, H. Thomas, III, Bryan Black, and Marc D. Abrams

2004   A Witness Tree Analysis of the Effects of Native American Indians on the Pre-

European Settlement Forests in East-Central Alabama. *Human Ecology* 32(1): 27–47.

Foster, J. W.

1864 Ancient Relics in Missouri. *Smithsonian Institution, Annual Report* 1863:383–84.

Fox, Gregory L.

1992 *A Critical Examination of the Interpretive Framework of the Mississippian Period in Southeast Missouri.* Ph.D, dissertation, Department of Anthropology, University of Missouri-Columbia. University Microfilms, Ann Arbor.

1998 An Examination of Mississippian-Period Phases in Southeastern Missouri. In *Changing Perspectives on the Archaeology of the Central Mississippi Valley,* edited by Michael J. O'Brien and Robert C. Dunnell, pp. 31–58. University of Alabama Press, Tuscaloosa.

Fredlund, Glen G.

2001 Inferring Vegetation History from Phytoliths. In *The Historical Ecology Handbook,* edited by Dave Egan and Evelyn A. Howell, pp. 335–362. Island Press, Washington, D.C.

Freeman, John F.

1965 University Anthropology: Early Departments in the United States. *Kroeber Anthropological Society Papers* 32:78–90.

Frink, Douglas S.

1992 The Chemical Variability of Carbonized Organic Matter through Time. *Archaeology of Eastern North America* 20:67–79.

1994 The Oxidizable Carbon Ratio (OCR): A Proposed Solution to Some of the Problems Encountered with Radiocarbon Data. *North American Archaeologist* 15:17–29.

1999 The Scientific Basis of Oxidizable Carbon Ratio (OCR) Dating. *Society for American Archaeology Bulletin* 17(5):32–37.

Fritz, Gayle J.

1986 *Prehistoric Ozark Agriculture: The University of Arkansas Rockshelter Collections.* Ph.D. Dissertation, University of North Carolina, Chapel Hill.

1990 Multiple Pathways to Farming in Precontact Eastern North America. *Journal of World Prehistory* 4:387–435.

1993 Early and Middle Woodland Period Paleoethnobotany. In *Foraging and Farming in the Eastern Woodlands,* edited by C. Margaret Scarry, pp. 39–56. University Press of Florida, Gainesville.

1995 Ethnobotanical Remains. In *Manifest East: Cultural Resources Investigations Along Portions of Louisiana Highway 8, Catahoula Parish, Louisiana,* by Donald G. Hunter, Gayle J. Fritz, Whitney J. Autin, and Kam-biu Liu, pp. 185–194. Report submitted to Louisiana Department of Transportation and Development, Baton Rouge, by Coastal Environments, Inc., Baton Rouge.

1997 Archaeological Plant Remains from the Birds Creek Site. In *Archaeological Data Recovery at the Birds Creek Site (16CT416), Catahoula Parish, Louisiana,* edited by Jill-Karen Yakubik, pp. 11:1–11. Report submitted to Louisiana Department of Transportation and Development, Baton Rouge, by Earth Search, Inc., New Orleans.

1999a Gender and the Early Cultivation of Gourds in Eastern North America. *American Antiquity* 64:417–429.

1999b Plant Remains from the Oliver Site. Report submitted to John Connaway, Mississippi Department of Archives and History, Clarksdale, Mississippi.

2007 Keepers of Louisiana's Levees: Early Moundbuilders and Forest Managers. In *Rethinking Agriculture: Archaeological and Ethnoarchaeological Perspectives*, edited by Tim Denham, Jose Iriarte, and Luc Vrydaghs. In Press. Left Coast Press, Walnut Creek.

Fritz, Gayle J., and Tristram R. Kidder
1993 Recent Investigations into Prehistoric Agriculture in the Lower Mississippi Valley. *Southeastern Archaeology* 12(1):1–14.

Fullen, Steven R.
2005 *Temporal Trends in Tchula Period Pottery in Louisiana.* Masters Thesis, Department of Geography and Anthropology, Louisiana State University.

Fuller, John William
1981 *Developmental Change in Prehistoric Community Patterns: The Development of Nucleated Village Communities in Northern West Virginia.* Unpublished Ph.D. dissertation, Department of Anthropology, University of Washington.

Fuller, Richard S.
1992 *Archaeological Recovery and Analysis of an Indian Dugout Canoe (Site 22 WS776) Discovered in the Bank of Steele Bayou, Swan Lake, Washington County, Mississippi.* Report submitted to the U.S. Army Corps of Engineers, Vicksburg District, by Coastal Environments, Inc., Baton Rouge, Louisiana.

Funkhouser, W. D., and W. S. Webb
1932 *Archaeological Survey in Kentucky.* Reports in Archaeology and Anthropology Vol. 2. University of Kentucky, Lexington.

Futato, Eugene M.
1987 *Archaeological Investigations at Shell Bluff and White Springs, Two Late Woodland Sites in the Tombigbee River Multi-Resource District.* University of Alabama, Alabama State Museum of Natural History, Office of Archaeological Research, Report of Investigations 50, Tuscaloosa.

Fye, Falko K., David W. Stahle, and Edward R. Cook
2003 Paleoclimatic Analogs to Twentieth-Century Moisture Regimes Across the United States. *Bulletin of the American Meteorological Society* 84:901–909.

Gaffney, Chris, and John Gater
2003 *Revealing the Buried Past: Geophysics for Archaeologists.* Tempus Publishing, Ltd., Stroud, U.K.

Gaffney, V., and M. van Leusen
1995 Postscript: GIS and Environmental Determinism: A Parallel Text. In *Archaeology and Geographic Information Systems*, edited by Gary Lock and Zoran Stancic, pp. 367–382. Taylor and Francis, London.

Galaty, Michael L.
2001 A Petrographic Analysis of Middle Woodland Ceramics from the Cork Site,

Oktibbeha County, Mississippi. Report on file at the Cobb Institute of Archaeology, Mississippi State University, Starkville.

Galloway, Patricia K.

1993 Ethnohistory. In *The Development of Southeastern Archaeology*, edited by Jay K. Johnson, pp. 78–108. University of Alabama Press, Tuscaloosa.

Gardner, Paul S.

1982 Analysis of Plant Remains from the Possum Trap Site (3DE37), Desha County, Arkansas. Report on file, Paleoethnobotanical Laboratory, Washington University, St. Louis.

Garrow, Patrick H.

1992 *Archaeology and History of the Rum Boogie Site, Memphis Tennessee.* Garrow and Associates, Atlanta.

2000 Urban Archaeology in Tennessee: Exploring the Cities of the Old South. In *The Archaeology of Southern Urban Landscapes*, edited by Amy L. Young, pp. 192–216. University of Alabama Press, Tuscaloosa.

Garrow, Patrick H., John Hopkins, and Linda Kennedy

1998 *Working on the Railroad: The Archaeology and History of the MATA North End Terminal Site, Memphis, Tennessee.* TRC Garrow Associates, Inc., Atlanta.

Genheimer, Robert

2000 Archaeology at Covington, Kentucky: A Particularly "Northern-looking" Southern City. In *The Archaeology of Southern Urban Landscapes*, edited by Amy L. Young, pp. 69–91. University of Alabama Press, Tuscaloosa.

George, D., C. Labadia, J. Strait, R. B. Draughon, Jr., and W. P. Athens

2001 *Phase II National Register Testing and Evaluation of Nine Archeological Sites (22Co573, 22Co726, 22Co773, 22Co774, 22Co775, 22Co776, 22Co777, 22Co778, and 22Co781), Coahoma County, Mississippi.* Report submitted to the Mississippi Department of Transportation, Jackson, by R. Christopher Goodwin & Associates, Inc., New Orleans.

Gertjejansen, Doyle J., J. Richard Shenkel, and Jesse O. Snowden

1983 Laboratory Simulation of Tchefuncte-Period Ceramic Vessels from the Pontchartrain Basin. *Southeastern Archaeology* 2:37–63.

Gibson, Jon L.

1973 *Social Systems at Poverty Point: An Analysis of Intersite and Intrasite Variability.* Unpublished Ph.D. Dissertation, Southern Methodist University, Dallas.

1982 *Archeology and Ethnology on the Edges of the Atchafalaya Basin: A Cultural Resources Survey of the Atchafalaya Protection Levees.* Report submitted to the U.S. Army Corps of Engineers, New Orleans District, by the University of Southwestern Louisiana Center for Archaeological Studies, Lafayette.

1985 Punctuating Lower Mississippi Valley Prehistory: A Hyphen or a Period Between Troyville and Coles Creek. In *The Emergent Mississippian: Proceedings of the Sixth Mid-South Archaeological Conference, June 6–9, 1985,* edited by Richard A. Marshall, pp. 71–84. Cobb Institute of Archaeology, Mississippi State University Occasional Papers 87–01, Starkville.

1987a Poverty Point Reconsidered. *Mississippi Archaeology* 22(2):14–31.

1987b   *The Ground Truth about Poverty Point: The Second Season, 1985.* Report No. 6, Center for Archaeological Studies, University of Southwestern Louisiana, Lafayette.

1993   Ceramics. In *The Development of Southeastern Archaeology,* edited by Jay K. Johnson, pp.18–35. University of Alabama Press, Tuscaloosa.

1994a   Before Their Time? Early Mounds in the Lower Mississippi Valley. *Southeastern Archaeology* 13:162–186.

1994b   Empirical Characterization of Exchange Systems in Lower Mississippi Valley Prehistory. In *Prehistoric Exchange Systems in North America,* edited by Timothy G. Baugh and Jonathon E. Ericson, pp.127–176. Plenum Press, New York.

2005   Mississippi Beads, Louisiana Beads: What Difference a River Makes. Paper presented at the Mississippi Archaeological Association Annual Meeting, Vidalia, Louisiana.

Gibson, Jon L. (editor)

1989   *Digging on the Dock of the Bay(ou): The 1988 Excavations at Poverty Point.* Report No. 8, Center for Archaeological Studies, University of Southwestern Louisiana, Lafayette.

Gibson, Jon L., and Phillip J. Carr (editors)

2004   *Signs of Power: The Rise of Cultural Complexity in the Southeast.* University of Alabama Press, Tuscaloosa.

Gibson, Jon L., and Mark A. Melancon

2004   In the Beginning: Social Contexts of First Pottery in the Lower Mississippi Valley. In Early Pottery: Technology, Function, Style, and Interaction in the Lower Southeast, edited by Rebecca Saunders and Christopher T. Hays, pp.169–192. Tuscaloosa: University of Alabama Press.

Gibson, Jon L., and J. R. Shenkel

1988   Louisiana Earthworks: Middle Woodland and Predecessors. In *Middle Woodland Settlement and Ceremonialism in the Mid-South and the Lower Mississippi Valley,* edited by Robert C. Mainfort, pp. 8–18. Archaeological Report No. 22. Mississippi Department of Archives and History, Jackson.

Glascock, Michael D.

1992   Characterization of Archaeological Ceramics at MURR by Neutron Activation Analysis and Multivariate Statistics. In *Chemical Characterization of Ceramic Pastes in Archaeology,* edited by Hector Neff, pp. 11–26. Prehistory Press, Madison, Wisconsin.

Glascock, Michael D., and Hector Neff

2003   Neutron Activation Analysis and Provenance Research in Archaeology. *Measurement Science & Technology* 14:1516–1526.

Goldstein, Lynn G.

1980   *Mississippian Mortuary Practices: A Case Study of Two Cemeteries in The Lower Illinois Valley.* Scientific Papers No. 4. Northwestern University Archaeological Program, Evanston, Illinois.

Goman, Michelle, and David S. Leigh

2004   Wet Early to Middle Holocene Conditions on the Upper Coastal Plain of North Carolina. *Quaternary Research* 61:256–264.

Gonzales, John Edmund

1973   Flush Times, Depression, War, and Compromise. In *A History of Mississippi*, Vol. 1, edited by Richard Aubrey McLemore, pp. 284–309, University and College Press of Mississippi, Hattiesburg.

Goodyear, Albert C.

1995   *The Brand Site: A Technofunctional Study of a Dalton Site in Northeast Arkansas*,
[1974] 2nd edition. Arkansas Archeological Survey, Research Series No. 7, Fayetteville.

Gray, Bruce

1996   *Cultural Resources Survey of Proposed Widening/Relocation of U.S. Highway 61 from the Bolivar-Coahoma County Line to U.S. Highway 49 (MDOT Project No. 98-0009-04-004-10), Coahoma County, Mississippi.* Environmental Division, Mississippi Department of Transportation, Jackson.

Gray, Bruce J., Philip J. Carr, and Cliff Jenkins

1997   *Cultural Resources Survey of Proposed Welcome Center at U.S. Highways 49 and 61 and Alternate Location at U.S. Highway 49 and Mississippi Highway 1 (MDOT Project No. 79-0057-01-003-10), Coahoma County, Mississippi.* Environmental Division, Mississippi Department of Transportation, Jackson.

Greengo, Robert E.

1964   *Issaquena: An Archaeological Phase in the Yazoo Basin of the Lower Mississippi Valley.* Society for American Archaeology, Memoirs 18, Salt Lake City.

Greenlee, Diana

1998   Prehistoric Diet in the Central Mississippi River Valley. In *Changing Perspectives on the Archaeology of the Central Mississippi Valley*, edited by Michael J. O'Brien and Robert C. Dunnell, pp. 299–324. University of Alabama Press, Tuscaloosa.

Greig-Smith, P.

1952   The Use of Random and Contiguous Quadrats in the Study of Plant Communities. *Annals of Botany, London* 16:293–316.

Gremillion, Kristen J.

1995a   *Archaeological and Paleoethnobotanical Investigations at the Cold Oak Shelter, Kentucky.* Report submitted to the National Geographic Society (Grant No. 5226-94).

1995b   Comparative Paleoethnobotany of Three Native Southeastern Communities of the Historic Period. *Southeastern Archaeology* 14:1–16.

1996   Diffusion and Adoption of Crops in Evolutionary Perspective. *Journal of Anthropological Archaeology* 15:183–204.

2002   The Development and Dispersal of Agricultural Systems in the Woodland Period Southeast. In *The Woodland Southeast*, edited by David G. Anderson and Robert C. Mainfort, Jr., pp. 447–501. University of Alabama Press, Tuscaloosa.

Griffin, G. M.

1962   Regional Clay-Mineral Facies—Products of Weathering Intensity and Current Distribution in the Northeastern Gulf of Mexico. *Geological Society of America Bulletin* 73:737–768.

Griffin, James B.

1941   *The Fort Ancient Aspect.* University of Michigan Press, Ann Arbor.

1952   Prehistoric Cultures of the Central Mississippi Valley. In *The Archeology of Eastern United States*, edited by James B. Griffin, pp. 226–238. University of Chicago Press, Chicago.

Griffin, James B. (editor)

1952   *Archeology of Eastern United States*. University of Chicago Press, Chicago.

Grine, Fred E.

1987   Quantitative Analysis of Occlusal Microwear in *Australopithecus* and *Paranthropus*. *Scanning Microscopy* 1:647–656.

Grissinger, E. H., J. B. Murphey, and W. C. Little

1982   Late-Quaternary Valley-Fill Deposits in North-Central Mississippi. *Southeastern Geology* 23:147–162.

GSRI (Gulf South Research Institute)

1975   *Red River Waterway, Louisiana, Texas, Arkansas, and Oklahoma. Vol. V, Archeology, History and Culture*. Gulf South Research Institute, Unpublished report submitted to the U.S. Army Corps of Engineers, New Orleans District, by Gulf South Research Institute, Baton Rouge.

Guccione, Margaret J.

1987   Geomorphology, Sedimentation, and Chronology of Alluvial Deposits, Northern Mississippi County, Arkansas. In *A Cultural Resources Survey Testing and Geomorphic Examination of Ditches 10, 12, and 29, Mississippi County, Arkansas*, by Robert H. Lafferty, Margaret J. Guccione, Linda J. Scott, D. Kate Aasen, Beverly J. Watkins, Michael C. Sierzchula, and Paul F. Baumann, pp. 67–99. Mid-Continental Research Associates, Report 86-5, Lowell, Arkansas.

Guilday, John E., and Paul W. Parmalee

1975   Appendix I: Faunal Remains from the Zebree Site. In *Report of Excavations at the Zebree Site 1969*, by Dan F. Morse, pp. 228–234. Research Report 4, Arkansas Archeological Survey, Fayetteville.

Gunderson, Lance H., and C. S. Holling (editors)

2002   *Panarchy: Understanding Transformations in Human and Natural Systems*. Island Press, Washington, D.C.

Gunn, Charles R., Thomas M. Pullen, Earl A. Stadelbacher, James M. Chandler, and Joel Barnes

1980   *Vascular Flora of Washington County, Mississippi, and Environs*. U.S. Department of Agriculture, Science and Education Administration, New Orleans.

Gunn, Joel D.

1994   Global Climate and Regional Biocultural Diversity. In *Historical Ecology: Cultural Knowledge and Changing Landscapes*, edited by Carole L. Crumley, pp. 67–97. School of American Research Press, Santa Fe.

1996   A Framework for the Paleoindian/Early Archaic Transition. In *The Paleoindian and Early Archaic Southeast*, edited by David G. Anderson and Kenneth E. Sassaman, pp. 415–420. University of Alabama Press, Tuscaloosa.

1997   A Framework for the Middle-Late Holocene Transition: Astronomical and Geophysical Conditions. *Southeastern Archaeology* 16:134–151.

Guralnik, David B., and Joseph H. Friend (editors)

1968   *Webster's New World Dictionary of the American Language.* World Publishing, Cleveland.

Guthe, Carl E.

1930   *Guide Leaflet for Amateur Archaeologists.* Reprint and Circular Series of the National Research Council, No. 93. National Research Council, Washington, D.C.

1952   Twenty-Five Years of Archaeology in the Eastern United States. In *Archeology of Eastern United States,* edited by James B. Griffin, pp. 1–12. University of Chicago Press, Chicago.

Haag, William G.

1952   Archaeological Survey of the Grenada Reservoir in Mississippi. Report prepared for the National Park Service. On file at the Mississippi Department of Archives and History, Jackson.

1985   Federal Aid to Archaeology in the Southeast, 1933–1942. *American Antiquity* 50:272–280.

1986   Field Methods in Archaeology. In *American Archaeology: Past and Future,* edited by David J. Meltzer, Don Fowler, and Jeremy A. Sabloff, pp. 63–76. Smithsonian Institution Press, Washington, D.C.

Haddy, Alice, and Albert Hanson

1981   Relative Dating of Moundville Burials. *Southeastern Archaeological Conference Bulletin* 24: 97–99.

1982   Nitrogen and Fluorine Dating of Moundville Skeletal Samples. *Archaeometry* 4:37–44.

Haggett, Peter

1965   *Locational Analysis in Human Geography.* Edward Arnold, London.

Hahn, Thurston H. G., III, Sammy Cranford, and Charles E. Pearson

1994   *Historical and Archaeological Investigations of Doro Plantation, Bolivar County, Mississippi.* Report Submitted to the U.S. Army Corps of Engineers, Vicksburg District, by Coastal Environments, Inc., Baton Rouge, Louisiana.

Haley, Bryan S.

2002   *Airborne Remote Sensing, Image Processing, and Multisensor Data Fusion at the Hollywood Site, A Large Late Mississippian Mound Center.* Unpublished master's thesis, Department of Sociology and Anthropology, University of Mississippi, Oxford.

Haley, Bryan S., and Jay K. Johnson

2006   Pit Feature Detection Using Magnetic Characteristics. Poster presented at the 63rd Annual Southeastern Archaeological Conference, Little Rock, Arkansas.

Haley, Bryan S., Jay K. Johnson, and Richard Stallings

2002   *The Utility of Low-Cost Thermal Sensors in Archaeological Research.* Report Submitted to the Office of Naval Research by the Center for Archaeological Research, University of Mississippi, Oxford.

Hamilton, Kenneth M.

1991   *Black Towns and Profit: Promotion and Development in the Trans-Appalachian West, 1877–1915.* University of Illinois Press, Urbana.

Harbottle, G.

1976   Activation Analysis in Archaeology. *Radiochemistry* 3:33–72.

Hargrave, Michael L.

2006   Ground Truthing the Results of Geophysical Surveys. In *Remote Sensing in Archaeology: An Explicitly North American Perspective,* edited by Jay K. Johnson, pp. 269–304. University of Alabama Press, Tuscaloosa.

Harmon, Anna M., and Jerome C. Rose

1989   Bioarcheology of the Louisiana and Arkansas Study Area. In *Archeology and Bioarcheology of the Lower Mississippi Valley and Trans-Mississippi South in Arkansas and Louisiana,* by Marvin D. Jeter, Jerome C. Rose, G. Ishmael Williams, and Anna M. Harmon, pp. 323–354. Arkansas Archeological Survey Research Series No. 37, Fayetteville.

Harris, Suzanne E.

1982   Preliminary Ethnobotanical Analysis. In *The Mangrum Site: Mitigation Through Excavation and Preservation in Northeast Arkansas,* by Timothy C. Klinger, pp. 101–108. Arkansas Archeological Survey Research Series 20, Fayetteville.

1983   Floral Remains. In *Brougham Lake: Archaeological Mitigation of 3CT98 Along the Big Creek Enlargement and Diversion, Item 1 Crittenden County, Arkansas,* by Timothy C. Klinger, Steven M. Imhoff, and Roy J. Cochran, Jr., pp. 390–408. Historic Preservation Associates Reports 83-7, Fayetteville, Arkansas.

Hart, John P., Hetty Jo Brumbach, and Robert Lusteck

2007   Extending the Phytolith Evidence for Early Maize (*Zea Mays* ssp. *mays*) and Squash (*Cucurita* sp.) in Central New York. *American Antiquity* 72:563–583.

Hart, John P., and Nancy Asch Sidell

1997   Additional Evidence for Early Cucurbit Use in the Northern Eastern Woodlands of the Allegheny Front. *American Antiquity* 62:523–537.

Hart, John P., David L. Asch, C. Margaret Scarry, and Gary W. Crawford

2002   The Age of the Common Bean (*Phaseolus vulgaris* L.) in the Northern Eastern Woodlands of North America. *Antiquity* 76:377–385.

Harvey, Dennis E.

1977   Preliminary Analysis of Wood Utilization at Two Mississippi Sites. *The Missouri Archaeologist* 38:272–278.

Hathcock, Roy

1976   *Ancient Indian Pottery of the Mississippi Valley.* Hurley Press, Camden, Arkansas.

1983   *The Quapaw and Their Pottery.* Hurley Press, Camden, Arkansas.

Hays, Christopher T., and Richard A. Weinstein

2000   Perspectives on Tchefuncte Cultural Chronology: A View from the Bayou Jasmine Site, St. John the Baptist Parish, Louisiana. *Louisiana Archaeology* 23:49–89.

2004   Early Pottery at Poverty Point: Origins and Functions. In *Early Pottery: Technology, Function, Style, and Interaction in the Lower Southeast,* edited by R. Saunders and C. Hays, pp.150–168. University of Alabama Press, Tuscaloosa.

Heartfield, Price and Greene, Inc.

1987   *Data Recovery at the Milner (22YZ515) and O'Neil Creek (22YZ624) Sites, Yazoo*

County, Mississippi. Report submitted to the U.S. Army Corps of Engineers, Vicksburg District, by Heartfield, Price and Greene, Inc., Monroe, Louisiana.

Hegmon, Michelle

1995   *The Social Dynamics of Pottery Style in the Early Puebloan Southwest*. Occasional Paper No. 5, Crow Canyon Archaeological Center, Cortez, Colorado.

Heinrich, P. V.

1991   A Sedimentological Explanation for the Distribution of Archaeological Sites in a Meander Belt as Stated by the "Relict Channel Rule." *Transactions of the Gulf Coast Association of Geological Societies* 41:320.

Helama, Samuli, Mauri Timonen, Markus Lindholm, Jouko Meriläinen, and Matti Eronen

2005   Extracting Long-period Climate Fluctuations from Tree-ring Chronologies over Timescales of Centuries to Millennia. *International Journal of Climatology* 25:1767–1779.

Held, Pollyanna

2004   *The Search for the Elusive Fort Maurepas in Southern Mississippi*. Unpublished M.A. thesis, University of Mississippi, Oxford.

Hermann, Janet Sharp

1979   *The Black Community at Davis Bend: The Pursuit of a Dream*. Unpublished Ph.D. dissertation, Department of History, University of California, Berkeley.

1981   *The Pursuit of a Dream*. Oxford University Press, Oxford.

Hietala, Harold J., and Paul A. Larson

1984   *Intrasite Spatial Analysis in Archaeology*. Cambridge University Press, Cambridge.

Hietala, Harold J., and Dominique S. Stevens

1977   Spatial Analysis: Multiple Procedures in Pattern Recognition Studies. *American Antiquity* 42:539–559.

Higgs, Eric S., and Claudio Vita-Finzi

1972   Prehistoric Economies: A Territorial Approach. In *Papers in Economic Prehistory*, edited by Eric S. Higgs, pp. 27–36. Cambridge University Press, Cambridge.

Hill, Bunker

1969   University of Mississippi 1969 Summer Digs: Excavations at 22-Co-516. *Newsletter of the Mississippi Archaeological Association* 4(9):1.

Hill, Mary C.

1981   Analysis, Synthesis, and Interpretation of the Skeletal Material Excavated for the Gainesville Section of the Tennessee-Tombigbee Waterway. In *Biocultural Studies in the Gainesville Lake Area*, by Gloria M. Caddell, Anne Woodrick, and Mary C. Hill, pp.211–334. Office of Archaeological Research, University of Alabama, Report of Investigations No. 14, Tuscaloosa.

Hilliard, Sam Bowers

1984   *Atlas of Antebellum Southern Agriculture*. Louisiana State University Press, Baton Rouge.

Hillman, Mitchell

1990   Paleoindian Settlement on the Macon Ridge, Northeastern Louisiana. *Louisiana Archaeology* 12:203–218.

Hodder, Ian

1982   *Symbols in Action.* Cambridge University Press, Cambridge.

Hodder, Ian, and Clive Orton

1976   *Spatial Analysis in Archaeology.* Cambridge University Press, Cambridge.

Hoffman, Michael P.

1999   Ancient Races of Giants, Moundbuilders, and Hero Collectors: Newspaper Accounts of Archeology 1870–1930 in Arkansas Archeology. In *Arkansas Archaeology: Essays in Honor of Dan and Phyllis Morse,* edited by Robert C. Mainfort and Marvin D. Jeter, pp. 245–258. University of Arkansas Press, Fayetteville.

Hoffman, Robert W.

1998   The Faunal Material. In *Toltec Mounds and Plum Bayou Culture: Mound D Excavations,* edited by Martha A. Rolingson, pp. 84–94. Research Series 54, Arkansas Archeological Survey, Fayetteville.

Hogue, S. Homes

2000   Burial Practices, Mortality, and Diet in East-Central Mississippi: A Case Study from Oktibbeha County. *Southeastern Archaeology* 19:63–81.

2003a   The Application of a Small-mammal Model in Paleoenvironmental Analysis. In Evan Peacock and Timothy Schauwecker (editors), *Blackland Prairies of the Gulf Coastal Plain: Nature, Culture, and Sustainability,* pp. 48–63. University of Alabama Press, Tuscaloosa.

2003b   Corn Dogs and Hush Puppies: Diet and Domestication at Two Protohistoric Farmsteads in Oktibbeha County, Mississippi. *Southeastern Archaeology* 22:185–195.

2006   Evaluating the Reliability of Fluoride Dating at Two Prehistoric Mound Sites in Mississippi. *Journal of Field Archaeology* 31:307–315.

Hogue, S. Homes, April Boyd, and Jodi Jacobson

1995   A Secondary Burial from the Rolling Hills Subdivision in Starkville, Mississippi: Osteological and Archaeological Interpretations. *Mississippi Archaeology* 30(1):1–22.

Hogue, S. Homes, Suzanne Bufkin, and Heather Rushing

1996   European Contact, Burial Behavior, Health and Diet: A Case Study from Starkville, Mississippi. *Mississippi Archaeology* 31(2):1–22.

Hogue, S. Homes, and Vincent Dongarra

2002   Biomechanical Changes in Long-Bone Structure: A Study of Preagricultural and Agricultural Populations in Northeastern Mississippi and Northwestern Alabama. *Midcontinental Journal of Archaeology* 27:1–21.

Hogue, S. Homes, and William Erwin

1993   A Preliminary Analysis of Diet Change Using Small Burial Samples from Three Sites in Mississippi. *Mississippi Archaeology* 28(1):1–19.

Hogue, S. Homes, and Evan Peacock

1995   Environmental and Osteological Analysis at the South Farm Site (22OK534), A Mississippian Farmstead in Oktibbeha County, Mississippi. *Southeastern Archaeology* 14:31–45.

Hollenbach, Kandace D.

2005   Beyond Nuts and Fruits: The Role of Gatherers in Late Paleoindian and Early Archaic Foraging Groups in Northwest Alabama. Paper presented at the 70th Annual Meeting of the Society for American Archaeology, Salt Lake City, Utah.

Holliday, Vance T.

1990   Pedology in Archaeology. In *Archaeological Geology of North America,* edited by Norman P. Lasca and Jack Donahue, pp. 525–540. Geological Society of America, Centennial Special Volume 4, Boulder, Colorado.

Holling, C. S., Lance H. Gunderson, and Donald Lugwig

2002   In a Quest for a Theory of Adaptive Change. In Lance H. Gunderson and C. S. Holling (editors), *Panarchy: Understanding Transformations in Human and Natural Systems,* pp. 3–22. Island Press, Washington, D.C.

Holloway, Richard G.

1983   Pollen Analysis. In Jay K. Johnson, Abigayle Robbins, and John T. Sparks, *Excavations at the Mud Island Creek Archaeological Complex and the Gordon Mounds Site, Jefferson County, Mississippi,* pp. 210–213. University of Mississippi, Center for Archaeological Research, Archaeological Papers No. 4, Oxford.

Holloway, Richard G., and Sam Valastro

1983a   Palynological Investigations Along the Yazoo River, Item 3. Appendix I in *Cultural Resources Survey of Items 3 and 4, Upper Yazoo River Projects, Mississippi, With a Paleoenvironmental Model of the Lower Yazoo Basin,* by Robert M. Thorne and Hugh K. Curry, pp. 161–204. Report submitted to the U.S. Army Corps of Engineers, Vicksburg District, by the University of Mississippi, Center for Archaeological Research, Oxford.

1983b   Palynological Investigations Along the Yazoo River, Item 4. Appendix II in *Cultural Resources Survey of Items 3 and 4, Upper Yazoo River Projects, Mississippi, with a Paleoenvironmental Model of the Lower Yazoo Basin,* by Robert M. Thorne and Hugh K. Curry, pp. 207–243. Report submitted to the U.S. Army Corps of Engineers, Vicksburg District, by the University of Mississippi, Center for Archaeological Research, Oxford.

Holmes, William Henry

1884   Illustrated Catalogue of a Portion of the Collections Made by the Bureau of Ethnology during the Field Season of 1881. In *Third Annual Report of the Bureau of American Ethnology, 1881–1882,* edited by John Wesley Powell, pp. 427–510. U.S. Government Printing Office, Washington, D.C.

1886a   Ancient Pottery of the Mississippi Valley. *Fourth Annual Report of the Bureau of Ethnology, 1882–1883,* pp. 361–436. Smithsonian Institution, Washington, D.C.

1886b   The Pottery of the Ancient Pueblos. In *Fourth Annual Report of the Bureau of Ethnology, 1882–1883,* pp. 257–360. Smithsonian Institution, Washington, D.C.

1886c   Origin and Development of Form and Content in Ceramic Art. *Fourth Annual Report of the Bureau of Ethnology, 1882–1883,* pp 437–465. Smithsonian Institution, Washington, D.C. Reprinted in Meltzer and Dunnell 1992.

1892   Notes upon Some Geometric Earthworks with Contour Maps. *American Anthropologist* 5:363–373.

1903   Aboriginal Pottery of the Eastern United States. In *Twentieth Annual Report of the Bureau of American Ethnology, 1898–1899,* pp. 1–237. Smithsonian Institution, Washington, D.C. Reprinted in Meltzer and Dunnell 1992.

Hony, William

1985   Test Excavations at the Murphey Site, 19–0–21. In *Anthology of Mississippi Archaeology 1966–1979,* edited by Patricia Galloway, pp. 112–114. Mississippi Department of Archives and History, Jackson.

Hopkins, John L., and Guy G. Weaver

1993   *Literature and Records Search for the Proposed AutoZone Corporate Site, County Lots 488 and 489, Blocks 16 and 17, Memphis, Shelby County, Tennessee.* Garrow and Associates, Memphis, Tennessee.

Houck, Louis

1908   *A History of Missouri from the Earliest Explorations and Settlements until the Admission of the State into the Union* (3 vols). R. R. Donnelly & Sons, Chicago.

House, John H.

1982   *Powell Canal: Baytown Period Occupation on Bayou Macon in Southeast Arkansas.* Arkansas Archeological Survey Research Series No.19, Fayetteville.

1987   Kent Phase Investigations in Eastern Arkansas, 1978–1984. *Mississippi Archaeology* 22(1):46–60.

1991   *Monitoring Mississippian Dynamics: Time, Settlement, and Ceramic Variation in the Kent Phase, Eastern Arkansas.* Unpublished Ph.D. Dissertation, Department of Anthropology, Southern Illinois University, Carbondale.

1995   Mississippian Farmstead Testing in the Lower St. Francis Basin Spring 1995. *Field Notes* 266:7–11.

Howell, John

1985   Human Bones Unearthed at King's Crossing. In *Anthology of Mississippi Archaeology 1966–1979,* edited by Patricia Galloway, p. 270. Mississippi Department of Archives and History, Jackson.

Hrdlička, Ales

1908   Report on a Collection of Crania from Arkansas. *Journal of the Academy of Natural Sciences of Philadelphia* 13:558–563.

1909   Report on an Additional Collection of Skeletal Remains from Arkansas and Louisiana. *Journal of the Academy of Natural Sciences of Philadelphia* 14:174–249.

1912   Report on Skeletal Remains from a Mound on Haley Place, near Red River, Miller County, Arkansas. *Journal of the Academy of Natural Sciences of Philadelphia* 14:639–640.

Hudson, Charles

1985   De Soto in Arkansas: A Brief Synopsis. *Field Notes: Newsletter of the Arkansas Archeological Society* 205:3–12.

1987   *The Uses of Evidence in Reconstructing the Route of the Hernando de Soto Expedition.* De Soto Working Paper No. 1, University of Alabama, State Museum of Natural History, Tuscaloosa.

Hudson, Charles, Marvin T. Smith, and Chester B. DePratter

1990   The Hernando de Soto Expedition: From Mabila to the Mississippi River. In

Towns and Temples Along the Mississippi, edited by David H. Dye and Cheryl A. Cox, pp. 181–207. University of Alabama Press, Tuscaloosa.

Hudson, John C.
1982 The Yazoo-Mississippi Delta as Plantation Country. In *Proceedings, Tall Timbers Ecology and Management Conference,* February 22–24, 1979, pp. 66–87. Tall Timbers Research Station, Tallahassee, Florida.

Hunter, Donald G., Gayle J. Fritz, Whitney J. Autin, and Kam-biu Liu
1995 *Manifest East: Cultural Resources Investigations Along Portions of Louisiana Highway 8, Catahoula Parish, Louisiana.* Report submitted to the Louisiana Department of Transportation and Development by Coastal Environments, Inc., Baton Rouge, Louisiana.

Hurt, Teresa D., and Gordon F. M. Rakita
2001 *Style and Function: Conceptual Issues in Evolutionary Archaeology.* Bergin & Garvey, Westport.

Huxtable, Joan, Martin J. Aitken, and J. C. Weber
1972 Thermoluminescence Dating of Baked Clay Balls of the Poverty Point Culture. *Archaeometry* 14:269–275.

Hyatt, Robert D.
1990 *Cultural Resources Survey of Proposed Bridge Replacements on U.S. Highway 61 at the Hushpuckena River and Alligator Lake (MSHD Project No. 79-0009-03-048-10), Bolivar County, Mississippi.* Environmental Division, Mississippi Department of Transportation, Jackson.

1991 *Clearing Survey of Proposed Widening of U.S. Highway 61 between Shutersville and Barbee (MSHD Project No. 17-0009-04-016-10), Coahoma County, Mississippi.* Environmental Division, Mississippi Department of Transportation, Jackson.

1992 *Cultural Resources Survey of Proposed Widening of U.S. Highway 61 from Mississippi Highway 4 East to Six Miles North of Tunica (MSHD Project No. 97-0009-05-021-10), Tunica County, Mississippi.* Environmental Division, Mississippi Department of Transportation, Jackson.

Ingbar, Eric E.
1994 Lithic Material Selection and Technological Organization. In *The Organization of North American Prehistoric Chipped Stone Tool Technologies,* edited by Philip J. Carr, pp. 45–56. International Monographs in Prehistory, Archaeological Series No. 7, Ann Arbor, Michigan.

Irion, Jack, Susan Barrett Smith, Paul V. Heinrich, Science Kilner, William P. Athens, and David Beard
1995 *Historical Assessment and Magnetometer Survey for Construction at Two Locations Along the Mississippi River, Jefferson and Issaquena Counties, Mississippi and East Carroll and Tensas Parishes, Louisiana.* R. Christopher Goodwin & Associates, Inc., New Orleans, Louisiana.

Ivester, Andrew H., David S. Leigh, and D. I. Godfrey-Smith
2001 Chronology of Inland Eolian Dunes on the Coastal Plain of Georgia, U.S.A. *Quaternary Research* 55:293–302.

Jackson, David H., Jr.

2000   Charles Banks: "Wizard of Mound Bayou." *Journal of Mississippi History* 62(4): 269–294.

Jackson, H. Edwin

1981   Recent Research on Poverty Point–Period Subsistence and Settlement Systems: Test Excavations at the J. W. Copes Site in Northeast Louisiana. *Louisiana Archaeology* 8:73–86.

1986   *Sedentism and Hunter-Gatherer Adaptations: Subsistence Strategies during the Poverty Point Period.* Unpublished Ph.D. dissertation, University of Michigan, Ann Arbor.

1989   Poverty Point Adaptive Systems in the Lower Mississippi Valley: Subsistence Remains from the J. W. Copes Site. *North American Archaeologist* 10:173–204.

1998   Little Spanish Fort: An Early Middle Woodland Enclosure in the Lower Yazoo Basin, Mississippi. *Midcontinental Journal of Archaeology* 23:199–220.

2005   "Darkening the Sun in the Flight": A Zooarchaeological Accounting of Passenger Pigeons in the Prehistoric Southeast. Paper presented at the 70th Annual Meeting of the Society for American Archaeology, Salt Lake City, Utah.

Jackson, H. Edwin, and Susan L. Scott

1995   Mississippian Homestead and Village Subsistence Organization: Contrasts in Large Mammal Remains from Two Sites in the Tombigbee Valley. In *Mississippian Communities and Households,* edited by J. Daniel Rogers and Bruce D. Smith, pp. 181–200. University of Alabama Press, Tuscaloosa.

2001   Archaic Faunal Utilization in the Louisiana Bottomlands. *Southeastern Archaeology* 20:187–196.

2002   Woodland Faunal Exploitation in the Mid-South. In *The Woodland Southeast,* edited by David G. Anderson and Robert C. Mainfort, Jr., pp. 461–482. University of Alabama Press, Tuscaloosa.

James, Stephen R.

1994   *Historical Assessment and Magnetometer Survey for Revetment Construction at Three Locations Along the Mississippi River.* Report submitted to the U.S. Army Corps of Engineers, Vicksburg District, by Panamerican Consultants, Inc., Memphis, Tennessee.

Jefferson, Thomas

1801   *Notes on the State of Virginia.* Furman and Loudan, New York.

Jeffreys, Thomas

1760   *The Natural and Civil History of the French Dominions in North and South America.* Printed for Thomas Jeffreys at Charing Cross, London.

Jelinek, Arthur J.

1976   Form, Function and Style in Lithic Analysis. In *Cultural Change and Continuity,* edited by Charles E. Cleland, pp. 19–34. Academic Press, New York.

Jelks, Edward B. (editor)

1966   *The Gilbert Site, a Norteño Focus Site in Northeastern Texas.* Bulletin of the Texas Archeological Society 37.

Jenkins, Ned J.

1982   *Archaeology of the Gainesville Lake Area: Synthesis.* University of Alabama, Office of Archaeological Research, Report of Investigations 23, Tuscaloosa.

Jennings, Jesse D.

1986   American Archaeology, 1930–1985. In *American Archaeology: Past and Future,* edited by David J. Meltzer, Don Fowler, and Jeremy A. Sabloff, pp. 53–62. Smithsonian Institution Press, Washington, D.C.

Jeter, Marvin D.

1990   Review of *Tunica Archaeology,* by Jeffrey P. Brain. *Southeastern Archaeology* 9:147–151.

2001   Edward Palmer and Other Victorian Pioneers in Midsouth Archeology. In *Historical Perspectives on Midsouth Archaeology,* edited by Martha A. Rolingson, pp. 23–50. Arkansas Archeological Survey, Research Series 58, Fayetteville.

2002   From Prehistory through Protohistory to Ethnohistory in and near the Northern Lower Mississippi Valley. In *The Transformation of the Southeastern Indians, 1540–1760,* edited by Robbie Ethridge and Charles Hudson, pp. 177–223. University Press of Mississippi, Jackson.

Jeter, Marvin D. (editor)

1990   *Edward Palmer's Arkansaw Mounds.* University of Arkansas Press, Fayetteville.

Jeter, Marvin D., Jerome C. Rose, G. Ishmael Williams, and Anna M. Harmon

1989   Adaptation Types. In *Archeology and Bioarcheology of the Lower Mississippi Valley and Trans-Mississippi South in Arkansas and Louisiana,* by Marvin D. Jeter, Jerome C. Rose, G. Ishmael Williams, and Anna M. Harmon, pp. 355–378, Arkansas Archeological Survey Research Series No. 37, Fayetteville.

Johannessen, Sissel

1988   Plant Remains and Culture Change: Are Paleoethnobotanical Data Better than We Think? In *Current Paleoethnobotany,* edited by Christine A. Hastorf and Virginia S. Popper, pp. 145–166. University of Chicago Press, Chicago.

1993   Farmers of the Late Woodland. In *Foraging and Farming in the Eastern Woodlands,* edited by C. Margaret Scarry, pp. 57–77. University Press of Florida, Gainesville.

Johnson, Frederick (editor)

1946   *Man in Northeastern North America.* Papers of the Robert S. Peabody Foundation, Vol 3. Andover.

Johnson, Glenn

1985   A Burial from Quitman County. In *Anthology of Mississippi Archaeology 1966–1979,* edited by Patricia Galloway, p. 11. Mississippi Department of Archives and History, Jackson.

Johnson, Gregory A.

1972   A Test of the Utility of Central Place Theory in Archaeology. In *Man, Settlement and Urbanism,* edited by Peter J. Ucko, Ruth Tringham, and G. W. Dimbleby, pp. 769–785. Duckworth, London.

1980   Rank-Size Convexity and System Integration: A View from Archaeology. *Economic Geography* 56:234–247.

Johnson, Jay K.

1980   Poverty Point Period Social Organization in the Yazoo Basin, Mississippi: A Pre-
        liminary Examination. In *Caddoan and Poverty Point Archaeology: Essays in Honor
        of Clarence Hungerford Webb,* edited by Jon L. Gibson, pp. 251–281. *Louisiana Ar-
        chaeology* 6.

1986   Rocks, River Channels and Prehistory on the Lower Yalobusha. *Mississippi Archae-
        ology* 21(1):2–27.

1989   The Utility of Production Trajectory Modeling as a Framework for Regional
        Analysis. In *Alternative Approaches to Lithic Analysis,* edited by Donald O. Henry
        and George H. Odell, pp. 119–138. Archaeological Papers of the American Anthro-
        pological Association Number 1.

1991   Settlement Patterns, GIS, Remote Sensing and the Late Prehistory of the Black
        Prairie in East Central Mississippi. In *Applications of Space-Age Technology in An-
        thropology,* edited by Clifford Behrens and Thomas Sever, pp. 111–119. National
        Aeronautics and Space Administration, Science and Technology Laboratory,
        John C. Stennis Space Center, Mississippi.

1993a   Preface. In *The Development of Southeastern Archaeology,* edited by Jay K. Johnson,
        pp. ix-xii. University of Alabama Press, Tuscaloosa.

1993b   Lithics. In *The Development of Southeastern Archaeology,* edited by Jay K. Johnson,
        pp. 36–52. University of Alabama Press, Tuscaloosa.

1993c   Poverty Point Period Crystal Drill Bits, Microliths, and Social Organization in the
        Yazoo Basin, Mississippi. *Southeastern Archaeology* 12:59–64.

2000   Beads, Microdrills, Bifaces, and Blades from Watson Brake. *Southeastern Archae-
        ology* 19:95–104.

2001   An Obituary: The Twin Lakes Phase. *Mississippi Archaeology* 36(1):17–36.

2002   One Hundred Years of Archaeology in Mississippi. In *Histories of Southeastern
        Archaeology,* edited by Shannon Tushingham, Jane Hill, and Charles H. McNutt,
        pp. 183–193. University of Alabama Press, Tuscaloosa.

2006   A Comparative Guide to Applications. In *Remote Sensing in Archaeology: An Ex-
        plicitly North American Perspective,* edited by Jay K. Johnson, pp. 305–320. Univer-
        sity of Alabama Press, Tuscaloosa.

Johnson, Jay K. (editor)

1993   (editor) *The Development of Southeastern Archaeology.* University of Alabama
        Press, Tuscaloosa.

Johnson, Jay K., Gena M. Aleo, Rodney T. Stuart, and John Sullivan

2002   *The 1996 Excavations at the Batesville Mounds: A Woodland Period Platform
        Mound Complex in Northwest Mississippi.* Mississippi Department of Archives
        and History, Archaeological Report No. 32, Jackson.

Johnson, Jay K., and Bryan S. Haley

2004   Multiple Sensor Applications in Archaeological Geophysics. In *Proceedings of
        SPIE Vol. 5234, Sensors, Systems, and Next-Generation Satellites VII,* edited by
        Roland Meynart, Steven P. Neeck, Haruhisa Simoda, Joan B. Lurie and Michelle L.
        Aten, pp. 688–697. SPIE: The International Society for Optican Engineering,
        Bellingham, Washington.

2006   A Cost-Benefit Analysis of Remote-Sensing Application in Cultural Resource
       Management Archaeology. In *Remote Sensing in Archaeology: An Explicitly North
       American Perspective*, edited by Jay K. Johnson, pp. 33–45. University of Alabama
       Press, Tuscaloosa.

Johnson, Jay K., and Carol A. Raspet
1980   Delta Debitage. *Mississippi Archaeology* 15(1):3–11.

Johnson, Jay K., Thomas L. Sever, Scott L. H. Madry, and Harry T. Hoff
1988   Remote Sensing and GIS Analysis in Large Scale Survey Design in North Missis-
       sippi. *Southeastern Archaeology* 7:24–131.

Johnson, Jay K., Richard Stallings, Nancy Ross-Stallings, R. Berle Clay, and V. Stephen
Jones
2000   *Remote Sensing and Ground Truth at the Hollywood Mounds Site in Tunica County,
       Mississippi.* Report submitted to the Mississippi Department of Archives and His-
       tory by the Center for Archaeological Research, University of Mississippi, Oxford

Jolley, Robert D.
1984   *An Archaeological Assessment of the Proposed Peabody Place Mall and Office
       Complex, Memphis, Tennessee.* Cultural Resource Consultants, Inc., Nashville,
       Tennessee.

Jones, Charles C., Jr.
1999   *Antiquities of the Southern Indians, Particularly of the Georgia Tribes.* Edited and
[1873] with an introduction by Frank T. Schnell, Jr. University of Alabama Press, Tusca-
       loosa. Originally published by D. Appleton & Co., New York.

Jones, Dennis, and Carl Kuttruff
1998   Prehistoric Enclosures in Louisiana and the Marksville Site. In *Ancient Earthen
       Enclosures of the Eastern Woodlands*, edited by Robert C. Mainfort and Lynne P.
       Sullivan, pp. 31–56. University Press of Florida, Gainesville.

Jones, Reca
2005   Troyville Factoids. (mimeo/xerox). On file, Louisiana Department of Culture,
       Recreation & Tourism, Division of Archaeology, Baton Rouge, Louisiana.

Jones, Volney H.
1953   Plant Materials from the Fuller Site. In *A Report of Excavations Made at the T. O.
       Fuller Site, Shelby County, Tennessee, between March 8, 1952 and April 30, 1953*, ed-
       ited by Kenneth L. Beaudoin, pp. 15–21. Memphis Archaeological and Geological
       Society, Memphis.

Joseph, Joseph W.
1986   *Archaeological Testing at the Site of the Peabody Place Mall and Office Complex,
       Memphis, Tennessee.* Garrow and Associates, Atlanta, Georgia.

Joutel, Henri
1998   *The La Salle Expedition to Texas: The Journal of Henri Joutel*, edited by William
[1713] C. Foster. Texas State Historical Association, Austin. First, abbreviated version of
       journal published in 1713 by Chez E. Robinot, Paris.

Joyce, Arthur A.
1988   Early/Middle Holocene Environments in the Middle Atlantic Region: A Revised

Reconstruction. In *Holocene Human Ecology in Northeastern North America*, edited by George P. Nicholas, pp. 185–214. Plenum Press, New York.

Justice, Noel D.

1987   *Stone Age Spear and Arrow Points of the Midcontinental and Eastern United States.* Indiana University Press, Bloomington.

2002a   *Stone Age Spear and Arrow Points of California and the Great Basin.* Indiana University Press, Bloomington.

2002b   *Stone Age Spear and Arrow Points of the Southwestern United States.* Indiana University Press, Bloomington.

Justice, Noel D., and Suzanne K. Kudlaty

2001   *Field Guide to Projectile Points of the Midwest.* Indiana University Press, Bloomington.

Kaczor, Michael J., and John Weymouth

1981   Magnetic Prospecting: Preliminary Results of the 1980 Field Season at the Toltec Site, 3LN42. In *Bulletin 24, Proceedings of the 37th Southeastern Archaeological Conference,* edited by Vernon J. Knight and Jerald T. Milanich, pp. 118–123.

Katzenberg, M. Anne

1989   Stable Isotope Analysis of Archaeological Faunal Remains from Southern Ontario. *Journal of Archaeological Science* 16:319–329.

Katz-Fishman, Walda, and Jerome Scott

2002   The South and the Black Radical Tradition: Then and Now. *Critical Sociology* 28:169–199.

Keck, Charlene

1997   Subsistence Strategies in the Middle to Late Mississippian Transition at the Parkin Site. Paper presented at the 54th Annual Meeting of the Southeastern Archaeological Conference, Baton Rouge, Louisiana.

Keel, Bennie C. (editor)

1988   *Advances in Southeastern Archeology 1966–1986: Contributions of the Federal Archaeological Program.* Southeastern Archaeological Conference, Special Publication Number 6.

Kehoe, Alice B.

1990   The Monumental Midwestern Taxonomic Method. In *The Woodland Tradition in the Western Great Lakes: Papers Presented to Eldon Johnson,* edited by Guy E. Gibbon, pp 31–36. University of Minnesota Publications in Anthropology 4, Minneapolis.

Keller, John E., and L. Janice Campbell

1983   *Cultural Resources Survey of Catahoula Parish, Louisiana.* Report submitted to the Lousiana Department of Culture, Recreation and Tourism, Division of Archaeology, by New World Research, Inc. New World Research, Inc., Report of Investigations 90.

Kelly, John E., Steven J. Ozuk, and Joyce A. Williams

1990   *The Range Site 2: The Emergent Mississippian Dohack and Range Phase Occupations.* University of Illinois Press, Urbana.

Kelly, Lucretia S.

1990   Faunal Remains from the Priestly Site. In *Excavations at the Priestly Site (3Po490), An Emergent Mississipian Community in Northeastern Arkansas*, edited by David W. Benn, pp.327–361. CAR-740, Center for Archaeological Research, Southwest Missouri State University, Springfield.

1992   Moon Site Faunal Analysis. In *Excavations at the Moon Site (3Po488), A Middle Mississipian Village in Northeastern Arkansas*, edited by David W. Benn, pp.225–248. CAR-780, Center for Archaeological Research, Southwest Missouri State University, Springfield.

Kelly, Lucretia S, and Martha Rolingson

2003   Mound S at the Toltec Mounds Site: A Locus of Special Activity. Paper presented at the 59th Annual Meeting of the Southeastern Archaeological Conference, Biloxi, Mississippi.

Kelly, Robert L.

1988   The Three Sides of a Biface. *American Antiquity* 53:717–734.

Kelso, Gerald K.

1994   Pollen Percolation Rates in Euroamerican-Era Cultural Deposits in the Northeastern United States. *Journal of Archaeological Science* 21:481–488.

Kelso, Gerald K., D. Ritchie, and N. Misso

2000   Pollen Record Preservation Processes in the Salem Neck Sewage Plant Shell Midden (19-ES-471). *Journal of Archaeological Science* 27:235–240.

Kesel, Richard H., and Elaine G. Yodis

1992   Some Effects of Human Modifications on Sand-Bed Channels in Southwestern Mississippi, U.S.A. *Enviromental Geology and Water Sciences* 20:93–104.

Kesel, Richard H., Elaine G. Yodis, and David J. McGraw

1992   An Approximation of the Sediment Budget of the Lower Mississippi River Prior to Major Human Modification. *Earth Surface Processes and Landforms* 17:711–722.

Keyes, Charles Reuben

1925   Progress of the Archaeological Survey of Iowa. *Iowa Journal of History and Politics* 23:339–352.

1928   The Hill-Lewis Archaeological Survey. *Minnesota History* 9:96–108.

1930   A Unique Survey. *Palimpsest* 9:214–226.

Kidder, Alfred V., Jesse D. Jennings, and Edwin M. Shook

1946   *Excavations at Kaminaljuyu.* Carnegie Institution, Publication 561. Washington, D.C.

Kidder, Tristram R.

1988   The Koroa Indians of the Lower Mississippi Valley. *Mississippi Archaeology* 23(2):1–42.

1996a   Perspectives on the Geoarchaeology of the Lower Mississippi Valley. *Engineering Geology* 45:305–323.

1996b   New Directions in Poverty Point Settlement Archaeology: An Example from Northeast Louisiana. In *The Poverty Point Culture: Local Manifestations, Subsistence Practices, and Trade Networks*, edited by Kathleen M. Byrd, pp. 27–53. *Geosciences and Man.* Vol. 29. Louisiana State University, Baton Rouge, Louisiana.

1998   The Rat that Ate Louisiana: Aspects of Historical Ecology in the Mississippi River
        Delta. In *Advances in Historical Ecology,* edited by William Balée, pp. 141–168. Co-
        lumbia University Press, New York.

2002   Woodland Period Archaeology of the Lower Mississippi Valley. In *The Woodland
        Southeast,* edited by David G. Anderson and Robert C. Mainfort, Jr., pp. 66–90.
        University of Alabama Press, Tuscaloosa.

2004   Prehistory of the Lower Mississippi Valley after 800 B.C. In *Handbook of North
        American Indians, Volume 14, Southeast,* edited by Raymond D. Fogelson and
        William Sturtevant, pp. 545–559. Smithsonian Institution Press, Washington, D.C.

2006   Climate Change and the Archaic to Woodland Transition (3000–2500 Cal B.P.) in
        the Mississippi River Basin. *American Antiquity* 71:195–231.

Kidder, Tristram R., and Gayle J. Fritz

1993   Subsistence and Social Change in the Lower Mississippi River Valley: The Reno
        Brake and Osceola Sites, Louisiana. *Journal of Field Archaeology* 20:281–297.

Kidder, Tristram R., Gayle J. Fritz, and Christopher J. Smith

1993   Emerson (16TE104). In *1992 Archaeological Test Excavations in Tensas Parish, Loui-
        siana,* by Tristram R. Kidder, pp. 110–137. Tulane University, Center for Archae-
        ology, Archaeological Report 2, New Orleans, Louisiana.

Killick, David J., A. J. T Jull., and G. S. Burr

1999   A Failure to Discriminate: Querying Oxidizable Carbon Ratio (OCR) Dating. *So-
        ciety for Ameican Archaeology Bulletin* 17(5):32–36.

King, Frances B.

1982   Archeobotanical Remains. In *Powell Canal: Baytown Period Occupation on Bayou
        Macon in Southeast Arkansas,* by John H. House, pp. 63–65. Fayetteville: Arkansas
        Archeological Survey Research Series No. 19.

1985   Early Cultivated Cucurbits in Eastern North America. In *Prehistoric Food Produc-
        tion in North America,* edited by Richard I. Ford, pp. 73–98. Anthropological Pa-
        pers 75. Museum of Anthropology, University of Michigan, Ann Arbor.

King, Frances B., and Russel W. Graham

1981   Effects of Ecological and Paleoecological Patterns on Subsistence and Paleoenvi-
        ronmental Reconstructions. *American Antiquity* 46:128–142.

King, Frances B., and James E. King

1996   Interdisciplinary Approaches to Environmental Reconstruction: An Example
        from the Ozark Highland. In *Case Studies in Environmental Archaeology,* edited
        by Elizabeth J. Reitz, Lee A. Newsom, and Sylvia J. Scudder, pp. 71–85. Plenum
        Press, New York.

King, James E.

1981   Late Quaternary Vegetational History of Illinois. *Ecological Monographs* 51:43–62.

King, James E., and William H. Allen, Jr.

1977   A Holocene Vegetation Record from the Mississippi River Valley, Southeastern
        Missouri. *Quaternary Research* 8:307–323.

King, Thomas F.

2005   *Doing Archaeology: A Cultural Resource Management Perspective.* Left Coast Press,
        Inc., Walnut Creek, California.

Kipfmueller, Kurt F., and Thomas W. Swetnam

2001   Using Dendrochronology to Reconstruct the History of Forest and Woodland Ecosystems. In *The Historical Ecology Handbook,* edited by Dave Egan and
Evelyn A. Howell, pp. 199–228. Island Press, Washington, D.C.

Klemptner, Lori J., and Paul F. Johnson III

1985   An Analytical Approach to the Technological Development of Mississippian Pottery. In *Ancient Technology to Modern Science,* edited by W. David Kingery, pp. 101–
112. The American Ceramic Society, Inc., Columbus, Ohio.

Klinger, Timothy C.

1975   Mississippian Communities in the St. Francis Basin: A Central Place Model. *Arkansas Academy of Science Proceedings* 29:50–51.

1976   The Problem of Site Definition in Cultural Resource Management. *Arkansas
Academy of Science Proceedings* 30:54–56.

Klippel, Walter E.

2001   Sugar Monoculture, Bovid Skeletal Part Frequencies, and Stable Carbon Isotopes:
Interpreting Enslaved African Diet at Brimstone Hill, St. Kitts, West Indies. *Journal of Archaeological Science* 28:1191–1198.

Klippel, Walter E., and William B. Turner

1991   Terrestrial Gastropods from Glade Sere and the Hayes Shell Midden in Middle
Tennessee. In *Beamers, Bobwhites, and Blue-Points: Tributes to the Career of
Paul W. Parmalee,* edited by James R. Purdue, Walter E. Klippel, and Bonnie W.
Styles, pp. 177–188. Illinois State Museum Scientific Papers Vol. 23, Springfield, and
the University of Tennessee, Department of Anthropology, Report of Investiga-
tions 52, Knoxville.

Kniffen, Fred B.

1936   A Preliminary Report of Mounds and Middens of Plaquemines and St. Bernard
Parishes, Lower Mississippi River Delta. *Louisiana Department of Conservation,
Geological Bulletin* 8:407–444.

Knox, J. C.

1976   Concept of the Graded Stream. In *Theories of Landform Development,* edited
by William N. Melhorn and Ronald C. Flemal, pp. 169–198. Allen and Unwin,
London.

1983   Responses of River Systems to Holocene Climates. In *Late-Quaternary Environments of the United States,* edited by Herbert E. Wright, Jr., pp. 26–41. University of
Minnesota Press, Minneapolis.

Kolchin, Peter

1992   The Tragic Era? Interpreting Southern Reconstruction in Comparative Perspective. In *The Meaning of Freedom: Economics, Politics, and Culture after Slavery,* edited by Frank McGlynn and Seymour Drescher, pp. 291–311. University of Pittsburgh Press, Pittsburgh.

Koldehoff, Brad H.

1990   *Household Specialization: The Organization of Mississippian Chipped-Stone-Tool
Production.* Unpublished M.A. thesis, Department of Anthropology, Southern Illinois University, Carbondale.

Krech, Shepard, III

1999   *The Ecological Indian*. W. W. Norton, New York.

Krieger, Alex D.

1944   The Typological Concept. *American Antiquity* 3:271–288.

Kroeber, Alfred L.

1916   *Zuni Potsherds*. Anthropological Papers of the American Museum of Natural History 18(1) (whole issue). New York.

1919   On the Principle of Order in Civilization as Exemplified by Changes of Fashion. *American Anthropologist* 21:235–263.

1940   Statistical Classification. *American Antiquity* 6:29–44.

Krogman, William Marion

1978   *The Human Skeleton in Forensic Medicine*. Charles C. Thomas Publisher, Springfield, Illinois.

Küchler, A. W.

1964   *Potential Natural Vegetation of the Coterminous United States*. American Geographical Society Special Publication 36, New York.

Kuttruff, Carl, Michelle Hutchins, David B. Kelley, and Laurie A. Wilkie

1995   *Archaeological Test Excavations at Eight Sites in the Upper Steele Bayou Basin, Washington County, Mississippi*. Report submitted to U.S. Army Corps of Engineers, Vicksburg District by Coastal Environments, Inc., Baton Rouge, Louisiana.

Kutzbach, John E.

1987   Model Simulations of the Climatic Patterns During the Deglaciation of North America. In *North America and Adjacent Oceans During the Last Glaciation*, edited by W. Ruddiman and H. Wright, Jr., pp. 425–446. The Geological Society of America, The Geology of America, Volume K-3, Boulder.

Kutzbach, John E., and Thompson Webb III

1991   Late Quaternary Climatic and Vegetational Change in Eastern North America: Concepts, Models, and Data. In *Quaternary Landscapes*, edited by Linda C. K. Shane and Edward J. Cushing, pp. 175–217. University of Minnesota Press, Minneapolis.

Kvamme, Kenneth L.

2001   Current Practices in Archaeogeophysics: Magnetics, Resistivity, Conductivity, and Ground Penetrating Radar. In *Earth Sciences and Archaeology*, edited by Paul Goldberg, Vance T. Holliday, and C. Reid Ferring, pp. 353–384. Kluwer Academic/Plenum Publishers, New York.

2003a   Geophysical Surveys as Landscape Archaeology. *American Antiquity* 68:435–458.

2003b   Multidimensional Prospecting in North American Great Plains Village Sites. *Archaeological Prospection* 10:131–142.

Kvamme, Kenneth L., Jay K. Johnson, and Bryan S. Haley

2006a   Integration and Interpretation of Multiple Instrument Applications. In *Remote Sensing in Archaeology: An Explicitly North American Perspective*, edited by Jay K. Johnson, pp. 205–234. University of Alabama Press, Tuscaloosa.

2006b   Multiple Methods Surveys: Case Studies. In *Remote Sensing in Archaeology: An Ex-*

plicitly North American Perspective, edited by Jay K. Johnson, pp. 251–267. University of Alabama Press, Tuscaloosa.

Lafferty, Robert H., III

1977   *The Evolution of Mississippian Settlement Patterns and Exploitative Technology in the Black Bottom of Southern Illinois.* Ph.D. dissertation, Department of Anthropology, Southern Illinois University at Carbondale.

1998   Landscape Change and Settlement Location in the Cairo Lowland of Southeastern Missouri. In *Changing Perspectives on the Archaeology of the Central Mississippi Valley,* edited by Michael J. O'Brien and Robert C. Dunnell, pp. 124–147. University of Alabama Press, Tuscaloosa.

Lafferty, Robert H. III, and James E. Price

1996   Southeast Missouri. In *Prehistory of the Central Mississippi Valley,* edited by Charles H. McNutt, pp. 1–45. University of Alabama Press, Tuscaloosa.

Lambert, Patricia M.

2000   *Bioarchaeological Studies of Life in the Age of Agriculture.* University of Alabama Press, Tuscaloosa.

Lapham, I. A.

1855   *The Antiquities of Wisconsin.* Smithsonian Contributions to Knowledge 7 (Article 4.), Smithsonian Institution, Washington, D.C.

Larsen, Clark Spencer

1997   *Bioarchaeology: Interpreting Behavior from the Human Skeleton.* Cambridge University Press, Cambridge.

Larsen, Clark Spencer, Christopher B. Ruff, Margaret J. Schoeninger, and Dale L. Hutchinson

1992   Population Decline and Extinction in La Florida. In *Disease and Demography in America,* edited by John W. Verano and Douglas H. Ubelaker, pp. 25–39. Smithsonian Institution Press, Washington, D.C.

Lauro, James

1993   *Cultural Resources Survey and Testing on the Pearl River in the Jackson Metropolitan Area, Jackson, Mississippi.* Report submitted to the Pearl River Basin Development District by Archaeology Mississippi, Inc. On file, Mississippi Department of Archives and History, Jackson.

Lauro, James, and Geoffrey R. Lehmann

1982   *The Slate Site: A Poverty Point Lapidary Industry in the Southern Yazoo Basin, Mississippi.* Mississippi Department of Archives and History, Archaeological Report No. 7, Jackson.

Leader, Jonathan M.

1990   The Humber-McWilliams Site Brass Headdress: Preliminary Evidence for the Reuse of European Metal by Contact Period Native Americans in Mississippi. *Mississippi Archaeology* 25(2):63–69.

Leeds, Leon L.

1979   *Surface Sampling and Spatial Analysis: The Study of a Major Mississippian Ceremonial Center at the Rich Woods Site in Southeaster Missouri.* Unpublished Ph.D. dissertation, University of Washington.

Leese, M. N., and P. L. Main
1994   The Efficient Computation of Unbiased Mahalanobis Distances and Their Interpretation in Archaeometry. *Archaeometry* 36:307–316.

Lehmann, Geoffrey R.
1982   *The Jaketown Site: Surface Collection from a Poverty Point Regional Center in the Yazoo Basin Mississippi.* Mississippi Department of Archives and History, Archaeological Report No. 9, Jackson.

1991   A Summary of Poverty Point Investigations in the Yazoo Basin, Mississippi. In *The Poverty Point Culture: Local Manifestations, Subsistence Practices, and Trade Networks,* edited by Kathleen M. Byrd, pp. 3–6. *Geosciences and Man,* vol. 29. Louisiana State University, Baton Rouge.

Lengyel, Stacey N.
2004   *Archaeomagnetic Research in the U.S. Midcontinent.* Unpublished Ph.D. dissertation, University of Arizona, Tucson.

Lengyel, Stacey N., Jeffrey L. Eighmy, and Lynne P. Sullivan
1999   On the Potential of Archaemagnetic Dating in the Mid-Continent Region of North America: Toqua Site Results. *Southeastern Archaeology* 18:156–171.

Leone, Mark P., Cheryl Janifer LaRoche, and Jennifer J. Babiarz
2005   The Archaeology of Black Americans in Recent Times. *Annual Review of Anthropology* 34:575–598.

Lewarch, Dennis E., and Michael J. O'Brien
1981   Effect of Short Term Tillage on Aggregate Provenience Surface Pattern. In *Plowzone Archaeology: Contributions to Theory and Technique,* edited by Michael J. O'Brien and Dennis E. Lewarch, pp. 7–49. Vanderbilt University, Publications in Anthropology 27.

Lewis, Barbara
1997   Tchefuncte Use of Animal Bone with Inferences for Tchefuncte Culture, Ritual, and Animal Cosmology. *Louisiana Archaeology* 22:31–70.

Lewis, R. Barry
1996   The Western Kentucky Border and the Cairo Lowland. In *Prehistory of the Central Mississippi Valley,* edited by Charles H. McNutt, pp. 47–75. University of Alabama Press, Tuscaloosa.

Lewontin, Richard C.
1974a   *The Genetic Basis of Evolutionary Change.* Columbia University Press, New York.

1974b   Darwin and Mendel—the Materialist Revolution. In *The Heritage of Copernicus: Theories Pleasing to the Mind,* edited by Jerzy Neyman, pp. 166–183. MIT Press, Cambridge.

Lipo, Carl P.
2001a   *Science, Style, and the Study of Community Structure: An Example from the Central Mississippi River Valley.* British Archaeological Reports, International Series No. 918, Oxford.

2001b   Community Structures among Late Mississippian Population of the Central Mississippi River Valley. In *Posing Questions for a Scientific Archaeology,* edited by Terry L. Hunt, Carl P. Lipo, and Sarah L. Sterling, pp. 175–216. Bergin & Garvey, Westport.

Lipo, Carl P., Robert C. Dunnell, and Daniel O. Larson

2004   Studying the Evolution of Complex Societies: Recent Geophysical Studies in the Mississippi River Valley. *Missouri Archaeologist* 65:68–106.

Lipo, Carl P., James K. Feathers, and Robert C. Dunnell

2005   Temporal Data Requirements, Luminescence Dates, and the Resolution of Chronological Structure of Late Prehistoric Deposits in the Central Mississippi River Valley. *American Antiquity* 70:527–544.

Lipo, Carl P., Mark E. Madsen, Robert C. Dunnell, and Tim Hunt

1997   Population Structure, Cultural Transmission, and Frequency Seriation. *Journal of Anthropological Archaeology* 6:301–333.

Litwack, Leon F.

1979   *Been in the Storm So Long: The Aftermath of Slavery.* Alfred A. Knopf, New York.

Livingood, Patrick

2003   Plaquemine Cooking: Using Digital Image Analysis to Find Plaquemine Paste Recipes. Paper presented at the 60th Annual Meeting of the Southeastern Archaeological Conference, Charlotte, North Carolina.

2004   Digital Image Analysis of Ceramic Thin-Sections: Present and Future. Paper presented at the Southeastern Archaeological Conference/ Midwestern Archaeological Conference, St. Louis.

Lock, G.

1995   Archaeological Computing, Archaeological Theory and Moves Towards Contextualism. In *Computer Applications and Quantitative Methods in Archaeology, 1994,* edited by J. Huggett and N. Ryan, pp. 13–18. BAR International Series 600, Tempus Reparatum, Oxford.

Lockhart, J. J., and Thomas J. Green

2006   The Current and Potential Role of Archaeo-Geophysics in Cultural Resource Management in the United States. In *Remote Sensing in Archaeology: An Explicitly North American Perspective,* edited by Jay K. Johnson, pp. 17–32. University of Alabama Press, Tuscaloosa.

Logan, William N.

1907   *Clays of Mississippi.* Mississippi State Geological Survey Bulletin No. 2. Brandon Printing Company, Nashville.

1908   *Clays of Mississippi.* Part II. Brick Clays and Clay Industry of Southern Mississippi. Mississippi State Geological Survey Bulletin No. 4. Brandon Printing Company, Nashville.

1909   *The Pottery Clays of Mississippi.* Mississippi State Geological Survey, Bulletin No. 6. Brandon Printing Company, Nashville.

Lopinot, Neal H.

1995   Archaeobotanical Remains. In *Woodland and Mississippian Occupations at the Hayti Bypass Site, Pemiscot County, Missouri,* edited by Michael D. Conner, pp. 221–262. Southwest Missouri State University, Center for Archaeological Research, Special Publication No. 1, Springfield.

Lopinot, Neal H., and Gina Powell

2003   Ethnobotanical Analyses. In *Phase II Archaeological Testing at Sites 22LF551 and*

22LF552, Leflore County, Mississippi, by Charles H. McNutt, Jr., pp. 161–176. Report prepared for U.S. Army Corps of Engineers, Vicksburg District, by Panamerican Consultants, Inc, Memphis.

Lopinot, Neal H., and Larissa A. Thomas

2003   Archeobotany. In *Mississippian Transitions at John's Lake: Data Recovery Excavations of Three Buried Sites in Northeast Arkansas,* by C. Andrew Buchner, Eric S. Albertson, Neal H. Lopinot, Larissa A. Thomas, Emanuel Breitburg, and Jerome V. Ward, pp. 140-151. Arkansas Archeological Survey, Research Series 60, Fayetteville.

Lopinot, Neal H., and William I. Woods

1993   Wood Overexploitation and the Collapse of Cahokia. In *Foraging and Farming in the Eastern Woodlands,* edited by C. Margaret Scarry, pp. 206–231. University Press of Florida, Gainesville.

Lorenz, Karl G.

1990   Archaeological Survey and Testing Within a Five Kilometer Radius of the Old Hoover Platform Mound in the Big Black River Valley. *Mississippi Archaeology* 25(1):1–42.

1996   Small-Scale Mississippian Community Organization in the Big Black River Valley of Mississippi. *Southeastern Archaeology* 15:145–171.

Lubbock, Sir John

1872   *Prehistoric Times.* Appleton & Co., New York.

Lumb, Lisa Cutts, and Charles H. McNutt, Sr.

1988   *Chucalissa: Excavations in Units 2 and 6, 1959–67.* Memphis State University Anthropological Research Center, Occasional Papers 15.

Lyman, R. Lee

1985   On the Concepts of "Significance" and "Site": Implications for Inventorying Archaeological Resources. In *Archaeological Inventory and Predictive Modeling in the Pacific Northwest,* edited by R. F. Darsie, J. D. Keyser and S. Hackenberger, pp. 31–90. U.S.D.A. Forest Service, Pacific Northwest Region. Studies in Cultural Resource Management No. 6, Portland, Oregon.

2003a   *W. C. McKern and the Midwestern Taxonomic Method.* University of Alabama Press, Tuscaloosa

2003b   The Influence of Time Averaging and Space Averaging on the Application of Foraging Theory in Zooarchaeology. *Journal of Archaeological Science* 30:595–610.

Lyman, R. Lee, Michael J. O'Brien, and Robert C. Dunnell

1997   *The Rise and Fall of Culture History.* Plenum Press, New York.

Lynott , Mark J., Thomas W. Boutton, James E. Price, and Dwight E. Nelson

1986   Stable Carbon Isotope Evidence for Maize Agriculture in Southeast Missouri and Northeast Arkansas. *American Antiquity* 51: 51–65.

Lynott, Mark J., Hector Neff, James E. Price, James W. Cogswell, and Michael D. Glascock

2000   Inferences About Prehistoric Ceramics and People in Southeast Missouri: Results of Ceramic Compositional Analysis. *American Antiquity* 65:103–126.

Lyon, Edwin A.

1996   *A New Deal for Southeastern Archaeology.* University of Alabama Press, Tuscaloosa.

MacCord, H.

1988   Where Do You Draw The Line? *American Society for Conservation Archaeology, Report* 15(1):6–15.

MacNeish, Richard S.

1952   *Iroquois Pottery Types.* National Museum of Canada, Bulletin 124, Ottawa.

Madry, Scott L. H., and Carole L. Crumley

1990   An Application of Remote Sensing and GIS in a Regional Archaeological Settlement-Pattern Analysis: The Arroux River Valley, Burgundy, France. In *Interpreting Space: GIS and Archaeology,* edited by Kathleen M. S. Allen, Stanton W. Green, and Ezra B. W. Zubrow, pp. 364–380. Taylor & Francis, London.

Magdol, Edward

1977   *A Right to the Land: Essays on the Freedmen's Community.* Greenwood Press, Westport, Connecticut.

Magne, M. P. R.

1985   *Lithics and Livelihood: Stone Tool Technologies of Central and Southern Interior British Columbia.* Archaeological Survey of Canada Mercury Series 133, Ottawa.

Maher, Thomas O.

1983   *Ceramic Exchange in the Southeastern United States: An Examination of Three Methods for Mineralogically Characterizing Aboriginal Ceramics from Archaeological Sites in Alabama, Louisiana, and Mississippi.* Unpublished M.A. thesis, SUNY Binghamton, Department of Anthropology.

Mainfort, Robert C., Jr.

1994   *Archaeological Investigations in the Obion River Drainage: The West Tennessee Tributaries Project.* Tennessee Department of Environment and Conservation, Division of Archaeology, Research Series No. 10.

1996   Late Period Chronology in the Central Mississippi Valley: A Western Tennessee Perspective. *Southeastern Archaeology* 15:172–181.

1999   Late Period Phases in the Central Mississippi Valley: A Multivariate Approach. In *Arkansas Archaeology: Papers in Honor of Dan and Phyllis Morse,* edited by Robert C. Mainfort, Jr., and Marvin D. Jeter, pp. 143–167. University of Arkansas Press, Fayetteville.

2003a   Late Period Ceramic Rim Attribute Variation in the Central Mississippi Valley. *Southeastern Archaeology* 22:33–46.

2003b   An Ordination Approach to Assessing Late Period Phases in the Central Mississippi Valley. *Southeastern Archaeology* 22:176–184.

2005   A K-Means Analysis of Late-Period Ceramic Variation in the Central Mississippi Valley. *Southeastern Archaeology* 24:59–69.

Mainfort, Robert C., Jr., and J. Shawn Chapman

1994   West Tennessee Ceramic Typology, Part I: Tchula and Middle Woodland Periods. *Tennessee Anthropologist* 19(2):148–179.

Mainfort, Robert C., Jr., James W. Cogswell, Michael J. O'Brien, Hector Neff, and Michael D. Glascock

1997   Neutron Activation Analysis of Pottery from Pinson Mounds and Nearby Sites in

Western Tennessee: Local Production vs. Long-Distance Importation. *Midcontinental Journal of Archaeology* 22: 43–68.

Mainfort, Robert C., Jr., and Charles H. McNutt

2004   Calibrated Radiocarbon Chronology for Pinson Mounds and Middle Woodland in the Midsouth. *Southeastern Archaeology* 23:12–24.

Mainfort, Robert C., Jr., and Michael C. Moore

1998   Graves Lake: A Late Mississippian Period Village in Lauderdale County, Tennessee. In *Changing Perspectives on the Archaeology of the Central Mississippi Valley,* edited by Michael J. O'Brien and Robert C. Dunnell, pp. 99–123. University of Alabama Press, Tuscaloosa.

Mariaca, Maria Teresa

1988   *Late Marksville/Early Baytown Period Subsistence Economy: Analysis of Three Faunal Assemblages from Northeastern Louisiana.* Unpublished M.A. thesis, Department of Archaeology, Boston University.

Marquardt, William H.

1994   The Role of Archaeology in Raising Environmental Consciousness. In *Historical Ecology: Cultural Knowledge and Changing Landscapes,* edited by Carole L. Crumley, pp. 203–221. School of American Research Press, Santa Fe.

Marshall, Richard A.

1986   Comments on Geomorphological Implications on the Development of the Late Tchula/Early Marksville Settlement Pattern in the Upper Yazoo Basin, Mississippi. In *The Tchula Period in the Mid-South and Lower Mississippi Valley,* edited by David H. Dye and Ronald C. Brister, pp. 63–69. Mississippi Department of Archives and History, Archaeological Report No. 17, Jackson.

1987   A Brief Comparison of Two Early Mississippi Substage Settlement Patterns in Southeast Missouri and Northwest Mississippi. In *The Emergent Mississippian: Proceedings of the Sixth Mid-South Archaeological Conference, June 6–9, 1985,* edited by Richard A. Marshall, pp. 160–166. Mississippi State University, Cobb Institute of Archaeology, Occasional Papers 87–01, Starkville, Mississippi.

1988   *Preliminary Archaeological Testing Near Mound A, Buford (22TL501) Site, Tallahatchie County, Mississippi.* Mississippi State University, Cobb Institute of Archaeology, Report of Investigations No. 5.

Martin, Paul Sidney, George I. Quimby, and Donald Collier

1947   *Indians before Columbus: Twenty Thousand Years of North American History Revealed by Archeology.* University of Chicago Press, Chicago.

Mason, Otis T.

1878a   *Circular 316 In Reference to American Archaeology.* Smithsonian Institution, Washington, D.C.

1878b   Anthropology. In *Annual Record of Science and Industry for 1877,* edited by S. F. Baird, pp. 255–274. Harper and Brothers, New York.

1881   Abstracts of the Smithsonian Correspondence Relative to Aboriginal Remains in the United States. *Annual Report of the Board of Regents of the Smithsonian Institution for the year 1880,* pp. 441–448. Washington, D.C.

Mason, Ronald J.

1970   Hopewell, Middle Woodland, and the Laurel Culture: A Problem in Archaeological Classification. *American Anthropologist* 72:802–815.

Matson, Frederick R.

1965   Ceramic Ecology: An Approach to the Study of the Early Cultures of the Near East. In *Ceramics and Man,* edited by Frederick R. Matson, pp. 161–177. Viking Fund Publications in Archaeology, Chicago.

May, R. V.

1988   Broadside from the West: Response to Howard MacCord. *American Society for Conservation Archaeology* 15(2):10–14.

Mayer, Frederick J.

1989   Appendix D: Ground Penetrating Radar (GPR) Subsurface Testing, Poverty Point. In *Digging on the Dock of the Bay(ou): The 1988 Excavations at Poverty Point,* edited by Jon L. Gibson., pp. 211–227. University of Southwestern Louisiana, Center for Archaeological Studies Report No. 8, Lafayette.

Mayer-Oakes, William J.

1955   *Prehistory of the Upper Ohio Valley: An Introductory Study.* Annals of the Carnegie Museum, No. 34, Pittsburgh.

Mayr, Ernst

1959   Darwin and the Evolutionary Theory in Biology. In *Evolution and Anthropology: A Centennial Appraisal,* edited by Betty J. Meggers, pp. 509–512. Anthropological Society of Washington, Washington, D.C.

1982   *Growth of Biological Thought: Diversity, Evolution, and Inheritance.* Belknap Press, Cambridge.

McAlester, Virginia, and Lee McAlester

1986   *A Field Guide to American Houses.* Alfred A. Knopf, New York.

McCain, William D.

1953   *The Story of Jackson.* J. F. Hyer Publishing, Jackson.

McGahey, Samuel O.

1986   A Compendium of Mississippi Dugout Canoes Recorded Since 1974. *Mississippi Archaeology* 21(1):58–70.

1987   Paleo-Indian Lithic Material: Implications of Distribution in Mississippi. *Mississippi Archaeology* 22(2):1–13.

1996   Paleoindian and Early Archaic Data from Mississippi. In *The Paleoindian and Early Archaic Southeast,* edited by David G. Anderson and Kenneth E. Sassaman, pp. 354–384. University of Alabama Press, Tuscaloosa.

1999   Use and Avoidance of Kosciusko Quartzite in Prehistoric Mississippi Flaked Stone Assemblages. In *Raw Materials and Exchange in the Mid-South,* edited by Evan Peacock and Samuel O. Brookes, pp. 1–11. Mississippi Department of Archives and History, Archaeological Report 29, Jackson.

2000   *Mississippi Projectile Point Guide.* Mississippi Department of Archives and History, Archaeological Report 31, Jackson.

2002   The Short #3 Site (22Pa750): Phase Two Investigations. *Mississippi Archaeology* 37(1):1–43.

McGimsey, Charles R., III

1996 *Points, Pits, and Potholes: Archaeology in Southwestern Louisiana.* University of Southwestern Louisiana, Department of Sociology and Anthropology, Regional Archaeology Program, Management Unit III, 1995/96 Annual Report, Lafayette.

2001 Headwaters of How the Federal Government Became Involved in Archaeology in the Midsouth and Elsewhere after World War II. In *Historical Perspectives on Midsouth Archaeology,* edited by Martha A. Rolingson, pp. 93–102. Arkansas Archeological Survey, Research Series 58, Fayetteville.

2003 The Rings of Marksville. *Southeastern Archaeology* 22:47–62.

McGimsey, Charles R., III, and Hester A. Davis

1968 Modern Land Use Practices and the Archeology of the Lower Mississippi Alluvial Valley. *The Arkansas Archeologist* 9:28–36.

McGlade, James

1995 Archaeology and the Ecodynamics of Human-Modified Landscapes. *Antiquity* 69:113–132.

McKee, Larry

1992 The Ideals and Realities behind the Design and Use of 19th-Century Virginia Slave Cabins. In *The Art and Mystery of Historical Archaeology: Essays in Honor of James Deetz,* edited by Anne E. Yentsch and Mary C. Beaudry, pp. 195–214. CRC Press, Boca Raton.

1999 Food Supply and Plantation Social Order: An Archaeological Perspective. In *"I, Too, Am America": Archaeological Studies of African-American Life,* edited by Theresa A. Singleton, pp. 218–239. University Press of Virginia, Charlottesville.

McKern, W. C.

1939a The Midwestern Taxonomic Method as an Aid to Archaeological Culture Study. *American Antiquity* 4:301–313.

1939b Application of the Midwestern Taxonomic System. *Bulletin of the Archaeological Society of Delaware* 3(3):18–21.

1943 Regarding the Midwestern Archaeological Taxonomy. *American Anthropologist* 45:313–315.

McLean, John P.

1879 *The Moundbuilders of Butler County, Ohio.* R. Clarke and Company, Cincinnati.

McMillen, Neil

1989 *Dark Journey: Black Mississippians in the Age of Jim Crow.* University of Illinois Press, Urbana.

McNutt, Charles H., Jr.

2003 Test Excavations at 22Lf551, a Late Woodland Site in LeFlore County, Mississippi. In *Proceedings of the 19th Mid-South Archaeological Conference: Papers in Honor of Charles H. McNutt, Sr.,* edited by C. Andrew Buchner and David H. Dye, pp. 101–120. Panamerican Consultants, Inc., Special Publication No. 3, and University of Memphis, Anthropological Research Center, Occasional Paper No. 22, Memphis.

McNutt, Charles H., Sr.

1996 The Upper Yazoo Basin in Northwest Mississippi. In *Prehistory of the Central Mis-*

sissippi Valley, edited by Charles H. McNutt, pp. 155–185. University of Alabama Press, Tuscaloosa.

McNutt, Charles H., Sr., and Gerald P. Smith

1982   Salvage Excavations at Adams and Riverside Drive, Memphis, Tennessee. *Tennessee Anthropologist* 7:151:175.

Medford, L. D.

1972   Site Destruction Due to Agricultural Practices in Northeast Arkansas. *Arkansas Archeological Survey, Research Series* No. 3, Fayetteville.

Meggers, Betty

1957   *Archaeological Investigations in the Mouth of the Amazon.* Bureau of American Ethnology, Bulletin 160. Washington, D.C.

Meltzer, David J.

1998   Introduction: Ephraim Squier, Edwin Davis, and the Making of an American Archaeological Classic. In *Ancient Monuments of the Mississippi Valley,* by Ephraim G. Squier and Edwin H. Davis, edited by David J. Meltzer, pp.1–98. Smithsonian Classics of Anthropology, Smithsonian Institution, Washington, D.C.

Meltzer, David J., and Robert C. Dunnell (editors)

1992   *The Archaeology of William Henry Holmes.* Smithsonian Institution Press, Washington, D.C.

Metcalf, Ashley

1992   Materials Analysis of Sand-Tempered Pottery from Northeast Mississippi. *Mississippi Archaeology* 27(1): 19–43.

Michod, Richard E.

1999   *Darwinian Dynamics: Evolutionary Transitions in Fitness and Individuality.* Princeton University Press, Princeton.

Millard, A. R.

2006   Bayesian Analysis of Pleistocene Chronometric Measures. *Archaeometry* 48:359–375.

Miller, Steven F.

1993   Plantation Labor Organization and Slave Life on the Cotton Frontier: The Alabama-Mississippi Black Belt, 1815–1840. In *Cultivation and Culture: Labor and the Shaping of Slave Life in the Americas,* edited by Ira Berlin and Philip D. Morgan, pp. 155–169. University Press of Virginia, Charlottesville.

Million, Michael G.

1975   Ceramic Technology and the Nodena Phase People (ca. 1400–1700). *Southeastern Archaeological Conference Bulletin* 18:201–208.

Mills, G. B.

1978   *Of Men and Rivers: The Story of the Vicksburg District.* U.S. Army Corps of Engineers, Vicksburg, Mississippi.

Misner, Elizabeth J.

1991   Vertebrate Faunal Remains from Pump Canal, Southern Louisiana. Paper presented at the 48th Annual Meeting of the Southeastern Archaeological Conference, New Orleans.

Mississippi Department of Transportation (MDOT)

2004 Project Report, Interstate 69: Section 11—Robinsonville to Benoit. Electronic document, http://www.gomdot.com/newsprojects/section11.htm, accessed September 21, 2004.

Mitchell, Nancy Ross

1977 *Paleopathology in Archaeology: The Humber Site (22-CO-601) as a Case Study.* Unpublished M.A. thesis, Department of Sociology and Anthropology, University of Mississippi, Oxford.

Mitchem, Jeffrey M., and Bonnie G. McEwan

1988 New Data on Early Bells from Florida. *Southeastern Archaeology* 7:39–49.

Mooney, James P., Susan K. Wilkerson, Troy Mead, and James P. Wilson

2004 *Cultural Resource Phase III Mitigation of Sites 22Co573/773 and 22Co778 for the Construction of the Coahoma Welcome Center at the Interchange of U.S. Highway 49 and U.S. Highway 61, Coahoma County, Mississippi.* Report submitted to Environmental Division, Mississippi Department of Transportation, Jackson, Mississippi, by Michael Baker Jr., Inc., White Hall, Arkansas.

Moore, Clarence B.

1908 Certain Mounds of Arkansas and Mississippi. *Journal of the Academy of Natural Sciences of Philadelphia* 13:481–557, 564–605.

1909 Antiquities of the Ouachita Valley. *Journal of the Academy of Natural Sciences of Philadelphia* 14:7–170.

1910 Antiquities of the St. Francis, White, and Black Rivers, Arkansas. *Journal of the Academy of Natural Sciences of Philadelphia* 14:255–364.

1911 Some Aboriginal Sites on Mississippi River. *Journal of the Academy of Natural Sciences of Philadelphia* 14(3):365–480.

1912 Some Aboriginal Sites on the Red River. *Journal of the Academy of Natural Sciences of Philadelphia* 14:422–638.

1916a Some Aboriginal Sites in Louisiana and Arkansas. *Journal of the Academy of Natural Sciences of Philadelphia* 16:1–98.

1916b Some Aboriginal Sites on Green River, Kentucky; Certain Aboriginal Sites on Lower Ohio River; Additional Investigations on Mississippi River. *Journal of the Academy of Natural Sciences of Philadelphia* 16: 431–511.

Moore, Glover

1973 Separation from the Union. In *A History of Mississippi,* Vol. 1, edited by Richard Aubrey McLemore, pp. 420–446. University and College Press of Mississippi, Hattiesburg.

Moore, Lawrence E.

2006 CRM: Beyond Its Peak. *The SAA Archaeological Record* 6(1):30–35.

Moran, Emilio F.

1990 Ecosystem Theory in Biology and Anthropology: A Critical Assessment. In *The Ecosystem Approach in Anthropology,* edited by Emilio F. Moran, pp. 3–40. University of Michigan Press, Ann Arbor.

Morgan, David T.

1988 22-Ho-654: Another Puzzle to the Pieces. *Mississippi Archaeology* 23(2):43–52.

1992　The Post-Archaic Prehistory of Mississippi. Draft for Comprehensive State Planning Document. Manuscript on file, Mississippi Department of Archives and History, Jackson, Mississippi.

1996　*The Mississippi de Soto Trail-Mapping Project.* Mississippi Department of Archives and History, Archaeological Report No. 26, Jackson.

Morgan, David T., and Carol A. Raspet

1979　*Archaeological Salvage of a Portion of the Lightline Lake Site (22LF504), Teoc Creek Levee, Leflore County, Mississippi.* Report submitted to the U.S. Army Corps of Engineers, Vicksburg District.

Morse, Dan F.

1971　Recent Indications of Dalton Settlement Pattern in Northeast Arkansas. *Southeastern Archaeological Conference Bulletin* 13:5–10.

1973　Dalton Culture in Northeast Arkansas. *Florida Anthropologist* 26(1):23–38.

1975　Reply to Schiffer. In *The Cache River Archaeological Project: An Experiment in Contract Archaeology,* assembled by Michael B. Schiffer and John H. House, pp. 113–119. Arkansas Archeological Survey, Fayetteville.

1977　Dalton Settlement Systems: Reply to Schiffer (2). *Plains Anthropologist* 22:149–158.

1986　McCarty (3-Po-467): A Tchula-Period Site near Marked Tree, Arkansas. In *The Tchula Period in the Mid-South and Lower Mississippi Valley,* edited by David H. Dye and Ronald C. Brister, pp. 70–92. Mississippi Department of Archives and History, Archaeological Report No. 17, Jackson.

1997　*Sloan: A Paleoindian Dalton Cemetery in Arkansas.* Smithsonian Institution Press, Washington, D.C.

Morse, Dan F., and Phyllis A. Morse

1980　*Zebree Archaeological Project: Excavation, Data Interpretation, and Report on the Zebree Homestead Site, Mississippi County, Arkansas.* Arkansas Archeological Survey. Report submitted to the U.S. Army Corps of Engineers, Memphis.

1983　*Archaeology of the Central Mississippi Valley.* Academic Press, New York.

1996　Northeast Arkansas. In *Prehistory of the Central Mississippi Valley,* edited by Charles H. McNutt, pp. 119–135. University of Alabama Press, Tuscaloosa.

Morse, Dan F., and Phyllis A. Morse (editors)

1998　*The Lower Mississippi Valley Expeditions of Clarence Bloomfield Moore.* University of Alabama Press, Tuscaloosa.

Morse, Phyllis A.

1981　*Parkin.* Arkansas Archeological Survey Research Series No. 13, Pine Bluff, Arkansas.

1990　The Parkin Site and the Parkin Phase. In *Towns and Temples Along the Mississippi,* edited by David H. Dye and Cheryl A. Cox, pp. 118–134. University of Alabama Press, Tuscaloosa.

Morton, Samuel

1839　*Crania Americana, or a Comparative View of the Skull of the Various Nations of North and South America.* J. Dobson, Philadelphia.

Mueller, James W.

1981　*A Cultural Resources Survey of the Red River Waterway from Shreveport, Louisiana to the Mississippi River.* Report submitted by Commonwealth Associates, Inc., for the U.S. Army Engineer District, New Orleans.

Nassaney, Michael S., and Kendra Pyle

1999   The Adoption of the Bow and Arrow in Eastern North America: A View from Central Arkansas. *American Antiquity* 64:243–263.

National Research Council

1932   *Conference on Southern Pre-History.* National Research Council, Washington, D.C.

Neff, Hector

1994   RQ-mode Principal Components Analysis of Ceramic Compositional Data. *Archaeometry* 36:115–130.

2000   Neutron Activation Analysis for Provenance Determination in Archaeology. In *Modern Analytical Methods in Art and Archaeology,* edited by Enrico Ciliberto and Giuseppe Spoto, pp. 81–134. John Wiley and Sons, Inc., New York.

2002   Quantitative Techniques for Analyzing Ceramic Compositional Data. In *Ceramic Production and Circulation in the Greater Southwest: Source Determination by INAA and Complementary Mineralogical Investigations,* edited by Donna M. Glowacki and Hector Neff, pp. 15–36. Monograph 44, Cotsen Institute of Archaeology at UCLA, Los Angeles.

Neff, Hector, Frederick J. Bove, Brenda Lou, and Michael F. Piechowski

1992   Ceramic Raw Materials Survey in Pacific Coastal Guatemala. In *Chemical Characterization of Ceramic Pastes in Archaeology,* edited by H. Neff, pp. 59–84. Madison: Prehistory Press.

Neff, Hector, James W. Cogswell, and Michael D. Glascock

1996   Compositional Analysis of Caddoan Ceramics from Northeast Texas. Unpublished report on file, University of Missouri Research Reactor Center (MURR).

Neff, Hector, and Michael D. Glascock

2000   Compositional Variation in Caddoan and other Ceramics from Northeastern Texas: Update on Results from Instrumental Neutron Activation Analysis. Unpublished report on file, University of Missouri Research Reactor Center (MURR).

Neff, Hector, Michael D. Glascock, and James W. Cogswell

1995   Late Woodland and Mississippian Pottery Production and Exchange in the Western Lowlands and Adjacent Ozark Uplands of Southeast Missouri, Phase III. Unpublished report on file, University of Missouri Research Reactor Center (MURR).

1996   Compositional Analysis of Pottery and Clays from Southeastern Arkansas. Unpublished report on file, University of Missouri Research Reactor Center (MURR), University of Missouri, Columbia.

Neff, Hector, Michael D. Glascock, and Kathryn S. Stryker

1996   Chemical Characterization of Moundville Pottery. Unpublished report on file, University of Missouri Research Reactor Center (MURR).

Neff, Hector, and Donna M. Glowacki

2002   Ceramic Source Determination by Instrumental Neutron Activation Analysis in the American Southwest. In *Ceramic Production and Circulation in the Greater*

Southwest: Source Determination by INAA and Complementary Mineralogical Investigations, edited by Donna M. Glowacki and Hector Neff, pp 1–14. Monograph 44, Cotsen Institute of Archaeology at UCLA, Los Angeles.

Neff, Hector, and Daniel O. Larson

1997 Methodology of Comparison in Evolutionary Archaeology. In *Rediscovering Darwin: Evolutionary Theory and Archaeological Explanation,* edited by C. Michael Barton and Geoffrey A. Clark, pp. 75–94. Archaeological Publications of the AAA, No. 7. American Anthropological Association, Washington, D.C.

Neiheisel, James, and Charles E. Weaver

1967 Transport and Deposition of Clay Minerals, Southeastern United States. *Journal of Sedimentary Petrology* 37: 1084–1116.

Neitzel, Robert S.

1965 *Archeology of the Fatherland Site: The Grand Village of the Natchez.* American Museum of Natural History, Anthropological Papers 51, Pt. 1, New York.

1983 *The Grand Village of the Natchez Revisited: Excavations at the Fatherland Site, Adams County, Mississippi, 1972.* Mississippi Department of Archives and History, Archaeological Report No. 12, Jackson.

Nelson, Margaret C.

1991 The Study of Technological Organization. In *Archaeological Method and Theory,* Vol. 3, edited by Michael B. Schiffer, pp. 57–100. University of Arizona Press, Tucson.

Neuman, Robert W.

1984 *An Introduction to Louisiana Archaeology.* Louisiana State University Press, Baton Rouge.

Neumann, Georg K.

1952 Archaeology and Race in the American Indian. In *Archeology of Eastern United States,* edited by James B. Griffin, pp. 13–34. University of Chicago Press.

1959 Origins of the Indians of the Middle Mississippi Area. *Proceedings of the Indiana Academy of Science* 69:66–69.

Newsom, Lee A.

1993 Plants and People: Cultural, Biological, and Ecological Responses to Wood Exploitation. In *Foraging and Farming in the Eastern Woodlands,* edited by C. Margaret Scarry, pp. 115–137. University Press of Florida, Gainesville.

2002 The Paleoethnobotany of the Archaic Mortuary Pond. In *Windover: Multidisciplinary Investigations of an Early Archaic Florida Cemetery,* edited by Glen H. Doran, pp. 191–210. University Press of Florida, Gainesville.

Nicholas, George P.

1988 Ecological Leveling: The Archaeology and Environmental Dynamics of Early Postglacial Land Use. In *Holocene Human Ecology in Northeastern North America,* edited by George P. Nicholas, pp. 257–296. Plenum Press, New York.

Noël Hume, Ivor

1962 An Indian Ware of the Colonial Period. *Quarterly Bulletin, Archeological Society of Virginia* 17(1):3–14.

Nuttall, Thomas

1980   *A Journal of Travels into the Arkansas Territory During the Year 1819*, edited by Savoie Lottinville. University of Oklahoma Press, Norman

Oakley, Kenneth P., and C. Randall Hoskins

1950   New Evidence on the Antiquity of Piltdown Man. *Nature* 165:379–382.

O'Brien, Michael J.

1993   Late-Period Phases and Assemblage Variation in Southeastern Missouri. Paper presented at the 58th annual meeting, Society for American Archaeology, St. Louis, Missouri.

1994a *Cat Monsters and Head Pots: The Archaeology of Missouri's Pemiscot Bayou.* University of Missouri Press, Columbia.

1994b The Physical Environment. In *Cat Monsters and Head Pots: The Archaeology of Missouri's Pemiscot Bayou,* by Michael J. O'Brien, pp. 95–140. University of Missouri Press, Columbia.

1995   Archaeological Research in the Central Mississippi Valley: Culture History Gone Awry. *The Review of Archaeology* 16:23–36.

1996a The Historical Development of an Evolutionary Archaeology: A Selectionist Approach. In *Darwinian Archaeologies,* edited by Herbert Donald Graham Maschner, pp. 17–32. Kluwer Academic/Plenum, New York.

1996b *Paradigms of the Past: The Story of Missouri Archaeology.* University of Missouri Press, Columbia.

2001   *Mississippian Community Organization: The Powers Phase in Southeastern Missouri.* Kluwer Academic/Plenum, New York.

O'Brien, Michael J., James W. Cogswell, Robert C. Mainfort, Jr., Hector Neff, and Michael D. Glascock

1995   Neutron-Activation Analysis of Campbell Appliquéd Pottery from Southeastern Missouri and Western Tennessee: Implications for Late Mississippian Intersite Relations. *Southeastern Archaeology* 14:181–194.

O'Brien, Michael J., and Robert C. Dunnell

1998   A Brief Introduction to the Archaeology of the Central Mississippi River Valley. In *Changing Perspectives on the Archaeology of the Central Mississippi Valley,* edited by Michael J. O'Brien and Robert C. Dunnell, pp. 1–30. University of Alabama Press, Tuscaloosa.

O'Brien, Michael J., Thomas D. Holland, Robert J. Hoard, and Gregory L. Fox

1994   Evolutionary Implications of Design and Performance Characteristics of Prehistoric Pottery. *Journal of Archaeological Method and Theory* 1: 259–304.

O'Brien, Michael J., and R. Lee Lyman

1998   *James A. Ford and the Growth of Americanist Archaeology.* University of Missouri Press, Columbia.

1999a *Measuring the Flow of Time: The Works of James A. Ford, 1935–1941.* University of Alabama Press, Tuscaloosa.

1999b *Seriation, Stratigraphy, and Index Fossils: The Backbone of Archaeological Dating.* Kluwer Academic/Plenum Publishers, New York.

2000   *Applying Evolutionary Archaeology: A Systematic Approach.* Kluwer Academic/ Plenum Publishers, New York.

2001   Introduction. In *Setting the Agenda for American Archaeology: The National Research Council Conferences of 1929, 1932, and 1935,* edited by Michael J. Obrien and R. Lee Lyman, pp.1–83. University of Alabama Press, Tuscaloosa.

O'Brien, Michael J., and R. Lee Lyman (editors)

2001   *Setting the Agenda for American Archaeology: The National Research Council Conferences of 1929, 1932, and 1935.* University of Alabama Press, Tuscaloosa.

O'Brien, Michael J., R. Lee Lyman, and John Darwent

2000   Time, Space and Marker Types: James A. Ford's 1936 Chronology for the Lower Mississippi Valley. *Southeastern Archaeology* 19:46–62.

O'Brien, Michael J., R. Lee Lyman, and Michael B. Schiffer

2005   *Archaeology as a Process: Processualism and Its Progeny.* University of Utah Press, Salt Lake City.

O'Brien, Michael J., Roger D. Mason, Dennis E. Lewarch, and James A. Neely

1982   *A Late Formative Irrigation Settlement Below Monte Alban: Survey and Excavation on the Xoxocotlan Piedmont, Mexico.* University of Texas Press, Austin.

O'Brien, Michael J., and W. Raymond Wood

1998   *The Prehistory of Missouri.* University of Missouri Press, Columbia.

Odell, George H.

1989   Experiments in Lithic Reduction. In *Experiments in Lithic Technology,* edited by Daniel S. Amick and Raymond P. Mauldin, pp. 163–197. British Archaeological Reports International Series 528, Oxford.

1996a   Economizing Behavior and the Concept of "Curation." In *Stone Tools: Theoretical Insights into Human Prehistory,* edited by George H. Odell, pp. 51–80. Plenum Press, New York.

1996b   *Stone Tools and Mobility in the Illinois Valley: From Hunter-Gatherer Camps to Agricultural Villages.* International Monographs in Prehistory, Anthropological Series 10, Ann Arbor.

Odell, George H., and Frank Cowan

1987   Estimating Tillage Effects on Artifact Distributions. *American Antiquity* 52:456–484.

Odess, Daniel

1998   The Archaeology of Interaction: Views from Artifact Style and Material Exchange in Dorset Society. *American Antiquity* 63:417–435.

O'Hara, Sarah L., F. Alayne Street-Perrott, and Timothy P. Burt

1993   Accelerated Soil Erosion around a Mexican Highland Lake Caused by Prehistoric Agriculture. *Nature* 362:48–51.

Olsen, Stanley J.

1971   Report of Faunal Analysis. In *Archaeological Excavation at the Boyd Site, Tunica County, Mississippi,* by John M. Connaway and Samuel O. McGahey, pp. 67–77. Mississippi Department of Archives and History, Technical Report No. 1, Jackson.

Olson, Alan P.

1962   A History of the Phase Concept in the Southwest. *American Antiquity* 27:457–472.

Orser, Charles E., Jr.

1988   *The Material Basis of the Postbellum Plantation: Historical Archaeology in the South Carolina Piedmont.* University of Georgia Press, Athens.

1996   *A Historical Archaeology of the Modern World.* Plenum Press, New York.

Ortmann, Anthony, and Tristram R. Kidder

2004   Petrographic Thin-Section Analysis of Poverty Point Ceramics. In *Early Pottery: Technology, Function, Style and Interaction in the Lower Southeast,* edited by Rebecca Saunders and Christopher T. Hays, pp. 193–209. University of Alabama Press, Tuscaloosa.

Ortner, Donald J., and Walter G. J. Putschar

1985   *Identification of Pathological Conditions in Human Skeletal Remains.* Smithsonian Institution Press, Washington, D.C.

O'Shea, John M.

1984   *Mortuary Variability: An Archaeological Investigation.* Academic Press, Orlando.

Otvos, Ervin G.

2005   Holocene Aridity and Storm Phases, Gulf and Atlantic Coasts, U.S.A. *Quaternary Research* 63:368–373.

Parker, Arthur C.

1929   The Value to the State of Archaeological Surveys. In *Report on the Conference on Midwestern Archaeology, Held in St. Louis Missouri, May 18, 1929,* edited by K. Dunlap, pp. 31–41. Bulletin of the National Research Council, No. 74, Washington, D.C.

Parker, Kathryn E.

1989   Archaeobotanical Assemblage. In *The Holding Site: A Hopewell Community in the American Bottom,* by Andrew C. Fortier, Thomas O. Maher, Joyce A. Williams, Michael C. Meinkoth, Kathryn E. Parker, and Lucretia S. Kelly, pp. 429–464. American Bottom Archaeology FAI-270 Site Reports, Vo1.19. University of Illinois Press, Urbana.

Parker, Robert H.

1956   Macro-Invertebrate Assemblages as Indicators of Sedimentary Environments in East Mississippi Delta Region. *Bulletin of the American Association of Petroleum Geologists* 49(2):295–376.

Parkinson, William A.

1999   Integration, Interaction, and Tribal 'Cycling': The Transition to the Copper Age on the Great Hungarian Plain. In *The Archaeology of Tribal Societies,* edited by William A. Parkinson, pp. 391–438. International Monographs in World Prehistory, Archaeological Series 15, Ann Arbor.

Parsons, Jeffrey R.

1972   Archaeological Settlement Patterns. *Annual Review of Anthropology* 1:127–150.

Patterson, William A., III, and Kenneth E. Sassaman

1988   Indian Fires in the Prehistory of New England. In *Holocene Human Ecology in*

Northeastern North America, edited by George P. Nicholas, pp. 107–135. Plenum Press, New York.

Pauketat, Timothy R.

1998   Refiguring the Archaeology of Greater Cahokia. *Journal of Archaeological Research* 6:45–89.

Peabody, Charles

1904   *Exploration of Mounds, Coahoma County, Mississippi.* Papers of the Peabody Museum of American Archaeology and Ethnology 3(2). Harvard University, Cambridge.

1908   The Exploration of Bushey Cavern, Maryland. *Phillips Academy Bulletin* 4:5–24. Andover.

Peabody, Charles, and Warren K. Moorehead

1904   Exploration of Jacob's Cavern, McDonald County, Missouri. *Phillips Academy Bulletin* 1 (whole issue). Andover.

Peacock, Evan

1993   Reconstructing the Black Belt Environment Using Leaf Impressions in Daub. *Southeastern Archaeology* 12:148–154.

1994   Twenty-Five Years of Cultural Resource Management on the National Forests of Mississippi. *Mississippi Archaeology* 29(2):72–81.

1996   Tchula Period Sites on the Holly Springs National Forest, North-Central Mississippi. In *Proceedings of the 14th Annual Mid-South Archaeological Conference*, edited by Richard Walling, Camille Wharey, and Camille Stanley, pp. 13–23. Panamerican Consultants, Inc., Special Publications 1, Tuscaloosa.

1997   Woodland Ceramic Affiliations and Settlement Pattern Change in the North Central Hills of Mississippi. *Midcontinental Journal of Archaeology* 22:237–261.

1998a   *Fresh-Water Mussels as Indicators of Prehistoric Human Environmental Impact in the Southeastern United States.* Unpublished Ph.D. thesis, Department of Archaeology and Prehistory, University of Sheffield, England.

1998b   Historical and Applied Perspectives on Prehistoric Land Use in Eastern North America. *Environment and History* 4:1–29.

2001   Review of *Setting the Agenda for American Archaeology: The National Research Council Archaeological Conferences of 1929, 1932, and 1935*, edited by Michael J. O'Brien and R. Lee Lyman, University of Alabama Press, Tuscaloosa, 2001. *Journal of Alabama Archaeology* 47:157–161.

2002   Shellfish Use during the Woodland Period in the Middle South. In *The Woodland Southeast*, edited by David G. Anderson and Robert C. Mainfort, Jr., pp. 444–460. University of Alabama Press, Tuscaloosa.

2003   Excavations at Stinking Water (22WI515/516), a Prehistoric Habitation Site in the North Central Hills Physiographic Province of Mississippi. *Mississippi Archaeology* 38(1):3–91.

2005a   Investigating the Hypsithermal Climatic Optimum through Morphometric and Chemical Analyses of Freshwater Mussels. Paper presented at the International Congress of Archaeozoology, Archaeomalacology Working Group Conference, Gainesville, Florida.

2005b   *Mississippi Archaeology Q & A.* University Press of Mississippi, Jackson.

n.d.   Freshwater Mussels, Land Snails, and Aquatic Snails. In *The Oliver Site (22-Co-503), Coahoma County, Mississippi: Collected Papers,* edited by John M. Connaway, Jay K. Johnson, and Patricia Galloway. Mississippi Department of Archives and History, Jackson. Volume in preparation.

Peacock, Evan, and Shawn Chapman

2001   Taphonomic and Biogeographic Data from a Plaquemine Shell Midden on the Ouachita River, Louisiana. *Southeastern Archaeology* 20:44–55.

Peacock, Evan, and David W. Fant

2002   Biomantle Formation and Artifact Translocation in Upland Sandy Soils: An Example from the Holly Springs National Forest, North-Central Mississippi, U.S.A. *Geoarchaeology: An International Journal* 17:91–114.

Peacock, Evan, and Jochen Gerber

2008   Using Land Snails and Freshwater Mussels to Chart Human Transformation of the Landscape: An Example from Northeast Mississippi, U.S.A. In *Case Studies in Environmental Archaeology,* 2nd edition, edited by Elizabeth J. Reitz, C. Margaret Scarry, and Sylvia J. Scudder, pp. 123–141. London: Springer Science Business Media.

Peacock, Evan, Wendell R. Haag, and Melvin L. Warren, Jr.

2005   Prehistoric Decline in Freshwater Mussels Coincident with the Advent of Maize Agriculture. *Conservation Biology* 19(2):547–551.

Peacock, Evan, and Thomas R. James

2002   A Prehistoric Unionid Assemblage from the Big Black River Drainage in Hinds County, Mississippi. *Journal of the Mississippi Academy of Sciences* 47:119–123.

Peacock, Evan, Hector Neff, Janet Rafferty, and Thomas Meaker

2007   Using Laser Ablation–Inductively Coupled Plasma-Mass Spectrometry (LA-ICP-MS) to Source Shell in Shell-tempered Pottery: A Pilot Study from North Mississippi. *Southeastern Archaeology* 26(2):319–329.

Peacock, Evan, and Rebecca Melsheimer

2003   Terrestrial Gastropods from Archaeological Contexts in the Black Belt Province of Mississippi. In *Blackland Prairies of the Gulf Coastal Plain: Nature, Culture, and Sustainability,* edited by Evan Peacock and Timothy Schauwecker, pp. 27–47. University of Alabama Press, Tuscaloosa.

Peacock, Evan, and Janet Rafferty

2007   Cultural Resource Management Guidelines and Practice in the United States. In *Quality Management in Archaeology,* edited by Willem J. H. Willems and Monique van den Dries. Oxbow Books, pp. 113–134. Oxford.

Peacock, Evan, Janet Rafferty, and S. Homes Hogue

2005   Land Snails, Artifacts, and Faunal Remains: Understanding Site Formation Processes at Prehistoric/Protohistoric Sites in the Southeastern United States. In *Archaeomalacology: Molluscs in Former Environments of Human Behavior,* edited by Daniella Bar-Yosef Mayer, pp.6–17. Oxbow Books, Oxford.

Peacock, Evan, and Mary Celeste Reese

2003   A Comparison of Three Methods of Paleoenvironmental Analysis at an Archaeological Site on the Mississippi Black Prairie. In *Blackland Prairies of the Gulf Coastal Plain: Nature, Culture, and Sustainability*, edited by Evan Peacock and Timothy Schauwecker, pp. 64–79. University of Alabama Press, Tuscaloosa.

Pearsall, Deborah M.

1989   *Paleoethnobotany*. Academic Press, San Diego.

1992   Analysis of Plant Remains from the Moon Site (3PO488). In *Excavations at the Moon Site (3PO488, a Middle Mississippian Village in Northeast Arkansas*, edited by David W. Benn, Vol. 1, pp. 249–345. Southwest Missouri State University, Center for Archaeological Research 780, Springfield.

2000   *Paleoethnobotany: A Handbook of Procedures*. Academic Press, New York.

Pearsall, Deborah M., and Andrea A. Hunter

1990   Analysis of Plant Remains from the Priestly Site. In *Excavations at the Priestly Site (3PO490), An Emergent Mississippian Community in Northeastern Arkansas*, edited by David W. Benn, Vol. 2, pp. 362–419. Southwest Missouri State University, Center for Archaeological Research 740, Springfield.

Pearson, Charles E.

1980   Rank-Size Distributions and the Analysis of Prehistoric Settlement Systems. *Journal of Anthropological Research* 36:453–462.

Pearson, Charles E., Wayne P. Glander, David B. Kelley, and Sherwood M. Gagliano

1982   *A Terrestrial Magnetometer Survey for Cultural Resources Along the Red River, Louisiana*. Report submitted to the U.S. Army Corps of Engineers, Vicksburg District, by Coastal Environments, Inc., Baton Rouge, Louisiana.

Pearson, Charles E., Allen R. Saltus, Jr., and David B. Kelley

1992   *Cultural Resources Assessment of Two Possible Shipwreck Locations in the Yazoo River at Belzoni, Mississippi*. Report submitted to the U.S. Army Corps of Engineers, Vicksburg District, by Coastal Environments, Inc., Baton Rouge, Louisiana.

Pearson, Osbjorn M., and Daniel E. Lieberman

2004   The Aging of Wolff's "Law": Ontogeny and Responses to Mechanical Loading in Cortical Bone. *Yearbook of Physical Anthropology* 47:63–99.

Peebles, Christopher S.

1983   *Prehistoric Agricultural Communities in West-Central Alabama: Excavations in the Lubbub Creek Archaeological Locality, Volume 1*. Report submitted to the U.S. Army Corps of Engineers, Mobile District. National Technical Information Services, Springfield, Virginia.

1988   Federal Archeology in the Southeast: Practice, Product and Promise. In *Advances in Southeastern Archaeology 1966–1986: Contributions of the Federal Archaeology Program*, edited by Bennie C. Keel, pp. 53–60. Southeastern Archaeological Conference Special Publication No. 6.

Penman, John T.

1977   *Archaeological Survey in Mississippi, 1974–1975*. Mississippi Department of Archives and History, Archaeological Report No. 2, Jackson.

1983   Appendix II. Faunal Remains. In *The Grand Village of the Natchez Revisited*, by Robert S. Neitzel, pp. 146–165. Mississippi Department of Archives and History, Archaeological Report No. 12, Jackson.

Perino, Gregory

1968   *Guide to the Identification of Certain American Indian Projectile Points.* Special Bulletin No. 3, Oklahoma Anthropological Society, Oklahoma City.

1971   *Guide to the Identification of Certain American Indian Projectile Points.* Special Bulletin No. 4, Oklahoma Anthropological Society, Oklahoma City.

Perlman, I., and Frank Asaro

1969   Pottery Analysis by Neutron Activation Analysis. *Archaeometry* 11:21–52.

1971   Pottery Analysis by Neutron Activation. In *Science and Archaeology,* edited by Robert H. Brill, pp. 182–195. MIT Press, Cambridge.

Perrault, Stephanie, Elizabeth L. Davoli, Carey L. Coxe, and William Cash

1999   *Cultural Resources Inventory, Upper Steele Bayou Project, Swan Lake Mitigation Area, Washington County, Mississippi.* Report submitted to the U.S. Army Corps of Engineers, Vicksburg District, by Coastal Environments, Inc., Baton Rouge, Louisiana.

Perrault, Stephanie L., Sylvia Timmons Dennison, Charles E. Pearson, and Tom Wells

1995   *Historical Assessment and Magnetometer Survey for Dike Construction at Thirteen Location Along the Mississippi River.* Report submitted to the U.S. Army Corps of Engineers, Vicksburg District, by Coastal Environments, Inc., Baton Rouge, Louisiana.

Perrault, Stephanie L., and Roger T. Saucier

2000   *National Register Eligibility Testing at the Hollybrook Site (16EC85), MRL-485-R, East Carrol Parish, Louisiana.* Report submitted to the U.S. Army Corps of Engineers, Vicksburg District, by Coastal Environments, Inc., Baton Rouge, Louisiana.

Perttula, Timothy K.

2002   Archaeological Evidence for the Long-Distance Exchange of Caddo Indian Ceramics in the Southern Plains, Midwest, and Southeastern United States. In *Geochemical Evidence for Long-Distance Exchange,* edited by Michael D. Glascock, pp. 89–107. Bergin and Garvey, Westport, Connecticut.

Peukert, John N.

2002   *Ground Penetrating Radar at Hollywood, 22TU500.* Unpublished M.A. thesis, Department of Sociology and Anthropology, University of Mississippi.

Philip, G., D. Donoghue, A. Beck, and N. Galiatsatos

2002   CORONA Satellite Photography: An Archaeological Application from the Middle East. *Antiquity* 76(291):109–118.

Phillips, Philip

1939   *Introduction to the Archaeology of the Mississippi Valley.* Unpublished Ph.D. dissertation, Harvard University, Cambridge.

1958   Application of the Wheat-Gifford-Wasley Taxonomy to Eastern Ceramics. *American Antiquity* 24:117–125.

1970   *Archaeological Survey in the Lower Yazoo Basin, Mississippi, 1949–1955, Parts 1 and 2.* Papers of the Peabody Museum of Archaeology and Anthropology, Harvard University, Vol. 60, Cambridge.

Phillips, Philip, James A. Ford, and James B. Griffin

2003   *Archaeological Survey in the Lower Mississippi Alluvial Valley, 1940–1947.* Reprinted

[1951] with an introduction and edited by Stephen Williams by the University of Alabama Press, Tuscaloosa. Originally printed as Papers of the Peabody Museum of Archaeology and Ethnology, Harvard University, Vol. 25, Cambridge.

Phillips, Philip, and Gordon R. Willey

1953 Method and Theory in American Archaeology: An Operational Basis for Culture-Historical Integration. *American Anthropologist* 55:615–633.

Pierce, Christopher

1998 Theory, Measurement, and Explanation: Variable Shapes in Poverty Point Objects. In *Unit Issues in Archaeology: Measuring Time, Space, and Material,* edited by Ann F. Ramenofsky and Anastasia Steffen, pp. 163–190. University of Utah Press, Salt Lake City.

Pillar, James J.

1973 Religious and Cultural Life: 1817–1860. In *A History of Mississippi,* Vol. 1, edited by Richard Aubrey McLemore, pp. 378–419. University and College Press of Mississippi, Hattiesburg.

Piperno, Dolores R.

1988 *Phytolith Analysis: An Archaeological and Geological Perspective.* Academic Press, New York.

Pirazzoli, Paolo Antonio

1991 *World Atlas of Holocene Sea-Level Changes.* Elsevier Oceanography Series No. 58. Elsevier, New York.

Plog, Stephen

1976 Measurement of Prehistoric Interaction between Communities. In *The Mesoamerican Village,* edited by Kent V. Flannery, pp. 255–272. Academic Press, New York.

Plog, Stephen, Fred Plog, and Walter Wait

1978 Decision Making in Modern Surveys. In *Advances in Archaeological Method and Theory, Volume 1,* edited by Michael B. Schiffer, pp. 383–421. Academic Press, New York.

Porter, James W.

1962 *Temper in Bluff Pottery from the Cahokia Area.* Research Report, No. 1. Lithic Laboratory, Southern Illinois University Museum, Carbondale.

1964 Comment on Weaver's "Technological Analysis of Lower Mississippi Ceramic Materials." *American Antiquity* 29:520–521.

Potter, P. E., D. Heling, N. F. Shimp, and W. Van Wie

1975 Clay Mineralogy of Modern Alluvial Muds of the Mississippi River Basin. *Bulletin du Centre de Recherches de Pau* 9:353–389.

Potter, W. B.

1880 Archaeological Remains in Southeastern Missouri. In *Contributions to the Archaeology of Missouri, by the Archaeological Section of the St. Louis Academy of Science,* pp. 1–19. vol. Part 1: Pottery. Bates, Salem.

Potts, Thomas D., and Samuel O. Brookes

1981 The Bobo Site (22-Co-535). *Mississippi Archaeology* 16(1):2–24.

Powdermaker, Hortense

1993 *After Freedom: A Cultural Study of the Deep South.* University of Wisconsin Press, Madison. Originally published in 1939.

Powell, Mary Lucas

1983 Biocultural Analysis of the Human Skeletal Remains from the Lubbub Creek Locality. In *Prehistoric Agricultural Communities in West Central Alabama,* Volume 2, edited by Christopher S. Peebles, pp. 430–477. Report submitted to the U.S. Army Corps of Engineers, Mobile District. National Technical Information Service, Washington D.C.

1988 *Status and Health in Prehistory: A Case Study of the Moundville Chiefdom.* Smithsonian Institution Press, Washington, D.C.

1992 Health and Disease in the Late Prehistoric Southeast. In *Disease and Demography in America,* edited by John W. Verano and Douglas H. Ubelaker, pp. 41–53. Smithsonian Institution Press, Washington, D.C.

Powell, Mary Lucas, Patricia S. Bridges, and Ann Marie Wagner Mires (editors)

1991 *What Mean These Bones? Studies in Southeastern Archaeology.* University of Alabama Press, Tuscaloosa.

Praetzellis, Adrian

1993 The Limits of Arbitrary Excavation. In *Practices of Archaeological Stratigraphy,* edited by Edward C. Harris, Marley R. Brown, III, and Gregory J. Brown, pp. 68–86. Academic Press, New York.

Praus, A. A.

1945 The Midwestern Taxonomic Method. *Bulletin of the Archaeological Society of Connecticut* 18:13–15.

Preston, C. H.

1877– [Minutes of] April 27, 1877—Regular Meeting. *Proceedings of the Davenport*
1880 *Academy of Natural Sciences* 2:127–128.

Price, James E., and James B. Griffin

1979 *The Snodgrass Site of the Powers Phase of Southeast Missouri.* Museum of Anthropology, University of Michigan, Anthropological Papers No. 66, Ann Arbor.

Price, James E., and Cynthia R. Price

1981 *Changing Settlement Systems in the Fourche Creek Watershed in the Ozark Border Region of Southeast Missouri and Northeast Arkansas.* Southwest Missouri State University, Center for Archaeological Research, Report 251, Springfield.

Purdue, James R.

1991 Dynamism in the Body Size of White-Tailed Deer (*Odocoileus virginianus*) from Southern Illinois. In *Beamers, Bobwhites, and Blue-Points: Tributes to the Career of Paul W. Parmalee,* edited by James R. Purdue, Walter E. Klippel, and Bonnie W. Styles. pp. 277–283. Illinois State Museum Scientific Papers 23 and University of Tennessee, Department of Anthropology, Report of Investigations 52, Springfield.

Putnam, Frederick Ward

1875a List of Items from Mounds in New Madrid County, Missouri, and Brief Description of Excavations. *Harvard University, Peabody Museum, Eighth Annual Report:*16–46.

1875b The Pottery of the Mound Builders. *The American Naturalist* 9:321–328, 393–409.

1881 Ancient American Pottery. *Scientific American Supplement* No. 216, pp. 4161–4163.

1887 The Proper Method of Exploring an Earthwork. *Ohio Archaeological and Historical Quarterly* 1:60–62.

Quimby, George I., Jr.

1942 The Natchezan Culture Type. *American Antiquity* 7:255–275.

R. Christopher Goodwin & Associates, Inc.

2000 *A Cultural Resources Remote Sensing Survey of Items 3B-2 and 4 of the Upper Yazoo River Project, Leflore County, Mississippi.* R. Christopher Goodwin & Associates, Inc., New Orleans.

Rafferty, Janet

1986 A Critique of the Type-Variety System as Used in Ceramic Analysis. *Mississippi Archaeology* 21(2):40–50.

1994 Gradual or Step-Wise Change: The Development of Sedentary Settlement Patterns in Northeast Mississippi. *American Antiquity* 59:405–425.

2001 Determining Duration at Prehistoric Sites: Short-Term Sedentary Settlement at Josey Farm, N.E. Mississippi. *Journal of Field Archaeology* 28:347–366.

Rafferty, Janet, Jeffrey Alvey, S. Homes Hogue, Evan Peacock, and Robert McCain

2005 *Archaeological Testing at the Pocahontas Mound A Site (22HI500), Hinds County, Mississippi.* Report submitted to the Mississippi Department of Transportation, Jackson, by the Cobb Institute of Archaeology, Mississippi State University.

Rafferty, Janet, and Michael Galaty

2002 Point-Counting, Petrography, and Context: Analysis of Ceramics from a Middle Woodland Site in Eastern Mississippi. *La Tinaja: A Newsletter of Archaeological Ceramics* 14(1): 2–6. Available at http://www.millsaps. edu/socio/lati.shtml.

Rafferty, Janet, Thomas R. James, Kevin McMahon, Jeffrey Alvey, and Evan Peacock

2003 Geophysical Evidence Bearing on the Community Plan at a Mississippian Mound Site, Oktibbeha County, Mississippi. Paper presented at the 60th Southeastern Archaeological Conference, Charlotte, North Carolina.

Ramenofsky, Ann F.

1986 The Persistence of Late Archaic Subsistence-Settlement in Louisiana. In *Foraging, Collecting, and Harvesting: Archaic Period Subsistence and Settlement in the Eastern Woodlands,* edited by Sarah W. Neusius, pp. 289–312. Southern Illinois University at Carbondale, Center for Archaeological Investigations Occasional Paper 6.

1987 *Vectors of Death: The Archaeology of European Contact.* University of New Mexico Press, Albuquerque.

1990 Loss of Innocence: Explanations of Differential Persistence in the Sixteenth-Century Southeast. In *Columbian Consequences, Vol. 2, Archaeological and Historical Perspectives on the Spanish Borderlands East,* edited by David Hurst Thomas, pp. 31–48. Smithsonian Institution Press, Washington, D.C.

1991 Investigating Settlement Strategies at Cowpen Slough, a Late Archaic–Poverty Point Site in Louisiana. In *The Poverty Point Culture: Local Manifestations, Subsistence Practices, and Trade Networks,* edited by Kathleen M. Byrd, pp. 159–172. Geosciences and Man 29. Louisiana State University, Baton Rouge.

Ramenofsky, Ann F., and Anastasia Steffen (editors)

1998 *Unit Issues in Archaeology: Measuring Time, Space, and Material.* University of Utah Press, Salt Lake City.

Rau, Charles

1876 The Archaeological Collections of the United States National Museum in Charge of the Smithsonian Museum, Washington D.C. *Smithsonian Contributions to Knowledge* 22(4):8–12.

Rawick, George

1977 The American Slave: A Composite Autobiography. *Contributions to Afro-American and African Studies,* No. 35. Supplement Series 2, Volume 5, pp. 16–92. Greenwood Press, Westport, Connecticut.

Read, Dwight W.

1977 Some Comments on Typology in Archaeology and an Outline of a Method. *American Antiquity* 39:216–242.

1982 Toward a Theory of Archaeological Classification. In *Essays on Archaeological Typology,* edited by Robert Whallon and James A. Brown, pp. 56–91. Center for American Archaeology Press, Evanston, Illinois.

Read, Dwight W., and Glen Russell

1996 A Method for Taxonomic Typology Construction and an Example: Utilized Flakes. *American Antiquity* 61:663–684.

Redfield, A.

1971 *Dalton Project Notes: Volume One.* Museum of Anthropology, University of Missouri–Columbia, Museum Brief 13, Columbia.

Redman, Charles L.

1999 *Human Impact on Ancient Environments.* University of Arizona Press, Tucson.

2005 Resilience Theory in Archaeology. *American Anthropologist* 107:70–77.

Rees, Mark A.

2001 Mississippian Culture History: The Contributions of Phillips, Ford, and Griffin. In *Historical Perspectives on Midsouth Archaeology,* edited by Martha A. Rolingson, pp. 85–92. Arkansas Archeological Survey, Research Series 58, Fayetteville.

Reitz, Elizabeth J.

1993 Zooarchaeology. In *The Development of Southeastern Archaeology,* edited by Jay K. Johnson, pp. 109–131. University of Alabama Press, Tuscaloosa.

Renfrew, Colin

1977 Alternative Models for Exchange and Spatial Distribution. In *Exchange Systems in Prehistory,* edited by T. K. Earle and J. E. Ericson, pp. 71–90. Academic Press, New York.

Reynolds, William R.

1991 Discrimination of Kaolinite Varieties in Porters Creek and Wilcox Sediments of North-Central Mississippi. *Clays and Clay Minerals* 39:316–323.

Rhodes, E. J., C. Bronk Ramsey, Z. Outram, C. Batt, and L. Willis

2003 Bayesian Method Applied to the Interpretation of Multiple OSL Dates: High-Precision Sediment Ages from Old Scatness Broch Excavations, Shetland Islands. *Quaternary Science Reviews* 22:1231–1244.

Riley, Thomas, Gregory R. Walz, Charles J. Bareis, Andrew C. Fortier, and Kathryn E. Parker

1994   Accelerator Mass Spectrometer (AMS) Dates Confirm Early *Zea mays* in the Mississippi River Valley. *American Antiquity* 59:490–498.

Rindos, David

1984   *The Origins of Agriculture: An Evolutionary Perspective.* Academic Press, New York.

Rittenour, Tammy M., Ronald J. Goble, and Michael D. Blum

2003   An Optical-Age Chronology of Late Pleistocene Fluvial Deposits in the Northern Lower Mississippi Valley. *Quaternary Science Reviews* 22:1105–1110.

Rivet, Phillip G.

1991   A Brief History of the Archaeological Site Survey in Louisiana. *Louisiana Archaeology* 18:122–129.

Robbins, Maurice

1936   Survey Methods. *American Antiquity* 1:220–221.

Roberts, Katherine M.

1999a   Plant Remains. In *Excavating the Past: Archaeology and the Marksville Site (16AV1)*, by Charles R. McGimsey, pp. 72–81. Louisiana Division of Archaeology, Annual Report of the Regional Archaeology Program, Management Unit III, Baton Rouge.

1999b   Plant Remains. In *Archaeology along the Lower Tensas: Cultural Resources Investigations Relating to Items 2A and 2B of the Sicily Island Levee Project, Catahoula Parish, Louisiana,* by D. G. Hunter, D. B. Lee, W. J. Autin, C. L. Coxe, and K. M. Roberts, pp. 261–168. Report submitted to U.S. Army Corps of Engineers, Vicksburg District, by Coastal Environments, Inc., Baton Rouge.

2004   Plant Remains. In *Data-Recovery Excavations at the Hedgeland Site (16CT19)*, *Catahoula Parish, Louisiana,* edited by Joanne Ryan, pp. 207–226. Report submitted to the U.S. Army Corps of Engineers, Vicksburg District by Coastal Environments, Inc., Baton Rouge.

2005a   *Optimal Foraging and Prehistoric Food Production in the Lower Mississippi Valley: An Examination of Subsistence in the Tensas Basin, Northeast Louisiana.* Unpublished Ph.D. dissertation, Department of Anthropology, Washington University in St. Louis.

2005b   Plant Remains. In *Lake Providence: A Terminal Coles Creek Culture Mound Center, East Carroll Parish, Louisiana,* edited by Richard A. Weinstein, pp. 431–489. Two volumes. Report submitted to the U.S. Army Corps of Engineers, Vicksburg District, by Coastal Environments, Inc., Baton Rouge.

Rolingson, Martha A.

1985   An Assessment of the Significance of Clay-Tempered Ceramics and Platform Mounds at the Toltec Mounds Site. In *The Emergent Mississippian: Proceedings of the Sixth Mid-South Archaeological Conference, June 6–9, 1985,* edited by Richard A. Marshall, pp. 107–116. Cobb Institute of Archaeology, Mississippi State University Occasional Papers 87-01.

1999   The Toltec (Knapp) Mounds. In *Arkansas Archaeology: Essays in Honor of Dan and Phyllis Morse,* edited by Robert C. Mainfort and Marvin D. Jeter, pp. 119–142. University of Arkansas Press, Fayetteville.

2001 Archeology of the Midsouth Region to 1960. In *Historical Perspectives on Midsouth Archaeology,* edited by Martha A. Rolingson, pp.1–22. Arkansas Archeological Survey, Research Series 58, Fayetteville.

2004 Prehistory of the Central Mississippi Valley and Ozarks after 500 B.C. In *Handbook of North American Indians, Volume 14, Southeast,* edited by Raymond D. Fogelson and William Sturtevant, pp. 534–544. Smithsonian Institution Press, Washington, D.C.

Rolingson, Martha A. (editor)

2001 *Historical Perspectives on Midsouth Archaeology.* Arkansas Archeological Survey, Research Series 58, Fayetteville.

Rollins, Harold B., Daniel H. Sandweiss, and Judith C. Rollins

1990 Mollusks and Coastal Archaeology: A Review. In *Archaeological Geology of North America,* edited by Norman P. Lasca and Jack Donahue, pp. 467–478. Geological Society of America, Centennial Special Volume 4, Boulder.

Rose, Jerome C.

1984 Bioarchaeology of the Cedar Grove Site. In *Cedar Grove: An Interdisciplinary Investigation of a Late Caddo Farmstead in the Red River Valley,* edited by Neal L. Trubowitz, pp. 227–256. Arkansas Archeological Survey Research Series No. 23, Fayetteville.

Rose, Jerome C. (editor)

1999 *Bioarchaeology of the South Central United States.* Arkansas Archeological Survey Research Series No. 55, Fayetteville.

Rose, Jerome C., Barbara A. Burnett, Mark W. Blaeurer, and Michael S. Nassaney

1984 Paleopathology and the Origins of Maize Agriculture in the Lower Mississippi Valley and Caddoan Culture Areas. In *Paleopathology at the Origins of Agriculture,* edited by Mark N. Cohen and George J. Armelagos, pp. 393–425. Academic Press, Orlando.

Rose, Jerome C., Keith W. Condon, and Alan H. Goodman

1985 Diet and Dentition: Developmental Disturbances. In *The Analysis of Prehistoric Diets,* edited by Robert I. Gilbert, Jr., and James H. Mielke, pp.281–305. Academic Press, New York.

Rose, Jerome C., and Anna M. Harmon

1986 Enamel Microwear and Prehistoric North American Diets. *American Journal of Physical Anthropology* 69:257 (abstract).

1989 History of Bioarcheology and Bioarcheological Resources of the Louisiana and Arkansas Study Area. In *Archeology and Bioarcheology of the Lower Mississippi Valley and Trans-Mississippi South in Arkansas and Louisiana,* by Marvin D. Jeter, Jerome C. Rose, G. Ishmael Williams, and Anna M. Harmon, pp. 291–322. Arkansas Archeological Survey Research Series No. 37, Fayetteville.

1999 Louisiana and South and Eastern Arkansas. In *Bioarchaeology of the South Central United States,* edited by Jerome C. Rose, pp. 35–82. Arkansas Archeological Survey Research Series No. 55, Fayetteville.

Rose, Jerome C., and Murray K. Marks

1985 Bioarcheology of the Alexander Site. In *The Alexander Site, Conway County, Ar-*

kansas, edited by E. Thomas Hemmings and John H. House, pp. 76–98. Arkansas Archeological Survey Research Series No. 24, Fayetteville.

Rose, Jerome C., Murray M. Marks, and Larry L. Tieszen

1991   Bioarchaeology and Subsistence in the Central and Lower Portions of the Mississippi Valley. In *What Mean These Bones? Studies in Southeastern Bioarchaeology,* edited by Mary Lucas Powell, Patricia S. Bridges, and Ann Marie Wagner Mires, pp. 7–21. University of Alabama Press, Tuscaloosa.

Ross, Stephen T.

2001   *Inland Fishes of Mississippi.* University Press of Mississippi, Jackson.

Ross-Stallings, Nancy A.

1989   Treponemal Syndrome at the Austin Site (22TU549): A Preliminary Report. *Mississippi Archaeology* 24(2):1–16.

1992   A.D. 800–1200 in the Upper Delta: Evidence from Northwest Mississippi. Paper presented at the 49th Southeastern Archaeological Conference, Little Rock, Arkansas.

1995   Of Headless Bodies and Disembodied Heads: Decapitation and Trophy Skulls in Prehistoric North Mississippi. Paper presented at the 52nd Annual Southeastern Archaeological Conference, Knoxville, Tennessee.

1997   Treponemal Syndrome in the Mississippi Delta Revisited: A Case from the Barner Site (22Co542) and a Probable Case of Congenital Treponemal Syndrome from the Austin Site (22TU549). In *Results of Recent Archaeological Investigations in the Greater Mid-South,* edited by Charles H. McNutt, pp. 95–109. University of Memphis, Anthropological Research Center Occasional Paper No. 18, Memphis.

2002   The People of the Oliver Site (22Co503): A Late Prehistoric/Contact-Period Site on the Sunflower River. Paper presented at the 59th Southeastern Archaeological Conference, Biloxi, Mississippi.

2003   Just a Canoe Ride Downriver: A Comparison of Mortuary Practices at the Wickcliffe Mounds with Sites in the Northern Mississippi Delta, ca. A.D. 1200–1250. Paper presented at the Midsouth Archaeological Conference, Murray State University, Murray, Kentucky.

Rouse, Irving B.

1939   *Prehistory in Haiti: A Study in Method.* Yale University Publications in Anthropology, Vol. 21, New Haven.

1960   The Classification of Artifacts in Archaeology. *American Antiquity* 25:313–323.

Rovner, Irwin

1983   Plant Opal Phytolith Analysis: Major Advances in Archaeobotanical Research. In *Advances in Archaeological Method and Theory* 6:225–266, edited by Michael B. Schiffer. Academic Press, New York.

2001   Phytolith Evidence for Large-Scale Climatic Change in Small-Scale Hunter-Gatherer Sites of the Middle Archaic Period, Eastern USA. In *Phytoliths: Applications in Earth Sciences and Human History,* edited by J. D. Meunier and F. Colin, pp. 303–313. A. A. Balkema Publishers, Lisse, Netherlands.

Rowe, John Howland

1961   Stratigraphy and Seriation. *American Antiquity* 26:324–330.

Rowland, Dunbar (editor)

1927   A Symposium on the Place of Discovery of the Mississippi River by Hernando de Soto. Publications of the Mississippi Historical Society, Special Bulletin No. 1, Jackson.

Royall, P. Daniel, Paul A. Delcourt, and Hazel R. Delcourt

1991   Late Quaternary Paleoecology and Paleoenvironments of the Central Mississippi Alluvial Valley. Geological Society of America Bulletin 103:157–170.

Ruff, Christopher B., and Clark Spencer Larsen

1990   Postcranial Biomechanical Adaptations to Subsistence Changes on the Georgia Coast. In Archaeology of Mission Santa Catalina de Guale 2. Biocultural Interpretations of a Population in Transition, edited by Clark Spencer Larsen, pp. 94–120. Anthropological Papers of the American Museum of Natural History 68.

Ruff, Christopher B., Clark Spencer Larsen, and Wilson C. Hayes

1984   Structural Changes to the Femur with the Transition to Agriculture on the Georgia Coast. American Journal of Physical Anthropology 64:125–136.

Russell, Emily W. B.

1997   People and the Land Through Time. Yale University Press, New Haven.

Russo, Michael

1996   Southeastern Archaic Mounds. In Archaeology of the Mid-Holocene Southeast, edited by Kenneth E. Sassaman and David G. Anderson, pp. 177–199. University Press of Florida, Gainesville.

Rust, H. N.

1877   The Mound Builders in Missouri. Western Review of Science and Industry 1:531–535.

Ryan, Joanne

1995   Archaeological Survey and Testing Within Items 3-A, 3-B, and Portions of Items 4-A and 4-B, of the Sicily Island Levee Project, Catahoula Parish, Louisiana. Report submitted to the U.S. Army Corps of Engineers, Vicksburg District, by Coastal Environments, Inc., Baton Rouge.

Ryan, Joanne, and Katherine M. Roberts

2003   Coles Creek–Period Native Seed Use in the Tensas Basin, Louisiana. In Proceedings of the 19th Mid-South Archaeological Conference: Papers in Honor of Charles H. McNutt, Sr., edited by C. Andrew Buchner and David H. Dye, pp. 83–94. Memphis, Tennessee: Panamerican Consultants, Inc., Special Publication No. 3, and University of Memphis, Anthropological Research Center, Occasional Paper No. 22.

Ryan, Joanne, Douglas C. Wells, Richard A. Weinstein, David B. Kelley, and Sara A. Hahn

2004   Cultural Resources Survey of the Proposed Route of Interstate 69 Between Robinsonville and Benoit—Bolivar, Coahoma, Tunica, and Sunflower Counties, Mississippi. Submitted to Neel-Schaffer, Inc., for the Environmental Division, Mississippi Department of Transportation, Jackson, Mississippi, by Coastal Environments, Inc., Baton Rouge.

Sabloff, Jeremy A., and Robert E. Smith

1970   The Importance of Both Analytic and Taxonomic Classification in the Type-Variety System. American Antiquity 34:115–118.

Saikku, Mikko

2005   *This Delta, This Land: An Environmental History of the Yazoo-Mississippi Flood-plain.* University of Georgia Press, Athens.

Saltus, Allan R., Jr.

1977a   Appendix B: Exploratory Magnetic Survey of a Portion of the Yazoo River (Silver City to Yazoo City, MS). In *Cultural Resources Survey, Item I, Upper Yazoo Projects, Yazoo River, Mississippi, Between SRM 75.6 and 107.8,* edited by Robert M. Thorne, pp. 162–169. Report submitted to the U.S. Army Corps of Engineers, Vicksburg District, by the Center for Archaeological Research, University of Mississippi, University, Mississippi.

1977b   Appendix C: In-site Magnetic Survey of a Portion of the Yazoo River in the Vicinity of Yazoo City, MS. In *Cultural Resources Survey, Item I, Upper Yazoo Projects, Yazoo River, Mississippi, Between SRM 75.6 and 107.8,* edited by Robert M. Thorne, pp. 170–183. Report submitted to the U.S. Army Corps of Engineers, Vicksburg District, by the Center for Archaeological Research, University of Mississippi, University, Mississippi.

1979a   Appendix A: Exploratory Magnetic Survey of a Portion of the Yazoo River (Statute River Miles 107 to 131). In *Cultural Resources Survey, Item II, Upper Yazoo Projects, Yazoo River, Mississippi, Between SRM 107.268 and 131.5,* edited by Robert M. Thorne. Report submitted to the U.S. Army Corps of Engineers, Vicksburg District, by the Center for Archaeological Research, University of Mississippi, University, Mississippi.

1979b   Appendix B: Intensive Magnetometer Mapping of a Portion of the Yazoo River in the Vicinity of Belzoni, Mississippi. In *Cultural Resources Survey, Item II, Upper Yazoo Projects, Yazoo River, Mississippi, Between SRM 107.268 and 131.5,* edited by Robert M. Thorne. Report submitted to the U.S. Army Corps of Engineers, Vicksburg District, by the Center for Archaeological Research, University of Mississippi, University, Mississippi.

Sassaman, Kenneth E.

1993   *Early Pottery in the Southeast: Tradition and Innovation in Cooking Technology.* University of Alabama Press, Tuscaloosa.

Saucier, Roger T.

1974   *Quaternary Geology of the Lower Mississippi Valley.* Arkansas Archeological Survey Research Series No. 6, Fayetteville.

1977   Geological Analysis. In John M. Connaway, Samuel O. McGahey, and Clarence H. Webb, *Teoc Creek: A Poverty Point Site in Carroll County, Mississippi,* pp. 9–105. Mississippi Department of Archives and History, Archaeological Report No. 3, Jackson.

1978   Sand Dunes and Related Eolian Features in the Lower Mississippi River Alluvial Valley. *Geoscience and Man* 19:23–40.

1981   Current Thinking on Riverine Processes and Geologic History as Related to Human Settlement in the Southeast. *Geoscience and Man* 22:7–18.

1985   *Fluvial Responses to Late Quaternary Climatic Change in the Lower Mississippi Valley.* Boulder, Colorado: Geological Society of America, South Central Section, Abstracts of 1985 Annual Meeting in Fayetteville, Arkansas.

1994   *Geomorphology and Quaternary Geologic History of the Lower Mississippi Valley.* Two Volumes. Vicksburg: U.S. Army Corps of Engineers Waterways Experiment Station.

1997   Late Quaternary Geologic History of the Western Lowlands. In *Sloan: A Paleo-indian Dalton Cemetery in Arkansas,* by Dan F. Morse, pp. 96–102. Smithsonian Institution Press, Washington, D.C.

2001   History of Archeology in the Midsouth: Geoarchaeology. In *Historical Perspectives on Midsouth Archaeology,* edited by Martha Ann Rolingson, pp. 59–72. Arkansas Archeological Survey Research Series 58, Fayetteville.

2002   Paleogeography and Geomorphology in the Lower Mississippi Valley. In *Histories of Southeastern Archaeology,* edited by Shannon Tushingham, Jane Hill, and Charles H. McNutt, pp. 51–60. University of Alabama Press, Tuscaloosa.

2004   Geomorphic and Geoarchaeological Overview of the Big Sunflower Watershed, Yazoo Basin, Mississippi. In *Archaeological Investigations Within the Big Sunflower River Watershed: A Synthesis of Terrestrial and Maritime Intensive Phase I Surveys, 1992–1996,* by Shawn Chapman, Richard Walling, Stephen R. James, Jr., C. Andrew Buchner, and Roger T. Saucier, pp. 45–90. Report submitted to the U.S. Army Corps of Engineers, Vicksburg District, by Panamerican Consultants, Inc., Memphis, Tennessee.

n.d.   Physiographic Setting and Geologic History of the Sunflower River Drainage, Yazoo Basin, Mississippi, as Related to the Oliver Site. In *The Oliver Site (22-Co-503), Coahoma County, Mississippi: Collected Papers,* edited by John M. Connaway, Jay K. Johnson, and Patricia Galloway. Mississippi Department of Archives and History, Jackson. Volume in preparation.

Saunders, Joe W., and Thurman Allen

1994   Hedgepeth Mounds: An Archaic Mound Complex in North-Central Louisiana. *American Antiquity* 59:471–489.

2003   Jaketown Revisited. *Southeastern Archaeology* 22:155–164.

Saunders, Joe W., Thurman Allen, Dennis LeBatt, Reca Jones, and David Griffing

2001   An Assessment of the Antiquity of the Lower Jackson Mound. *Southeastern Archaeology* 20:67–77.

Saunders, Joe W., Thurman Allen, and Roger T. Saucier

1994   Four Archaic? Mound Complexes in Northeast Louisiana. *Southeastern Archaeology* 13:134–153.

Saunders, Joe W., Rolfe D. Mandel, C. Garth Sampson, Charles M. Allen, E. Thurman Allen, Daniel A. Bush, James K. Feathers, Kristen J. Gremillion, C. T. Hallmark, H. Edwin Jackson, Jay K. Johnson, Reca Jones, Roger T. Saucier, Gary L. Stringer, and Malcolm F. Vidrine

2005   Watson Brake, a Middle Archaic Mound Complex in Northeast Louisiana. *American Antiquity* 70:631–668.

Saunders, Joe W., Rolfe D. Mandel, Roger T. Saucier, E. Thurman Allen, C. T. Hallmark, Jay K. Johnson, Edwin H. Jackson, Charles M. Allen, Gary L. Stringer, Douglas S. Frink, James K. Feathers, Stephen Williams, Kristin J. Gremillion, Malcom F. Vidrine, and Reca Jones

1997   A Mound Complex in Louisiana at 5,500–5,000 Years before Present. *Science* 277:1796–1799.

Sayre, Edward V.

1975 *Brookhaven Procedures for Statistical Analyses of Multivariate Archaeometric Data.* Brookhaven National Laboratory Report BNL-23128, New York.

Scarborough, William K.

1973 Heartland of the Cotton Kingdom. In *A History of Mississippi,* Vol. 1, edited by Richard Aubrey McLemore, pp. 310–350. University and College Press of Mississippi, Hattiesburg.

Scarry, C. Margaret

1993 Variability in Mississippian Crop Production Strategies. In *Foraging and Farming in the Eastern Woodlands,* edited by C. Margaret Scarry, pp. 78–90. University Press of Florida, Gainesville.

1995 Plant Remains. In *The Rock Levee Site: Late Marksville through Late Mississippi Period Settlement, Bolivar County, Mississippi,* by Richard A. Weinstein, Richard S. Fuller, Susan L. Scott, C. Margaret Scarry, and Sylvia Timmons Duay, pp. 263–285. Report submitted to the U.S. Army Corps of Engineers, Vicksburg District, by Coastal Environments, Inc., Baton Rouge.

2003 Patterns of Wild Plant Utilization in the Prehistoric Eastern Woodlands. In *People and Plants in Eastern North America,* edited by Paul E. Minnis, pp. 50–104. Smithsonian Books, Washington, D.C.

Scarry, C. Margaret, and Elizabeth J. Reitz

2005 Changes in Foodways at the Parkin Site, Arkansas. *Southeastern Archaeology* 24:107–120.

Scarry, C. Margaret, and John F. Scarry

2005 Native American 'Garden Agriculture' in Southeastern North America. *World Archaeology* 37(2):259–274.

Scarry, C. Margaret, and Vincas P. Steponaitis

1997 Between Farmstead and Center: The Natural and Social Landscape of Moundville. In *People, Plants, and Landscape: Studies in Paleoethnobotany,* edited by Kristen J. Gremillion, pp. 107–122. University of Alabama Press, Tuscaloosa.

Scarry, Margaret, and Elizabeth Reitz

2000 Changes in Foodways at the Parkin Site, Arkansas. Paper presented at the 57th Southeastern Archaeological Conference, Macon.

Schambach, Frank F.

1970 *Pre-Caddoan Cultures in the Trans-Mississippi South: A Beginning Sequence.* Ph.D. dissertation, Harvard University, Cambridge. University Microfilms, Ann Arbor.

Schiffer, Michael B.

1972 Archaeological Context and Systemic Context. *American Antiquity* 37:156–165.

1975a An Alternative to Morse's Dalton Settlement Pattern Hypothesis. *Plains Anthropologist* 20:253–266.

1975b Some Further Comments on the Dalton Settlement Pattern Hypothesis. In *The Cache River Archaeological Project: An Experiment in Contract Archaeology,* edited by Michael B. Schiffer and John H. House, pp. 103–112. Arkansas Archeological Survey, Fayetteville.

1988 The Structure of Archaeological Theory. *American Antiquity* 53:461–485.

Schmidt, Christopher W.

2001 Dental Microwear Evidence for a Dietary Shift between Two Nonmaize-reliant Prehistoric Human Populations from Indiana. *American Journal of Physical Anthropology* 114: 139–145.

Schoeninger, Margaret J.

1984 Reconstructing Prehistoric Human Diet. In *The Chemistry of Prehistoric Human Bone,* edited by T. Douglas Price, pp. 38–67. Cambridge University Press, Cambridge.

1995 Stable Isotope Studies in Human Evolution. *Evolutionary Anthropology* 4(3):83–98.

Schoeninger, Margaret J., and Michael J. DeNiro

1984 Nitrogen and Carbon Isotopic Composition of Bone Collagen from Marine and Terrestrial Animals. *Geochimica Cosmochimica Acta* 48:625–639.

Schoeninger, Margaret J., and Mark R. Schurr

1998 Human Subsistence at Moundville: The Stable Isotope Data. In *Archaeology of the Moundville Chiefdom,* edited by James Vernon Knight, Jr. and Vincas P. Steponaitis, pp. 120–132. Smithsonian Institution Press, Washington, D.C.

Schuldenrein, Joseph

1996 Geoarchaeology and the Mid-Holocene Landscape History of the Greater Southeast. In *Archaeology of the Mid-Holocene Southeast,* edited by Kenneth E. Sassaman and David G. Anderson, pp. 3–27. University Press of Florida, Gainesville.

Schurr, Mark

1989 Fluoride Dating of Prehistoric Bones by Ion Selective Electrode. *Journal of Archaeological Science* 16:265–270.

Scientific American

1848 The Smithsonian Institute [sic]. *Scientific American* 3:157 (unsigned editorial).

Scott, Susan

1983 Analysis, Synthesis, and Interpretation of Faunal Remains from the Lubbub Creek Archaeological Locality. In *Prehistoric Agricultural Communities in West Central Alabama, Vol. 2: Studies of Material Remains from the Lubbub Creek Archaeological Locality,* edited by Christopher S. Peebles, pp. 272–390. Museum of Anthropology, University of Michigan, Ann Arbor.

1995 Vertebrate Faunal Remains. In *The Rock Levee Site: Late Marksville through Late Mississippi Period Settlement, Bolivar County, Mississippi,* by Richard A. Weinstein, Richard S. Fuller, Susan L. Scott, C. Margaret Scarry, and Sylvia Timmons Duay, pp. 243–262. Report prepared for the U.S. Army Corps of Engineers, Vicksburg District, by Coastal Environments, Inc, Baton Rouge.

1996 Faunal Remains. In *Test Excavations at the Faulkner Lake Sites: 3PU115, 3PU163, and 3PU410, Pulaski County, Arkansas,* by Randall L. Guendling. Report submitted to the Arkansas Highway and Transportation Department by the Arkansas Archeological Survey, Fayetteville.

2005 Vertebrate Remains. In *Lake Providence: A Terminal Coles Creek Culture Mound Center, East Carroll Parish, Louisiana,* edited by Richard A. Weinstein, pp. 411–430. Two volumes. Report submitted to the U.S. Army Corps of Engineers, Vicksburg District, by Coastal Environments, Inc., Baton Rouge.

Scott, Susan L., and H. Edwin Jackson

1990   Faunal Remains from the Goldsmith-Oliver Site (3PU306). In *Archeological Investigations of the Goldsmith-Oliver Site (3PU306), Pulaski County, Arkansas,* edited by Marvin D. Jeter. Arkansas Archeological Survey, Fayetteville.

2004   Faunal Remains. In *The Chickasaws: Economics, Politics, and Social Organization in the Early 18th Century,* by Jay K. Johnson, John W. O'Hear, Robbie Etheridge, Brad Lieb, Susan L. Scott, H. Edwin Jackson, Keith Jacobi, and Donna Rausch, pp. 6.1–6.23. Report submitted to the National Endowment for the Humanities by the Center for Archaeological Research, University of Mississippi, Oxford.

Scull, B. J., C. J. Felix, S. B. McCaleb, and W. G. Shaw

1966   The Inter-Discipline Approach to Paleoenvironmental Interpretations. *Transactions of the Gulf Coast Association of Geological Societies* 16:81–117.

Sellars, Wilfred

1963   Philosophy and Scientific Image of Man. In *Science, Philosophy and Reality,* edited by Wilfred Sellars, pp. 1–40. Routledge and Kegan Paul, London.

Seltzer, Jennifer

2005   Daub: The Data Set Left Behind. Paper presented at the Annual Meeting of the Mississippi Archaeological Association, Vidalia, Louisiana.

Setzler, Frank M.

1940   Archeological Perspectives in the Northern Mississippi Valley. *Smithsonian Miscellaneous Collections* 100:253–290.

Setzler, Frank M., and W. D. Strong

1936   Archaeology and Relief. *American Antiquity* 1:301–309.

Sever, Thomas, and James Wiseman

1985   *Remote Sensing and Archaeology: Potential for the Future.* Earth Resources Laboratory, National Aeronautics and Space Administration, Stennis Space Center, Mississippi.

Shea, Andrea B.

1978   Botanical Remains. In *The Peripheries of Poverty Point,* edited by Prentice Thomas, Jr., and L. Janice Campbell, pp. 245–260. New World Research Report of Investigations 12.

1996   Archaeobotanical Remains from the Fulmer Site (40SY527). Appendix B In *Archaeological Investigations at Three Sites near Arlington, State Route 385 (Paul Barrett Parkway), Shelby County, Tennessee,* by Guy G. Weaver, Mitchell R. Childress, C. Andrew Buchner, and Mary E. Starr. Report submitted to the Tennessee Department of Transportation Environmental Planning Office, Nashville, by Garrow & Associates, Inc., Memphis, Tennessee.

1999   Floral Remains. In *Archaeological Data Recovery at the McNight Site (22CO560), Coahoma County, Mississippi,* by Richard Walling and Shawn Chapman, pp. 239–247. Report submitted to the Mississippi Department of Transportation, Jackson, by Panamerican Consultants, Inc., Memphis, Tennessee.

Shea, Andrea B., and Robert C. Mainfort, Jr.

1994   Archeobotany. In *Archaeological Investigations in the Obion River Drainage: The West Tennessee Tributaries Project,* by Robert C. Mainfort, Jr., pp. 167–169. Tennessee Department of Environment and Conservation, Division of Archaeology, Research Series 10.

Sheehan, Mark C., Donald R. Whitehead, and Stephen T. Jackson

1985   *Late Quaternary Environmental History of the Richard B. Russell Multiple Resource Area.* U.S. Department of the Interior, National Park Service, Interagency Archeological Services, Atlanta.

Shepard, Anna O.

1956   *Ceramics for the Archaeologist.* Publication 609, Carnegie Institution of Washington, Washington, D.C.

1964   Temper Identification: "Technological Sherd-Splitting" or an Unanswered Challenge. *American Antiquity* 29:518–520.

1976   *Ceramics for the Archaeologist.* Sixth Printing. Carnegie Institution of Washington, Washington, D.C.

Shetrone, H. C.

1920   The Culture Problem in Ohio Archaeology. *American Anthropologist* 22:144–172.

Shott, Michael J.

1989   On Tool-Class Use Lives and the Formation of Archaeological Assemblages. *American Antiquity* 54:9–30.

1994   Size and Form in the Analysis of Flake Debris: Review and Recent Approaches. *Journal of Archaeological Method and Theory* 1:69–110.

1995   Reliability of Archaeological Records on Cultivated Surfaces: A Michigan Case Study. *Journal of Field Archaeology* 22:475–490.

Sidey, Hugh

1991   Sad Song of the Delta. *Time* June 24, 1991, Vol. 137, Issue 25.

Simek, Jan F.

1994   The Organization of Lithic Technology and Evolution: Notes from the Continent. In *The Organization of North American Prehistoric Chipped Stone Tool Technologies,* edited by Philip J. Carr, pp. 118–122. Archaeological Series No. 7, International Monographs in Prehistory, Ann Arbor.

Simmons, Ian G.

1989   *Changing the Face of the Earth.* Basil Blackwood, Ltd., Oxford.

Simon, Mary L.

2002   Red Cedar, White Oak, and Bluestem Grass: The Colors of Mississippian Construction. *Midcontinental Joural of Archaeology* 27:273–308.

Sims, Douglas C., and John M. Connaway

2000   Updated Chronometric Database for Mississippi. *Mississippi Archaeology* 35:208–269.

Skinner, Alanson, and Max Schrabisch

1913   *Preliminary Report of the Archaeological Survey of the State of New Jersey.* Geological Survey of New Jersey, Bulletin No. 9, Trenton.

Smart, Tristine Lee, and Ellen S. Hoffman

1988   Environmental Implications of Archaeological Charcoal. In *Current Paleoethnobotany,* edited by Christine A. Hastorf and Virginia S. Popper, pp. 167–205. University of Chicago Press, Chicago.

Smith, Bruce D.

1975   *Middle Mississippi Exploitation of Animal Populations.* Anthropological Papers 57. Museum of Anthropology, University of Michigan, Ann Arbor.

1978   Variation in Mississippian Settlement Patterns. In *Mississippian Settlement Patterns,* edited by Bruce D. Smith, pp. 479–503. Academic Press, New York.

1985   The Role of *Chenopodium* as a Domesticate in Pre-Maize Garden Systems of the Eastern United States. *Southeastern Archaeology* 4:51–72.

1986   The Archaeology of the Southeastern United States: From Dalton to de Soto, 10,500–500 B.P. *Advances in World Archaeology* 5:1–92. Academic Press, Orlando.

1992   The Floodplain Weed Theory of Plant Domestication in Eastern North America. In *Rivers of Change: Essays on Early Agriculture in Eastern North America,* by Bruce D. Smith, pp. 19–33. Smithsonian Institution Press, Washington, D.C.

2000   Guilá Naquitz Revisited: Agricultural Origins in Oaxaca, Mexico. In *Cultural Evolution: Contemporary Viewpoints,* edited by Gary M. Feinman and Linda Manzanilla, pp. 15–60. Plenum Press, New York.

Smith, Buckingham (translator)

1866   *Narratives of the Career of Hernando de Soto in the Conquest of Florida as Told by a Knight of Elvas and in a Relation by Luis Hernandez de Biedma, Factor of the Expedition.* Bradford Club, New York.

Smith, Eugene A.

1963   Report of a Geological Reconnaissance of Parts of the Counties of Yazoo, Issaquena, Washington, Holmes, Bolivar, Tallahatchie, and Coahoma, Mississippi, During the Months of October and November, 1870. Mississippi Geological, Economics, and Topographic Survey, *The Mississippi Geological Survey, A Centennial Bulletin 100,* Jackson.

Smith, Gerald P.

1978   *Final Report, Archaeological Excavation, The Rivervale Site, 3PO395, Fall 1977, Poinsett County, Arkansas.* Report submitted to the U.S. Army Corps of Engineers, Memphis District, by GAI Consultants, Inc., Pittsburgh, Pennsylvania.

1979   *Archaeological Surveys in the Obion-Forked Deer and Reelfoot–Indian Creek Drainages: 1966 Through Early 1975.* Memphis State University, Anthropological Research Center, Occasional Paper No. 9.

1990   The Walls Phase and its Neighbors. In *Towns and Temples along the Mississippi,* edited by David H. Dye and Cheryl A. Cox, pp. 135–169. University of Alabama Press, Tuscaloosa.

Smith, H. I.

1910   *The Prehistoric Ethnology of a Kentucky Site.* American Museum of Natural History, New York.

Smith, Maria O.

1993   Physical Anthropology. In *The Development of Southeastern Archaeology,* edited by Jay K. Johnson, pp. 53–77. University of Alabama Press, Tuscaloosa.

Smith, Marvin T.

1976   The Route of de Soto through Tennessee, Georgia, and Alabama: The Evidence from Material Culture. *Early Georgia* 4(1–2):27–48.

1977　The Early Historic Period (1540–1670) on the Upper Coosa River Drainage of Alabama and Georgia. *The Conference on Historic Site Archaeology Papers 1976*, 11:151–167.

1987　*Archaeology of Aboriginal Culture Change in the Interior Southeast: Depopulation during the Early Historic Period.* Ripley P. Bullen Monographs in Anthropology and History No. 6. University Press of Florida, Gainesville.

Smith, Robert E., Gordon R. Willey, and James C. Gifford

1960　The Type-Variety Concept as the Basis for the Analysis of Maya Pottery. *American Antiquity* 25:330–340.

Smith, Samuel D.

1982　*Archaeological Excavations in Search of the Site of Fort San Fernando de las Barrancas, Memphis, Tennessee.* Tennessee Historical Commission, Tennessee Department of Conservations Planning and Development Division, and the Shelby County Historical Commission, Memphis.

Snowden, Jesse Otho, and Richard R. Priddy

1968　*Loess Investigations in Mississippi.* Jackson: Mississippi Geological, Economic, and Topographical Survey, Bulletin 111.

Sober, Elliot

1980　Holism, Individuals, and the Units of Selection. *Proceedings of the Philosophy of Science Association* 1980:2.

Sokal, Robert R., and P. H. A. Sneath

1963　*Numerical Taxonomy.* W. H. Freeman, San Francisco.

Solis, Carlos, and Richard Walling

1982　*Archaeological Investigations at the Yarborough Site (22C1814), Clay County, Mississippi.* Report of Investigations 30. Office of Archaeological Research, University of Alabama, Tuscaloosa.

South, Stanley

2005　*Archaeology on the Roanoke.* Research Laboratories of Archaeology, University of North Carolina, Monograph No. 4, Chapel Hill.

Spaulding, Albert C.

1953　Statistical Techniques for the Discovery of Artifact Types. *American Antiquity* 18:305–313.

1968　Explanation in Archaeology. In *New Perspectives in Archaeology*, edited by Sally R. Binford and Lewis R. Binford, pp. 33–41. Aldine Publishing Company, Chicago.

Speakman, Robert J., and Hector Neff (editors)

2005　*Laser Ablation ICP-MS in Archaeological Research.* University of New Mexico Press, Albuquerque.

Spencer, William H., and Jean Shipley Perry

1978　*The Dragline Site: A Problem in Cultural Classification in the Lower Tensas Basin, Louisiana.* Report submitted to the Louisiana Delta Plantation, Jonesville, Louisiana, by Southern Archaeological Research, Inc., Baton Rouge.

Spier, Leslie

1917　*An Outline for a Chronology of Zuni Ruins.* Anthropological Papers of the American Museum of Natural History 18(3) (whole issue), New York.

Sponheimer, Matt, Benjamin H. Passey, Darryl J. de Ruiter, Debbie Guatelli-Steinberg, Thure E. Cerling, and Julia A. Lee Thorp

2006 Isotopic Evidence for Dietary Variability in the Early Honinin *Paranthropus robustus*. *Science* 324:980–982.

Springer, James W.

1980 An Analysis of Prehistoric Food Remains from the Bruly St. Martin Site, Louisiana, with a Comparative Discussion of Mississippi Valley Faunal Studies. *Midcontinental Journal of Archaeology* 5:193–224.

Squier, Ephraim G., and Edwin H. Davis

1998 *Ancient Monuments of the Mississippi Valley*. Reprinted in 1998, edited and with an
[1848] introduction by David J. Meltzer, by the Smithsonian Institution Press. Originally printed as Smithsonian Contributions to Knowledge, Vol. 1. Smithsonian Institution, Washington, D.C.

SSRC The Social Science Research Council Summer Seminar on Acculturation

1954 Acculturation: An Exploratory Formulation. *American Anthropologist* 56(6), Pt. 1:973–1002.

Stahl, Peter W.

1996 Holocene Biodiversity: An Archaeological Perspective from the Americas. *Annual Review of Anthropology* 25:105–126.

Stahle, D. W., M. K. Cleaveland, and J. G. Hehr

1985 A 450-year Drought Reconstruction for Arkansas, United States. *Nature* 316:530–532.

1988 North Carolina Climate Change Reconstructed from Tree Rings: A.D. 372 to 1985. *Science* 240:1517–1519.

Stahle, David W., and Malcolm K. Cleaveland

1992 Reconstruction and Analysis of Spring Rainfall over the Southeastern U.S. for the Past 1,000 Years. *Bulletin of the American Meteorological Society* 73(12):1947–1961.

1994 Tree-Ring Reconstructed Rainfall over the Southeastern U.S.A. During the Medieval Warm Period and Little Ice Age. *Climatic Change* 26:199–212.

Stahle, David W., Edward R. Cook, Malcolm K. Cleaveland, Matthew D. Therrell, David M. Meko, Henri D. Grissino-Mayer, Emma Watson, and Brian H. Luckman

2000 Tree-Ring Data Document 16th Century Megadrought over North America. *Eos, Transactions of the American Geophysical Union* 81:121–125.

Stahle, David W., Roy B. VanArsdale, and Malcolm K. Cleaveland

1992 Tectonic Signals in Baldcypress Trees at Reelfoot Lake, Tennessee. *Seismological Research Letters* 63(3):439–447.

Stallings, Richard

1989 Factors in Interpreting the Prehistoric Use of the Citronelle Gravels in Mississippi. *Mississippi Archaeology* 24(1):35–58.

1994 Final Report of Investigations at the Hollywood Site (22TU500). Paper presented at the 51st Annual Meeting of the Southeastern Archaeological Conference, Lexington, Kentucky.

Stallings, Richard, and Nancy A. Ross-Stallings

1996 Analysis of the Human Skeletal Remains. In *1993 Investigations at Hollywood*, edited by Richard Stallings and Nancy A. Ross-Stallings, pp. 6–10. Cultural Horizons, Inc., Harrodsburg, Kentucky.

Stark, Miriam

1998   Technical Choices and Social Boundaries in Material Culture Patterning: An Introduction. In *The Archaeology of Social Boundaries,* edited by Miriam Stark, pp. 1–11. Smithsonian Institution Press, Washington, D.C.

Starr, Mary Evelyn

1984   The Parchman Phase in the Northern Yazoo Basin: A Preliminary Analysis. In *The Wilsford Site (22-Co-516), Coahoma County, Mississippi: A Late Mississippi Period Settlement in the Northern Yazoo Basin of Mississippi,* by John M. Connaway, pp. 163–209. Archaeological Report No. 14. Mississippi Department of Archives and History, Jackson.

1992   Preliminary Report on Ceramic Vessels from the 1991 Oliver Salvage. *Mississippi Archaeology* 27(2):40–55.

1997   Powell Bayou (Part II) and Dockery: Two Mississippian Components in the Sunflower Basin of Mississippi. *Mississippi Archaeology* 32(2):79–97.

2003   CRM's Contribution to Late Prehistoric Studies in the Southern Central Mississippi Valley. In *Proceedings of the 19th Mid-South Archaeological Conference: Papers in Honor of Charles H. McNutt, Sr.,* edited by C. Andrew Buchner and David H. Dye, pp. 17–38. Panamerican Consultants, Inc., Special Publication No. 3 and University of Memphis, Anthropological Resarch Center, Occasional Paper No. 22, Memphis.

Stein, Julie K., and Angela R. Linse (editors)

1993   Effects of Scale on Archaeological and Geoscientific Perspectives. *The Geological Society of America, Special Paper* 283.

Steinbock, R. Ted

1976   *Paleopathological Diagnosis and Interpretation.* Charles C. Thomas, Springfield.

Steponaitis, Vincas P.

1983   *Ceramics, Chronology, and Community Patterns: An Archaeological Study of Moundville.* Academic Press, New York.

Steponaitis, Vincas P., and M. James Blackman

1981   Chemical Characterization of Mississippian Pottery. Paper presented at the 38th Annual Southeastern Archaeological Conference, Asheville, North Carolina.

Steponaitis, Vincas P., M. James Blackman, and Hector Neff

1996   Large-Scale Patterns in the Chemical Composition of Mississippian Pottery. *American Antiquity* 61:555–572.

Steponaitis, Vincas P., and Jeffrey P. Brain

1976   A Portable Differential Proton Magnetometer. *Journal of Field Archaeology* 3:455–463.

Steponaitis, Vincas P., Jeffrey P. Brain, and Ian W. Brown

1983   Glossary of Ceramic Types and Varieties. In *The Grand Village of the Natchez Revisited: Excavations at the Fatherland Site, Adams County, Mississippi, 1972,* by Robert S. Neitzel, pp. 139–145. Mississippi Department of Archives and History, Archaeological Report No. 12. Jackson.

Steward, Julian H.

1954　Types of Types. *American Anthropologist:* 56:54–57.

Stewart, Thomas D.

1979　*Essentials of Forensic Anthropology.* Charles C. Thomas, Springfield.

Stewart-Abernathy, Leslie

1986　Urban Farmsteads: Household Responsibilities in the City. *Historical Archaeology* 20(2):5–15.

1998　A Reply to "Concerning Cutoff Dates for State Archaeological Inventories," by Jack D. Elliott, Jr. *Mississippi Archaeological Association Newsletter* 33(4):6–11.

1999　From Famous Forts to Forgotten Farmsteads: Historical Archaeology in the Mid-South. In *Arkansas Archaeology: Essays in Honor of Dan and Phyllis Morse,* edited by Robert C. Mainfort, Jr., and Marvin D. Jeter, pp. 225–244. University of Arkansas Press, Fayetteville.

Stoddard, Amos

1812　*Sketches, Historical and Descriptive, of Louisiana.* Mathew Carey, Philadelphia.

Stoltman, James B.

1989　A Quantitative Approach to the Petrographic Analysis of Ceramic Thin Sections. *American Antiquity* 54:147–160.

1991　Ceramic Petrography as a Technique for Documenting Cultural Interaction: An Example from the Upper Mississippi Valley. *American Antiquity* 56:103–120.

2004　Did Poverty Pointers Make Pots? In *Early Pottery: Technology, Function, Style, and Interaction in the Lower Southeast,* edited by R. Saunders and C. Hays, pp.210–222. University of Alabama Press, Tuscaloosa.

Stoltman, James B., and Robert C. Mainfort, Jr.

2002　Minerals and Elements: Using Petrography to Reconsider the Findings of Neutron Activation in the Compositional Analysis of Ceramics from Pinson Mounds, Tennessee. *Midcontinental Journal of Archaeology* 27:1–33.

Stone, Anne C.

2000　Ancient DNA from Skeletal Remains. In *Biological Anthropology of the Human Skeleton,* edited by M. Anne Katzenberg and Shelley Saunders, pp.351–371. Lilley Liss, New York.

Story, Dee Ann, Janice A. Guy, Barbara A. Burnett, Martha Doty Freeman, Jerome C. Rose, D. Gentry Steele, Ben W. Olive, and Karl J. Reinhard

1990　*The Archeology and Bioarcheology of the Gulf Coastal Plain.* Arkansas Archeological Survey, Research Series No. 38, Fayetteville. Two volumes.

Stout, Charles

1991　Adams Meets St. Francis: Lower Mississippi Valley Site Classification. In *The Human Landscape in Kentucky's Past: Site Structure and Settlement Patterns,* edited by Charles Stout and Christine K. Hensley, pp. 128–138. Kentucky Heritage Council, Frankfort.

Struever, Stuart

1968　Woodland Subsistence-Settlement Systems in the Lower Illinois valley. In *New Perspectives in Archeology,* edited by Sally R. Binford and Lewis R. Binford, pp. 285–312. Aldine de Gruyter, Chicago.

Stuiver, Minze, Paula J. Reimer, and Ron Reimer
1998   INTCAL98 Radiocarbon Age Calibration, 24,000-cal BP. *Radiocarbon* 40:1041–1083.

Styer, Kenneth F.
1991   *An Evaluation of Controlled Surface Collections from Three Potential de Soto Contact Sites in Western Mississippi.* Unpublished M.A. thesis, Department of Sociology and Anthropology, University of Mississippi, University.

Styles, Bonnie W.
1994   The Value of Archaeological Faunal Remains for Paleodietary Reconstruction: A Case Study for the Midwestern United States. In *Paleonutrition: The Diet and Health of Prehistoric Americans,* edited by Kristin D. Sobolik, pp. 34–54. Occasional Paper 22. Center for Archaeological Investigations, Southern Illinois University, Carbondale.

Sullivan, Alan P., and Kenneth C. Rozen
1985   Debitage Analysis and Archaeological Interpretation. *American Antiquity* 50:755–779.

Swallow, George C.
1857   Indian Mounds in New Madrid County, Missouri. *Transactions of the Academy of Science of St. Louis* 1:36–37.

Swanton, John R.
1911   *Indian Tribes of the Lower Mississippi Valley and Adjacent Coast of the Gulf of Mexico.* Smithsonian Institution, *Bureau of American Ethnology, Bulletin* No. 43, Washington, D.C.

Swanton, John R. (editor)
1985   *Final Report of the United States de Soto Expedition Commission.* Smithsonian Institution Press, Washington, D.C. Originally published 1939, U.S. House of Representatives Document No. 71, 76th Congress, 1st Session, Washington D.C.

Swartz, B. K., Jr.
1996   The McKern Taxonomic System and Archaeological Culture Classification in the Midwestern United States: A History and Evaluation. *Bulletin of the History of Archaeology* 6:3–9.

Talbott, P.
1984   Prospecting for Clay. *Journal of the American Ceramic Society* 63:1047–1050.

Tanner, William F.
1991   The "Gulf of Mexico" Late Holocene Sea Level Curve and River Delta History. *Transactions of the Gulf Coast Association of Geological Societies* 41:583–589.

Teaford, Mark F.
1988a   A Review Of Dental Microwear And Diet In Modern Mammals. *Scanning Microscopy* 2:1149–1166.

1988b   Scanning Electron Microscope Diagnosis of Wear Patterns versus Artifacts on Fossil Teeth. *Scanning Microscopy* 2:1167–1175.

1991   Dental Microwear: What Can It Tell Us about Diet and Dental Function? In *Advances in Dental Anthropology,* edited by Marc. A. Kelley and Clark Spencer Larsen, pp. 341–356. Willey-Liss, Inc., New York.

Teltser, Patrice A.

1998   Nonsite Survey in the Cairo Lowland of Southeastern Missouri. In *Changing Perspectives on the Archaeology of the Central Mississippi Valley,* edited by Michael J. O'Brien and Robert C. Dunnell, pp. 148–168. University of Alabama Press, Tuscaloosa.

Tennessee Department of Transportation (TDOT)

2004   Interstate 69 Legislation. Electronic document. http://www.tdot.state. tn.us/information-office/I-69/linkage.html, accessed August 1, 2004.

Tesar, Lewis D.

1976   *The Humber-McWilliams Site: Pre-Columbian Indian Burial Ground, Coahoma County, Mississippi: Exploration and Analysis 1975–1976.* Port Caddo Press, Marshall, Texas.

Tesar, Lewis D., and Donna L. Fichtner

1974   A Preliminary Report on Archaeological Investigations Conducted at the Humber Site (22Co601) in Westcentral Coahoma County, Mississippi. *Cottonlandia Notes* 1(1) (whole number). Cottonlandia Educational and Recreational Foundation, Inc., Greenwood, Mississippi.

Thomas, Cyrus

1891   *Catalogue of Prehistoric Works East of the Rocky Mountains.* Smithsonian Institution, Washington, D.C.

1985   *Report on the Mound Explorations of the Bureau of Ethnology.* Smithsonian Insti-
[1894] tution Press, Washington, D.C. Originally published as the *Twelfth Annual Report of the Bureau of American Ethnology, 1890–1891,* U.S. Government Printing Office, Washington, D.C.

Thomas, David Hurst

1979   *Archaeology.* 1st edition. Holt, Rinehart, and Winston, Austin.

1981   How to Classify the Projectile Points from the Monitor Valley, Nevada. *Journal of California and Great Basin Anthropology* 3:7–43.

1986   Points on Points: A Reply to Flenniken and Raymond. *American Antiquity* 51:617–627.

Thompson, Raymond H.

1956   An Archaeological Approach to the Study of Cultural Stability. *Society for American Archaeology Memoirs* 11:31–57.

Thorne, Robert M. (editor)

1977   *Cultural Resources Survey, Item I, Upper Yazoo Projects, Yazoo River, Mississippi, Between SRM 75.6 and 107.8.* Report submitted to the U.S. Army Corps of Engineers, Vicksburg District, by the Department of Sociology and Anthropology, University of Mississippi.

1988   Archeological Data Recovery in Transition: Observations from Mississippi. In *Advances in Southeastern Archaeology 1966–1986: Contributions of the Federal Archaeology Program,* edited by Bennie C. Keel, pp. 30–33. Southeastern Archaeological Conference Special Publication No. 6.

Thorne, Robert M., and Bettye J. Broyles

1968   *Handbook of Mississippi Pottery Types.* Bulletin of the Southeastern Archaeological Conference, No. 2, Morgantown.

Thorne, Robert M., and Hugh K. Curry

1983   *Cultural Resources Survey of Items 3 and 4, Upper Yazoo River Projects, Mississippi, with a Paleoenvironmental Model of the Lower Yazoo Basin.* Report submitted to the U.S. Army Corps of Engineers, Vicksburg District, by the University of Mississippi Center for Archaeological Research.

Thornes, J. B.

1985   The Ecology of Erosion. *Geography* 70(3):222–235.

Thruston, G. P.

1890   *The Antiquities of Tennessee.* Robert Clarke and Co., Cincinnati.

Thunen, R. L.

1988   Geometric Enclosures in the Mid-South: An Archaeological Analysis of Enclosure Form. In *Middle Woodland Settlement and Ceremonialism in the Mid-South and the Lower Mississippi Valley,* edited by Robert C. Mainfort, pp. 99–116. Archaeological Report No. 22. Mississippi Department of Archives and History, Jackson.

Tivy, Joy

1990   *Agricultural Ecology.* Longman Scientific and Technical, New York.

Torrence, Robin

1994   Strategies for Moving on in Lithic Studies. In *The Organization of North American Prehistoric Chipped Stone Tool Technologies,* edited by Philip J. Carr, pp. 123–131. Archaeological Series No. 7, International Monographs in Prehistory, Ann Arbor.

Toth, Alan

1988   *Early Marksville Phases in the Lower Mississippi Valley: A Study of Culture Contact Dynamics.* Mississippi Department of Archives and History, Archaeological Report 21, Jackson.

Toth, Alan, and Samuel O. Brookes

1977   The Martin #1 Site (22Tu533), Tunica County, 1976. *Mississippi Archaeology* 12(1):8–13.

Trachtenberg, Samuel

1999   *Macrobotanical Remains from the Raffman Site (16MA20).* Unpublished M.A. thesis, Department of Anthropology, Tulane University, New Orleans.

Trigger, Bruce G.

1989   *A History of Archaeological Thought.* Cambridge University Press, Cambridge.

Turner, Jocelyn, and Gayle J. Fritz

n.d.   Plant Remains from the Wallace Bottom Site, the First Arkansas Post. Ms. on file, Paleoethnobotany Laboratory, Department of Anthropology, Washington University in St. Louis.

Tushingham, Shannon, Jane Hill, and Charles H. McNutt (editors)

2002   *Histories of Southeastern Archaeology.* University of Alabama Press, Tuscaloosa.

Ubelaker, Douglas H.

1978   *Human Skeletal Remains: Excavation, Analysis, Interpretation.* Aldine Publishing Company, Chicago.

Underwood, John R., Dennis B. Blanton, W. Jason Cline, David W. Lewes, and William H. Moore

2004   *Systematic Archaeological Survey of 6,000 Acres, Naval Weapons Station Yorktown,*

Virginia. Report submitted to Atlantic Division, Naval Facilities Engineering Command, Norfolk, Virginia, by the William and Mary Center for Archaeological Research, Williamsburg, Virginia.

Ungar, Peter S.

1994   Incisor Microwear of Sumatran Anthropoid Primates. *American Journal of Physical Anthropology* 94:339–364.

Ungar, Peter S., and Mark A. Spencer

1999   Incisor Microwear, Diet, and Tooth Use in Three Amerindian Populations. *American Journal of Physical Anthropology* 109:387–396.

Ungar, Peter S., and Mark F. Teaford

1996   Preliminary Examination of Non-Occlusal Dental Microwear In Anthropoids: Implications of The Study of Fossil Primates. *American Journal of Physical Anthropology* 100:101–113.

Usner, Daniel H., Jr.

1983   A Cycle of Lowland Forest Efficiency: The Late Archaic–Woodland Economy of the Lower Mississippi Valley. *Journal of Anthropological Research* 39:433–444.

Vale, Thomas R. (editor)

2002   *Fire, Native Peoples, and the Natural Landscape.* Island Press, Washington, D.C.

Vance, Rupert B.

1935   *Human Geography of the South.* Second Edition. University of North Carolina Press, Chapel Hill.

Verano, John W., and Douglas H. Ubelaker

1992   *Disease and Demography in the Americas.* Smithsonian Institution Press, Washington, D.C.

Vidrine, Malcolm F.

1993   *The Historical Distributions of Freshwater Mussels in Louisiana.* Gail Q. Vidrine Collectibles, Eunice, Louisiana.

1997   Report on Shells from Hedgeland Place Site 16CT19 in Catahoula Parish, Louisiana. Report submitted to Coastal Environments, Inc., Baton Rouge, Louisiana, by Louisiana State University at Eunice.

Vogt, Evon Z.

2004   Gordon Randolph Willey 1913–2002 Biographical Memoirs. *National Academy of Science of St. Louis, Transactions* 84:399–415.

Voss, James A., and Robert L. Young

1995   Style and Self. In *Style, Society, and Person,* edited by Christopher Carr and Jill E. Neitzel, pp. 77–100. Plenum Press, New York.

Wadleigh, Linda, and Kevin W. Thompson

1989   *Proton Magnetometer Survey of Site 3MS105, Eaker Air Force Base, Arkansas.* Archaeological Service, Western Wyoming College, Rock Springs, Wyoming.

Wagner, Gail E.

1994   Corn in Eastern Woodlands Late Prehistory. In *Corn and Culture in the Prehistoric New World,* edited by Sissel Johannessen and Christine A. Hastorf, pp. 335–346. Westview Press, Boulder.

2005   Anthropogenic Changes at the Carlston Annis Site. In *Archaeology of the Middle*

Green River Region, Kentucky, edited by William H. Marquardt and Patty Jo Watson, pp. 213–242. University of Florida, Institute of Archaeology and Paleoenvironmental Studies, Monograph 5, Gainesville.

Walling, Richard, and Shawn Chapman

1999   *Archaeological Data Recovery at the McNight Site (22CO560), Coahoma County, Mississippi.* Report submitted to the Mississippi Department of Transportation, Jackson, by Panamerican Consultants, Inc., Memphis, Tennessee.

Walling, Richard, and Erwin Roemer

1993   *A Cultural Resources Inventory Survey of Portions of the Big and Little Sunflower Rivers, Issaquena, Sharkey, and Yazoo Counties, Mississippi—Volume I.* Report submitted to U.S. Army Corps of Engineers, Vicksburg District by Panamerican Consultants, Inc., Memphis, Tennessee.

Walthall, John A.

1992   Aboriginal Pottery and the Eighteenth-Century Illini. In *Calumet and Fleur-de-Lys: Archaeology of Indian and French Contact in the Midcontinent,* edited by John A. Walthall and Thomas E. Emerson, pp. 155–174. Smithsonian Institution Press, Washington, D.C.

Ward, Heather D.

1998   The Paleoethnobotanical Record of the Poverty Point Culture: Implications of Past and Current Research. *Southeastern Archaeology* 17:166–174.

Ward, Jerome V.

1999   Pollen Analysis. In Richard Walling and Shawn Chapman, *Archaeological Data Recovery at the McNight Site (22CO560), Coahoma County, Mississippi,* pp. 249–250. Report submitted to the Mississippi Department of Transportation, Jackson, by Panamerican Consultants, Inc., Memphis, Tennessee.

Wardle, H. Newell

1913   The People of the Flints: Recent Archaeological Discoveries along Red River Arkansas. *Harper's Monthly Magazine* 126:291–300.

1956   Clarence Bloomfield Moore (1856–1936). *Bulletin of the Philadelphia Anthropological Society* 9(2):9–11.

Warren, Robert E.

1990   *UNIO: A Spreadsheet Program for Reconstructing Aquatic Environments Based on the Species Composition of Freshwater Mussel (Unionacea) Assemblages.* Illinois State Museum Technical Report No. 89-000-29, Springfield.

1991   Freshwater Mussels as Paleoenvironmental Indicators: A Quantitative Approach to Assemblage Analysis. In *Beamers, Bobwhites, and Blue-Points: Tributes to the Career of Paul W. Parmalee,* edited by James R. Purdue, Walter E. Klippel, and Bonnie W. Styles pp. 23–66. Illinois State Museum Scientific Papers Vol. 23, and University of Tennessee, Department of Anthropology, Report of Investigations 52, Knoxville.

Waselkov, Gregory A.

1997   Changing Strategies of Indian Field Location in the Early Historic Southeast. In *Peoples, Plants and Landscapes: Studies in Paleoethnobotany,* edited by Kristen J. Gremillion, pp. 179–194. University of Alabama Press, Tuscaloosa.

Watson, Patty Jo

1985   The Impact of Early Agriculture in the Upland Drainages of the Midwest and Midsouth. In *Prehistoric Food Production in North America,* edited by Richard I. Ford, pp. 99–147. University of Michigan, Museum of Anthropology, Anthropological Papers No. 75, Ann Arbor.

1990   Trend and Tradition in Southeastern Archaeology. *Southeastern Archaeology* 9(1):43–54.

Watson, Richard A.

1991   What the New Archaeology Has Accomplished. *Current Anthropology* 32:275–291.

Watts, William A.

1980   The Late Quaternary Vegetation History of the Southeastern United States. *Annual Review of Ecology and Systematics* 11:387–409.

Watts, William A., Eric C. Grimm, and T. C. Hussey

1996   Mid-Holocene Forest History of Florida and the Coastal Plain of Georgia and South Carolina. In *Archaeology of the Mid-Holocene Southeast,* edited by Kenneth E. Sassaman and David G. Anderson, pp. 28–40. University of Florida Press, Gainesville.

Wauchope, Robert

1966   *Archaeological Survey of Northern Georgia.* Society for American Archaeology Memoir No. 21, Salt Lake City.

Weaver, Elizabeth C.

1963   Technological Analysis of Prehistoric Lower Mississippi Ceramic Materials: A Preliminary Report. *American Antiquity* 29:49–56.

Weaver, Guy G.

1988   *Archaeological Testing at the Site of the Peabody Place Mall and Office Complex, Memphis, Tennessee: Phase II Construction.* Report submitted to the City of Memphis, Division of Housing and Community Development, by Garrow and Associates, Atlanta, Georgia.

Weaver, Guy G., Brian Collins, and Gerald P. Smith

1997   *Supplemental Phase III Archaeological Data Recovery of Feature 85, MATA North End Terminal Site, Memphis, Shelby County, Tennessee.* Report submitted to the Memphis Area Transit Authority by the University of Memphis, Memphis, Tennessee.

Weaver, Guy G., and John L. Hopkins

1991   *Archaeological Data Recovery at the Rum Boogie Site (40SY494), Peabody Place Mall and Office Complex, Memphis, Tennessee.* Report submitted to the City of Memphis, Division of Housing and Community Development, by Garrow and Associates, Memphis, Tennessee.

1996   *Phase I Cultural Resources Survey and Assessment of the North End Terminal Property Memphis, Shelby County, Tennessee.* Report submitted to the Memphis Area Transit Authority by Garrow and Associates, Memphis, Tennessee.

Weaver, Guy G., John Hopkins, and Marsha Oats

1994   *The Tom Lee Monument Relocation Project at Beal Street Landing (Site 40SY352),*

Memphis, Shelby County, Tennessee, Phase II Archaeological Testing and Evaluation. Report submitted to the City of Memphis, Division of Engineering, by Garrow and Associates, Inc., Memphis, Tennessee.

Weaver, Guy G., John Hopkins, Marsha Oats, and Gary Patterson

1996 *The Memphis Landing Cultural Resource Assessment and Preservation Plan, City of Memphis, Shelby County, Tennessee.* Two volumes. Report submitted to the City of Memphis, Division of Engineering, by Garrow and Associates, Memphis, Tennessee.

Weaver, Guy G., John Hopkins, Louella Whitson Weaver, Jane P. Kowalewski, and Mitchell R. Childress

1996 *Cultural Resource Investigation at the AutoZone Corporate Headquarters Site (40SY528), Memphis, Shelby County, Tennessee.* Report submitted to the City of Memphis, Division of Housing and Community Development and the Division of Engineering, by Garrow and Associates, Memphis, Tennessee.

Weaver, Guy G., and Louella Whitson Weaver

1985a Archaeological Investigations at the Magevny House, Memphis, Tennessee. Manuscript on file, Memphis Museums, Memphis, Tennessee.

1985b The Tale of Two Wells: Historical Archaeology in Memphis. Paper presented to the American Institute of Archaeology, Mid-South Chapter, Memphis, Tennessee.

Webb, Clarence H.

1970 Settlement Patterns in the Poverty Point Cultural Complex. In *The Poverty Point Culture,* edited by Bettye J. Broyles and Clarence H. Webb, pp. 3–12. Bulletin 12. Southeastern Archaeological Conference, Morgantown, Louisiana.

1982 The Poverty Point Culture. *Geoscience and Man* 17 (whole issue). Lousiana State University School of Geoscience, Baton Rouge.

1991 Poverty Point Culture and Site: Definitions. In *The Poverty Point Culture: Local Manifestations, Subsistence Practices, and Trade Networks,* edited by Kathleen M. Byrd, pp. 3–6. *Geoscience and Man* 29 (whole issue). Louisiana State University, Baton Rouge.

Webb, William S.

1938 An Archaeological Survey of the Wheeler Basin on the Tennessee River in Northern Alabama. *Bureau of American Ethnology* Bulletin 122.

1951 *The Parrish Village Site.* Lexington. Reports in Anthropology 7(6), University of Kentucky, Lexington.

Webb, William S., and David L. DeJarnette

1942 *An Archaeological Survey of Pickwick Basin in the Adjacent Portions of the States of Alabama, Mississippi, and Tennessee.* Bureau of American Ethnology Bulletin No. 129, Washington, D.C.

Weigand, Phil C., Garman Harbottle, and Edward V. Sayre

1977 Turquoise Sources and Source Analysis: Mesoamerica and the Southwestern U.S.A. In *Exchange Systems in Prehistory,* edited by Timothy K. Earle and Jonathon E. Ericson, pp. 15–34. Academic Press, New York.

Weinstein, Richard A.

1981a Meandering Rivers and Shifting Villages: A Prehistoric Settlement Model in the

Upper Steele Bayou Basin, Mississippi. *Southeastern Archaeological Conference Bulletin* 24:37–41.

1981b   *Archaeological Investigations Along Moores Creek, Alcorn County, Mississippi.* Report submitted to the National Park Service, Southeast Regional Office, Interagency Archeological Services Division, by Coastal Environments, Inc., Baton Rouge.

1985   Some New Thoughts on the de Soto Expedition through Western Mississippi. *Mississippi Archaeology* 20(2):2–24.

1991   *Cultural Resources Survey of Four Disposal Areas, Three Water-Control Structures, and a Portion of the Tallahatchie River, Tallahatchie County, Mississippi.* Report submitted to the U.S. Army Corps of Engineers, Vicksburg District, by Coastal Environments, Inc., Baton Rouge.

2004a   Previous Archaeological Research within the I-69 Corridor. In *Cultural Resources Survey of the Proposed Route of Interstate 69 Between Robinsonville and Benoit Bolivar, Coahoma, Tunica, and Sunflower Counties, Mississippi,* by Joanne Ryan, Douglas C. Wells, Richard A. Weinstein, David B. Kelley, and Sara A. Hahn, pp.3:1–170. Report submitted to Neel-Schaffer, Inc., Jackson, Mississippi, and the Environmental Division, Mississippi Department of Transportation, Jackson, by Coastal Environments Inc., Baton Rouge.

2004b   Aboriginal Cultural Sequence within the I-69 Corridor. In *Cultural Resources Survey of the Proposed Route of Interstate 69 between Robinsonville and Benoit, Bolivar, Coahoma, Tunica, and Sunflower Counties, Mississippi,* by Joanne Ryan, Douglas C. Wells, Richard A. Weinstein, David B. Kelley, and Sara A. Hahn, pp. 4:1–39. Report submitted to Neel-Schaffer, Inc., Jackson, Mississippi, and the Environmental Division, Mississippi Department of Transportation, Jackson by Coastal Environments, Inc., Baton Rouge.

Weinstein, Richard A. (editor)

2005   *Lake Providence: A Terminal Coles Creek Culture Mound Center, East Carroll Parish, Louisiana.* Two volumes. Report submitted to the U.S. Army Corps of Engineers, Vicksburg District, by Coastal Environments, Inc., Baton Rouge.

Weinstein, Richard A., Susan D. deFrance, and David B. Kelley

1985   *Cultural Resources Survey in the Vicinity of Sunflower Landing: Investigations Related to the Rena Lara Landside Berm, Item L-628, Coahoma County, Mississippi.* Report submitted to the U.S. Army Corps of Engineers, Vicksburg District, by Coastal Environments, Inc., Baton Rouge.

Weinstein, Richard A., Richard S. Fuller, Susan L. Scott, C. Margaret Scarry, and Sylvia Timmons Duay

1995   *The Rock Levee Site: Late Marksville through Late Mississippi Period Settlement, Bolivar County, Mississippi. The Lake Beulah Project Levee Project: Archaeology and History, Vol. III.* Report submitted to the U.S. Army Corps of Engineers, Vicksburg District, by Coastal Environments, Inc., Baton Rouge.

Weinstein, Richard A., Wayne P. Glander, Sherwood M. Gagliano, Eileen K. Burden, and Kathleen G. McCloskey

1979   *Cultural Resources Survey of the Upper Steele Bayou Basin, West-Central Missis-*

sippi. 3 vols. Report submitted to the U.S. Army Corps of Engineers, Vicksburg District, by Coastal Environments, Inc., Baton Rouge, Louisiana.

Weiss, Kenneth M.

1973   Demographic Models for Anthropology. *Memoirs of the Society for American Archaeology* 27.

Welch, Paul D.

1990   Mississippian Emergence in West-Central Alabama. In *The Mississippian Emergence,* edited by Bruce D. Smith, pp. 197–225. Smithsonian Institution Press, Washington, D.C.

1991   *Moundville's Economy.* University of Alabama Press, Tuscaloosa.

Wells, Douglas C., and Sara A. Hahn

2005   *Addendum: Survey of the Preferred Alternate Route for the Proposed Interstate 69 between Robinsonville and Benoit—Bolivar, Coahoma, and Tunica Counties, Mississippi.* Report submitted to the Mississippi Department of Transportation by Coastal Environments, Inc., Baton Rouge.

Wetterstrom, Wilma

1978   Plant Foods from the Gypsy Joint Site. In *Prehistoric Patterns of Human Behavior: A Case Study in the Mississippi Valley,* by Bruce D. Smith, pp. 101–115. Academic Press, New York.

Whallon, Robert

1972   A New Approach to Pottery Typology. *American Antiquity* 37:13–33.

1973   Spatial Analysis of Occupation Floors: The Application of Dimensional Analysis of Variance. In *The Explanation of Culture Change: Models in Prehistory,* edited by Colin Renfrew, pp. 115–130. Duckworth, London.

Whallon, Robert, and James A. Brown (editors)

1981   *Essays on Achaeological Typology.* Center for American Archaeology, Northwestern University, Evanstown.

Whatley, John S.

2002   An Overview of Georgia Projectile Points and Selected Cutting Tools. *Early Georgia* 30:7–133.

Wheat, Joe B., James C. Gifford, and William W. Wasley

1958   Ceramic Variety, Type Cluster, and Ceramic System in Southwestern Pottery Analysis. *American Antiquity* 24:34–47.

Whitbread, Ian K.

1995   *Greek Transport Amphorae: A Petrological and Archaeological Study.* British School at Athens, Fitch Laboratory Occasional Paper 4.

White, Tim D.

2000   *Human Osteology.* Second edition. Academic Press, San Diego.

Whitehead, Donald R., and Mark C. Sheehan

1985   Holocene Vegetational Changes in the Tombigbee River Valley, Eastern Mississippi. *American Midland Naturalist* 113:122–137.

Whitney, Gordon G., and Joseph P. DeCant

2001   Government Land Office Surveys and Other Early Land Surveys, pp. 147–172, in

The Historical Ecology Handbook, edited by Dave Egan and Evelyn A. Howell. Island Press, Washington, D.C.

Whyte, Thomas R.

1991 Small-animal Remains in Archaeological Pit Features. In *Beamers, Bobwhites, and Blue-Points: Tributes to the Career of Paul W. Parmalee,* edited by James R. Purdue, Walter E. Klippel, and Bonnie W. Styles, pp. 163–176. Illinois State Museum Scientific Papers Vol. 23, and University of Tennessee, Department of Anthropology, Report of Investigations 52, Knoxville.

Willer, David, and Judith Willer

1973 *Systematic Empiricism: Critique of a Psuedoscience.* Prentice-Hall, Englewood Cliffs.

Willey, Gordon R.

1949 Archeology of the Florida Gulf Coast. *Smithsonian Miscellaneous Collections* 113 (whole issue), Washington, D.C.

1953 *Prehistoric Settlement Patterns in the Viru Valley, Peru. Bureau of American Ethnology Bulletin* 155, Washington, D.C.

Willey, Gordon R., and Philip Phillips

1955 Method and Theory in American Archaeology, II: Historical-Developmental Interpretation. *American Anthropologist* 57:723–819.

2001 *Method and Theory in American Archaeology,* edited by R. Lee Lyman and Michael
[1958] J. O'Brien. University of Alabama Press, Tuscaloosa. Originally published by University of Chicago Press, Chicago.

Willey, Gordon R., and Jeremy A. Sabloff

1970 *A History of American Archaeology.* W. H. Freeman, San Francisco.

1980 *A History of American Archaeology.* 2nd ed. W. H. Freeman, San Francisco.

1993 *A History of American Archaeology.* 3rd ed. W. H. Freeman, San Francisco.

Williams, G. Ishmael, Jr.

1993 Environmental Setting. In *Caddoan Saltmakers in the Ouachita Valley: The Hardaman Site,* edited by Ann M. Early, pp. 15–28. Arkansas Archeological Research Series No. 43.

Williams, J. Mark

1984 A New Resistivity Device. *Journal of Field Archaeology* 11:110–114.

Williams, J. Raymond

1967 *Land-Leveling Salvage Archaeological Work in Southeast Missouri: 1966.* National Park Service, Region 2, Omaha.

1968 *Southeast Missouri Land-Leveling Salvage Archaeology: 1967.* National Park Service/University of Missouri Archaeological Research Division, Columbia.

1972 *Land-Leveling Salvage Archaeology in Missouri: 1968.* National Park Service/University of Missouri Archaeological Research Division, Columbia.

Williams, Michele L.

1993 *Plant Remains from the Parkin (3CS29) Archaeological Site.* Unpublished M.A. thesis, Department of Anthropology, Washington University in St. Louis.

Williams, Stephen

1949 *An Archaeological Study of the Sandy Woods Site, Scott County, Missouri.* Undergraduate thesis, Anthropology, Yale University, New Haven. Univeristy Microfilms, Ann Arbor.

1954   *An Archaeological Study of the Mississippian Culture in Southeast Missouri.* Unpublished Ph.D. dissertation, Department of Anthropology, Yale University.

1963   The Eastern United States. In *Early Indian Farmers and Villages and Communities,* edited by William G. Haag, pp. 267–325. National Park Service, Washington, D.C.

1967   On the Location of the Historic Taensa Villages. *Conference on Historic Sites Archaeology Papers, 1965–1966,* 1:3–13.

1990   The Vacant Quarter and Other Late Events in the Lower Valley. In *Towns and Temples Along the Mississippi,* edited by David H. Dye and Cheryl A. Cox, pp. 170–180. University of Alabama Press, Tuscaloosa.

2003   Introduction to the 2003 Edition. In Philip Phillips, James A. Ford, and James B. Griffin, *Archaeological Survey in the Lower Mississippi Alluvial Valley, 1940–1947,* edited by Stephen Williams, pp. xi–xxxii. University of Alabama Press, Tuscaloosa. Original edition published in 1951 by the Peabody Museum of American Archaeology and Ethnology, Harvard University, Cambridge.

Williams, Stephen (editor)

2003   *Archaeological Survey in the Lower Mississippi Alluvial Valley, 1940–1947.* University of Alabama Press, Tuscaloosa. Original edition published in 1951 by the Peabody Museum of American Archaeology and Ethnology, Harvard University, Cambridge.

Williams, Stephen, and Jeffrey P. Brain

1983   *Excavations at the Lake George Site, Yazoo County, Mississippi, 1958–1960.* Papers of the Peabody Museum of Archaeology and Ethnology 74. Harvard University, Cambridge.

Williams, Stephen, W. Kean, and Alan Toth

1966   *The Archaeology of the Upper Tensas Basin.* Lower Mississippi Survey, Peabody Museum, Harvard University, Bulletin No. 1, Cambridge.

Willoughby, Charles C.

1897   An Analysis of Decorations upon Pottery from the Mississippi Valley. *Journal of American Folk-Lore* 10(36):9–20.

Wilson, Robert C.

1987   Analysis of Faunal Remains from the French Site 22HO565/19P, Holmes County, Mississippi. In *The Emergent Mississippian: Proceedings of the Sixth Mid-South Archaeological Conference,* edited by Richard A. Marshall, pp. 38–62. Mississippi State University, Cobb Institute of Archaeology, Occasional Papers 87–01.

Wilson, Thomas

1899   Arrowpoints, Spearheads, and Knives of Prehistoric Times. *Annual Report of the United States National Museum for 1897,* Part I:811–988.

Wing, Elizabeth S., and Antoinette B. Brown

1979   *Paleonutrition: Method and Theory in Prehistoric Foodways.* Academic Press, New York.

Winterhalder, Bruce

1994   Concepts in Historical Ecology: The View from Evolutionary Ecology. In *His-*

torical Ecology: Cultural Knowledge and Changing Landscapes, edited by Carole L. Crumley, pp. 17–41. School of American Research Press, Santa Fe.

Winterhalder, Bruce, and Carol Goland

1999   An Evolutionary Perspective on Diet Choice, Risk, and Plant Domestication. In *People, Plants and Landscapes: Studies in Paleoethnobotany,* edited by Kristen J. Gremillion, pp. 123–160. University of Alabama Press, Tuscaloosa.

Wintle, Ann G.

1996   Archaeologically-Relevant Dating Techniques for the Next Century: Small, Hot, and Identified by Acronyms. *Journal of Archaeological Science* 23:123–138.

Wissler, Clark, A. W. Butler, Ronald B. Dixon, F. W. Hodge, and Bertold Laufer

1923   *State Archaeological Surveys: Suggestions in Method and Technique.* National Research Council, Washington, D.C.

Wobst, Martin

1977   Stylistic Behavior and Information Exchange. In *For the Director: Research Essays in Honor of James B. Griffin,* edited by Charles E. Cleland, pp. 317–342. University of Michigan Museum of Anthropology, Ann Arbor.

Wolverton, Steve

2005   The Effects of the Hypsithermal on Prehistoric Foraging Efficiency in Missouri. *American Antiquity* 70:91–106.

Woodman, Harold D.

1997   Race, Class, Politics, and the Modernization of the Postbellum South. *Journal of Southern History* 63(1):3–22.

Woods, William I., and George R. Holley

1991   Upland Mississippian Settlement in the American Bottom Region. In *Cahokia and the Hinterlands: Middle Mississippian Cultures of the Midwest,* edited by Thomas E. Emerson and R. Barry Lewis, pp. 46–60. University of Illinois Press, Urbana.

Worsaae, J. J. A.

1849   *Primeval Antiquities of Denmark* (translated by W. J. Thoms). John Henry Parker, London.

Wyman, Jefferies

1863   An Account of the Fresh-Water Shell-Heaps of the St. John's River, Florida. *American Naturalist* 2:393–403,449–463.

1875   *Fresh Water Shell Mounds of the St John's River, Florida.* Memoirs of the Peabody Academy of Science, No. 4, Salem.

Yerkes, Richard W.

1987   *Prehistoric Life on the Mississippi Floodplain.* University of Chicago Press, Chicago.

1989   Lithic Analysis and Activity Patterns at Labras Lake. In *Alternative Approaches to Lithic Analysis,* edited by Donald O. Henry and George H. Odell, pp. 183–212. Archaeological Papers of the American Anthropological Association, Washington, D.C.

Young, Amy L.

1997   Risk Management Strategies among African-American Slaves at Locust Grove Plantation. *International Journal of Historical Archaeology* 1:5–37.

1999   Archaeological Investigations of Slave Housing at Saragossa Plantation, Natchez, Mississippi. *Southeastern Archaeology* 18:57–68.

2000   *Preliminary Report of Phase II Archaeological Investigations at 22WA933.* Report submitted to the Mississippi Department of Transportation, Jackson.

2002a   From Slavery to Freedom: Archaeological Investigations at Peachwood, Wayne County, Mississippi. Paper presented at the Society for Historical Archaeology, Mobile, Alabama.

2002b   Archaeological Testing at Two African-American Midwives Home Sites in South Mississippi. Paper presented at the South Central Historical Archaeology Conference, Jackson, Mississippi.

2003a   Getting Into Paradise: Literacy in Slave-Quarter Communities. Paper presented at the 60th Annual Meeting of Southeastern Archaeological Conference, Charlotte, North Carolina.

2003b   An Examination of Literacy in Slave Communities. Paper presented at the South-Central Historical Archaeology Conference, Natchitoches, Louisiana.

2004   From Farms to Forests to Cities: Landscapes Toward Freedom in the Mississippi Piney Woods, 1880–1950. Paper presented at the Southern Anthropological Society, Decatur, Georgia.

2005   *Archaeological and Historical Investigations at The Oaks, Jackson, Mississippi.* Report submitted to The Oaks, and to Mississippi Department of Archives and History, Jackson.

2006   Archaeological and Historical Investigations in Turkey Creek, Harrison County, Mississippi. Department of Anthropology and Sociology, The University of Southern Mississippi, Hattiesburg.

Young, Amy L., Philip J. Carr, and Joseph E. Granger

1997   How Historical Archaeology Works: A Case Study of Slave Houses at Locust Grove. *The Kentucky Register* 96(2):167–194.

Young, Amy L., Michael Tuma, and Cliff Jenkins

2000   The Role of Hunting to Cope with Risk at Saragossa Plantation, Natchez. *American Anthropologist* 103:692–704.

Young, Amy L., and Irmgard H. Wolfe

1998   *Report of Investigations at Auvergne Plantation: 1996 Field Season.* Report on File, Kentucky Heritage Council, Frankfort, Kentucky.

Young, Amy L., and Charles Wright

2001   *Exploring African-American and Euroamerican Rural Life in the Pine Hills of Mississippi: Phase II Investigations at Peachwood, 22WA933.* Report submitted to Mississippi Department of Transportation, Environmental Division, Jackson.

Zeidler, J. A.

1995   *Archaeological Inventory Survey Standards and Cost-estimation Guidelines for the Department of Defense.* U.S. Army Corps of Engineers Research Laboratories Special Report 96/40, Volume 1, Vicksburg.

Contributors

Ian Brown received a B.A. degree from Harvard University in 1973 and a Ph.D. from Brown University in 1979. He served as Assistant Director of Harvard University's Peabody Museum for many years. He is currently a Distinguished Teaching Fellow of the College of Arts and Sciences and Professor of Anthropology at the University of Alabama. He is also Curator of Gulf Coast Archaeology at the Alabama Museum of Natural History. He specializes in the archaeology and history of Southeastern Indians, and has spent over thirty-five years excavating sites in Louisiana, Mississippi, and Alabama.

Kevin L. Bruce is the current Planning Team Leader on the McKenzie River Ranger District, Oregon. He received his Master's degree in anthropology from the Eastern New Mexico University in 2001. His research interests include prehistoric hunter-gatherer lifeways, stone tool technologies, GIS, and geophysical survey techniques and applications.

Philip J. Carr is Associate Professor of Anthropology and Associate Director of the Center for Archaeological Studies, University of South Alabama, with research interests in stone tools, hunter-gatherers, and the organization of technology.

Robert C. Dunnell received a B.A. degree from the University of Kentucky in 1964 and a Ph.D. from Yale University in 1967. He worked for thirty years at the University of Washington, including thirteen years as department chair. He is currently Professor Emeritus at the University of Washington and Adjunct Professor at Mississippi State University and the University of Tennessee; he is also Affiliate Curator at the Yale Peabody Museum. His research interests include Mississippi valley archaeology, dating, and archaeological theory, especially evolutionary theory.

James Feathers is the Director of the Luminescence Dating Laboratory and a research associate professor at the University of Washington. His main research is in the application of luminescence dating in archaeological contexts.

Gayle J. Fritz is Professor of Anthropology in the Department of Anthropology at Washington University in St. Louis. General research interests include ethnobotany, paleoethnobotany, and agricultural origins and developments, with primary involvement in the North American Southeast and Midwest, as well as the southwestern U.S. and northwestern Mexico.

Michael L. Galaty is associate professor of anthropology at Millsaps College in Jackson, Mississippi. He conducts field research in both Europe and North America. His research interests include the origins of complex societies and prehistoric political economy. He is a ceramic analyst who employs chemistry and petrography to better understand systems of pre- and Protohistoric ceramic manufacture, distribution, and consumption.

S. Homes Hogue received her Ph.D. from the University of North Carolina, Chapel Hill, in 1988. She is currently Professor of Anthropology and Department Chair at the Department of Anthropology, Ball State University. Research interests include bioarchaeology and zooarchaeology of the southeastern United States.

H. Edwin Jackson is Professor of Anthropology at the University of Southern Mississippi, where he teaches Southeastern prehistory, cultural resources policy, and methods of analysis. His research focuses on Mississippian-period chiefdoms, in particular the role animal exploitation plays in economic, social, and ideological systems of prehistoric societies.

Jay K. Johnson is a Professor of Anthropology and the Director of the Center for Archaeological Research at the University of Mississippi. He received his Ph.D. from Southern Illinois University, Carbondale. Research interests include remote sensing, GIS, lithic analysis, and ethnohistory.

Carl P. Lipo is Associate Professor of the Department of Anthropology and Research Scientist at the Institute for Integrated Research in Materials, Environments, and Society at California State University, Long Beach. His research interests include the use of evolutionary theory to explain human cultural change in the archaeological record, cultural transmission, remote sensing, geophysics, luminescence dating, and quantitative methods.

Hector Neff is Professor of Anthropology and Research Scientist at the Institute for Integrated Research in Materials, Environments, and Society at California State University, Long Beach. One focus of his research is the application of chemical characterization to prehistoric craft production and exchange systems. He has pursued this interest through ceramic-sourcing studies in Mesoamerica, North America, and many other regions of the world.

Evan Peacock is Associate Professor of Anthropology and Senior Research Associate at the Cobb Institute of Archaeology, Mississippi State University.

He is an environmental archaeologist with interests in evolutionary theory, paleobiogeography, cultural resource management, and the application of "hard science" methods in archaeology.

Janet Rafferty is a Professor of Anthropology and Senior Research Associate at the Cobb Institute of Archaeology, Mississippi State University. Her research has focused on understanding prehistoric settlement pattern change in northeast Mississippi through an evolutionary framework.

James H. Turner is currently an Archaeologist for the Environmental Division, Mississippi Department of Transportation. He received his Master's in anthropology from Mississippi State University in 2006. His research interests include bioarchaeology, human osteology, Southeastern prehistoric archaeology, cultural resource management, and ethnohistory.

John R. Underwood is currently the Chief Archaeologist for the Environmental Division, Mississippi Department of Transportation. He received his Master's in anthropology from the College of William and Mary in 1998. Research interests include cultural resources management, Historic artifact studies, ethnohistory, and Southeastern prehistoric and historic archaeology in general.

Amy L. Young is an Associate Professor in the Department of Anthropology and Sociology at the University of Southern Mississippi. Her research interests in historical archaeology include African-American archaeology, gender, vernacular architecture, and inequality.

Index